ANCIENT EGYPT IN THE MODERN IMAGINATION

ANCIENT EGYPT IN THE MODERN IMAGINATION

ART, LITERATURE AND CULTURE

Edited by
Eleanor Dobson and Nichola Tonks

BLOOMSBURY ACADEMIC
LONDON • NEW YORK • OXFORD • NEW DELHI • SYDNEY

BLOOMSBURY ACADEMIC
Bloomsbury Publishing Plc
50 Bedford Square, London, WC1B 3DP, UK
1385 Broadway, New York, NY 10018, USA
29 Earlsfort Terrace, Dublin 2, Ireland

BLOOMSBURY, BLOOMSBURY ACADEMIC and the Diana logo
are trademarks of Bloomsbury Publishing Plc

First published in Great Britain 2020
Paperback edition first published 2021

Copyright © Eleanor Dobson, Nichola Tonks and contributors, 2020

Eleanor Dobson and Nichola Tonks have asserted their right under the Copyright, Designs and Patents Act, 1988, to be identified as Editors of this work.

Cover design by Adriana Brioso
Cover image © The New York Public Library Digital Collections. 1895.

All rights reserved. No part of this publication may be reproduced or transmitted in any form or by any means, electronic or mechanical, including photocopying, recording, or any information storage or retrieval system, without prior permission in writing from the publishers.

Bloomsbury Publishing Plc does not have any control over, or responsibility for, any third-party websites referred to or in this book. All internet addresses given in this book were correct at the time of going to press. The author and publisher regret any inconvenience caused if addresses have changed or sites have ceased to exist, but can accept no responsibility for any such changes.

A catalogue record for this book is available from the British Library.

A catalog record for this book is available from the Library of Congress.

ISBN: HB: 978-1-7883-1339-1
PB: 978-1-3501-9380-2
ePDF: 978-1-7867-3670-3
eBook: 978-1-7867-2664-3

Typeset by Newgen KnowledgeWorks Pvt. Ltd., Chennai, India

To find out more about our authors and books visit
www.bloomsbury.com and sign up for our newsletters.

For my parents, Georgia and Mike

E. D.

For Toby & Phyllipa – without whom I could not exist

For Lynda & Barry – without whom I would not exist

N. T.

CONTENTS

List of Figures ix
Notes on Contributors xi

Introduction 1
Eleanor Dobson and Nichola Tonks

PART I The Egyptological Imaginary 11

1 'Wonderful Things' in Kingston upon Hull 13
    Gabrielle Heffernan

2 'Let Sleeping Scarabs Alone': When Egypt Came to Stonehenge 29
    Martyn Barber

3 'Mummy First: Statue After': Wyndham Lewis, Diffusionism, Mosaic Distinctions and the Egyptian Origins of Art 47
    Edward Chaney

4 Ancient Egypt in William S. Burroughs's Novels 75
    Riccardo Gramantieri

5 Between Success and Controversy: Christian Jacq and the Marketing of 'Egyptological' Fiction 89
    Vassilaki Papanicolaou

PART II Death and Mysticism 103

6 Egyptomania, English Pyramids and the Quest for Immortality 105
    Jolene Zigarovich

7 Obituaries and Obelisks: Egyptianizing Funerary Architecture and the Cemetery as a Heterotopic Space 117
    Nichola Tonks

Contents

8 Tutankhartier: Death, Rebirth and Decoration; Or, Tutmania in
   the 1920s as a Metaphor for a Society in Recovery after World War One   127
   Lizzie Glithero-West

9 Celtic Egyptians: Isis Priests of the Lineage of Scota   145
   Caroline Tully

10 Jack the Ripper and the Mummy's Curse: Ancient Egypt in *From Hell*   161
   Eleanor Dobson

PART III Gender and Sexuality   181

11 From Sekhmet to Suffrage: Ancient Egypt in Early Twentieth-Century
   Women's Culture   183
   Mara Gold

12 'The Use of Old Objects': Ancient Egypt and English Writers around 1920   199
   R. B. Parkinson

13 Women Surrealists and Egyptian Mythology: Sphinxes, Animals and Magic   213
   Sabina Stent

14 Egyptian Excesses: Taylor, Burton and *Cleopatra*   229
   Siv Jansson

15 The Mummy, the Priestess and the Heroine: Embodying and Legitimating
   Female Power in 1970s Girls' Comics   247
   Nickianne Moody

Notes   261
Bibliography   333
Index   361

FIGURES

1.1	The Gold Throne. © Hands on History, Hull Museums.	18
1.2	The Footstool. © Hands on History, Hull Museums.	20
1.3	The Golden Shrine. © Hands on History, Hull Museums.	22
2.1	The scarab from Stonehenge Aerodrome. Line drawings by R. S. Newall originally published in Engleheart & Collignon 1936.	36
2.2	Aerial view of Stonehenge and the First World War aerodrome, the latter in the process of being dismantled. The photograph was taken on 12 July 1928, two months before the scarab was found, almost certainly on the site of the hangar seen at the top of the photograph. CCC 11796/4519, reproduced by permission of the Historic England Archive.	36
2.3	The scarab from Collingbourne Wood (or Ludgershall). Salisbury Museum acc. no. 1935/31 ('On deposit from Mr James'. Max. length 107 mm, max. height 37 mm). Reproduced by permission of Salisbury Museum.	38
2.4	One of Alexander Keiller's 1930s concrete obelisks at Avebury. This is an example of his 'Mark 2' design. Photo: M Barber.	45
3.1	Tut (1931). Sketch by Wyndham Lewis. Pencil, charcoal and wash, 11 × 9¼ in. By permission of the Wyndham Lewis Memorial Trust (a registered charity).	71
6.1	Francis Douce Mausoleum (c. 1748), Lower Wallop, Hampshire. Courtesy of The Mausolea & Monuments Trust.	111
6.2	John 'Mad Jack' Fuller, 'The Pyramid' (c. 1811), Brightling Churchyard. Courtesy of the Mausolea & Monuments Trust.	112
6.3	Burton Pyramid (c. 1837), St. Leonards, East Sussex. This image is in the public domain.	113
6.4	Kilmorey Mausoleum (c. 1850), St. Margarets, Richmond upon Thames. Courtesy of the Mausolea & Monuments Trust.	114
6.5	Courtoy Mausoleum (c. 1850), Brompton Cemetery, London. This image is in the public domain.	114
7.1	'Aerial View of Hamilton Mausoleum', © A.P.S. (UK)/Alamy Stock Photo.	124
7.2	'Hamilton Mausoleum', © paulskinner25/Stockimo/Alamy Stock Photo.	125
8.1	'What the great find in Egypt may bring: a 3000-year old pharaoh "coming forth into the day" with the contemporary garlands which adorned his mummy'. © Illustrated London News Ltd/Mary Evans.	132
8.2	Scarab brooch, Cartier London, 1924. Vincent Wulveryck, Collection Cartier © Cartier.	136
8.3	Scarab brooch, Cartier London, 1925. Nils Herrmann, Collection Cartier © Cartier.	137

Figures

8.4 Egyptian sarcophagus vanity case. Cartier, 1925 VC 70 A25. Photo: Nick Welsh, Cartier Collection © Cartier. 140

8.5 Egyptian sarcophagus vanity case. Cartier, 1925 VC 70 A25. Nils Herrmann, Cartier Collection © Cartier. 141

8.6 Execution drawing, Paris, 1923. Graphite pencil and gouache on transparent paper. Cartier Archives, Paris. Cartier Archives © Cartier. 142

9.1 MacGregor and Moina Mathers in Egyptian costume. From Frederic Lees, 'Isis Worship in Paris: Conversations with the Hierophant Rameses and the High Priestess Anari', *The Humanitarian* 16/2 (1900), 82–7. 148

9.2 MacGregor Mathers as the Hierophant Rameses. From André Gaucher, 'Isis à Montmartre', *L'Echo du merveilleux: Revue bimensuelle* 94, 95 (1900). 150

9.3 Moina Mathers as the High Priestess Anari. From André Gaucher, 'Isis à Montmartre', *L'Echo du merveilleux: Revue bimensuelle* 94, 95 (1900). 151

9.4 Olivia and Lawrence Durdin-Robertson, Huntingdon Castle, County Carlow, Ireland. The Marsden Archive/Alamy Stock Photo. 158

10.1 The detailed view of the Unlucky Mummy, *From Hell*, ch. 5, p. 39. FROM HELL © Alan Moore and Eddie Campbell. 166

10.2 The detailed view of Cleopatra's Needle, *From Hell*, ch. 4, p. 20. FROM HELL © Alan Moore and Eddie Campbell. 170

10.3 Jabulon, *From Hell*, chapter 2, p. 26. FROM HELL © Alan Moore and Eddie Campbell. 176

11.1 Sarah Bernhardt (1844–1923), French, actress in the role of Cleopatra. Ca. 1891, Mary Evans/Everett Collection. 186

11.2 'Salomé – Robe du soir de Paul Poiret', plate 28 from *Gazette du Bon Ton*, Volume 1, No. 3, Boston Museum of Fine Arts. 187

11.3 Claudette Colbert in *Cleopatra*, directed by: Cecil B. DeMille, USA 1934, Mary Evans/SZ Photo/Scherl. 189

11.4 British New Kingdom type low chair, 1920s, from the Egyptian Revival Sale, Bonhams, 23 January 2008, Lot 8. 190

11.5 English Art Deco 'Egyptianesque' Bakelite and Celluloid necklaces, 1930s. From The Egyptian Revival Sale, Bonhams, 23 January 2008, Lot 135. 192

11.6 Egyptian trinkets from 1,500 to 3,000 years old adapted as modern jewellery, © Illustrated London News Ltd/Mary Evans. 194

12.1 H. Rider Haggard's 'Sherd of Amenartas' (front; Norwich Castle Museum 1917.68.7.1). © Norfolk Museums Service. 201

12.2 Sir Wallis Budge, by 'Quiz' (Powys Evans; 1899–1981), from the *Saturday Review*, 24 February 1923, p. 251. 206

12.3 The beginning of the Papyrus of Ani (P. BM EA 10470.1), showing Ani and his wife worshipping the Sungod, with Budge's name above the museum registration number. © The Trustees of the British Museum. 207

12.4 Anthony Roth Costanzo as Akhnaten, at the English National Opera, 2016. © Richard Hubert Smith. 211

CONTRIBUTORS

Martyn Barber works for Historic England, specializing in archaeological aerial photographic inspection. Prior to this, he worked for the Royal Commission on the Historic Monuments of England. He is the author of *A History of Aerial Photography and Archaeology: Mata Hari's Glass Eye and Other Stories* (2011), as well as numerous articles on the history of archaeology in the nineteenth and twentieth centuries. His current research focuses on the landscapes around Avebury and Stonehenge.

Edward Chaney is Emeritus Professor at Solent University and Honorary Professor at UCL. He has published on the Grand Tour, Anglo–Italian cultural relations, the history of collecting, Inigo Jones, twentieth-century British art and the legacy of ancient Egypt in the early modern period. His books include *The Evolution of the Grand Tour* (revised ed. 2000), *The Jacobean Grand Tour: Early Stuart Travellers in Europe* (2014 – with Timothy Wilks) and *Genius Friend: G.B. Edwards and The Book of Ebenezer Le Page* (2015). He is currently writing a book entitled *Shakespeare and Egypt*.

Eleanor Dobson is Lecturer in Nineteenth Century Literature at the University of Birmingham. Her work focuses on culture of the nineteenth and early twentieth centuries, specifically focusing on representations of Egypt and Egyptology across this period. She has published articles in *Victorian Literature and Culture* and *Journal of International Women's Studies*, and an essay on representations of the ghost of Oscar Wilde in *Ghosts – or the (Nearly) Invisible: Spectral Phenomena in Literature and the Media* (2016). Recent work includes essays on jewel imagery in Bram Stoker's *Dracula*, supernatural stories set in Egyptian hotels as well as Egyptian artefacts and spirits materializing during early twentieth-century séances.

Lizzie Glithero-West is Chief Executive of the Heritage Alliance, the biggest alliance of heritage interests in the UK, set up to promote the central role of the independent movement in the heritage sector. Her previous career has been mainly in the civil service and she has expert knowledge of a wide range of policy areas including archaeology, heritage protection, museums and tourism. She has also spent time on secondment to English Heritage and to the National Museum Directors' Council. Glithero-West has a degree in Archaeology and Anthropology from Oxford, and an MA in History of Art from Birkbeck, where she focused on Egyptian Revival in the Regency and Art Deco Periods. In 2014 she was elected a Fellow of the Society of Antiquaries.

Mara Gold is a doctoral candidate at the University of Oxford, working on gender and sexuality in nineteenth- and twentieth-century reception of the ancient world and women in archaeology. She has previously studied at the UCL Institute of Archaeology, Central School of Speech and Drama, and Victoria University of Wellington.

Riccardo Gramantieri is the author of a number of books addressing literature, science and science fiction. He is the author of *Metafisica dell'evoluzione in A. E. Van Vogt* (2011), *William Burroughs: manuali di sopravvivenza, techniche di guerriglia* (2012), *Post 11 settembre: Letterature e trauma* (2016), and 'Re-emergence of the Death Instinct in Wilhelm Reich's Last Experiment' in *Psychoanalysis and History* (2016), among others.

Gabrielle Heffernan is Assistant Curator of Designated Collections at Hull Museums; based in the archaeology museum, she works with a range of British and world archaeology collections. She was previously a Future Curator Trainee at the British Museum, where she worked on the reinterpretation of the Egyptian Sculpture Gallery, and at the Burrell Collection where her role focused on the research and redisplay of the Egyptian and Near Eastern collections. She completed her PhD in Egyptology at the University of Birmingham, where her thesis focused on cultural memory and identity in the Egyptian Eighteenth Dynasty, with relation to memorial cults and royal ancestors.

Siv Jansson has taught at Imperial College, Royal Holloway and the Open University. Until 2014, she lectured at the University of Auckland. She currently teaches at Birkbeck College, University of London. Jansson has written on the figure of the 'angel in the house' and Elizabeth Gaskell, art, gender, and desire.

Nickianne Moody is Principal Lecturer in Media and Cultural Studies at Liverpool John Moores University. She acts as convenor for the Association for Research in Popular Fictions. She has published in *Nineteenth Century Gender Studies*, *Popular Narrative Media*, and essays on gothic, science fiction, and popular female authors from the nineteenth century onwards.

Vassilaki Papanicolaou is a member of the TELEM Research Team at Bordeaux-Montaigne University, having completed his doctorate in General and Comparative Literature. His work primarily deals with theoretical, epistemological and cultural topics in the area of the historical novel of the nineteenth and twentieth centuries, with a focus on fictions set in antiquity. He has published articles on historical novelists such as Gore Vidal, Gary Jennings, Hermann Hesse, Hermann Broch, Amin Maalouf and Odile Weulersse. Papanicolaou's work has appeared in *Journal of American Studies of Turkey*, and *The German Historical Novel since the Eighteenth Century: More than a Bestseller* (2016).

R. B. Parkinson is Professor of Egyptology at the University of Oxford. His research interests centre round the interpretation of ancient Egyptian literature, especially the poetry of the classic age (1940–1640 BC). As well the philological study of manuscripts, he works on material contexts, actors' perspectives, literary theory ('new historicist' and 'material philology' practices) and modern receptions in literature, art and film. He is interested in issues of performance practice, cultural power and sexuality in ancient Egyptian culture. Parkinson enjoys the experience of attempting an integrated reading of ancient texts, thinking about their context in the landscape, their performance and their emotional and intellectual impact on their audiences (including us).

Sabina Stent is an independent researcher with a doctorate from the University of Birmingham. Her doctoral thesis is entitled *Women Surrealists, Fetish, Femininity and Female Surrealism*. She has published articles including 'Fetishizing the Feminine: The Surreal Fashion of Elsa Schiaparelli', and given public talks on jewellery design and fairy tales.

Nichola Tonks is an AHRC-funded doctoral candidate in History and the Co-Editor of the *Journal of History and Cultures* at the University of Birmingham. Her research interests include the reception of ancient Egypt in nineteenth- and twentieth-century Britain, with a particular focus on spiritualism and notions of life after death. Tonks's forthcoming work includes an essay on C. S. Lewis and spirituality in the First World War.

Caroline Tully is a lecturer in the School of Historical and Philosophical Studies at the University of Melbourne, Australia. She has qualifications in Classics, Archaeology and Fine Art and her doctoral research focused upon tree worship in the Bronze Age Aegean, eastern Mediterranean and Egypt. She has published on modern paganism, Aleister Crowley and artefacts in the British Museum with supernatural connotations.

Jolene Zigarovich is an associate professor in the Department of Languages and Literatures at the University of Northern Iowa. She has also taught at Cornell University and Claremont Graduate University. Her recent book publications include *Writing Death and Absence in the Victorian Novel: Engraved Narratives* (2012) and she is editor of *Sex and Death in Eighteenth-Century Literature* (2013) and *TransGothic in Literature and Culture* (2017). Zigarovich's work has been published in *ANQ*, *Dickens Quarterly*, *Dickens Studies Annual*, *Eighteenth-Century Life*, *Studies in the Novel*, and *Women's Studies*. Her current work in progress examines death and the popularity of the eighteenth-century novel.

INTRODUCTION
Eleanor Dobson and Nichola Tonks

In 2016, we hosted a two-day conference entitled 'Tea with the Sphinx: Ancient Egypt in the Modern Imagination' at the University of Birmingham. This was followed by another event, 'Tea with the Sphinx: Defining the Field of Ancient Egypt Reception Studies', the next year. These activities were a delight to host: bringing together academics at various career stages working on subject material under this broad umbrella facilitated connections and ideas for future projects which are testament to increasing academic interest in the field, working in tandem with a widespread popular interest in ancient Egypt and its depictions by the general public, as fervent today (if not more so) in our native Britain, at least, as it was when the British Museum opened its doors to all visitors in 1857. This collection showcases some of the most exciting work that emerged over the course of the first two conferences, expanding on ideas which were presented and discussed in an atmosphere characterized by intellectual generosity and passionate debate. It also contains essays by other scholars working at the forefront of this discipline, who have contributed their own pieces as part of a collection which is truly multidisciplinary in its focus.

Few multi-authored books have yet been produced on the subject of ancient Egypt's reception in the modern world. The handful of such studies that have emerged include most of the eight volumes of the landmark series *Encounters with Ancient Egypt* (2003; 2007) edited by Peter Ucko and *Histories of Egyptology: Interdisciplinary Measures* (2014) edited by William Carruthers.[1] These works, like the single-authored books that have laid a rigorous foundation for future efforts – focusing on British perspectives, titles that range from Stephanie Moser's works on ancient Egypt and the British Museum (2006), the Crystal Palace (2012), and in the paintings of Lawrence Alma-Tadema, Edward Poynter and Edwin Long (2019) to David Gange's *Dialogues with the Dead: Egyptology in British Culture and Religion, 1822–1922* (2013), and modern Egyptian perspectives in Donald Malcolm Reid's *Whose Pharaohs?* (2002) and Elliott Colla's *Conflicted Antiquities: Egyptology, Egyptomania, Egyptian Modernity* (2007)[2] – are testament to a growing interest in the subject in academic circles. As the single-authored volumes have clear methodological approaches, the multi-authored studies have likewise tended to adopt a focused theoretical framework derived from a single discipline. All of these books are excellent in achieving their aims, but – as one of the manuscript's anonymous reviewers kindly highlighted – the present volume stands out by making a more conscious effort to combine theories of different disciplines within each individual essay. This, we should note, could not have been achieved without the stellar work of our aforementioned and esteemed colleagues, whose own efforts have carved out the central paths from which the contributors in this study branch.

Ancient Egypt in the Modern Imagination

Bringing together scholars from a variety of backgrounds, this current volume explicitly seeks to break down conventional disciplinary boundaries between fields such as history, classics, art history, fashion, film, archaeology, Egyptology and literature to further a nuanced understanding of ancient Egypt in cultures across the period that these essays consider: from the eighteenth century to the present day, predominantly in the 'Western' world – the British Isles, Europe and the Americas. Ancient Egypt Reception Studies, as evidenced by the diverse work presented at the 'Tea with the Sphinx' conferences, is leading the way in blending critical theory from different fields and applying such theory to non-traditional subject matter. The result, in this volume, is a series of new perspectives upon incidents within and beyond the world of Egyptology, some familiar but presented in a new light, others little-known and introduced here to a wider readership. This book thus provides a timely examination of a selection of such incidents that have been previously overlooked by scholars, or received inadequate or else superficial attention, prompting an exciting realization that many more Egyptianizing phenomena in our history await rediscovery and explanation.

The essays that pursue this common goal are divided in three sections: 'The Egyptological Imaginary', 'Death and Mysticism' and 'Gender and Sexuality'. Each section comprises five essays (arranged chronologically in terms of subject matter) which relate to these themes. In structuring the work in this way, we seek to highlight shared ideas between the chapters' different authors and their subject matter, emphasizing the cross-disciplinarity that is the hallmark of Ancient Egypt Reception Studies. Rather than grouping essays by media or subject specialism, we intend for the structure to concentrate upon the tracing of connections, rather than divisions, between academic fields. We hope that by structuring the work in this manner, parallels might be more readily drawn between the pieces grouped together: while the essays necessarily all have points of connection, such a structure will aid the reader in finding the connections linking the pieces in which they have a particular interest, emphasizing how some of the various meanings of ancient Egypt to modern people have traversed time and media.

The Egyptological imaginary

In the section devoted to 'The Egyptological imaginary', the component essays are particularly concerned with the influence that Egyptology had upon the arts – an influence that the arts themselves, at times, reciprocated. Some detail how the arts spread contemporary Egyptological theories, including some that were later discredited. Distinctions are drawn between 'pure' Egyptology, which attempts to discover what happened in the past and which has historically itself unknowingly championed misconceptions and inaccuracies, and popular ideas about Egypt that imitate some elements of Egyptological knowledge for the sake of authenticity, but deviate from archaeological knowledge for creative and political ends. Such a focus has already produced exceptional scholarly work, trailblazed by the late Dominic Montserrat in, for example, his *Akhenaten: History Fantasy and Ancient Egypt* (2000).[3] The chapters that make up this section follow Montserrat's lead, navigating Egyptological fact and imaginative fancy, notions of authenticity, reproduction, forgery, influence and misinterpretation to probe the space of overlap between history, interpretation and imagination.

The first essay both within this collection and this section, Gabrielle Heffernan's '"Wonderful Things" in Kingston Upon Hull', addresses the replicas of the objects discovered by Howard Carter's team in the tomb of Tutankhamun that were displayed at the British Empire Exhibition of 1924. Now housed in a museum known as Hands on History in the Old Grammar School in the city of Hull, these objects are part of a narrative which begins back in ancient Egypt itself where their originals were produced, continues in 1922 when these objects were rediscovered, develops again in 1924 when the replicas themselves were made and originally displayed, and continues in the present day as the replicas reside in their current home. Heffernan's chapter scrutinizes the replicas, relates how they were exhibited, understands them as products of their time as well as copies from an ancient civilization, and uses this as a starting point for a broader consideration of the role of replicas more generally in modern museums and heritage sites.

Martyn Barber's essay also addresses objects on the peripheries of Egyptology as a scholarly discipline: two limestone scarabs, both inscribed with the cartouche of Tuthmosis III. Barber's case study considers these items, discovered in Wiltshire in 1928 (one of them found just a few hundred yards from Stonehenge), in relation to the so-called hyperdiffusionist theories of Grafton Elliot Smith and William Perry, which envisioned ancient Egypt as the sole source of archaic civilization and the ancient Egyptians as the carriers of civilization across the known world. The scarabs were held by some archaeologists (including O. G. S. Crawford) as genuine ancient Egyptian items, while others (such as Percy Newberry and Margaret Murray) identified them as nineteenth-century fakes. Reviewing the surviving accounts of the objects' discovery, and drawing on unpublished archives associated with some of the key protagonists, this chapter not only uses the contemporary debate surrounding the scarabs to reassess the impact of hyperdiffusionist ideas on interwar understanding of what were regarded as the key achievements of Neolithic and Bronze Age society in Britain, and belief (or otherwise) in the likely presence of ancient Egyptians in prehistoric Wessex, but also explores the largely unrecognized legacy of these ideas into the twenty-first century. This legacy, Barber shows, survives not just as orphaned fragments of Smith's and Perry's ideas hidden within later narratives of prehistoric Britain, but also in physical form, marking the British landscape itself.

In Chapter 3, Edward Chaney further considers the influence of diffusionist ideas of Grafton Elliot Smith, specifically examining their impact on the writer and artist Wyndham Lewis. In his essay, Chaney argues that Lewis's encounter with Smith's controversial accounts of Egyptian art and its 'diffusion' throughout the ancient world was crucial to the development of his ideas, citing Smith's belief that mummification led to portrait sculpture, which in turn led to architecture in the form of mortuary temples.

Scrutinizing Lewis's *The Dithyrambic Spectator* (1931) among other writings, paintings and drawings, Chaney demonstrates the impact of Smith's writings on Lewis, and that ancient Egypt was crucial for Lewis's theory of art and its origins.

Riccardo Gramantieri's essay addresses ancient Egypt and its mythology in the novels of William Burroughs. Gramantieri claims that Burroughs's use of ancient Egypt in his later works might be read as a rewriting of this ancient culture for a modern audience, adapting aspects of ancient Egyptian mythology and civilization to correspond with his contemporary world. Specifically, Gramantieri analyses Burroughs's 'hieroglyphic' method of writing in his experimental works of the 1970s, as well as his extensive use of ancient Egyptian settings and mythological characters in his works of the 1980s, including his memoirs. Gramantieri shows how, through such writings, Burroughs reimagined ancient Egyptian culture through a modern lens, conceiving of the ancient Egyptian journey to the afterlife as a kind of space travel, perceiving deities as forms of energy, and envisaging scribes with technologically advanced tools. Ultimately, this reinterpretation of antiquity, Gramantieri claims, allowed Burroughs to comprehend the ancient Egyptian pantheon as an alternative to modern western religions, cementing its relevance in the modern world.

In the essay that concludes the works on the 'Egyptological Imaginary', Vassilaki Papanicolaou focuses on the French Egyptologist and novelist Christian Jacq, one of the most prominent and prolific writers of fiction set in pharaonic times. Perhaps as a result of his widespread success, and the methods by which he has appealed to such a broad market, Jacq has received little critical attention besides some ephemeral reviews, short references and rare interviews. Papanicolaou's essay fills this scholarly lacuna, offering a comprehensive analysis of the role played by ancient Egypt and Egyptology in Jacq's worldwide success, and reconciling the scholarly Egyptological and popular 'Egyptomaniac' aspects of both his writing and persona.

Collectively, these chapters navigate the tensions between the purportedly factual narratives of scholarly Egyptology and creative processes across the twentieth century. Barber's and Chaney's essays chart the influence of ideas of ancient Egyptians and Britons being in contact, traversing the landscape of the archaeological dig through to the world of modern art. Chaney and Gramantieri, moreover, both outline how ancient Egypt is used as an antidote to problems with the modern world: from Lewis's perception of the blandness of modern abstract art to Burroughs's mistrust of modern languages and the sinister ways in which he believed that they might be wielded. Heffernan's and Papanicolaou's chapters further explore the overlap between scholarly Egyptology and creative media, detailing – respectively – the creation of replica artefacts for the sake of popular spectacle and the creation of fictionalized narratives based on an Egyptological foundation, again to appeal to a broad public audience. Encompassing both exclusive and accessible cultural forms, these essays illuminate the permeable boundaries between the scholarly and the amateur, speaking to Egyptology's cultural esteem as well as its firm entrenchment within the imagination on a much larger scale, across Britain, France and the United States.

Introduction

Death and mysticism

Ancient Egypt has long been held as a civilization fixated on death. This assertion has several bases, predominantly relying upon public fascination with funerary relics above other materials unearthed by archaeology, and the relatively excellent condition of this paraphernalia as a result of its being carefully packed and sealed within tombs. While Egyptologists often lament such generalizations, this longstanding supposition has resulted in a rich infusion of ancient Egyptian symbolism into cultures of death and mysticism in the West, dating back centuries. Florian Ebeling has, for instance, detailed ancient Egypt's place in the history of Hermeticism while, in line with the temporal parameters of the current study, others have taken up the mantle in exploring ancient Egypt's significance in the nineteenth century's occult circles, most notably Roger Luckhurst in his *The Mummy's Curse: The True History of a Dark Fantasy* (2012), and subsequently in essays on the likes of Aleister Crowley by Caroline Tully, and Steve Vinson and Janet Gunn.[4] However, while thorough studies such as those by James Stevens Curl have documented revivals of ancient Egyptian style and their infiltration into spaces and goods associated with death and mourning, the deeper meanings and reasonings behind such employment have been left to scholars to tease out within this volume, and within this section specifically.[5]

This section opens with Jolene Zigarovich's essay on 'Egyptomania, English Pyramids and the Quest for Immortality'. Zigarovich's essay explores how ancient Egyptian embalming practices and pyramidal imagery shaped eighteenth-century British culture. She observes the influence of the surgeon Thomas Greenhill's *Nekpokhdeia, or The Art of Embalming* (1705), and its connections to contemporary cultures of mummy 'unrollings'. Greenhill's work, Zigarovich notes, both responded to and encouraged public fascination with ancient Egyptian culture. Simultaneously, she claims that *Nekpokhdeia* stimulated public interest in embalming, and the protection of bodies from signs of decay. Zigarovich reads eighteenth- and nineteenth-century embalming practices and heart and viscera burials in light of contemporary fascination with ancient Egyptian mortuary culture, further connecting this to pyramidal tombs and monuments. Ultimately, she argues that such ancient Egyptian influences on embalming and burial culture are material reminders of Britain's imperial ventures, as well as a desire for immortality: a point of overlap in Christian and ancient Egyptian religious beliefs.

Nichola Tonks's essay, 'Obituaries and Obelisks: Egyptianising Funerary Architecture and the Cemetery as Heterotopic Space', extends on some of the issues that Zigarovich raises. She turns to the funeralia of the Victorian period, observing how ancient Egyptian motifs and iconography were increasingly incorporated into the material culture of burial and, concurrently, how such appropriation moved beyond a mere reflection of contemporary fashion. Arguing that nineteenth-century British engagement with ancient Egyptian imagery was both personal and meaningful as opposed to superficial, Tonks pays particular attention to the 10th Duke of Hamilton, an individual who was interred in an ancient Egyptian sarcophagus. Hamilton's use of the relic has hitherto been examined as an eccentric employment of an artefact in response to the fashion of Egyptomania, and often read as an 'orientalist' practice. His use of this artefact, this essay argues, instead illuminates a deeper engagement in the culture and practices of the ancients which transcends the merely decorative and constitutes a real and sustained interest in ancient culture.

In Chapter 8, Lizzie Glithero-West explores items produced by the jeweller Cartier subsequent to the discovery of the tomb of Tutankhamun in 1922, commenting on the symbolic meanings behind the imagery adopted by the jewellery designers and purchased by consumers. She begins her essay by establishing the connections between Tutankhamun's body and the bodies of the war dead in the aftermath of First World War, particularly pertinent after it was revealed that the pharaoh was a young man at the time of his death. Glithero-West claims that the imagery of revival, such as scarab beetles, lotus flowers and sunburst motifs, adopted by contemporary jewellers appealed to a society in mourning, seeking comfort so soon after the loss of their loved ones. Highlighting particular examples produced by Cartier allows Glithero-West to showcase the heretofore unexplored meanings of such pieces and their cultural potency.

Caroline Tully's chapter, entitled 'Celtic Egyptians: Isis Priests of the Lineage of Scota', analyses the use of ancient Egyptian religion by the founders of two modern manifestations of the worship of the goddess Isis: the rites of Isis in *fin-de-siècle* Paris overseen by Samuel Liddell MacGregor Mathers and Moina Mathers – key figures in the Hermetic Order of the Golden Dawn – and the Fellowship of Isis, created by Lawrence Durdin-Robertson, Pamela Durdin-Robertson and Olivia Durdin-Robertson in early 1970s Ireland. Tully shows how both groups – though temporally and geographically distinct – claimed an authentic connection to ancient Egypt through the mythological Egyptian queen Scota, claimed as an ancestor of the Irish and Scottish peoples. Her essay demonstrates how both groups favoured an ahistorical construction of Isis, while simultaneously asserting their legitimacy through connections to Scota's mythology. Her essay both establishes the ways in which Isis has been appropriated for modern esoteric ends via Scota and the significant employment of Scota as a figure at once Egyptian and Celtic, a conduit between the East and the West, and the modern and ancient worlds.

The essay that concludes the 'Death and Mysticism' section, Eleanor Dobson's 'Jack the Ripper and the Mummy's Curse: Ancient Egypt in *From Hell*', also discusses nineteenth- and early twentieth-century occultism and esotericism and its ripples in the late twentieth century. Dobson scrutinizes Alan Moore and Eddie Campbell's celebrated graphic novel *From Hell* (1999), and its employment of textual and illustrative references to ancient Egypt: allusions to E. A. Wallis Budge, the Keeper of Egyptian and Assyrian Antiquities at the British Museum, 1893–1924; ancient Egyptian artefacts, ranging from the British Museum's 'Unlucky Mummy' to the obelisk known as 'Cleopatra's Needle' situated on London's Embankment; and depictions of ancient Egyptian deities including Osiris and Horus. She recognizes that in such allusions Moore and Campbell engage with nineteenth-century Egyptiana and esotericism and suggest the extension of such magic into the modern world in which their work was published. Real ancient Egyptian artefacts are markers of occult potency, but they also tether the narrative in reality, collapsing time and blurring the lines between real and fictional spaces.

The essays in this section, when considered alongside one another, scrutinize the aforementioned longstanding associations between ancient Egypt, death and mysticism in the cultural consciousness, enriching our understanding of how and why these connections prove so indelible through specific case studies. Zigarovich and Tonks build upon survey works such as Curl's which have charted the presence of ancient Egypt in British funerary contexts, providing deeper analyses as to the shared and personal significances of such symbolism's employment: evoking imperial might and immortality, in Zigarovich's interpretation, and personal fascination beyond superficial fashion in Tonks's. Glithero-West sees these eighteenth- and nineteenth-century employments of ancient Egyptian symbolism in mourning culture evolve in the twentieth century in the context of the Great War, where ancient Egypt imagery provides comfort to the bereaved. Tully and Dobson, meanwhile, both illuminate nineteenth- and twentieth-century engagements with ancient Egypt in mystical contexts, detailing the concurrent use and misuse of Egyptological sources, as well as twentieth-century returns to nineteenth-century conventions. All of the chapters, while suggesting change over time influenced by the rise and fall of British imperialism, burgeoning female empowerment in many contexts but specifically within occult groups, along with other major social and historical shifts, also reinforce a sense of stasis in terms of our understanding of the employment of ancient Egypt over the past few centuries; familiar ideas are returned to with remarkable regularity, and perceived links between Egypt, death and magic are shown ultimately to be reinforced rather than challenged.

Gender and sexuality

Preoccupations with gender and sexuality have long guided the reception of ancient Egypt, stretching back to antiquity itself. In modern academia, meanwhile, the rise of feminist and later queer theory revolutionized the study of these concepts, and the scrutiny of how ancient Egypt has historically intersected with these themes has recently resulted in the first full length work on the reception of ancient Egypt in women's writing: Molly Youngkin's *British Women Writers and the Reception of Ancient Egypt, 1840–1910: Imperialist Representations of Egyptian Women* (2016), subsequent to Judith E. Tucker's social-historical exploration of *Women in Nineteenth-Century Egypt* (2009).[6] Other scholars central to discussions of gender, sex and sexuality in depictions of ancient Egypt include Jasmine Day, and subsequently Nolwenn Corriou, who have read certain mummy narratives involving gendered attacks on the bodies of the female dead as evoking rape.[7] Lynn Meskell and Bradley Deane have detailed the connection between fascination with Egypt and the eroticization of the ancient Egyptian body, and Angie Blumberg and Eleanor Dobson have both begun to interrogate the 'queering' of ancient Egypt since the late nineteenth century in literary and theatrical contexts.[8]

Building upon this developing body of work, this section opens with Mara Gold's 'From Sekhmet to Suffrage: Ancient Egypt in Early Twentieth-Century Women's Culture.' Gold explores the plentiful but understudied connections between the reception of ancient Egypt and concepts of femininity and feminism during the early twentieth century. She identifies appropriations of ancient Egyptian motifs, concepts and historical figures (including Nefertiti and Hatshepsut), employed by modern women to construct and perform their own gender identities. Drawing upon specific archaeological discoveries and a wealth of publications – from fashion magazines and suffrage publications to respected national newspapers – Gold examines how women interpreted the ancient past to corroborate their concept of the 'ideal' woman, bolstered by and sensitive to an ever-increasing body of archaeological data.

Chapter 12, R. B. Parkinson's ' "The Use of Old Objects": Ancient Egypt and English Writers around 1920', addresses issues of literary style and sexuality in literature with ancient Egyptian subject matter in the years bookending 1920. Parkinson draws examples from diverse literary genres, from Sax Rohmer's supernatural novel *Brood of the Witch Queen* (1918) to the higher-brow fictional and non-fictional works of E. M. Forster. He reads 'queerness' in Rohmer's and Forster's texts; in Rohmer's novel, the queer stands for theatrical otherness, while in Forster the queer represents something far more personal to the author. Parkinson connects Forster's queer empathy with the ancient Egyptian past to his falling in love with an Egyptian man. Queer sexualities, Parkinson demonstrates – in both Forster's case and in the works of his near-contemporaries – can be read as intimately connected to criticism of British Egyptological 'authority'.

In her essay, 'Women Surrealists and Egyptian Mythology: Sphinxes, Animals and Magic', Sabina Stent investigates the ancient Egyptian iconography employed by female Surrealist artists, paying particular attention to Lee Miller, Remedios Varo and Leonor Fini. Academic discussion of ancient Egyptian influences on these artists has thus far been limited to Fini; Stent introduces assessments of ancient Egypt in a broader corpus of works by Fini and other female Surrealists to extrapolate commonalities. In doing so, she proposes that ancient Egypt represented feminine and female power for all of these artists, with goddesses, sphinxes and animal-familiars embodying the magical abilities reserved only for the woman.

Siv Jansson's essay focuses on *Cleopatra* (1963), concentrating on the film's stars, Elizabeth Taylor and Richard Burton, and the myriad ways in which their lives, love affair and personalities mirrored – or were perceived to mirror – those of the historical characters that they played. Jansson emphasizes the 'celebrification' not only of Taylor and Burton but also of Cleopatra and Antony, exploring how the modern actors and the film that they worked to create have subsequently impacted on the popular perceptions of their earlier counterparts and the world of ancient Egypt. This film, she shows, has had a lasting impact on ancient Egypt as it is depicted in later media, with Taylor contributing to an image of Cleopatra VII sometimes at odds with the real Egyptian queen. Due to Taylor's portrayal of the last of the Ptolemies more than any other before her, 'Cleopatra' became cemented as a byword for bewitching beauty, 'black widowhood' and decadent indulgence.

Introduction

The final essay in this section and in the collection as a whole, Nickianne Moody's 'The Mummy, the Priestess and the Heroine: Embodying and Legitimating Female Power in 1970s Girls' Comics', turns to *Spellbound* (1976–7) and *Misty* (1978–9) to analyse how narratives for girls in the mid to late 1970s used horror, mystery and supernatural narrative structures and imagery in comics with ancient Egyptian subject matter. Moody specifically examines the young female protagonists' relationships with elderly priestesses, observing matriarchal structures of power in which these young women become embroiled. Ultimately, she illuminates this genre's consideration of ancient Egypt as a fictional space for the exploration of feminine power and the limitations that were placed upon this by duty, feminine appearance and deportment, secrecy and intrusion into the mundane world.

Together, these chapters illuminate a sustained connection between ancient Egypt, gender, sexuality and power across the twentieth century. From Gold's chapter which explores how women at the beginning of this era looked to the past for feminist icons, through Stent's essay which demonstrates how women artists also turned to ancient Egypt as symbolic of feminine authority, Jansson's work which emphasizes the cultural indivisibility of Cleopatra and Elizabeth Taylor as decadent *femmes fatales*, and Moody's chapter which posits Egyptian magic as within the grasp of young women on the brink of adulthood, a thread is charted which implies an unwavering tradition of celebrating ancient Egypt for the authority it conferred upon its queens and priestesses. Alongside this, there exists a degree of fear roused by the sexually appealing and, at times, unsettling bodies of Egypt, as detailed in Parkinson's and Jansson's chapters – bodies which threaten sexual norms, incite extramarital affairs, promise not only sex but also, with it, death. The essays in this section are concerned with power, hierarchies, autonomy and control, and they also capture the tension between the stalwarts of Egyptology and those with other claims on Egypt, who harness ancient Egypt's cultural capital to express deeply personal identities and desires.

***

The essays that comprise this volume are wide-ranging in their chronology and scope; however, together they draw on themes most pertinent to the burgeoning field of Ancient Egypt Reception Studies to demonstrate the wide variety of ways in which ancient Egypt has pervaded Western society over the course of the previous few centuries and beyond. Egyptomania is a diverse phenomenon, encompassing a wide range of media and genres, and stretching across ancient, medieval and modern history. No one study can fully capture this range in detail, but this volume contains an eclectic sample of incidents drawn from the eighteenth to the twentieth centuries that are suggestive of the span of media in which Egyptomania has operated, and the varying, even conflicting ideologies that have harnessed Egyptian objects and symbols. The interpretations of ancient Egyptian culture included in this volume range from those of writers, artists and archaeologists to filmmakers, religious cultists and undertakers. These chapters are testament to both the multiplicity and the patterning of popular responses to ancient Egypt, as well as the longevity of this phenomenon and its relevance today.

Ancient Egypt in the Modern Imagination

As the centenary of the discovery of Tutankhamun approaches in 2022, ancient Egypt may very well experience yet another revival in the tastes of the West. The strands that this volume identifies were significant prior to the Tutankhamun discovery, were revitalized by the significance of the find and continue to have a lasting impact on engagements with ancient Egypt and Egyptology to this day. Ancient Egypt is associated with death and mysticism, sexual decadence, pharaonic masculinity and queenly femininity, and has been for centuries, responsive all the while to Egyptology as the discipline that seeks to understand it. With this significant centenary looming, to better understand how these imaginative engagements with ancient Egyptian culture materialized and will surely continue to do so, another revival likely on the horizon, it is essential to look to the past.

PART I
THE EGYPTOLOGICAL IMAGINARY

CHAPTER 1
'WONDERFUL THINGS' IN KINGSTON UPON HULL
Gabrielle Heffernan

The Old Grammar School in the city of Hull houses a museum known as Hands on History. The ground floor gallery imitates a Victorian schoolroom, complete with desks and a working blackboard. Upstairs, galleries tell the recent history of Hull, as well as highlight significant figures in the building of the city, its value as a key fishing port and the local dressmaker Madam Clapham. Yet in another room on the first floor there is an exhibit that is a little more unexpected. One is confronted by a larger-than-life pharaoh, his crown sitting upon his head, before catching sight of gleaming 'golden' chairs covered with Egyptian scenes, huge funerary beds and intricate 'alabaster' vases. One might be forgiven for thinking one had accidentally wandered through a portal to the Egyptian Museum in Cairo, for these are some of the 'wonderful things' from the tomb of the Egyptian pharaoh, Tutankhamun. Of course, these are not the original artefacts (which are still safely displayed in the Egyptian capital). Instead, they are replicas of the objects that were discovered by Howard Carter's team and excavated in the years following that great discovery.[1] But what brought these replicas to Hull? To answer this question, we must first look at the events of that incredible discovery in 1922, as well as occurrences slightly closer to home.

This essay looks at the replicas themselves, discussing why they were made and how they were originally displayed in the British Empire Exhibition of 1924. Building upon this case study, it discusses the topic of replicas more generally;[2] why were, and are, replicas created and what part can they play in modern museums and heritage sites? While some studies of the Tutankhamun discovery and its cultural aftermath mention the exhibition, discussion has often been restricted to the most basic information, and details on the replicas themselves have usually been omitted.[3] This essay, therefore, not only illuminates the fascinating history of these objects, but also contributes to the debate on the nature of replicas. It looks at the original exhibition and its replicas as an example of British culture and colonialism, and also considers them in their modern context, as well as the wider use of replicas by cultural institutions today. In doing so, it raises questions about modern interactions with ancient Egypt, thus encouraging consideration of what the implications may be for the future of such encounters.

The discovery of Tutankhamun's tomb

On 5 November 1922, an excavation led by the Egyptologist Howard Carter discovered the entrance to a previously unknown tomb in the Valley of Kings, situated on the

West Bank of the Nile at modern-day Luxor in southern Egypt. Carter wrote in his diary, 'Here before us was sufficient evidence to show that it really was an entrance to a tomb, and by the seals, to all outward appearances that it was intact.'[4] Many had hypothesized that there was nothing left to find in the valley and so this discovery was, for many, both exciting and surprising. The seals identified it as belonging to a then little-known New Kingdom pharaoh of the name Tutankhamun. Once the entrance had been identified it was necessary to report the find to the Egyptian authorities and await the arrival of representatives of the Egyptian Antiquities Service, and so the excavation of the tomb was delayed for a short while. Once the necessary individuals had been gathered, on 25 November, Carter and his patron, Lord Carnarvon, were finally able to enter the tomb.

After the passageway was cleared, Carter looked inside the first room. When asked if he could see anything, he is reported to have replied with that now famous phrase, 'Yes, wonderful things.' As more of the tomb was excavated it became clear that although it had been partially robbed in antiquity, it was far more intact that any other excavated royal tomb and contained a wealth of treasures, the like of which had never been seen before. Hundreds of pieces of tomb furniture were removed in an excavation that would take approximately ten years to complete.[5] Each object was meticulously recorded and photographed, before being taken from the tomb and packed ready to be transported to Cairo.

Visitors and press jostled at the site to catch a glimpse of some of the objects, or possibly even steal a moment inside the tomb. People across the world became swept up in the magic of Tutankhamun, the mysterious boy-king whose tomb contained riches beyond imagination. It should be noted, however, that the relationship between the excavators and the press was, at best, strained.[6] *The Times* had rights to exclusive information, and Carter did his best to ensure that they received scoops ahead of their rivals. Carter's own notebooks record his irritation at the interruptions to his work caused by interested journalists, where he wrote on 2 October 1925 of being 'pestered by correspondents of local and foreign papers'.[7] Members of the press sometimes went over Carter's head to gain access to information about the excavation. In one article, Arthur Weigall – a *Daily Mail* journalist whose role in this story will soon become clear – wrote:

> I think it may be of interest to mention that I was the first press representative to enter the tomb of the pharaoh Tut-ankh Amen in the Valley of the Kings since the inner chamber was opened on Friday. I did so not at the invitation of the monopolists [excavators], but at the invitation of the Egyptian government, which thus asserted its unquestioned proprietorship. At the time of writing the representatives of *The Times* have not yet been admitted.[8]

Clearly there was little love lost between Weigall and both the excavators of the tomb and the favoured *Times* newspaper.

The British Empire Exhibition at Wembley

At a similar time as these events were taking place in Egypt, plans were afoot in London to develop an exhibition that would showcase Britain and its place as the leader of a great empire. Britain in the early 1920s was part of a changing world. Approximately one million British servicemen had been killed in the horrors of the First World War and many more had been permanently injured. This left many families devastated personally, because of their immediate loss, and financially, in the long term. Furthermore, women had taken on many of the roles traditionally filled by men during the years of fighting; they worked in factories supporting the war effort, and they held their families together in the absence of male patriarchs. In the years after the war, calls for equal women's suffrage grew following the granting of suffrage to women over the age of 30 in the 1918 Representation of the People Act. The social implications of this shift towards equal voting rights were potentially huge and threatened the traditional systems of government and control.

It was in the midst of this changing and challenging cultural maelstrom that the idea for a British Empire Exhibition was revisited (previous discussion had taken place before the outbreak of war). The exhibition would showcase the wonders of the British Empire, cement trade links and foster new ventures. Furthermore, it would revitalize the British sense of pride in its own history and achievements.

The exhibition opened in 1924 at Wembley and was visited by more than 25 million people.[9] It displayed the cultures of 56 British territories ranging from Canada to British Guiana (now Guyana) to India. Alongside pavilions demonstrating the culture and industry of each territory there were huge displays of British science, engineering, transport and communication. The organizers even built a sports stadium (then called the Empire Stadium but better known now as the original Wembley Stadium, which stood until 2003 on the outskirts of London). In her review of the event, Amelia Deffries of the *American Magazine of Art* suggested that 'a visitor might see all there is to see at the Exposition if he devoted his whole time for three weeks to nothing else', such was its scale.[10] It was, all things considered, a tremendous display of power and achievement by a truly global empire.

But what of Tutankhamun? Egypt was never a formal part of the British Empire and so, arguably, should not have had a place at the Wembley exhibition. However, it can be reasonably assumed that Carter's British nationality, alongside that of his patron Carnarvon, made the discovery seem somewhat 'British' to many of those in positions of power. Ignoring the fact that the excavation had taken place in Egypt, was largely peopled by Egyptian workmen, and had discovered the tomb of an Egyptian pharaoh, the presence of a small number of influential British individuals at the site gave the organizers of the exhibition enough reason to include the tomb discovery among their British triumphs. Thus, the decision was made to include a replica of the tomb as part of the exhibition. The tomb was to be included as a paid-for exhibit in the amusement park that adjoined the main event, which made its inclusion possible without wrongly placing it among British territories. Additionally, it could help to raise income, another main aim of the British Empire Exhibition.

Having decided to include the replica tomb, the first task was to develop the displays. A London-based sculptor, William Aumonier, was engaged to create the replicas. The son of a sculptor (also called William), Aumonier was a respected artisan and a member of the company William Aumonier and Son, founded by his father. During the course of his career he worked on several high-profile projects, including in Hull where he created a war memorial for the grounds of the Reckitt factory in Dansom Lane.

As Aumonier was not particularly familiar with the subject matter, it was also decided to engage an expert in ancient Egypt to advise and oversee the project. Arthur Weigall was, therefore, hired to work alongside Aumonier. As an Egyptologist, Weigall had an understanding of the objects and of the culture that they represented. In addition to his Egyptological background, Weigall had also worked for some time in set design for both stage and film.[11] This gave him an excellent understanding of the needs of a display such as that proposed for the replica tomb, as well as experience in developing designs. As Weigall had been in Egypt during the excavation of the tomb working as a journalist, he had seen first-hand some of the objects as they were removed from the tomb. In the absence of many detailed photographs, this knowledge would have been crucial. Weigall's experience, therefore, made him ideal for the job; his Egyptological experience, his knowledge of Tutankhamun's tomb, his knowledge of creating stage sets and his interest in film and theatre[12] ensured that he both understood the context of the original tomb and that he recognized the importance of recreating this unique find in a way that would appeal to the paying public.[13] His dramatic flair is demonstrated in his report about the opening of the royal tomb:

> There are … few sensations so thrilling as that of entering a royal tomb which has been concealed for thousands of years … the excavators gaze around them at the beds, chairs, tables, vases and other objects buried with the dead, all apparently new and untouched by the hand of time; and it is with beating hearts that they pass on into the dark chamber where the mummy lies in its golden coffin.[14]

Although the aim of the exhibit was to create a replica of the entire tomb of Tutankhamun, in reality it was only possible to develop replicas based on objects excavated from the first room: the antechamber. At the time that the Wembley exhibition was being developed, this was the only part of the tomb that had been fully excavated.[15]

The absence of detailed images of the objects was a great challenge for the team. While Carter's excavation photographer, Harry Burton, had worked tirelessly taking detailed photographs of each of the objects, these images were not readily available beyond the permitted newspaper articles and features.[16] No full publication containing details and images from the tomb was yet forthcoming, and publicity was tightly controlled. All that Aumonier's team had as reference points were press photographs and sketches; while these were useful, accurate replication of the finer details of the objects was more difficult. Of course, this makes the quality and accuracy of the replicas even more impressive and is testament to the skill of both Weigall and the sculpting team.

'Wonderful Things' in Kingston upon Hull

The replicas took approximately eight months to make in a studio in central London. Aumonier was assisted by two of his sons along with up to twelve additional artists and craftsmen.[17] They required almost £1,000 worth of gold and gold leaf to give colour to certain replicas.[18] The organizers' intention was to create a replica tomb. Visitors would have the opportunity to enter and feel that they were re-enacting the 'wonderful' experience that Carter had described when he first gazed upon the contents of Tutankhamun's tomb in Egypt. Between April 1924 and its closure the next year it was one of the star attractions at the exhibition, with adults paying 1s 3d and children 8d for the privilege of admittance. Visitors entered through a white tent-like structure emblazoned with the words 'Tomb of Tut-ankh-Amen', which resembled the white cliffs found on the west bank of Luxor. They were then able to view the antechamber, in which the replicas were displayed, before continuing along a corridor to see the golden shine, unopened because, of course, the original shrine in Egypt was unexcavated at the time that the exhibition had been developed.[19] In order to ensure true 'authenticity',[20] visitors were guided by a gentleman dressed in a fez. Further additions of sand and even a camel completed the experience.

Shortly before the opening of the exhibition, Carter heard about the planned replica tomb. Far from being supportive of the effort, he instead filed a lawsuit to prevent its ever opening to the public. The lawsuit claimed that the replicas were a breach of copyright, based on the argument that they could not possibly have been created without access to restricted photographs of the originals. Furthermore, and somewhat contrarily, argued the lawsuit, the replicas were simply not very good. Despite Carter's efforts, his lawsuit proved unsuccessful and the replica tomb opened on schedule.[21]

After the exhibition

After the exhibition closed the replicas were put up for sale at auction, where they were bought by Albert Reckitt, a prominent Hull businessman. Reckitt was already aware of the work of Aumonier – including Aumonier's war memorial on Dansom Lane in Hull – and it was possible that this inspired him to buy the replicas.[22] Alternatively he could, like many others, have had an interest in the tomb of Tutankhamun and the culture of ancient Egypt. It may well have been a combination of the two. Regardless, Reckitt donated the replicas to the city of Hull in 1936, and they were originally displayed in the city's Mortimer Museum.[23] While a large number of objects in the Hull Museums collection were sadly destroyed in the bombings of the Second World War, the replicas survived[24] and eventually, following the creation of a museum in the Old Grammar School in Hull's Holy Trinity Square, they were installed in a permanent display in a first floor gallery where they remain to this day.

There are a range of objects represented by the replicas, including thrones, stools, beds, boxes and vases. Each object is a direct copy of an object that was excavated from the antechamber of Tutankhamun's tomb. Despite the challenges faced by the team – predominantly not having access to the objects themselves and having to work instead

Ancient Egypt in the Modern Imagination

from limited press photographs and sketches – the replicas are incredibly accurate both in their details and their colours. Paint and gold leaf have been used to pick out many of the details, often imitating other materials such as glass. In this chapter it is not possible to discuss every piece; thus, I turn to three objects in the collection that highlight the quality as well as some interesting physical details of the replicas.

The gold throne

One such piece is the gold throne (Fig. 1.1), the original of which was found beneath one of the large funerary couches in the antechamber, although whether this was its original position or if it had been moved there by ancient looters is uncertain.[25] It was made of wood overlaid with gold and inlaid with glass and faience. The replica is also made of wood, overlaid with gold leaf. The sides of the throne are carved into the shape of a winged uraeus.[26] On its head the cobra wears a double crown, which represents the kingship of both Upper and Lower Egypt. On the replica, the feathers that make up the

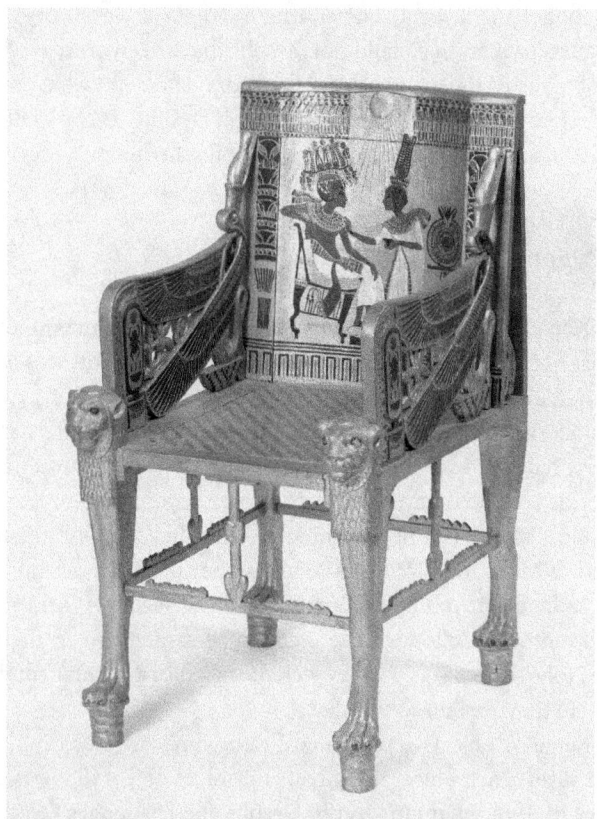

Figure 1.1 The Gold Throne. © Hands on History, Hull Museums.

wings are painted blue, each one picked out individually. This paint imitates the blue glass that was used to emphasize the feathers of the original throne. The feet of the chair are shaped as lions' feet, with the heads of the lions visible at the edge of the seat. Lions were also a symbol of Egyptian kingship: as the king of animals they represented power and strength and so were a suitable symbol for the pharaoh.

The backrest features a painted depiction of Tutankhamun himself, seated, with his wife, Ankhesenamun. Above them is a sun-disc, its rays stretching towards them. The sun-disc is a reminder of Tutankhamun's young life at Amarna, the capital city of the pharaoh Akhenaten. Instead of paying homage to the traditional gods of Egypt, Akhenaten placed focus on a single entity, the sun-disc (or Aten), which he worshipped as the only divine being.[27] The Aten was depicted in art as a sun-disc with its rays reaching down, often terminating in hands or ankh-signs. In fact, the object record cards written during the excavation of the tomb note that some of the cartouches on the throne actually contained Tutankhamun's childhood name – Tutankhaten, or 'Living image of the Aten' (thus linking him with the religion of Akhenaten) – instead of his new name, Tutankhamun, which honoured instead the god Amun ('Living image of Amun').[28] Others had been altered to read 'Tutankhamun', presumably from 'Tutankhaten'. This suggests that the chair was made in the early years of Tutankhamun's reign, before the state-led rejection of Akhenaten's religion of the Aten that began after Akhenaten's death. The depiction of the royal pair on the backrest of the replica is deeply evocative of the scene on the original throne, with details such as the cartouche and the crown of Tutankhamun – a triple *Atef*-crown, rams' horns, uraei and sun-discs[29] – rendered with great accuracy and skill. The chair reflects the wealth of the objects from the tomb of Tutankhamun and must have had a powerful effect on visitors to the 'tomb' at Wembley.

Significantly, the back of the throne is undecorated. This may, at first, seem strange given the effort that had been put into decorating its other parts. The original throne had an intricately decorated back, with four uraei with sun-discs atop their heads, texts and other decoration covering the bulk.[30] Yet if we consider how the replica throne was used, the reason becomes clear. Despite its obvious high quality, the throne was essentially part of a set. It was used to recreate the antechamber from Tutankhamun's tomb, thus giving visitors a sense of entering the place and re-tracing the steps of Carter himself. The replicas were not, however, accessible to visitors, who followed a set route and viewed them from designated spots. Some parts of the replicas, therefore, were presumably hidden from view (possibly as they were placed against another object or away from any of the viewpoints). Consequently, it had no effect on the visitors' experience if these hidden sides were left undecorated. It would therefore make sense, to reduce time and cost, to leave these parts bare. These objects were not created to be scientific replicas, or for research purposes, but were intended to populate a stage-set for a specific exhibition. While their accuracy was clearly of interest to those involved in making them – and their high quality attests to this – the necessity of limiting costs and of completing the replicas within a given timeframe may have led to corners being cut where these omissions would not negatively affect the experience of visitors to the exhibit. This object, therefore, highlights the care that was taken in creating the replicas but also the

Ancient Egypt in the Modern Imagination

fact that they were not intended to be scientifically accurate; they were, instead, part of a set and were treated as such. Their purpose was to impress and intrigue visitors who saw them at a set distance and from specific angles.

A footstool

The stool (Fig. 1.2) is a copy of one found opposite the doorway in the tomb's antechamber.[31] The original stool was made of ebony inlaid with ivory,[32] while the replica is made of wood painted to emulate the original materials. It is shaped in the style of a folding stool, although the seat appears to be rigid. The legs are carved in the shape of ducks' heads, a popular form for furniture. Using the same materials was not, therefore, a priority for the builders of the replicas; the focus was on the visual effect. The seat itself is covered in an asymmetrical pattern of cream marks on a black background, intended to represent leopard-skin, albeit in negative (leopard skin instead consisting of dark spots on a light background). By Tutankhamun's reign, leopards were no longer found in Egypt. They were, however, often included in tribute from foreign envoys – examples of which can be found in reliefs showing the presentation of tribute from foreign lands to Queen Hatshepsut[33] – and were a mark of wealth and power.

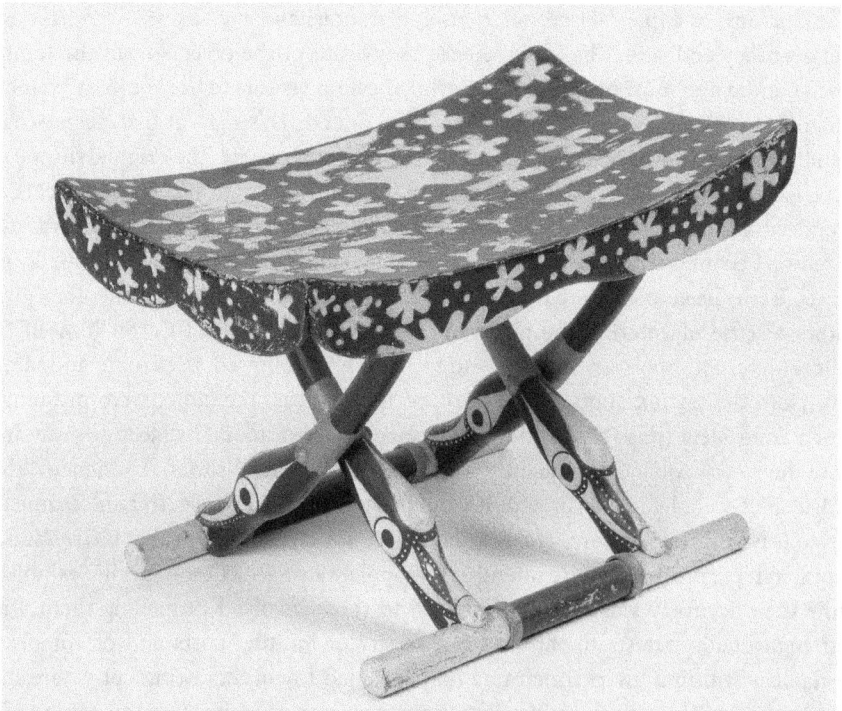

Figure 1.2 The Footstool. © Hands on History, Hull Museums.

Furthermore, leopard skin was symbolic of the role of a lector priest (or *Xry-Hb*), the man who was responsible, among other things, for reciting texts during the funerary rituals. For this reason, it was particularly suitable for inclusion in a royal tomb. It not only symbolized the place of the pharaoh as ruler of all the known world, and of the animals within it, but also linked with funerary ritual and recitation. This replica, therefore, allowed visitors to the British Empire Exhibition to encounter aspects of Egyptian culture and belief that may have otherwise remained unknown to them; while the replicas were included to create a visual effect, each one told its own story, although it is likely that the deeper symbolism would not have been recognized by many of the visitors to the Wembley tomb. This stool demonstrated the skill of the craftsmen who made the original, but it also represented specific funerary and ritual beliefs of the ancient Egyptians.

The original stool had a tail hanging down at one end, which increased its similarity to genuine leopard-skin.[34] One is left to question if there were originally paws protruding over the edges of the seat, which would have completed the picture. If this were the case, then they appear to have been removed by robbers. Interestingly, the tail has not been included on the replica. It is possible that the tail was not visible from the images that were available to Aumonier and his team. This again, reminds us that Aumonier was copying the replicas from photographs without ever having seen the original object. The replicas may be impressive copies of the originals, but some details are omitted. While in some cases omissions are intentional (in the case of the back of the throne), in this case, meanwhile, this appears to be an oversight, as a result of a lack of sufficient data to fully recreate the piece.

A golden shrine

A third object of interest in the collection is a replica of a shrine upon a sled (Fig. 1.3), also found in the antechamber, although the position is recorded in Carter's object cards simply as 'not original'.[35] The shrine, tall and narrow with a sloping roof, has two doors which were held closed by wooden pegs. The lintel above the doors is decorated with a winged sun-disc, while the jambs are covered in texts. Both the shrine and the sled are covered in gold leaf. The texts around the doors have been copied with a high level of accuracy on the replica, presumably testament to Weigall's guidance and the copying skill of the sculptors. However, the original shrine was also decorated with images incised in the gold leaf.[36] These images, found on each outer face of the shrine, showed various scenes of Tutankhamun; these include the king hunting, receiving offerings from the queen and scenes of libation. These scenes are not copied onto the replicas. Again, it is possible that they were not visible from the photographs, although the accuracy of the copied hieroglyphs suggests that at least some details of the shrine must have been available. Possibly, then, it was felt that the carved scenes would not be easily visible to those who viewed the replicas and so the time and funds needed to copy them would not have been the most valuable use of resources.

Ancient Egypt in the Modern Imagination

Figure 1.3 The Golden Shrine. © Hands on History, Hull Museums.

The inner floor of the original shrine was marked in such a way as to suggest that it originally held two small statues.[37] Additionally, a stand for one of these statuettes was found inside of the shrine, supporting the hypothesis that it originally contained such objects. The base of the stand is made of ebony, while the rest, like the shrine itself, consists of wood covered in gesso and gold leaf. Further objects found inside the shrine included a necklace and pendant depicting a deity in the form of a snake, as well as parts of a collar and corselet.[38] Clearly the shrine had been entered by thieves in antiquity, who removed the statues and damaged other objects. The replica shrine does not contain any such objects, or even a representation of the statues that would once had stood within it, as the shrine was displayed with its doors closed, so any objects within would not have been seen by visitors.

These three replicas, therefore, highlight various aspects which are pertinent to the discussion of replicas and copies more generally. They were created for a specific purpose and were made to fulfil this. The emphasis was on the visual, rather than on exact replication and, for this reason, certain decisions were made regarding decoration and materials; painted wood was substituted for ivory and some surfaces were left undecorated. This does not mean that attempts were not made to faithfully copy the originals when it was considered worthwhile to do so; the detailed hieroglyphs on the golden shrine demonstrate this. Furthermore, the focus on creating a 'scene' does not

'Wonderful Things' in Kingston upon Hull

preclude the replicas from playing an important role in introducing Egyptian culture to a new audience; the details in the objects, such as the leopard print on the stool or the winged uraeus on the throne, gave visitors a rich sense of the beliefs and iconography of the ancient Egyptians.

Replicas and copies

This case study questions the role of replica objects in displays, museums and on archaeological sites. The role of such objects can be usefully divided into two categories: replicas that are created for research and scientific interest, and those that are developed for visitor experience. As already noted, the Tutankhamun replicas were developed specifically for visitors to an exhibit. They were not intended to be exact scientific replicas, although their accuracy – in terms of what could be seen – was important to ensure authenticity for those who visited the display. For this reason, here I examine only the importance of replicas for display purposes.

Replicas, in this instance, take the place of the real object in the context of the display. Ideally, they give visitors a sense of the genuine article by imitating its size, materials and design. Many of the dinosaurs displayed at the Natural History Museum in London, for example, are in fact casts of originals. This use of replicas, made necessary by incomplete original specimens and conservation needs, does not dull the excitement of visitors as they encounter dinosaur skeletons that tower over them.[39] Indeed, as Rosmarie Beier de Haan observes, replicas – frequently in the form of casts – in the nineteenth century were often viewed not as lesser copies, but as representing an appreciation of the artistic qualities of sculpture; it was the artistic merit and not the authenticity of the object that was of interest.[40] This attitude, she claims, survived after the Victorian era drew to a close. Perhaps, therefore, for visitors to the Wembley tomb, the replicas elicited the same aesthetic appreciation that the originals would have done.

It is important, at this stage, to consider what constitutes a replica. Presumably a modern copy of a historical or archaeological object can be classified as such; it is a separate object, most often made by different individuals and perhaps consisting of different raw materials. But what happens when an object consists of sections of the original pieces augmented with new parts? How much of an object can be replaced before it is termed a 'replica'?[41] While this does not apply to the Tutankhamun replicas, this issue is a significant one in the broader context of ancient Egyptian objects in the modern world. Many Egyptian temples contain areas that have been reconstructed in modern times alongside sections that have survived intact from ancient times. Furthermore, some temples have been entirely reconstructed. One such example is Abu Simbel, an iconic Egyptian temple in southern Egypt. The entire temple complex was dug up in the 1960s – as part of a mission to rescue sites that would be flooded by the new Aswan Dam – and moved upstream, where it was rebuilt brick by brick. So, while it consists of ancient stones carved thousands of years ago, the temple, as it stands today, was therefore technically 'built' by modern hands. Furthermore, the tomb of Horemheb

23

at Saqqara – close to modern Cairo – contains stelae and doorjambs as part of its decoration. Some of these, however, are copies, the originals actually being housed in the British Museum;[42] they are, to all intents and purposes, modern replicas.[43] Whether such sites are not perceived as less authentic, through being augmented, moved or even created by modern hands is dependent on the individual viewer.[44] It would seem that to most, however, both proximity to the historical or archaeological context and ancient manufacture both lend an air of authenticity to objects, though it is not vital for both of these criteria to be fulfilled in order for visitors to view artefacts as 'real'. Perhaps it is for this reason that outside the Wembley tomb, sand and camels were laid out to set the scene: mimicking the archaeological context in which the tomb was discovered as well as the tomb itself, significant in creating a more authentic experience.

This leaves open for discussion those objects that are both modern *and* displayed away from the context of the original (despite, in the case of the Tutankhamun replicas, some contextual 'dressing'). What is their purpose? This next section discusses replicas which have been created entirely in modern times[45] and are displayed away from the context of the original, as exemplified by the Tutankhamun replicas, reflecting on the inspiration behind such projects, and their effect on visitors. There are three main motivations behind the development of such replicas: access, conservation and, arguably, income.[46]

The role of replicas

Replicas can play a central role in providing or enhancing access to objects that, for various reasons, would otherwise be restricted. These restrictions can either be due to the needs of the objects themselves, or to their physical distance from audiences.

Physical distance is of particular relevance when looking at the Tutankhamun tomb replicas. The majority of those who visited the Wembley tomb would have been unable to travel to Egypt to see the original; even if the distance and related cost of travel was itself manageable, access to the tomb was strictly controlled during the decade of excavation. For these people, therefore, the Wembley exhibit was their only opportunity to 'experience' the wonders of an Egyptian tomb and of the treasures buried within. The replica tomb, therefore, provided access for a far wider cross-section of society than would otherwise have been the case. Of course, we should not assume that this was a main aim of the exhibit which was, in all likelihood, focused more on profit than philanthropy. Today, however, social inclusion and diversity are two key aims in museums' work. Providing access to objects and stories for those who have experienced barriers to access is increasingly prioritized; such barriers might include financial restrictions, social barriers and disabilities. Including replica objects within museum displays places them in an accessible space, thus potentially helping to overcome such barriers.

Additional factors can prevent individuals from accessing sites and objects. Hundreds of sites are currently located in unsafe areas, or in warzones, and are, therefore, inaccessible. Sites in Syria and Iraq, for example, are deemed unsafe for travel due to sectarian violence. In Egypt itself, the UK Government advises against travel to parts of the Sinai Peninsula, which includes St. Catherine's Monastery. Similar situations are found across the globe, making large amounts of heritage and culture inaccessible at any given time. Perhaps, then, replicas can provide at least some access to these sites, and their histories, until such a time as they become physically accessible again.

The physical accessibility of objects is also important when looking at the postcolonial legacy of exploration and excavation. While the furniture from Tutankhamun's tomb remained in Egypt, many objects that had been excavated in Egypt in the late nineteenth and early twentieth centuries were shipped back to colonial powers, in particular Britain, France and Germany, as well as the United States; this has left gaps at Egyptian archaeological sites. The Eighteenth Dynasty tomb of Horemheb at Saqqara, for example, originally contained standing stelae which were transported to the British Museum for display. While the original objects remain in London, replica stelae have been created and erected at the site in Egypt. In this way, the site has retained its original character despite the historical loss of some of its architecture. While the use of replicas has solved a practical problem, namely that the originals are not available, this does not mean that some visitors' experiences of the site are not altered because of this loss of original architecture. Although the relatively small size of the stelae in the tomb likely means that that the effect for most visitors is minimal, it does not reduce ethical questions surrounding collecting in the colonial era.

An arguably similar, although less controversial, approach to collecting can also be found closer to home. In Hull's archaeology museum there are replicas of the Folkton Drums – three unique chalk 'drums' which were found in the tomb of a child, dating to the Neolithic period, near Folkton in North Yorkshire.[47] After their excavation in the late nineteenth century they, too, were transported to London where they have remained. While the original objects cannot be displayed in Yorkshire, the replicas ensure that their story is accessible to the communities for whom the drums represent part of their own local culture. While not relating to the ancient history of Hull, the Tutankhamun replicas have also become a part of the city's heritage. Their connection to Albert Reckitt and, through him, the local Reckitt business, gives them an intrinsic link with the community, while their prominent display in Hull Museums has made them a much-loved part of local culture.

The creation of replicas can also help with the long-term conservation of objects (or sites) by reducing the need for visitors to access the original. Archaeological sites, while having often survived for thousands of years, are susceptible to atmospheric changes caused by visitors. Replicas, therefore, can allow tourists to experience the 'site' without causing further damage to the original. The Lascaux Caves in France, for example, contain numerous prehistoric paintings, one of the earliest and finest examples of the art of early humans; the high numbers of tourists visiting the site after its opening to the public in 1948, however, risked causing serious damage to the paintings due to the resulting changes in heat, air humidity, carbon dioxide levels and other similar effects. Consequently, a replica cave was created to showcase some of the paintings and the original site was closed to visitors. The replica site has proven very popular, so much so that similar damage has now been recorded at the replica cave, which has led to the need to develop further replicas.

Similarly, a replica of the tomb of Tutankhamun itself was opened recently in 2014. Again, the long-term effects of high tourist numbers at the original tomb were potentially damaging to the paintings, and so the tomb was laser scanned in high detail and an exact replica created. Although the original tomb has remained open, tourists are encouraged to visit the replica instead. By situating it next to Carter's house – and including entrance to the tomb in the ticket price – the Antiquities Service has endeavoured to develop an appealing attraction, which focuses on the history of the excavation of the tomb as well as the replica itself. Panels attached to the walls of the replica tomb offer information about the excavation of the original. This provides visitors with an experience that does not simply replicate that of visiting the original tomb, but enhances it, inviting tourists to expand their understanding of the site in ways that are not possible at the ancient site. Replicas, therefore, do not have to be mere duplicates, but can provide new and enhanced experiences, in part *because* they are copies; as such, they are not necessarily restricted by conservation and heritage concerns in the same way that the genuine artefact or site might be.

While the Wembley exhibit was not developed for these reasons, one must question if attractions such as this, which show the tomb as it was before it was emptied of its treasures, might provide a suitably appealing alternative to original tombs so as to reduce tourist numbers to the Valley of the Kings, without the corresponding loss of revenue, and help with the long-term conservation of the site. The Tate's recent reconstruction of Modigliani's studio demonstrates the public interest in this approach; the popular exhibit provides visitors with a virtual reality visit to the artist's workroom which has been carefully reconstructed based on detailed research.[48] This example is not physical but digital, however; visitors access it via a virtual reality headset. Perhaps, therefore, physical reconstructions may well be increasingly replaced by digital ones, thus reducing the spatial requirements for such ventures and allowing for experiences to be more flexible, and more easily updated, in terms of content.

A final consideration, and one that is clearly relevant in the case of the Wembley replicas, is income generation. The Wembley tomb charged an entrance fee (close to a couple of pounds in today's money), thus using the fame and intrigue of Tutankhamun to raise income. While many modern museums in the UK do not charge entry fees, they rely on visitor figures both to advocate for public funding and to boost sales in shops and cafés. Highlight objects, whether genuine or replica, therefore, can help with this. Hull Museums has its own Rosetta Stone replica which stands in the Egyptian gallery alongside the Wembley replicas, perhaps to further increase the appeal of the gallery by showcasing objects with which potential visitors are familiar. Replicas can help to fill gaps in displays, act as a highlight object to advertise galleries or provide a focus for displays. While the object itself may be a replica, the stories it tells are as real as those of the original.

Replicas or copies?

Given that there are multiple motivations for developing replicas of historical and archaeological objects, are these replicas simply shadows of the original, copies of real objects? As Beier de Haan asks, 'Is the copy the "poor sister" of the resplendent original?'[49] One could argue that the replicas for sale in the shops of so many museums fall into this category. Walter Benjamin writes that

> the authenticity of a thing is the quintessence of all that is transmissible in it from its origin on, ranging from its physical duration to the historical testimony relating to it. Since the historical testimony is founded on the physical duration, the former, too, is jeopardized by reproduction, in which the physical duration plays no part.[50]

This would reduce any replica to a lesser copy of a unique original, lacking in the authenticity which is founded in its history as an object. While the original object may be hundreds, if not thousands, of years old – Tutankhamun's tomb had been hidden for more than 3,000 years at the time of its rediscovery – replicas are often comparatively recent. The paint on the Wembley replicas barely had time to dry before they were displayed. How, then, can they hope to evoke the same sense of wonder as those objects that have survived the test of time? Surely it is this idea of building a bridge across time that contributes to ancient objects' appeal; this is something that replicas simply cannot do. As Benjamin observes, 'In even the most perfect reproduction, one thing is lacking: the here and now of the work of art – its unique existence in a particular place.'[51]

Yet, surely some distinction should be made between mass-produced objects doled out to sites and museums simply for their aesthetic value, such as those often sold in gift shops, and those objects made by skilled artists for a specific purpose. Anthony Hughes reminds us that even so-called original sculpture can vary in its integrity; while Michelangelo's *Atlas Slave* stands as a unique original, emphasized by its unfinished nature, Rodin's *La Pensée* (*Thought*) was originally created by the artist in clay and then carved by a stonemason.[52] Equally Rodin's *Le Penseur* (*The Thinker*), bronze versions of which can be found in several galleries across the globe, surely cannot be seen as one unique piece. While commonly considered as original sculptures, these pieces could, in fact, be viewed as copies of a concept conceived by Rodin and then recreated in another form. Such practice stands in stark contrast to Michelangelo's single carved example of *Atlas Slave*. Where, then, should the line between 'original' and 'replica' be drawn? Can such a line be clearly marked? While some pieces may clearly be designated as replicas or copies, others may be open to more scrutiny.

Ultimately, replicas can still conjure up narratives about original objects – and the related cultures – to be re-imagined in a heritage or museum setting. The history of the original still exists (and is still evoked) even if the object is a copy. Hillel Schwartz even suggests that it is possible to remove the original entirely and yet retain its essence in the duplicate item.[53] Replicas are not simply static objects. They are intricately linked with the original, referring to a common history. Furthermore, replicas are objects in their own right, with their own histories. The display of the replica throne in Hands on History, for example, acknowledges and encourages the contemplation of its own story, the unfinished back of the throne inviting consideration of its original purpose, rather than being hidden from visitors so all that they can see are the lavishly decorated aspects.

Ancient Egypt in the Modern Imagination

The aim of this chapter has been to establish the story of the Wembley Tutankhamun replicas, demonstrating their interest as copies of the original objects, but also as historical objects themselves. Their relevance in understanding British culture and society of the post-war period, their links with the rise of Tutmania following the excavation of the pharaoh's tomb[54] and their importance as examples of high quality sculpture make them important artefacts and not simply copies. We should, therefore, stop looking at replicas such as those found in Hull as lesser versions of original objects and, instead, as re-imagined objects in their own right, that enhance existing stories but that also tell stories of their own. Not only do they evoke the ancient world in which Tutankhamun lived, and the momentous opening of his tomb by Carter following the discovery of its steps by an Egyptian member of his team, they evoke a narrative of twentieth-century manufacture, local history, and invite questions as to the place of the replica in the modern museum both now and in the future.

CHAPTER 2
'LET SLEEPING SCARABS ALONE': WHEN EGYPT CAME TO STONEHENGE
Martyn Barber

Ancient Egypt is well-trodden ground as far as the world of pseudo-archaeology is concerned. In particular, much has been written over the last few centuries exploring the possibility that Egyptians actually set foot in prehistoric Britain – that the builders of the pyramids had some connection with the builders of Stonehenge.[1] As a body of work, there is a distinct lack of consistency and coherence; recent books on this theme pay little or no attention to previous writers, while establishing a demonstrable connection with available and current archaeological evidence seldom seems of any great concern. In fact, arguing against perceived current archaeological orthodoxy is a more typical standpoint.

Archaeologists today rarely pay much attention to this literature, but for a few years in the early twentieth century, mainstream archaeology in Britain openly flirted with one particular set of ideas that offered a connection between ancient Egypt and prehistoric Britain, ideas that saw Egypt as the sole source of civilization in the ancient world and consequently saw a direct Egyptian influence on key developments in the Neolithic of the British Isles. These ideas are today considered, at best, unorthodox – as pseudoscience, even – but they nonetheless influenced processes of knowledge creation about the distant past. Beginning around 1911, the theory that key social, cultural and technological innovations had a single source of origin in ancient Egyptians both appealed and appalled, but by the late 1920s there were few archaeologists seemingly willing to support it, although ironically it was at that point that it was threatening to gain wider public attention and acceptance.

Around this time, a pair of Egyptian artefacts came to archaeological attention, one of them found very close to Stonehenge. They were quickly dismissed as fakes and appear not to have been mentioned in print for over eighty years. However, correspondence relating to investigations into their authenticity highlights some problems in regarding the whole debate about Egypt as the source of key developments in prehistory as an aberration of little relevance to contemporary and later archaeological practice. The possibility that these objects were genuine antiquities that had arrived in the British Isles in prehistory attracted the attention of individuals on both sides of the argument. The lines drawn between archaeology and pseudo-archaeology by subsequent historians of the discipline were far more permeable than is often claimed.

Ancient Egypt in the Modern Imagination

Introducing the scarabs

In the autumn of 1928, two Egyptian limestone scarabs, both inscribed with the cartouche of Tuthmosis III, were found in Wiltshire within a few weeks and a few miles of each other. One of them was reportedly discovered at a spot in or near the small town of Ludgershall on the eastern edge of the county, close to the border with Hampshire. The other was apparently picked up just a few hundred yards west of Stonehenge. Accounts of both scarabs, detailing the circumstances of their discovery and discussing matters of authenticity, were published a few years later. The first, in *Man*, the journal of the Royal Anthropological Society, appeared in 1935, while a considerably more detailed treatment was printed the following year in the *Wiltshire Archaeological and Natural History Magazine*, the annual journal of the Wiltshire Archaeological Society.[2] There appears to be no subsequent published discussion of either object.

Both scarabs were deposited with Wiltshire museums in 1935. The curators' concerns over their provenance, circumstances of discovery, authenticity and especially ownership mean that a quantity of correspondence also found its way to these museums.[3] The two published articles appeared to offer the final word on both objects, the second article in particular combining considerable detail from intensive investigation, including the questioning of the finders, eye-witnesses and others connected to the discoveries, as well as examination of the reported findspots and the soliciting of expert opinion on the scarabs themselves. However, while the presentation of accumulated detail appears persuasive, the surviving correspondence highlights problems with much of that detail.

Neither of the published articles offers much in the way of reflection on one key question: how the scarabs came to be in Wiltshire, at their respective findspots, in the first place. Both discoveries occurred at an interesting time in terms of contemporary acceptance of possible direct connections between ancient Egypt and prehistoric Britain. Although by 1936 it was believed by most (though not all) of those involved that the scarabs were of recent date, manufactured perhaps in the nineteenth century AD in Egypt for sale to tourists, responses to their discovery both before and after confirmation that they were not antiquities throws some intriguing light on attitudes towards the idea of Egyptian influence on developments in British prehistory. Individuals who are generally acknowledged to have been opposed to the notion of direct Egyptian involvement in key sociocultural innovations in the British Neolithic were nonetheless interested in the possibility that these scarabs had arrived in the British Isles in antiquity.

Ancient Egypt and prehistoric Britain

The idea that ancient Egyptians may have set foot in prehistoric Britain was hardly new, but the so-called hyperdiffusionists – Grafton Elliot Smith, William J. Perry, W. H. R. Rivers and their followers[4] – paid little attention to existing literature in bringing their ideas to an academic, as well as a wider public, audience.[5] It is not necessary to summarize those ideas in any detail here – there are plenty of recent and not-so-recent accounts of the inception, reception and rejection of their brand of diffusion – but particularly pertinent here is Adam Stout's account in his book *Creating Prehistory* (2008), set as it is within a discussion of the growing institutionalization and professionalization of British archaeology, and particularly prehistory, between the two world wars.[6]

While the hyperdiffusionist thesis is often reduced to the idea that civilization arose within, and spread out from, a single source – ancient Egypt – the fifteen or so years that these ideas were a focus of academic debate saw important developments in their efforts to explain the causes of both the rise and diffusion of civilization. The First World War – and especially Smith's and Rivers's experiences of treating victims of shell-shock at Maghull – was particularly significant. As Stout observes, the idea of civilization spreading from a single centre was 'the least interesting aspect of their argument. To them, civilisation was very much a mixed blessing, driven by warfare and imposed by a warrior elite on a humanity that was otherwise peaceful'.[7] Their central argument, Stout shows, '[i]s not the detailed process of culture change outlined in their vulnerable conjectural history, but the notion that civilization was imposed by force of arms upon a species that was essentially peaceful by nature.'[8]

The story of the 'Children of the Sun', as Perry labelled them, began with Smith's studies of excavated mummies in Egypt, and his growing belief that mummification practices encountered elsewhere in the world – notably an example from the Torres Straits – were too close in detail and presumed practice to represent anything other than direct Egyptian influence. Meanwhile, Perry's analyses of the geographical distributions of particular phenomena, especially an apparent correlation between the locations of megalithic tombs and the presence of metal ores, offered the basis of an explanation. The development in ancient Egypt of ideas about the afterlife and, importantly, how to ensure a successful passage to it, prompted widespread and ultimately near-global exploration in search of the raw materials – the 'givers of life' – essential to the process, the explorers imposing 'civilisation' on those they encountered.

The archaeological details of their conjectural history were indeed vulnerable, and major weaknesses were highlighted at the time. However, the broad thesis of diffusion from Egypt proved attractive to some at least. Diffusion of a less extreme kind was already accepted as a key component of culture change, and would continue to be so for some time. 'Hyperdiffusion' was coined as a pejorative term by British prehistorian Glyn Daniel in the 1950s, partly to distinguish the ideas of Smith and his colleagues from more orthodox positions, such as his own.[9] Daniel's own studies, from the late 1930s onwards, of megalithic tombs across Europe relied heavily on a diffusionist framework to explain key aspects of their evolution and distribution, and although he occasionally looked somewhat vaguely to the 'eastern Mediterranean' for influential developments, he saw no role for Egypt. Smith and Perry, of course, had placed Egypt at the head of their evolutionary scheme for the development of megalithic forms, arguing that what was widely considered the earliest megalithic tomb type – the dolmen – was ultimately derived from the Egyptian mastaba.[10]

As Stout records, a key archaeological objection came in 1924 in the form of a review by O. G. S. Crawford of several recent publications from Smith and his colleagues.[11]

Writing for the *Edinburgh Review*, Crawford described them as 'a band of scientific adventurers ... skirmishing over regions of the past', but attacked them over what was for him relatively firm ground.[12] The question of the innate peacefulness of pre-megalithic populations, and the warlike nature of their civilized subjugators, was barely acknowledged. Crawford's ire was piqued in particular by Perry's use of essentially geographical techniques to establish his arguments. In fact, in *The Children of the Sun*, Perry explicitly rejected a key element of Crawford's own vision of prehistory:

> in dealing with the problem of the distribution of the various forms of culture, and particularly with the settlements of the archaic civilization itself, I urge that the important factor is the human mind with its desires and aims. Men in the past have imposed their will on their surroundings, and have not been forced by them into any line of action. Given certain desires, men will do their utmost to satisfy them, and it is to this dynamic attitude that is attributed the development and spread of the archaic civilization. This will hardly tally with the commonly accepted doctrines of the modern school of geographers, who appear, explicitly or implicitly, to ascribe such importance to 'Geographic Control' as a causative factor in the development of various forms of human culture, instead of looking at these phenomena as the outcome of processes at work in society itself.[13]

He insisted that

> The views advanced here, if correct, serve to establish a continuity in human society from the very earliest stages, so that, from the days of palaeolithic man settlement has been made in certain localities because men chose to live there, and not because they were forced to do so by the climate or some other geographical cause.[14]

In contrast, for Crawford, from the earliest times, the natural environment presented a strong influence on human society and culture: 'primitive man selected those regions which were free from dense forest and marsh and which also provided good open pasture land to graze his flocks and herds upon'.[15] He viewed the 'history of civilization' as 'the history of the gradual reversal of man's place in nature',[16] the gradual 'wane of the influence of environment on man, and the growth of his control over the environment'.[17] When Perry wrote dismissively of the 'modern school of geographers' who ascribed such significance to 'Geographic Control', he was effectively dismissing the ideas of the geographers – Crawford, Herbert Fleure, Harold Peake and others – responsible for introducing and developing such geographical approaches to the study of prehistory.[18]

It was, nonetheless, that geographical approach that held sway among prehistorians, underpinning landmark studies such as Cyril Fox's *The Personality of Britain* (1932), and it was to be some time before the underlying ideas began to be questioned either on theoretical or empirical grounds. Meanwhile, as the academic support that had existed for 'hyperdiffusionism' waned, its public profile continued to rise partly through the publications of Smith and Perry – both of whom wrote books for a general audience – but perhaps most notably through the work of the writer H. W. Massingham, who spent several years in the mid-1920s as a research assistant to Smith and Perry.[19] In 1926 he published *Downland Man*, a detailed exploration of Egyptian influence on Neolithic Britain. Massingham's reputation and ability as a writer meant that *Downland Man* attracted an audience far beyond that which his more orthodox archaeological contemporaries could reach.

Into the 1930s, however, even the public audience was dwindling. Academically, few archaeologists or anthropologists were willing to follow Smith and Perry any further, the field being left, in the main, to a handful of followers and outsiders. One particularly prolific individual was J. Rendel Harris, a retired biblical scholar of note who had first encountered Smith and Perry by March 1916 at the latest.[20] By the mid-1920s, now retired, he turned his attention to the issue of cultural migration in prehistory, producing books such as *The Builders of Stonehenge* (1932) in which he argued that Stonehenge was a monument built to both Osiris and Ra, and offered detailed etymological argument for its proposed architect, Merlin, also being Egyptian.[21] Following Smith and Perry, he accepted ancient Egypt as the source of civilization. His favoured form of evidence was different to theirs, but fully in keeping with his philological approach to biblical studies: he focused on place-names. However, his approach was somewhat idiosyncratic – overly simplistic, in fact – with a heavy reliance on simple phonetic resemblances between ancient Egyptian and modern British place-names rather than any detailed analysis of their respective origins and development. Perhaps the best example of this somewhat unscientific approach is his discussions of occurrences of the place-name 'Egypt' in England.[22]

Harris published prolifically on the subject from the mid-1920s for around a decade before old age and blindness slowed him down. He died in 1941. He inspired a small but enthusiastic band of followers, however, the most prominent of which was one Pierre Louis Collignon. Collignon, influenced by the discovery of faience beads in British barrows – 'clearly of Mediterranean origin and similar, in fact very similar, to some found in Egypt' – developed a theory that there had been:

> in remote times what I called a Masonic civilization without which culture could not have spread as it did. It must have had initiation ceremonies, high Secrets, which were learned at progressive degrees of initiation, and those secrets of the Masonic craft must have included a high degree of mathematical knowledge, including geometry, astronomies, and, above all, building and architecture. I was sure that Stonehenge was of Egyptian origin.[23]

Enthusiastically combining Harris's prolific output with his own researches, Collignon ultimately began contributing articles in the late 1940s for the journal *Atlantean Research*, in which he wrote at length about Harris's work while also – as his choice of vehicle for publication suggests – contemplating the idea that Egypt may not have been the original source of civilization after all. By now, clearly, there was little common ground at all between orthodox archaeology and those who championed a direct Egyptian influence on British prehistory.

The scarabs: Discovery and investigation

Investigation into the scarabs occurred mainly at the instigation of George Engleheart (1851–1936). Engleheart had been vicar of Chute Forest, on the borders of Hampshire and Wiltshire, during the final decades of the nineteenth century before converting to Catholicism. Following a move to Dainton near Salisbury in 1901, he appears to have devoted much of his time to two particular interests: horticulture and archaeology. He became heavily involved with the Wiltshire Archaeological and Natural History Society, and was also Wiltshire secretary of the Society of Antiquaries.[24]

The scarabs were brought to his attention in 1930 by Mr W. E. Wright, 'a personal friend of my own'.[25] Wright was a school inspector who had 'endeavoured to interest the masters and pupils of Wiltshire village schools in objects such as flint implements, fossils, coins, etc., picked up locally'.[26] The Stonehenge scarab had been spotted on 2 December 1929 during a visit by Wright and his colleague Dr J. Leicester to Shrewton School. The second scarab was collected from Ludgershall School on 16 July 1930, Wright being accompanied on that occasion by a Mr E. J. Walsh.

The surviving correspondence in Salisbury Museum suggests that between 1930 and 1935 Engleheart, by now an octogenarian and suffering bouts of ill-health and restricted mobility, made several attempts to investigate the circumstances of discovery of both scarabs, apparently in the hope that they were genuine antiquities that had reached their respective findspots in the prehistoric rather than recent past. By late 1934 he had met someone willing and able to undertake a far more detailed and intensive investigation than he himself could manage: Pierre Louis Collignon.

Collignon (1896–1952) had enlisted in 1917, serving the final stages of the First World War in the Labour Corps.[27] After the war, he headed to Keble College, Oxford, taking the shortened degree course in history offered to former servicemen. College records suggest that he was not regarded as ideal student material on arrival, but improved considerably over the two years he was there. In 1921, he left Keble for Witney, Oxfordshire and a post as a schoolmaster at the boys' grammar school there, but by the late 1920s he was undertaking doctoral research at University College, London under the supervision of W. J. Perry. His thesis, on 'The Ritual Significance of Water', was submitted in June 1929 and was essentially concerned with 'the nature of magico-religious beliefs' with respect to 'water and other liquids', which he suggested were of the greatest importance in magical and religious rites. His study focused on ancient Egypt, but his overall approach owed more to Frazer and Tylor than to Smith and Perry, essentially offering a comparative study of literature and inscriptions that drew on Egyptian belief systems to illustrate the rites and beliefs of other cultures rather than simply seeing Egypt as their ultimate source.[28]

After submitting his thesis, he seems to have returned to full-time teaching at Witney. He also began his own programme of research investigating reported discoveries of ancient Egyptian objects in the British Isles.[29] The lack of any unequivocal examples of Egyptian material culture from prehistoric Britain was a common objection to Smith's and Perry's theories, so Collignon's research may have begun as an effort to address this. However, he eventually concluded that there were no such finds. It may have been this lack of material evidence that led him to Harris and his place-name studies.

Collignon seems to have come to Engleheart's attention after contacting Devizes Museum for information on any Egyptian antiquities with a claimed British provenance in their collections. Engleheart was certainly impressed with his efforts, initially at least: 'It is the most thorough piece of work I've ever come across', he wrote to O. G. S. Crawford:

> he ought to be retained at a large salary by Scotland Yard or the combined archaeological authorities as a sleuthhound. He is a curious personality; he started writing to me as one of the 'Egyptian' cranks, but is quite teachable. He offered to take the scarab business … off my hands: he came here and I took quite a liking to him.[30]

Collignon spent several days in January 1935 visiting the findspots and meeting or corresponding with as many individuals connected to both discoveries as possible. Engleheart left much of Collignon's research out of the *Man* article, but Collignon's report was included in full in the following year's *Wiltshire Archaeological Magazine* article, compiled after Engleheart's death.

The Stonehenge scarab

According to Engleheart's account in *Man*, the Stonehenge scarab (Fig. 2.1) was found by 'A lad who had lately left Shrewton School … [while] employed on the demolition of the Stonehenge Aerodrome.'[31] There had been an active military aerodrome adjacent to Stonehenge between late 1917 and early 1921, although the subsequent removal of hangars and other buildings dragged on well into the 1930s (Fig. 2.2).[32] Apparently, while

> filling up a deep foundation-trench in October 1928, he saw, protruding from the spoil heap excavated from it when the aerodrome was built, a scarab. Thinking it was some form of 'Shepherd's Crown' fossil he sent it by his brother to Shrewton School where it lay unnoticed among other odds and ends on a shelf.[33]

Engleheart's account in the following year's *Wiltshire Archaeological Magazine* article was slightly different. This time the lad, named as Charles Palmer, had been 'engaged in removing (blasting out) foundations of the derelict aerodrome close to Stonehenge'.[34] The scarab was apparently 'thrown up from the bottom of the trench sunk for foundations before the building or occupation of the aerodrome'.[35]

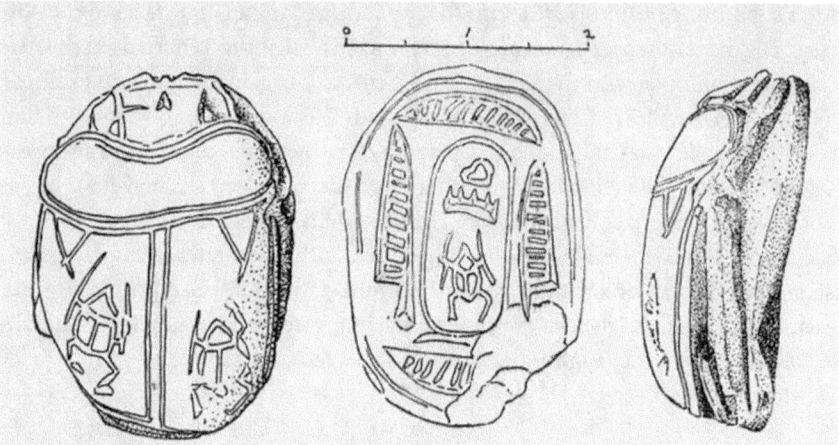

Figure 2.1 The scarab from Stonehenge Aerodrome. Line drawings by R. S. Newall originally published in Engleheart & Collignon 1936.

Figure 2.2 Aerial view of Stonehenge and the First World War aerodrome, the latter in the process of being dismantled. The photograph was taken on 12 July 1928, two months before the scarab was found, almost certainly on the site of the hangar seen at the top of the photograph. CCC 11796/4519, reproduced by permission of the Historic England Archive.

Engleheart's revised version appears to have been based on the outcome of Collignon's investigation. Collignon had visited Shrewton on 8 January 1935, when he spoke to Palmer, now twenty-four years old and working as a farm labourer. Palmer

> told me that towards the end of 1928, about October, he was temporarily employed on blasting out the foundations of the aerodrome. After one explosion he watched the debris falling and caught sight of the scarab ... lying among it. It was, he said, thickly coated with chalk, and it was a wonder that he noticed it at all. He took it home, where he scrubbed it and scraped it.[36]

Collignon accepted this version of events, although the correspondence in Salisbury Museum highlights some problems. In a letter written to Engleheart in 1933, Wright pointed out that 'the youth has little definite mental record of the find, particularly as the schoolmaster seems to have taken no special notice of it at the time and merely dumped it with a motley collection of flints and "Shepherd's Crowns".'[37] This issue – of pursuing details of an event that none thought particularly significant at the time – may account for the variations between the 1935 and 1936 articles, or, in other words, between the story told to Collignon in 1935 and the version originally given five years earlier. However, Collignon himself reported different versions of what Palmer told him. For example, in a note dated 10 January 1935 – two days after Collignon met with Palmer – Collignon wrote that: 'After an explosion [Palmer] saw the scarab lying among the debris. It was thinly covered with chalk, indicating that it had been blown out of the ground.'[38] An additional (albeit unsigned) note, dated to 6 June 1935, states that Palmer found the scarab while shovelling rubble back into the foundation trenches.[39]

Collignon also visited the findspot on 8 January 1935, following Palmer's directions. According to Collignon, the aerodrome 'was on the south side of the road running between Stonehenge and the barrows on Normanton Down'.[40] In fact, the building foundations being dynamited in 1928 were the other side of the road, so Collignon investigated the wrong site. South of the road, he 'found the surface soil to be about eight inches deep, and beneath it a fine dusty chalk which cakes in the manner described by Palmer'.[41]

The Ludgershall scarab

The other scarab presents more problems. Between its sighting in Ludgershall School in 1930 and the publication of Collignon's investigation in 1936, almost every detail surrounding its discovery and subsequent passage to the classroom changed at least once. In 1930, the finder insisted that he had picked it up in Collingbourne Wood, a little to the north of Ludgershall, and even showed people the actual spot. By 1935 he was equally insistent that it had been found somewhere else.

Engleheart's brief account in *Man* stated that the scarab (Fig. 2.3) had 'been unearthed by a boy ferreting for rabbits in Collingbourne Wood ... in October 1928, nearly 3 feet deep in black soil, which adhered to it when found'.[42] However, 'The boy's story was

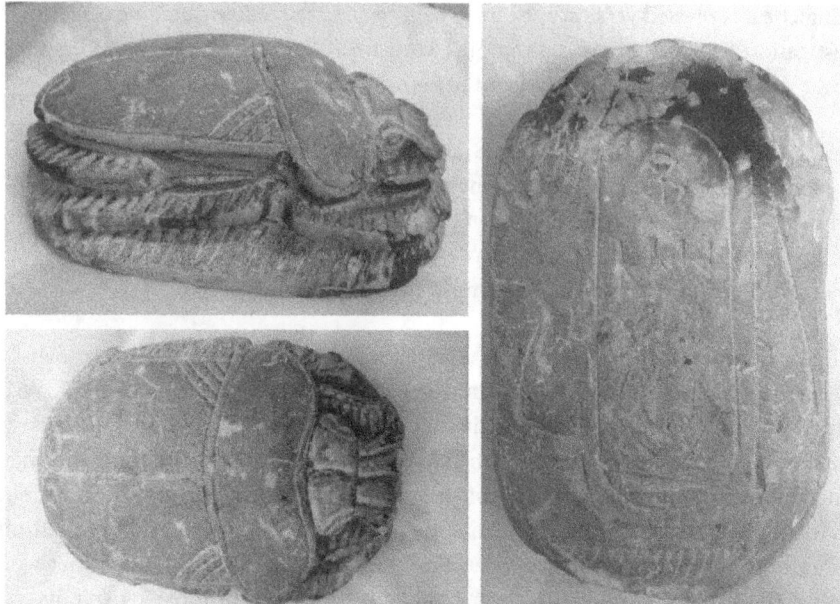

Figure 2.3 The scarab from Collingbourne Wood (or Ludgershall). Salisbury Museum acc. no. 1935/31 ('On deposit from Mr James'. Max. length 107 mm, max. height 37 mm). Reproduced by permission of Salisbury Museum.

difficult to verify at first because he had evidently been poaching, but the schoolmaster has no doubt of its truth.'[43]

When Collignon arrived in January 1935, he was confronted with two different stories – the original account of the discovery in Collingbourne Wood, and a second, of which there were several versions, that it had been found in Ludgershall itself. Arriving in the town on 7 January, he met first with the schoolmaster, Mr James, who

> took me to the spot in Collingbourne Wood which had been pointed out to him as the place where the find was first made. We dug down three feet in order to ascertain whether there were any signs of black ash or black earth. The scarab was partially covered with a black ashy substance when originally brought to Mr James, and the brother of the finder had told him that it had been found in that kind of substance. No trace whatever of black soil or ash was found in Collingbourne Wood, so we returned to Ludgershall.[44]

This lack of 'black soil or ash' was a key factor in Collignon's rejection of the Collingbourne Wood story. In response, James wrote an account of his original visit to the findspot in 1930. He was taken there by the brother of the finder. He gave its location as:

> A short distance (150 yards approx) south of Fairoak Gate in Collingbourne Wood and about 250 yds west of the earthwork known locally as the 'Grimsditch'. It was

found at a depth of 2'10" to 3'. The surface soil is blackish, can contain many small flints. I give a diagram from memory.[45]

Here he offered a sketch section of the stratigraphy that he recalled encountering when digging at the spot in 1930: an upper layer of 'Blackish soil', then a layer of 'Clay with large flints', below which was a narrow layer of 'apparently burnt material' overlying 'Clay'. The scarab had reportedly been found at the interface between the last two layers.[46]

Later that day Collignon visited Mr Fuzzard, the father of the finder. Fuzzard insisted that the scarab had been discovered by his son Alec 'in Mr Bowers' yard at Bell Street, Ludgershall'. Alec told Collignon that he had found it while 'levelling the yard in question after a large wooden shed and its contents had been destroyed by fire. This involved sifting a good deal of material, and while doing it the scarab came to light. It was about two feet, perhaps a little more, below the level of the upper end of the yard'.[47] Mr Bowers himself, 'a gipsy with a local reputation for complete honesty and sharpness of wit',[48] had no clear recollection of the scarab being found in his yard, but remembered one of the Fuzzard boys picking up something from the ground when he was levelling.

Collignon again investigated the alleged findspot. He wrote:

The scarab, when I had it, was burned and had black ash on it. I dug at the spot indicated in Collingbourne Wood and found no ash at all. I also dug in Mr Bowers' yard in Ludgershall where one of the witnesses told me to dig, and I found identical ash there. The burning was caused by a fire in the Bowers' yard which is remembered by everyone in Ludgershall.[49]

He made no reference to James's report of encountering 'apparently burnt material' in Collingbourne Wood. The explanation offered for the change of provenance was confusion. Alec Fuzzard claimed that his brother had confused the scarab with another object found in Collingbourne Wood around the same time – 'a metal thing – a boat I think it was'. Collignon and James both questioned Frank Fuzzard about it, with Frank initially supporting his brother's story before 'becoming confused himself', but nonetheless remaining 'quite certain that one of the objects found by Alec came from Mr Bowers' yard'.[50]

Collignon accepted the yard as the place where the scarab was found. The surviving correspondence, however, suggests that the change in provenance had only occurred once Engleheart began to encourage further investigation. Reasons offered by James and Engleheart centred around the fact that Alec had probably been poaching when the scarab was found in the woods, and also that Alec's father, as a result of the interest being shown, believed that the scarab might be valuable.[51] James also mentioned that before the Bowers' yard story emerged, he had also been told that the scarab had been found while digging foundations for a house.[52]

Ancient or modern?

In *Man*, Engleheart had noted the apparent scarcity of genuine Egyptian objects from prehistoric or Roman contexts in Britain. However, he also pointed to the presence of 'objects of Mediterranean provenance, such as the well-known faience beads and gold-rimmed amber brooches' found in Wiltshire barrows, arguing that 'there is no antecedent reason against the importation of scarabs, of which so many thousands were made in Egypt from before 2,000 B.C. into the Ptolemaic period and were abundantly imported and copied throughout South-eastern Europe'.[53] Unfortunately, by the time he wrote this, he had already received plenty of expert opinion telling him that the scarabs were almost certainly of recent date.

First to be consulted was Dr Henry Hall, Keeper of the Department of Egyptian and Assyrian Antiquities at the British Museum. Hall, who died in October 1930, had only seen the Stonehenge scarab. Apparently, 'at first sight [Hall] pronounced it to be a probable forgery'.[54] This was not what Engleheart wanted to hear. However, 'on further consideration, after hearing details of its discovery, [Hall] said he would like it to be submitted to other experts for confirmation'.[55] The opinion of those other experts, whom Engleheart did not name, was summarized as follows: 'if either scarab was genuine it was the smaller (Stonehenge) one'.[56]

Egyptologist Percy Newberry was consulted much later. His initial assessment seems to have been based on drawings or photographs, and in a note attached to the *Man* article, he wrote that:

> [both items] appear to me much more like the scarabs I saw at Thebes forty years ago, and I was told that they had been made by a Kurnawi forger named Adam. The material, limestone, was very rarely employed for making scarabs in ancient times, but during the last hundred years it has often been used for large scarabs of this kind.... If these specimens are modern (and I believe they must be) they were probably brought to England by some traveller from Egypt during the years between 1820 and 1860, if not later.[57]

In a shorter note added to the end of the article Newberry related, 'Since writing the above I have seen the actual scarabs and am confirmed in my opinion about their being modern forgeries.'[58]

It seems to have been Collignon who showed Newberry the scarabs. After concluding his investigations in Wiltshire, Collignon wrote that:

> On Friday and Saturday [11 and 12 January 1935] I visited Dr Margaret Murray and Professor Percy E Newberry, the great authority on scarabs. Miss Murray said that there is no known example of limestone scarabs like these. They always have inscriptions, not cartouches. The scarabs came from Luxor, she thought, where they are manufactured and sold to tourists as mementoes. They are not even

supposed to be genuine …. Professor Newberry said that limestone scarabs are most rare, and that these were manufactured at a place near Luxor. He recognized the technique of a particular maker, being able to do so after an exhaustive study of forgeries. He has a collection of forgeries especially made for him.[59]

Engleheart then sent both scarabs to Herbert H. Thomas of the Geological Survey of Great Britain along with a third: a tourist souvenir given to Engleheart by a friend. Thomas was familiar to archaeologists as the man who had, a decade or so earlier, first identified the Preseli Mountains in Wales as the source of the Stonehenge bluestones.[60] In *Man*, Thomas was quoted as saying that all three scarabs sent to him had been 'carved out of the native limestone deposit', prompting Engleheart to conclude that 'The Wiltshire examples are therefore not English imitations.'[61] As for their authenticity as genuine antiquities, Thomas appears to have been led by Engleheart. There was no visible distinction between the material used for the three scarabs, and so 'I have very little doubt from what you tell me that they are genuine for as you say it seems very futile to have had to plant fakes in places where they would remain undetected for goodness knows how long.'[62] In fact, on the basis of their discussions, Engleheart came to believe that his own tourist piece might also be a genuine antiquity.

The 1936 article in the *Wiltshire Archaeological Magazine* was compiled after Engleheart's death. An earlier version of the latter's text had been rejected by the editor, E. H. Goddard, on the grounds that 'it didn't quite meet the occasion'.[63] In that earlier version, written in 1935 after Collignon's investigations had taken place, Engleheart had dwelt at length on his reasons for considering still that both scarabs were genuine antiquities:[64]

(i) As far as the circumstances of their discovery were concerned, 'No time or pains has been spared in their closest investigation. The persons concerned are all well known and transparently truthful; the actual unearthing was in each case as purely accidental as was the recognition of the scarabs … after their disposal in the school collections'.

(ii) There was 'no antecedent improbability of contemporary scarabs of Thothmes iii having come by trade routes to Salisbury Plain', pointing again to the presence in the area of items of gold, faience and amber.

(iii) 'that they are not of English fabrication has been proved'.

(iv) The existence of another scarab from southern England, found in Alton in Hampshire 'in association with brooches of the Villanova, Earliest Italian Iron Age, and assigned by Dr Wallis Budge to the same period, the 26th Dynasty'.

Writing to Collignon before the latter began his investigations, Engleheart insisted that 'it is all very well for Newberry and others to put these scarabs down as fakes, but I can't get them to address the obvious question "where then were or are the genuine archetypes from which the imitations must necessarily have been copied"'.[65]

How did the scarabs reach their findspots?

With hindsight, the few suggestions made at the time to explain how both scarabs arrived at the places where they were found can appear remarkably simplistic. However, they do largely reflect contemporary understanding of the processes by which material culture entered the archaeological record. These tended to focus around loss, discard or failure to retrieve concealed items.

On 14 January 1935, O. G. S. Crawford wrote to Collignon suggesting that 'No doubt at some time a tourist who came to reside later in Ludgershall had acquired these objects in Egypt and at his death or departure they were thrown away or buried.'[66] Collignon seems to have agreed, adding in support that while in the area

> it occurred to me to see whether I could locate any more imitation scarabs of the same kind, and rather to my surprise I found two! They both came from Cairo bazaars. One belonged to a Ludgershall resident, and the other to somebody who lives near Salisbury.[67]

A response to the *Man* article from Ludwig Glanert, curator of Perth Museum in Australia, highlighted another possibility:

> During the Great War, Australian troops were quartered on Salisbury Plain. Many of these spent a period of training in Egypt and collected momentoes [*sic*], which they either sent to their friends or retained in their possession. In this manner many would be brought to England where they might be lost or thrown away. During my own stay on the Plain I visited both Stonehenge and Collingbourne Wood and no doubt thousands of others did likewise.[68]

As for their being found at some depth, Collignon himself suggested that '[t]he existence of so many rabbit holes on the Plain seems to me to account for the scarabs being found below the surface of the ground'.[69]

Potentially more interesting is a letter in the archives of Devizes Museum written by Wiltshire archaeologist A. D. Passmore following the publication of the 1936 article.[70] Writing to Goddard on 20 June 1936, Passmore related that

> [w]hen I first saw the article about these Wiltshire finds, in Man, I intended to write and tell you the following, but it slipped my memory. The publication of the whole story of these scarabs, in the current issue of the Magazine, reminds me of it, and these facts may help to suggest how the scarabs came to be where they were.

He then recounted a story concerning his purchase of two scarabs at an auction in Newquay, Cornwall in May 1909.

The auction included the sale of items formerly belonging to 'local curio-hunter', George Hicks. Passmore was intent on buying 'a beautiful little stone Egyptian god ... of some green stone, and two large scarabs ... with cartouches cut on their sides',[71] but he found the former out of reach as two antiquities dealers bid against each other for it. The sale ended for the day before reaching the scarabs. Unable to return the next morning, Passmore asked to leave a bid, but was told that if he made a reasonable offer, he could have the scarabs. A bid of 11.5 pence each was accepted, and Passmore left with the scarabs thinking he had a bargain. 'Some years later I showed them to an expert and was told that they were only imitation ones .... I don't remember what the cartouches were, since, not being genuine, I lost interest in them.'[72] They became paperweights.

The remainder of the letter is, unfortunately, missing, which probably makes Passmore's offer to 'suggest how the scarabs came to be where they are' more ambiguous than was actually the case. The most obvious possibilities are that he was simply offering a scenario that might explain the Wiltshire pair, that is to say, that they had once belonged to a collector who thought them genuine, presumably a scenario which would see them discarded once it was realized that they were not antiquities; or that Passmore's two scarabs were the ones found in Wiltshire in 1928. On balance, the latter seems far less likely, but the absence of the end of the letter leaves just a little room for speculation.

Where are they now?

The scarab from Collingbourne Wood (or Ludgershall) is currently in the collections of Salisbury Museum, along with Engleheart's example. The whereabouts of the scarab from Stonehenge Aerodrome are unclear. All three were sent to Devizes Museum in March 1935 by Engleheart, who had apparently told the museum's curator, Maud Cunnington, that he was 'tired of them'.[73]

According to Cunnington, soon after the scarabs had arrived in Devizes, Mr Wright the School Inspector objected, insisting that Engleheart 'had no right to give them away',[74] and that the Collingborne Wood/Ludgershall scarab had in any case been promised to Salisbury Museum. After further correspondence and consultation, Maud Cunnington decided to retain the Stonehenge scarab and send the other two to Salisbury. However, as curator of Devizes Museum she still had a problem over officially accepting the gift, as it was unclear as to who any of the scarabs actually belonged. Engleheart, she suggested, 'really had no right to them at all'.[75] Consequently, no entry was made in the museum's accession records, and the receipt of the gift was not acknowledged, as would otherwise have happened, in the *Wiltshire Archaeological Magazine*. 'It seemed wiser to let sleeping dogs (scarabs) alone', she wrote.[76] There appears to be no record of what happened to it subsequently.

Conclusions

There seems little reason to doubt that both Charles Palmer and Alec Fuzzard found objects that turned out to be Egyptian scarabs of probable nineteenth-century AD date.

The matter of how each got to its respective findspot may never be resolved. That both were found in close proximity to each other in terms of time and place, and that both were then spotted during school inspections – with the same inspector present on both occasions – may well be remarkable coincidences. It is possible that both (and perhaps others) were planted as some kind of practical joke, perhaps intended to be at the expense of the hyperdiffusionists and their followers. If this were true, there can have been little guarantee that they would ever be found, let alone recognized as scarabs.

On one level, the story of these objects highlights the potential problems in taking published reports, however detailed and persuasive they may appear, at face value. The archived correspondence clearly reveals the inconsistencies and contradictions present among a collection of ostensibly first-hand accounts, as well as the choices made by Collignon in constructing his version of events. This is not just an issue with objects such as these scarabs, of course – when re-examining key finds from historic excavations, for example, reliable records of provenance and context can prove to be equally elusive.[77]

As far as the scarabs are concerned though, of particular interest here is the glimmer of additional light they shine on the complex responses to Smith's and Perry's theories. The effort that went into exploring the circumstances of objects that are clearly of no great age seems remarkable. George Engleheart may have initially considered Collignon to be 'one of the "Egyptian" cranks',[78] but he was obviously unhappy with the idea that neither scarab was a genuine antiquity.

It is unclear when O. G. S. Crawford first became aware of the scarabs.[79] He was clearly in communication about them with Engleheart at a time when Engleheart still believed that the Stonehenge example at least might be ancient. Crawford was also put in touch with Collignon before the latter's visit to Wiltshire. Crawford's interest should not really occasion surprise. As the early years of *Antiquity* showed, he was interested in archaeological hoaxes but, as already noted, his main objections to the heliocentric hypothesis were concerned with method, especially Perry's explicit rejection of the geographical approaches that Crawford was instrumental in introducing to the study of prehistory.

Crawford offered little in the way of objection to Smith's and Perry's diffusionist outlook. He was more concerned with their (single) point of origin. He concluded his 1924 review article by insisting that 'Generally speaking, it was Egypt that copied Babylonia, rather than the opposite. Indeed, it is to Babylonia that we must look for the origins of civilization.'[80] He expanded a little on this fifteen years later, in what was essentially an obituary to Smith:

> Our civilization has its roots in Sumeria and India as well as Egypt; and the early cultures of South America cannot yet be satisfactorily explained by the theory of diffusion. It may ultimately be found that Elliot Smith's theory was partially right, though his facts were often wrong; time and further research alone can make this clear.[81]

By the time he wrote this, many of Crawford's contemporaries probably felt that things were already perfectly clear.

'Let Sleeping Scarabs Alone'

Crawford had been following Smith's and Perry's work since at least 1915,[82] attracted by a shared interest in explaining the (assumed) westward and northward spread of both metallurgy and megalithic tombs. For Crawford, the diffusion of various phenomena across prehistoric Europe was a matter of lifelong interest, albeit one that only sporadically surfaced in print. However, his final book, *The Eye Goddess* (1957) focused on the diffusion in prehistory of particular motifs and the ideas they represented, its geographical scope extending across Europe, North Africa and the Near East, while his first appearance in print – in 1908, more than two decades before J. Rendel Harris was drawn to the same question – concerned occurrences in England of the place-name 'Egypt'.[83]

Glyn Daniel was a pioneer in writing about archaeology's own history, and his oft-cited and emphatic dismissals of the 'pan-Egyptian hyperdiffusionist delusion' have played a key role in enabling the view that this was something separable and distinguishable from a more orthodox, mainstream archaeology progressing steadily towards becoming a modern, scientific discipline.[84] Indeed, subsequent commentators have sought to further separate the hyperdiffusionists from mainstream archaeology by insisting that neither Smith nor Perry were, in fact, archaeologists. Smith, for example, was a scientist – an anatomist – who relied for authority on his reputation in other fields.[85] Consequently, it can appear as little more than a brief aberration with little lasting impact, yet some of Smith's and Perry's ideas and methods had significant consequences, the traces of which in subsequent mainstream archaeological discourse can appear as elusive as the origins of those scarabs. For example, Smith's insistence on the importance of the switch from food gathering to food production – the 'Neolithic Revolution' as Gordon Childe called

Figure 2.4 One of Alexander Keiller's 1930s concrete obelisks at Avebury. This is an example of his 'Mark 2' design. Photo: M Barber.

it, an 'epoch-making innovation ... rightly taken to mark in archaeology the beginning of a new age'[86] – was 'one of the many services rendered to prehistory by Prof. Elliot Smith'.[87] Even Daniel accepted that the hyperdiffusionists 'at least made prehistorians think clearly about the mechanisms of culture change'.[88] Crawford was just one of many archaeologists of the interwar period whose engagement with their ideas was more complex than recent assessments of the episode allow.

Fully assessing the longer-term influence of their work on ideas about what happened in prehistory is beyond the scope of this essay, but it is perhaps worth pointing out that the hypothesis of Egyptian influence on prehistoric Britain achieved concrete expression – quite literally – around the time that Engleheart and Collignon were grappling with the problem of the scarabs. Crawford had introduced Alexander Keiller to the prehistory of 'Wessex' in the early 1920s, and he quickly became involved with developments at Stonehenge and, to a much greater extent, Avebury. At Stonehenge, his architectural designs for a proposed museum were rejected. One of them was essentially a mastaba-like building constructed from megalithic components cast in concrete. In the mid-1930s, when he undertook his programme of excavation and restoration at Avebury, Massingham's Egyptian-influenced capital of Neolithic Britain, the locations of missing sarsens were marked with concrete obelisks (Fig. 2.4).[89]

CHAPTER 3
'MUMMY FIRST: STATUE AFTER': WYNDHAM LEWIS, DIFFUSIONISM, MOSAIC DISTINCTIONS AND THE EGYPTIAN ORIGINS OF ART

Edward Chaney

Wyndham Lewis was one of Britain's first modernists; yet, while maintaining a continuously high standard of artistic production, both critical and creative, he eventually became its most articulate anti-modernist and an apologist for a particular kind of classicism.[1] In a civilization evermore under threat, and with most contemporary art of an unprecedentedly banal quality, it seems worth exploring the reasons someone who worked so energetically in both painting and literature should have ended up lambasting *The Demon of Progress in the Arts*, the title of Lewis's anti-avant-gardist polemic of 1954. By the mid-1920s the polytheistically inclined Lewis had come to believe that art began with the ancient Egyptians and that it had not improved since their 3,000-year civilization had ceased to prevail. Where Edward Gibbon regretted the destructive effect of Christianity on the civilization of ancient Rome, Lewis lamented the longer-term legacy of Egypt which had been even more thoroughly 'obscured or destroyed by Christianity'.[2] By focussing upon the state of the arts of both ancient Egypt and the modern West Lewis illuminated both civilizations with rare insight.

In this essay I argue that Lewis's acquaintance with a particular account of the evolution of Egyptian art played a crucial role in the development of his ideas. The now largely (if somewhat exaggeratedly) discredited authors of this narrative were led by the remarkable Sir Grafton Elliot Smith (1871–1937).[3] As well as believing that civilization started in Egypt and spread thence throughout the world, Smith promoted the notion that mummification led to portrait sculpture, which in turn led to the development of architecture in the form of mortuary temples. Eventually (albeit millennia before the Greeks), the Egyptians brought their statues out of their serdabs into the open. Throughout the 1920s, while developing his thoughts on the role of the arts in the modern world, Lewis wrote enthusiastically about the Egyptocentric diffusionism of Smith and his colleagues. He learned enough to appreciate that the self-conscious avant-gardism of post-nineteenth-century art, evermore measured according to the extent of its progressive originality and concomitantly separated from mainstream society, indicated a mentality that pre-Christian Egyptians would have found incomprehensible.

Thus, having initially advocated iconoclastic advancedness, Lewis was ultimately won over by 'the Wisdom of the Egyptians'.[4] Given the relative youth and instability of fifth-century BC Greece, Plato had long since admired an apparently unchanging civilization in which the artistic conventions were displayed in the temples:

> And no painter or artist is allowed to innovate upon them, or to leave the traditional forms and invent new ones. To this day, no alteration is allowed either in these arts, or in music. ... And you will find that their works of art are painted or moulded in the same forms which they had ten thousand years ago; – this is literally true and no exaggeration – their ancient paintings and sculptures are not a whit better or worse than the work of today, but are made with just the same skill.[5]

If ancient Egyptian civilization did not in fact endure for ten millennia, it survived for more than three, arguably longer than the Chinese (if it is not too early to tell). Lewis came to admire both these profoundly conservative civilizations, but above all that of Egypt.

***

In the summer of 1938, having hitherto – even after the *Anschluss* – underestimated the extent of the Nazi threat to his life and work, the 82-year-old Sigmund Freud was finally persuaded to leave Vienna. He had written to his son Ernst, Lucian Freud's father: 'I sometimes compare myself with the old Jacob who, when a very old man, was taken by his children to Egypt.'[6] Ernst organized for his father to move into the Hampstead house that is now the Freud Museum, where he surrounded himself with his collection of Egyptian artefacts. Here he completed a short monograph entitled, in the English edition published by the Hogarth Press, *Moses and Monotheism*.[7] In this, Freud argues that Moses was an Egyptian priest who derived the idea of monotheism from the fourteenth-century BC pharaoh, Amenhotep IV, who changed his name to Akhenaten when he rejected the polytheism and powerful priesthood of his forefathers and singled out for exclusive worship of the universalist sun god, or Aten. Freud's Egyptology may be discredited but the question as to whether this top-down religious revolution ultimately encouraged 'the Mosaic Distinction' and the Judaic first commandment that: 'Thou shalt have no other gods before me' (and thus Christianity and Islam), remains (literally) fundamental.[8] Freud's principal source for the third and final part of his book was the enthusiastic account of Akhenaten by the great American Egyptologist, James Breasted in *The Dawn of Conscience* of 1933.[9] Seeking to understand the gradual shift in what Freud's rebellious follower, Carl Jung, called the collective unconscious away from something so sensible as polytheism – with its local gods, animals gods and female gods – towards a single, implicitly male and indeed 'jealous' god who rejects all other gods as false, is surely as vital as ever, with variously enthusiastic adherents of the world's major monotheistic religions still killing each other in the name of their particular and exclusive 'truth'. In view of the subsequent refutation of diffusionism in favour of evolutionary 'independent origins', 'psychic unity' or, as Elliot Smith disparagingly called it, 'spontaneous combustion', the extent to which Amarna's monotheistic moment may have proved influential is surely also still of great significance, not least because

Akhenaten was first the agent and then, posthumously, with the return to polytheism, the victim of iconoclasm.[10]

More specifically relevant where the history of art is concerned was the *second* commandment, that forbidding the making of 'any graven image or any likeness of any thing'.[11] In literal-minded obedience to this Judaic instruction and in competition with 'paganism' in general, the counter-religious if conversely superstitious early Christians so thoroughly eliminated 3,000 years' worth of Egyptian art that there was little left above ground for the similarly iconoclastic Muslims to destroy when they took control of Egypt in the seventh century.[12] Once it had secured its status as the official religion of the Roman and then Byzantine Empires, though traumatically divided and still periodically iconoclastic, Christianity eventually relaxed the ban on images enough to allow for the revival of elements of ancient iconography (and even theology) which, albeit transmuted via Graeco-Roman adaptations, ultimately derived from ancient Egypt.[13] The most obvious (albeit oddly understudied) instance of this 'return of the repressed' was the evolution and diffusion of the image of Isis breastfeeding her infant god Horus, via Venus and the virginal Diana, into that of the Virgin Mary nursing the Christ-child, a transformation which that reassertion of 'the Mosaic Distinction' we call the Reformation would denounce as Mariolatry. Even Lewis was still creating Madonna and Child images at the beginning of his career, subsequently celebrating humankind's tendency to persist in worshipping, 'if we worship, still the virgin-goddess' along with the Egyptian-sounding 'stars on the ocean, the break-of-day[and] the natural magic that inspired our earliest beliefs'.[14]

Beneath this re-emergence of pagan iconography, which became more self-consciously overt en route to the Renaissance, lay deeper debts owed by Christianity to Egyptian religion, relating above all to its obsession with immortality and the Last Judgement.[15] In *Moses and Monotheism*, Freud summarized the matter: 'No other people of antiquity did so much as the Egyptians to deny death or took such pains to make existence in the next world possible.'[16] Largely thanks to having absorbed 'the information brilliantly presented by Dr. Elliot Smith' in his *Evolution of the Dragon* (1919), Lewis had already written enthusiastically (and more amusingly) about the cultural consequences of this phenomenon:

> You only have to walk into a museum gallery devoted to Egyptian art to recognize at once that you are walking into a sort of churchyard or very curious sort of undertaker's shop. Thoth, in massive trutination, is weighing life against death. And, sure enough, the form life takes on this occasion, is that of *art*. Indeed in dynastic Egypt, *art* comes nearer to being *life* than at any recorded period: and apparently for the reason that it was *death*. ... The living death that is represented by Egyptian culture is the very atmosphere for the sculptor and painter to thrive in.[17]

When in reaction to the Renaissance revival of antiquity (albeit prompted by the very humanist textual criticism that underpinned it) Christian fundamentalism reared its literal-minded head again, iconoclasm reasserted itself, above all in Northern Europe.[18]

This was exported via trouble-making Puritans (along with a revived obsession with witchcraft) to North America, the South meanwhile becoming evermore Catholic, thereby benefitting from the scepticism of the early modern Spanish theologians who vetoed the death penalty for witchcraft one and half centuries before the Scots and Americans.[19] The death penalty for sorcery survives, however, in countries like Saudi Arabia and there have been renewed calls for the destruction of the remains of ancient Egypt, including the Pyramids, from the likes of Salafist leader, Murgan Salem al-Gohary.[20]

In sixteenth- and seventeenth-century Northern Europe, while the Grand Tour to Italy emerged as a more acceptably secular version of pilgrimage, new, non-religious artistic genres were developed to satisfy aesthetic appetites. While churches were whitewashed and their statues and stained-glass windows sold or smashed, still-life, landscapes and portraits emerged and flourished, particularly in the United Provinces, where they graced civic and domestic buildings alike. What might be described as an underlying discomfort with imagery persisted, however, encouraging, it could be argued, some of the abstract ideology that characterized the so-called Enlightenment.[21]

The progressive philosophy of Hegel (and consequently Marx) encouraged an idealist theory of history rather than one that prioritized the quest for truth through art.[22] It is surely no accident that, in conformity with Hegel's essentially self-fulfilling prophecy by which art would become pure, self-expressive Geist, abstraction and eventually conceptualism flourished nowhere more than in post-Reformation cultures. Though less enthusiastic than Flinders Petrie and Breasted, Freud's promotion of Akhenaten suggests something of the same when he describes the resultant monotheism as having 'risen to the heights of sublime abstraction'.[23] It was this idealist (and effectively determinist) tendency to believe in the inevitability of abstraction that Lewis would warn against in the *Demon of Progress*, for the Absolute (the ground of 'Everything') can only be its opposite: 'Nothing'. Lewis thought that human beings are, and should be, 'surface creatures', and attempts to burrow down to ultimate abstraction result in self-destruction ('Zero') in art as in life.[24] In 1940, in the March issue of *The New Republic*, Lewis had optimistically proclaimed 'The End of Abstract Art' (it had 'died of acute boredom … on the part of both public and artist'); yet Expressionism was then about to merge with Surrealism to produce what the progressivist Clement Greenberg would promote as the New York School.[25]

Meanwhile back in Edwardian Bloomsbury, Freudian patricidal proclivities, a Protestant (Quaker) background and snooty Francophilia would combine in a compromisingly elitist campaign to replace traditionalist Victorian values with Fabianism and Clive Bell's 'Significant Form.'[26] As his rather feeble NPG portrait of Bell demonstrates, Roger Fry was neither a radical nor indeed a very talented artist. As an entrepreneurial art historian and theorist, however, while writing sensitively enough on Cezanne, he advocated a more extreme, meaning-less and narrative-free aesthetic which proved all too influential. In his *Last Lectures* Fry critiqued the inconsistency of Egyptian sculpture, extolling 'Negro art' in preference, and concluding that 'modern art owes more to the Negros than to any other tradition'.[27]

Initially, Lewis went along with Fry's project as compatible with his own more radical, Paris-based artistic theory and practice as well as his modernist literary aspirations. He soon, however, found reason to break free from Fry's *Omega Workshop*, which he now disparaged as 'a family party of strayed and dissenting aesthetes', and established himself as leader of a more authentically revolutionary movement.[28] In March 1914 he founded the Rebel Art Centre and a few months before the outbreak of the First World War published the first of two editions of *Blast*. Experience of real war and the death of brilliant colleagues such as T. E. Hulme and Henri Gaudier-Brzeska made the infighting between competing avant-gardisms seem relatively trivial. As the ancient Egyptians themselves tended to do when their civilization was in danger of degeneration, Lewis began exploring ways of picking things up where they had gone wrong.

In *Blast 1*, under the influence of Willhelm Worringer and a post-Bergsonian Hulme as much as of Lewis and Ezra Pound, Gaudier had issued a diffusionist manifesto entitled simply 'Vortex', based on his vision of the history of sculpture: 'The HAMITE VORTEX of Egypt: the land of plenty – Man succeeded in his far reaching speculations – Honour to the divinity!'[29] 'Hamite' derived from Noah's son, Ham, whose descendants were supposed to be both Egyptians and Berbers (a notion that may have encouraged Lewis's travels to the Maghreb; see below):

> Religion pushed him to the use of the VERTICAL which inspires awe. His gods were self made, he built them in his image. ... He preferred the pyramid to the mastaba. The fair Greek felt his influence across the middle sea. ... HIS SCULPTURE WAS DERIVATIVE his feeling for form secondary. ... Gothic sculpture was but a faint echo of the HAMITO-SEMITIC energies through Roman traditions, and it lasted half a thousand years, and it wilfully divagated again into the Greek derivation from the land of Amen-Ra.[30]

Hulme had promoted Egyptian art as tending towards the abstract while appreciating its complementary capacity to depict the essence of the real world. Having discussed the latest German aesthetic concepts, including 'empathy', which Aby Warburg and Worringer borrowed from the Vischers and Theodor Lipps, Hulme was especially influenced by Worringer's *Abstraktion und Einfühlung*, which he summarized in his posthumously published *Speculations*:

> The characteristics of archaic art are not due to incapacity. In Egypt, at the time when the monumental sculpture showed a stylification as great as any we find in archaic art, the domestic art of the period exhibited a most astonishing realism. In pure technical ability in mastery of raw material, the Egyptians have never been surpassed. It is quite obvious that what they did was intentional.[31]

In *Blast 2*, Lewis reorders Hulme's previous triumvirate to prioritize Egypt:

> It may be objected that all the grandest and most majestic art in the world, however (Egyptian, Central African, American) has rather divested man of his vital plastic qualities and changed him into a more durable, imposing and in every way harder machine; and that is true. ... This dehumanizing has corresponded happily with the unhuman character, the plastic, architectural quality of art itself.[32]

Beneath his apparently assertive exterior Lewis seemed less certain than either Gaudier or Hulme about which direction to move in or even whether to concentrate on writing or painting. Inasmuch as he opted for the latter he would be all the more interested in Egypt and this fed back into further refinement of his cultural criticism. In *Blast 1*, he had included excerpts from Kandinsky's *Über das Geistige in der Kunst*, as introduced and translated by Edward Wadsworth, who presented it as 'a most important contribution to the psychology of modern art'.[33] In this version, the cosmopolitan Kandinsky, a follower of both Hegel and the Egyptophile Rudolph Steiner, asserts that there are 'three mystical fundamentals' required for the modern work of art, rooted as this must be in 'Inner Necessity'. The first is that the artist 'has to express himself'; the second, that he has 'to express what is particular to this epoch'; and the third that he 'has to express what is particular to all art'.

> Only the third element of the eternal and pure qualities remains ever alive. It does not lose its strength with time, but continually acquires more. An Egyptian statue astounds us certainly more to-day than it could have astounded its contemporaries: for them it was associated much too strongly with characteristics and personalities of the period, which weakened its effect. Today we hear in it the exposed timbre of eternal art.[34]

Familiar with German (and Munich), Lewis would no doubt have read Kandinsky's 1910 treatise soon after its original publication. Partly due to Hulme's promotion of Egyptian art, Lewis was no doubt prepared to approve of its highlighting here but by the following year, writing for his second, War Issue of *Blast*, while categorizing Kandinsky as 'the only PURELY abstract painter in Europe', he critiqued him as 'at the best, wandering and slack. You cannot make a form more than it is by the best intentions in the world'.[35] Albeit conscious of the 'eternal' nature of Egyptian art, Lewis reminded his readers that even 'in his most seemingly abstract paintings' the artist must always be representing the world in some way.[36] He nevertheless concludes the list of rules in this 'Review of Contemporary Art', in revolutionary, albeit jocular, mode:

> 12. There should be a bill passed in Parliament at once FORBIDDING ANY IMAGE OF RECOGNIZABLE SHAPE TO BE STUCK UP IN ANY PUBLIC PLACE ...
> 13. Only after passing a most severe and esoteric Board and getting a CERTIFICATE, should a man be allowed to represent in his work Human Beings, Animals or Trees.[37]

It is surely relevant that such supposedly radical modernism so closely echoed the Old Testament's second commandment which may itself have been indebted to an iconoclastic pharaoh. *Pace* the likes of Rowan Williams who criticized Freud's thesis on the origins of Judaism (and therefore Christianity) as: 'painfully absurd',[38] the superior Egyptologist Jan Assmann saw psychoanalysis as providing the new, universalist paradigm, superseding both diffusionism and those alternative explanations for cultural flourishings which the diffusionists' opponents argued evolved spontaneously in diverse locations as merely coincidental. Assmann's argument for psychoanalytical supersession of a debate in which 'the only problem was to determine the source of diffusion: was Israel or Egypt the origin [of monotheism]?' leaves Freud as a master diffusionist in a great mnemonic tradition with Egypt triumphant.[39]

If Lewis, rather like D. H. Lawrence, avoided acknowledging Freud, he was (surreptitiously) similarly susceptible to his influence (see, e.g. the discussion of *The Enemy of the Stars* below), while a passage in *Time and Western Man* reveals him as sounding surprisingly Assmann-like, albeit more critically where a mnemonic 'picture' of the past is concerned:

> The 'historic' picture is in reality a description of the Unconscious, as exactly as is the teaching of [Karl Robert Eduard] von Hartmann or of Freud. When it is brought to life by time-consciousness, it exists only as *immense image*. So there is in the life of the time-conscious individual a crushing preponderance of image-material.[40]

Lewis here critiques the Bergsonian, time-bound, historicist view of the modern world, favouring instead 'the extremely "ahistorical" Chinese [who] are more troublesome than the Greeks for the chronological philosopher. The ancient Egyptians are as bad'. In thus preferring the Egyptians and Chinese, Lewis signals his paleo-conservative preference for permanence and stability over 'progress', and pacificism over Heraclitian flux with its 'clockwork rising and falling of empires, with the regular oscillations of great wars, plots and massacres'.

Pioneeringly conscious of both the virtues and limitations of abstraction as well as its dependence upon what he feared would be a shrinking if plutocratic clientele, Lewis was already deeply concerned about artistic patronage.[41] He may have heard about the display in New York in 1917 of a urinal, attributed to Marcel Duchamp.[42] The following year, Duchamp painted his last picture, *Tu m'*, designed to demonstrate that painting was dead, 'to underscore the limitations of the medium', *Tu m'* being either short for 'Tu m'emmerdes' or 'tu m'ennuies' (you're boring or crapping on me).[43] As such gestures pass their centenaries, critics still strive to maintain their iconoclastic and radical *raisons d'être* even when these one-time avant-garde challenges to authority have themselves become stultifying orthodoxies. According to Jonathan Jones, the art of Modigliani (a signatory of Gaudier's manifesto and remembered by Anna Akhmatova as 'completely carried away by the great Egyptian art'),[44] 'shows why, in 1917, Duchamp had to put a urinal in an exhibition; Modernism was getting far too respectable by then'.[45]

A worthier justification for Duchamp's iconoclastic gestures would have been Dadaist disillusion with a civilization that had degenerated into an appalling world war (he abandoned Paris for New York in 1915). Such disillusion was reflected in diffusionist advocacy of ancient Egypt as a stable, highly civilized yet essentially anti-imperialist state.[46] Rather than taking the Duchampian road to facetious nihilism (ending up playing chess with naked women), Lewis was encouraged by Grafton Elliot Smith in particular to see Egypt as having not only invented and exported art, but having brought it to a state of perfection that would never be surpassed. This would still allow a 'revisionist-modernist' to, in T. S. Eliot's terms, 'construct something upon which to rejoice' in emulation of, as well as competition with, the past, while encouraging an emphasis on the creative concern with death and dualism that Lewis associated with Egypt and the 'Ka' which inhabits the sculpture that permanently replicated the mummy. Several of Lewis's best portraits convey the impression of being invested with their sitter's Ka.

In *The Caliph's Design*, Lewis returned to chiding the Futurists for their 'mythical attitude towards a racing-car, or workshop where big guns (or Teddy bears) are made', proposing instead 'a reasoned enthusiasm for the possibilities that lie in this new spectacle of machinery; of the uses it can be put to in art'. 'Machinery should be regarded as a new pictorial resource' he wrote, 'there to be exploited'. Lewis might almost be referring to the celebrated urinal when he writes that once an efficient, shiny piece of machinery 'is absorbed into the aesthetic consciousness ... its meaning would be transformed':

> It is of exactly the same importance, and in exactly the same category as a wave on a screen by Korin, an Odalisque of Ingres, a beetle of a sculptor of the XVIII. dynasty.[47] Ingres lived in the midst of a great appetite for the pseudo-classic: the Egyptian sculptor lived in the presence of a great veneration for the beetle ... the Beetle and the Odalisque are both sleek and solid objects! Ingres probably did not believe in the Odalisque as an Odalisque, although realising the admirable uses to which she could be put. The Egyptian probably found the beetle objectionable until transformed into stone.[48]

Following this final remark, with its suggestion of a theory of religion related to Warburg's 'serpent ritual', Lewis appeals for an alternative to current, failing forms of patronage:

> If the world *would only build temples to Machinery* in the abstract then everything would be perfect. The painter and sculptor would have plenty to do, and could, in complete peace, and suitably honoured, pursue their trade without further trouble.[49]

Lewis's somewhat unconvincing tone here is only reinforced by his faltering, quasi-fatalistic concluding question which returns us to where we began, both with monotheism and its discontents, and where we are now, encumbered with the likes of Gilbert and George RA, Tracey, Damien and Marina Abramovic, or indeed the infantilizing swings and slides of Tate Modern:

Else what is the use in taking all the useful Gods and Goddesses away, and leaving the artist with no role in the social machine, except that of an entertainer, or a business man?[50]

It becomes clear that Lewis agreed with Nietzsche (if not perhaps as exclusively) that the abandonment of 'the Great Benefit of Polytheism' – resulting in 'the belief in one standard god next to whom there could only be false gods – posed the greatest danger to humanity. It threatened to stop humanity short'.[51]

Perhaps significantly, the paragraph that followed Lewis's preceding quotation from *The Caliph's Design* references Freud's pioneering XVIII-dynasty monotheist: 'Imagine Koyetzu, Signorelli, or the sculptor who carved the head of Akhenaton or of the wife of the Sheik-el-Beled, alive, painting and carving today'. The so-called 'wife of Sheikh-el-Beled' is in fact the c. 2475 BC (V dynasty) bust of the wife of the lector-priest Ka-Aper, who was thus named by Auguste Mariette's Egyptian workmen who excavated her and her husband from his mastaba in Saqqara and thought he looked like their local mayor.[52] Lewis may have recalled the publicity that succeeded the excavation of the couple in the 1890s when he painted and named his 'Sheik's Wife' in 1936.[53] His fine painting and what remains of this superb sculpture share the same serene smile familiar from so much Egyptian portraiture. More generally, Lewis's major portraits share a particular quality of stasis, even 'deadness', with much Egyptian figure sculpture.

Lewis may not have approved of Akhenaten for banishing all but one of 'the useful Gods and Goddesses' but he clearly admired him as a patron of exceptionally individualist portraiture. Elsewhere in the *Caliph's Design*, while ridiculing Roger Fry's pronouncement that a man's head is 'no more and no less important than a pumpkin', he proclaims his preference for paying close attention to the carapace or exterior in order better to illuminate the interior.[54] Far from inclined to follow Kandinsky's advice to express either himself, his sitters or his *Zeitgeist* too overtly, Lewis instead invested not merely heads but entire bodies, including nudes, with a kind of metaphysical isolation more austerely Egyptian and erect than Lucian Freud's comparatively painterly figures, who recall his grandfather's supine analysands rather than the Egyptian statuary he admired.[55] Freud's one-time friend, Francis Bacon, meanwhile agreed with Lewis that 'Egyptian art is the greatest I think that has happened so far.'[56] It seems that like Lewis, Bacon also subscribed to a diffusionist view of Egyptian influence: 'I could never dissociate myself from the great European images of the past – and by "European" I mean to include Egyptian, even if the geographers wouldn't agree with me.'[57] Based on such statements and pictures of both Egyptian- and Greek-style sphinxes, the Bergson-admiring Gilles Deleuze wrote that 'Bacon renders to Egypt the homage of the sphinx and declares his love for Egyptian sculpture.'[58] Both Freud and Bacon may have been encouraged in their Egyptophilia by Lewis, who pioneeringly praised Bacon as: 'one of the most powerful artists in Europe today' both in *The Listener*, from 1946 on,[59] and in *The Demon of Progress* a decade later as 'at the opposite pole to the pretentious blanks and voids of *Réalités Nouvelles*'.[60]

Interestingly, Bacon and Lucian Freud both used a book by James Breasted (a major inspiration for Sigmund Freud) as a source for their prints and pictures. Bacon tore out of the German edition of *A History of Egypt* (*Geschichte Aegyptens*) of 1936), plate 120 which is entitled 'Mannerkopf (Konig Amenhotep III.?). Gipsmaske. aus der Werkstatt des Bildhauers Thutmose in Amarna. 18. Dynastie, um 1400 v. Chr. Berlin, Ägyptisches Museum'.[61] Freud etched and at least twice painted the opening of his own battered copy that features both this and (opposite) the photograph of another head discovered in the same Amarna workshop of Thutmose, 'the sculptor who carved the head of Akhenaten' mentioned by Lewis.[62] Amenhotep III was Akhenaten's father and the detailed analysis of his mummy by Smith is still cited as authoritative.[63] Lucian Freud received his copy of this book in 1939 when he enrolled at an English art school and began to use it as a source more or less immediately, choosing to be photographed (by Julia Auerbach) with it lying in front of him fifty years later.[64] This was the same year that *Moses and Monotheism* was published, the young Lucian's Exodus from Nazism in the company of his parents having taken place in advance of his grandfather's.[65] Given this experience of exile and his use of the book from soon after Sigmund ended his life it seems likely he was precociously aware of its implications. He would later recall reading about Akhenaten, imagining 'The terrific loneliness of the king. Not many monotheists around: all these little gods and then one god only': 'My grandfather didn't endear himself to the Jews by suggesting that Moses was an Egyptian, an Egyptian floating down the river. An outrageous book: his final kick at the Talmud.'[66]

A parallel pairing of Egyptophile authors can likewise be adduced, of D. H. Lawrence and James Joyce, rivals rather than otherwise to Lewis, but united to various extents in their use of Freud senior. According to Cynthia Lewiecki-Wilson: 'Each writer's use of Egyptian myth reveals a different attitude to patriarchy'.[67] In a temporally broader discussion of patriarchy, published three years before Freud completed *Moses and Monotheism*, yet predictive of what he already calls 'the second world war', Lewis problematizes the 'axiom almost of western thought that the advantages of the judaic religion over almost others is its primitive monotheism'.[68] Having described how 'the patriarchal divinity of the early Israelites' had evolved beyond the pagan partly through focussing upon the 'personality' that such natural phenomena as rivers and the sun have in common, Lewis articulated his Nietzschean reservations about monotheism by analogy with art. Here one can see how deeply rooted was his view, subsequently articulated in *The Demon of Progress in the Arts*, that the artist should not surpass the limit 'beyond which there is nothing':[69]

> Just as a picture ceases to be a picture, but becomes a spot and then becomes *nothing*, when it is removed beyond the reach of our vision; so the mind can neither imagine nor see anything *perfectly* except at a certain fixed distance from it. The only way it can imagine infinitude is as NOTHING. (There is an intermediate stage at which it can imagine it as a featureless spot). The only real logical God of man is the exact opposite in every respect of him – the infinity of his finitude, the

eternity of his life-in-time: in short, his support and explanation. For the only total explanation of anything finite is its total opposite.

This is Spinoza's god; which, whatever way you turn, is nothing but a Blank. His is true monotheism; and it was a Jew who most perfectly expressed it.[70]

Thus even before Freud's book, Lewis, at least implicitly, had posed the problem that Assmann would address in *Moses the Egyptian*: how did Egypt lose its historical reality and turn into an inverted image of Israel, despite having previously shared much in common? Instead, 'Israel is the negation of Egypt, and Egypt stands for all that Israel has overcome.'[71]

If Lewis was too much of a polytheist to identify with Akhenaten, Sigmund Freud certainly identified with the pharaoh's supposed successor Moses, 'learned in all the wisdom of the Egyptians, and ... mighty in words and deeds' (and that's just the *New Testament*).[72] In Rome he spent hours contemplating Michelangelo's giant statue of the Prophet, subsequently publishing an essay on the image which even included sketches thought to be his own. Freud chose a photograph of the bearded face of Michelangelo's God-like Moses to fill the front cover of his *Moses and Monotheism*.[73] Before his quarrel with Jung he wrote to his protégé: 'If I am Moses then you are Joshua, and will take possession of the promised land of psychiatry.'[74] Elsewhere, Freud facetiously addressed Jung as Alexander the Great, which carried unfortunately patricidal connotations given that Alexander was rumoured to have had his father Philip II assassinated. This in turn reminds one of a case Freud would surely have written up had he known of it, the painter Richard Dadd's murder of his father on the imagined instructions from Osiris after returning from Egypt in the summer of 1843.[75] Lewis's own unhappy relations with his father have recently been the subject of academic speculation.[76]

Moses features prominently in Freud's analysis as remembered by H. D., who indeed dreams of the Egyptian princess who finds him in the Nile bulrushes, thereby seeming to anticipate his completion of *Moses and Monotheism*:

> She is peculiarly 'his' Princess for this is a life wish, apparently, that I have projected into or unto an image of the Professor's racial, ancestral background. ... Around us are the old images or 'dolls' of pre-dynastic Egypt, and Moses was perhaps not yet born when that little Ra or Nut or Ka figure on the Professor's desk was first hammered by a forger-priest of Ptah on the banks of the Nile.[77]

That most underestimated of twentieth-century artists, R. B. Kitaj, likewise increasingly identified with Moses.[78] He also owned 'a whole shelf of Wyndham Lewis' and told me he 'was very moved by him'.[79] In 1969 he had selected the cover of Lewis's *Caliph's Design* to be one of his *In our Time* screenprints. Prior to this he had been inspired by Aby Warburg and the *Journal* published in his name. Though his career progressed, Kitaj suffered diverse personal blows. He became evermore conscious of his Jewishness but remained resistant to its aniconism, aspiring instead to 'invent a Jewish style like the

Egyptian figure style'.[80] The last entry, number 615, in Kitaj's *Second Diasporist Manifesto*, published six weeks before he committed suicide, reads as if he were still anxious about the Hebrew proscription of idolatry: ironically, the legacy of the Great Hymn of the Aten, 'Sole God beside whom there is none', parts of which made their way into Psalm 104:

> As I make to die, here's <u>my 615th: EASEL-PAINTING ARE NOT IDOLS</u>, so, JEWISH ART IS OK to do without consulting your Rabbi, so do it! It's good and universal!

David Hockney, upon whom Kitaj was probably the most significant contemporary influence, was precociously Egyptophile even when they were still at the Royal College of Art together.[81] Outdoing Egyptophile predecessors from Alma-Tadema to Gauguin (and both Freuds), Hockney actually visited Egypt, obtaining sponsorship from *The Sunday Times Magazine* in September 1963. He returned there in early 1978 while finalizing his Egyptianizing designs for Glyndebourne's *Zauberflöte*.[82] He wrote:

> Egypt is one of the most thrilling countries I've ever been to in the sense that these monuments are the oldest known buildings anywhere. After all, when Cleopatra showed Julius Caesar the pyramids, they were already two thousand years and more. It is quite awe-inspiring; not even in China are there things older, and I think you feel connected with them, whoever you are.[83]

Lewis had no doubt also been aware of Egyptian art since his art school days at the Slade, not least because of its proximity to the British Museum. In *Blast 2*, he included a short section on the Museum's 'Egyptian Gallery' by his protégée Jessica Dismorr, who could almost be describing William Strang's wonderful etching of an elderly man embracing a young woman beneath a row of sculptures of Sekhmet:

> In a rectangular channel of space light drops in oblique layers upon rows of polished cubes sustaining gods and fragments. … Seductive goddesses, cat-faced and maiden-breasted sit eternally stroking smooth knees.[84]

Appearing immediately after *The Caliph's Design*, it is evident from Lewis's subsequent writings that Smith's *Evolution of the Dragon* greatly enhanced Lewis's enthusiasm for the art of ancient Egypt. Meanwhile Smith and Lewis shared a great admiration for what the former praised as William Lethaby's 'brilliant little book', *Architecture: An Introduction to the Art and Theory of the Art of Building* (1912), and this in Smith's case despite Lethaby's 'wholly unwarranted assumption that Egypt learnt its art from Babylonia'.[85]

In October 1922 T. S. Eliot launched *The Criterion*, the journal to which Lewis became a regular contributor. One cannot be sure whether Lewis suggested the idea but on 28 May 1923 Eliot wrote to Smith asking whether he would contribute to his new journal, enhancing the invitation by informing him that the great Sir James Frazer would also be contributing.[86] Eliot unctuously repeated the request on 10 March 1924 but only in the following November finally extracted the promise of an article entitled 'The Glamour of Gold' which appeared in the April 1925 issue (though nothing by Frazer was ever published in the journal).[87] Meanwhile, in late 1924 Lewis submitted a 20,000-word typescript entitled 'The Perfect Action', a preliminary section of his projected, 500,000-word 'Man of the World', a work that never materialized as a single publication, appearing instead as several books, including *The Art of Being Ruled* (1926) and *Time and Western Man* (1927). Eliot's polite refusal to publish what would have been '*over twice as long* as anything we have ever published' (though confusingly a version was proofed and advertized as forthcoming), led to irascible letters from Lewis culminating instead in his fascinating account of what he described as 'Elliot Smith's account of the Egyptian origins of art' in the April and May 1925 issues of the *Calendar of Modern Letters* as 'The Dithyrambic Spectator: an Essay on the Origins and Survivals of Art'.[88] This eventually reappeared in *The Diabolical Principle and the Dithyrambic Spectator* in 1931 but meanwhile relations with the ever-loyal Eliot survived in good enough shape for Lewis to review three more recent books for *The Criterion*: Smith's *Essays on the Evolution of Man*, Smith and Warren R. Dawson's *Egyptian Mummies*, and *Medicine, Magic and Religion*, by fellow diffusionist, W. H. R. Rivers.[89] Given how critical this self-styled 'Enemy' tended to be, Lewis wrote with extraordinary enthusiasm about all aspects of Smith's approach and conclusions, commending him, in the *Essays*, for his Nietzschean will in tackling such 'dangerous issues'.[90] For *Egyptian Mummies*, benefitting as this co-authored work did from Smith's very detailed account of *The Royal Mummies* of 1912 (see above), Lewis likewise has only praise, even if he says he would have preferred a photographic record (as per the 2000 reprint of *The Royal Mummies*) to the woodcuts by the young Arthur H. Gerrard and his wife Kaff (K. Leigh Pemberton), 'good and dramatic as the execution of the plates certainly is'.[91]

Lewis also reveals that he had already been reading Smith's younger University College London colleague, W. J. Perry (1887–1949), with whom he agreed at the profoundest level, not least on the 'progressive' causes of war. In this review he records that

> Professor Perry shows how, from the point of view of this school [human culture] has been collapsing ever since the ancient Egyptian dynasties came to an end. The rest of the world has been living ever since on what was reached at that time, parcelling it out and debasing it. There is no *independent* evolution of human society; and a trick of ritual occurring in a subarctic American tribe and also among bushman probably has a common source. Dr Rivers slowly came to that conclusion also.[92]

Perry and Rivers were both persuaded by Smith to adopt what is now disparaged as 'hyper-diffusionism', but what Lewis prefers to call 'historicism'.

A man of extraordinary energy and talent, by 1900, aged just 29, the Australian-born Dr Elliot Smith had been appointed Professor of Anatomy in Cairo. His burgeoning interest and expertise in mummies soon led to him working with the University of California's Hearst Egyptological Expedition.[93] By 1919 he was able to establish a research institute as the first Professor of Anatomy at UCL but had long since become what Lewis calls 'this fanatical egyptologist.' The extent to which Lewis was impressed by this fanaticism is evident in his enthusiastic summary of Smith's career:

> It may in a sense be a doctor's dream, of civilization growing up around the operating-table. His own brilliant theoretic structure has originated after that manner. ... While in the Cairo hospital, many desiccated bodies that had been buried five thousand years before ... were brought to him for dissection. He would find in the intestines of the proto-Egyptian the bones of the fish off which he had made his last meal, and would discover in the throat of a child the skinned body of a mouse, administered in this way when it was in extremis.[94]

Ironically, as someone who had revolutionized brain morphology in his 20s, Smith would have been well-placed to inform Lewis that his failing eyesight was caused by a brain tumour rather than by his teeth, all of which were removed as a result of this false diagnosis.[95] Where teeth are concerned he might also have recommended caution to Zawi Hawass when in 2007, he announced the discovery of Hatshepsut's mummy on the basis of a stray molar that seemed to fit a gap in KV-60's mouth.[96]

As has been said, 'The Dithyrambic Spectator' was reprinted as part two of *The Diabolical Principle and the Dithyrambic Spectator* in 1931. In his biography of Lewis, Jeffery Meyers states that 'The second part attacked the anthropological theories of Jane Harrison and Elliot Smith which stressed the primitive origins of art.'[97] This could hardly be less true where Smith is concerned, a similarly succinct but in this case correct summary being offered by the late-lamented Andrew Causey who, referring to Lewis's tendency to polarize to the point of caricature, writes that 'his approbation for Elliot Smith was matched by a stinging attack on Harrison.'[98] A more detailed account is provided by Paul Edwards in his superior monograph on Lewis. Interestingly he also references the extent to which Lewis might, despite his protestations to the contrary, have been influenced by Freud.[99] Relating this topic to Lewis's 1933 drawing of *Athanaton* and his painting of *Inca and the Birds*, done in the same year, Edwards migrates to the subject of diffusionism, focussing in particular on Perry's *Children of the Sun* (1923) and his *Growth of Civilization* (1924) which Lewis quotes in his 'Creatures of Habit'.[100] The irony is that, apparently inspired by W. H. Prescott's *History of the Conquest of Peru* of 1847, Lewis was highlighting what is now considered one of the weakest links in the diffusionist hypothesis.[101] Indeed, only recently on BBC Radio 4, Neil MacGregor was proclaiming the prior ancestry of Peruvian mummies over Egyptian ones.[102] Where the supposedly un-Egyptian Peruvian custom of keeping mummies in the house is concerned, however, a passage from Diodorus Siculus quoted by Lewis in his *Criterion* review from Smith and Dawson's *Egyptian Mummies* suggests that that the Egyptians also followed this practice.[103] Moreover, the sacred birds, the Coraquenque, whose two feathers were 'placed upright in the scarlet tasselled fringe of a large turban' as symbols of 'authority deriving from the heavens',[104] bear an uncanny similarity to the two feathers that feature in headdresses of Egyptian lector priests, which may have contributed to the iconography of the two-horned Moses that so fascinated Freud.[105]

By dying in 1937 Smith was spared the indignity of having much of his life's work apparently discredited by radiocarbon dating. Less than a decade later, Willard Libby proposed a method for dating organic materials by measuring their content of carbon-14, carbon's radioactive isotope. Prior to this discovery, the most effective undermining of Smith's diffusionist proselytizing was confined to comments about the unlikelihood of the natives of those lands that adopted the superior ways of the ancient Egyptians failing to adopt such phenomena as the wheeled vehicle. In this and other instances, however, Smith turned the objection back on his critics, questioning these advocates of 'psychic unity' as to why such a 'happy thought' as the wheel had not spontaneously occurred to native Americans.[106]

Putting Smith, Perry and Rivers together with a surprisingly Freudian reading of Schopenhauer on the subject of the erotic unconscious (and the '*genius* or double'), Lewis felt evermore confident that it was by the banks of Nile that 'all civilization saw the light':

> In touch in an organized way with a supernatural world of whose potentialities we can form no conception, the art of Egypt is as rare and irreplaceable a thing as would be some communication dropped upon our earth from another planet.[107]

In particular, Smith's 'exhilarating and adventurous treatise', *The Evolution of the Dragon*, encouraged Lewis to assert that the Egyptians invented art by creating statues of the deceased to supplement and ultimately supersede their mummification.[108]

> Experience of dreams led men to believe that the 'soul' [or 'Ka'] could also leave the body temporarily and enjoy varied experiences. But the concrete-minded Egyptian demanded some physical evidence to buttress these intangible ideas of the wandering abroad of his vital essence. He made a statue for it to dwell in after his death, because he was not able to make an adequately life-like reproduction of the dead man's features upon the mummy itself or its wrappings. Then he gradually persuaded himself that the life-substance could exist apart from the body as a 'double' or 'twin' which animated the statue.[109]

According to Smith, in his earliest attempt to interpret these phenomena, he

> adopted the view that the making of portrait statues was the direct outcome of the practice of mummification. But Dr. Alan Gardiner, whose intimate knowledge of the early literature enables him to look at such problems from the Egyptian's own point of view, has suggested a modification of this interpretation. Instead of regarding the custom of making statues as an outcome of the practice of mummification, he thinks that the two customs developed simultaneously, in response to the two-fold desire to preserve both the actual body and a representation of the features of the

dead. But I think this suggestion does not give adequate recognition to the fact that the earliest attempts at funerary portraiture were made upon the wrappings of the actual mummies.[110]

Lewis refers specifically to this passage, coining a facetiously Freudian phrase by way of summary:

> In *The Migrations of Early Culture*, Dr. Elliot Smith attributed the making of statues the practice of mummification. And in spite of Dr. Alan Gardiner, he is still disposed to stick to his order – namely, *mummy first, statue after*: though his distinguished colleague would prefer that they were placed abreast of each other.[111]

That Lewis seems to follow Smith in preference to the great Alan Gardiner is worthy of note, though for him the virtue of both mummification and sculpture was the freezing of time. In *The Story of Art* it is as if Ernst Gombrich has merged the two accounts, albeit implicitly erring on the side of Smith and thus of Lewis whose *Demon of Progress* he elsewhere acknowledges:

> The Egyptians held the belief that the preservation of the body was not enough. If the likeness of the king was also preserved, it was doubly sure that he would continue to exist forever. So they ordered sculptors to chisel the king's head out of hard, imperishable granite, and put it in the tomb where no one saw it, there to work its spell and to help his soul to keep alive in and through the image. One Egyptian word for sculptor was actually 'He-who-keeps-alive'.[112]

Quoting himself quoting Gardiner in 1915, Smith had already said as much in his *Migrations*:

> The sculptor who carved the portrait-statues for the Egyptian's tomb was called *sa'nkh*, 'he who causes to live', and 'the word to fashion' (*ms*) a statue is to all appearances identical with (*ms*), 'to give birth.'[113]

Smith argued that both mummification and this secondary, even more sophisticated practice spread throughout an increasingly civilized world from Egypt in the third millennium BC. Lewis built upon both this as also Smith's thesis that the beginnings of monumental architecture developed out of this practice, the deceased and their statues requiring mortuary temples to accommodate them and provide facilities for priests and access to worshippers when pharaohs and other key figures, such as the architect-sage, Imhotep, became gods.[114]

In 1922, in the second and last issue of *The Tyro*, Lewis contrasted progress in science with (ideally) its absence in the visual arts. Having provided examples of our ever-improving scientific knowledge he concluded that:

There is reason to believe that we shall soon be still better informed. In painting, on the other hand, a masterpiece of Sung or of the best sculpture of Dynastic Egypt is, as art, impossible to improve on, and very little has been produced in our time that could bear comparison with it.[115]

In both *Time and Western Man* and *Paleface*, Lewis continued to argue for the static and permanent as against the historic and progressive, and in specifically artistic terms, against the organic, ostensibly life-like naturalism of the ancient Greeks. In 1934, in *Men without Art*, Lewis confirmed his critical view of the 'chronological philosophy' of the Greeks (however beneficial to science), which culminated artistically in Rodin, 'that much-overrated master of the Flux':

If you ask me what I suggest you should place over against the perverted cascades of sleek, white, machine-ground stone of the Bergsonian sculptor, well, there is a wide choice. Neither the Greeks, not yet the Renaissance masters (except here and there) afford a quite effective contrast. The naturalist stream started flowing in Hellas, and it has gone on flowing ever since. Only now, at last, has it begun to dry up. I should direct you to Egypt, to China or Japan, to select the monumental counterblast to this last vulgar decadence of the original Hellenic mistake.[116]

'This can be put another way', writes Lewis: 'The massive sculpture of the Pharaohs is preferable to the mist of the automatic or spirit-picture.'[117] Lewis recommends 'the *external* approach to things (relying upon the evidence of the eye rather than of the more emotional organs of sense)'. Even when returning to praise Egyptian art as the only hope for the future of civilization he cannot refrain from suggestive ridicule of the Romantic alternative. The external approach, he writes:

can make of 'the grotesque' a healthy and attractive companion. Other approaches cannot do this. The scarab can be accommodated – even a crocodile's tears can be relieved of some of their repulsiveness. For the requirement of the new-world order this is essential.[118]

If Lewis failed to follow Smith and Perry as far as America in his diffusionism, Smith at least seems to have encouraged him to seek out Egyptian influence in the Maghreb.[119] When, somewhat surprisingly, in the spring of 1931 Lewis visited Morocco with his long-suffering (and unacknowledged) wife, Froanna, his prior reading helped him recognize the full range of ancient improvement:

as a result of this preliminary preparation, I knew before I put my legs across its back or had ever clapped eyes on it, that the ass of which the Berbers make such extensive use is of Egyptian origin.[120]

On a more elevated front, Lewis surveyed the origins of the earliest building types including the so-called Kasbahs. In the preface to the second edition of *The Ancient Egyptians and the Origins of Civilization* (1923), Smith had written that he 'became convinced that the rude stone monuments of the Mediterranean litoral were crude copies of the more finished and earlier monuments of the Pyramid Age'. In the original 1911 edition he discussed the western direction of Egyptian diffusion into Mauretania, 'where the art of building megalithic structures took root and developed exceedingly, specializing along lines peculiarly distinctive of this real home of the dolmen, as distinct from its Egyptian forerunner, the more finished, but far more ancient, stone tomb and mortuary temple.'[121] Had he read Inigo Jones's treatise on *Stonehenge* he would no doubt have approved of the early Stuart architect's notion that this ancient monument was Roman, given that Jones's hypothesis was underpinned by his admiration of Egyptian engineering, as confirmed in his annotated copy of Herodotus:

> Those, which made this wonder [the Temple of Latona at Buto on the Nile] would have much more admired, if they could have seen the *Obelisk* raised in times of old by King *Ramesis* at *Heliopolis*, in that part of *Aegypt* anciently called *Thebais*, in height one hundred twenty one Geometrical feet (which of our measure makes one hundred thirty six feet) of one entire stone.[122]

Appended to Cy Fox's 1983 edition of his *Filibusters in Barbary* are two articles Lewis extracted from an unpublished book originally intended to succeed it. The most relevant of these for our purposes was published in January 1933 in *The Architectural Review* under the title 'The Kasbahs of the Atlas'. This was illustrated by a selection of Lewis's drawings of the said buildings. That his fascination with these endured is confirmed by the presence of one such image on the wall of his studio in the background of his 1938 portrait of 'John Macleod' now in the Yale Center for British Art.[123] Immediately behind the sitter, to the left of his head, Lewis has depicted a slightly abstracted cluster of buildings, at least one of which is a Kasbah, featuring a distinctively Egyptian cavetto cornice and rooftop corner finials. A clumsier depiction of a Kasbah is included in a similar background position in the generally somewhat awkward pencil and watercolour drawing of a 'Berber woman'.[124] In the section on 'Kasbah-Art', Lewis is keen to emphasize the Berber's proud history of avoiding the iconoclastic puritanism of Islam. Lewis writes that the Berber:

> is anything ... but in a position of abject submission to a High God. Even, I should guess, he is essentially the reverse – true worship of the Berber peasant being the saint-cult of the Koubah, rather than the more abstract devotions indicated by the mosque.[125] And in his Kasbah-art he seems to have put at the disposal of Man, and brought into the service of his personal egotism, all the resources of a monumental aesthetic developed originally for some far more abstract and lofty purpose. The effect is rather that of a cathedral organ being employed to accompany a Tango. These towers that are pharaonic *pylons* may be partly responsible for this sensation, which forces itself upon one's consciousness.[126]

Noting that 'The great Kasbahs of the Atlas are a formidable explosion of Berber power,' Lewis asks: 'if the Berber tradition is an ancient one, how did it withstand the assaults of Arab taste?' The latter is characterized as the victim of 'the barren rigours of the Koranic compulsions, which stamped out organic form, and put a *Verbot* upon life altogether, and for which, of course, the body of a lion in stone would be a trespass) – most people would even concede that this Hispano-Arabian pastry [the Alhambra] was the reverse of a great art-form.'[127]

In his *Architectural Review* essay Lewis answers his own question with an idea derived from Émile-Félix Gautier (1864–1940), 'a person with the utmost sense':

> It is because of *the dual soul of Maghreb* – the *nomadic* and the *sedentary*. That is why Maghreb was never one.
> The imported religion – and such a religion too, one of the most ferocious and Fantastic engines of mass-bigotry that the world has to show, anywhere in its well-stocked Chamber of Horrors – *that* gave them one 'dual soul'.[128]

Lewis's second answer to his own question returns us to diffusionist Egyptology:

> the absence of the written word ... has been the most powerful factor of any in mummifying a tradition that may be coeval with Knossos, or the early history of the Nile Valley. But the Kasbah art is also a part, essentially, of the scene in which it occurs.[129]

He describes the Kasbahs as

> the wild fruit of these particular short scorched plains or volcanic gorges; as they descend towards the Sahara from the central crater of Sirwa, the Kasbahs become more and more magnificent.[130]

Sirwa or more usually Siwa is the name of the ancient oasis celebrated for its temple to Amun-Ra which Alexander the Great visited when he conquered Egypt (or liberated it from the Persians) in 332 BC, going on to found Alexandria to the North East.[131]

Emphasizing on the one hand the naturalness of the Kasbahs and the fact that the surviving examples are not ancient due to being made of mudbrick, he nevertheless continues in a mode that reminds one of the special scope Egyptian artefacts afford the intelligent observer of interpreting their ancient legacy, given the relative absence of documentary evidence:

> They could not have been produced without the existence of some very splendid tradition of building. ... The first architectural oddity to strike the observer is the strange appearance – that is like a trick of perspective – of all these towers drawing together as they rise into the air. This in fact is the case; the flanking towers are tapered from the base up. In some cases, in the course of an ascent

of say, forty or fifty feet they may lose as much as a quarter of their girth. This obliquity of the Egyptian pylon, recalling immediately the ancient temples of the valley of the Nile, is probably a first clue to the ancestry of these buildings. The diminishing silhouette of the pylon (only two or three times as high) – in place of the sharply-projecting cavetto of the former, if the tower is high, there is a combed and martial crest – found again everywhere in the heart of the Atlas.[132]

Lewis comments on the 'designs of animals' that are seen, for example 'two rock carvings of a ram, with the solar disk between its horns flanked with the uraeus'.

In Karnak, Gautier tells us, and in the temples of Upper Egypt, it is impossible to see the criocephalic Ammon-Ra, represented so often in the wall paintings, without immediately being struck with the analogy between Ammon-Ra and the Ram of the Atlas. 'It is exactly the same profile of the same head,' he tells us. 'bearing the same disk, similarly flanked – the solar disk, in short. A necklace adds still further to the resemblance.'

Lewis continues:

And *Ammon* is the god of the Saharan oases. So it is natural that his image should be found at Figuig, the gate of the Sahara. Ammon is not a very old god. The cult of Ammon-Ra dates from the eighteenth dynasty (that is to say, roughly 1,500 years before Christ). So we are well inside the temporal frontiers assigned by history to the Berber races.

And he repeats:

Nowhere else in the world, as far as I know, is there any monumental building of this order, with a façade of dual towers, tapering in the manner of the Egyptian pylon, and producing exactly this effect, except the Kasbah of the Atlas. And in spite of the Libyan Desert and the Sahara, the Atlas is, after all, the next-door neighbour of the Nile.[133]

***

'One thing however is certain,' wrote the normally more astutely (less optimistically) prophetic Lewis in *Blasting and Bombardiering*:

Apart from the gallant rear-guard actions spasmodically undertaken in the British Isles by literary sharpshooters steeped in the heroic 'abstract' tradition, usually still termed 'avant-garde' for want of a more appropriate word; and save possibly for the rather untidy sunset, for a few years yet, in the 'new' American Fiction, by the end of this century the movement to which, historically, I belong will be as remote as predynastic Egyptian statuary.[134]

This was published in 1937, by which time it seems that his enthusiasm for ancient Egypt, or at least for Smith's diffusionist account of it, had cooled somewhat if only because it involved too much attention being paid to the past which, even as he critiqued Freud, he associated with the buried unconscious. Meanwhile, the quasi-Surrealist paintings he produced throughout this period belied his classicizing polemics. A passage in *Time and Western Man* summarizes his considered opinion by way of conclusion. Given Freud's favourite analogy between archaeology and psychoanalysis it might reference buried Egyptiana in all but name, and is perhaps relevant to other essays in this volume:

> Freud's teaching has resuscitated the animal past of the soul, following upon Darwin, and hatched a menagerie of animal, criminal and primitive 'complexes' for the Western Mind. All these approaches stress *the Past*, the primitive, all that is *not* the civilized Present. There is no revolutionary theory or movement that does not ultimately employ itself in bringing to life ghosts, and putting the Present to school with the Past.
>
> But there is nothing so 'new' and so startling as the Past for most people. All the supreme novelties come from the most distant epochs; the more remote the more novel, of course.[135]

Despite, or perhaps (as with Freud?) because of his familiarity with early twentieth-century Germany and Austria, Wyndham Lewis was reluctant to dwell on the danger of Nazism as distinct from that of another world war, though he at least realized that Nazism was in large part a reaction to Communism and a bigger threat to civilization than the Catholic church, about which Freud was still complaining as late as 1938.[136] Lewis's book on Hitler was written in 1930 in the wake of the latter's declaration that he would seek election through democratic means and before he became Chancellor. By the following year he was critiquing Paris, which had 'had its life squeezed out of it by the Machine-Age': 'Berlin could beat it if it were not for Hitler.'[137] Lewis's visit to Germany and Poland in 1937 confirmed his negative reading of *Mein Kampf* and by 1939 he had published the critical *Hitler Cult* and the unfortunately titled: *The Jews: Are They Human?* The latter is still cited as evidence of Lewis's anti-Semitism, despite its argument for the opposite, urging the admission of Jewish refugees and praised as such by *The Jewish Chronicle*.[138] In *The Mysterious Mr Bull* Lewis in fact wrote that 'The average Jew is twice as intelligent as the average Englishman', but like Smith he tended to disassociate race from culture.[139] Though he had been planning to leave England since at least as early as December 1938 when he wrote to Pound about plans for an exhibition in New York, Lewis, his wife and pet dog ended up sailing from Southampton for North America the day before war was declared and a fortnight before Freud ended his life with help from his doctor and his daughter.[140] All four of Freud's sisters would die during a Holocaust that was clearly the worse for war, Stalin's mass-murdering being well-underway before war began.

Though they were both inspired by common sources including Egypt and (despite Freud's denial that he ever read him), Nietzsche, inasmuch as Lewis acknowledged Freud he critiqued him as symptomatic of the pessimistic post-Romantic flux that was dragging Western civilization into what Smith and Perry described as 'degeneracy'. If in *The Mysterious Mr Bull* Lewis somewhat surprisingly praises Freud as a scientist, he otherwise tended to scoff, writing that: 'Freud explains everything by *sex*: I explain everything by *laughter*.'[141] The latter approach was consistent with Lewis's advocacy of a kind of moral and aesthetic detachment and also applies to Lewis's satirical choice of names. In the present context I conclude with two examples of his deflationary (satirical) exploitation of Egyptian nomenclature, the coining of 'Hotshepsot', who Beckett-like (but more brutally amusing) features in the revised, 1927 edition of Lewis's play, *The Enemy of the Stars*, and the name he gave his Sealyham dog.[142]

Given my recent documentation of (at least) a meeting between Lewis and the Scots poet, Joseph Macleod, who took over the Cambridge Festival Theatre from Egyptologist and literary impresario, Terence Gray, it is noteworthy that in 1920, the 25-year-old Gray published *The Life of the King of the South and North Kamaria, Daughter of the Sun, Hatshepsut, A Pageant of Court Life in Old Egypt in the Early XVIIIth Dynasty, Reconstructed from the Monuments*.[143]

Given that it was, in his own words, 'circa 1924–5' that Lewis worked on his 'Candide-like piece' he may have had Gray's play in mind when writing *Hoodopip*.[144] The futuristic setting for this incomplete manuscript on the life of a Tyro is a kingdom called 'O', located on a distant planet which has developed a culture at least superficially inspired by ancient Egypt:

> there were by this time schools of Egyptology: it was a subject in the ordinary school curriculum, and a great many Egyptian words and even grammatical forms were to be found in the official language of O. All this had originated in a long series of Musical Comedies with touring companies in all the provincial cities of O, which had had the Egypt of our antiquity as a setting.[145]

This theatrical theme extends to a proto-Freudian reference to the similarity between the finding of a pharaonic Moses (in all but name) and the protection of Horus from Seth by Isis:

> At birth a child was carried in a specially prepared cradle to the river bank, & concealed among the bullrushes for some hours. This survival of the Osiris myth was a source of considerable danger to the new born KNAP, but also one of very great sentimental efficacy in the life of the woman.[146]

Bands of men

> got up to represent the soldiery of Dynastic Egypt, pretended to scour the river banks. ... On recovering what was assumed to be his usual appearance [he had

been exposed on the river too long by accident], he was noticed to have the assured eye of a perfect little Pharaoh.

Still in satirical mode, 'BES' is also referenced as, 'the name of an Egyptian deity of African origin'. Lewis writes that:

> He is represented in the form of a bald and paunchy dwarf Satyr, bearded, with a panther skin round the body, and a tiara of feathers on the head. He was the god of the Birth House of the Egyptian temple. Subsequently he was regarded as the especial entertainer of the child. He is also the patron of dancing and music. The BES with whom Hoodopip was first brought into contact was a rather peculiar one. He was named Hapopop (Hap being the Egyptian for Bull).[147]

Where *The Enemy of the Stars* is concerned, 'Hotshepsot' first appears quite casually in Lewis's 1927 enlargement of his 1914 play. She then makes a more memorable entrance:

> She is a big girl with a big roll in the hips and carrying her head erect and without movement in contrast to her revolving middle, as if it had been used to oriental pitchers and the desert palm wells. She has ear-rings of beaten gold.[148]

She strikes Arghol heavily across the mouth 'with a thick white fist with divers rings'.[149]

Later, as if in connection with Hanp threatening to slit the throat of the snoring Arghol, Lewis inserts the following stage instructions:

> (A head rises above the floor-level at the rear of the hut, out of the trap descending to the player's quarters. It is Hotshepsot. She remains a head only, of an observer dropped up to watch for a spell, she does not come up any more out of the trap.)[150]

Hotshepsot's head then engages in a facetious tragi-comic dialogue with Hanp, beginning with: 'The devil is asleep!' For all his tendency to dismiss Freud and to a lesser extent Frazer, the nature of Lewis's long-standing interest in this play encourages us to read its characters as versions of his patricidal self (as Hanp), his feckless father (as Arghol) and tougher-than-expected mother ('Miss Hotshepsot'), albeit with considerable qualifications.[151] Hotshepsot's head then disappears 'with a grimace of contumelious scorn and parting snort from lips of red disdain' reminding one of Shelley's wilful misreading of Rameses II's Ozymandian smile (which he never saw) as a 'sneer of cold command'.[152] For some, the comedy in all this may since have been enhanced by Zahi Hawass's discovery of Hatshepsut's mummy.[153] Lewis, meanwhile, has Hanp notice the chopper 'which has flown out of the hand of Hotshepsot, when he tumbled her into the companion-hatch'.[154] Hanp eventually kills Arghol with this chopper and then commits suicide from a nearby canal bridge.

Many a detached head of Hatshepsut might have inspired Lewis, notably in the museums of Munich (where he rented a studio in 1906), Berlin, Cairo, New York and

Brooklyn. But since the association of Hotshepsot with Hatshepsut has now been independently made in a fine essay on the Freudian implications of Lewis's relations with his father (and in terms of his alleged homophobia) I now turn to the relatedly humorous topic of Tut, the name that Mr and Mrs Lewis gave their pet dog.

In November 1922, having been searching for some thirty years, Howard Carter finally discovered the tomb of Tutankhamun. Ever energetically up-to-the-minute, in January and February of 1923, Elliot Smith published a series of eight interpretative articles on the subject for *The Daily Telegraph* and a few months later merged these in a 133-page, illustrated book on *Tutankhamen and the Discovery of his Tomb by the late Earl of Carnarvon and Mr. Howard Carter*. Such publications encouraged familiarization with both the buried treasure and the teenaged pharaoh, contributing to him becoming a household name. There were 'King Tut' balls held in New York and the 1924 British Empire exhibition in Wembley Stadium featured a full-size replica of the tomb's treasure-filled antechamber.[155] The premature death of Lord Carnarvon in the previous year, widely interpreted as a result of the pharaoh's curse, only added to what became known as 'Tut-mania'.[156]

Lewis had referenced the discovery of Tut's tomb and its supposed curse in September 1927 in *The Enemy 2* while making fun of D. H. Lawrence's dark consciousness (albeit acknowledging him as 'one of the most justly celebrated of english [*sic*] novelists'):

> We are almost reminded of the superstitions associated with the tombs of the Egyptian dead, and the belief in the *unlucky* nature of the enterprise of the excavator the Late Lord Carnarvon and Tutankamen, for instance. His death seemed to come very suddenly after disturbing Tutankamen.

Lewis then references (if more facetiously) the analogy between archaeology and psychoanalysis promoted by Freud:

> The White Man has unearthed and brought to light an enormous historical rubbish-heap: there is nothing he has not excavated and brought into his own 'consciousness for examination'.[157]

Despite being the subject of several of Lewis's most (uncharacteristically) charming sketches (e.g. Fig. 3.1), so far as I am aware only a single reference has been made to the likelihood that the dog which his wife, and to a surprising extent, he too doted upon was named after the pharaoh Smith called 'this youthful nonentity'.[158] Tutankhamun was so ubiquitously celebrated that from an initially exotic pharaoh he became King Tut and was then further familiarized as 'Mr Tut' or plain 'Tut' (which was indeed the first part of the tripartite name Tut-Ankh-Amon).[159] Given Lewis's satirical style and his intense, at least decade-long interest in things Egyptological documented above, it now seems obvious that Lewis further diminished Akhenaten's teenaged son/son-in-law by naming his pet Sealyham after him.[160] Given the Lewises' further familiarization (and feminization?) of their dog's pharaonic name to 'Tutsi' he came to bear an unfortunate

'Mummy First: Statue After'

Figure 3.1 Tut (1931). Sketch by Wyndham Lewis. Pencil, charcoal and wash, 11 × 9¼ in. By permission of the Wyndham Lewis Memorial Trust (a registered charity).

resemblance to the victim of Lewis's alter ego, Richard Beresin, in his brilliant but brutal, 1918 short story 'The War Baby': 'Titsy, as she was called, was a diminutive of Lutitia. Tets appeared to Beresin to sum her up.'[161] She is a rather gullible, inarticulate girl who is impregnated by the caddish soldier, Beresin, who then leaves for Egypt. He thinks of himself in Nietzschean terms but of her with just enough affection to continue corresponding from Egypt after he learns that 'Tets must expect a child'. 'Tets' he writes, 'was small and pathetic. ... But Tets was enthroned; for although one of several, she was softly sculpting a Totem, whereas others [that is, other casual relationships] had not had that art – or craft. He wrote her a sort of love-letter'.[162] By return her parents wrote 'in injured and more or less injurious tones that their daughter was dead'.[163]

The extent of Tutankhamun's popularity was such that a hit song in jollified Egyptomaniac style was launched by Billy Jones and Ernie Hare under the title: 'Old King Tut (Was a Wise Old Nut)'. Evelyn Waugh thought it all most vulgar but having married Lord Carnarvon's niece and visited 'the Tutankhamen discoveries' with her he was 'overwhelmed by [their] beauty'.[164] President Herbert Hoover thought 'King Tut' an appropriate name for their celebrated Belgian shepherd.[165] Still in the process of being analysed, the tomb's treasures confirmed Smith and many of his readers, including Lewis, in their belief that ancient Egypt was the unrivalled source of modern civilization.

> The dazzling display of skill and luxury has forced the scholar and the man in the street to recognize in some measure the vastness of the achievements of ancient Egyptian civilization and to ask themselves whether this vigorous and highly developed culture could have failed to exert a much more profound influence upon its neighbours than is generally admitted. When it is recalled that Egypt herself devised the ships and developed the seamanship which created the chief bond of union with Syria and Crete, East Africa and Arabia, the Persian Gulf and beyond, we should be in a better position to realize the plain meaning of the evidence that points to Egypt as the dominating factor in shaping the nascent civilization of the world.[166]

The Lewises acquired their Sealyham terrier soon after returning from their adventures in Morocco in August 1931 when they migrated to 27 Ordnance Road (now Ordnance Hill, London NW8). The acquisition of a dog was no doubt a placatory gesture of domesticity after what must have been an arduous time for Lewis's childless wife.[167] The sketches of Tut that survive seem to date from soon after his acquisition, between 1931 and 1933.[168] Though relatively indifferent to his various illegitimate children, Lewis expressed concern for Tut during their transatlantic crossing in September 1939.[169] Having abandoned what Freud had so recently hailed as 'beautiful, free and generous England' for his own native land, by January 1944, self-exiled in Canada where he and his wife experienced the quasi-Kafkaesque decline in their morale most poignantly described in his novel *Self Condemned*, the decline and death of Tut so added to their woes that Lewis sounded, by his standards, almost sentimental:

> We are on the grim side just now. The death of our hirsute gremlin has left an ugly gap. You will understand that people never forgive you for possessing more of anything than themselves. ... By coming to Canada – in the middle of a world-war – ... my wife has had to pay as well as myself. So this small creature, which stood for all that was benevolent in the universe, sweetened the bitter medicine for her. Like the spirit of a simpler and saner time, this fragment of primitive life

confided his destiny to her, and went through all the black days beside us. She feels she has been wanting in some care – for why should this growth in his side, almost as big as his head, have gone undetected? Such are the reflections that beset her. Whereas I am just another human being – by no means a well of primitive *joie-de-vivre*: so not much comfort![170]

Given his reputation as 'that lonely old volcano of the Right', Lewis's early identification with Timon of Athens's post-philanthropical misanthropy (and perhaps less consciously with Timon's ungrateful clients?) might be relevant here.[171] In Plutarch's life of Mark Antony, after Cleopatra's flight from Actium, Antony resolves to lead a life like Timon's, 'because he had the like wrong offered him, that was before offered unto Timon.' In Dryden's *All for Love* (1,i), Antony retires to Isis Temple. In *Timon of Athens*, which Lewis illustrated in 1913 with 'artificial strife ... livelier than life', a surely depressive Shakespeare (inasmuch as he was sole author) used the word 'dog' pejoratively throughout, but has Timon prefer to 'be a beggar's dog than Apemantus'. In superb style, anticipating both Vorticism and his enthusiasm for Egyptian art, Lewis's *Thebaid* depicts the moment that Timon informs Alcibiades: 'I am *misanthropos*, and hate mankind. / For thy part, I do wish thou wert a dog, that I might love thee something.'[172] Lewis's naming of his diminutive pet after a magnificently memorialized pharaoh is consistent with his sometimes similarly facetious, yet ultimately serious support of the diffusionists and their advocacy of the Egyptian origins of art and indeed civilization.

CHAPTER 4
ANCIENT EGYPT IN WILLIAM S. BURROUGHS'S NOVELS
Riccardo Gramantieri

The American author and artist William S. Burroughs described control as a sort of occult and subliminal form of domination, the features of which closely resemble those established in the relationship between a submissive faithful and a deity. This control permeates his novels. His works contain descriptions both of situations in which such control occurs and the techniques used to implement it. Indeed, Burroughs meant his novels to act as deconditioning works and wrote them to combat such control. In his most famous works such as *Naked Lunch* (1959) and *Nova Trilogy* (*The Soft Machine*, 1961; *The Ticket That Exploded*, 1962; *Nova Express*, 1964), Burroughs put 'The Order of Mayan Priests' at the top of the theocratic system that controls the population of the entire planet. In his later works, however, Burroughs abandoned the Mesoamerican divinities and started referring to the world of ancient Egypt, Egyptian methods of writing and Egyptian mythology. This change in perspective was due to his increasing interest in the subject of immortality, which he considered an alternative to theories of evolution heralded in the 1970s.[1] Instead, he depicted the seven souls, the hellish River Duad and the Western Lands as the ultimate end of man. Despite Burroughs's place in the canon of American literature, and recent academic interest in assessing the reception of ancient Egypt in modern culture, ancient Egypt in Burroughs's works has not yet been established; this chapter rectifies this, establishing his use of a 'hieroglyphic' writing process and ancient Egyptian mythology, which he adapted for the modern world in which he found himself.

Egyptian mythology had always been among Burroughs's first interests; hieroglyphs had captured his attention in the late 1930s as a method of writing with symbols which (unlike modern alphabets) imitate natural objects and can encompass magical meanings.[2] For this reason, Burroughs considered hieroglyphs a communication system that was difficult to 'control'. As hieroglyphs are based on images they cannot be subject to modification. Words can be distorted, truncated or altered; symbolic images cannot. Burroughs also held that a language based on symbols could not contain the concept of identity. If the word 'is' is abolished, language is independent from preordained identities; it is more precise and less easily manipulated.

In 1936, Burroughs obtained a bachelor's degree from Harvard in anthropology, having written a thesis on Mayan archaeology.[3] In 1939, he attended seminars in general semantics led by the Polish philosopher Alfred Korzybski in Chicago. He also attended a new course in anthropology at Harvard in the autumn of that year, during which he became interested in Egyptian hieroglyphs. He studied the subject in greater depth when, in 1942, 'in Chicago Burroughs … turned his interest in language to learning Egyptian hieroglyphs, a subject he had approached earlier when he was studying Mayan hieroglyphs.'[4] Ancient Egypt was a mysterious world which harmonized with his pseudoscientific interests and the image that Burroughs, as a self-styled intellectual bohemian, wanted to project. In 1953, when Burroughs and Allen Ginsberg visited the Metropolitan Museum, the poet took a picture of his friend in front of a sphinx, naming him 'Brother Sphinx' because of his air of 'authority on ancient secrets, a master of inscrutable wisdom'.[5]

Burroughs had an anti-academic attitude. He was expressly in favour of any theory developed outside of the scientific establishment. In the 1950s, for example, he was a convinced admirer of Wilhelm Reich's concept of orgone.[6] Therefore, it is not surprising that in the 1940s Burroughs was attracted to all that was innovative or definable as 'alternative', that is, not to be ascribed to a strictly classified system. General semantics was innovative, and not yet recognized by universities. Early proponents of the field claimed that words affect health: language manipulation may condition behaviour and, hence, the person's body and mind. A lack of understanding due to a general linguistic abstraction and, of course, manipulation, may help strengthen coercion and control over a human being. Interested in both general semantics and hieroglyphic scripts during these formative years, Burroughs fused these two unorthodox interests in his later literary output.

William Burroughs and word control

Alfred Korzybski's general semantics met with great popularity between the late 1930s and the early 1950s in the United States. Many writers of that time, especially authors who were active in the field of science fiction such as A. E. Van Vogt, Robert A. Heinlein and Robert Moore Williams took an interest in it and referred to it, directly or indirectly, in their work.[7] Heinlein's and Williams's biographer, H. Patterson, wrote that Korzybski 'was in exactly the right time and place to exploit this particular paradigm shift'.[8] Many intellectuals and artists saw in general semantics, which was unveiled in *Science and Sanity: An Introduction to Non-Aristotelian Systems and General Semantics* (1933), not only a possible method to improve oneself (it was meant to be a mental health technique) but also a set of communication techniques applying specifically to the writer's profession. Indeed, it was intended to offer a new way to communicate based on the suppression of the third person singular of the verb 'to be': 'is'. After 2,000 years, general semantics set out to destroy Aristotle's principle of identity. According to Korzybski, this change was necessary since the discoveries of twentieth-century physics had opened the doors to a microscopic model of matter that had led man to see everyday life as an electro-colloidal process:

> Our knowledge today indicates that all life is electro-colloidal in character, the functioning of the nervous system included. We do not as yet know the intrinsic

mechanisms, but from an electro-colloidal point of view every part of the brain is connected with every other part and with our nervous system as a whole. With such a foundation, even though it becomes necessary to investigate different aspects of the processes of abstracting for purposes of analysis, we should be aware that these different aspects are parts of one whole continuous process of normal human life.[9]

In this new model of thought, the notion of identity (as an abstract generalization) is discarded. While it is true that this concept had enabled the development of modern science, it had strongly contributed to the imprecision of modern language. In *Science and Sanity* Korzybski claimed that the way in which we see reality is influenced by our use of words. Stratification of inaccurate and generic meanings of words had resulted in an imprecise vision of reality and, consequently, an imperfect way of thinking. The wrong use of words was also the cause of behavioural issues, from petty daily incidents to wars. Communication dysfunctions also led to the development of psychosis.[10]

Burroughs became convinced by Korzybski's theories; in particular the idea that words can influence an individual in a direct manner captured his attention. The manipulative potential of words could be harnessed to alter human behaviour: to control. Therefore, Burroughs concluded that words are dangerous, and that government systems use words to control 'the masses' through newspapers, television and advertising. According to Burroughs, each word is ambiguous and 'To speak is to lie – to live is to collaborate.'[11] There is no defence against the word but silence. Burroughs believed that the human being thinks and speaks in terms of written words, which are then uttered (spoken). By altering the words, whether written or spoken, orders can be transmitted which can subliminally force others to perform compulsive behaviour. By modifying the words, information becomes false or unintelligible. The method applies as a means of control implemented by the government and multinationals to maintain the status quo and to propagate coercion.

Burroughs's concept of control directly derives from Orwellian technology. His novel *Naked Lunch* (1959) describes 'The Switchboard', a mechanism that is halfway between a computer and an electroshock device:

Electric drills that can be turned on at any time are clamped against the subject's teeth; and he is instructed to operate an arbitrary switchboard, to put certain connections in certain sockets in response to bells and lights. Every time he makes a mistake the drills are turned on for twenty seconds. The signals are gradually speeded up beyond his reaction time. Half an hour on the switchboard and the subject breaks down like an overloaded thinking machine.[12]

In the novel, the doctors paid by the plutocrats governing the state of Interzone control all possible opponents using physical torture and controlling thought as well as behaviour. In his subsequent novels, the implementation of this control is described as induced in a more subliminal manner, for example, through the maintenance of urges for drugs and sex, as well as through word manipulation.

Burroughs believed that drugs and sex were the tools used to control drug addicts and homosexuals respectively, two demographics that he saw as potentially dangerous to the government. Word manipulation, however, was a more general control technique which might be applied to the entirety of humankind. Controlling words means controlling information. Subliminal methods involving pre-recording and the sequencing of special sentences can drive compulsive behaviours. In Burroughs's opinion, the modified word acts as a virus which settles in the nervous system and takes hold of the human host, thus becoming a sort of double. Burroughs names this 'word virus' the 'Other Half':

> the 'Other Half' is the word. The 'Other Half' is an organism. Word is an organism. The presence of the 'Other Half' a separate organism attached to your nervous system on an air of words can now be demonstrated experimentally. One of the most common 'hallucinations' of subject during sense withdrawal is the feeling of another body sprawled through the subject's body at an angle ... yes quite an angle it is the 'Other Half' worked quite some years on a symbiotic basis. From symbiosis to parasitism is a short step. The word is now a virus. The flu virus may once have been a healthy lung cell. It is now a parasitic organism that invades and damages the lungs. The word may once have been a healthy neural cell. It is now a parasitic organism that invades and damages the central nervous system.[13]

According to Burroughs, the word is not a human innate characteristic. It was fixed in the human host in prehistory and, under certain conditions, can have certain effects on the nervous system, facilitating control.

Burroughs wrote extensively about word control in his *Nova Trilogy*. These novels were written according to a literary technique that he called 'cut-up', and which he claimed was meant to disrupt word control. Inspired by his friend, the Surrealist painter Brion Gysin, this method involves cutting up sentences or paragraphs of heterogeneous texts, by himself and other authors (Burroughs often used Beckett, Kafka, Conrad and science fiction novels) and rearranging them in a new order:

> when you cut and rearrange words on a page, new words emerge. And words change meaning. The word 'drafted' as into the Army, moved into a context of blueprints or contracts, gives an altered meaning. New words and altered meanings are implicit in the process of cutting up, and could have been anticipated. Other results were not expected. When you experiment with cut-ups over a period of time, some of the cut and rearranged texts seem to refer to future events.[14]

Cut-up destructs the logical discourse. The text that emerges from it can be understood only if the reader is not under the word virus's control. The teleological aspect of cut-up is compensatory: texts already written (belonging to the past), when manipulated, produce new texts (belonging to the future). They become orders to be executed, actions to be performed. They are dispatches for the Nova police. Burroughs thus identifies the writer as a police officer, a private detective or an astronaut: characters who will execute orders encoded in modified texts.

Nova Trilogy describes a war fought by, and between, the Nova Police, represented by agent William Lee, and Nova Mob, alien viruses aiming at invading planet Earth. The viruses use the three forms of control outlined by Burroughs, taking the guise of drug dealers, prostitutes and modified words. This latter type of virus stimulates reception errors; they deceive about hearing things that were never said, delete real messages and cause bureaucracy to thrive.[15]

The final scene of the *Trilogy* does not appear at the end of the third novel, but instead the middle of the second: the Nova Police burst into the 'reality studio' where the tapes recording the words that are meant to control mankind are cut and re-edited, and where the biological movie (the pre-recordings that dictate a person's life) is made. The machine that edits the audio and video tapes must be destroyed to disrupt this control. In the end, the 'control machine is disconnected – Word fell out of here through the glass and metal streets – God of Panic pipes blue notes through dying peoples – The law is dust – The wired structure of reality went up in slow-motion flashes'.[16] The editing chamber, the reality studio, is dismantled. No movie can be re-cut and silence reigns at last. Mankind is free from the virus because it is free from words.

Hieroglyphs as the anti-control weapon

To counteract control over words, the only possible weapon – aside from silence and word manipulation – is the use of a type of functional communication that is not based on words. Syntax contributes to words' meanings. The greater the gap between the word and the entity to which it refers, the greater the control that can be exerted through it. If the word is the very image of the entity to be represented, however, then there is no way to control it. In his interview-book, *The Job* (1969), Burroughs cites this example:

> The study of hieroglyphic languages shows us that a word is an image … the written word is an image. However, there is an important difference between hieroglyphic and a syllabic language. If I hold up a sign with the word 'ROSE' written on it, and you read that sign, you will be forced to repeat the word 'ROSE' to yourself. If I show you a picture of a rose you do not have to repeat the word. You can register the image in silence. A syllabic language forces you to verbalize in auditory patterns. A hieroglyphic language does not.[17]

Hence, the deconditioning is obtained via the 'hieroglyphic silence', of which Burroughs made explicit use with experimental works in the late 1970s. *The Book of Breeething* (1974), an *ante-litteram* graphic novel, makes explicit reference to the ancient Egyptian Books of Breathing (funerary texts aiding the deceased in their journey to the afterlife) in the very title. It also includes modern hieroglyphic drawings/writings by Robert Gale and graphic references to ancient Egypt. In *The Third Mind* (1978), which Burroughs wrote with Brion Gysin, he points out the advantage of using hieroglyphs as a strategy to resist virus-words. In the chapter entitled 'Hieroglyphic silence', he states:

> No matter what the spoken language may be, you can read hieroglyphs, a picture of a chair or what have you; makes no difference what you call it, right? You don't need subvocal speech to register the meaning of hieroglyphs. Learning a hieroglyphic language is excellent practice in the lost art of inner silence. 'It would be well, today, if children were taught a good many Chinese ideograms and Egyptian hieroglyphs as a means of enhancing their appreciation of our alphabet.' If you are able to look at what is in front of you in silence, you will be able to write about it from a more perceptive viewpoint.[18]

Spoken language is based on single letters making up an alphabet. Such complexity facilitates controllability and manipulability. The word must be read for the meaning to become apparent, a filter between man and reality. On the contrary, the symbolic image is immediately recognizable. Ideograms are immediately connected to the object, circumventing this filter.

The Third Mind marked the close of Burroughs's 'technical' period. Until then, the writer had only used ancient Egypt to inform his method of writing, which enabled him to put his theories on word control into practice. The exemplification of an anti-control writing method required Burroughs to be a language technician first, and then a writer. In the 1980s, however, he abandoned his experimental style, using ancient Egypt instead as the setting for his novels.

The ancient Egyptian afterlife

During his studies Burroughs likely came across a classic study by the German Egyptologist Alfred Wiedemann, who wrote that:

> in Egypt we have the unique spectacle of one of the most elaborated forms of the doctrine of immortality side by side with the most elementary conception of higher beings ever formulated by any people. We do not know whether the belief in immortality which prevailed in the valley of the Nile is as old as the Egyptian religion in general, although at first sight it appears to be so.[19]

Ancient Egyptian beliefs in the immortal soul and its journey to the afterlife have reached us through numerous sources, dating back to various eras in the civilization's history. Although differing in some regards, they all refer to a journey to the afterlife in a perilous land. The *Pyramid Texts* – papyrus copies of scripts engraved at Sakkara in the pyramids of pharaohs reigning from the Fifth (Unas, 2315 BC) to the Sixth Dynasties (Teti, Phiopos I, Phiopos II, 2181 BC) – contain spells that enable the pharaoh to reach the afterlife.

The *Coffin Texts* – reproductions of hieroglyphs engraved on wooden sarcophagi of the first intermediate period (2181–2060 BC) – relate spells meant for the deceased of the upper echelons of society (but not royalty) who, in the afterlife, must overcome hunger and several perils. These spells are, essentially, based on the spells found in the *Pyramid Texts*, with the addition of new material.[20]

Portrayals of the afterlife can be found in many texts such as the *Book of Am-Tuat*, the *Book of Gates*, the *Book of Day*, the *Book of Caverns*, the *Book of Night* and the *Book of Two Ways*. The latter reproduces texts engraved on coffins of the Eleventh Dynasty (2133–2191 BC) and describes the pilgrimage to the Land of the Dead as a route that starts from a lake of fire from which two roads branch out: one on land (leading to the entrance to Osiris's world), and one on water (leading to a lake at Ro-Stau). The *Book of Am-Tuat* (i.e. the book about Duat, the afterlife) describes the world of the dead as crossed by a river and divided into twelve regions, each corresponding to one hour of the world of the living. In this world, the deceased follows the sun god Ra on a journey across twelve realms.[21] The *Book of Breathings* is the most important book among those written later in ancient Egyptian history. Its composition can be dated back to between 1 BC and AD 1. This text returns to elements already found in the *Pyramid Texts* and the *Book of the Dead*, featuring expressions and concepts occurring previously on the stelae and coffins of the Middle and New Kingdoms. It repeats the formulae from which other funerary religious texts were derived and invigorates ancient concepts with a sense of novelty.[22]

These various books have enabled scholars to reconstruct the ancient Egyptian underworld and envisage the journey of the soul after death. The soul leaves the grave and sets out across the Western Desert. There it meets goddess Hathor to offer her food and water; if the goddess accepts the offering, the soul is not allowed to turn back. Next there are tests to overcome: the soul meets crocodile-headed demons and snakes that endeavour to devour it. Then, there is a river with boiling water to be crossed and from which the soul is bound to drink. It then sets out towards marshes where monkeys throw pots to catch lost souls. To avoid being caught, the soul must recite magic spells and formulae from the *Book of the Dead*. The soul thus identifies with given deities who enable it to reach the shores of the lake, beyond which the kingdom of Osiris can be seen. According to *The Pyramid Texts* the lake can be crossed in two ways: in one, Thoth, in the form of an ibis, carries the soul on its wings; in the other, a boat driven by a celestial ferryman transports the deceased.[23] Finally, after reaching the kingdom of Osiris, the soul is brought before the Tribunal of Osiris.

The most perilous lands are those in the region of Duat (also spelled 'Duad' or 'Tuat'; Burroughs uses 'Duad' so I adopt this spelling when referring to his texts, rather than ancient Egyptian ones), named after the river that crosses the area. It is a narrow circular valley, surrounded by mountains, in whose recess the river flows. The Duat was the abode of many deities, including Anubis, Osiris (Lord of the Duat) and Apophis. It was 'filled with numerous supernatural beings who were inimical not only to the deceased, but to Osiris as well. In addition to Seth and his associates, who continued to pose a threat to Osiris in the Duat, there were the forces of chaos led by Apophis, who is envisioned as an endless snakelike creature'.[24]

Ancient Egypt in the Modern Imagination

The popular imaginary of ancient Egyptians and their beliefs in the afterlife is inseparably linked to mummies. The preservation of the body was an essential requirement of ancient Egyptian funerary belief, since only on this basis could the soul set off on its journey to Duat. Ancient Egyptians could not imagine a survival without a physical substratum. Man without a body seemed incomplete and ineffectual; he required his body in perpetuity, hence, the development of mummification practices.[25] Both the unearthly journey and the practice of mummification are crucial to the re-invention that Burroughs accomplishes in his novel *The Western Lands*.

The Western Lands and mummification

Mythological situations and characters from ancient Egypt feature heavily in Burroughs's last novel, *The Western Lands* (1987), as well as in his autobiographical texts, *My Education: A Book of Dreams* (1995) and *Last Words* (2000). He uses these characters and situations for three reasons: firstly, to resume the theme of the evolutionary leap into cosmic space he had advanced in the *Nova Trilogy* (although in this instance the leap would be in time rather than space: 'Ancient Egypt is the only period in history when the gates to Immortality were open, the Gates of Anubis');[26] secondly, to associate the multiple identities of his characters with the metaphor of the seven souls always in conflict with one another (in doing so, he was able to rewrite in novel form the scenarios of resident control); thirdly, to use an alternative to Mayan mythology, already employed in the *Nova Trilogy*, and an alternative to monotheistic Jewish-Christian-Islamic belief systems. Burroughs wanted to establish a 'magical Universe': 'MU is a universe of many gods, often in conflict. So the paradox of an all-powerful, all-knowing God who permits suffering, evil and death, does not arise.'[27]

The Western Lands completes a trilogy that includes *Cities of the Red Night* (1981) and *The Place of Dead Roads* (1983). Although it has few connections with the first novel except for the description of the pre-historical settlement of Waghdas, this final novel resumes the narration where the previous one had ended and reveals the identity of the killer of gunman Kim Carsons. Yet, while the previous novel was a Western (albeit an atypical one) set in nineteenth-century America, this new book describes the experiences the souls of various characters must go through in the Western Lands in order to achieve immortality. The *Western Lands* is an adventure novel whose characters were defined by Burroughs as a group of 'Chauceresque pilgrims'.[28] The protagonists are all deceased: Kim Carsons was killed in the gun duel, cyborg Joe the Dead is his killer and, as his name denotes, is already deceased. Being dead enables Burroughs's characters' souls to be free from their bodies, as required by Egyptian mythology. They face numerous dangers along the way to the Land of the Dead. The characters of *The Western Lands* move in an otherworldly territory and thus have semi-divine characteristics, similar to the protagonists of the *Nova Trilogy* (the demigod Mr Bradly Mr Martin) or of *Ah Pook Is Here* (the magnates Bickford and Hart, who reappear in *The Western Lands*).

Burroughs did not use the cut-up technique to write the novel, but continued to refer to other authors' texts. Instead of directly referencing the Egyptian holy books, however, he consulted a literary response to them in Norman Mailer's *Ancient Evenings* (1983). This novel is historical only in part: it describes a flashback to life in ancient Egypt during the reign of Ramses II. The narrative frame recounts the reincarnation of Menenhetet II, who lived at the time of Ramses IX, whose Ka meets that of his great-grandfather Menenhetet I. Evoking Harold Bloom, Mailer describes an Egypt made of 'scatology, buggery and the war between women and men'.[29] Moreover, 'For Mailer, Egypt is "one of the places where magic was being converted into social equivalence, in effect used as an exchange." '[30] If this statement applies to Mailer's Egypt, it applies even more to Burroughs's. A war between controllers is like a war between magicians. Burroughs, like Mailer, chose ancient Egypt for its links to magic. Other similarities include the theme of the seven souls fighting each other: Burroughs makes them characters, controllers of human beings. He was so delighted that he shared with Mailer:

> First, in the views of these writers, most Americans are spiritually dead. … Second, the borrowed eschatologies do not separate post-mortem existence from life in the manner ingrained in Western thought. This continuity creates new ways of reading meaning into life. Third, these foreign models for afterlife permit the authors to reclaim existence beyond death without having to accept the static soul, whose ability to develop and change ceases at the moment of death.[31]

Burroughs's indebtedness to Mailer is conspicuous in his descriptions of the infernal river and in his rehabilitation of the cycle of the seven souls freed from the body. Ancient Egyptian texts relate that 'the afterlife was predominantly celestial, with an important subterranean complement represented by the Duat'.[32] Metaphysicality is important in this model. Nevertheless, Burroughs followed Mailer's novel, which expressed its own down-to-earth corporeality. He did not write of fire or boiling water, that is, images that would have recalled an Occidental hell, but of excrement. The river of faecal waters and the ranking of the souls were concepts that Burroughs borrowed from Mailer. Mailer refers to this latter concept at length at the beginning of *Ancient Evenings*, when Menenhetet II feels his souls leave his body, one by one. Burroughs assigned a 'modern' function to each of the souls:

> The ancient Egyptians postulated seven souls. Top soul, and the first to leave at the moment of death, is Ren, the Secret Name. This corresponds to my Director. He directs the film of your life from conception to death. The Secret Name is the title of your film. When you die, that's where Ren came in. Second soul, and second one off the sinking ship, is Sekem: Energy, Power, Light. The Director gives the orders, Sekem presses the right buttons. Number three is Khu, the Guardian Angel. He, she, or it is third man out … depicted as flying away across a full moon, a bird with luminous wings and head of light. Sort of thing you might see on a screen in an Indian restaurant in Panama. The Khu is responsible for the subject and

can be injured in his defence – but not permanently, since the first three souls are eternal. They go back to Heaven for another vessel. The four remaining souls must take their chances with the subject in the Land of the Dead. Number four is Ba, the Heart, often treacherous. This is a hawk's body with your face on it, shrunk down to the size of a fist. Many a hero has been brought down, like Samson, by a perfidious Ba. Number five is Ka, the Double, most closely associated with the subject. The Ka, which usually reaches adolescence at the time of bodily death, is the only reliable guide through the Land of the Dead to the Western Lands. Number six is Khaibit, the Shadow, Memory, your whole past conditioning from this and other lives. Number seven is Sekhu, the Remains.[33]

To access the lands of the dead, the four mortal souls need to be strong enough to withstand the first three during post-mortem conflict. The decay of ancient Egyptian civilization, in Burroughs's view, stemmed from mummification techniques, which had resulted in a conflict between souls. In the 1960s, while also writing about word control, Burroughs claimed that

> any sort of physical immortality is going in the wrong direction. It is a question of separating whatever you choose to call it – the soul – from the body, not perpetuating the body anyway. I think any perpetuation of the body is a step in the wrong direction. The Egyptians made their mummies and the preservation of the mummies was essential to their immortality. I think you want to get away from the body, not get into it.[34]

To evade control, you need to escape into outer space where silence reigns; that is, where there are no words, where the word-virus cannot spread. To become immortal, you need to escape the body. It is this goal that the two leading characters of the novel, Kim and the scribe Neferti, set themselves, striving to reach the Western Lands without mummification.

The plot of the novel, which presents a variety of situations and characters in different timeframes, can be reduced to a quest. Kim Carsons, who has just been killed in a duel, is instructed by the District Supervisor to find the Western Lands, the place of immortality and, as a result, discovers why ancient Egyptian civilization collapsed. This would not have been possible if, in ancient times, the Western Lands had actually been reached.

The solution that Burroughs advanced in his novel resumed the theories of control and the algebra of need that he had framed earlier in his *Nova Trilogy*. At that time, he had expressed his idea of control through the algebra of need: control was achieved through drugs, sex or words.[35] In his new novel, Burroughs introduced the same mechanism to mummification techniques and their effect on immortality. The holy books referred to two paths (land and water); in this case, Burroughs conceived of two possible ways to achieve immortality: one is fast and straight, the other slow and crooked. The fast option involves facing death directly, a route that various characters take at Last Chance through the duel. The slow and crooked path is the vampire's way chosen by the Ren controllers: it involves dying by degrees. Burroughs's thesis was that an increase in mortality led to saturation in the mummification market. As with drugs, if addicts get to the point where they are no longer able to absorb doses, in the end there will be no more drug addicts to control. The virus must keep its host alive. If this fails to happen, the controller-controlled system implodes. The same must have happened in ancient Egypt: with a view to maintaining their immortality, the Ren controllers needed to absorb mortal souls; these were created via mummification. Making this process cheaper would produce more mummies, that is, more souls (though of an increasingly inferior quality). The reiteration of the process implied the end of immortality, and thus the disappearance of the Western Lands and the Egyptian civilization. Kim, together with Neferti, has to destroy the assembly line of cheap mummification and set up new Western Lands to which access was granted through an alternative process avoiding the control exerted by mummification by converting the corporeal into the spiritual.

These transfigurations of bodies into souls are similar to the mutation that Burroughs described in *Nova Trilogy*. In these novels he hoped that humanity could leave the earth and move towards cosmic space. In *The Ticket That Exploded* Burroughs had described the dead roads that are Planet Earth. Dead Roads are streets without exit, but they also are the roads of death, where the characters are all deceased. Cosmic space, where silence reigns; that is where there are no words and, hence, there is no control. A transfiguration of the cosmic space is 'the land of the Dead, the frontier beyond time, learning how to deal with space condition'.[36] Thus, the space programme portrayed in the *Nova Trilogy* of the 1960s develops into a time programme.[37] It implies the search for immortality, that is, the cancellation of time.

The city of Waghdas – a space port – is the beginning of the journey in *The Western Lands*. Burroughs describes it in the novel *Cities of the Red Night* as a dangerous place. Its alleys are the setting of many violent deaths and duels are the order of the day. Each character ends up a gunman. Those who survive Waghdas are able to reach Last Chance, another old city resembling those of the Far West. The journey from there to the Land of the Dead is short, providing they are not killed. Then comes Duat, the river of faecal waters that separates the lands they have covered so far from the Western Lands. Not everybody can make it; Joe, Kim and Neferti fail to cross the line. Despite having found a way to face death through the duel (a method that avoids mummification), they are overcome. William Seward Hall (Kim's clone) is still alive, but close to the final duel. When they reach the Grand Hotel des Morts, the environment is a mixture of the Old West and the Paris of the 1950s. The rooms are unkempt, and the corridors are deserted. Joe the Dead, who dies – for the second and definitive time – right there, meets soldiers there who had died in Vietnam and Ian Sommerville, an old lover of Burroughs's. Yet, he cannot cross the Duat. Only the writer William Seward Hall could make it, but he hesitates. 'Hurry up, please. It's time',[38] he says. Still, he holds on.

Ancient Egypt in the Modern Imagination

Crossing the Duad: The books of memories

At the end of *The Western Lands* Hall feels like a soldier abandoned at the front line in a war that is now over. This feeling of insecurity appears again in *My Education*, a record of dreams across decades of his life, and *Last Words*, diaries from his final year. Burroughs had long drawn inspiration from his dreams. *My Education: A Book of Dreams* in its very title refers to dreams as a method of divination of ancient Egypt: 'in Egypt divination through dream was officially recognized. The "Egyptian Book of the Dead" takes account of the "world of dreams" and its interpretation'.[39] Significantly, Burroughs also relates how dreams were part of his own education, his first source of inspiration; they are also images and messages from the Western Lands: 'The dreams are the lifeline to our possible biological and spiritual destiny. Dreams sometimes approximate space conditions.'[40] The book is a collection of Burroughs's vivid and intense dreams and memories. When he feels he is very close to the Duad, Burroughs portrays himself as Seward Hall in the conclusion of *The Western Lands*: a guest in the hotel of the Land of the Dead. He remarks that:

> the people are all dead and known to me, Mother, Dad, Mort, Brion Gysin, Ian Sommerville, Antony Balch, Michael Portman (Mikey), Kells Elvins. There is always difficulty in obtaining breakfast or nay food for that matter. The set in usually some section, three or four blocks of Paris, Tangier, London, New York., St. Louis. And what is outside this dreary claustrophobic area? What lies beyond the Expanding Universe? Answer: Nothing. But??? No but. That is all you-I-they … can see or experience with their senses, their telescopes, their calculations.[41]

Burroughs was old, and the feeling of being close to death haunted him, possibly because his friends Allen Ginsberg and Brion Gysin had died before him. The Land of the Dead is a 'grey, empty city [that] is more real than my real life here in Lawrence'.[42] He senses that the time to cross the Duad is very close at hand. The territory of death seems to appear to him more real than his present life, now empty because of ended love affairs and sporadic fellowships. It is therefore symptomatic that the Hotel of the Land of the Dead gives him that peace of mind that his home, at Lawrence, no longer provides. The hotels, the rented rooms, in which he has spent most of his days as a writer, remain his only connection to life, the room key in his pocket his only tether to existence. The Hotel where Joe the Dead had been a regular guest gradually transforms into Burroughs's New York loft apartment, his Bunker of the 1970s: a place of hectic meetings, old friends and interviews for a recovered narrative vein. This is the reason why Burroughs – the character – spends his time in this hotel of dreams: to meet again the people of old, those he had loved over the years. Yet, he is already tormented by disturbing omens. He sees a long line of people at the reception desk; they are all souls waiting for a room. In other words, he observes a crowd of dead akin to that in his novel. Moreover, he smells:

a familiar odor. ... Piss? Piss!! The lake is piss. Years and years of strong yellow piss. And slowly the full desolate horror of that stagnant place hits him like a kick in the stomach.

'Fishing, anyone?' The scales are encrusted with crystals of yellow piss, the flesh yellow and oily with piss. Where is the plane? No plane here. He tries to reach the top of the basin. Keeps sliding back on white stones, smooth and slippery. Where is the pilot? No pilot here. The sun is not moving. Just a steady glow in the golden distance, on the great brown-yellow river of shit and piss.

The Duad! Out of basin!? Beyond the basin? There is nothing beyond the basin!

A deep slough of clear, yellow urine, seepage of centuries from the Duad, there in the western distance, bathed in the golden glow of sun that never sets.

Eternal vigilance and skill in the use of weapons that will never be needed here in this yellow stalemate where it is always late afternoon.[43]

Once again, Burroughs waits. At the end of *The Western Lands*, the old writer anticipates death in front of the lake; at the end of *My Education*, Burroughs describes the lake near his home in Kansas. He is on the dock and looks at the waters where catfish are catching and above which flying saucers have been sighted. He wishes that aliens would abduct him, but it does not happen. As if before the Duad, he lingers. Like the mummies he described in *The Western Lands*, he is now out of time.

Conclusion

Ancient Egyptian religious texts convey the idea that even the living could gain access to the world of the dead in special circumstances. This condition of liminality is the same as that experienced by Burroughs's characters. Burroughs had, in his early career, developed an interest in hieroglyphs, and the world of ancient Egyptians, but then turned his attention to other phenomena and mythologies. The exigency to represent the danger of control in narrative fiction had led him to prefer the association of Mayan priests to that of occult theocrats. While the cycle of works dealing with Mesoamerican deities (*Nova Trilogy*, 1961–4) was drawing to a close, Burroughs resumed his interest in hieroglyphic writing, which he had studied towards the end of his time at Harvard. Hieroglyphs seemed to him the ideal vehicle to eradicate word control.

The idea of a language through images proved useful to Burroughs's anti-control theories, which find their own theoretical expression in the two experimental works of the 1970s, *The Book of Breeething* and *The Third Mind*. In the 1980s, Burroughs began to meditate on old age and death. In his novels, this subject became increasingly prevalent, to the extent that in the last novel, *The Western Lands*, the author's viewpoint was no longer that of a youthful character, as it was in the case of Kim Carsons in *The Place of the Dead Roads*, but that of two adult or elderly people: cyborg-gunman Joe the Dead and writer William Steward Hall. In *The Western Lands*, and in the succeeding autobiographical writings, Burroughs resumed the theory of control and applied it to immortality, turning to ancient Egyptian civilization. Through *The Western Lands*, Burroughs tried to solve the problems left unsolved in his two previous novels. In them, the various characters formed communities (the pirates in *Cities of the Red Night*; the Johnson gunmen in *The Place of Dead Roads*). In the third novel there are no more communities; the characters are lone wolves. The only conception of a group is that conveyed by the aggregate of seven souls residing in every individual:

> Burroughs's refrains throughout *The Western Lands*, 'every man for himself' and '*sauve qui peat*' … might appear to mark the end of his revolutionary reconstitutional project, but since 'every man' is already a conglomeration of conflicting souls, they merely mark that project's metamorphosis.[44]

Every man stands alone in his quest for immortality. In Burroughs's *Nova Trilogy* of the 1960s, this mission to reach cosmic space had proved unachievable for the protagonists. Their quest for silence, the no-word state, had only been reached through the destruction of the reality studio where the biological movie was cut. The evolutionary leap, from man to creature able to live in outer space had not been realized. If the space programme had failed, now Burroughs depicted a time programme. The protagonists of *The Western Lands* all search for their own immortality, but as was the case in the *Nova Trilogy*, their goals are only achieved on a fractional scale. They arrive at Last Chance and at the faecal river Duad but stop there. At the novel's conclusion, the writer William Steward Hall's situation parallels Burroughs's own; he 'had reached the end of words, the end of what can be done with word'.[45] This might suggest that Hall and/or Burroughs did not have any fictional material left (*The Western Lands* was Burroughs's last novel), but it also means that they had reached the end of words, that is, hieroglyphs. They both approach the Western Lands, the place where there is no need of words, where silence reigns and no more control exists.

For more than two centuries, ancient Egypt has been an object of interest to Western culture. The fascination that emanates from its mythology and its ideogrammatic writing, so different from alphabetic writing, has ignited the imagination of innumerable authors and artists, of which Burroughs is one. In the late 1930s he became interested in hieroglyphs because they seemed to be able to respond to his need to look for a method of communication not subject to control from external sources. In the 1980s and 1990s, the theme of death became almost an obsession for him, and his recourse to Egyptian mythology seems almost obligatory. In the Western imagination, the ancient Egyptian people, with their mummies and funerary rituals, are the ones that, more than any others, seemed capable of living in two worlds: one terrestrial and one otherworldly, and both perfectly real. Death was only a transition. Burroughs makes this fascination his own, adapting it to his own theories about the nature of human language and behaviour.

CHAPTER 5
BETWEEN SUCCESS AND CONTROVERSY: CHRISTIAN JACQ AND THE MARKETING OF 'EGYPTOLOGICAL' FICTION

Vassilaki Papanicolaou

Flatteringly nicknamed 'Monsieur Egypte',[1] or 'the Egyptian Alexandre Dumas',[2] Christian Jacq is unquestionably one of the most prominent and prolific writers of fiction set in ancient Egypt. His works span almost half a century (from 1971 to the present day) and consist of over 100 publications about ancient Egypt, ranging from scientific essays to historical novels, detective fictions and esoteric works. Translated into 30 languages, Jacq's books have reputedly sold twenty-seven million copies,[3] ranking him among the world's fifteen most popular writers.[4] Jacq has become a household name in his native country, France, where he is renowned for his literature, and imagery of ancient Egypt;[5] his name is almost a synonym for 'Egyptomania'.[6]

Jacq is largely ignored by the academic community, despite having earned a doctorate in Egyptology from Université Paris-Sorbonne, due to the 'popular' nature of many of his works. Except for some ephemeral reviews, occasional references and sporadic interviews, he has received sparse critical attention. This scholarly lacuna, which this essay remedies, is the result of the author's controversial market-oriented strategies and risky compromises, the historical novel genre and ancient Egyptian material woven into its fabric. Jacq's historical novels conceived of explicitly as a consumer product sought to satiate demand for ancient Egyptian escapism and transcendentalism. Averaging 1,600 pages per year,[7] Jacq – in his hyperactivity – exemplifies the adage 'quantity over quality', and the so-called 'acceleration of history' stimulating the hyper-commercialism of popular literature.[8] These factors explain the relative structural emptiness of his historical novels, characterized by a wealth of dialogue, short sentences and one-dimensional characters, aligning his work with the modern-day soap opera.[9] Jacq's approach to the historical novel has also provoked criticism for its 'historical re-enactment' relying heavily upon 'pyramidal exoticism'.[10]

Following in the footsteps of Georg Ebers, Arthur Weigall and Barbara Mertz, Jacq has risen to eminence by deftly combining his dual professions as Egyptologist and novelist. The success of his fictions is tied to the ways in which they are influenced by Egyptology, the latest archaeological discoveries and extensive historical readings. Seeking to reach the largest possible audience, Jacq offers easy access to his scholarly knowledge for non-expert readers by adopting a pleasantly didactic style and jargon-free language, while his clever use of the historical novel's protean ability to mutate into other popular genres (such as the thriller, detective or adventure novel) guarantees the entertaining quality of his fictions. Yet, this simplified and popularizing treatment of historical material is viewed as 'sacrilegious' by the scholarly community, which regards Jacq as its 'black sheep'.[11]

Concomitant to this issue is Jacq's sometimes imaginative representation of the past. Blamed for misleading readers, his historical novels periodically showcase an alternative archaeology promoting an esoteric and parapsychological vision of ancient Egypt for commercial ends.[12] The Egyptological community also distance themselves from Jacq because of his associations with an Egyptian-themed Masonic Lodge.[13] According to Jean-François Colosimo, the author's most controversial aspect lies in his utopian version of ancient Egypt as a happy and peaceful place, which he disparages as a 'New Age type of regression'.[14] Like Théophile Gautier in the nineteenth century, Jacq seeks to bring out a sharp contrast with modern decadence, seeing ancient Egypt as a value system capable of embodying resistance to current 'tyrannical technology'.[15] Yet, his high regard for ancient Egypt also includes a sui generis view of the civilization as mother of all existing religions and a latent endorsement of the old pharaonic propaganda, which have both provoked angry responses from biblical scholars.[16]

Jacq's success has, thus, sparked intense multidisciplinary debates which have undoubtedly played a role in the underappreciation of his oeuvre and jeopardized his place in the literary canon. Is there any validity to these criticisms? Has the author been subjected to unfair animadversion? Any objective discussion of these issues requires a preliminary understanding of the circumstances leading to Jacq's ascension to the rank of bestselling novelist, as well as Egyptologist. This biographical preamble prepares the ground for an in-depth examination of the significance of ancient Egypt and Egyptology in the author's worldwide success. The arguments presented are substantiated by scrutinizing Jacq's historical novels, particularly his most representative work: the *Ramsès* pentalogy. This magnum opus has been praised as 'the most sustained and successful twentieth-century series of archaeologically-inspired historical fantasies'.[17] This essay ultimately offers a long overdue appraisal of Jacq's oeuvre as the starting-point for a broader reflection on how marketization affects the critical reception and literary status of fictions that re-enact the past, and argues that Jacq has been underestimated as a writer by the scholarly community, his work consistently undervalued. His contribution to popular interest in Egyptology and Egyptomania, through his fictional works, can be seen as 'out-reach' on an enormous scale.

Jacq: Egyptologist and novelist

Christian Jacq was born in the seventeenth arrondissement of Paris to a Breton pharmacist and a Polish mother, on 28 April 1947. He was raised by his grandmother, who instilled in him an eclectic taste for reading.[18] His first encounter with ancient Egypt was literary; specifically, he read the fourth and fifth books of Belgian artist Edgar P. Jacobs's comic series *Blake et Mortimer* (*Blake and Mortimer*): *Le Papyrus de Manethon*

(*Manetho's Papyrus*, 1954) and *La Chambre d'Horus* (*The Chamber of Horus*, 1955). These books constitute a two-volume 'cross-genre' piece entitled *Le Mystère de la Grande Pyramide* (*The Mystery of the Great Pyramid*), an entertaining blend of detective and adventure-fantasy story dealing with Akhenaten's reign and the 'Amarna heresy', among various Egyptological themes.[19] Yet Jacq's passion for ancient Egypt truly ignited when he encountered a scholarly work: the Belgian Egyptologist Jacques Pirenne's *Histoire de la civilisation de l'Egypte ancienne* (*History of Ancient Egyptian Civilization*, 1961-3).[20] Pirenne's account of the Egyptian dynastic history, biographies of pharaohs, translations, archaeological descriptions of temples and rituals, illustrated with black-and-white rotogravure pictures, made a lasting impression on the then 13-year-old Jacq, who soon thereafter attempted to teach himself hieroglyphs.[21]

The works of French and German Romantics such as Stendhal, Alfred de Musset, Gérard de Nerval, Hermann Hesse, and of historians such as Mircea Eliade and Heinrich Zimmer, aroused Jacq's lifelong interest in orientalism, mysticism and myth. At the age of 16, he had already completed a novel, several poems and even an opera libretto. Despite his Catholic education, he also departed from the discursivism of monotheist religion; he became increasingly attracted to the ancient Egyptians' rectitude and symbolic way of thinking. In 1964, he spent his honeymoon with his wife Françoise in Egypt.[22] Jacq was deeply affected by the centrepiece of the Memphis Museum: a gigantic colossus of Rameses II, which he vowed to bring to life through the power of fiction.[23] The imposing 27-ton statue carved in limestone heavily influenced his decision to become an Egyptologist.

Jacq pursued graduate studies in philosophy, classics and art history at Paris Nanterre University, which led him to publish, from 1971 onwards, several esoteric essays on astrology, Freemasonry and the influence of ancient Egypt on the art of cathedrals. In 1973, he branched out into archaeology and Egyptology at the Sorbonne, where he attended lectures by Jean Leclant and Paul Barguet. It was not until 1979 that Jacq defended his doctoral thesis on the burial customs of ancient Egypt, later published under the title *Le voyage dans l'autre monde selon l'Egypte ancienne: épreuves et metamorphoses du mort d'après les Textes des Pyramides et les Textes des Sarcophages* (*The Journey through the Netherworld as Perceived in Ancient Egypt: The Trials and Metamorphoses of Death According to the Pyramid and Coffin Texts*, 1986). Jacq chose not to follow the usual route to becoming a member of the French Institute for Eastern Archaeology in Cairo, which would have enabled him to complete his training as a field Egyptologist and to take part to major scientific projects. He felt uncomfortable working at dusty excavation sites with the professional archaeologist's toolkit and so confined himself to the role of expert observer. Jacq found his true calling as a tireless transmitter of knowledge and facilitator of learning. Besides teaching at the Sorbonne, he assiduously contributed to making Egyptology accessible to the public through the regular publication of popular scientific works, including nearly thirty historical studies, learning guides and *vade mecums*. His essay *L'Egypte des grands pharaons* (*Great Pharaohs of Egypt*, 1981), was awarded the Prix Broquette-Gonin of the French Academy in 1982, even succeeding in drawing the attention of the literary elite.[24]

His career as a novelist also took off in the 1980s. A great admirer of Arthur Conan Doyle and Agatha Christie, Jacq began publishing detective novel series under various pseudonyms: five as Célestin Valois (1980–1), forty-four as J. B. Livingstone (1984–97) and seven as Christopher Carter (1998–2002).[25] He later became a historical novelist, almost by accident, with his *Champollion l'égyptien* (*Champollion the Egyptian*, 1987). This book was intended to be a biographical work on Jean-François Champollion which retraced the steps leading to his decipherment of Egyptian hieroglyphs, until Jacq unearthed Champollion's forgotten travel notes from the cellars of the Collège de France. The notebooks revealed Champollion to be a genuine 'Egyptian Indiana Jones',[26] and Jacq's biography transformed into an adventure novel with a historical foundation. *Champollion l'égyptien* marked a turning-point in Jacq's literary career as the first work in which his two professional facets – the novelist and the Egyptologist – fused. The novel enjoyed such success that Jacq was subsequently invited to translate the hieroglyphs of the Luxor Obelisk live on the first national French television channel (TF1).

After the success of *Champollion*, Jacq took steps towards becoming a full-time writer. In 1988, he and his wife moved from Paris to Aix-en-Provence into a library-house containing over 10,000 books. Here, he produced two other notably successful stand-alone historical novels: *La Reine Soleil* (*The Sun Queen*, 1988), the improbable story of the fate of Akhenaten's daughter Ankhesenamun, later adapted into animation in 2007; and *L'affaire Toutankhamon* (*The Tutankhamun Affair*, 1992), a faithful account of Howard Carter's and Lord Carnarvon's discovery of the nearly intact tomb of the ancient Egyptian king and his rumoured subsequent 'curse'. These works won, respectively, the Prix Jean d'Heurs du roman historique and the Prix des Maisons de la Presse.

Yet Jacq's greatest accomplishments and international recognition came with the adoption of the serial form for his 'Egyptianising' fictions. From 1993 to 2015, he published eight cycles of historical novels.[27] Each cycle is built upon an ancient Egyptian value (justice, power, art, truth, freedom) or stereotype (mystery, curse, magical artefact), treated in depth through the lives of famous Egyptologists, pharaohs or queens, or via the lenses of politics, history and mythology. The first cycle sold over 300,000 copies and catapulted Jacq onto the French bestseller lists where he remained for a year; together the second, third and fourth sold 23 million copies worldwide,[28] breaking several records in France. Enthroned as 'the Pharaoh of French publishing' since the mid-1990s, Jacq is believed to be 'the most widely read French living writer in the world'.[29]

Despite his immense popularity, Jacq keeps a low profile and remains an active writer. His phenomenal success acts as a catalyst to further consolidate his legacy with new literary ventures. In addition to recent reissues of his older works, Jacq has produced several thrillers, novellas, comics, books for children as well as an anthology of poetic fables, short satires and suspense tales entitled *Que la vie est douce à l'ombre des palmes: Dernières Nouvelles d'Egypte* (*Life Is Sweet under the Shade of the Palm Trees: Egyptian Short Stories*, 2005). Very few literary genres have thus far escaped his ever-expanding narrative penchant for ancient Egypt.

The *Ramsès* pentalogy: Anatomy of a blockbuster

One work, however, stands out within Jacq's massive body of literary production: *Ramsès*. With over 11 million copies sold, the series is widely considered Jacq's 'best "bestseller"'.[30] It had been over three decades in the making, though its 1,922 pages were written in just two years. This five-volume historical novel is entirely devoted to Rameses II. As Jacq explains in the first volume's afterword, 'Mes rencontres avec Ramsès' ('My Meetings with Rameses'), each part of the quintet represents an important stage in the king's illustrious fate: the opening volume, *Le Fils de la lumière* (*The Son of Light*, 1995), recounts Rameses's youth, his education supervised by his father Sethi I, the rivalry with his elder brother and his accession to the throne; the second, *Le Temple des millions d'années* (*The Eternal Temple*, 1996), deals with his intensive building campaign; the third and the fourth, *La Bataille de Kadesh* (*The Battle of Kadesh*, 1996) and *La Dame d'Abou Simbel* (*The Lady of Abu Simbel*, 1996), recall the challenges he faced against the Hittites, how he forced them to come to a peace settlement and the shocking death of the Royal Spouse, Queen Nefertari; the final volume, *Sous l'acacia d'Occident* (*Under the Western Acacia*, 1996), depicts the end of his 66-year reign and acquisition of wisdom. The series met with immediate large-scale success. Its rights were sold internationally to Warner (United States), Rowolt (Germany), Mondadori (Italy) and Planeta (Spain). The five volumes became readily available in libraries and on supermarket shelves, before rapidly going out of stock, compelling Jacq to publish a spin-off product: a collection of captioned photographs titled *Sur les pas de Ramsès* (*In the Footsteps of Rameses*, 1996).

The dazzling success of the pentalogy is due to a combination of factors, one of which is Jacq's judicious decision to write about one of history's 'Great Men'. Though dead for thousands of years, the pharaohs remain very much alive in the popular imagination. They count among France's all-time favourite personalities. The country has a long history with Egypt, at least since the Napoleonic invasion in 1798. Napoleon Bonaparte's scientific expedition left an indelible mark on Parisian urbanism, with the Luxor Obelisk, the fountains du Fellah and du Palmier, numerous Neo-Egyptian style buildings and street names. Under the influence of Champollion, Auguste Mariette and Vivant Denon and their successors, Christiane Desroches Noblecourt and Jean-Yves Empereur, Egyptology has been a resurgent fashionable topic. The success of the Tutankhamun exhibition in Paris (1967) triggered a new wave of Egyptomania, peaking around the time *Ramsès* was published.[31] The Louvre was renovating its Department of Egyptian Antiquities; courses in hieroglyphic decipherment provided by the Kheops Institute were gaining renewed interest; Egyptophile clubs and societies were proliferating at an astounding rate; a boom in ancient Egypt-related literature occurred, with over 500 books published since 1990.[32] *Ramsès* hit the 'jacq-pot' during this cultural frenzy.

Bernard Fixot, former editor at Robert Laffont and founder of Jacq's current publishing house XO Editions, was instrumental in envisioning and managing the commercial potential of the pentalogy. His marketing methods are inspired by entrepreneurship, today's disposable consumer culture and the realities of the book industry; strategic planning is based on the fundamental goal of increasing sales instead of accruing literary prizes.³³ Jacq soon agreed to publish the five volumes of *Ramsès* on a quarterly basis, relying on Fixot's ambition 'to reinvent the nineteenth-century serialised novel'.³⁴ To meet this timetable, Jacq allegedly wrote 14 hours per day, seven days a week,³⁵ a 'Stakhanovist' pace justified by his desire to satisfy the customers' demand for immediacy.³⁶ Since the twentieth century, the world has witnessed rapid progress and events that have accelerated the course of history; authors write historical novels as an attempt to appropriate history before it slips through their fingers. *Ramsès* is part of Jacq's career-long project to 'novelise' every era of ancient Egyptian civilization.³⁷ His holistic fictional re-enactment of ancient Egypt is grounded on the urgency to rescue a historical heritage from oblivion, reflecting his dual vocation as archaeologist and raconteur of stories.

Popularization of Egyptology and scholarly concerns

Nevertheless, according to Jacq, historical novels, especially bestsellers, often stir up jealousy and suspicion among scholars and historians.³⁸ The mixture of genres raises professional and ethical issues: can the historian be a practitioner of the historical novel and subject his own field to the scrutiny of fiction? Jacq's solution lies in tailoring content and form to mass readership, widely using Egyptological material tempered with radical poetic concessions. The author is known for his simple, minimalistic writing style, which he adopted from Anatole France.³⁹ Readers are engaged in effortless reading, though Jacq spared no efforts to achieve that end. In *Ramsès*, his vocabulary eschews idioms, ethnic and learned words; scientific terminology is merged with everyday language; metalinguistic functions are rarely used; unpronounceable ancient Egyptian names are abbreviated to facilitate their reading. Additionally, chapters, paragraphs and sentences are consistently brief; depictions of Egyptian landscapes and sites remain concise; syntax is clear and limpid; narration extends itself as an easy flow.

These linguistic and stylistic simplifications not only help to make the pentalogy a real 'page-turner', but also greatly facilitate the popularization of scholarly knowledge. Due to its narrow meaning and pejorative connotation, the term 'popularisation', however, is deemed inappropriate by Jacq; unlike some of his Egyptologist colleagues, the transmission of knowledge, he believes, deserves better consideration.⁴⁰ Reluctant to share the fruits of its labour with a 'lay' audience, French Egyptology on the whole rejects popularization: the simplification of scholarly knowledge inevitably gives rise to historical shortcuts, inaccuracies and misinterpretations; the historical novelist is given too much leeway to present their own theories as verified facts.⁴¹ More broadly, 'creative' histories and novels are eschewed by the scholarly community as a whole; academia seems intolerant of those that like to put their own spin on (what scholars think of as) 'the truth'. The arguments made by historians which sneer at such popular offerings are generally centred around the public assuming that the book will be 'fact' and becoming 'misinformed'; they do not appear to think that the public can distinguish a novel from a textbook. In his attempt to defuse this criticism, Jacq recalls the basic distinction between the factuality of epistemological essays and the creativity of novels. He argues that scientific objectivity is impossible, since the experimenter cannot be independent of experience;[42] likewise, fiction necessarily derives from personal experience.[43] Jacq's reasoning implies that his knowledge-broking mission concerns ancient Egypt, and not Egyptology. His educational impulse is particularly evident in the *Ramsès* series. Etymological explanations, romanticized ethnographic and mystagogic discourses, hieroglyphic initiation and multi-sectorial division of chapters are some of the recurring pedagogical tools employed in the five volumes. Common pitfalls of historical novels such as hypertrophied didacticism and overuse of paratextual notes are avoided. Without realizing it, readers cultivate their minds and exceed their horizon of expectations.

Yet, this pleasant consequence could not operate without an emphasis on the Romanesque aspect of the pentalogy. For Jacq, ancient Egypt does not belong to the past but to the present; it is an integral part of his daily life. Preferring a resurrectional approach to his characters, he is convinced, like Michel Lisse, that fiction is the 'prosthesis of history', an artificial supplement that helps history come to life.[44] In the foreword of *Le Fils de la lumière*, he writes:

Ce que la mort physique refuse à Ramsès, la magie du roman a le pouvoir de le lui accorder. Grâce à la fiction et à l'égyptologie, il est possible de partager ses angoisses et ses espérances, de vivre ses échecs et ses succès.[45]

What physical death has stolen from Rameses, the magic of the novel can restore. Thanks to fiction and Egyptology, it is possible to share his fears and hopes, to experience his failures and successes.[46]

Jacq imagines himself more a scribe than a writer,[47] with the power to transform death into life. The substantial quantity of conversational writing in the pentalogy is consistent with his intent to revitalize history.[48] *Ramsès*, a Manichean series, has stereotypical characters moved by emotion and political ambition, is melodramatic in tone and features a clear storyline spread over several episodes which leads to comparisons with soap operas such as *Dallas* and *Dynasty*.[49] Jacq transposes present-day situations into ancient Egypt, using modern language to erase temporal distance and ease the process of his reader's identification with the characters. This method has been unfairly criticized for its lack of verisimilitude and linguistic authenticity. Jacq's 'modern' lines are in fact literal translations of mastaba inscriptions,[50] and his direct quotations from Ptahhotep's *Maxims* and Homer's *Iliad* are irrefutable evidence of distinctive archaic linguistic colouring in the series. Jacq skilfully succeeds in aggregating historical material to offer a realistic representation of the everyday lives of ancient Egyptians.

His concern for historical accuracy derives from a desire to satisfy his audience. This writer-reader contract also includes a plausible fictitious anastylosis of the sites and monuments of ancient Egypt, geared to quench the readers' thirst for archaeological exoticism. This restoration project takes shape through the voice of Jacq's narrator, who offers clinical descriptions of sacred sites. One salient example lies in his imaginary evocation of the Temple of Millions of Years:

le monarque s'attarda dans les salles du Ramesseum entouré d'une enceinte longue de trois cents mètres, abritant deux grandes cours avec des piliers représentant le roi en Osiris, une vaste salle à quarante-huit colonnes, profonde de trente et un mètres et large de quarante, et un sanctuaire où résidait la présence divine. Marquant l'accès au temple, des pylônes hauts de soixante-dix mètres dont les textes disaient qu'ils montaient jusqu'au ciel; sur le côté sud de la première cour, le palais. Autour du lieu saint, une vaste bibliothèque, des entrepôts, un trésor contenant des métaux précieux, les bureaux des scribes et les maisons des prêtres. Cette ville-temple fonctionnait jour et nuit, car le service des dieux ne connaissait pas de repos.[51]

[The] king lingered in the halls of the Ramasseum, surrounded by a 300-metre long enclosure with two great courtyards where pillars depicted the king as Osiris, a vast hall, 31 metres deep and 40 metres wide, with 48 columns, and a sanctuary where the divine presence resided. Access to the temple was through 70-metre high pylons, inscribed with texts saying that they rose to the heavens; on the south side of the forecourt stood the palace. Around the holy site were an extensive library, storerooms, a treasury containing precious metals, the scribes' offices, and the priests' quarters. This temple complex hummed with activity night and day, for the service of the gods knew no rest.

Here, Jacq demonstrates the methodological and intellectual rigour of the archaeologist. With carefully chosen geometrical data, he provides an accurate three-dimensional representation of the main structural characteristics of the sacred place; ethnographic commentary, inspired by translations of ancient texts, informs about the functioning and life-history of the temple complex. More precise than Gautier's *Le Roman de la momie* (*The Mummy's Tale*, 1858), such archaeological description is a clear demonstration of authorial authority with the purpose of impressing and reassuring readers about his historical exactitude. Other re-enacted complexes, such as Abydos, Pi-Ramses, Babylon, Memphis, Abu Simbel, Giza, Luxor, Karnak and the Valley of the Kings are scattered throughout the five volumes and appear to be a pretext to a virtual tourist circuit encompassing the most famous sites of ancient Egypt. Yet, this Grand Tour has a valid historical justification: Rameses's fame is tied to his exuberant building activity, which includes regular commemorative visits of temples devoted to his own self-glorification. This re-enacting process is also motivated by jubilatory writing, which Jacq sees as an alternative to the 'sadness of museums and archaeological pieces'.[52] Breathing life into historical archives stimulates writerly and readerly euphoria. Describing the great audience chamber at Pi-Rameses the narrator relates:

[C']était l'une des merveilles de l'Égypte. On y accédait par un escalier monumental, orné de figures d'ennemis terrassés. Ils incarnaient les forces du mal, sans cesse renaissantes, que seul Pharaon pouvait soumettre à Maât, la loi d'harmonie, dont la reine était le visage vivant. Autour de la porte d'accès, les noms de couronnement du monarque, peints en bleu sur fond blanc, et placés dans des cartouches, formes ovales évoquant le cosmos, le royaume de Pharaon, fils du créateur et son représentant

sur terre. Quiconque franchissait le seuil du domaine de Ramsès en découvrait, émerveillé, la sereine beauté.[53]

[It] was one of the wonders of Egypt, accessible through a monumental stairway, lined with scenes of slain enemies, who represented the ever-present forces of evil that only Pharaoh could subjugate. They must be brought in line with Ma'at, the principle of harmony and justice with the queen as its living face. Around the entryway, the monarch's coronation names were painted in blue on a white background, placed inside oval cartouches symbolising the cosmos over which Pharaoh ruled as the creator's son and earthly representative. Whoever crossed the threshold of Rameses's domain was stunned by its serene beauty.

This colourful architectural description reveals the evocative power of symbol as a means of emphasizing the magnificence and metaphysical attractiveness of ancient Egyptian art, which lies in the representation of Pharaoh as an omnipotent universal monarch. Jacq obviously seeks to ignite sublime feelings in his readers. This transcendental style also applies to his account of Egypt's natural landscape, where emphatic rhetoric, neo-Romantic emotionalism and ecological sensibility actively solicit the audience's admiration. This mixture of fictionalism and sensationalism efficiently instrumentalizes the public's fascination with ancient Egypt.

Transgenericity: Filling the historiographical gaps

Additionally, Jacq harnesses the entertaining potential of the historical novel's generic mutability. This transformative tendency results from the progressive blurring of temporal and generic boundaries around the notion of 'historical writing', and has been exploited by many historical novelists to ensure the popularity of their fictions.[54] Inspired by *Comte de Monte-Cristo* (*The Count of Monte Cristo*, 1844) by Alexandre Dumas, Jacq conducted a transgeneric experiment with *L'affaire Toutankhamon*, blending historical detective fiction with the adventure novel, whodunit and novel of manners. While fundamentally a historical novel, *Ramsès* incorporates elements from epic, myth and crime fiction, with a pinch of eroticism. Detective fiction makes a particularly prominent generic contribution to the pentalogy. To make *Ramsès*'s story entertaining, suspenseful and cryptic, dramatic events such as attempted murders and conspiracies (plotted by courtiers and secret societies) constantly deflect the biographical trajectory of the series. Shaanar and Dolora, the brother and sister of the pharaoh, are based on the historical assumption of a conspirator among the royal family, whose name has been erased from history as part of their punishment. These characters were also inspired by various testimonies left by the wise men of ancient Egypt.[55] Jacq's ulterior motive is to reveal, *in fine*, the relativity and perenniality of human nature, a common characteristic of the historical detective fiction under its 'form of *littérature engagée*'.[56]

'Transgenericity' – which might be understood as a kind of fluidity when it comes to the adoption of conventions of genre, as well as the use of one or more genres within another – is also a convenient device for filling the gaps left by historical accounts. Rameses's reign, as Roger Caratini has noted,[57] is largely uneventful, except for the Battle of Kadesh (1274 BC), whose veracity is questionable.[58] Although Egyptologists do not contest the pharaoh's victory over the Hittites, the account of this feat of arms is regarded as a sort of 'Egyptian *Iliad*', which served to promote the 'invincibility' of the pharaonic regime. This Homeric analogy and the lack of reliable historical sources pushed Jacq to write an epic, conceived as a superior, extended form of historical novel. In the pentalogy, Rameses appears as a heroic figure who single-handedly defeats thousands of Hittites thanks to his Herculean strength. This choice of characterization has been castigated by Christiane Desroches Noblecourt as a deceit vis-à-vis the general public, who have no way to verify the 'unthinkable' actions that Jacq assigns to Rameses.[59] Noblecourt, the 'female Pharaoh' of French Egyptology, felt obliged to propose a more realistic portrayal of the king in her book *Ramsès II: la veritable histoire* (*Rameses II: The True Story*, 1996).

The palimpsestic narrative technique Jacq employs to recount the legendary exploits of Rameses is another source of misunderstanding. He takes inspiration from the two primary ancient Egyptian versions of the battle of Kadesh found inscribed across temples in Egypt – the *Poem* of *Pentaur* (a written account of the battle of Kadesh by a courtier that was intent on the glory of his king, Rameses II),[60] and the *Bulletin* (which stresses the divine nature of Rameses's power)[61] – without much creative license, blurring the line between novel and monograph. Such a confusion also emerges from implausible stories partially attested by verifiable historical sources. For instance, the visit of Menelaus and Helen in Egypt may look like a surrealistic anecdote at first glance. Most readers familiar with Homer probably feel the presence of these historical characters during Rameses's reign as 'alien' and take it to be pure invention. Yet, this episode is part of an alternative Egyptian version of the Trojan War recorded by Herodotus in his *Histories*.[62] Many similar examples in the *Ramsès* series make it a true challenge for readers to separate real history from fiction; they end up putting their instinct for validation on standby, reduced to a position of blind faith in the author. Jacq's tour de force is thus to persuade readers that the improbable is probable, to give free rein to a resolutely mythological narrative under the aegis of history.

Supernaturalism and Masonic controversy

These intellectual gymnastics with fact and fiction aim less at manipulating readers than at introducing them to the in-between notion of mystery, a conceptual no man's land at the heart of the fascinating world of ancient Egypt. In *Ramsès*, readers are invited to decode '*les secrets de la vie et de la mort*' ('the secrets of life and death'), to explore '*les mystères de l'univers*' ('the mysteries of the universe') that the wise men have transcribed into hieroglyphs and transmitted to the next generations.[63] This sort of parapsychological literature usually embraces the philosophy of a 'forbidden archaeology', a common marketing device exploiting the public's hunger for the unresolved mysteries of ancient civilizations and the secret side of history.[64] A salient proof that Jacq is no stranger to this trend lies in his esoteric belief that temples are reservoirs of positive energy. Throughout the pentalogy, he explains that ancient Egyptian gods reside in an ocean of energy and the temples that the pharaoh offers to them; in return, temples increase the *ka* (vital energy) of the pharaoh so that magic (the divine weapon made for mankind to ward off future contingent events) can be activated.[65] Nevertheless, according to Jacq, this magic – a supernatural element at the boundaries of reality – is no fantasy, but 'historically accurate', for it had an important role in the political decision making of the pharaonic state.[66]

Rameses's Egypt is idealistically depicted as a utopian society of individuals living in harmony. Magic is used as a prophylactic tool to keep this 'fulfilled dream' intact, the construction of temples a necessary measure to secure a long-standing peace. Ancient Egyptians, Jacq argues, were neither warriors nor conquerors, for their only preoccupation was to maintain a perpetual state of overflowing happiness.[67] War meant a brutal return to reality; hence, their military policy was '*tu[er] la guerre*' ('to kill war') and impose a mutually beneficial armistice.[68] The Battle of Kadesh is interpreted as a victory, for it helped to implement a non-aggression pact between the two nations.

Meanwhile, Rameses faces an 'invisible war' against destructive forces: opponents to his politics, and dark magi, relentlessly attempt to dethrone him. Jacq represents ancient Egyptians as deeply aware of the fragility of life. To avoid political chaos, they put their faith in the balance between fragility and power regulated by the concept of *Ma'at*, the universal law of love and justice. Half-god-half-human Rameses endeavours to consolidate *Ma'at* as the guarantor power of the continuity of happiness. To this end, the *homo duplex* uses pseudoscience (radiesthesia, lithotherapy) and superhuman abilities (sungazing, magnetism, telekinesis, intuitive omniscience). After some initiatory training, he learns from Seti the secret chiasmatic nature of power: '*Pharaon est bâti par l'Égypte, Pharaon bâtit l'Égypt*' ('Pharaoh is built by Egypt, Pharaoh builds Egypt').[69]

The original secret of the builders, the ordeals of initiation, the will to give his life for the sake of the community, the commitment to existential pacifism, are clichés of Freemasonry.[70] In his essay *La franc-maçonnerie: histoire et initiation* (*Freemasonry: History and Initiation*, 1975), Jacq attempted to demonstrate that this fraternal organization was created in ancient Egypt. Critics have ignored his theory and lambasted him for conveying Masonic ideology (in line with his extraliterary activities) through his historical fiction.[71] Jacq is the founder of three Egyptophile organizations: a parent company, the *Ramses Institute*, whose aim is to save the visual heritage of ancient Egypt by collecting all existing photographic documents from sites and monuments; and two subsidiaries: *Naos*, an association chaired by his wife, and *Maison de vie*, a society created in 1992 for aficionados of Nilotic linguistics and spirituality,[72] which publishes transcriptions of Egyptian texts and hieroglyphs in addition to research studies on Freemasonry.[73]

In 1996, the French satirical journal *Charlie Hebdo* claimed that Jacq hijacked *Maison de vie* to create an independent Masonic Lodge functioning as a sect.[74] Inspired by ancient Egyptian rituals, this Lodge was allegedly based on a 'structure of absolute power' and directed by a 'Pharaonic Royal Couple' – Jacq and his wife as the worshipful master and chancellor – who subjugated a group of officers.⁷⁵ The values of the Masonic Lodge are a hodgepodge of controversial views on various values: humanism is described as a creeping and viscous doctrine responsible for the worst tragedies of the twentieth century; freedom is no more than a false concept since no one can ever be free; slavery, in contrast, is seen as a useful way of domesticating human beings. Jacq acknowledged the existence of this rule of procedure, but denied being its author.⁷⁶

There is no clear evidence to suggest that the dangerous ideology of the Lodge is mirrored in the pentalogy. Certainly, Jacq emphasizes the very close bond between Rameses and Nefertari, but the royal couple show no signs of abusing their authority. Furthermore, humanism is not a toxic notion, but an idealistic aspiration. Rameses is portrayed as a generous benefactor protecting the most vulnerable, a diplomatic genius and a gifted peacekeeper. Jacq goes so far as to say that the pharaoh can still be an influential role model for today's generation; he sees the historical novel as a modern metaphor, whose past can instruct the present through temporal reverberation.⁷⁷

Ancient Egypt: An anti-tyrannical model?

The author lays a claim for contemporaneity, yet the legitimacy and efficiency of the message he wants to convey remains questionable. His vision of an illusory past regime aims to contrast with a disillusioning political present, but, in doing so, he indirectly points out the 'powerlessness' to change the order of things in a globalized world.⁷⁸ More specifically, Jacq often expresses a sense of war-weariness, though his message is exaggeratedly optimistic. He overemphasizes the glorious traits of Rameses's Egypt to hide the despicable ones.⁷⁹ And, when these disgraceful aspects disrupt the linear flow of his utopian narrative, he simply eliminates them. For instance, Rameses does not adhere to the Lodge's scandalous view on thraldom, affirming that *'[i]l n'y a pas d'esclavage en Égypte'* ('slavery is non-existent in Egypt').⁸⁰ This goes against the common historical bias which views the civilization as a land of servitude and triumphalist idolatry.⁸¹

Freedom, on the other hand, is faithful to its status of fundamental virtue and is used profitably to highlight present day issues, such as the feminist cause.⁸² Ancient Egyptian women are described as having more civil liberties, rights and political involvement than women living in the present day. Rameses, who considers Egypt as *'mon épouse'* ('my wife'),⁸³ acknowledges Nefertari as his equal. The queen is not only his special advisor but acts as the interim ruler when Rameses is on a military campaign. This power-sharing exists as women have liberated Egypt from occupying forces in the past, and successfully negotiated peace treaties with foreign courts.

A second topical issue pertaining to freedom is the enslavement of individuals by technological tyranny. Jacq is a proponent of ancient Egyptian conservatism and peaceful modus vivendi, the only alternatives he sees to the ever-increasing manipulation of mass communication and ever-decreasing quality of life today.⁸⁴ His recent thriller *Sphinx* (2016) tells the story of billions of persons enslaved by a parameterized unjammable 'Machine'. Technological advancement is described as the deviant, uncontrollable offspring of demonic capitalism, denoting human regression. In *Ramsès*, Shaanar attempts several times to find political allies to move Egypt in the direction of state capitalism, but systematically fails in his plan, hence expressing Jacq's rejection of progressivism.

The author is also an active fighter of religious tyranny. According to Jacq, the main attractiveness of ancient Egypt does not necessarily lie in the esoteric traditions but is born from a Western crisis in faith and the search for Eastern spiritual serenity. He argues that Egyptian religion is not a religion per se, but a system of thought, which has never been responsible for fanatical fundamentalism or interreligious wars.[85] His view of the Egyptians' religious tolerance seems to be contradicted at least twice in the pentalogy, firstly, when he recounts Rameses's decision to eradicate all lasting traces of the City of the Horizon of Aton. This political move is clearly intended to eliminate the threat of an Egyptian Monotheistic resurgence. He also promotes a sort of Egyptocentrism; according to Raphaël Draï, Jacq is the adept of a neo-Egyptian religion, which encroaches upon the Bible's domain. In Jacq's historical novels, he argues, a pure ancient Egyptianism is elevated to the rank of indisputable matrix of world religions, while a plagiarist Hebraism is disparaged as a feeble simulacrum of the first.[86] Several problematic elements support Draï's interpretation. Moses is portrayed as a traitor of the pharaonic regime, indoctrinated and brainwashed into fanatic Hebraism; the plagues of Egypt are no more than a concatenation of natural phenomena; the Exodus is also a demystified reinterpretation of the Old Testament. Christianity is portrayed as an alternative to Judaism, however, in sharp contrast, the Egyptian cult is self-engendered and affirms its primacy. Jacq not only espouses Champollion's argument of a primitive monotheistic system headed by the pharaoh and assisted by his priests, he unconsciously re-enacts the pharaonic propagandist ideology while caricaturing Egyptology as a mystical gnosis and a totalitarian pseudo-scientific field.[87]

Nevertheless, Jacq asserts that his intent is less ideological than logical. He has no interest in engaging in the kind of revisionist approach of postmodernist historiographic metafiction. Since the pentalogy focuses on the life of an Egyptian pharaoh, it appears natural to provide the Egyptian version of history.[88] Verisimilitude even forces the author to adopt such a point of view. On the other hand, nothing forces him to regard the Pentateuch as an official Egyptological source. And yet, in the final chapter of the series, he pays homage to Moses's historical contribution to Rameses's reign:

Moïse... L'un des architectes de Pi-Ramsès, l'homme dont la foi avait triomphé de nombreuses années d'errance, le prophète à l'enthousiasme indestructible! Moïse, fils de l'Égypte et frère spirituel de Ramsès, Moïse dont le rêve était devenu réalité.[89]

Moses. ... One of the architects of Pi-Ramses, the man whose faith had triumphed over endless years of wandering, the indomitable prophet. Moses, son of Egypt and Rameses's spiritual brother. Moses, whose dream had become reality.

While not wholly unfounded, the assumption of an Egyptian absolutist agenda is undermined by this eulogy.

Conclusion

Jacq's attitude towards ancient Egypt is decidedly sphinx-like. He is a mysterious, inscrutable personality, whose position as a writer and archaeologist remains equivocal. His uncanny work walks a thin line between literature and paraliterature, history and parahistory, Egyptolophilia and bibliophobia. A cloud of suspicion surrounds the ideology he conveys in his re-enactment of pharaonic times. One thing is sure, however: Jacq is an expert in literary marketing mechanisms; he knows thoroughly how to handle the tricky issues in historically related literature; he fends off every attack with counterarguments. Dominique Legrand wrote that Jacq is a remarkable communicator above all.[90] Thus, it is clear that Jacq's contribution to the scholarly field of Egyptology has been vastly underestimated; a discipline will only survive as long as new knowledge is in demand, and Jacq's level of interaction with the public through his historical novels ensures that this demand is not only sustained, but increases. The burgeoning field of Ancient Egypt Reception Studies, as seen at conferences such as Tea with the Sphinx at the University of Birmingham, is recognizing the valuable contributions of authors such as Jacq who pique the interest of a readership and begin life-long love affairs with Egypt's ancient past; the future of Egyptology has a lot to thank Christian Jacq for.

PART II
DEATH AND MYSTICISM

CHAPTER 6
EGYPTOMANIA, ENGLISH PYRAMIDS AND THE QUEST FOR IMMORTALITY
Jolene Zigarovich

For centuries ancient Egypt remained largely inaccessible to Europeans. However, with the opening of portions of the East in the late eighteenth century, and the French campaign in the Ottoman territories of Egypt and Syria (1798–1801), Egyptomania became fuelled by Western discovery, scientific enterprise and travel. This essay specifically explores how Egyptian embalming practices and pyramidal imagery entered the eighteenth-century British cultural landscape. Ancient Egyptian mourning and burial rituals intrigued eighteenth-century eccentrics, who embraced Egyptian sepulchral culture; science and medicine explored various forms of modern embalming practices; and, as the British Empire spread to the East, Egyptomania and its materiality migrated to Britain.[1] By examining early interest in embalming, the popularity of mummy 'unrollings', and the rise of Egyptian style funerary architecture, this essay argues that British interest in Egypt influenced undertaking and commemorative practices. This fascinating and curious history ultimately contributes to an understanding of a culture's attitudes towards death, the body and commemoration.[2]

For this discussion, it is important to observe the eighteenth-century interest in ancient Egyptian burial practices and their modernization in Britain. Perhaps the most significant and widely published early book on the sole subject of embalming is surgeon Thomas Greenhill's *Nekpokhdeia, or The Art of Embalming; Wherein is Shewn the Right of Burial, the Funeral Ceremonies, and the several Ways of Preserving Dead Bodies in Most Nations of the World* (1705). Here Greenhill discusses theological, medical and political reasons for embalming, and includes numerous illustrations of Egyptian sarcophagi. This lengthy work defends the craft of the embalmer and, according to Clare Gittings, describes embalming as 'one facet of an increasing preoccupation with the preservation of the individual after death.'[3] It also reflects the growing public interest in Egyptology. In fact, Greenhill's *Art of Embalming* shows the usual method of bandaging based on knowledge gained from contemporary public mummy unrollings. The eighteenth century witnessed a widespread public interest in Egyptology which manifested in numerous public mummy unrollings in which surgeons and anatomists publicly dissected mummified bodies in order to unmask the ancient secrets of death and preservation, but also to help demystify the superstitions associated with the corpse.

As a form of advertisement for embalming, Greenhill's volume represents the interests not only of those prominent surgeons who already practiced embalming, such as Sir Hans Sloane (to whom Greenhill dedicates the book) and Francis Douce, but also of those who supplied the proper chemicals to surgeons, as noted in the extensive list of subscribers. This lengthy work defends the craft of the embalmer and 'reflected one facet of an increasing preoccupation with the preservation of the individual after death'.[4] While Greenhill's work unwrapped the mysteries of Egyptian embalming, experimenters criticized the Egyptian embalming methods as they worked to develop more successful techniques. Such criticism did little to dampen public interest in mummy unrollings, however; often these proceedings were witnessed by both professional and non-professional audiences and published in both professional and non-professional periodicals.

The *Philosophical Transactions of the Royal Society* of January 1764, for example, includes 'An Account of a Mummy, inspected at London 1763'.[5] In a letter to William Heberden, John Hadley records that he invited several surgeons (including William Hunter) and a reverend to participate in the unrolling to be performed in his home. Given to him by the Museum of the Royal Society, the mummy was examined in order to investigate the 'manner in which this piece of antiquity had been put together; to compare it with the accounts given of these preparations by ancient authors; and to see, whether there were any traces left of the softer parts; and, if so, by what means they had been preserved'.[6]

A few decades later, on 10 April 1794, Dr John Blumenbach read his 'Observations on some Egyptian Mummies opened in London' which details the opening and examining of several Egyptian mummies attended by the president of the Royal Society and many of its members.[7] Of the five mummies unrolled in 1782, three were done in the homes of private collectors who offered their mummies for investigation, and two were from the Sloanian collection at the British Museum.[8] Four of the mummies were of children, and one believed to be that of a baby was discovered to be the skeleton of an ibis. Blumenbach's account is one of many; together they attest to the significant market for mummies by private collectors and public museums, and the scientific interest in deconstructing ancient preservation methods.

Greenhill espouses embalming as a mortuary practice and seeks potential consumers by inciting fears concerning the disturbance of the corpse (he recommends embalming as an alternative to earth burial, where a corpse could be attacked by 'voracious animals'). He goes so far as to paraphrase Sir Thomas Browne's *Hydriotaphia: Urne-Buriall, or a Discourse of The Sepulchrall Urns Lately Found in Norfolk* (1658), by asking, 'Who knows the Fate of *his* Bones, or how often he is to be bury'd? Who has the Oracle of his Ashes, or where they are to be scatter'd?'[9] In fact, Greenhill's volume marks a point in history where social and medical attitudes towards the body and death were changing, intimating that it was natural to seek to preserve the bodies of the highly revered from corruption. Greenhill emphasizes this by remarking that God wants man to be preserved and uncorrupted for the final judgment: 'Besides, we *Christians* ought to esteem *Embalming* a pious Work, acceptable to GOD, because it frees us from that Corruption which he so much detests.'[10] What better marketing tool than to quote Psalms 16:10 and suggest that Christ was '*embalm'd* in order to his Resurrection' and was 'exempt from the Laws of Corruption'; we should, therefore, follow his example.

Greenhill also defends the art of embalming from being practiced by charlatans and quacks, adding that 'the noble *Art of Embalming* has been entirely ruin'd by the Undertaker'.[11] Indeed, the occupational role of the undertaker had been emerging from the late-sixteenth century. This rise in funeral contracting is evidenced in the annals of the barber-surgeons who for centuries exercised strict domain over the right to embalm and who, in the seventeenth century, took measures to see that their members were fit to carry out the practice of surgery, 'of which embalming was an important subordinate skill'.[12] In order to maintain strict control over embalming practice and to pass down methods and traditions, the barber-surgeons of London decided to apply for a new charter in 1604, the sixteenth clause declaring the

> openinge searinge and imbalmeinge of the dead corpes to be pply [solely] belongeinge to the science of Barbery and Surgery, And the same intruded into by Butchers Taylors Smythes Chaundlors and others of mecanicall trades unskillfull in Barbery or Surgery, And unseemely and unchristian lyke defaceinge disfiguringe and dismembringe the dead Corpes.[13]

These charter rights demonstrate the growing concern over the rise of the embalming trade by untrained wax chandlers, butchers and tailors, possibly stemming from the expensive procedures performed by the barber–surgeons.[14] Yet, by the end of the seventeenth century, the duties of the undertaker grew more complex, and they eventually assimilated the task of embalming, if in a crude form. In Richard Steele's scathing comedy *The Funeral, or Grief-a-la-Mode* (1701), an undertaker asks his assistants if they have 'brought the Saw-dust and Tarr for Embalming?',[15] demonstrating the integration of the art into his duties (sawdust, tar, bran and rosemary were inexpensive materials for lining coffins). In 1751, Frederick, Prince of Wales, was the first member of the British royal family to be embalmed by a professional undertaker.[16]

Greenhill's *Art of Embalming* indicates the rise of the undertaker, the growth in the market for embalming (even among non-aristocrats), an increased concern over the dissolution of the body and a literal interpretation of Christian-era preservation and bodily resurrection.[17] In fact, the belief that the bodies of Christian saints and other venerated individuals are incorruptible is ancient; the preserved body was often seen as a sign that the individual was holy or was favoured by God. The Church of England never took an official position towards embalming, but seventeenth- and eighteenth-century sermons and inspirational texts often focused attention on the state of the interred corpse, perhaps suggesting embalming as a means of maintaining a corpse fit for resurrection. This, coupled with the aristocrat practice of preservation, distinctly contributes to contemporary interest in mummies and ancient Egyptian preservation techniques. And as the cult of sensibility favoured a beautiful death, medical practices looked to modernize ancient Egyptian preservation methods. Eighteenth-century physicians often collected Egyptiana, conducted mummy unrollings, and, like Greenhill, included discussions of ancient embalming methods in their medical textbooks.

While Greenhill's text attempts to unearth the mysteries of ancient Egyptian embalming practices, techniques described following numerous mummy unrollings in the late seventeenth century, public mummy unrollings continued well into the nineteenth century. In 1821, physician Augustus Bozzi Granville FRS unwrapped and dissected an ancient Egyptian mummy, presenting the results at the Royal Society in 1825. He commissioned artist Henry Perry to draw the process in stages, and the drawings were subsequently engraved for publication in *Philosophical Transactions*. Egyptianizing embalming practices continued among the wealthy: Alexander, 10th Duke of Hamilton (d. 1852), for example, was embalmed by physician and mummy expert Thomas 'Mummy' Pettigrew and buried in a genuine Egyptian sarcophagus of the Ptolemaic period in a lavish mausoleum (c. 1858) on his family estate in Scotland.[18]

During the eighteenth and early nineteenth centuries, the practice of heart and viscera burial also continued among the wealthy. Many eighteenth-century wills mention the deceased's request for embalming. An early example is the lengthy will of draper and philanthropist Francis Bancroft (d. 1727), which was published in its entirety the year following his death. Specifying his own funeral and burial arrangements, Bancroft writes, 'My Body I desire may be embalmed within six Days after my Death, and my Entrails to be put in a Leaden Box, and included in my Coffin, or placed in my Vault next the same, as shall be most convenient.'[19] He directs that he be buried in a vault within 'ten Days after my decease',[20] and that his funeral 'shall not exceed the Sum of Two Hundred Pounds'.[21] Bancroft's will demonstrates that the management of death shifted from the church to the individual and professional undertakers. Excerpts of the draper's will were published several years later in the *Ladies Magazine*, which comments on its remarkable detail and seems to support Bancroft's planning and meticulous orders for his posthumous endurance.[22]

The practice of burying the heart separately to the corpse was common, particularly in relation to the funerals of kings and warriors.[23] Indeed, in the Middle Ages, many followed the growing custom of burying the heart at a favourite church or shrine, or even requested heart burial in the Holy Land.[24] In addition to many British royals and religious figures having their hearts and viscera separately buried, aristocrats, poets and military members also have a tradition of burying their hearts under monuments, in family vaults, or at other locations with personal significance. A notable eighteenth-century example is that of the poet and satirist Paul Whitehead who ordered that his heart be wrapped in lead and enshrined in an urn, costing £50, with the inscription:

Paul Whitehead of Twickenham, Esq., ob. 1775.
Unhallowed hands, this urn forbear,
No gems, nor orient spoil
Lie hear concealed; but what's more rare,
A heart that knows no guile.[25]

The ceremonial at the heart burial included grenadiers, flute players, bassoon players and fifers. Whitehead's urn was borne by six soldiers and placed on a pedestal in the

Dashwood mausoleum in West Wycombe churchyard. Apparently, his heart was sometimes taken out to show to visitors, until 1829, when it was stolen. Heart burial occurred throughout the eighteenth and nineteenth centuries (the heart burials of Lord Byron and Percy Shelley are notable examples), and embodying not only the extravagant emotional response to the loss of a loved one, but reflecting ancient Egyptian practices and the interest in preserving the mortal body for the afterlife. Since the Egyptians believed that a person's soul disconnected from the body at death, but could be reanimated in the afterlife, preservation, prayers and rituals were necessary to this process. Realising that the era and status of the deceased affected embalming rituals, it is helpful to have a general sense of the Egyptian process. The brain could be removed, especially in the case of royalty. The viscera were removed and often preserved in separated jars or wrapped and reinserted in the body (though the heart was at times left in place).[26] Important in this intricate process was that the desiccated body would still resemble how the person looked while alive, and that the body was protected from dangers that may occur on the journey to the afterlife. These concerns regarding the body and the afterlife are of course reflected in Christian tradition as well.

Egyptiana also infiltrated the cemetery landscape in the eighteenth century, where noted eccentrics erected obelisks, folly pyramids, as well as mausoleums with Egyptian-style subterranean burial vaults. Giovanni Piranesi's designs and drawings helped to popularize the use of Egyptian features and symbols not only in British interiors, but also in cemetery landscape. For example, his illustration (c. 1748) of the pyramidal tomb of Caius Cestius in Rome (c. 18–12 BC) was especially influential, inspiring replicas not only as follies in the eighteenth-century British landscape, but also in cemetery landscapes and burial practices (such as subterranean vaults). True Egyptian-style monuments, rather than those modelled on ancient Roman ones like the pyramid of Cestius, had already been built, but the popularity of the style was encouraged by well-known Egyptologists. The British Museum held and exhibited ancient Egyptian statuary sent back to England by the pioneer Egyptologist Giovannni Belzoni (1778–1823). In 1830, Thomas Willson noted disease and pestilence of the dead permeated London spreading disease and filth. He infamously proposed an 18-acre mega pyramid in Primrose Hill to house '5 million individuals' made up of 'catacombs', each holding up to twenty-four coffins. Though never built, the 'metropolitan cemetery' was designed like a car park, with coffins gradually raised to the higher catacombs, its pyramidal shape allowing for drainage and maximum space.[27]

Willson even formed a Pyramid General Cemetery Company in which people could invest, estimating large profits, mostly from tourism. The concept was eventually turned down for more conventional cemetery designs. Cemetery designer Stephen Geary would later be inspired by the funeral specimens brought back to the British Museum by Belzoni. In fact, Geary designed The London Cemetery Company's North London or Highgate cemetery, consecrated 20 May 1839. One of its most popular features was the Egyptian Avenue, which 'pandered to the craze for Egyptiana'.[28] Here the dead were interred in a line of sixteen family vaults, each brick-lined and with enough shelf-room for twelve coffins (small in comparison with Willson's mega pyramid, but still sizeable).

In front of each door was an inverted torch, the symbol of life extinguished. 'As we enter the massive portals', wrote William Justyne in his *Guide to Highgate Cemetery* (1865), 'and hear the echo of our footsteps intruding on the awful silence of this cold, stony, death-palace, we might also fancy ourselves treading through the mysterious corridors of an Egyptian temple'.[29]

It seems appropriate that the Victorians (who embraced a cult of mourning) should turn to ancient Egyptian culture for inspiration and incorporate pagan symbolism of Egypt into the familiar rituals of Anglican burial. As David Gange observes, for the deeply religious mid-Victorians, biblical history somehow coexisted with Egyptian archaeology and colonialist Egyptology, yet by 1870 'a new Egyptology played a part in the more general backlash against scientific and theological latitude'.[30] For many, the knowledge revealed by archaeologists became a social and religious threat. Yet for others, the religious continuity that characterized Egyptian religion was now 'interpreted not as conservative failings, but as some of the Egyptians' most admirable qualities'.[31] The tendency to entwine Egyptian religion with the Christian present was often used by the Victorians to support biblical Christianity.[32] Yet this craze, of course, pre-dated the Victorians.

Previous to the Egyptiana craze inspired by Belzoni's exhibitions, there are numerous early examples of the ancient Egyptian style infiltrating mausolea. With the Enlightenment came an aristocratic interest in melancholy and remembrance, seen manifested in mausoleum commemoration. Castle Howard reflects this shift in the erection of the first English mausoleum (c. 1729) by Nicholas Hawksmoor, and for its folly pyramid (c. 1728) (also designed by Hawksmoor) celebrating the memory of Lord William, founder of the Howard dynasty.[33] The pyramid is designed with recessed spaces used to accommodate inscriptions to the memory of the 3rd Earl's ancestors. In 1724 John Lethieullier (d. 1737) built a subterranean vault at St. Mary's Little Ilford that housed his lead coffin and viscera jar, as well as those of his sons. The daughter of John Hobart (the 2nd Earl of Buckinghamshire) erected a pyramid for her father who died in 1793 and is buried there with his two wives. The Chambers family erected a pyramid at Clapham churchyard in 1733.

According to Matthew Craske, surgeon Francis Douce (d. 1760), who also practiced embalming, was preoccupied to the point of obsession with the preservation of his body after death. He goes to the unusual lengths in his will of requesting a specific undertaker to handle his corpse: 'Mr. Hazaldine at the Mitre in Pudding Lane should be employed and, should he be dead, Mr. Keele at Upholsterer's Hall in Leadenhall Street'.[34] In an eccentric nod to ancient Egyptian embalmers, Douce and his architect John Blake designed a pyramid-style vault, which was built in 1748 in Lower Wallop, Hampshire (Fig. 6.1). While others built Romanesque and Egyptian-style burial vaults, Douce's monument is unique in that it is also a tomb that contains internal burial rooms holding the bodies of both Douce and his wife.[35] This extravagant burial was clearly inspired by ancient Egyptian embalming and burial practices. Douce was, notably, one of the subscribers to Thomas Greenhill's *The Art of Embalming*, and together Douce and Greenhill were members of the Company of Surgeons and embalming practitioners themselves.

Figure 6.1 Francis Douce Mausoleum (c. 1748), Lower Wallop, Hampshire. Courtesy of The Mausolea & Monuments Trust.

While Douce built a functioning Egyptian-style mausoleum, most of these pyramidal structures were built as follies for design impact.[36] As noted above, the Earl of Carlisle had a pyramid built in 1728 at Castle Howard to commemorate his ancestors; a pyramid was built by Vanbrugh in Stowe School (c. 1725) that is now destroyed; and Knill's Steeple in St. Ives, Cornwall is home to a pyramid mausoleum (unoccupied) (c. 1782) for John Knill, a former mayor of St. Ives. John 'Mad Jack' Fuller (d. 1834), a Sussex eccentric, built a folly mausoleum 'The Pyramid' (c. 1811) under which he was buried and which still stands in the Brightling Churchyard next to his former home (Fig. 6.2). William Mackenzie's Pyramid (c. 1868) in the Church of Saint Andrew, Liverpool and the Killigrew Monument (c. 1738) Falmouth, Cornwall are other pyramid shaped monuments erected as follies. James Burton (d. 1837) and other members of the Burton family are buried beneath the Burton Pyramid (c. 1837) St. Leonards, East Sussex (Fig. 6.3). The Gillow Mausoleum (c. 1830) is designed in the Egyptian style with carved columns, capitals and papyrus leaf decorations (interments are above-ground). The Egyptian Revival style Kilmorey Mausoleum (c. 1850) in St. Margarets, Richmond upon Thames, contains the bodies of the 2nd Earl of Kilmorey (d. 1880) and his mistress (Fig. 6.4).

Built by the company founded by MacDonald, it is said to have cost £30,000 (about £1.5 million at modern prices). In *Up to a Point – In Search of Pyramids in Britain and Ireland* (2009), David Winpenny features ten pyramids in Gloucestershire, including an eighteenth-century example at Stanway House, a small pyramid in St. Mary's churchyard, Prestbury to commemorate the Dyer family, and the pyramidal tomb of stonemason John Bryan in Painswick churchyard.[37] In addition, numerous obelisks were erected in the eighteenth and nineteenth centuries, including Fuller's Brightling Needle (erected

Figure 6.2 John 'Mad Jack' Fuller 'The Pyramid' (c. 1811), Brightling Churchyard. Courtesy of the Mausolea & Monuments Trust.

to commemorate Nelson's victory at Trafalgar or Wellington's victory over Napoleon in 1815), the Wellington Obelisk (c. 1861) and the Bulkeley Memorial (c. 1882). Topped with a pyramidion, the obelisk has been used for thousands of years as a commemorative structure. Used to adorn various monuments, including tombs, since ancient times, the obelisk has been interpreted as a monument to the dead. Following the Battle of the Nile and defeat of Napoleon, the obelisk was an especially poignant symbol of British imperial power and victory. And with the popularity of Egyptian-style monuments in the nineteenth century, we see the erection of monolithic obelisks in Victorian cemeteries (such as Highgate) to commemorate war dead and mark tombs.

When the 'Magnificent Seven' cemeteries were built in the mid-nineteenth century, Highgate and Abney Park incorporated Egyptian-style buildings (Abney Park boasted an entrance in this style). Well-known Victorian sculptor and Egyptologist Joseph Bonomi the Younger (who designed the entrance to Abney Park as well as the folly Egyptian Springs) supposedly designed the Courtoy Mausoleum (c. 1850) in Brompton Cemetery, London (where Bonomi Jr is buried as well). With its pyramidal peak and mysterious hieroglyphs inscribed in the walls of the tomb, the Courtoy Mausoleum (Fig. 6.5) holds the bodies of Hannah Courtoy (d. 1849) and her three daughters.

Figure 6.3 Burton Pyramid (c. 1837), St. Leonards, East Sussex. This image is in the public domain.

Bonomi Jr also designed an Egyptian facade for John Marshall's Temple Works in Leeds (c. 1841). Though many such as architect Augustus Charles Pugin criticized the Egyptian Revival as pagan and inappropriate for England as a Christian country, the monument style proliferated well into the early twentieth century.[38] Greek and Roman styles were popular among the aristocratic, and the funeral monuments of the wealthy reflected this. The McLennan Monument (c. 1893) erected in Anfield Cemetery in the form of an Egyptian pylon is a notable later example that includes engraved Egyptian-style decoration. Yet despite the increasing interest in ancient Egypt during the nineteenth century, compared with other funerary styles Egyptian monuments and commemorative statues in cemeteries were relatively rare, exotic and costly. The continuance of this style into the early twentieth century, and the survival of these monuments into the twenty-first, signals an ongoing curiosity surrounding memorials and the Egyptian style in Britain.

These mausoleums and monuments symbolize both the rage for all things Egyptian as well as the extravagance of their erectors. The British pyramid reflects the desire for the

Figure 6.4 Kilmorey Mausoleum (c. 1850), St. Margarets, Richmond upon Thames. Courtesy of the Mausolea & Monuments Trust.

Figure 6.5 Courtoy Mausoleum (c. 1850), Brompton Cemetery, London. This image is in the public domain.

dead body to be somehow symbolically more prepared for the afterlife. It is the ultimate British funerary expression of wealth, detachment and imperial egotism. This is reflected in the growing interest in preservation techniques as seen in mummy unrolling, medical practice and undertaking. Members of the aristocracy and wealthy middle and upper classes certainly had access to and sought out the preservation of their remains. And though never popular or frequent, embalming spread beyond royal tradition, infiltrating the burial rites of the aristocratic and wealthy in an effort to posthumously preserve social distinction. By the late-eighteenth century, the association between ancient Egypt, death and the survival of the soul was well-established in Britain. James Cavanah Murphy's *Plans, Elevations, Sections and Views of the Church of Batalha* (1795) includes a compelling passage about British Egyptomania and the pyramid. Reviewer Jurgis Baltrusaitis summarizes Murphy's view:

> Murphy sees pyramids everywhere: on the façades of Westminster Abbey and York Cathedral, on transept towers and buttresses of medieval churches. The 'pyramidal tendency' dominates the overall layout of the building, down to the canopies above the niches. ... The pyramid was sacred to the subjects of Pharaoh, who used its shape to express the origin of all things. They erected it in their ceremonies, as do the Christians, to signify the immortality of the soul. Like the flame, it represents the spirit of the dead leaving the body and mounting to divine repose. The Gothic cathedral, in its elements and as a whole, the symbolism of its forms, is a transposition of an Egyptian mode.[39]

The oddities erected by Douce and others reflect this Christian transposition that Murphy describes. The English pyramid intersects both ancient symbol of immortality with the Christian belief in the afterlife. Whether found on the façade of a medieval church in London, or erected in the garden of a country estate, the English pyramid was indeed 'everywhere' in the eighteenth and nineteenth centuries. However, the increasing secularization of British society, and the rise of other undertaking forms such as cremation, meant that the fall of the monument, and decline in mausoleum popularity, were inevitable. Extravagant burial and funeral practices declined, and along with this came the necessary decline of Egyptiana in this context.

Together, the culture's embracing of Egyptomania and the mysticism surrounding death and funerary architecture and sculpture represents an apparent festishization and commodification of imperial interests. This reverse colonization of cultural materialism finds its apex in the ancient symbol of the pyramid (and pyramid-like structures). Embraced by eighteenth- and nineteenth-century eccentrics, aristocrats and landed gentry, English embalming practices, the English pyramid and other forms of interest in Egyptiana are material reminders of not only these imperial ventures and commemorative symbologies, but of the persistent idealization of the human pursuit of immortality.

CHAPTER 7
OBITUARIES AND OBELISKS: EGYPTIANIZING FUNERARY ARCHITECTURE AND THE CEMETERY AS A HETEROTOPIC SPACE
Nichola Tonks

Double me up! Double me up!

These were, reportedly, some of the anguished final words of Alexander Hamilton – the 10th Duke of Hamilton – as he lay on his death bed in 1852, anxious that his final wishes for his burial be carried out.[1] A request to be 'doubled up' in this context seems somewhat strange, however the Duke knew that his chosen casket would, in fact, be too small for his frame. He had purchased an ancient Egyptian sarcophagus which, being made from Egyptian syenite, was impossible to alter or lengthen in order to accommodate his body. This instance of an artefact being incorporated into a burial is but one of many ways in which the influence of ancient Egypt was threaded through the material culture of British funerals and resting places.

I argue that the uses of ancient Egyptian imagery and artefacts are representative of how the British cemetery performs as a heterotopic space in which ancient cultures can be engaged with, and appropriated, in ways that would not be permissible in the same manner elsewhere.[2] The Egyptian revivals of the nineteenth century coincided with the rise of the cemetery company in Britain. Burials became increasingly more ostentatious and flamboyant affairs.[3] Edwin Chadwick noted in his *Interment Report* of 1843 that 'the average cost of funerals of persons of every rank above pauper [was …] £14 19s 9d' but that the funerals of 'persons of rank and title' could cost up to £1500 with the average for funerals of 'gentry of the better condition' being £400.[4] Chadwick estimates that £4.8 million was spent annually in England on Wales on funerals (excluding mourning) yet the actual cost of the burials was closer to £1 million, leading him to conclude that the rest of the money was merely being 'thrown into the grave, at the expense of the living'.[5] It seems that no expense was spared.[6] Thus, one can suppose that it was inevitable that in a society which associated ancient Egypt with luxury and opulence that this imagery would find its way into rituals that required those characteristics. The cemetery, and the burials and funerals which took place within it, became an environment in which the culture and imagery of ancient Egypt could be embraced. As the pharaohs enjoyed a legacy that lasted for thousands of years, so too could those who chose to include ancient Egypt in their own burial. In essence, the Egyptianizing material culture of British cemeteries speaks of a society which longed to be remembered and looked to an iconic past civilization which was still drawing people's interest thousands of years after its tombs had been sealed.

The new privatized cemeteries allowed for a more personal flair to be exacted in death, making the spaces a heterotopic cornucopia of cultural appropriation and individuality which deviated from the previously prescribed 'good Christian death'.[7]

The transference of burials from churchyards to cemeteries allowed individuals, or their grieving families, to choose headstones, monuments and plots; if one had the means to pay, then no demand was too much. In this way, the space within the cemetery became a 'heterotopia' whereby the trend for the Egyptian revival style could be embraced among an eclectic array of styles from earlier burials. The societal pressure to have 'the best send-off' one could afford was immense, and this encouraged even the most frugal to hang the expense, influenced, of course, by what was deemed fashionable, as styles came in and out of vogue.

In this chapter, I draw upon Michel Foucault's concept of the heterotopia to examine the cemetery as a heterotopic space for the expression of 'Egyptomania'. I pay specific attention to Alexander Hamilton's final resting place as a case study of particular interest, in order to demonstrate that the changes in the locations of British burials in the nineteenth century allowed for the deceased to immortalize themselves in individualistic ways that previously, within churchyards, had been somewhat stifled. The use of ancient Egyptian imagery, iconography and, indeed, artefacts themselves could be used by those who wished for their name to live on to secure their place in notable British burials.

Michel Foucault's concept of the heterotopia is complicated; this particular notion was never extensively clarified. Thus, it is possible to explore Foucault's notion of a heterotopia with a degree of flexibility. He suggests that a heterotopia is a place which has the inordinate power to modify the ways in which humans behave within a space, a space in which conventions can be broken and the 'everyday' is, to an extent, subverted.[8] Foucault defines two separate types: 'crisis heterotopias, i.e., there are privileged or sacred or forbidden places, reserved for individuals who are, in relation to society and to the human environment in which they live, in a state of crisis: adolescents, menstruating women, pregnant women' and 'heterotopias of deviation: those in which individuals whose behaviour is deviant in relation to the required mean or norm are placed'. This essay suggests that the cemetery acts as a heterotopia in both of these ways; it becomes both a privileged place of those in crisis (the dead and the grieving), and also a space within which it is permissible to deviate from previously prescribed social mores. Ancient Egypt was often seen as exotic, mystical and, quite often, deviant in many ways in the nineteenth century; part of the West's fascination for Egypt is expressed through the 'othering' of a mystical, exotic, and sometimes, erotic culture.[9] The newly commercialized cemetery became a unique space in which this fascination could be embraced without fear or reprisal. Being buried in a cemetery was not an unusual occurrence, nor was choosing a fitting monument for remembrance; however, I argue that the cemetery allows for deviance from the normative cross and angel of the churchyard, and for ancient Egypt to encroach upon the British landscape.

The Egyptian revivals of the nineteenth and early twentieth centuries pervaded many aspects of British culture: jewellery, fashion, film and architecture to name but a few.[10] Ancient Egypt and the 'Nile style' experienced waves of popularity throughout the period as the British embraced their fascination with this ancient culture. Robert Southey (1774–1843), a poet of the Romantic school, notably criticized the pervasiveness of ancient Egypt, demonstrating the extent to which the culture was being adopted. He wrote, in 1836:

> Everything now must be Egyptian: the ladies wear crocodile ornaments, and you sit upon a sphinx in a room hung round with mummies, and with the long black lean-armed long-nosed hieroglyphical men, who are enough to make children afraid to go to bed.[11]

Southey's comment captures the zeitgeist of the Egyptian revivals in the nineteenth century. His suggestion of the ubiquity of the trend demonstrates the widespread incorporation of ancient Egyptian imagery into British design and décor – from women's jewellery, to chairs, to wallpaper.

It was this omnipresence of ancient Egypt that led to the use of the term 'Egyptomania' to encapsulate the fervour with which the culture was received. Noreen Doyle's essay on the term notes that 'The origin of the word "Egyptomania" has been traced back to the phrase "Egyptian mania," employed by Sir John Soane (1753–1837). ... The word "l'égyptomanie" seems to have debuted in a German book of 1808, ... its English equivalent, "Egyptomania," appeared [in 1809]. But the coinage predates all of these publications by more than a decade.'[12] When first used, the term was used simply to describe the prevalence of design inspired by ancient Egypt.

Yet, the term itself now seems to suggest that engagements with the culture of ancient Egypt are somewhat frivolous or over-zealous; the adoption of the word 'mania' is, in many ways, representative of the views of scholars such as Ronald H. Fritze, and James Stevens Curl who have explored the Egyptian revivals within Britain. Their work suggests that such revivals are shallow, superficial and one-dimensional. Curl's work on the art of the movement illuminates various ways in which the West has engaged with ancient Egypt's imagery as an element of design history and proffers excellent details on the revivals, but does not seek to explore the cultural underpinning of the use of these motifs, or the term Egyptomania.[13] Conversely, Fritze, in his introduction, seeks to interrogate what Egyptomania could mean.[14] Yet, during his exploration of the term he posits that 'the term "Egyptomania" could give the impression of being concerned with a form of mental illness. Some people who go to extremes with their interest in Egypt might well be mentally ill, and the name "Egyptopaths" has been suggested for them'.[15] This statement, in and of itself, is remarkably problematic. Not only does it suggest that engagements with ancient Egyptian culture are frivolous – indeed Fritze suggests that, for the majority, their encounters with Egyptomania are 'an enjoyable interest in a manner similar to the way that other people enjoy golf, period melodramas such as *Downton Abbey*, or NASCAR'[16] – but it also calls into question the mental health of those who have an extreme interest in ancient Egypt. Fritze's assessment demonstrates the extent to which Egyptomania is oft purported to be somewhat simplistic, lacking in depth and, quite frankly, a bit 'mad', even to scholars of the phenomenon.

More recent scholarship has begun to dip beneath the surface of the West's engagements with ancient Egypt to illuminate how the fascination can be demonstrative of broader issues within society. For example, Eleanor Dobson's work on science and magic in the Victorian period establishes the ways in which ancient Egypt was used throughout nineteenth-century literature and meticulously argues that authors such as H. Rider Haggard and Bram Stoker influenced modern attitudes to ancient Egypt through their writing.[17] Indeed, Dobson posits that 'ancient Egypt and the most remarkable scientific discoveries of the present day became unlikely bedfellows' as the notion that 'ancient Egypt may have been more scientifically advanced than modern Western civilization was, by the late nineteenth century, a familiar idea'.[18] Furthermore, Sara Brio, whose work also interrogates the influence of ancient Egypt in the Victorian period, has posited that 'archaeological digs which appropriated ancient Egypt [were seen] as a precursor to Christianity' and 'the polytheistic religion of the ancient Egyptians [was] not ... a distant and alien concept, but [was] instead ... an active participant in the shaping of Victorian faith'.[19] This perception that ancient Egyptian civilization was as sophisticated, if not more so, than contemporary society is key to understanding nineteenth-century engagements with the ancient culture. Far from being ridiculed or mocked, ancient Egyptians were held in esteem, their knowledge revered, and their beliefs (particularly regarding burial) scrutinized and imitated. Matthew Coniam notes that 'the very term "Egyptomania" became established as the marker of a phenomenon of which intellectual sobriety is not necessarily to be expected',[20] and that 'even as a boy [he] knew there was something fundamentally incompatible between the seriousness of Egyptology and the frivolity of mummy movies'.[21] His study, *Egyptomania Goes to the Movies: From Archaeology to Popular Craze to Hollywood Fantasy* (2017), recognizes that Western uses of ancient Egypt are far from superficial – while acknowledging derision of the subject – and seeks to uncover what such fascination means.

These perceived boundaries that exist between 'serious' Egyptology and the study of the reception of ancient Egypt are increasingly being worn away by the significant work being done by scholars such as Dobson. The conference series *Tea with the Sphinx* based at the University of Birmingham sought, in 2017, to 'define the discipline' of ancient Egypt reception studies. Scholars are increasingly becoming aware that 'popular' engagements with ancient Egypt are as worthy of scholarly attention as the artefacts that hail from the 'Land of the Pharaohs' themselves. This essay ultimately seeks to contribute to that growing body of scholarship on Egyptomania that seeks to push beyond surface-level analysis of the use of ancient Egypt in the modern world, instead seeking to unearth the cultural significances that lie beneath.

The cemetery as heterotopic space

The places in which the dead were buried changed significantly during the nineteenth century. Concerns regarding public health and cholera outbreaks had been linked to overflowing churchyards where rotting corpses were becoming exposed due to over filling.[22] Before the nineteenth century, the cyclical use of burial grounds meant that graves over a century old were reused and bones dug up to create new space; however, with the widespread introduction of permanent stone monuments as attitudes surrounding remembrance and commemoration shifted, the creation of new spaces in which to inter the dead became a crucial and pressing matter.[23] To combat the crisis a series of legislations (collectively known as the Burial Acts) were passed in the 1850s which were intended to relieve the pressure put on church burial grounds.[24] Population growth in urbanized areas in the 1840s and 1850s spurred the trend of establishing expensive cemeteries on the outskirts of towns, while newly created burial boards provided public cemeteries.[25] Until the end of the century, the cemetery companies were in charge of British burials, until the Local Government Acts of 1894 and 1899 saw the control of cemeteries pass to the newly formed local authorities.[26] Sarah Rutherford argues that cemeteries developed in the Victorian period were 'a new type of burial ground for the dead, bringing innovation in the assemblage of landscape design, architecture, planting and social use, and became a countrywide asset'.[27] These new spaces allowed for personal creativity, individual design and a way to move away from traditionalist funerary architectural forms. The cemetery of the nineteenth century became a heterotopic space in which imagery and cultures could be embraced in ways that Christian churchyards and conventional burial spaces have previously not permitted.

Far from being solely created to solve the problem of overcrowding, the new cemeteries were designed with aesthetics in mind, and proponents of the new ventures looked to France for inspiration as the height of taste and respectability. Père Lachaise, opened in 1804, contains a plethora of memorials reminiscent of ancient Egypt and provided a model of sophisticated elegance that British cemetery designers were desperate to emulate. George Frederick Carden was one of the first to suggest public cemeteries in England in the nineteenth century after travelling to Paris in the 1820s.[28] In 1830, he wrote in his prospectus for the General Cemetery Company that the planned cemetery would be 'laid out and planted, (after the manner of the celebrated cemetery of *Père-la-Chaise*, in the neighbourhood of Paris)'.[29] The prospectus also contains a seven-page description of Père Lachaise: it records that 'on either side of the finely-coloured gravel walk, neatness and gaudiness alternately attract the attention of the visitor'.[30] It is clear that Carden was rather taken with the burial ground and his intentions were to replicate the splendour of the Parisian cemetery in his home country. His choice to use the word 'visitor' rather than 'bereaved', or 'those in mourning', is indicative of the extent to which cemeteries were spaces that were more than a resting place for the dead.

With their serpentine paths and structured planting, cemeteries were also places of recreation: a space in which one could see and be seen – in life and in death. Memorial monuments would not only be seen by the bereaved family but also by the society that chose to walk the paths of the cemetery for years to come.[31] The misconception that all pharaohs chose to build a pyramid for their everlasting resting place was ubiquitous in the nineteenth century and, thus, taking inspiration from ancient Egypt, one could say a lot – even from the grave – through the choice of such a monument for the memorialization of one's remains. The Victorian trend for a lavish funeral and a fitting 'send-off' could be seen as vulgar in the eyes of the church, and so, private burial grounds provided the perfect milieu for egoism, pomp and ceremony; it was only fitting, then, that the same attention to detail could be lavished on the memorial. 'As at Paris, so in the British Burial Ground', Carden wrote, 'the public will be at liberty to erect what description of monuments they please'.[32] The new cemeteries offered the opportunity to personalize the grave, to incorporate a design to the deceased (or family's) preference, and presented a way to display wealth and status in a way churchyards had not. The taste for designs which echoed ancient Egypt made an impression with Carden in Père Lachaise and, as such, he detailed how people could ensure their names lived on by appropriating the imagery of the past. He wrote:

> Man, indeed, conscious of the shortness of his natural existence, has in all ages endeavoured to perpetuate, beyond the grave, the recollection of his journey upon the earth; and sculpture, in remoter times, was nurtured by this legitimate exercise of the art, and it has been the delight of succeeding ages, and the height of their ambition, to copy after, and endeavour to equal, the many monuments of antiquity.[33]

Thus, Carden proposes his plans for the new cemeteries to be a space in which one's name can live on and emulate the immortality achieved by those of antiquity: the great pharaohs, and ancient Greek and Roman emperors. In this way, then, the cemetery was a heterotopic space in which one could deviate from traditional burial, have a monument of one's own choosing which would stand the test of time, quite unlike churchyards which offered limited space and cyclical plots in which it was possible that your grave would be reused and, as such, your legacy be erased from the annals of history forever.

Immortality, it seems, could be achieved with the erection of a suitable obelisk, pyramid or draped urn, cast in stone for posterity. The new cemeteries flourished and, over the course of the 1830s and 1840s, the use of churchyards became almost redundant.[34] Vast, picturesque burial grounds offering a space within which the grandest of burials could be achieved were created the length and breadth of the country: Glasgow Necropolis, the 'Magnificent Seven' in London, Gravesend Cemetery in Kent, Liverpool Necropolis, Dean Cemetery in Edinburgh, and Leeds General Cemetery to name but a few. In such locations, the wealthy had a space in which they could shape their funerary architecture to their own specifications, and move beyond the constrictions of the Christian churchyard.

Individualism was not only contained within cemeteries, however. The landed gentry also saw fit to build striking memorials on their own land and within their private cemeteries. Once the remit of the estate chapel grounds, landowners could increasingly venture out across the estate to create their own heterotopic space within which to be interred and deviate from preceding traditions.

How Hamilton lost his feet

One of the most ostentatious examples of the ways in which ancient Egypt was woven into the fabric of the new individualistic British burials is the case of Alexander Hamilton, 10th Duke of Hamilton, who died in 1852. Hamilton was a man with his own idea of magnificence; he had many titles (Marquis of Hamilton, Marquis of Douglas and Clydesdale, Earl of Angus, Baron Hamilton, Duke of Brandon in Suffolk, and Baron Dutton, Co. Chester, and Duke of Châtelherault in France) and used most of his titles rather than preferring just one which earned himself the nickname 'El Magnifico'.[35] He also claimed to be the rightful heir to the Scottish throne, insisting that James VI had, in fact, been killed while still an infant and had been replaced with a pretender.[36] Hamilton was indeed one of Scotland's premier peers, with most of his engagements being reported in *the Morning Post*; the minutiae of the Duke's everyday life were laid bare for all to read – even down to incidents such as him falling off his horse in an accident in which 'his head was sent completely through his hat'.[37] Rather than articles reporting such events in a mocking manner the tone is one of quiet concern for the Duke's wellbeing; this reverence demonstrates the extent to which the Duke was esteemed within his society. His titles, his monarchical ties and the status afforded to him by the community in which he lived all reinforced his air of self-aggrandizement which ultimately contributed to the manner in which he saw fit to plan for his demise.

Hamilton was a collector of fine arts and antiquities and amassed quite the fortune by investing in art and artefacts, to the extent that Godfrey Evans made his collecting the subject of his doctoral thesis in which he argued that Hamilton was 'the greatest collector in the history of Scotland'.[38] Hamilton's collection did not contain many Egyptian artefacts – these being limited to two sarcophagi and a smattering of Egyptian porphyry vases – though he was an avid enthusiast of ancient Egyptian mummies, and had subscribed to Thomas Pettigrew's volume on the subject, *A History of Egyptian Mummies* (1834).[39] Although Hamilton had not purchased a great many Egyptian artefacts, being buried in an original ancient Egyptian sarcophagus speaks volumes of the ways in which he saw ancient Egypt's status within British Victorian society. To align oneself with the rulers of such a forward-thinking ancient civilization such as Egypt is a brazen statement in and of itself. Hamilton makes his wishes to be placed in his sarcophagus very clear in his will, and he repeats himself more than once to ensure that his point is made.[40]

Hamilton was mummified by Thomas Pettigrew in a replication of an ancient Egyptian ceremony, and interred in a sarcophagus that was 3,000 years old.[41] Despite evident planning on Hamilton's part, he did not actually fit – and thus it is said that his feet were cut off to make his corpse an appropriate size for the basalt encasement.[42] The grisly details of his feet being removed are absent from his obituary; however, it does go into detail about the sarcophagus itself. His obituary in *The Gentleman's Magazine* reads:

> The late Duke Alexander ... is not destined to lie in the same vault with his noble kindred, but in the chapel above, in a costly sarcophagus, which his Grace procured about thirty years ago from the Pyramids of Egypt. ... This sarcophagus

is made of the hardest basalt, and covered with hieroglyphics, which are almost as fresh as the day they were executed. The lid contains a beautiful female face, and it is believed that the sarcophagus originally contained the body of an Egyptian queen or princess; but the late Duke had the cavity chiselled out and extended, so as to serve as the sepulchre for his own body. Everything had been prepared by the orders of the late Duke before his death, and the sarcophagus rested in the niche of the chapel opposite the entrance, upon two splendid blocks of black marble.[43]

The sarcophagus, purchased in 1836, required an adequate tomb in which it could reside after the Duke's passing; the family chapel vaults were not satisfactory for Hamilton's interment and, in 1842, Hamilton began to construct a new mausoleum.[44] The mausoleum was colossal; it stands at an imposing height of 120 feet.[45]

The Gentleman's Magazine describes it as the 'most costly and magnificent temple for the reception of the dead that was ever erected – at least in Europe'.[46] Its height and imposing design dwarfed the trees and woodlands around it on the Hamilton estate – a luxury which would not have been possible in a churchyard – and it contained vaults for deceased family members (which Hamilton had transferred) and a 14-foot plate glass window which, when the light came through, would illuminate the place where Hamilton's sarcophagus was to rest.[47]

This display of wealth, extravagance and utter self-importance runs counter to the Christian beliefs of a humble 'good death'. As his family lay below in the vaults

Figure 7.1 'Aerial View of Hamilton Mausoleum', © A.P.S. (UK) / Alamy Stock Photo.

of the mausoleum, Hamilton lay above them on his 'splendid black marble', clearly demonstrating where he placed himself in life as in death: above everyone else. It is important to note that there were many more pharaohs buried in secluded tombs than have been found to be buried in pyramids; increasingly pharaohs chose to be interred in places such as the Valley of the Kings as they were much 'less obvious and more readily guarded against tomb-robbers'.[48] Yet, we can see that Hamilton is mirroring his perception of the practices of the ancient Egyptian pharaohs, constructing a monument to himself and placing himself at the very centre. By choosing to emulate the kings of Egypt, as he saw them, Hamilton ensured that his death would be grand, spectacular, extravagant, to the point that his burial would dominate the space in which it lay. He did not want to be placed under the ground, or in the vaults below, but centre stage bathed in light from the open glass circular ceiling.

This behaviour is so far removed from the traditional picture of the coffin being lowered into the grave as family look on and mourn; it is deviant, not only in its difference, but in the ways in which it pushes back against social mores and ideas surrounding what a burial should be. Hamilton took the burial space and made it his own. The obituary notes that the hieroglyphs on the sarcophagus were 'almost as fresh as the day they were executed', suggesting that they were made to last forever. Carved from 'hardest basalt' it is clear that the sarcophagus had lasted for thousands of years by the time Hamilton purchased it, and it would last for thousands more with him within it. It was the perfect vessel to carry Alexander Hamilton's name on throughout history and into legend.

Figure 7.2 'Hamilton Mausoleum', © paulskinner25/Stockimo/Alamy Stock Photo.

As Victorian funerals became more extravagant, so too did the spaces in which they took place, and Hamilton's was one of the grandest of them all. What else would be fitting for the heir to the Scottish throne? The mausoleum was not quite finished when Hamilton died in 1852, yet his wishes were carried out and he was interred there until the mausoleum began to collapse and his sarcophagus was relocated to Bent Cemetery. The pedestal upon which the 10th Duke resided in death still, to this day, bears a faint outline of his sarcophagus.[49]

Hamilton's burial offers a unique insight into the ways in which the landed gentry constructed their own burial sites in accordance with their own wishes, rather than those that conform strictly to their faith. Hitherto, it would not have been possible for Hamilton to be buried in his sarcophagus had he been interred in a churchyard. The changing nature of British burials from a church-dominated practice to a commercially led venture allowed the Duke to deviate from a more traditional burial. The sarcophagus, *The Gentleman's Magazine* purports, was made for a female, and as such Hamilton's frame would not fit within it without chiselling out the basalt. The existing site for burials on the Hamilton estate was not grand enough, in the Duke's opinion, for the artefact which was to carry his corpse to be housed, which led to the construction of the mausoleum. In this way, then, Hamilton is creating a new heterotopic space for his remains to reside after his death. He replaces the old with the new, and the new with the old. The size of the mausoleum demonstrates the extent to which Hamilton was set on having his name immortalized, emulating the pharaohs and capitalizing upon the radical transformations in the ways in which Britain dealt with its dead during the nineteenth century.

It is clear, then, that cemeteries and burial sites in Britain became heterotopic spaces in which people could challenge accepted practices and traditions to form their own unique memorial which would last forever. They were places in which the culture of ancient Egypt began to take precedence over the once ubiquitous cross and weeping angel of the British grave-side monument. The particular way that the landscaping was designed allowed for individuality according to means and financial situation, thus, expanding the options available to the person, or family, making the decisions surrounding the monument that would bear their memorial. Within the confines of the cemetery, amid the sinuous pathways and the ubiquitous yew trees lay catacombs, pyramids and winged solar discs that evoked that ancient culture of the past, calling out with a desire to be remembered as the pharaohs were in this modern age. The materiality of the cemetery of Britain became more diverse and allowed for levels of individuality in death that would not be deemed acceptable in other spaces. Therefore, the cemetery became a heterotopia for the wealthy in Britain during the nineteenth and early twentieth centuries, a place and space in which they could hope to be remembered forever.

CHAPTER 8
TUTANKHARTIER: DEATH, REBIRTH AND DECORATION; OR, TUTMANIA IN THE 1920S AS A METAPHOR FOR A SOCIETY IN RECOVERY AFTER WORLD WAR ONE

Lizzie Glithero-West

On 26 November 1922 Howard Carter first created a small opening in the sealed door of the tomb of Tutankhamun in Egypt. He could barely have predicted, when he looked around in amazement and saw 'emerging slowly from the mist; the strange animals, statues, and everywhere the glint of gold', that these 'wonderful things' would quickly become endowed with a plethora of collective and individual meanings for an unprecedentedly broad public.[1] Whether the inhabitants of Paris, London and New York saw an archaeological triumph, a commercial opportunity, artistic inspiration or a doorway to an exciting or frightening spiritual world, what seems most apparent is that a society in mourning, plagued with uncertainty and recovering from the First World War, looked hopefully into the face of Tutankhamun and saw themselves, and in so doing perceived a means of recovery.

The tomb revealed little new textual or architectural information, and the wall art was sparse, but it was uniquely intact. It was a time-capsule: both a frozen funerary assemblage, giving unprecedented insights into mortuary ritual and belief, and a treasure trove of the ancient decorative arts. It therefore seems natural that the greatest impact of such a visually rich assemblage was on fashion and jewellery. The consequent 'Tutmania' which took the world by storm was, however, by no means purely an aesthetic craze. I propose in this essay that the discovery of a young boy lying amidst the remains of his funeral, and 'resurrected' after 3,000 years of obscurity, tapped into deeper preoccupations of the time. Here was a society trying to attribute meaning to the loss of so many of its young at war and looking for the means to revive itself, emotionally, socially and economically. Observers not only saw the dusty remains of a long extinct civilization in Tutankhamun's tomb, but something uncannily reminiscent of their own circumstances.

There have been three challenges for scholarship on these issues. First, as Bridget Elliott has suggested, serious theoretical discussion of the impact of Egyptian art on the period has often been sacrificed to the tendencies of leading modernist thinkers, who rejected the traditional, including theatricalized and spectacular spaces, ornament and decoration. She argues convincingly that the Egyptian-revival artefact of the twenties should be 'credited with as much cultural resonance as Le Corbusier's white ripolin walls'.[2] Second, the study of Egyptian-revival art in the 1920s has often been met with aesthetic snobbery. *Art and Archaeology* magazine reassured readers in 1923 that 'fortunately for the true lover of art all this is but a passing fancy rather amusing while it lasts',[3] while more recently the *New York Times* of 25 February 1990 mused that 'The Tutankhamun discovery must have boosted the Egyptian business but its aesthetic benefits seem dubious.'[4] Daniel Miller suggests that the 'humility' of certain more subtle artefacts means that by their very reticence they are more easily 'assimilated into unconscious and unquestioned knowledge'.[5] Criticized or excluded from the canon of art for their public and fashionable appeal, it is indeed these qualities which make Egyptian-revival items of the utmost value in revealing the preoccupations of their consumers. Finally, a wealth of literature has been produced about Tutankhamun, the decorative arts of the 1920s, Egyptomania and the First World War, but rarely do accounts consider the connections between them.[6] Texts on Tutankhamun hardly mention the impact of the discovery beyond the media hype. Most studies of Art Deco see Egyptian influence merely as part of the exotic melting-pot of inspiration that shaped the style. Most disappointingly, a number of works on the Egyptian revival discuss the range of forms inspired by the discovery,[7] but only a handful attempt to explain why the impact of the discovery on the arts was so profound.[8] As Helen Whitehouse has argued, 'Egyptomania has been amply documented in its visible manifestations; the focus should now shift to a more penetrating analysis of the mental constructs of Egypt that lie behind this selective use of its imagery'.[9]

In this essay I explore the reasons behind the wide application of themes around death and resurrection in 1920s design, through the branch of the decorative arts which most directly relates to the particular flavour of Tutankhamun's tomb: jewellery and accessories.[10] One jeweller stands out in this area; Cartier was not only one of the most innovative and insightful firms of the day, but their deep understanding of Egyptian symbolism was also used to infuse meaning into beautifully crafted items that reflected the identity and concerns of their wearers. I turn to specific items that Cartier created to explore the appropriation of Egypt in the 1920s as a metaphor for a society in recovery. Ultimately, I use a combination of anthropological and art historical approaches to look beyond the aesthetic reception of these Egyptian-revival items and see their value as meaningful indicators, imbued with meaning and intention, which reveal a society in flux.

Mourning and rebirth

Nearly every family was in mourning in the aftermath of the First World War and the bodies of over 200,000 loved ones were never found or returned.[11] Society was left in a state of irresolution. Until 1920 no private exhumations from France or reburials were allowed and public debate in Europe focused on appropriate resting places for the dead and the rights of families to be able to treat their loved ones in their own distinctive way.[12] Starting in the summer of 1922 around 300,000 of the war dead were returned home.[13] The French and Americans were very committed to the return of their deceased, but the British ruled it out on grounds of expense and equality. Instead, communities went to great expense to pay for memorials (some of which took the form of obelisks), which not only marked the spot where the dead were symbolically brought home, but where communities were reunited, national identity was reconfigured and acceptance of loss could be ritualized and concretized.[14]

The spiritual welfare and destination of the dead were also concerns. The return of bodies was both longed for and feared. Myths and tales of spiritual encounters helped to reorder the world, and experiences in trenches led many men to trust in amulets and charms.[15] For many, conventional religion failed to provide sufficient answers or solace. Spiritualism spread rapidly during this period as a means of reaching out to the dead or responding to the verdict of 'missing' through an alternative search.[16]

In 1909, Arnold van Gennep proposed a universal tripartite structure in rites of passage such as death. Beginning with separation, the transition through a liminal phase where dead and mourners are 'betwixt and between' normal social roles, and finally ending with social re-aggregation. This liminal period is often characterized by changes in dress and behaviour, and spiritual searching. These were certainly characteristics of the 1920s, where bereavement became a universal experience and the dead continued to coexist with the living in several ways. In 1973, Clifford Geertz wrote that 'Death and its rituals not only reflect social values, but are an important force in shaping them.'[17] As people seek to understand death they redefine themselves, while leaving traces of this preoccupation in the objects they produce. Daniel J. Sherman, discussing the practice of commemoration, cites Sigmund Freud's belief that in the aftermath of war, societies both enact and attempt to control individual mourning through the transfer of desire for the deceased to some new object or abstraction.[18] Jay Winter identifies two contrasting routes for this process of remembering and recovery: first through a new language of truth-telling about war in literature and the arts, and second through a focus on 'glory', the 'hallowed dead' and a re-affirmation of traditional values.[19] These seemingly opposing positions worked in tandem, weaving between the spheres of public and private mourning, providing vents for stability in memory and new expression in grief. Death was tamed and translated into material form, asserting order and eternal memory in the face of disorder and transience. The search for an appropriate language of commemoration looked to the past, while taking on new meanings and manifestations. This was nowhere more evident than in Egyptian-revival design.

Post-war Paris was recovering from excessive French mortality of 1.4 million, and an urgent need to rebuild France: morally, commercially, symbolically and physically. France sought a re-invigorated self-image based not on outside forces, but from within. Charles Morice, writing in *L'Homme Libre* in December 1917 saw the writer and artist as 'healers, judges, awakeners of souls, and good fighters in their fashion', making art with the glory of nation, civilization and eternity in mind,[20] while the luxury trade was perceived as a major means of Parisian recovery. In America, there had been fewer dead, but its losses were still shocking at 100,000. New York now eclipsed London as the financial capital of the world and, over the next few years, it would become one of the most commercially and culturally creative places on earth.[21] Finally, in Britain, mortality was near incomprehensible with 950,000 dead, the country was in debt to America, and there were political problems in Ireland. Britain was occupied with its empire, trade and industry, erring on the side of conservatism and historicism in design. Near universally, however, people were determined that the world must never again go to war, demanding instead reform, pleasure and luxury. As a phoenix from the fields of Flanders, society began to be re-invigorated. Sexual and familial relationships were re-negotiated, social structures re-defined and this cultural upheaval was reflected in art, design and radical fashions. As Charlotte Benton, Tim Benton and Ghislaine Wood record, hope lay in novelty; 'never was fantasy so functionally necessary for survival, whether to industry or the individual'.[22]

James Laver has argued that 'Post-crisis epochs always have certain things in common; dance mania, an inflated currency, a wave of female emancipation, and general promiscuity ... reflected with astonishing faithfulness in the clothes women wore.'[23] It is therefore tempting to see the 1920s as a time of resurrection, though in Britain this theme was deeply entwined with what David Cannadine describes as a 'massive all-pervasive pall of death'.[24] Freud claimed that death could no longer be denied: 'we are forced to believe in it',[25] but here we see the development of a culture which hid the experience of death and dealt with it in other ways: through objects, memorials and spiritual exploration. Additionally, individual mourning and recovery progressed at differing paces. This was not a re-aggregated society, but one in transitional limbo. What better outlet for this grief restrained than through the appropriation of the symbolism of a culture best known for its belief in life-eternal? It was with impeccable timing then that a symbolic figure, representing the dead and feeding the desires of the living, was revived.

Most simply, Tutankhamun fulfilled the public desire for entertainment and novelty. Arthur Merton of *The Times* described the carnivalesque atmosphere in Luxor:

> His name is all over the town. It is shouted in the streets, whispered in the hotels. While in the local shops Tutankhamun advertises everything. ... Every hotel in Luxor had something on the menu à la Tut. ... There is a Tutankhamun dance tonight at which the first piece is to be a Tutankhamun Rag.[26]

With the exclusive rights to the news as it emerged, *The Times* left other newspapers floundering until Lord Carnarvon died. The media seized on this morbid opportunity, citing prior warnings given to Carnarvon, theories about vengeful elementals, or poisons hidden in the tomb, and rumour and suspicion took over. For some this was frightening, and the British Museum received a torrent of donations of antiquities from a superstitious public. For others, it confirmed their belief in a spirit world or added to the excitement and sensationalism surrounding the discovery.

Of the huge press interest in the discovery Carter commented: 'One must suppose that ... the general public was in a state of profound boredom with news of reparations, conferences and mandates, and craved for some new topic of conversation.'[27] This thrill of buried treasure and excitement of a curse, which through nineteenth-century mummy novels was already ingrained in the public imagination, allowed adults to indulge in fantasy. Carter, however, had failed to recognize that the discovery had a deeper-seated resonance. Tutankhamun was not pure entertainment or academic endeavour, and the multiplicity of personalities he displayed, both ancient and surprisingly modern, ensured his swift adoption as an icon of the age and the subject of the longest running news saga of modern times.

To the grieving, Tutankhamun must have been strikingly reminiscent of the lost young men of the war.[28] Of the men who died on active military service, 76 per cent had been under the age of thirty.[29] For those still longing for news of loved ones, the discovery of the pharaoh's tomb was a tale of reward for hope and perseverance. The world now waited with bated-breath for two years to see if Tutankhamun was to be found within his sarcophagus. The ancient Egyptians firmly believed that life continued beyond the grave and 'Tut', as he was affectionately known, seemed to personify this hope.

The war had dulled the romance of death. Corpses had been used to patch-up the sides of trenches, graves were robbed, games played with skulls and bones,[30] and 'the full panoply of public mourning had become the exception'.[31] However, here ancient human care and sentiment was re-affirmed as Tutankhamun was discovered surrounded by the remains of flowers and golden tributes. During the war, in Mesopotamia, a decent grave was unmarked, in order to reduce the risk of bodies being unearthed in a search for clothes and blankets.[32] Tutankhamun had only been preserved because his grave, too, had been covered and forgotten. For families in limbo this fact might have provided some comfort. Tutankhamun was also the last of his line. Many mourning parents also had no one to carry on the family name. The figure of Tut became a global inheritance, a universal child, and just as cenotaphs had provided a channel for grief, Tutankhamun allowed society to meditate on a safe personification of death and rebirth to which they could relate.

The media clearly understood the layers of symbolism. The *New York Times* of 10 February 1923 observed that:

> As the objects have been brought out spectators have remarked that from the manner in which they were bandaged and transported with almost tender care on the stretcher-like trays, they reminded one of casualties being brought out of the trenches or casualty clearing stations. As a matter of fact, great quantities of surgical bandages, cotton wool and surgical safety pins are actually being used.[33]

The *Illustrated London News* led with an imagined illustration of 'a 3000-year old pharaoh "coming forth into the day" with the contemporary garlands which adorned his mummy'.[34] The depiction bore a closer resemblance to an honoured war casualty than a mummy (Fig. 8.1).

However, when people looked at Tutankhamun they not only saw their dead, but themselves. Tutankhamun was sold as the 1920s man, 'a man of fashion',[35] both a devoted husband and a lover of life. Carter wrote: 'We recognise in the royal sportsman, the dog-lover, the young husband and the slender wife, creatures in human taste, emotion and

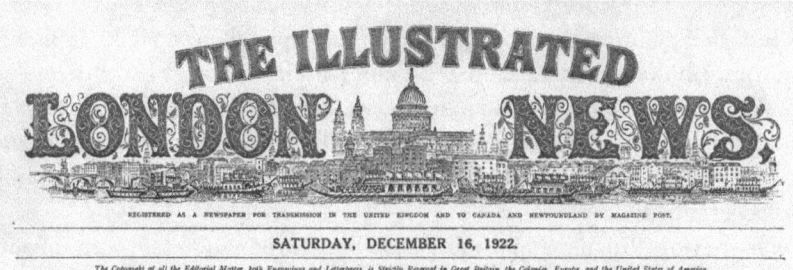

Figure 8.1 'What the great find in Egypt may bring: a 3000-year old pharaoh "coming forth into the day" with the contemporary garlands which adorned his mummy'. © Illustrated London News Ltd/Mary Evans.

affection, very like ourselves.'[36] Wartime experiences led to an increased yearning among the male sex for domesticity,[37] and Tutankhamun provided an appealing model of a luxurious life characterized by family togetherness. Alternatively, for those in mourning, Tutankhamun's wife, Ankhesenamun, perhaps embodied for the modern widow the spirit of feminine grace and identity. This strong woman did not despair; she set out to find a new husband to continue her dynasty. Finally, Tutankhamun as commodity took form. The discovery had wide appeal, and now it could be owned and translated into popular culture and design. Carter's favourite line about the wider cultural impact of the discovery came from Pope Pius XII who insightfully commented, 'It is not an exhumation, it is a resurrection.'[38]

The initial impact on the arts was most explosive in fashion. Pierre Cartier rightly predicted on 8 February 1923 that 'the discovery of the tomb will bring in some sweeping changes in fashion in jewellery'.[39] On the same day *the New York Times* observed that museums were crowded with designers, and The *Jewelers' Circular of* 19 September 1923 reported that 'Jewellery designers and others in the wholesale line are evolving "new" patterns, copied from mummy cases, vases and other very ancient material to be found in the cellars of the museum of the Louvre.'[40] Then, as a number of publications emerged after the Tutankhamun discovery, further accurate sources for inspiration were added to the spectrum of others already in use. Carter's descriptions of decorated robes covered in beadwork and gold sequins, sandals with a lotus thong between the toes, a necklace of enormous beads, furniture and a life-sized mannequin almost read like a contemporary fashion magazine. These items could be (and were) easily adopted and adapted for the modern day.

Deeper analysis reveals that although at times these Egyptianizing 'artefacts' may have been created for commercial reasons alone, many of them display a preoccupation with questions of life and death. As I now explore through the lens of Cartier the jeweller, Tutankhamun's value to 1920s society as a personification of rebirth is most vividly expressed when mapped onto the objects that people chose as their closest identifiers, and most highly prized possessions.

Cartier: The epitome of style

Edward VII described Cartier as 'the jeweller of kings as well as the king of jewellers'.[41] Arguably, Cartier did for the late nineteenth and early twentieth centuries what ancient artisans had done for Tutankhamun. As the jeweller of choice for the upper echelons of society (and those who aspired to be so), Cartier played a prominent role in the ceremonies of life while creating *objets d'art* that could be passed down through generations. These masterworks of skill took extensive time and effort to create, and in the words of Louis Cartier, 'would mark the wealth of an exceptional era'.[42] Cartier not only represented tradition and luxury, however, but also creativity and innovation. Their creations shaped the tastes of a society which followed their fashionable lead. Kathryn Bonanno describes the 1920s as the great epoch of the 'Master Jeweller'.[43] This was indeed the period when jewellery became closely connected with fashion and an art-form in its own right, and Cartier's work, particularly under the creative leadership of Louis Cartier, provided a perfect amalgam of the artistic and cultural spirit of the times with its obsession with ancient Egypt. In this Cartier was unique for several reasons.

Firstly, Louis Cartier had his finger on the pulse of fashion and was extremely intuitive when it came to society's desires. Headed by three brothers in London, Paris and New York, Cartier branches were at the vanguard of changing styles, constantly observing and adapting to taste. Following the war, Cartier's clientele changed and broadened with the collapse of monarchies and the growth of a new bourgeoisie, coupled with the discovery of diamond mines in South Africa which made fine jewellery more affordable. Cartier had always been able to balance tradition with innovation, and this new market was open to new ideas and wanted new kinds of jewels that were both useful and tailored to their needs.

Secondly, Cartier's designs were interesting and original. The designer Charles Jacqueau, who joined the firm in Paris in 1909, favoured eclectic mixtures of oriental and traditional references, including Egyptian motifs, and new combinations of colours such as blue and green inspired by the Ballets Russes. In 1919 the art dealer René Gimpel recognized that Cartier had set in motion a renaissance in the art of jewellery.[44] The firm became one of the most important creators of the Art Deco period, but they also understood their materials and how changing fashions could be successfully adapted within their objects.

Finally, Cartier's designers were grounded in a coherent and sound philosophy of the interplay between taste, object and meaning. The three brothers were collectors of Egyptian antiquities and had studied them in depth. Therefore, when it came to Egyptian-revival styles, their objects were not only innovative and sophisticated, reflecting Cartier's philosophy of harmony, balance, colour in design and technical brilliance in creation, but were rooted in knowledge of ancient Egyptian culture and belief. Young designers were personally tutored by the Cartier brothers from their large libraries of design books and collections of antiques.[45] These included Edme-François Jomard's *Description de l'Égypte* (1809–29) and pattern books such as Owen Jones's *Grammar of Ornament* (1856). Louis Cartier constantly encouraged his draughtsmen to wander through Paris to note down aspects of historical detail in architecture and Jacqueau was fond of prowling the Louvre with his sketchbook.[46] Cartier strove to 'transform and somehow "refract" historical material through the prism of its own outlook, combined with the aesthetic requirement of the twentieth century',[47] and in this the firm was highly successful.

There are two main types of Cartier's Egyptian-creations (comprising jewellery, accessories and clocks) differing in the materials chosen for their construction. The first was longest lived, beginning in 1913 and continuing into the 1930s, and was crafted from modern materials. The second group, which dates from 1923, combined ancient Egyptian themes and motifs with authentic ancient artefacts or pieces of faience acquired from Parisian dealers. These pieces are particularly important. As Nuno Vassallo e Silva and João Cavalho Dias have suggested, these 'exotic, and sometimes bizarre inventions were much more than mere personal ornament for they encapsulated a part of the culture that inspired them, with all its symbolic and talismanic qualities'.[48] Aside from the astute presentation of designs in fashionable form, which reflected society's search for spiritual enlightenment and its desire for rebirth, Louis Cartier believed he was also doing something new for the objects themselves. He held that these ancient constituents, in being re-contextualized, were being given new life and meaning, and perhaps even improved worth: literally a resurrection.[49] It is, therefore, no surprise that some of Cartier's regular clients – from film stars to aristocrats – were also collectors who appreciated his particular vision.[50] These creations were unique in Art Deco jewellery, and for this reason they stand apart from the range of other themed items in competition. Louis Cartier understood society, he knew Egypt and he was willing to experiment, making his firm the single most enlightening case study of the deeper reasons as to why Tutankhamun became an icon of the age.

Scarab brooches: Jewellery and the death and rebirth of the individual

Cartier produced a range of Egyptian revival jewellery, particularly using pylons, the lotus – a symbol of resurrection – deities such as Horus and Sekhmet and, most interestingly, scarabs. Beginning in 1923, Cartier London began to produce a series of scarab brooches, which could often also double-up as belt-buckles. These were usually of the winged-scarab variety and either contained a modern scarab set in ancient blue-faience wings (Fig. 8.2), or a genuine ancient scarab with modern jewelled wings (Fig. 8.3). The designs appeared in many unique variations of material and colour, and unlike the ancient Egyptians, who did not have stones such as diamonds, Cartier was able to contrast the opacity of some materials with the glitter of others. The two best examples of winged scarab brooches (Figs 8.2 and 8.3) were produced in London in 1924 and 1925, respectively. The first, with ancient blue-faience wings dating from the first millennium BC, is made of platinum, with a smoky quartz scarab with emerald eyes, diamonds and black enamel. The second contains a blue-faience scarab with elaborate wings of diamonds, onyx, emeralds, rubies, topaz and citrine.

The largest number of jewels set with Egyptian faience was made by Cartier London. Scarabs had been popular in jewellery since the mid-nineteenth century and Cartier had been producing variations on the theme since 1852. The rootedness implied by the incorporation of ancient elements, combined with new incarnations of familiar motifs, must have appealed to an English audience who were somewhat nervous of the 'hard chic' of French decorative jewellery, which was considered showy.[51] Carnarvon himself had said in 1921 that when 'beauty and historic interest are blended in a single object the interest and delight of possession are more than doubled'.[52] Cartier, too, seems to have strongly believed in this philosophy.

Scarabs were common amulets in Egypt. They represented the god Khepri, the self-created God and the guarantor of resurrection and immortality. The scarab laid its eggs in protective balls of cattle-dung, from which new scarabs could later be seen emerging.[53] The Egyptians equated this process with re-birth and the daily renewing

Figure 8.2 Scarab brooch, Cartier London, 1924. Vincent Wulveryck, Collection Cartier © Cartier.

of the earth. As the heart was central to eternal life, in most New Kingdom burials it is protected by a winged-scarab in the wrappings on the chest. There were many such scarabs adorning the body of Tutankhamun. Jewels in ancient Egypt were imbued with magical meaning, protecting the wearer from hostile powers and ensuring eternal life.[54] Some even endowed their wearers with the specific powers or attributes of the deities concerned.[55] Winged scarabs were often inscribed with texts from the *Book of the Dead* to ensure that the heart did not testify against its owner at the last judgement. For the ancient Egyptians, death was not the end, and jewellery played an essential role in this.

Archival research into the *Jewelers' Circular* publications in 1923 reveals that, although some jewellers were accused of using motifs unthinkingly, many designers had a good understanding of the symbolism that they were appropriating. In the nineteenth century there had been several significant jewellery caches found, and the symbolism of certain motifs and colours was very much already in designers' vocabulary.[56] The *Jewelers' Circular* also sought to continually improve knowledge through scholarly articles, and sparked lively debate over the use of certain symbols. The winged-scarab proved to be a

Figure 8.3 Scarab brooch, Cartier London, 1925. Nils Herrmann, Collection Cartier © Cartier.

very popular form and was produced by many jewellers in everything from diamonds to Bakelite, or plastic costume jewellery. Some contributors described its use as taboo as it was employed entirely for funeral rites; others, however, clearly disagreed: 'Some declare that the open winged scarab represents death ... [but] its Egyptian name means creator, never death. Arguing from the funeral aspect some say the jeweller should refrain from using that scarab form. The writer differs totally from this view and would recommend its use even as signifying a sombre fact we must all face.'[57] This contemporary source highlights the crux of my argument, namely that people often chose to wear the scarab because they wanted to remember their dead, and in adopting the positive eschatological symbolism of a society which believed in immortality, they too could display the hope that their jewellery represented. In resurrecting these ancient scarabs from the tombs of the dead, Cartier, I believe, tapped into their sublime beauty to give them new meaning and purpose in resurrecting the hearts of the women they now adorned.

As previously discussed, post-war society was still in limbo, having been robbed of the full capacity to mourn, and death was increasingly underplayed in public ceremonies. At

Easter 1918, Dean Inge of St Paul's Cathedral 'pleaded with his listeners to stop parading bereavement'.[58] However, it seems mourners did find an outlet for expressions of grief. Following the precedent set by previous generations they were aided by designers such as Cartier, in a new and creative fashion, to map their memories and hopes onto the item closest to their own bodies: their jewellery. John T. Irwin suggests that 'in sacrifice man attempts to transform death from something passively suffered into something actively controlled' and this can be achieved by a person's rebirth through an image.[59] Whether as a reminder that death was not the end, a symbol of their own survival, or as a talisman of protection for a broken heart, the image of the scarab could become a controlled channel for reflection as well as a highly fashionable symbol for a 1920s woman.

Perhaps the most hopeful suggestion of the scarab brooch was the resurrection of the living. The world was full of widows, orphans and those whose lives had been either socially or economically altered by the war, but there was also a sense of hope. In this sense, the self-creation symbolism of the scarab could have represented a vivid badge for an individual who had to endure, and to reconstruct their life. The scarab brooches could also have tapped into the wider spiritual undercurrents evident among the living. Rumours of a curse protecting Tutankhamun's tomb, and the long association of Egypt with magic, may have inspired and furthered belief in the power of such ancient objects. As mentioned previously, amulets, charms and protective tunics were popular during the war, including in the trenches, and people genuinely believed in their protective powers. Scarabs and other Egyptian objects had even been documented as 'appearing' in spiritualist séances.[60] At the time, the popular novelist and ancient Egypt enthusiast H. Rider Haggard tried to counter such beliefs, telling an audience of Rotarians that 'All this nonsense about Lord Carnarvon having been brought to his end by magic is dangerous nonsense. Dangerous because it goes to swell the rising tide of superstition which at present seems to be overflowing the world.'[61] The idea of a curse, T. G. H. James argues, was needed by many people to satisfy a kind of deep-seated expectation of supernatural evil.[62] Perhaps this went some way to explaining the otherwise inexplicable losses in the previous decade. The power of amulets, worn in ancient Egypt to protect their wearers from such hostile powers, was harnessed anew. One example involves Cartier's use of Sekhmet, the goddess with a reputation for the destruction of mankind. Christopher Frayling documents that it was a custom for American and English ladies to go and try to appease her statue at Karnak.[63] The cynic could perhaps accuse Cartier, with their large range of amuletic items, of exploiting sorrow as a commodity.

The vanity case: The jeweller's art and the rebirth of society

There is evidently a second layer of meaning inherent in the resurrection imagery of the jewelled scarab, and one that comes across even more vividly in this second case study: that of the death and rebirth of society, and in particular the re-configuration of gender roles. It was during this period that old-fashioned attitudes about the role of women were being debated, challenged and eroded. Changing fashions such as short hair, bare arms and more revealing clothing gave jewellers new freedoms with their designs, and women became bolder in their tastes. The industry was re-invigorated, jewellery itself was reborn as art, and the inventive Cartier brooches were clearly a product of this trend. The scarab jewellery became a metaphor for its own craft. A second, and even more radical, change affecting the jeweller was the increased adoption of make-up and smoking by women. The vanity-case or 'nécessaire' became a symbol of the age and the new-found freedom of women, and Cartier's Egyptian interpretations of the genre brought with them a host of fascinating references to death and rebirth. Again, I suggest that Cartier was entirely considered in the selection of these themes, marketing products to an audience who understood their references to beauty, new-life and eternity.

After the First World War, the use of cosmetics became more respectable and indeed fashionable in some quarters. Cosmetics became a flourishing business and in 1921 Helena Rubenstein opened her Paris salons. Following the war, women became more mobile and independent. The advent of the vanity-case bridged these two trends and freed the modern woman to carry her make-up with her, allowing her to appear perfectly groomed while on the go. Cartier, finger ever on the pulse, produced many highly imaginative Egyptian-style cases.

In 1923, less than a year after the discovery of Tutankhamun's tomb, Cartier's Parisian-based Henri Lavabre designed a vanity-case in the form of a sarcophagus, the interior of which was fitted with a folding mirror, a comb and a lipstick holder (Figs 8.4 and 8.5). The piece, which was eventually produced in 1925, is layered with complex symbolism denoting youth and beauty, femininity and eternal life, and it is entirely appropriate therefore that it was purchased by Mrs George Blumenthal, a leader of fashion and wife of a New York banker whose situation had improved greatly since the war. The case is richly decorated and was probably modelled on a combination of Twenty-Sixth Dynasty coffins and the perfume and jewellery boxes discovered in Tutankhamun's tomb or on display in museums.[64] The antique lid of Persian ivory depicts a girl among lotus flowers, and the base continues this theme, with a female offering-bearer surrounded by lotus stems and an ibis (Fig. 8.6). Rudoe suggests that the ibis may have referred to Thomas Moore's poem *Alciphron* (1840).[65] This poem recounts the search for eternal life; Alciphron is told: 'Go, and beside the sacred Nile. You'll find the Eternal Life you seek.'[66] The sides are equally bursting with resurrection symbolism. Two of the sides are enamelled, with coloured lotus flowers, daisies and grapes, whereas the other two depict a pharaoh looking strikingly reminiscent of Tutankhamun as a sphinx,[67] with the face and paws engraved on an emerald and the head crowned with a sapphire and gold *nemes* headdress. The floral patterns appear to have been inspired by Jones's *The Grammar of Ornament*, which championed the underlying principles of Egyptian conventionalized design and the use of symbolic and ideal representations. Though not all designers understood these sophisticated theories, Cartier's designers clearly did, combining established nineteenth-century motifs and interests with those associated with the new discovery.

Cartier's use of colour here also betrays a deep understanding of the magical significance ancient Egyptians attributed to certain colours. Osiris, the god of the

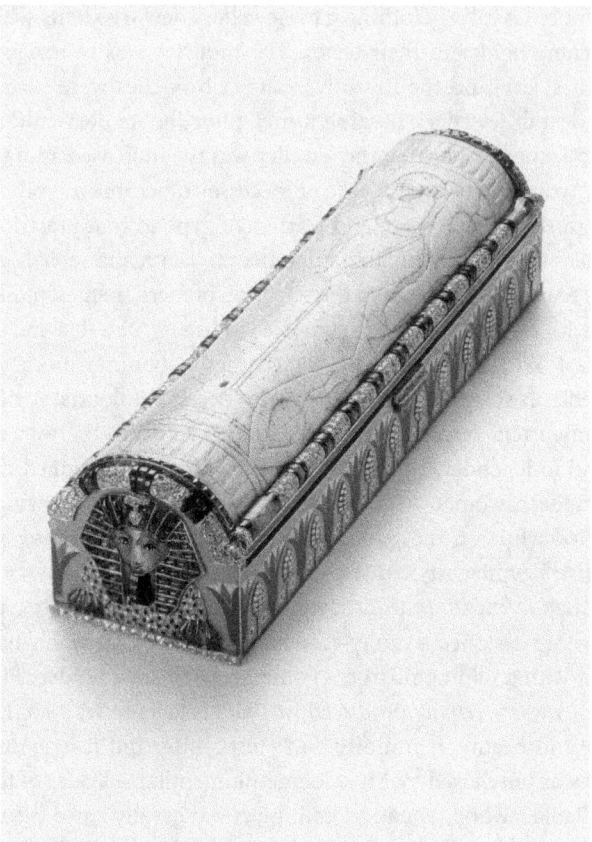

Figure 8.4 Egyptian sarcophagus vanity case. Cartier, 1925 VC 70 A25. Photo: Nick Welsh, Cartier Collection © Cartier.

dead was usually depicted with green flesh, as shown on the vanity case in the sphinx-like Tutankhamun. Myth records that Osiris was cut into pieces by his brother, then reconstituted and brought back to life by his sister Isis, becoming both immortal and judge of the dead. His followers believed that they would enjoy everlasting life in a perfectly constituted body.[68] Green, to the ancient Egyptians, signified fertility, health, new life and resurrection, all extremely appropriate for the embellishment of an object which epitomized the idea of a 1920s fashionable female.[69] In a post-war world, where broken bodies were common, the hope Osiris represented must have resonated deeply.[70] Perhaps also worthy of note in the case of this object is that Alfred Cartier died in 1925. Was the house of Cartier, in its depiction of a god-like figure adorned with jewels, thinking about its own mortality?

The vanity-case as an emblem of social renewal suggests several contrasting ideas about gender divisions and the emancipation of women. 1920s women became more aware of their rights, moved more freely, and designers reflected this ideal of liberation

Figure 8.5 Egyptian sarcophagus vanity case. Cartier, 1925 VC 70 A25. Nils Herrmann, Cartier Collection © Cartier.

through dress and accessories. Women wore a philosophy as well as a fashion. Michael North describes the primary value of Egyptian-style accessories as references or allusion. They both advertised the owner's inspired relationship with a prominent news event, and complimented that of any observer chic enough to notice.[71] In ancient Egypt, certain articles of jewellery served as badges of rank, and aptly here their appropriation signified social awareness. Furthermore, as Tag Gronberg suggests, 'The nécessaire played a role in rendering the female body spectacular.'[72] She sees the transformative role of the nécessaire in feminizing Paris and moving the processes of the feminine toilette from a private into a public ritual.[73] It is therefore no surprise that Cartier chose exotic themes for these cases.

The Cartier sarcophagus vanity-case did not serve merely to transform activity or to remind women of their 'resurrection', it also provided a precedent and vindication by

Figure 8.6 Execution drawing, Paris, 1923. Graphite pencil and gouache on transparent paper. Cartier Archives, Paris. Cartier Archives © Cartier.

reminding women that femininity and adornment were rooted in antiquity. Cosmetic boxes like Cartier's were discovered in Tutankhamun's tomb. Cleopatra and Nefertiti, the ancient paradigms of mystery and beauty, were evoked to advertise female products and now every woman could attempt to attract men as Cleopatra had ensnared Antony. Both henna and kohl were swiftly re-adopted in the 1920s. Ancient cosmetics, here connected with the mortician's art of beautifying corpses, are paradoxically translated from a ritual of death into an emblem of new life for the 1920s woman. The widow, Ankhesenamun, would also have struck other chords with the women of the day. By Egypt's standards both she, and her predecessor Queen Nefertiti, represented the original emancipated woman. The art which depicts them is freer and more filled with emotion. They are not sculpted as miniature characters at the feet of their husbands; both share his throne, more as partner than commodity.

These differing perspectives are indicative of the debate about a woman's proper role, further reflected, in France at least, by the fact that this supposed liberation went hand in hand with widespread Natalist rhetoric, including social policies that linked the commitment to motherhood to national security and the future of France.[74] As Mary Louise Roberts has suggested, gender was central to how change was understood in the post-war decade, exemplified by the obsession with female identity. Perhaps here the art of Tutankhamun's reign provided another parallel: that of the beautiful, yet dutiful, wife and mother. The obvious flipside of liberating feminine adornment is the possession implied by expensive jewellery. The bejewelled woman becomes decoration for the male and the showcase of his wealth and power. Within the pages of *Vogue* in early September 1923, is a revealing article entitled: 'A career for women: being beautiful'.[75] The author exhorts readers in '*the* career in which women have always excelled', warning that as ladies take on other roles, the 'Beautiful Young Man', the 'perfect parasite' with his waved hair, pearl studs and jewelled cigarette cases is ready to usurp their birth-right. This article gives a fascinating insight into beauty as a duty and the changing relationship between the sexes. The *Vogue* article also implies that for some men the Egyptian vanity or cigarette-case may have held deeper meanings too. The war had highlighted the innocent young soldier dying in Flanders, and the warrior-hero personified by Kitchener, but for some, Tutankhamun's adornment and the love of life his tomb goods implied, may have also supported a move to alternative possibilities for masculinity.

The second resurrection-theme highlighted by the vanity-case was the role of luxury firms such as Cartier in the rebirth of Paris. I have previously discussed the ways in which jewellery became a metaphor for the revitalization of its own industry; here, the woman and the accessories she carried become a metaphor for the recovery of the city. Gronberg's study of the 1925 Paris Exposition reveals its mission and symbolic force to reconstruct Paris. She also discusses the way in which the female body was transformed into a spectacle of luxury which itself represented the feminized city it decorated. She sees the seductive boutique, simultaneously pantomime and tabernacle, as a means and manifestation of post-war reconstruction.[76]

Conclusion

Society throughout the 1920s was in transition, constantly changing and developing, and Cartier provided people with objects for meditation, expression and, for some, rebirth. Informed by fashion, but simultaneously inventive and intuitive, Cartier provided meaningful models for others to follow. Their creations show that themes of death and resurrection are vividly presented, both in overt imagery and underlying symbolism.

While some people must have bought Cartier's Egyptian-revival designs for fashionable reasons alone, it seems likely that others either consciously, or subconsciously, saw imbued in them some of the mysteries of the grave. Cartier's designers certainly understood what they were creating.

By the end of the decade, the preoccupations of society appear to have been different to what they had been in 1922, and while people could not have fully recovered from the war, they perhaps became more distanced from it, seemingly meditating more on the future. In all the arts, as direct references to Tutankhamun were shed, so often were the obvious references to death. As ancient Egyptian symbolism tended towards abstraction, themes such as the lotus and the sunburst seemed to retain the hope of resurrection without the morbid associations of the grave. This may signify a society in denial about the horrors of war, but it may equally denote one in recovery, emerging from a state of liminality. In *Ulysses*, published in 1922, James Joyce imagines a graveyard fitted with recording machines so that the bereaved might hear the voices of their loved ones.[77] Today's society's desire for preservation continues as it mummifies itself in its ideal form through film, photography and social media. Interest in Tutankhamun resurges with every major exhibition and each time we invent modern personalities for him. The Egyptian revival is far from a passing aesthetic fad; ancient Egyptian iconography makes its influence felt in recurring waves, providing great insight into any period that felt its deep resonance.

CHAPTER 9
CELTIC EGYPTIANS: ISIS PRIESTS OF THE LINEAGE OF SCOTA
Caroline Tully

Samuel Liddell MacGregor Mathers – the primary creative genius behind the famous British occult group the Hermetic Order of the Golden Dawn – and his wife Moina Mathers established a mystery religion of Isis in *fin-de-siècle* Paris. Lawrence Durdin-Robertson, his wife Pamela and his sister Olivia created the Fellowship of Isis in Ireland in the early 1970s. Although separated by over half a century and not directly associated with each other, both groups have several characteristics in common. Each combined their worship of an ancient Egyptian goddess with an interest in the Celtic Revival; both claimed that their priestly lineages derived directly from the Egyptian queen Scota, mythical foundress of Ireland and Scotland; and both groups used dramatic ritual and theatrical events as avenues for the promulgation of their Isis cults.

The Parisian Isis movement and the Fellowship of Isis were (and are) historically inaccurate syncretic constructions that utilized the tradition of an Egyptian origin of the peoples of Scotland and Ireland to legitimize their founders' claims of lineal descent from an ancient Egyptian priesthood. To explore this contention, this essay begins with brief overviews of Isis in antiquity, the Renaissance, her appeal for Enlightenment Freemasons and her subsequent adoption by the Hermetic Order of the Golden Dawn.[1] It then explores the Parisian cult of Isis, its relationship to the Celtic Revival, the myth of the Egyptian queen Scota, and examines the establishment of the Fellowship of Isis. The Parisian mysteries of Isis and the Fellowship of Isis have largely been overlooked by critical scholarship to date; the use of the medieval myth of Scota by the founders of these groups has hitherto been left unexplored. This essay considers the Parisian Isis cult and the Fellowship of Isis in tandem and argues that although both groups constructed their religions of Isis in an eclectic manner, rather than being anomalous, each built upon and contributed to the continuous reformation of the goddess Isis evident since antiquity. Scota functions as a shared marker of combined Egyptian and Celtic authenticity that links the Parisian mysteries of Isis and the Fellowship of Isis; association with this figure provided sanction for their founders' roles as Celtic priests of the Egyptian goddess Isis.

The goddess Isis

The ancient Egyptian goddess Isis is first recorded during the Fifth Dynasty (2494–345 BC) in the *Pyramid Texts*. Subsequent mythological literature portrays Isis as a powerful and important goddess with six distinct roles: as sister-wife of Osiris; mother and protector of Horus; mother of the pharaoh; the mourner, sustainer and protector of the deceased; goddess of cosmic associations; and goddess of magic.[2] During the Ptolemaic period (332–30 BC) in Alexandria, Isis was paired with a new, composite deity called Sarapis and along with their son, Harpocrates, and the god of the dead, Anubis, was exported out of Egypt via Greek settlements in the eastern Mediterranean, eventually reaching Rome in 90 BC. There, in contrast to pharaonic Egyptian religion, the cult of Isis became a mystery religion requiring initiation for membership and to obtain secret knowledge.[3] The worship of Isis spread throughout the Roman Empire and evidence for her veneration has been found as far north as England.[4] The Isis cult in Egypt itself continued until AD 535 – long after most of Egypt and the wider Roman world had converted to Christianity.[5]

During the many subsequent centuries until the first major steps in the translation of the Egyptian hieroglyphs were taken by Jean-François Champollion in 1822, Isis was known only from ancient Greek and Latin texts.[6] The Egyptian myth of Isis featuring the death of Osiris and the conception of Horus was familiar from Plutarch's *De Iside et Osiride*.[7] Diodorus Siculus presented Isis and Osiris as responsible for bringing culture to humankind in his *Library of History* (I. 14–16).[8] In the Greek aretalogies from the first century BC onwards, Isis is depicted in association with Hermes as the co-inventor of writing.[9] In the *Kore Kosmu*, part of the *Corpus Hermeticum*, psuedepigraphic texts believed to be authored by Hermes Trismegistus and which purported to expound ancient Egyptian wisdom; Isis and Osiris are portrayed as the originators of civilization.[10] According to Renaissance Humanist, Giovanni Boccaccio, Isis taught humankind agriculture, writing and law (*De claris mulieribus* VIII).[11] In the seventeenth century German Jesuit scholar and polymath, Athanasius Kircher, interpreted the story of Isis and Osiris as a precursor to the Holy Trinity of Christianity.[12]

In 1731 the Abbé Jean Terrasson, a Hellenist at the Collège de France, published a novel, *Sethos*, which purported to describe elaborate ancient Egyptian initiations and Isiac mysteries.[13] Widely reprinted and translated, the novel would prove to be extremely influential upon later Freemasonic and other secret societies. In 1787 Enlightenment philosopher and Freemason, Karl Leonhard Reinhold, proposed that an ancient Egyptian inscription on a veiled statue of Isis in a temple at Sais in the Egyptian Delta, recorded by Plutarch and Proclus – 'I am all that has been and is and will be; and no mortal has ever lifted my veil' – meant that Isis was the personification of Nature.[14] The inscription was subsequently considered, within literary, philosophical and artistic circles, to be an extremely profound and sublime metaphor for 'veiled truth', and the embodiment of Egyptian wisdom.[15]

Once hieroglyphs had been deciphered, texts written by the ancient Egyptians were able to be read; students of ancient Egypt no longer had to rely solely on Greek, Latin or Arabic writings about Egypt. Decipherment marked the creation of the discipline of Egyptology and its split from what Erik Hornung has termed 'Egyptosophy', 'the study of an imaginary Egypt viewed as the profound source of all esoteric lore'.[16] As the nineteenth century progressed, more was revealed about the original pharaonic goddess Isis; however, the centuries since antiquity had changed Isis permanently into a symbol of the mysteries of nature. The penetration of her secrets was the goal of seekers of hermetic wisdom.

One such collection of seekers was the Hermetic Order of the Golden Dawn, a secret society in the tradition of Freemasonry that taught its members ritual magic. Founded in 1888 by London coroner and Freemason Dr William Wynn Westcott (1848–1925), and fellow Freemasons, Samuel Liddell MacGregor Mathers (1854–1918) and Dr William Robert Woodman (1828–1891), the Golden Dawn augmented the hermetic Egyptosophical tradition with the latest findings from academic Egyptology.[17] Designed as a school whereby Western esoteric systems such as alchemy, astrology, tarot, kabbala, geomancy and ritual magic would be expounded through elaborate initiation rituals, the Order created ceremonies infused with Egyptian content.[18] While utilizing the long-accessible classical literature about Egypt, as well as the latest research from academic Egyptology, the Golden Dawn interpreted both types of material through a hermetic lens.

Aspects of Egyptian religion were suffused throughout the Golden Dawn's ritual programme. Members were initiated into the Order through the Neophyte Ceremony which combined echoes of Apuleius's description of the initiation into the Isis cult in *Metamorphoses* and vignettes from the more recently translated Egyptian *Book of the Dead*.[19] Higher degree members encountered the myth of Isis and Osiris, as told in Plutarch's *De Iside et Osiride* (13–19), in symbolic form through the mystical 'L.V.X. signs'.[20] These encapsulated the story of Osiris' murder by Typhon (the Egyptian Seth), the subsequent mourning of Isis, and Osiris' eventual resurrection, syncretizing this with Christianity by associating Osiris with the crucified Christ. Another set of gestures known as the 'Portal Sign', part of the 'Greater Ritual of the Pentagram', enabled initiates to rend and see beyond the 'veil of Isis', a prerequisite to entering the 'tomb of Osiris' within which, after experiencing a symbolic death, they were reanimated through a version of the 'Opening of the Mouth' ceremony.[21] The Order's biannually enacted Equinox Ritual incorporated the Isian myth of pharaonic succession; the officer, who had for the previous six months played the role of Hierophant in Golden Dawn ceremonies – representing Osiris who in Egyptian religion signified the deceased pharaoh – vacated his position in favour of a new officer representing Horus, the new pharaoh.[22]

The Isis movement

Isis's relative prominence within the Golden Dawn's rituals, as well as the Hermetic and Freemasonic traditions from whence the Order derived, undoubtedly contributed to the goddess being chosen to be the focus of a new cult founded by two prominent members of the Golden Dawn. Samuel Liddell MacGregor Mathers and his wife Moina (1865–1928) were the creative geniuses of the Order.[23] They met in 1887 in the Egyptian Sculpture Gallery of the British Museum where Moina was sketching statues.[24] The following year MacGregor co-founded the Golden Dawn and Moina became the first initiate; later she was the only female member to attain the highest degree within the Order's graded system of advancement.[25]

In 1892 MacGregor and Moina moved permanently to Paris where there was a flourishing occult scene, establishing a Paris branch of the Golden Dawn, the Ahathoor Temple, in 1894.[26] By 1896 the couple was heavily involved in the exploration of what they termed 'The Egyptian Mysteries' (Fig. 9.1). By 1898 they were 'restoring the Mysteries', while 1899 saw them putting on public performances of 'Rites of Isis' at the Théâtre Bodinière in Paris, having been 'converted to the strange and passionate mysticism of the worship of Isis during their travels in Egypt', a claim which was almost certainly untrue.[27] This led, in 1900, to their establishment of private initiations into the 'Mysteries of Isis'.[28] MacGregor Mathers's biographer, Ithell Colquhoun, suggests that the Isis religion may have been intended as a recruiting ground for postulants for the Paris branch of the Golden Dawn and/or as a way to make money.[29] The Isis cult was not, however, connected to the Golden Dawn and reflected the Matherses' long-standing interest in ancient Egyptian religion.

Figure 9.1 MacGregor and Moina Mathers in Egyptian costume. From Frederic Lees, 'Isis Worship in Paris: Conversations with the Hierophant Rameses and the High Priestess Anari', *The Humanitarian* 16/2 (1900), 82–7.

The Parisian Isis cult had an exclusive initiatory aspect as well as a public face. Administered from the Matherses' various rented residences, a large rural mansion and a public theatre, the couple constructed their Egyptian rituals using a combination of material from the available literature and their 'memories' of past lives in Egypt.[30] Decorating their lodgings with Egyptian-style art, according to journalist Frederic Lees:

> Their flat on the Rue Mozart in fashionable Passy had been renovated into a Temple of Isis. Her winged statue stood at the door to the temple room, with light, diffused by the shutters behind, forming an aureole around her. Flowers lay at her feet, their odour mingled with that of incense. Large drawings of Osiris, Nephthys, Horus and Harpocrates flanked an altar to the left, upon which was a triangular-shaped Tibetan lamp of green stone with a flame that was never extinguished.[31]

Another visitor, Ella Young, witnessed:

> The richest collection of Egyptian treasures I have ever seen outside a museum. ... Curtains, woven in Egypt make a background in one corner of the room for a small altar. [She also saw] frescoes in mosaic ... apparently, images of Egyptian deities.[32]

Lees reported that the soirées held at the Matherses' Egyptian-style residence were 'the most interesting in Paris ... [as the] people attending them [were] of nearly every shade of opinion and profession; Isis worshippers, Alchemists, Protestants, Catholics, doctors, lawyers, painters, and men and women of letters, besides persons of high rank.'[33] According to the Matherses' friend, William Butler Yeats, at such events Moina, dressed in ancient Egyptian costume, performed dances with 'devout eyes, obviously believing in what she does' and hymns to Isis, after which MacGregor gave lectures on Egyptian religion and magic, the great gods of Egypt and the magical power that they would bestow upon their worshippers.[34]

Journalist, Jules Bois, collaborated with the Matherses in the staging of rituals to Isis in their various dwellings. Noting the popularity of the cult, he suggested that they transfer their activities to the Théâtre Bodinière, a small theatre in the Rue Sainte-Lazare that mainly catered to aristocrats, grand bourgeois, and the intelligentsia, with himself as compère.[35] Initially disinclined to perform their Isis rituals in a public theatre, the Matherses reconsidered the proposal after a dream visitation from the goddess Isis herself encouraging them to proceed.[36]

The first public performance of the Rites of Isis occurred in March 1899. MacGregor was introduced as 'the Hierophant Rameses' and Moina as 'the High Priestess Anari' (Figs. 9.2 and 9.3). Lees evokes the visual impact of the event:

> In the center of the stage was the figure of Isis, on each side of the statue were gods and goddesses, and in front was a little altar, upon which was an ever-burning

Figure 9.2 MacGregor Mathers as the Hierophant Rameses. From André Gaucher, 'Isis à Montmartre', *L'Echo du merveilleux: Revue bimensuelle* 94, 95 (1900).

green stone lamp. The Hierophant Rameses and High Priestess Anari appeared in long white priestly robes with bracelets on their arms and ankles, and each with a wide *uskh*, or collar, around the neck. ... Rameses, almost a head taller than his High Priestess, had a zodiacal belt around his waist and a leopard skin fastened over his shoulders. A sidelock of hair was attached over his left ear as an emblem of youth. The High Priestess Anari let her long flowing hair fall loose to express the 'idea of rays of light radiating through the universe.' Upon her head she wore a lotus flower 'symbolic of purity and wisdom' and a cone 'symbolical of the Divine Spirit.'

The Hierophant Rameses, holding in one hand the sistrum, which every now and then he shook, and in the other a spray of lotus, said the prayers before the altar, after which the High Priestess Anari invoked the goddess in penetrating and passionate tones. Then followed the 'dance of the four elements' by a young Parisian lady, who, dressed in long white robes, had previously recited some verses in French in honour of Isis. ... Most of the ladies present in the fashionable Parisian audience brought offerings of flowers, whilst the gentlemen threw wheat on to the altar. The ceremony was artistic in the extreme.[37]

Figure 9.3 Moina Mathers as the High Priestess Anari. From André Gaucher, 'Isis à Montmartre', *L'Echo du merveilleux: Revue bimensuelle* 94, 95 (1900).

The theatrical component was already present in the Matherses' domestic Isis cult with its Egyptian curtains, large-scale drawings akin to a fabricated stage set and intimate audience. That their personal religious practice was scaled up for the public Rites of Isis at the Théâtre Bodinière is suggested by the presence of cult equipment from their home altar such as the Tibetan green stone lamp. Like the Golden Dawn ceremonies, the Rites of Isis were not authentic ancient Egyptian rituals, rather they were constructed from a combination of classical and pharaonic sources filtered through a Hermetic lens.[38] Nevertheless, as Irish political activist, Maude Gonne, then living in Paris, explained the performance 'astonished and delighted most people – people that mattered!'.[39] Indeed, such was the positive response that the Matherses expected that the Isis religion would presently be adopted by all artistic people.[40]

Not everyone was entirely impressed with the Rites of Isis, however. A correspondent from the *Sunday Chronicle* was scathing about MacGregor's French accent but went on to say that:

After the preliminary prayers, the High Priestess performed the ceremony of the 'unveiling of the gods', and then she invoked Isis with such passion and force in both voice and gesture that she quite saved the situation and assured the success of the performance which otherwise might have turned to the ridiculous. [She has a] graceful attitude and dignified manner. More than that, she is very handsome, she has a beautiful oval face with large black, mysterious eyes – and beauty always tells in Paris.[41]

The correspondent may have found Moina more authentic because her dark eyes made her look like an Egyptian. The Rites of Isis at the Théâtre Bodinière were an aesthetic, as much as a spiritual, success. As well as the exoteric theatre performances of the Rites of Isis, the couple performed esoteric initiations into the mysteries of Isis and Osiris away from the public at a rural mansion.[42] Journalist André Gaucher was privy to the private initiations. Blindfolded and taken by carriage to a secret location outside Paris, Gaucher witnessed the 'Isis Mysteries'; his description providing the impression of an elaborate and immersive event:

> When the rite began the priest and priestess knelt at the foot of the statue to light a diffuser of perfume, and the sanctuary was filled with the scent of benzoin and incense. Then they sprinkled grains of wheat and flowers on the floor and on the worshippers. The priest of Isis, with a slight yet triumphant gesture, removed the mysterious veil from the statue. The goddess appeared, smiling; the worshippers fell to their knees crying, 'Isis! Isis! Isis!' The priestess fell to her knees. The priest remained standing, his arms widespread, his head held high, ecstatic. Slowly, as if the floor beneath it were dropping away, the statue began to descend. The priest hastily covered it again with the veil. Then he gave out a terrible cry; the crowd answered with a mournful moan.
>
> The white veils and garlands along the walls fell with an ominous shiver and the walls were revealed to be covered in black. At the same time the torches were extinguished, as if by an invisible wind. The drapes at the rear of the hall tore apart with a sinister rustling. In the distance a shapeless, chaotic mass was slowly emerging from the blackness. The worshippers sat up, rigid, motionless, then cried out, three times: 'Osiris! Osiris! Osiris!' The enormous statue was in fact the Egyptian god, an enormous *pschent* on his head. ... From the top of the statue a luminous, phosphorescent beam circled the hall, inexplicably, bathing the worshippers in the changing light. One after the other, in the eye of the god, they fell in ecstasy or cataleptic fits. All around were sighs and convulsive cries. Bodies rolling on the ground, in the darkness, prey to terrible nervous spasms. Others stood up rigid, their faces drained of blood, their eyes haggard. A reddish glow lit the depths of the sanctuary with an infernal light, from behind the gigantic statue which seemed to be locked in a terrible grin.[43]

The participants were evidently responding in what they thought was an authentic manner although such behaviour does not approximate the description of ancient Isiac initiation in Apuleius's *Metamorphoses*. So popular did the Matherses' cult of Isis become that they eventually required a dedicated temple, which they claimed was being built in Paris; however, it is unclear whether it ever was.⁴⁴ In Frederick Lees's interview he asks Moina, 'Have you very many followers amongst the Parisians?', who answers, 'An increasing number, and quite as many as our little chapel will hold. A temple for our Egyptian ceremonies is now being built in Paris.'⁴⁵ In a letter to fellow Golden Dawn member, Florence Farr, MacGregor relates that 'My time is just now so enormously occupied with the arrangements for the Buildings and Decorations of the Egyptian Temple of Isis in Paris, as well as other matters, that I must write as briefly as possible.'⁴⁶ These snippets of information about a temple being built have since been conflated with John Brodie-Innes's eulogistic obituary of McGregor Mathers published in the *Occult Review* (1919), in which he claimed that:

> When he arranged a Temple of Isis for the Paris Exhibition, an Egyptologist whose name is world-famous said 'MacGregor is a Pharaoh come back. All my life I have studied the dry bones; he has made them live.'⁴⁷

Brodie-Innes refers to MacGregor working in an Egyptological capacity at the Paris Exposition of 1900. This idea, however, almost certainly derives from Brodie-Innes's misunderstanding of references to an 'Egyptian temple' being built for the Isis rituals mentioned in interviews and correspondence dating to 1900. According to James Curl, the Palais de l'Égypte at the Exposition Universelle of 1900 was designed by the French architect, Marcel Dourgnon, 'who juxtaposed an Arab Bazaar, a theatre in the *style égyptien polychromé*, and a temple in the *égyptien antique* style'.⁴⁸ While Mathers may conceivably have helped Dourgnon, there is no evidence to support this, nor that the Rites of Isis were performed in any of these structures.

Celtic connection

While performing as Egyptian priests of Isis, MacGregor and Moina also presented themselves as Scottish aristocrats. MacGregor claimed that his father was Highland Scottish from the Clan MacGregor and he had been calling himself the 'Comte de Glenstrae' from as early as 1877, declaring that the title had been bestowed by the King of France in recognition for family services to the French.⁴⁹ In 1885, under the influence of the Celtic Revival, he added the Scottish clan name to his birth name (Samuel Liddell Mathers) and Moina changed her name from the original 'Mina' when they married in 1890.⁵⁰ After moving to Paris the couple became known as the Count and Countess of Glenstrae.⁵¹ An American visitor, Max Dauthendey, described MacGregor as 'the last descendant of a Scottish king who was living in Paris as an Egyptologist'.⁵² According to Yeats, MacGregor spent most of his day in Highland costume 'to the wonder of his neighbours' and while so attired claimed that he 'feels like a walking flame'.⁵³ For the correspondent from the *Sunday Chronicle* who witnessed the Rites of Isis at the Théâtre Bodinière, MacGregor:

Looked for all the world like a North Yorkshireman or a Scotchman, And, sure enough, when I made enquiries after the performance a braw Highlander he proved to be. M'Gregor is his name, but whence he comes I know not. They call him 'Count M'Gregor' in one of the French newspapers, but this, M. Jules Bois says, is a mistake. 'Monsieur M'Gregor is only the chief of an old Scottish clan!' Really! How delightfully they mix things up on this side of the channel.[54]

The Celtic Revival, which began to flourish in the 1880s, was the result of increasing Irish nationalism during the nineteenth century. Mainly a literary movement, it was closely bound up with politics and Ireland's freedom. William Butler Yeats, Lady Gregory and George Russell, known as 'A. E.', were prominent members who provided a fresh and stimulating approach to Irish literature by drawing on native mysticism and visions of a Celtic past.[55] Yeats had a background in hermeticism and had co-founded the Dublin Hermetic Society with Charles Johnston in 1885. In 1886 the society became the Dublin Lodge of the Theosophical Society. Yeats joined the London Theosophical Society in 1887, resigning in 1889 because he found it too fanatical and was subsequently initiated into the Golden Dawn in 1890.[56]

Yeats had been able to observe the Matherses' Isis Movement in Paris as he had travelled there in order to seek MacGregor and Moina's help in formulating 'Celtic Mysteries ... based on the lore of the Druids'.[57] He began working on this project with the help of other Golden Dawn members in London in 1893 with the aim of restoring the link between holiness and beauty, lost because 'commerce and manufacture had made the world ugly; the death of pagan nature-worship had robbed visible beauty of its inviolable sanctity'.[58] Envisioned as a new Celtic Mystical Order that would 'find its manuals of devotion in all imaginative literature', the content of the mystery rituals was to be derived from group sessions of scrying into the Celtic Otherworld.[59] Rather than 'compose rites as if for the theatre', Yeats wanted the Order's symbols and rituals to be created by the ancient Celtic gods themselves, as communicated through visions; 'They must in their main outline be the work of invisible hands'.[60] In 1896 he journeyed to the west coast of Ireland for inspiration and returned 'wrapt in a faery whirlwind ... talk[ing] much of reviving the Druidic Mysteries'.[61] That same year he sought the input of MacGregor and Moina who had originally introduced him to the method of attaining knowledge through visions when he joined the Golden Dawn in 1890.[62]

The Matherses were interested in Celtic traditions for political purposes and as a source of magical power connected to the land, as they felt that Gaelic magic involved comradeship with nature and the Earth.[63] In 1897 they travelled to MacGregor's ancestral homeland of Scotland and on their return to Paris found an increased focus on Celtic religion within literary and artistic circles, with bookshop owner and publisher, Edmond Bailly, interested in making his magazine, *Isis Moderne*, an organ for the Celtic cause.[64] Thus, the Matherses were at work on both the Rites of Isis and the Celtic Mysteries by the time Yeats visited them in Paris. By early 1898, however, although still busy scrying the Celtic Otherworld, ascertaining kabbalistic correspondences for the Celtic deities and designing the first initiation ritual for the Celtic Mysteries, the Isis movement was demanding more attention. Eventually, the Matherses prioritized the Rites of Isis and the Celtic Mysteries project with Yeats fell by the wayside, although the Matherses maintained interest in Celtic paganism and Druidism well into the first decade of the twentieth century.[65] By 1903 Yeats had produced entire drafts of the rituals for the Celtic Mystical Order but later lost interest and allowed the project to lapse into permanent neglect.[66]

Celtic priests of Isis

France was the perfect place for MacGregor Mathers to perform his dual identities as a priest of the goddess Isis and a Scottish aristocrat because of its appropriation of both Egyptian and Celtic culture. Isis had been associated with Paris during the French Revolution when she was recast as the goddess of reason and nature intended to replace Christianity. After Napoleon Bonaparte's invasion of Egypt in 1798, Isis became the tutelary goddess of Paris, and Egyptian forms such as the pyramid, obelisk and sphinx became popular. Jacques Louis David's *Fontaine de la Régénération* which consisted of a statue of an Egyptian goddess with water streaming from her breasts was erected on the ruins of the Bastille, and there was even temporary employment of the Egyptian calendar.[67] The belief that the cult of Isis had been instrumental in the founding of the city of Paris became widespread, based on false etymology; the Egyptian 'par-Isis' meaning 'House of Isis' or 'Temple of Isis', was reminiscent of 'Paris', and it was believed that Isis had been worshipped at some of the older church locations such as St Germain-des-Prés and Notre Dame.[68] In 1811 Napoleon even added an image of Isis to the Paris coat of arms which had originally only depicted a ship.[69]

The association of France with the ancient Celts was also promoted during the French Revolution. The ancient Gauls were ethnically and linguistically Celtic, and in 1789 the Revolution was characterized as indigenous Gauls throwing off the control of the Frankish aristocrats. In 1804 Napoleon founded the Académie Celtique, and between 1860 and 1865 his nephew, Louis Napoleon (Napoleon III), sponsored an ambitious archaeological excavation of the battleground of Alesia where the Gaulish war leader Vercingetorix had made his last heroic stand against Rome.[70] Napoleon III also initiated the excavation of the principal *oppidum* of the Aedui at Bibracte (Mont Beuvray), and in 1863 opened a Museum of National Antiquities in Paris to house Celtic antiquities.[71] The promotion of Celtic identity was intended to foster a national Gaulish identity unified under the emperor.[72]

MacGregor was thus able to harmonize his interest in both Egyptian and Celtic religion with his residence and ritual practice in Paris. In his interview with Gaucher, he brought the Egyptian and Celtic streams together by claiming to be a member of an ancient Scottish lineage of the priesthood of Isis, explaining that:

A good long time before the Christian era ... a daughter of the Pharaohs, the queen Scota, carries to Scotland the Goddess' altars. The tradition has continued until today. I am the last link in this secret chain.[73]

Scota

The Egyptian queen 'Scota' is the founder of Ireland and Scotland according to Irish and Scottish mythology and pseudohistory, and is often invoked in Irish and Scottish sources in order to distinguish the Irish and Scottish peoples from the English and thence from English rule.[74] The legend of Scota is found in various medieval texts including the *Historia Brittonum* (*History of the Britons*) (c. 829), attributed to the Welsh priest Nennius, which tells of a series of successive colonizations from Iberia by the pre-Gaelic peoples of Ireland, as well as the origins of the Gaels and how they came to be the ancestors of the Irish; *The Book of Leinster* (c. 1160), which contains a redaction of the *Lebor Gabála Érenn* (*The Book of Invasions of Ireland*) (eleventh–twelfth century), relates that Ireland was settled six times by six groups of people: the people of Cessair, the people of Partholón, the people of Nemed, the Fir Bolg, the Tuatha Dé Danann and the Milesians. The version in the *Book of Leinster* was heavily influenced by biblical stories and traces all of the groups back to Noah.

The *Instructions* and the *Pleading of Baldred Bisset* (1301) written by the lawyer employed to refute Edward I's claims to the Scottish throne in a submission to the Pope, invoked the myth of Scota to demonstrate the great antiquity of the Scottish people. The better-known *Declaration of Arbroath* (1320) by Bernard of Kilwinning, which was sent to Pope John XXII in the wake of Robert the Bruce's victory at Bannockburn in 1314 in an effort to legitimize Scotland's independence from England, drew on Bisset's text. The *Chronica Gentis Scotorum* (*Chronicle of the Scottish Nation*) (1380) by John of Fordun; the *Scalacronica* (1363) by Thomas Grey; the *Oryginale Cronykil of Scotland* (c. 1420) by Andrew of Wyntoun; the *Scotichronicon* (1477) compiled by Walter Bower, which drew extensively on John of Fordun's earlier chronicle and which also includes the first illustrations of the Scota legends; and the *Historia Gentis Scotorum* (History of the Scottish People) (1527) by Hector Boece, also include various renditions of the Scota myth.

These texts present several variants of the story of Scota and combine remnants of traditional Irish historical sagas with biblical events and characters. Scota is said to be the daughter of the Pharaoh Nectanebus or the pharaoh Cincris (a name found only in Irish legend) who was purportedly a contemporary of Moses. One version has Scota married to a Babylonian language scholar named Niul, son of Fénius Farsaid and grandson of the biblical Gomer.[75] Scota and Niul's son, Gáedal Glas (Geythelos), the eponymous ancestor of the Gaels, invented the Gaelic language from the best features of the 72 languages of Babel. Sometimes Scota is married to Gáedal Glas, a Greek or Scythian king, who becomes the eponymous founder of the Scots and Gaels after being exiled from Egypt.[76] In other versions, Mil Espaine is Scota's husband, providing a connection to Iberia, and the sons of Mil and Scota settle in Ireland. Baldred Bisset linked the Stone of Destiny (Stone of Scone) upon which all Scottish kings were crowned with the Scota foundation legends. He argued that during the exodus of Moses, Scota had transported the Stone from Egypt to Scotland and therefore Scotland was Scota's original Celtic homeland.[77] Ireland can claim to be the resting place of Scota, however, as a 'grave of Scota' is located in a valley south of Tralee Town, Co. Kerry, in an area known as Glenn Scoithin, the 'Vale of the Little Flower', or Foley's Glen.

The Fellowship of Isis

Over seventy years after MacGregor Mathers claimed to be the last priest of Isis of the lineage of Scota, another priest and priestess of Isis – this time *bona fide* aristocrats rather than pretenders like MacGregor – would explicitly cite the pseudo-historical medieval texts in order to support their claim to be descendants of the Egyptian queen Scota. Lawrence Durdin-Robertson (1920–1994), his wife Pamela (1923–1987) and his sister Olivia (1917–2013) founded the Fellowship of Isis at Huntington Castle, Clonegal, County Carlow, in Ireland in 1976.[78] Lawrence had been a Christian minister but left the Church in 1957 because he had come to believe in the 'Divine Feminine', a Goddess that complemented the traditionally male God. By 1966 Lawrence was experiencing 'an influx of Goddess energy' and writing about the Great Mother Goddess, and in 1972 felt called to the priesthood of Isis. Olivia also favoured Isis, while Lawrence's wife Pamela had a more animistic approach, revering the goddess as Mother Earth.[79] Olivia visited Egypt in 1975, and the following year the three of them founded the Fellowship of Isis. Olivia outlived both Lawrence and Pamela by several decades and consequently became the guiding light of the Fellowship from the early 1990s until her death in late 2013 (Fig. 9.4).

Starting with only forty-four members in 1976, the Fellowship of Isis today has more than 27,000 members spread over 132 countries, partly as a result of its prominent internet presence.[80] While based in Ireland, the Fellowship is an international organization with most of its branches located in the United States. The organization aims to promote closer communion between the goddess and each member, in order that the individual experience personal transformation through identification with the divine, resulting in higher spiritual awareness.[81] It also has an ecological focus and members are encouraged to participate in the goddess's creative work of regenerating the planet.[82] The Fellowship is open to members of any religion and includes all sorts of contemporary pagans as well as spiritualists, Christians, Buddhists, Hindus, Taoists and Sufis.[83] There is no joining fee and prospective members are only required to be over eighteen and agree with the Manifesto.[84]

Unlike the religion of Isis founded by MacGregor and Moina Mathers in *fin-de-siècle* Paris, there is a plethora of information available about the beliefs and rituals of the Fellowship of Isis. The organization provides online access to many of their documents. Lawrence and Olivia wrote many liturgical and philosophical texts, and

Figure 9.4 Olivia and Lawrence Durdin-Robertson, Huntingdon Castle, County Carlow, Ireland. The Marsden Archive/Alamy Stock Photo.

Olivia provided monthly oracles, all of which are available on the main website. Although named after Isis, the Fellowship is not exclusively focussed on Egypt or Egyptian deities and does not seek to reconstruct Egyptian religion.[85] The Fellowship interprets Isis as a universal goddess, 'Isis of 10,000 names', a Divine Mother and the personification of Nature.[86] It describes itself as 'multi-religious, multi-racial, and multi-cultural,' honouring 'the religion of *all* the Goddesses and pantheons throughout the planet.'[87] The central temple of the Fellowship of Isis is located in the basement of Clonegal Castle and exemplifies the organization's syncretic religious view; in addition to Isis, various chapels are dedicated to other goddesses from diverse pantheons, as well as to the signs of the Zodiac.[88]

Like MacGregor and Moina Mathers, the founders of the Fellowship combined the worship of the Egyptian goddess Isis with Celtic paganism.[89] The Durdin-Robertsons were well aware of the Celtic Revival and had been personally acquainted with some of its key players such as William Butler Yeats and 'A. E.'.[90] Lawrence and Olivia identified as Druids as well as priests of Isis and claimed to have received direct initiation into indigenous Celtic pagan religion through an ancient hermit called Mr Fox who lived on the banks of the River Slaney and was the guardian of a prehistoric pagan site. According to Olivia, 'He was an absolutely wild man, but he had been to Egypt', Egypt in this instance an apparent marker of spiritual authenticity.[91] They had also received Druidic initiations from Ross Nichols, leader of the Order of Bards, Ovates and Druids.[92] Lawrence explained that because Isis is a universal goddess she can be venerated as Dana or Brigit in Ireland, and as such the Fellowship incorporates Celtic pagan sub-branches such as the Noble Order of Tara,[93] the Druid Clan of Dana[94] and the Circle of Brigid.[95]

Despite the syncretistic and multi-religious nature of the Fellowship of Isis, according to Olivia it was not a modern invention but based on the revival and adaptation of authentic ancient traditions. She stated in official documents of the organization that she and Lawrence were the true heirs of Isis, responsible for reviving the College of Isis after a break of 1,500 years,[96] and, like MacGregor Mathers, to have received their authority as priests of Isis from Scota.[97] In the Fellowship of Isis *Handbook* she explains that:

> The priestly line comes to Lawrence and Olivia Robertson from the Egyptian princess Scota – the dark One – daughter of the Pharaoh 'Cincris'. Scota was hereditary Daughter of Isis through her descent from Isis and Osiris, Queen and King of Egypt. Scota left Egypt with her Scythian husband Nel and gave her name to Scotland. The Gaelic race was named after her son Goadhal or Gaelglas.[98]

Olivia's claim of descent from Scota is repeated in the Preface to the *Ordination of Priestesses and Priests* and the information page on the Fellowship of Isis's priesthood.[99] In *The Line of Priesthood within the Fellowship of Isis* she asserts that:

> The Priesthood of the Fellowship of Isis is hereditary. It comes through the family of two of the co-founders of the Fellowship of Isis, Olivia Durdin-Robertson and her late brother, Lawrence Durdin-Robertson. ... The right to establish a line of Isian priests and priestesses comes to Lawrence and Olivia Durdin-Robertson through their direct descent from the St. Legers, a family who can claim descent from the Egyptian Princess Scota, the daughter of the Pharaoh Cincris and legendary Queen of the Scots. Scota as the daughter of Pharaoh Cincris held the hereditary title Daughter of Isis, the royal line of the kings of Egypt always claiming descent through Horus, the son of Isis and Osiris.[100]

In Olivia's understanding the queen Scota's lineage can be traced to the Egyptian gods themselves. Scota has been incorporated into the Fellowship of Isis's cosmology as an authenticating ancestress, and features in other Fellowship literature. She is a figure in the 33-degree 'Spiral of Alchemy' system; a divinity in a ritual called 'Cesara's Ark' which is part of a larger series called 'Fortuna, Creation through the Goddess'; and a heroic Egyptian queen in a dramatic ritual called 'Scota, the Heretic Princess', part of a group of rituals within the series, 'Sphinx, Goddess of Myths and Mysteries'.[101] One of the groves of the Druid Clan of Dana is named after Scota, and the design on the coat of arms of the Barony of Strathloch, held by Lawrence Durdin-Robertson and which is the basis for the Order of Tara, is proposed as further validation for the Fellowship's relationship to Scota.[102] In addition, Olivia painted various portraits of Scota,[103] suggesting that she was able to see her through visionary means.

Conclusion

MacGregor and Moina Mathers and Olivia Durdin-Robertson are important and influential figures within the British occult revival and the subsequent pagan movement whose spiritual legacies remain potent today. This study is the first to highlight the fantastic claims of these figures and to explain the source of their assertions of priestly descent. It is evident that both MacGregor Mathers, and to a much larger extent the founders of the Fellowship of Isis, used the Egyptian Queen Scota as a validating ancestress in order to endorse their claims to be authentic priests of the goddess Isis. As the founder of Scotland and Ireland, Scota also bestowed authentic Celtic identity on these figures through an ancient Egyptian lineage. For MacGregor Mathers and the Durdin-Robertsons, then, being Celtic and being Egyptian were essentially two complementary sides of the one coin that provided them with a doubly potent spiritual identity.

While they claimed lineal descent from an ancient cult of Isis, as is evident from their ritual performances, occult theatre, personal interviews, missives and explanatory texts, the Parisian Isis mysteries and the Fellowship of Isis were created according to the abilities and concerns of their founders. Both groups favoured an ahistorical construction of the goddess Isis as an eternal, mysterious, magical figure representative of universal harmony, unity and nature. Although consciously reconstructed through a mixture of study and creative imagination, the Parisian mysteries of Isis and the Fellowship of Isis can also be understood as valid expressions of a religio-philosophical tradition, evident since antiquity, in which the goddess Isis is appropriated and re-fashioned in order to serve as a symbol of the zeitgeist. For the Matherses and the Durdin-Robertsons, association with the figure of Scota authenticated the performance of Egyptian selfhood as an expression of Celtic heritage.

CHAPTER 10
JACK THE RIPPER AND THE MUMMY'S CURSE: ANCIENT EGYPT IN *FROM HELL*
Eleanor Dobson

The fifth chapter of Alan Moore and Eddie Campbell's celebrated graphic novel *From Hell* (1989–98; 1999) – a text which speculates on the identity and the motives of the murderer who has come to be known as Jack the Ripper, interweaving factual and fictional material – opens with several epigraphs. The second of these, attributed to 'Sir Earnest Budge, Keeper of Egyptian and Assyrian Antiquities at the British Museum, 1893–1924', relates to supernatural rumours surrounding one of the ancient Egyptian artefacts housed by the institution. The epigraphs and images with which Moore commences each chapter are usually accompanied by detailed references to their sources. This quotation, however, is not provided with a named source here; instead the reference is tucked away in Moore's notes at the back of the volume. 'Never print what I say in my lifetime, but that mummy-case caused the war', Budge is claimed to have uttered.[1] This almost certainly a fabricated statement – circulating before *From Hell* in unreliable publications, hence the lack of acknowledged source material alongside the epigraph – attributing the outbreak of war to a malign ancient Egyptian spirit, relates to a painted wooden mummy board, known as the Unlucky Mummy. This artefact, catalogued under British Museum number EA 22542,[2] was acquired by the museum in 1889, the year after the murder of Mary Jane Kelly, canonically held to be the Ripper's final victim. While late nineteenth-century mysticism and Freemasonry in *From Hell* have previously been scrutinized by critics, this quotation invites the reading of another facet of the late Victorian magical revival: the influence of ancient Egyptian mythology, magic and iconography on contemporary conceptions of the supernatural.[3]

This chapter addresses the employment of such imagery and symbolism in *From Hell*, focusing on the significance of the British Museum's ancient Egyptian artefacts (in particular, the Unlucky Mummy), the inclusion of a range of obelisks (including London's most famous obelisk, the ancient Egyptian monument known as Cleopatra's Needle installed on the Embankment) and ancient Egypt's place in the magical revival of the late nineteenth century, focusing in particular on Moore and Campbell's depiction of the three-headed Masonic god Jahbulon which assimilates the ancient Egyptian god Osiris, as well as a vision of the god Horus, Osiris's son.[4] Analysed in conjunction with pertinent intertextual allusions – including one to Oscar Wilde's short story 'Lord Arthur Savile's Crime' (1887), a tale of fortune-telling which also uses Cleopatra's Needle as emblematic of supernatural power – I demonstrate how Moore and Campbell engage with nineteenth-century Egyptiana across a variety of discourses. I argue that they recognize the significance of ancient Egyptian symbolism not merely in the city's geography (as psychogeographical approaches encourage), but thoroughly infiltrating Victorian hermeticism, literature and culture more broadly. The ancient Egyptian presences in *From Hell* contribute to a pervasive supernaturalism and spectrality, based upon a considerable foundation of research.

Using the quotation attributed to Budge as a point of diversion, I also demonstrate that Egyptian material, used to tether the narrative to the real, is also twisted for fantastic purposes, at times relying upon source material which Moore himself appears to have deemed dubious by confining such references to the volume's appendices. Sources, in such a work of fiction (albeit one tethered to real people, places and events), are manipulated for creative ends, especially with regards to the mystical thread that runs throughout. It is Egypt, in particular, in *From Hell*, that marks it as a work of 'Victoria-arcana', the term by which Christine Ferguson denotes neo-Victorian 'works of fiction' which

> take the occult as subject matter and incorporate its rituals into their narrative strategies, working not to re-present a pre-existent and ontologically accessible nineteenth century in a linear of 'authentic' fashion but rather to *incant* it into being from a series of chaotically assembled textual fragments, loosely defined cultural 'energies,' and historical detritus.[5]

Ferguson recognizes the archaeology behind Moore and Campbell's work: the digging into archives, the piecing together of fragments, the binding of these cultural shards with imagination, fantasy and magic. Of course, ancient Egypt is a suitable metaphor for this material and the process by which it might be assembled and comprehended, itself present in the modern world (as it was in the Victorian world) as a mass of archaeological matter waiting to be interpreted.

Real ancient Egyptian artefacts are recorded in *From Hell* with a striking degree of accuracy (even reproducing genuine hieroglyphic inscriptions, in some cases), yet Egypt is also a marker of the illusory and the imaginary. Occupying a nebulous space between the real and the fabricated, Egypt becomes symbolic of exaggeration and invention at the same time as its very artefacts serve to anchor *From Hell* in the real world. Existing simultaneously in the real Victorian London, the version of Victorian London as depicted in *From Hell* at the time of production, and also in readers' contemporary London, ancient Egyptian objects collapse time in such a way as to dissolve the boundaries between these real and fictional times and spaces. Simultaneously, they also complicate this relationship between reality and fantasy, past and present, surrounded, as they are, by superstition, mythology and rumour. In this sense, ancient Egypt might be read as the key with which we might unlock the complexity of Moore and Campbell's process in creating a fantastic narrative based around a real and well-known series of murders, incorporating details from psychogeographical sojourns around the city, research into British Museum artefacts and the reading of literature in the years surrounding the events that they depict. Ancient Egypt might also be considered the cipher to understanding the hallucinatory spirituality of *From Hell*, based, in part, on Freemasonry, on activities central to the late Victorian magical revival, and to peripheral beliefs about ancient Egyptian curses whose potency stretches into the modern world.

The unlucky mummy: Museum gothic

As Ruth Hoberman notes in *Museum Trouble: Edwardian Fiction and the Emergence of Modernism* (2011), 'From its earliest incarnation, the museum has seemed inseparable from the imagination of disorder.'[6] She continues: 'turn-of-the-century writers saw the museum encounter as an opportunity to … explore the relation between individuals and such larger forces as the state, the past, and those other cultures whose artifacts are on display'.[7] In *From Hell*, Moore and Campbell encourage the consideration of the relationship between the ancient past and the present through references to ancient Egyptian culture, hinting at a kind of supernatural potency which has survived for millennia. Of particular interest is the depiction of a mummy board (British Museum number EA 22542), acquired in 1889. Its place in this text, as I have already indicated, is slightly anachronistic, the final canonical Ripper murder having taken place in November 1888; Moore attempts to smooth over this temporal crack, noting in an appendix that the object 'arrived in London during 1888' though the suggestion that the mummy board was 'hurriedly passed on … throughout the auction houses of London' appears to be erroneous.[8] The inclusion of this genuine artefact in the narrative serves to anchor *From Hell* in reality, albeit a twisted reality which encompasses various temporal slippages and a strong emphasis on the supernatural.

Although the mummy board has no explicit influence on the plot and is visually represented only a few times across *From Hell*'s some 500 pages, it is clearly of enough significance to have a dedicated epigraph at the opening of the chapter in which it first appears. 'Never print what I say in my lifetime,' E. A. Wallis Budge, the Keeper of Egyptian and Assyrian Antiquities at the British Museum is claimed to have stated, 'but that mummy-case caused the war'.[9] Beneath this quotation Budge's name is given, along with his position at the pinnacle of his career at the British Museum: 'Sir Earnest Budge, Keeper of Egyptian and Assyrian Antiquities at the British Museum, 1893–1924.' Budge died on 23 November 1934, having indeed retired in 1924. By including the dates at which Budge worked in this authoritative position at the British Museum, the implication is that the war in question falls within this temporal range; we are encouraged to assume that he refers to the First World War.

Moore opts not to include his source underneath this epigraph (as he does for most other quotations which open chapters), instead listing his source as J. A. Brooks's *Ghosts of London: The West End, South and West* (1982) in an appendix.[10] Brooks's volume provides some further details to this rumour, and indeed confirms that Budge's statement about the 'mummy-case caus[ing] the War' refers to the First World War.[11] Brooks claims that the mummy board was 'blamed for the loss of the HMS *Hampshire* in 1916 which resulted in the death of Field-Marshal Earl Kitchener', and as such was referred to by some as 'the Ship Wrecker'.[12] Somewhat predictably, Brooks provides no source of his own for this information. Rumours surrounding Cleopatra's Needle – pertinent to the next section of this essay – are also included in this volume; Brooks relates 'a strange fact, known to the police': 'most suicide attempts [between Waterloo and Hungerford bridges] take place close to this column'.[13] Egyptian artefacts, in Moore's source material, are intimately connected with spirits and mysterious deaths. They are less concerned with facts and traceable citations than rumour, sensationalism and fantastical narrative.

The first panels in this chapter, however, contradict the reader's assumptions: contextualized alongside material relating to the Second World War, the implication is that the 'mummy-case' (or, rather, the mummy board) has a dark magical potency that makes its influence felt even further into twentieth-century history than first assumed. The fifth chapter opens with Klara and Alois Hitler engaged in sexual intercourse; she experiences a vision of Jews washed away by wave of blood, which bursts forth from church doors at the moment her husband climaxes. We are led to believe that her vision coincides with the conception of their son, Adolf. Alongside these panels the quotation ascribed to Budge seems eerily prophetic rather than superstitiously reflective. We, as readers with the benefit of hindsight, might attribute a series of wars to the artefact in question; its potency, this juxtaposition implies, stretches beyond the lifetimes of *From Hell*'s central characters, perhaps – through the choice of an artefact which can be seen in the British Museum to this day – even into the world of contemporary readers.

In the first image of the mummy board, the object appears tilted back, prostrate, eyes directed towards the ceiling while Gull looks on, hand partially outstretched. We are invited to see in this image an echo of a victim (or indeed, an omen of one, as none of the murders have yet taken place), passively reclining while activity is embodied in the figure of the would-be attacker.[14] Indeed, on the day of the first murder, Gull cuts short a conversation about his plan with Sir Charles Warren – the Chief Commissioner of the Metropolitan Police – by stating that 'Sotheby's have a mummy, lately come to England, that I wish to view'.[15] With its very name evoking maternity, the 'mummy' here represents the inert body of the female who must be dispatched as a result of her reproductive abilities (the murders, in Moore's version of events, must take place to contain knowledge of an illegitimate royal baby). The 'mummy', like the Ripper's prostitute victims, is 'bought' for money, objectified and her form subject to often professional male scrutiny (in the case of the victims, the police and coroners; in the case of the mummy board, museum professionals; and in both cases, Dr Gull). This object may well be far from inert, however. If we are to believe the rumours associated with this artefact, the female spirit connected to the mummy board is violent and vengeful, a serial murderess. She is a female Ripper on a much greater scale, driven to attack victims mostly of the opposite sex (including the victims of both World Wars). She may appear passive, but this façade conceals a far more dangerous presence.

A sign reading 'Lot 32' is discernible on the artefact itself, and in this and the following panel other items evidently up for auction are visible. This location is confirmed as 'Sotheby's Auction House'.[16] While Sotheby's did auction mummies, this is an invented history; the actual artefact was acquired by the British Museum in 1889 (the year after the murder of Mary Kelly, purportedly the final victim of the 'Ripper'), and in reality never appears to have passed through Sotheby's doors. Roger Luckhurst provides the most detailed account of the artefact's movements: it was 'donated to the Museum by Mrs Warwick Hunt on behalf of her brother, Arthur F. Wheeler' as part of 'a small private collection of Egyptian objects, including some mummified crocodiles and a human mummy hand with finger-ring still attached'.[17] Luckhurst summarizes the mummy board's supposed journey to Britain:

> Some time in the 1860s, a party of five English friends travelled down the Nile to Thebes. ... Mr D (Douglas Murray) [an amateur Egyptologist heavily involved in the establishment of the mummy curse narrative] decided to buy a memento of the trip, and Arab treasure hunters showed him the coffin lid. ... The purchase was made, but the Englishmen then decided to draw lots as to who was to have the case in England. The lottery was won by Mr W (Arthur Wheeler). Mr W ... 'found, on reaching Cairo, that he had lost a large part of his fortune.' Ruined, Mr W passed the case to his sister (Mrs Warwick Hunt), who displayed it in her house. In the 1880s, Madame Blavatsky, the notorious occultist and founder of the Theosophical Society, saw the lid and warned that it radiated evil intent. ... Mr D – or perhaps others – persuaded the sister to send it to the British Museum, where it was recorded as a gift in 1889.[18]

The artefact's labelling with an auction number recalls Arthur Conan Doyle's short story 'Lot No. 249' (first published in 1892), in which an ancient Egyptian mummy is reanimated in order to enact its reanimator's violent revenge. While mummy fiction extends back to Jane Webb's *The Mummy!: Or a Tale of the Twenty-Second Century* (1827), Doyle's was the best-known nineteenth-century reanimation narratives in which the mummy is revived through magical rather than scientific means.[19] This subtle allusion may suggest that we should look to a magical rather than scientific explanation for some of *From Hell*'s events. Hallucinations have mystical significances; visions of deities may be grounded in cosmic truth.

The auction number is also visible in the close-up view of the mummy board (Fig. 10.1). We are offered this clearer representation after the first murder has taken place. Gull seems to hallucinate this image as he enters his bedroom. Appearing just after a frame in which we see the sleeping Mrs Gull, we are encouraged to equate the two, and to remember the scenes of the recently witnessed murder. Freemasonry may be a powerful fraternity, but there is a sense of sorority in these links suggested between these female figures: a representation of the deceased ancient Egyptian woman, the living, then dying, then deceased body of Mary Ann 'Polly' Nicholls, and the sleeping form of Mrs Gull.[20] If the masculine is rational and living, the feminine is mystical and associated with more liminal states.

This image is, in many ways, a faithful reproduction of the details that appear on the mummy board itself, though the facial features have been altered slightly, presumably for effect. The 'head' is tilted on the 'neck', giving the illustration of the mummy board a somewhat more human, inquisitive posture, while the enlarged eyes, emphasized cheekbones, and narrow nose create a thinner or more skeletal appearance, furthered by

Figure 10.1 The detailed view of the Unlucky Mummy, *From Hell*, ch. 5, p. 39. FROM HELL © Alan Moore and Eddie Campbell.

the greyscale palette. The youthful, bronzed skin of the individual depicted on the board as the object appears in real life is not reproduced here. The neck is obscured by shadow so that the face itself is surrounded by darkness, appearing like an apparition emerging from the gloom. The illustration is faithful enough for the artefact to be recognizable; it is simultaneously different enough for the reader to observe that this is not an entirely faithful depiction of EA 22542, but a Gothicized version of the artefact, playing on its supernatural associations. Unlike the previous depiction of the artefact – prostrate, passive – this version looks out from the picture, no longer subject to the gaze but itself gazing out at the reader, and, possibly, at Gull.

This is our final view of the mummy board, though not the final allusion to it. In the ninth chapter, Gull discusses the artefact with a Keeper at the British Museum. When questioned as to whether 'the British Museum intend[s] to purchase' the item, the Keeper responds somewhat nervously: 'Ah, yes. Yes, I have heard of the, ah, of the item. Excellent piece. First class. Of course, there IS the matter of its, ah reputation, so to speak ... .'[21] Gull is apparently shocked 'that pagan curses daunt this noble institution', arguing that the mummy board should be kept 'here in this museum, next to Hawksmoor's

Bloomsbury church', and that 'Half London's mad for things Egyptian with the Royal Household held alike in thrall.'[22] While dismissing occult rumours surrounding the artefact he invokes the occult potency of Hawksmoor's church (significances known to a select minority), meanwhile emphasizing the sheer popularity of Egyptiana permeating all levels of society up to the royal family. We are invited to linger on the perceived divide between the exclusive and the well-known, the elite and the popular; the Unlucky Mummy appears to appeal to both. Subsequent rumours of a curse have attracted a widespread audience for over a century, while those involved in secret societies appear to have attached specific significances to this item. The object and its history are suspended between professional Egyptological discourse and popular 'phantasy'.

In reality, British Museum officials have long denied the rumours surrounding the Unlucky Mummy, though Budge was more ambivalent on the matter than most. Budge became Assistant Keeper of the Egyptian Rooms in 1891, upon the retirement of Peter le Page Renouf, and was made Keeper in 1894. The Keeper who greets Gull in *From Hell* appears to be a young Budge, rather than Renouf who would have been the more historically appropriate choice. Budge is, however, a far more appealing individual for a work so embroiled in secrecy and occult symbolism, and was known to relate rumours about the Unlucky Mummy seemingly as entertainment, albeit for select audiences.[23] In Moore's notes, this character is described as 'some sort of museum official' – 'a smartly dressed, plump and bespectacled gentleman in a suit' – and referred to rather less flatteringly in the script as 'Fat Official'.[24] The choice of Budge as a model likely came after these notes were made, either on Campbell's suggestion or, perhaps more likely, when Moore unearthed the quotation from Budge about the mummy case provoking war. Budge is a slippery individual when it comes to attempting to pin down his involvement in either the whipping up or denouncing of supernatural stories, including those to do with Egyptian artefacts.[25] Despite critiquing individuals involved in the establishment of 'mummy's curse' narratives, such as Marie Corelli, Budge enjoyed friendships with Edith Nesbit and Florence Farr, both members of the Hermetic Order of the Golden Dawn, an organization which drew upon ancient Egyptian religion and iconography in its own rituals.[26] Campbell depicts Budge according to Moore's notes: ensconced in an institution where 'tentative giant statues are arranged, seated or standing in their hieroglyphic poses'; 'the Egyptian exhibits loom, strange, alien and silent'; 'Colossal sleeping kings and jackal-headed deities [keep] their eternal silent vigil.'[27] The Museum is a space of tension, caught between rationality and reason and the mysterious aura of the Egyptian objects themselves.

In a note entitled 'King Tut' (evoking another famous 'mummy's curse') in *The From Hell Companion* (2013), Campbell comments, 'I sometimes think there should be more Egyptian detail in the art. At the time, however, I judged that it would make things more prosaic, more "midnight in the museum" than the majesty of eternity.'[28] The representations of the Unlucky Mummy differ from the vague and mysterious Egyptian shapes that populate the British Museum in their specificity. Evidently, Moore and Campbell demonstrate familiarity with this genuine artefact, either in person or through photographic images, and Moore has, similarly, clearly delved into its history and mythology, drawing upon the many threads of curse narratives with which it is entwined. Moore downplays cultural interest in the mummy board; in his notes to the section in which Gull visits the British Museum he documents: 'The mummy case referred to is that of the Theban court musician as discussed in the appendix notes to Book Three, to which I would refer the interested reader (I assume there's only one of you).'[29] While I may be the first to discuss the artefact's appearance in this graphic novel in an academic context, details about the Unlucky Mummy and its mysterious history continue to be discussed in popular and academic fora. Visitors still frequent the British Museum to see this artefact in person. Moore and Campbell's text thus becomes another thread in a web of documents which refer to this object, enriching its cultural afterlife and contributing to its perpetual suspension between factual and fictional worlds.

Cleopatra's needle: Psychogeography

Much scholarly work on *From Hell* is specifically interested in the graphic novel's relationship to psychogeography, and the fruitful ways in which psychogeographical approaches might be used to dissect and reveal its symbolism, encouraged by its themes of secrecy, and a close adherence to London's geographical landscape. Critics have read Gull himself as a kind of psychogeographer: 'Gull's occult knowledge', Monika Pietrzak-Franger notes, 'allows him to see the pagan culture thriving under the surface of civilized London'.[30] Such work has also turned to landmarks with ancient Egyptian histories and associations, including the ancient Egyptian obelisk known as 'Cleopatra's Needle', presented to Britain in 1819 but only installed in London in 1878. Elizabeth Ho offers the most significant psychogeographical analysis of Cleopatra's Needle's part in *From Hell*:

> Plagued by calamities and disaster in its journey back 'home' to England as an imperial prize, the Needle anchors a long history of struggle that stretches back 'fifteen hundred years before Christ's birth' when the stone was 'etched with hieroglyphic prayers that Atum, Egypt's sun god might increase his sovereignty.' While the shipwrecks and deaths that accompany the Needle's journey are a jab at England's imperial games, the Needle is also a tribute to Gull's alternate cartography. ... The seductiveness of psychogeography lies in its potential for unveiling counterhegemonic stories like the vanity of dragging an obelisk from Alexandria to London as imperial spoils.[31]

Indeed, the obelisk is dense with symbolism, representative of phallic, masculine power, paganism, Freemasonic pseudo-history, magical potency and death. It is also, as Ho identifies, representative of psychogeography itself.

Moore's occult psychogeography was inspired in part by Iain Sinclair's *Lud Heat: A Book of the Dead Hamlets* (1975).[32] As Niall Martin notes of *Lud Heat*, 'With the transmission of images from Ancient Egypt, London inscribes itself within a system ... international and inter-epochal', evoking Michel Foucault's concept of the 'heterotopia'.[33] This might apply, too, to *From Hell*, another text into which 'a scattering of Egyptian hieroglyphs' is integrated,[34] through the representation, in this case, of one of the pair of guardian sphinxes that flank Cleopatra's Needle. 'The hieroglyphic elements of Ancient Egyptian found in the *Lud Heat* maps', as Brian Baker observes, 'also signify the concept of a pictorial communication'.[35] *Lud Heat* is a multi-generic work comprising poetry, illustrations, essays, journal entries and maps; the hieroglyphs in *From Hell* also draw our attention to its status as graphic novel – itself a hybrid form – and specifically one which is a patchwork of fact and fiction, integrating its own map-like illustrations, and with its own elucidatory text (in the case of the 1999 edition with its appendices). The appearance of Egyptian iconography within *From Hell* thus invites an intertextual and psychogeographically inflected reading.

Much psychogeographical criticism of *From Hell* focuses on Gull and Netley's journey around the city, over the course of which they encounter numerous obelisks. These include that which marks Daniel Defoe's grave (and 'looms' over William Blake's much more modest headstone), 'styled upon stones consecrated to the Sun God Atum, raised at Heliopolis in ancient Egypt'.[36] Netley's observation that it might instead be 'styled on my John Thomas' encourages Gull to confirm that 'The obelisk is phallic, for the sun's a symbol of the male principle.' Obelisks, phalluses and knives stand in opposition to the feminine, the 'left brain', magic, mysticism and ancient matriarchy. A pause at St Luke's church designed by Hawksmoor with its obelisk-steeple further cements these somewhat transparent associations: 'He built an obelisk: Another altar to the Sun, and Masculinity, and Reason, with its cold erection stabbing at the sky.'[37]

Other obelisks and pyramid-like structures litter the text, and further references to ancient Egyptian physical presences in the city abound in *From Hell* itself and in Moore's annotations.[38] Moore justifies their inclusion through research, using creative license in one case where a street map of 1885 shows an obelisk 'clearly marked in a position ascribed to it' as it appears in *From Hell*, though a map of the same area in 1890 shows that the obelisk had been removed by this point. 'Being presently unable to locate street plans for 1888', Moore relates, 'I ... have opted to stick one in anyway.'[39] Grounding his text in as much geographical evidence as he can unearth, Moore adopts a playful tone when creatively filling the historical blanks.

These are real places infused with ancient Egyptian symbolism, albeit possibly slightly out-of-time in the case of the aforementioned obelisk, though this temporal dislocation is crucial to both psychogeography and *From Hell* itself in the various visions, hallucinations and prophecies experienced by several characters. Egyptian symbolism appears particularly potent and dominant, too, on both a macro and micro scale: as Gull relates, Hawksmoor's 'final labours raised two horns like jackals [sic] ears upon a monument at England's governmental heart' – Westminster Abbey – 'built upon the ancient temple-site of Anubis'.[40] Gestures to ancient Egypt permeate the country's seats of power and icons of 'Britishness'. On a much smaller level, obelisks become a vital part in Netley's narrative. Moore relates the research behind Netley's death in *From Hell*'s final chapter:

> It seems that Carman Netley, born in Paddington in 1860, died in an accident when his horse bolted and his carriage wheel struck the base of an obelisk on a

pedestrian refuse in Park Road. ... Whether the John Netley killed at Clarence Gate was indeed the sinister coachman and Ripper-accomplice as portrayed by Stephen Knight ... is, of course, a matter open to conjecture. Still, the obelisk was too good to pass up.[41]

The obelisk here is an object associated with fate and, considered subsequent to the Unlucky Mummy's murderous associations, we are left to ponder whether Netley's demise is an ironic accident or whether some ancient Egyptian force is in fact responsible. The magical associations of obelisks – in particular Cleopatra's Needle – certainly suggests that this monument, caught between existence in 1885 and inexistence in 1890, might harbour supernatural forces.

Cleopatra's Needle itself is the most imposing obelisk in the text, and about which the densest array of supernatural tales orbits. It is also the obelisk depicted in the most detail. In the clearest image (Fig. 10.2) the hieroglyphic inscriptions themselves are obscured, while Gull's speech surrounds the monument, overwriting this ancient text with the

Figure 10.2 The detailed view of Cleopatra's Needle, *From Hell*, ch. 4, p. 20. FROM HELL © Alan Moore and Eddie Campbell.

artefact's more recent story. As recorded in *From Hell*'s appendices, 'The information on these pages relating to Cleopatra's Needle is accurate, and drawn from various sources.'[42] Gull relays historical information relating to the Needle's origins ('Carved fifteen hundred years before Christ's birth and raised at Heliopolis by Thotmes, etched with hieroglyphic prayers that Atum Egypt's Sun god might increase his sovereignty. ... Removed to Alexandria in 12 BC)', its transport in the nineteenth century ('it was extricated; placed aboard a ship' 'which promptly sank', 'was rescued; placed inside a floating cylinder' 'cut ... loose' in a storm, 'drifted, [and] was finally recovered'), and the supernaturally charged rumours that emerge after its installation ('It is a haunt for suicides and ghosts').[43] Historical accuracy and superstitious embellishment collide in the same narrative.

The previous panel depicts one of the pair of nineteenth-century guardian sphinxes created to flank the obelisk, each bearing the cartouche of Thutmose III.[44] As in the panel of the Needle, here the ancient Egyptian presence dominates the frame, 'looming incongruously into the picture' and dwarfing the human figures.[45] Perspective has been used to suggest a much bigger sphinx than the sculpture actually appears: something as monumental as the Great Sphinx of Giza, with all of its connotations of enigmas, secrecy and occult knowledge (conflated, of course, with the mythology of ancient Greek sphinxes). Indeed, in Moore's notes for this frame, he suggests that the sphinx should '[smile] faintly ... although we cannot tell what it's smiling at', evoking something of the Great Sphinx's mystery.[46] The clarity of the hieroglyphs on the sphinx contrasts, however, with the haziness of the hieroglyphs on the obelisk itself. While modelled on ancient examples, the sphinx and its partner are Victorian constructions,[47] commissioned to accompany the obelisk: the nineteenth century hieroglyphs are in focus, while the ancient text evades clear scrutiny. Again, we might read this juxtaposition of clarity and obfuscation as representative of the graphic novel's engagement with ancient Egypt more widely: on the one hand, anchored in historical realism, and on the other, elusive, embellished and emblematic of the supernatural unknown.

Gull's misogynist understanding of the Needle as one of many masculine symbols neglects the Needle's connection to women, instead only discussing the Needle in relation to men: Christ, Thotmes, Atum, 'six seamen', 'a naked man'.[48] Any women who are part of his narrative are objectified and literally 'entombed': in Gull's gendered language we learn that 'Daguerrotypes [*sic*] of our epoch's most lovely women', among other objects, are buried under the Needle, beneath 'the stone pudenda of its base'.[49] And, while the Needle itself has a name suggestive of femininity, 'Cleopatra's Needle' gesturing to the most famous female Egyptian monarch as well as sewing (traditionally, 'women's work'), Gull only imagines the Needle in male hands: 'He who'd wield it would the BEST of tailors be, to do its work; increase the Sun God's sovereignty... .'[50] He himself is the bearer of this blade, as a medical professional presumably as adept with a needle as he is with a knife.

The Needle is, however, connected to both male and female visions with supernatural significances. The first to experience otherworldly hallucinations involving the obelisk is not Gull, but Polly Nicholls, her own experiences a far cry from Freemasonry and hermetic lore. Her dreams are solely founded on some kind of feminine intuition. 'They'll kill us', she states 'I've ad NIGHTMARES':

> I walked over Waterloo Bridge down the Embankment, and there were that MONUMENT; that NEEDLE thing. Standin' by it was me brother . . . [sic] 'e burned to death two year back when 'is paraffin lamp exploded. I called him, but ... but 'e just started BURNIN'' like when 'e DIED. I couldn't do anythin'[.] 'E put is arms around the needle ... and the NEEDLE burned too! That cold stone, afire... it looked so QUEER[.] I woke up an knew somethin' bad would 'appen.[51]

Polly's hallucinations relate to death (specifically the death of a man), and while these are not glimpses of the future as with Gull's visions, they appear to pre-empt destruction of some variety – 'somethin' bad would 'appen' – symbolized by the masculine solar symbol of the flaming obelisk.[52] Her visions come during sleep; one is reminded of the slumbering Mrs Gull and the Unlucky Mummy. This juxtaposition takes on new resonances when we pay particular attention to the crossovers between the feminine and the otherworldly in *From Hell*, side-lined as they are in favour of the masculine. Again, Moore provides justification for this detail: while he admits that Polly's nightmares are 'an invention', she 'did live on Stamford Street just a short walk over Waterloo Bridge from Cleopatra's Needle'.[53] Factual material is again used to suggest the possibility of the Egyptian fantastic.

Polly's hallucinations prefigure Gull's own, which also feature Cleopatra's Needle as a site of particular supernatural significance. Gull anticipates Sigmund Freud (who would likely have also read phallic significance into the obelisk) in his understanding of the Needle as 'solid, fixed and permanent in time' while around 'its base parade oblivious phantoms that I know to be the living, although not of any single night or century'.[54] In *Civilization and Its Discontents* (1930), Freud compares the psyche to an archaeological site, and which layers of memory continue to exist as the mind matures:

> Now let us, by a flight of imagination, suppose that Rome is not a human habitation but a psychical entity with a similarly long and copious past – an entity ... in which nothing that has once come into existence will have passed away and all the earlier phases of development continue to exist alongside the latest one.[55]

Freud uses a well-established archaeological metaphor that might apply equally as well to Egyptian sites, or even Victorian London. Numerous temporal strata coexist and overlap as 'we see a peculiar and ghostly procession ... as if we can see three of four different periods all coexisting at once, as flimsy overlays stacked one on top of each other';[56] in Gull's vision of the Needle: 'About its ageless beacon is the vaporous swirl of human life and time continued.'[57] Only the ancient Needle and its nineteenth-century guardian sphinxes remain 'sharp and defined'.[58] Mystical power is denoted through light in these panels: 'the needle's black stone glows unearthly white',[59] giving off a spectral 'aura'.[60] Its psychogeographical potency, its magical properties sustained by the layers of time through which it has existed, makes it a 'luminous and phosphorescent beacon', connected to a network of magical energy through lines of 'flickering white fire', 'white and glittering'.[61] This, Gull's final extended hallucination that makes up the most part of the final chapter, sees his spirit ascend, 'rising' 'into the gold', a pantheistic heaven, further aligning Cleopatra's Needle with death.[62] Here, Gull himself is revealed to be the naked man who jumps into the Thames, a ghost out of time. Paul Harrison relates rumours that this ghost 'was a late Victorian disciple of Rameses II who was driven insane by the spell of the Needle', and turned to murder, perpetrating the acts attributed to 'the Thames Torso Killer' – roughly contemporary with the Ripper crimes – before ending his own life.[63] Murder, the Needle and ancient Egyptian forces are evidently connected by decades of supernatural rumour. Gull as the acolyte of an ancient pharaoh is not incompatible with Moore and Campbell's own contributions to the web of mythmaking surrounding the enigmatic figure of the Ripper.

The clairvoyant visions associated with Cleopatra's Needle are complemented by an extract from Oscar Wilde's short story, 'Lord Arthur Savile's Crime' which, as Moore records, was 'first published in THE COURT AND SOCIETY REVIEW (1887)'.[64] This quotation is the only epigraph at the opening of the eleventh chapter, 'The unfortunate Mr. Druitt', in which we encounter Wilde himself at a party at his home in Tite Street, and in which we meet the eponymous Druitt who is dismissed from the school at which he works (as a result of an inappropriate relationship with one of his male pupils: we are encouraged to see the ill-fated relationship between Wilde and Lord Alfred Douglas in this, subsequent to the references to Wilde), and scapegoated by the Freemasons to alleviate suspicion from Gull. The passage adds further colour to the patchwork of associations surrounding Cleopatra's Needle. Furthermore, Moore's emphasis on the date of the story's publication, the year before the Ripper murders, suggests that Wilde is channelling something of the contemporary city's occult energy in his tale of murder (interpreted as suicide) in the shadow of the Needle itself:

> At two o'clock he got up, and strolled towards Blackfriars. How unreal everything looked! How like a strange dream! The houses on the other side of the river seemed built out of darkness. One would have said that silver and shadow had fashioned the world anew. The huge dome of St. Paul's loomed like a bubble through the dusty air. As he approached Cleopatra's Needle he saw a man leaning over the parapet, and as he came nearer the man looked up, the gaslight falling full upon his face. It was Mr Podgers, the chiromantist! No one could mistake the fat flabby face, the gold-rimmed spectacles, the sickly feeble smile, the sensual mouth. Lord Arthur stopped. A brilliant idea flashed across him, and he stole softly up behind. In a moment he had seized Mr Podgers by the legs, and flung him into the Thames. There was a coarse oath, a heavy splash and all was still. Lord Arthur looked anxiously over, but could see nothing of the chiromantist but a tall hat, pirouetting in an eddy of moonlit water. After a time it also sank, and no trace of Mr Podgers was visible. Once he thought that he caught sight of the bulky misshapen figure striking out for the staircase by the bridge, and a horrible feeling of failure came

over him but it turned out to be merely a reflection, and when the moon shone out from behind a cloud it passed away. At last, he seemed to have realized the decree of Destiny. He heaved a deep sigh of relief, and Sybil's name came to his lips. 'Have you dropped anything sir?' said a voice behind him suddenly. He turned round, and saw a policeman with a bull's eye lantern. 'Nothing of importance sergeant,' he answered, smiling, and hailing a passing hansom, he jumped in, and told the man to drive to Belgrade Square.[65]

The dream-like tone of this passage complements the mystique surrounding Cleopatra's Needle as it is depicted in *From Hell*. It also draws particular attention to the idea of 'Destiny', Podgers's fate to become a murderer being realized as he pushes the palm-reader who made this prediction, Mr Podgers, into the river. Wilde's text offers a darkly comic layer to the narratives of suicides at the Needle's feet, and also tethers the monument specifically to murder. We as readers know Wilde's fate, too, and with this knowledge comes the feeling that, living amidst a city dense with malignant ancient Egyptian presences, obelisks functioning as harbingers of death between the pages of *From Hell*, he himself might be yet another of the Needle's victims.

Collectively, the supernatural narratives spun around the nucleus of Cleopatra's Needle form a fractured and kaleidoscopic picture of occultism: obelisks are harbingers of death and downfall, symbols that appear in prophetic dreams, artefacts that channel spirits and about which ghosts from the past and future congregate. They are significant to both Freemasonry and the various occult groups active in the late nineteenth century, clouding the line that Gull seems so determined to draw between the two. As we shall see, ancient Egypt in particular and its continued potency in Gull's contemporary world upset such attempts.

Jahbulon: The magical revival

Freemasonry serves a tripartite purpose in *From Hell*. Firstly, it is true that many of the powerful and influential men implicated in the narrative were involved in Freemasonry (and hence many theories about the identity of Jack the Ripper), ergo its usefulness to the plot. For the purposes of the graphic novel, it serves as a secret society exclusively accessible to men, and as such functions as a homosocial brotherhood at odds with the 'sisterhood' of London's streetwalking women. Finally, its mystical associations contribute to an air of occult threat that pervades *From Hell*. Significantly, however, Freemasonry is far less historically embroiled in occult matters than many other groups had been at the *fin de siècle*.

Nevertheless, the Freemasonry depicted in *From Hell* is one which rests upon a bedrock of magical energy, idols of ancient deities and visions of these deities themselves. In the final section of this essay, I dissect ancient Egyptian references in *From Hell*'s depictions of occultism, and links between named individuals and Egyptian-flavoured supernatural experiences. I claim the significance of other late nineteenth-century groups and belief systems on Moore and Campbell's depiction of Freemasonry, and assess the significance of the Unlucky Mummy and Cleopatra's Needle as supernaturally charged entities working within this culture.

The establishment of the Hermetic Order of the Golden Dawn, a secret society founded by several individuals involved in Freemasonry, occurred in 1888 with the foundation of London's Isis Urania Temple.[66] Its nascence is contemporaneous to the Ripper murders, and its membership included (or was to include) several of the individuals present or referred to across the graphic novel. Two of the three founding members of the Golden Dawn – William Robert Woodman and Willian Wynn Westcott – are featured (though Moore misremembers 'Woodman' as 'Woodford'), and W. B. Yeats and Aleister Crowley, both initiates (though neither by 1888), make cameo appearances.[67] Other individuals involved in the Order require a little more digging in order to be unearthed; Florence Farr is referred to in Moore's annotations to the chapters, and while Oscar Wilde himself was not directly involved in the Order, his wife, Constance, was admitted in November 1888, a matter of weeks after the murder of Mary Kelly.[68]

There were, of course, several differences between Freemasons and the initiates of the Golden Dawn (one of the most oft-discussed being the Golden Dawn's admittance of women). The most telling, in terms of Campbell and Moore's use of Freemasonry, is that the rituals and symbolism of the Golden Dawn were, unlike those of the Masons, held to have genuine magical power. Freemasonry as depicted in *From Hell* draws upon the magical potency supposedly inherent in the undertakings of Golden Dawn members. Farr studied the artefacts at the British Museum with Budge's aid and, by the mid-1890s, had supposedly been in contact with at least one ancient Egyptian spirit connected to the Museum's artefacts.[69] When Gull appears to experience moments of connection with Unlucky Mummy, he reflects experiences of Golden Dawn members in tune with antiquities and the spirits associated with them on a higher plane. This, however, occurs on a far greater scale than in Golden Dawn rituals when Gull witnesses the Freemasonic 'god' Jahbulon.

Jahbulon is first introduced as 'the Great Architect of the Universe', a 'trinity' made up of 'JAHWEH, worshipped by the Hebrews', 'Osiris, known to ancient Egypt' and 'BAAL, the horned god of the Canaanites'.[70] Three alcoves in one of the interior walls of the Freemasons' temple sport a representation of each of these facets; Osiris is represented in a fashion that mimics ancient Egyptian art. He wears a *nemes* headdress, more evocative of representations of a pharaoh than the ancient Egyptian god of the dead. After being shown these idols, Gull is requested to provide medical care to Queen Victoria's grandson, Prince Albert Victor (Eddy), an honour bestowed upon him as a result of his ever-ascending position among the Freemasons. He has witnessed the ancient deities, including an idol of the ancient Egyptian god of the dead; now he must administer to a living prince who is himself the keystone of the killing at the heart of *From Hell*. Osiris is lord of the underworld, and Jack the Ripper (Gull) writes 'from Hell', aligning himself specifically with this deity.[71] It was the Golden Dawn rather than Freemasonry that placed such importance on the ancient Egyptian deities, though far more frequently referenced than Anubis and Osiris were figures such as Isis, more aligned with life than death. Occult Freemasonry in *From Hell* is thus the masculinized foil to the feminized Golden Dawn.

In Gull's opinion, the Golden Dawn is a mere 'little group', 'a splinter, split from the bough of Masonry'.[72] While his experiences in many respects chime with Golden Dawn rather than real Freemasonic activities, the god Jahbulon, with Osiris as one component, is more imposing than any other Egyptian presence in *From Hell*. Indeed, Jahbulon is granted the first full-page image in the graphic novel (Fig. 10.3), looming over Gull, the lone human figure. Supposedly hallucinating having suffered a stroke (a detail gleaned from Gull's biography), this moment is presented as a theophany. Baal (in the centre) is flanked by the two other deities in this trinity: Yahweh on the left, and Osiris on the right. Osiris is, as he is in the image of the idol, depicted holding the crook and flail, though the *nemes* is not present here. While he does not wear the *atef* crown as is customary in ancient Egyptian iconography, he does wear one of its components: the *hedjet* crown of Upper Egypt. The curved beard is another typical feature of depictions of Osiris. Where the idol conflates ancient Egyptian imagery, the 'god' conforms more clearly to accurate Egyptological detail, suggestive of the veracity of what Gull sees as opposed to the hollowness of performed rituals.

Figure 10.3 Jabulon, *From Hell*, chapter 2, p. 26. FROM HELL © Alan Moore and Eddie Campbell.

Gull's visions continue; as already noted, Cleopatra's Needle with all of its ancient Egyptian potency is a site of exceptional psychical force. Indeed, the actress and theosophist Mabel Collins – referred to in passing in the second appendix, 'Dance of the gull catchers', as the lover of a Ripper suspect and tangentially connected to Aleister Crowley[73] – experienced similar visions to Gull corresponding with the arrival of Cleopatra's Needle in London (though hers involved spirits of the past rather than those of the future): 'In 1878 … I saw Cleopatra's Needle brought up the river and set up upon the Embankment. A procession of superb Egyptian priests began from that time to come into my room.'[74] Freemasonry had many acolytes in common with spiritualism and theosophy, and thus the supposedly supernatural encounters that members of such alternative groups reported can be attributed to Freemasons without too much creative license on Moore's part.[75]

Indeed, other occultists who appear in *From Hell* have pertinent connections to the Needle. Crowley, who appears as a thirteen-year-old sucking on a candy cane tells Inspector Abberline that he's wrong to believe that magic does not exist.[76] This chapter opens with an epigraph from John Symonds and Kenneth Grant's *The Confessions of Aleister Crowley* (1979), relating that 'One theory of the motive of the [Ripper] murderer was that he was performing an Operation to obtain the Supreme Black Magical Power.'[77] Crowley was no stranger to rituals; as Paul Harrison records, Crowley 'was convinced that the Rameses II carvings [on Cleopatra's Needle] contained a magical spell that preserved the soul of the dead pharaoh within the stone'. Furthermore:

> Crowley was obsessed with the monument and was known to have acquired a human skeleton that he regularly took to the needle in the dark of night. There he would feed animal blood to the skeleton, in the belief that it would return to life with Rameses II's reincarnated spirit.[78]

With this in mind, Netley's death takes on suggestions of a sacrifice to otherworldly Egyptian forces. It is, perhaps significantly, only after Netley's death that Gull's transcendental experience at the foot of the Needle occurs. Despite the contempt with which Gull treats occultism outside of the boundaries of Freemasonry, his own experiences and activities chime with theosophist, Golden Dawn and spiritualist encounters with ancient Egypt, suggestive that Freemasonry in *From Hell* cannot be divided from its broader occult context.

The 'sweet masters' that Gull witnesses having been borne aloft by solar energy, channelled via the obelisk, include Horus who stands in the foreground of a row of deities (seemingly including Jesus and Bacchus) indicative of the pre-eminence of ancient Egyptian deities in a harmonious multi-religious pantheon.[79] Indeed, the presence of Christ in this panel makes clear the text's 'blurring [of] pagan/Christian binaries' as identified by Pietrzak-Franger;[80] I would add that comparisons between Horus and Jesus (often based upon similarities in the iconography of the Virgin Mary with the infant Jesus and Isis with the infant Horus) were the subject of impassioned debate in the nineteenth century.[81] There is a historical context to this collision between faith systems, with Freemasory in *From Hell* incorporating Christian belief but also responding to the late Victorian magical revival, and with it the explosion of interest in ancient and alternative religions. Horus points Gull to a vision of the real Mary Kelly who has survived his murderous intent. That she is surrounded by female children – possibly daughters – who appear to have been named after Gull's victims mark her out as a 'mummy', and that she can see Gull's spirit – commanding him to 'Clear off back to Hell' – implies that she has supernatural abilities of her own.[82] She is the feminine force in opposition to Gull's masculine; the gods he sees – led by Horus – are all male deities.

Gull disparages contemporary occult groups, despite the evident connections between the occult powers he respects and wields (the aforementioned scene evoking astral projection) and the place of movements such as spiritualism in the late Victorian magical revival. A suggestion of a bird wearing what looks to be a wig or a headdress similar to a *nemes* appears on a Ouija board in 'Dance of the gull catchers'. It seems that this is meant to be reminiscent of Qebehsenuef, one of the sons of Horus and guardian of the intestines, who is depicted wearing a similar headdress, most commonly on canopic jars, emphasising the interconnectedness of ancient Egypt, spiritualism and death in the popular imagination.[83] The reappearance of an ancient Egyptian bird-headed god here gestures back to Gull's vision of Horus: we are invited to question, was his vision as meaningless as the spiritualist communications he himself disparages? Gull laments,

> Reason's BESIEGED: For all our science we are become an age of table rappers, tealeaf readers and Theosophists; where Dr. Westcott founds his 'Golden Dawn,' mistaking hokum for the wisdom of antiquity! The seance-parlour's murmurings; the gutters' pandemonium … these threaten Rationality itself.[84]

The veracity of such 'hokum' is questioned throughout *From Hell*, most significantly – for the purposes of this essay – in the discourse surrounding ancient Egyptian artefacts. Spiritualism, for example, is interrogated through Moore's depiction of Robert James Lees, the individual with whom contact is purportedly made using the Egyptianized Ouija board. Lees was a spiritualist medium and, in *From Hell*, Queen Victoria's psychic adviser, who admits his fraudulent activity to Abberline, only to relate that everything that he invented 'all came true'.[85] While, on the one hand, Lees admits to deception and having never encountered any evidence of the existence of an afterlife, on the other, he relates prophetic dreams, including the same vision as Klara Hitler, accompanied by the 'awful grunting' of her husband.[86]

That Lees is contacted via the Egyptianized Ouija board is appropriate. While it is not directly alluded to in the graphic novel, Lees is himself connected to ancient Egyptian curse narratives. According to Paul Harrison,

> In private communications [Lees] stated that he believed in the curse of the Egyptian pharaohs, and had once visited a certain well-known London home in Portland Place and been asked to purge a malevolent Egyptian spirit that resided in a coffin-like artifact stored there. He had neither the power nor the authority to

do this, so advised the owner to be rid of the casket with all haste! Whether it was the mummy board of Amen-Ra or another artifact is not known.[87]

Perhaps Lees had his own encounter with the Unlucky Mummy.

Gull's damnation of Lees becomes all the more interesting if we parallel their interests in ancient Egyptian spirits. Certainly, as already recorded by Luckhurst, Madame Blavatsky, the matriarch of the Theosophical Society, is suggested to have been brought into contact with this dangerous artefact. Gull unwittingly – or unknowingly – becomes part of a community that he despises, populated by spiritualists, theosophists and members of the Golden Dawn. He is unable to reconcile his devotion to masculine rationality and his commitment to feminine magic. The phallic obelisk and the murderous mummy both demonstrate that, when ancient Egypt is concerned, magic and murder go hand in hand. Gull's refusal to admit that he is part of an inclusive occult climate, in which humble prostitutes have visions which rival his own, results in his swift excision. Having encountered his multi-cultural, masculine, Freemasonic pantheon, and seeing that he has failed in his missions to eradicate the women aware of the existence of Prince Eddy's daughter, he dies an undignified death. We as readers are transported too: away from the nineteenth century, through the twentieth and, once we finish the novel's epilogue, back into our own time. Cleopatra's Needle and the Unlucky Mummy are static objects that persist, eerie sentinels still keeping watch.

Conclusion

At the 1907 Museums Association conference, the president, John Maclauchlan, declared: 'all the world's a museum, and all the men and women merely specimens'.[88] Maclauchlan's statement invites us to consider the body as specimen, particularly pertinent given the widespread public display of bodies of the ancient Egyptian dead (in the nineteenth century and to this day). Despite not being a human body, the mummy board is frequently referred to as such (as in its moniker, the 'Unlucky Mummy'). Maclauchlan's quotation also draws our attention to the 'boxes' (panels) in which the events of the novel take place, displayed for our viewing, presenting us with living, dead and dying bodies alike. All of the characters in the novel are specimens, not just the victims, or Joseph Merrick (known as the 'Elephant Man'), who is also presented as a medical oddity in this text, but Gull himself, the other real and fictional characters. *From Hell* is, in some ways, a cabinet of curiosities: these real and fictional lives are presented to us as part of an eclectic and eccentric collection which includes pagan idols, mummy boards and obelisks.

We have, in *From Hell*, a world suffused with the Egyptian supernatural, where working-class prostitutes, upper-class Freemasons and fraudulent spiritualists alike have symbolic dreams and prophetic visions linked to ancient Egyptian artefacts. Over the course of this graphic novel we witness communications with ancient Egyptian gods, are led to attribute world wars to ancient Egyptian spirits and individual deaths to cursed obelisks, and observe uneasy officials and occultists working in close proximity at the British Museum. Ancient Egypt may not be a visible presence in most of *From Hell*'s thousands of frames, but look closely and you can see obelisks in many views of the city. Ancient Egypt lurks as an omnipresent layer beneath the nineteenth-century veneer, at times emerging and making its dangerous presence felt through several emissaries: Osiris and Horus, Cleopatra's Needle, and the spirit of the Unlucky Mummy itself. Upon completing *From Hell*, readers may be able to shrug off the Egyptian supernatural as conceived by the many real and fictional characters between its pages. What they cannot do is deny the continued existence of ancient Egypt in the modern world, artefacts which have survived for millennia, have generated ghostly rumours which have lingered – in their current situation, at least – for well over a century, and which will, likely, outlive them too.

PART III
GENDER AND SEXUALITY

CHAPTER 11
FROM SEKHMET TO SUFFRAGE: ANCIENT EGYPT IN EARLY TWENTIETH-CENTURY WOMEN'S CULTURE
Mara Gold

Gender and orientalism

Over the past two decades, an abundance of work has emerged relating to women and orientalism, much of it in response to the neglect of gender in Edward Said's influential 1978 volume of the same name. As Meyda Yeğenoğlu argues, studies of orientalism should not and cannot be devoid of gender theory.[1] From travel writing to popular culture, the Western world experienced a kind of mania for the orient during the nineteenth and early twentieth centuries. In particular, it seems that women were drawn to and aligned with orientalism. While the boom in women's travel to, and writing about, the orient can certainly be attributed to the new-found accessibility of the Middle East due to advances in rail and air travel, women's interest in the orient outside of the context of tourism is much more complex.

Most scholars working in this area agree that the Middle East was associated with femininity. Some, such as Yeğenoğlu and Dúnlaith Bird, suggest that the East was considered feminine in terms of its perceived inferiority to and subjugation by the West, while others, such as Billie Melman, suggest that it also represented femininity, glamour, freedom and sexuality in positive and empowering ways for women.[2] She further refers to a variety of orients, offering a version of orientalist fantasy that was individual to each woman but had the unifying quality of providing a sense of freedom and sensuality that was unavailable to them within the Victorian model of separate spheres.[3] Sara Mills and Mary Louise Pratt examine the complex relationship between imperialism and femininity, paying particular attention to women's travel to the Middle East. Noting the abundance of women's writing about the region, they claim that women were able to critique colonialism by drawing upon their own experiences of subjection.[4] On the other hand, Bird and Yeğenoğlu acknowledge women's views of the Middle East as operating both in opposition to and within a colonial framework, with Bird referring to travel to the Middle East by both men and women as 'the penetration of the feminised East'.[5]

While this essay does not focus on women's travel to the Middle East but rather on recreations of the ancient Near East in Britain, these concepts regarding the femininity of the orient, women's own subjugation by the state and the patriarchy, and orientalist fantasy as escapism are key to exploring how women used archaeology to construct and perform their own femininity and feminism.[6] Furthermore, this essay examines how this affinity between femininity and the orient relates to women's reception of the ancient world in Britain in the early twentieth century and to recent archaeological discoveries, a connection that has not yet been analysed.

Studies relating to this topic have been dominated by post-Tutankhamun Egyptomania, neglecting considerations of gender and the ever-popular legacy of Cleopatra, whose image has been used and manipulated (largely by men) since the height of the Roman Empire as a symbol of excess femininity and sexuality.[7] Jasmine Day is one of the few scholars who has considered the reception of Egyptian archaeology in a gendered manner. However, as she largely deals with receptions of ancient Egypt prior to 1881 (the beginning of the 'golden age' of Egyptology), many of the specific archaeological discoveries influencing women had not yet occurred. Building on the concept of the East as feminine, Day suggests that the patriarchal imagination feminized mummies in order to objectify and possess them in the same way that the West subjugated the East and man subjugated woman.[8] As a result of this feminization, she suggests, women saw similarities between their own treatment and the treatment of mummies, particularly through the analogy of rape, and were the chief instigators of the mummy motif in popular culture.[9] Although this parallel with theories on gender and orientalism is interesting, it is difficult to relate these ideas to early twentieth-century Egyptomania. Although colonialist oppression was ever-present, the decline of the British Empire and the rise of feminism allowed for new and gendered interpretations of Egypt. In fact, women's emulation of the ancient world seems to have been more concerned with femininity as a force of power and a way to express themselves in the modern world.

Until now, there has been no connection made between the development of archaeology as a discipline and ideas of femininity or the rise of feminism. However, as this essay argues, the abundance of discoveries during this period due to the institutionalization and professionalism of archaeology had a direct impact on women's fashion and beauty trends, as well as on concepts of 'positive' femininity.[10]

The Nile style

Fashion historian Karin J. Bohleke claims that the period between 1881 and the First World War represents the 'glory years' for archaeology; many discoveries and exhibitions prior to Tutankhamun had massive impacts on women's trends, which had included Egyptian motifs since the eighteenth century.[11] Although other fashion historians are correct in attributing the Egyptomania of this period to the 1922 discovery, they – as do Bob Brier and James Stevens Curl – attribute the Egyptomania of the 1920s solely to the discovery of Tutankhamun's tomb, neglecting to consider the influence of archaeology in the years and decades preceding that singular event.[12] In fact, the discovery of the tomb was merely the catalyst for the explosion of an obsession that had already existed for thousands of years, greatly aided by the ever-increasing dissemination of both information and pictures, and the manufacturing of clothing and beauty products.[13]

While the discovery had a huge impact on popular culture and was undoubtedly influential on style,[14] it lacked a special historical significance for women.

The widespread contemporary mass media coverage of these and other important discoveries reached a huge audience, spurring the craze for the 'Nile style'.[15] Nineteenth- and twentieth-century British colonialism and expansion in the Middle East irrefutably sparked a general interest in archaeology, but the enchantment of the ancient past particularly captured women's imaginations. Furthermore, if one considers Judith Butler's notion that femininity only exists through the repeated performance of gendered acts, then it makes sense that women would use established representations of past femininity as reference points for their own performance of gender.[16]

It would be remiss to ignore the strong tradition of orientalist stereotypes and women from antiquity appearing in popular culture, particularly in art, décor, dance, theatre and literature. Cleopatra has been used as a symbol of Eastern sexuality and decadence since her first contact with the Romans, soon becoming a representation of the dangers of femininity, an idea that lasted throughout the early modern period and beyond, largely thanks to Shakespeare.[17] Although fictional, Dido also received the same treatment, featuring in a play by Christopher Marlowe and numerous operas throughout the seventeenth, eighteenth and nineteenth centuries. The biblical Salome was also a favourite among artists since the Renaissance. It was during the latter half of the nineteenth century, however, particularly in *fin-de-siècle* literature, entertainment and art, that these female figures underwent a sustained and intense revival of interest. The resurgence of Salome in popular culture coincided with the development of biblical archaeology, wherein the search for biblical locations and personas (including her grandfather Herod's palace by the Palestine Exploration Fund during the 1880s) was one of the earliest motivations for archaeology as a discipline.[18]

They, and other eastern women from history and mythology, featured prominently in mid-to-late nineteenth-century orientalist painting, as well as Art Nouveau design (along with classical goddesses), in a newly eroticized and exoticized way. They also resumed their presence on the stage, becoming infamous theatrical figures of the era.[19] It was during this period that Cleopatra became orientalized, culminating in performances by both Lily Langtry and Sarah Bernhardt during the 1890s (see Fig. 11.1).[20] As Christine Peltre notes, orientalism in art became popular largely due to the rising interest in Egyptian art at the British Museum, as well as the development of ancient Near Eastern archaeology during the mid-nineteenth century, with Bernhardt's performance being directly influenced by such.[21] As the following paragraphs highlight, the influence of archaeology on theatre, film and other art forms was instrumental in disseminating ancient motifs into women's everyday lives.

During the first two decades of the twentieth century, these figures became overtly sexual symbols of oriental decadence. Their costuming became more risqué and more modern, which both reflected and influenced street fashions.[22] Although Juliet Bellow argues that stage costumes became more modern to mirror women's fashions, it is clear that fashion designers understood the power of theatre and film to affect women's trends and they incorporated many of the oriental and archaeological motifs found in costumes

Figure 11.1 Sarah Bernhardt (1844–1923), French, actress in the role of Cleopatra. Ca. 1891, Mary Evans/Everett Collection.

into their lines. Furthermore, top designers such as Paul Poiret and Jean Charles Worth, who were at the forefront of orientalist designs on- and offstage, concurrently produced theatrical costume designs and had their clothing advertised in theatre programmes.[23]

One such production was the Ballets Russes's 1918 *Cléopâtre*, which included costumes made by Poiret's atelier that were both modern and reflective of the decadent ancient Egyptian styles made familiar to the public through archaeological discoveries. One of the costumes (see Fig. 11.2) exhibits this combination perfectly, with colours, geometric patterns and a headdress very similar to those of mummy masks discovered during the late-nineteenth century, as well as an ultra-modern 'hobble' skirt (named for its narrow hemline).[24] British newspaper articles of the day directly compared the hobble skirt – supposedly invented by Poiret – to the type of skirt worn in depictions of the Egyptian queen Hatshepsut that were found during the early twentieth century; even supposedly modern fashion innovations were understood to have had ancient precedents.[25]

As Bellow notes, women become the target audience for theatre, film and consumer products in this period, meaning that advertisements 'manifested this newfound power in addressing themselves directly to a female gaze'.[26] This unprecedentedly opulent production of *Cléopâtre* made waves on its worldwide tour and was performed with great success for over ten years. Influencing women on both sides of the Atlantic, the production enhanced the 'contradictions surrounding women's prominent role as consumers of culture' through its reinvention of Cleopatra as a chic modern woman.[27] The costumes of this production explicitly aligned women with a source of ancient femininity and power to help them understand their new role in modern society.

Both costume design and fashion illustration were the perfect media with which to explore orientalist and archaeological motifs. These motifs' existence in both reality and fantasy allowed designers to experiment before creating everyday wearable garments.

Figure 11.2 'Salomé – Robe du soir de Paul Poiret', plate 28 from *Gazette du Bon Ton*, Volume 1, No. 3, Boston Museum of Fine Arts.

Despite Poiret's denial at the time, Peltzer argues that Poiret took direct inspiration from Bakst's 1908 costume sketches for *Salome* for his designs, once again highlighting the importance of the theatre as a link between archaeology and fashion. Poiret's 1914 Salome dress mirrors Bakst's layered, flowing fabrics but modernizes Bakst's concept into fancy attire rather than fancy dress.[28]

Peltzer attributes the revival of oriental-style fashion from 1900 onwards to Bakst and Poiret, particularly in terms of the way such pieces were gendered and eroticized, though she ignores many of the other cultural factors contributing to the trend such as colonialism and women's sense of affinity with the East.[29] Furthermore, Bakst's and Poiret's interest in antiquity played a key role in their designs, with Peltzer contending that their well-known love of antiquity manifested itself through oriental-style apparel.[30] She adds in a footnote that Poiret recognizes that much of his inspiration was drawn from a visit to Victoria and Albert's Asian Collections in 1908.[31]

Although Peltzer does not develop this point, the anecdote about the Victoria and Albert Museum is significant; it shows that as a British institution popular with women this museum had a direct impact on contemporary fashion and ideals of glamour. Moreover, fashion illustration still played an important role in maintaining notions of femininity that could transcend the boundaries of what was real and, according to Cheryl Buckley and Hilary Fawcett, be 'connected in important ways with the modernity of contemporary life'.[32] These fantastical fashion illustrations featured prominently in influential magazines, such as *Vogue* and *Harper's Bazaar* throughout the 1910s and 1920s, and were the ideal medium through which to explore the boundaries between reality and ancient Near Eastern aesthetics. The class-specific 'high femininity' presented by the magazines allowed for the decadence associated with the orient, even during the war.[33] As Buckley and Fawcett point out, the 'otherness' of these illustrations as exotic and oriental designs (in their example, harem trousers) brings an element of sexuality to an otherwise 'vulnerable' figure, reminiscent of cinematic images.[34]

The connection with cinema runs deep, particularly during the 1920s and 1930s. The Hollywood aesthetic of that era took considerable inspiration from the decadence of ancient Egypt; J. Gordon Edwards's 1917 film *Cleopatra* stunned British audiences with Theda Bara costumed in a variety of exotic and ever-more revealing ensembles. Adam Geczy notes that this representation is the first time Cleopatra is shown as an entirely Eastern symbol of sexuality, instead of the more historically accurate portrayals seen in previous centuries which were classically styled but with oriental elements.[35] Both this *Cleopatra* and Cecil B. DeMille's 1934 *Cleopatra*, starring Claudette Colbert (Fig. 11.3), were both heavily inspired by archaeological discoveries and had a massive impact on women's concepts of beauty.

Following these, and a host of other Egyptian- and ancient Near Eastern-inspired films, ancient women became almost synonymous with beauty and glamour.[36] Beauty products, ancient Near Eastern-inspired perfumes and advice reflecting on ancient femininity, were ubiquitous. For instance, Guerlain's perfume Shalimar, inspired by the woman for whom the Taj Mahal was built, was a number-one seller of the 1920s and 1930s.[37] Contemporaries also attributed the iconic bob haircut to cinematic

Figure 11.3 Claudette Colbert in *Cleopatra*, directed by: Cecil B. DeMille, USA 1934, Mary Evans/SZ Photo/Scherl.

representations of Cleopatra which, as previously mentioned, were not historically accurate but based on the imitations of pharaonic masks discovered during the late nineteenth and early twentieth centuries, such as the mummy mask of the high-profile Egyptian woman Satdjehuty.[38] Although many variations on the bob style emerged, the 'Cleopatra bob', as it was called, clearly has the same length and fringe style as the masks, proving that this early twentieth-century version of Cleopatra, which has influenced ideals of femininity and sexuality ever since, was created directly from the archaeological discoveries that were so popular at the time.

The influence of Hollywood did not end with actresses and costumes: films and cinema spaces also went on to influence ordinary British women in a multitude of ways.[39] Around 75 per cent of cinema audiences were female, so the cinematic experience was geared towards women, not just the way in which movie stars represented the ideal of beauty.[40] Jacky Stacey contends that 'the glamorous interiors of British cinemas … provided the cultural space for the consumption of Hollywood's glamorous femininity'.[41] These exteriors and interiors were heavily influenced by opulent 'otherness' and exoticism, most notably ancient Egyptian or North African motifs.[42]

Ancient Egypt in the Modern Imagination

Domestic opulence

Stacey picks up on the role of woman as responsible for the domestic space, along with her relatively new role as the chief consumer of the household, particularly among the middle classes, contending that the visual spectacle of the cinema space was enjoyed in a gendered way.[43] To replicate this style, Egyptian-style furniture became popular among the largely female domestic consumer market. For example, the 'Thebes' range of stools and chairs became a top seller for Liberty's for over thirty years.[44] Other popular furniture pieces, particularly during the 1920s, were replicas of actual ancient Egyptian and Near Eastern furniture found or displayed in museums during the period (see Fig. 11.4).[45]

If we consider recent scholarship regarding domestic interiors' effect on how middle-class British women performed their identities in the late nineteenth and early twentieth centuries, the fact that these ancient styles were so popular indicates that the ancient world played a huge part in identity formation and domestic femininity.[46] An article from 1923 states, 'no up-to-date Englishwoman's writing table is complete to-day without a copy of a little Egyptian god as a paper-weight', further solidifying the notion that in

Figure 11.4 British New Kingdom type low chair, 1920s, from the Egyptian Revival Sale, Bonhams, 23 January 2008, Lot 8.

order to be a modern woman, one had to look to the past.[47] Furthermore, as Judy Giles has argued, the early twentieth century saw the professionalization of the housewife and housework, which was also related to archaeological themes in periodicals, with advice given to women that included how to look after one's glassware like the Egyptians and Phoenicians.[48]

These correlations between fashion, cinema and the reception of the ancient world were part of a wider boom in women's consumerism during the early twentieth century. As Ruth Iskin has argued, shopping, particularly shopping in department stores, was a key factor in women's emergence from the private into the public sphere. The store environment allowed women to feel comfortable in a domestic-type interior within a public space.[49] Unsurprisingly, the ancient influence was not restricted to cinema interiors but also became a feature of department stores such as Selfridge's. On a smaller scale, an even more direct connection between archaeology and the influence of department stores on women and their tastes exists. In 1925, John Spedan Lewis hired Miss F. M. G. Lorimer, an Indian archaeology specialist with no experience in retail, as a buyer of Oriental artefacts at Peter Jones (now known as John Lewis).[50] Her experience in archaeology, including nine years' employment at the British Museum, influenced trends at the store heavily, as well as, presumably, those of other London department stores. The 'fascinating white silks' she introduced in 1926, for example, became extremely fashionable.[51]

Egyptian and ancient Near Eastern motifs dominated advertising during this period. Kathy Peiss has noted that 'advertisers created narratives about beauty culture throughout the ages, bypassing Graeco-Roman tradition in favour of Egypt and Persia', highlighting the fact that these ancient cultures were seen as the epitome of femininity.[52] This is not to say that advertising was the sole reason women associated themselves with the ancient Near East, however, they had been creating similar narratives related to femininity, and feminism, since the late nineteenth century. Yet the ubiquity of ready-to-wear clothing provided easier and cheaper access to fashion items for those below the upper and upper-middle classes. The rising interest in archaeology and the ancient world came at just the right time for its influence to spread to mass consumerism, allowing women to have a piece of luxury at a lower price, whether it be clothing, jewellery or home décor.

Jewellery

The growing interest in archaeology also coincided with cheaper jewellery production methods, thereby broadening the avenue through which women could experiment with archaeologically themed pieces. Curl notes that the 1920s allowed 'aspiring sisters' to follow the trends of their more privileged counterparts with 'less perfect jewellery'; although he does not go into detail, one can assume that he means the mass-produced jewellery that was newly available during the early twentieth century.[53]

A 1926 *Vogue* article entitled 'Jewels of the Ancients' explains that because of the predilection for ancient styles, it no longer mattered whether jewellery was made of precious or imitation materials if it was full of 'colour and adornment, charm and individuality'.⁵⁴ The invention of Bakelite in 1907 allowed for a greater number of women to purchase jewellery and home accessories that looked opulent at low prices. Bakelite became a key material for Egyptian revival pieces as it was the perfect durable material for emulating flashy oriental styles, particularly due to the variety of bright colours in which it could be made (see Fig. 11.5). In addition, its smooth finish was ideal for recreating the highly stylized strong lines and geometric motifs found in both ancient Egyptian and Near Eastern art and architecture, as well as in modernist design: Art Deco design and architecture too were influenced by their ancient counterparts.⁵⁵ Other inexpensive materials used included celluloid (invented in 1856) and chrome plating (first used during the 1920s), while items in pressed glass (particularly from Czechoslovakia) and silver provided an economic middle ground.

Figure 11.5 English Art Deco 'Egyptianesque' Bakelite and Celluloid necklaces, 1930s. From The Egyptian Revival Sale, Bonhams, 23 January 2008, Lot 135.

Although Egyptian revival jewellery had been fashionable in preceding decades, the expense of these items had made them unattainable for most women. Rather than emulating luxury, they were often made from truly precious materials themselves, Cartier's range being the most notable.[56] Judy Rudoe classifies these items into two types: those prompted by the opening of the Suez Canal in 1869 and the interest in the discoveries that followed, as well as revival of interest in earlier discoveries, and those appearing after the internationally renowned Franco-Egyptian exhibition at the Louvre in 1911.[57]

To distinguish their creations from the new influx of Egyptian-themed jewellery that emerged after the discovery of Tutankhamun's tomb, Cartier began producing an even more expensive and unique range of pieces during the mid-1920s that incorporated fragments of actual Egyptian antiquities (see Fig. 11.6). The *Illustrated London News* article on these pieces states: the 'women interested in Egyptology, who desire to be in the Tutankhamen fashion, can now wear real ancient gems in modern settings as personal ornaments', indicating that women's interest in Egyptology was not niche, but was a common enough interest for it to be mentioned without need for explanation. This strongly suggests that interest in archaeology was a widespread trend among women.[58] Women's desire to wear genuine ancient fragments indicates their reverence for archaeology or at least an interest in learning about it, rather than blindly following trends that simply included unrealistic ancient-style motifs. Furthermore, the ownership of antiquities by women relates to a wider trend of women being collectors, a holdover from the Victorian period.

Women had a long history of collecting and curating practices, which peaked during the Victorian period, as a way of taking ownership of something when they had no property rights of their own.[59] Even for those who could not afford such precious pieces, there still appears to have been a keen interest in exploring femininity through replicating genuine ancient jewellery and learning about how ancient women expressed their own femininity. For example, the *Vogue* article referred to above depicts a variety of 'feminine accessories ... to give one an idea of the amazing similarity between women's fads today and long ago'.[60] The fact that ancient and modern femininity are compared so directly further highlights the idea that during the early twentieth century, women were keen to align themselves with, or to emulate, their ancient counterparts.

Femininity and feminism

It was not only the femininity of exotic ancient women that the 1920s woman would have wanted to emulate; their rights and power would have also seemed attractive. While women's rights advocates often had their femininity stripped from them by their critics – particularly through depictions of the 'mannish' New Woman and comparisons to Amazons – they were able to consolidate feminism and femininity through ancient Egyptian and Near Eastern women who were considered both beautiful and powerful.

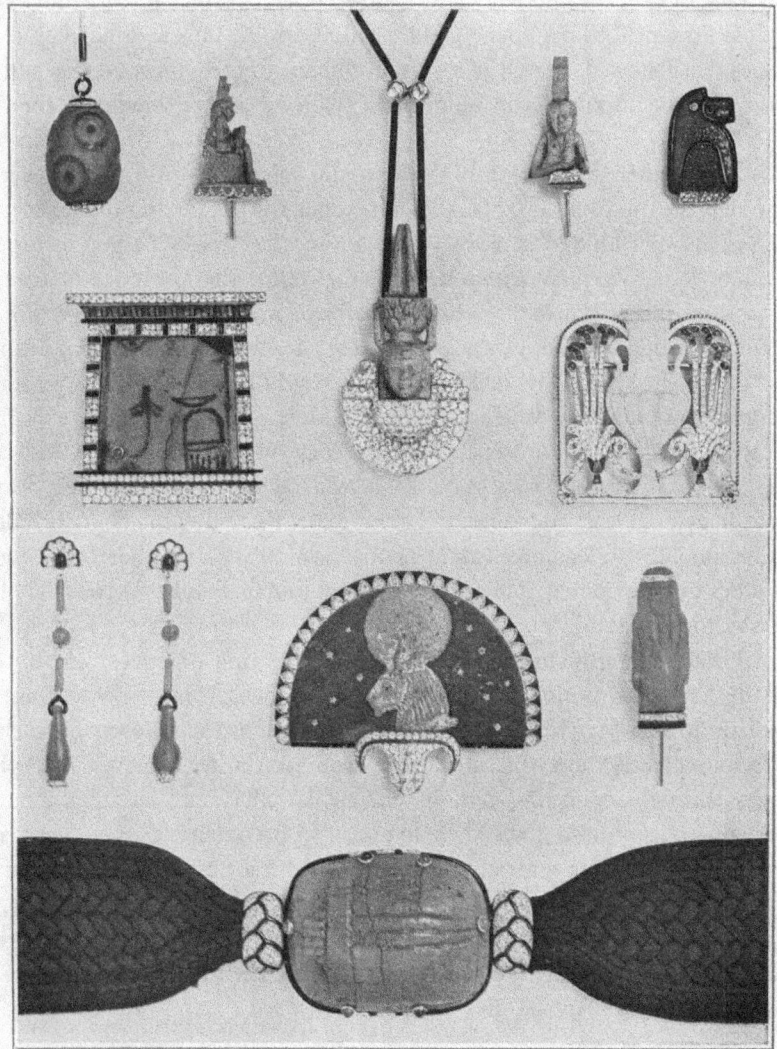

Figure 11.6 Egyptian trinkets from 1,500 to 3,000 years old adapted as modern jewellery, © Illustrated London News Ltd/Mary Evans.

The newly found interest in ancient women as a justification for women's rights was a direct result of new information gleaned from the very same archaeological discoveries that influenced not only design but also women's modern concepts of femininity. The discoveries of greatest interest to suffragists were those relating to Hatshepsut, whose mortuary temple was first excavated during the 1890s and was a continuing theme in early twentieth-century Egyptology, and the Code of Hammurabi, discovered in 1901, an ancient Babylonian law code of great significance that indicates a certain amount of equality and power for women. References to these artefacts and ancient women of standing pervade print media during the early twentieth century, both in specialist feminist or suffrage publications and in mainstream newspapers. The examples are too numerous to list, but the argument is always the same: if these ancient women had rights, then so too should the modern woman.[61]

As Melman argues, there was a growing interest in women's history from the mid-nineteenth century onwards, which coincided with the rise of first-wave feminism.[62] However, rather than merely writing women into history, these articles reinterpret the past from an explicitly feminist viewpoint, much like feminist history of the later twentieth century.[63] The fact that much of the knowledge gained was only recently discovered meant that it could be much more easily accommodated within a feminist agenda. Hatshepsut, a highly successful ruler and one of only a handful of true female pharaohs, was only rediscovered during the late nineteenth century because her name had been erased from the records by her successors. During a time when women had first systematically begun to construct feminist history, discoveries of such importance to women's history were perfectly suited to a feminist agenda. The first wave of feminism coincided with the development of archaeology as a discipline, and there were numerous links between the two.

One salient feature of these feminist ancient histories was the correlation between feminism and femininity. Barbara Caine contends that '[Victorian feminists] had sought particularly an end to the idea that womanliness or femininity necessarily involved physical and moral weakness, cowardice, and incompetence'; these ideals became more deep-rooted during the twentieth century, at the same time that knowledge of figures such as Hatshepsut was emerging from the past.[64] When the Egypt Exploration Fund (the Egypt Exploration Society, since 1919) excavated Hatshepsut's mortuary temple during the 1890s and following the renewal of the excavations in 1911 (and subsequent reconstruction), many women were drawn to Hatshepsut as a representation of their political goals given her power during her reign from c. 1478 to 1458 BC. Her beauty was equally praised.[65] Lectures about Hatshepsut were extremely popular among women, and some even treated her temple as a site of suffragette pilgrimage.

One early twentieth-century article contends that the 'New Woman' was not new at all, positing Hatshepsut herself as the original 'New Woman' who 'knew how to combine beauty and politics'.[66] In fact, a whole onslaught of early twentieth-century articles about ancient Egyptian and Near Eastern women in the popular press took the view that such women were on equal or almost equal terms with men. These articles regularly refer to beauty and femininity as going hand in hand with women's power, even down to describing their political successes in one paragraph and their beauty regimens in the next.[67] One could be both beautiful and politically active; perhaps they even infer that femininity and power were inextricably linked. In either case, the connection these articles make between feminine power and beauty in the past is perpetuated into the twentieth-century present by these very same articles. Michelle Tusan suggests that women were trying to actively promote the 'womanliness' of the 'New Woman', one component of which was motherhood.[68] Again, some articles reinforce ideas regarding femininity, motherhood and feminism in the past by indicating the high status enjoyed by mothers.[69] However, most interesting of all is that such articles repeatedly refer specifically to contemporary archaeological finds. Thus, not only were archaeology, feminism and femininity very much related during the early twentieth century, but in addition, due to the ubiquity of those themes, most well-read women would have been familiar with the connection.

Above all, the discovery of two breathtaking busts of Nefertiti in 1913 and 1933 sparked the largest cult following in terms of femininity and feminism. During the 1920s and 1930s, Nefertiti almost replaced Cleopatra as the symbol of Eastern beauty and power, but with one key difference: Nefertiti was a role model of intellectual value while Cleopatra remained a symbol of decadence and excessive sexuality. Lauded as both 'one of the most beautiful women in history' and as a 'feminist of 1375 BC', Nefertiti was completely novel to a modern audience and came to represent the ideal woman.[70]

A German team had discovered and retained the earlier polychrome bust, so no photographs of it were published in the British press until 1923, when they described the bust as having 'a haunting attraction surpassing the portraits of Cleopatra'.[71] In the years following, the British Museum and the Ashmolean Museum exhibited replicas of the bust, and Nefertiti's popularity grew, reaching a peak during the 1930s after a second quartzite bust of Nefertiti was found by British archaeologists on an Egypt Exploration Society excavation in 1933.[72]

Numerous periodicals featured fashion and beauty advice relating to Nefertiti, such as instructions on how to imitate her makeup, as well as portraying her as a feminist icon.[73] Interestingly, one of the justifications for her 'feminist' status was that archaeologists had deduced her high rank from the fact that she had the 'unusual honour' of being 'drawn to the same size and scale as the king [her husband Akhenaten]', again showing a direct connection between archaeology and women's culture.[74] By 1939, there was even a 'Nefertiti Club' formed for 'women suffering from one-eye defects' that encouraged them to embrace their beauty. The club emerged from theories positing that Nefertiti was blind in one eye, as the left eye on the polychrome bust lacks both pupil and iris.[75]

In the same year, an article in *Vogue* described the 'strange' new type of beauty that had become the ideal throughout the decade, 'very notably in Paris and London': an angular, unearthly and exotic enchantress with high cheek bones, often compared to Nefertiti.[76] Regarding the bust, the article states that 'no statue has, during the past twenty years, created so great a *furore*, so very many pictures and replicas, as that amazing polychrome head of Nefertiti', proving that women who were interested in performing femininity through the consumption of women's fashion and its associated publications were assumed to have been familiar with the queen.[77] Furthermore, the article describes Nefertiti's features as 'of the exotic order' and notes that depictions of Nefertiti are completely unlike the traditional forms of portraiture associated with ancient Egypt, indicating that the new style was partly responsible for the new ideals.[78] This style was, in fact, unique to the Amarna period, during which Nefertiti and Akhenaten reigned, and was characterized by elongated and particularly feminine features.[79] The style had only become widely known publicly during this period because of the bust, along with the Egyptian Exploration Society excavations from 1921 to 1936, making a strong case for the direct influence of archaeology on concepts of beauty and femininity.

Conclusion

During the early twentieth century, women actively engaged with ancient Egyptian and Near Eastern archaeology, using it to develop their sense of femininity and concepts of feminism. Closely related to women's relationships with colonialism and orientalism, the ancient world provided a myriad of influences for women's femininity, from innovations in fashion to traditions in domestic interiors. Archaeology and the ancient world featured heavily in theatre and cinema, both of which are of socio-historical importance for women. These media essentially acted as a means by which archaeological themes filtered into women's everyday lives and helped to reinforce ideals of ancient beauty and femininity. Furthermore, the rise in women's consumerism and the invention of new materials and techniques of mass production meant that archaeologically themed products and popular entertainments were increasingly accessible. With women being the prime target audience, their desire to emulate female figures of the ancient world was exploited. However, it was not just in superficial pursuits that women exhibited an interest in archaeology: powerful women who had been discovered through archaeological excavations during the late nineteenth and early twentieth centuries became symbols of the growing suffrage and women's rights movements. British women drew on ancient historical motifs to build on a sense of aesthetic, intellectual and social heritage, both in terms of how they performed gender and fought for greater rights and liberation.

CHAPTER 12
'THE USE OF OLD OBJECTS': ANCIENT EGYPT AND ENGLISH WRITERS AROUND 1920[1]
R. B. Parkinson

O fantastic and extraordinary land,
where art thou, where art thou?
E. M. Forster, The Egyptian Mail, 13 January 1918[2]

Pharaonic Egypt was notably influential for modernist visual art, as with Jacob Epstein (1880–1959) and Paul Nash (1889–1946),[3] but is not so evident in the contemporaneous modernist literary tradition. Here I suggest some issues of politics, literary style and genre that might help contextualize this absence through a reading of E. M. Forster's essay 'For the Museum's Sake'.[4] Gender and sexuality are also relevant: ancient Egypt was often regarded in nineteenth- and twentieth-century Europe as an over-sensuous culture, a troubling 'realm of unrestrained voluptuous excess', and responses reveal conflicting attitudes towards Egyptian masculinity, ranging from the oriental effeminate to the Arab stud.[5] A persistent sense of Egyptological unease about sexuality and gender can be traced back to early travellers. For example, James Burton (1788–1862) was intrigued to measure an intact ancient penis, his curiosity perhaps having been inspired by the sight of ancient ithyphallic deities: 'Some mummies or bodies of poorer orders only salted. I saw one of which penis remained of original length probably for it could not well be longer. It was full 6½ long in a depondant [*sic*, i.e. dependent, flaccid?] state, & had lost only its grossezza for its diam^r. flattened remained about 1½ inch.'[6] This essay outlines the context for English authors who chose to write about ancient Egypt around the year 1920, and the associations between ancient Egypt, decadence and sexuality that existed in the preceding decades. I focus on the work of E. M. Forster (1879–1970) who engaged with Egypt more deeply than many modernists. His responses to the country shunned 'popular' notions of pharaonic culture and were shaped not only by his anti-imperialist attitudes, but also by his sexuality and personal relationships.

Exoticism and decadence

One late nineteenth-century instance of orientalist attitudes to ancient Egypt is Oscar Wilde's *The Sphinx* (1894), published with illustrations by Charles Ricketts (1866–1931).[7] While Ricketts collected Egyptian art and also wrote perceptively about it,[8] the printed illustrations are not exclusively Egyptian (though a second series of illustrations commissioned in 1923 contain more extensively Egyptian motifs and details).[9] Both poem and illustrations create a generalized oriental exoticism, by merging Egyptian and un-Egyptian details. Unmanly sensuality is suggested through the sphinx, which is significantly female, rather than a positive male embodiment of royal might as in ancient Egyptian iconography.[10] This sphinx is aligned with sexual deviancy at odds with Christian norms in a way that contrasts with more culturally acceptable classical forms of homoeroticism:

> Get hence, you loathsome mystery! Hideous animal, get hence!
> You wake in me each bestial sense, you make me what I would not be.
> You make my creed a barren sham, you wake foul dreams of sensual life,
> And Atys with his blood-stained knife were better than the thing I am.[11]

Similar perceptions of ancient Egypt are embodied in popular narratives.[12] *She: A History of Adventure* by H. Rider Haggard (1856–1925) was serialized in *The Graphic* magazine in 1886–7.[13] The immortal 'She' is oriental, politically dangerous and seductive, the servant and embodiment of the Egyptian goddess Isis. Haggard's novels drew on his experiences as an administrator in Africa, and from a postcolonial perspective they include some rather troubling images and phrases, such as one illustration to *She* by Charles Kerr (1858–1907) where the blond hero battles a mass of Africans, captioned 'Up above them towered his beautiful pale face.'[14] Haggard also collected antiquities, and after the first magazine publication of *She*, he had the inscribed 'sherd of Amenartas', which is central to the novel's plot, manufactured by Agnes Barber, and drawings of it featured as the frontispiece in the book.[15] This artefact, which is now in the Norwich Castle Museum (Fig. 12.1),[16] is a striking fusion of colonialism, artefact, the occult and popular literature.[17] Popular literature provided an interpretative framework which even supposedly objective academic approaches and translations could not easily avoid. It is unsurprising that the Australian writer Guy Boothby (1867–1905) reshaped the Ancient Egyptian poem *The Tale of Sinuhe* into a sensationalist tale of reincarnation, 'A Professor of Egyptology' (1904),[18] and one reviewer in 1895 of Flinders Petrie's *Egyptian Tales: Translated from the Papyri* even considered that 'The Adventures of Sanehat [Sinuhe]' was 'the best tale in the collection … and, indeed, the story reminds the reader somewhat of Mr. Rider Haggard's ingenious African romances'.[19] Readers' responses to such fictional evocations of ancient Egypt, however, were varied. A review of his Second Intermediate Period romance *Queen of the Dawn: A Love Tale of Old Egypt* (1925)[20] is revealing of contemporaneous attitudes to such 'yarns':

> A love tale of old Egypt and its Shepherd King. The daughter of the real king is compelled to run away from the palace owing to the tyranny of the People of the Dawn. … There is vitality in this last yarn of ancient Egypt and of Babylon: also a plot of spirit, easy to follow. There are no eternal disquisitions, such as spoiled some few of the last books and made them heavy; nor is the heroine supernatural in any way; indeed, she is a modern flapper unmistakably, for all her queendom

'The Use of Old Objects'

Figure 12.1 H. Rider Haggard's 'Sherd of Amenartas' (front; Norwich Castle Museum 1917.68.7.1). © Norfolk Museums Service.

and her destiny. There is a supernatural element, but it does not overshadow all the story, which is of human people, acting humanly, and entirely easy and entertaining reading.[21]

From a later generation of writers, Sax Rohmer (1883–1959) is best known for his novels of Dr Fu-Manchu, an evil oriental enemy of the British Empire.[22] His *Brood of the Witch-Queen* of 1918 suggests how highly gendered and heteronormative such Egyptian tropes were.[23] In this 'standard pulp fare' tale of Oxford Egyptological student life,[24] the hero is the masculine Robert Cairn, 'a tall, thin Scotsman, clean-shaven, square jawed, and with the crisp light hair and grey eyes which often bespeak unusual virility'.[25] The villain is Antony Ferrara, the reborn child of Egypt's ancient Witch-Queen, who is first introduced as the hero and his friend talk:

'What is the matter with Ferrara?'.
'Well,' replied Cairn, 'he's queer'.[26]

Ferrara is a well-attested orientalist stereotype: 'the almond-shaped eyes, black as night, gleamed strangely beneath the low, smooth brow. The lank black hair appeared lustreless by comparison. His lips were very red. In his whole appearance there was something repellently effeminate';[27] 'there was something revoltingly effeminate; a sort of cat-like grace which had been noticeable in a woman, but which in a man was unnatural, and for some obscure reason, sinister'.[28] The contrast between modern manhood and the ancient east is strongly binary: 'No more singular anomaly could well be pictured than that afforded by the lean, neatly-groomed Scotsman, with his fresh, clean-shaven face and typically British air, in this setting of Eastern voluptuousness.'[29] The novel draws on Ancient Egyptian literary and funerary texts: the *Book of Thoth* is taken from the ancient Demotic magical tale of *Setne Khamwas and Naneferkaptah (Setne I)*,[30] and the priest Hortotef is based on Prince Hordjedef who features in *The Tale of Kheops' Court* and the *Book of the Dead*.[31] Despite such historical details, the novel is full of sinister orientalism: lotuses that sap the virgin heroine's life as they flower; human sacrifice inside a secret chamber in the Maidum pyramid, and even an elemental Thing (consistently capitalized). The modern masculine hero destroys both the occult book and the queer Ferrara, ensuring (as in *She*) that the sensuous dangers of the ancient East are rendered, in the book's final word, 'extinct'.[32] The choice of word affirms the triumphant incompatibility of the modern and ancient cultures.

The occult permeated the reception of ancient Egypt to the extent that a British Museum stela with a relatively conventional solar hymn could be rewritten as a vision of incestuous occult lust. The commemorative stela EA 826 was erected by twin officials Hor and Suty,[33] but these men were presented as also being lovers in 'The Twins' (1910), by the occultist Aleister Crowley (1875–1947). The poem opens with an allusion to the destruction of Sodom before turning to the text on the stela:

Look! In the polished granite,

Black as thy cartouche is with sins,

I read the searing sentence

That blasts the eyes that scan it:

'HOOR AND SET [Hor and Suty] BE TWINS.' …

Wherefore I solemnly affirm

This twofold Oneness at the term.

Asar on Asi [Osiris and Isis] did beget

Horus twin brother unto Set.

Now Set and Horus kiss, to call

The Soul of the Unnatural

Forth from the dusk; then nature slain

Lets the Beyond be born again.[34]

'The Use of Old Objects'

Crowley was prominent in the Hermetic Order of the Golden Dawn, an occult organization which was well established in Britain by the 1890s, although it fragmented at the turn of the century. The Order had links to professional Egyptology, and the Oxford Professor Battiscombe Gunn (1883–1950) was involved, acting as a consultant for Crowley in his youth.[35] Gunn had turned his back on the occult by the 1930s when he was elected to the chair, and he was cursed by an ancient princess for having doubted in 1937 the accuracy of her grammar. A lecture by 'Dr. F. H. Wood (Blackpool)' at the Oxford Psychic Centre on 13 April 1944 discussed Ancient Egyptian utterances by 'Telika-Ventiu (the Lady Nona)', spoken through a young medium from Blackpool named Rosemary. On a flyer all her utterances were translated, except one:

> 1217–1222 arooma-arooma di Gunn oo-e-ga! Asa! asa fon toot a(r) feren deen istia Gunn!
>
> N.B. 1217 – 1222 contain a forecast relating to our Oxford critic, Professor Gunn. Out of consideration for him, the translation must be withheld until it has been fulfilled.[36]

As Steve Vinson and Janet Gunn have remarked, 'in the late Victorian and Edwardian periods, the various scholarly disciplines that had emerged to study the past, and the systematic pursuit of occult knowledge, were flip sides of one coin'; Battiscombe Gunn's personal progress parallels a general movement towards greater scientificity, as the academic subject in part tried to differentiate itself from popular culture, as 'a project of demystification'.[37]

Egypt and Bloomsbury

The ancient past's possibilities of an alternative reality in terms of knowledge, sexuality and spirituality were not embraced by modernist writers, and there are comparatively few direct echoes of ancient Egypt in the secular Bloomsbury circle.[38] The motif representing a life's achievements in Virginia Woolf's *Jacob's Room* (1922) is characteristically a vision of the Athenian acropolis.[39] One allusion to Egypt in her *To the Lighthouse* (1927) is significantly covert and inexplicit. Lily Briscoe imagines:

> how in the chambers of the mind and heart of the woman ... were stood, like treasures in the tombs of kings, tablets bearing sacred inscriptions, which if one could spell them out, would teach one everything, but they would never be offered openly, never made public.[40]

This discreetly alludes to the supposed curse of Tutankhamun: the death of Lord Carnarvon in April 1923 was claimed to be the fulfilment of a curse written on 'an ordinary clay tablet' over the entrance to the tomb; the tablet was supposedly removed by Howard Carter who denied its existence in order not to hinder the excavation schedule.⁴¹ The story was apparently current when Woolf was writing: already in 1923, Arthur Weigall had written 'the story has been spread that there was a specific curse written upon a wall of the royal sepulchre',⁴² and by 1930, the existence of the tablet with the curse was so well established that:

> Dr. H. R. H. Hall, keeper of the Egyptian and Assyrian antiquities at the [British] museum, authorised 'The Daily Telegraph' to publish the following statement:
> ... As to the so-called inscription, 'Death shall come on swift wings to him that toucheth the tomb of a Pharaoh' no such inscription on the Royal or other tombs is known to me or to any Egyptologists.⁴³

The subsequent popularity of Egypt is perhaps alluded to in Woolf's *The Waves* (1931), where the insecure Australian Louis relates that 'as a boy I dreamt of the Nile'. In his speeches Egypt is presented un-mystically as an image of 'the long, long history that began in Egypt, in the time of the Pharaohs, when women carried red pitchers to the Nile'.⁴⁴ While Woolf avoided any mentions of esoteric Egypt, Egyptian occultism was referred to in T. S. Eliot's *Waste Land* (1922), and this allusion is revealingly satiric and indirect:

> Madame Sosostris, famous clairvoyante,
> Had a bad cold, nevertheless
> Is known to be the wisest woman in Europe.⁴⁵

Woolf's and Eliot's restraint contrasts with the tendency to melodramatic mysticism in the works of their popular contemporaries. The sheer popularity of ancient Egypt in fantastic fiction and the occult may have been a factor in the avoidance of that culture among many self-consciously literary stylists.⁴⁶

E. M. Forster (1879–1970) wrote extensively about Egypt, but largely about Hellenistic Egypt and the Graeco-Roman Alexandria of the ancient poets and the modern Constantine Cavafy (1863–1933),⁴⁷ culminating in *Alexandria, A History and A Guide* (1922) and associated essays including *Pharos and Pharillon* (1923).⁴⁸ Forster worked as a Red Cross volunteer in Alexandria during First World War (November 1915–January 1919), and on 29 December 1915, he wrote that Egypt was 'flat, unromantic, unmysterious, and godless – the soil is mud, the inhabitants are of mud moving, and exasperating in the extreme'.⁴⁹ His initial unempathetic response echoes the famous opening paragraph of *A Passage to India* – 'the very wood seems made of mud, the inhabitants of mud moving'.⁵⁰ In 1917, however, Forster fell in love with a young Egyptian man, Mohammed el-Adl, who worked as a tram conductor in Alexandria.⁵¹ This modified his reactions to the country, and in one article on 'photographic Egypt' he expressed his rejection of the romance of Egypt as 'a sumptuous and exotic country' – about which he stated 'it is doubtful whether such an Egypt ever existed' – in favour of the 'the little muddles and messes of the modern street'; in another article he referred to 'the Egypt of the Pharaohs which still moves tourists and *popular novelists*, but which means nothing to the resident' (my italics).⁵² Forster's experiences in Egypt shaped *A Passage to India*, and famously, he marked the fact that he had completed it with his dead Egyptian lover's pencil.⁵³ Egypt is, however, only explicit in the novel in its references to the Suez Canal through which Adela Quested and Fielding return to the Mediterranean, and where Forster met Mohamed as he travelled to and from India.⁵⁴ Fielding has a 'charming' impression of the country,⁵⁵ and Forster also used 'charming' of Egypt in his 1927 Cambridge lectures on the English novel, in which Henry James's characters are compared to 'the exquisite deformities who haunted Egyptian art in the time of Akhnaton – huge heads and tiny legs, but nevertheless charming. In the following reign they disappear'.⁵⁶ Like several of Henry James's characters, Akhenaten was a figure of some sexual ambiguity;⁵⁷ this mention suggests that Forster was aware of the sexual ambivalence of Pharaonic as well as Hellenistic Egypt, which makes his avoidance of it in his writings all the more notable, given his love for Mohammed el-Adl.

Forster and Budge

On 7 May 1920, Forster published an essay about Egyptian artefacts entitled 'The Objects' in *The Athenaeum*.⁵⁸ This review of the memoirs of the newly knighted Wallis Budge (1857–1934) was later republished as 'For the Museum's Sake' in *Abinger Harvest* (1936).⁵⁹ Budge expanded and curated the Egyptian and Assyrian collections of the British Museum, and his multitudinous guides and books on religious and funerary texts were influential for Egypt's public reception (Fig. 12.2). They were much used by fiction writers and occultists: he is the dedicatee of E. Nesbit's *The Story of the Amulet* (1906), in which an artefact acts as a gateway to ancient worlds,⁶⁰ and also of Haggard's *Morning Star* (1910).⁶¹ Present-day academics, however, regard, Budge as a controversial figure, largely due to the haste and inaccuracies of his scholarship, which disregarded contemporaneous advances in the subject, along with his discredited methods of collecting.⁶²

Forster's review opens with an overview of the history of Egyptian collecting, from the objects' source communities to their modern locations: 'The objects lay quiet for thousands of years, many of them in tombs where love or superstition had placed them.'⁶³ In Forster's account, the Renaissance's imaginative engagement with the past gives way to the interest of 'a new purchaser ... the modern European nation'.⁶⁴ Here Forsterian irony kicks in: ' "national possessions" they were now called, and it was important that they should outnumber the objects possessed by other nations, and should be genuine old objects, and not imitations, which looked the same, but were said to be discreditable'.⁶⁵ This passage recalls the scene in his 1914 novel *Maurice*, where Maurice Hall dismissively describes the contents of the British Museum to his gamekeeper lover as 'old things belonging to the Nation'.⁶⁶

The review centres on the acquisition in 1888 of the Papyrus of Ani (P. BM EA 10470), one of Budge's most spectacular purchases (Fig. 12.3).⁶⁷ The reliability of

Ancient Egypt in the Modern Imagination

The Saturday Review, 24 February, 1923

DRAMATIS PERSONÆ, No. 35

SIR E. A. WALLIS BUDGE

Figure 12.2 Sir Wallis Budge, by 'Quiz' (Powys Evans; 1899–1981), from the *Saturday Review*, 24 February 1923, p. 251.

'The Use of Old Objects'

Figure 12.3 The beginning of the Papyrus of Ani (P. BM EA 10470.1), showing Ani and his wife worshipping the Sungod, with Budge's name above the museum registration number. © The Trustees of the British Museum.

Budge's own account of finding the papyrus 'in a rectangular niche in the north wall of the sarcophagus chamber, among a few hard stone amulets', has been questioned by modern Egyptologists, and there is little evidence that his claims to have entered an intact tomb are plausible.[68] Forster, although unaware of these issues, describes Budge's ostensibly non-fictionalized account as a 'yarn', allying it with the fiction that was so influenced by Budge's publications. Forster's retelling of the episode significantly starts with an evocation of Ani's life, transforming the yarn into the life-story of the artefact.[69] Ani's ancient beliefs are affectionately mocked (as 'superstition'), but without any sense of the occult: the mythological location 'Re-stau' is misspelled 'Restan' in all editions, suggesting that Forster paid no more attention to any occult names than to the name of the Cairo director Eugène Grébaut (1846–1915), which he consistently misspelled as Grébaud.[70]

The museum artefact here is not a magical gateway like Nesbit's amulet, or a revelation like Haggard's sherd, but an expression of an entirely human (and un-occult) history: Forster claims that Ani acquired it because 'his memory was but human; so, buying a strip of papyrus eighty feet long, he had it inscribed with all he would have to say' in the otherworld.[71] Modern communication with the ancient past was not the result of any mystic ability but of humanistic imaginative empathy. This anti-fantastic preference is not unique to him at this period: the 1925 review quoted above distinguished the supernatural from the human aspects of Haggard's novels, and preferred 'human people, acting humanly'.[72] The same humanistic sensibility is found in Forster's essay 'Malconia

207

Shops' of 1903, in which the author's own thematic analysis of the decoration on the fourth century BC Cista Ficorini from Praeneste is dismissed by the shade of its ancient owner Dindia Malconia with the angry comment 'I bought the thing because it was pretty, and stood nicely on the chest of drawers'.[73] From a modern academic perspective, this emphasis on a common humanity underplays cultural difference, but the anachronism of 'the chest of drawers' suggests that this is a self-conscious strategy to produce a shock of recognition in the reader.

Forster criticizes not Ani's religious beliefs, but the colonialist attitudes evident in the acquisition of the papyrus for the British Museum. The papyrus was taken from an Egypt which was itself 'a nation, and had so far advanced as to have a museum at Cairo and a Director, M. Grébaud',[74] who had died a few years earlier in 1915. Budge claimed he had removed the papyrus from the intact tomb, 'and from that moment Ani was dumb. His voice, his "Book of the Dead" was taken and he can no longer reply to questions in the Under World'.[75] Budge removed it with military assistance as 'property of the British Government' to England, 'where he gave it to the British Museum. It may not be on display, but we have it, which is what matters. It would be humiliating to think it was on exhibit in Cairo'.[76] This attitude is very distinct from that of Haggard who, in the view of Roger Luckhurst, 'clearly had no conception of Egyptian ownership or wider cultural rights'.[77] Forster's anti-colonialist stance is more explicitly stated here than in *Alexandria*, which he was working on as he wrote the review.[78] Forster states that Budge

> has written a most delightful book, and yet he leaves an impression of vulgarity at the close. The vulgarity is not personal. It emanates from the system that he so ably serves. The dreariness and snobbery of the Museum business come out strongly beneath this tale of derring-do. ... It is fine if you think the modern nation is, without qualification, fine; but if you have the least doubts of your colossus, a disgust will creep over you and you will wish that the elderly gentlemen [like Budge] were employed more honestly.[79]

The mention of 'colossus' in this context perhaps evokes the tyranny of Shelley's *Ozymandias* (1818), inspired by another artefact in the British Museum.[80]

> After all, what is the use of old objects? They breathe their dead words into too dead an ear. It was different in the Renaissance, which did get some stimulus. It was important that the Laocoon should be found ... [but] our age is industrial, ... its interest in the past is mainly faked.[81]

One can compare Forster's attitude to the Demeter of Cnidos, another nineteenth-century discovery. This statue was a personal icon for him: it features as a symbolic motif in *The Longest Journey* (1907) and is, in many ways, a mythic archetype for his mature female characters who embody an instinctive wisdom that sees beyond gender conventions.[82] The Demeter is also in the collections of the British Museum where – as he noted in another essay – she is 'dusted twice a week', but although she was removed from Cnidos, she 'must know that she has come among people who love her'.[83] Budge's papyrus, in contrast, is simply masculine nationalist plunder and unloved. Although he praises Budge's 'sense of fun and ... of beauty',[84] he notes that there is 'something of the Renaissance desperado about him', like the archaeology heroes of popular 'derring-do' fiction. The review concludes scathingly:

> we part from him with admiration, but without tenderness, and with an increased determination to rob the British Museum. 'The Keeper of the Egyptian Antiquities is understood to be entirely prostrated as a consequence of the daring theft of the celebrated Papyrus of Ani.' Would that one was in a position to write such a sentence and to post it to M. Grébaud for his use in the Under World![85]

No mention is made of returning the papyrus to Egypt or Ani's tomb, but the modern Franco-Egyptian opponents of Budge are implicitly allied with Ani in the underworld. Budge is presented as a male, 'swagger[ing]' 'filibuster' who is determined to acquire 'national possessions'.[86] Despising 'honesty and simplicity',[87] he acts so as to make antiquity the 'property of the British Government'.[88]

Personal responses to Egypt

Forster's dislike of Budge's celebration of his own 'unending triumph' had an additional personal reason, which had to remain unspoken.[89] In the essay he noted that the 'natives' who found the papyrus turned to Budge 'because he paid more than M. Grébaud, although they risked imprisonment and torture'.[90] Significantly, Mohammed el-Adl had himself been imprisoned by the authorities in May 1919, news of this reaching Forster by August.[91] Before this, in March, Forster had already written to the *Manchester Guardian* with a growing sense of personal involvement in Egyptian political affairs, noting that

> we can never replace the fellahin whom we have so needlessly destroyed, but we can perhaps enter into the feelings of the survivors and realize why the present disturbances have occurred.[92]

He continued in 1920 to write the political 'Notes on Egypt' for *The Government of Egypt: Recommendations by a Committee of the International Section of the Labour Research Department*, which are as critical of British attitudes as his review.[93]

At that time, pharaonic culture was featuring in Egyptian national consciousness,[94] but it appears remarkably little in Forster's unpublished accounts of his love-affair or his published work. The 'writing out of El-Adl' is understandable given social attitudes to sexuality at the period,[95] but it is paralleled by a writing out of pharaonic Egypt. One mention, however, is resonant. In the memoir that he wrote after Mohammed's death in 1922, he recounted a trip apparently made in 1918 when he stayed with him in Mansourah:

you called out my name at Bebbit el-Haga station after we had seen that ruined temple about ten miles from it that no one else seems to have seen. It was dark and I hear an Egyptian shouting who had lost his friend: Margan, Margan – you calling me and I felt we belonged to each other, you had made me an Egyptian.[96]

The unvisited temple (Behbeit el-Hagar) was a famous temple of Isis, surely known to Forster from guidebooks, and mentioned as such in Haggard's *Ayesha: The Return of She* (1905).[97] There are several parallels with *A Passage to India*: the incident of calling for an absent friend recalls the motif of Professor Godbole's song, and the homoerotic implications of the word 'friend' are explicit in *Maurice*.[98] The phrase 'you had made me an Egyptian' parallels the first meeting of Aziz and Mrs Moore in a dark and partially ruined mosque when he remarks 'then you are an oriental', and again to Ralph Moore at the emotional climax of Chapter 36.[99] Here, the unvisited ruin features in a highly evocative passage, suggesting that, in different cultural circumstances, pharaonic culture might have featured in Forster's imaginative world as the highly valorized Italian and Indian culture did. However, when Mohammed features (posthumously and discreetly) in Forster's published writings, it is in the dedication to *Pharos and Pharillon* (1923) as the Greek 'Hermes psychopompos',[100] uniting the ancient Hellenistic past of his country with modern humanity. He is not evoked as any *Egyptian* deity, as if this would have contaminated him with the homophobic nationalistic 'vulgarity' of Egyptology; in a letter Forster had described him as 'a person uncontaminated by Nile mud'.[101] To my knowledge, Pharaonic Egypt only re-surfaces in Forster's work in his unpublished short story 'The Obelisk' of 1939, involving a closeted school teacher, a provocatively vulgar sailor and an extremely large obelisk.[102]

In 1920, for Forster, it seems that any possibilities of such cross-cultural empathy with Egypt being expressed in terms of the pharaonic past were negated by English cultural attitudes towards ancient Egypt, like Budge's. Ancient Egypt was, like the museum artefacts that represented it to the public, irrevocably entangled with colonialist politics, occultism, and (in terms of literary genres) heteronormative adventure 'yarns' and 'tales of derring-do'. The queer Forster sided with the Egyptian – with all the sexual ambiguity that could imply – and with the subaltern, but he did this through the Hellenistic past and modern village life, and not through the 'vulgarity' of popular and/or academic Egyptology.

Two years after 'The Objects', the tomb of Tutankhamun was discovered, which increased the popularity of ancient Egypt phenomenally through the 1920s and 1930s.[103] *Brood of the Witch-Queen* was republished in 1923 with a more obviously Egyptian title, *It Came Out of Egypt*, presumably in order to cash in on this phenomenon.[104] In Forster's subsequent discussion of the Amarna Period in *Aspects of the Novel*, there is a no mention of the tomb or its art-works, apart from the telling remark, 'I do not want the art of Akhnaton to extend into the reign of Tutankhamen.'[105] In the following decades popularized treatments of ancient Egypt often became the dominant forms of cultural representation, and this popularization can perhaps be sensed in two buildings in Oregon, from the pre- and post-Tutankhamun eras: the austerely elegant masonic Abbey Hope Mausoleum (1914) was designed by Ellis F. Lawrence, the first Dean of the University of Oregon's School of Architecture and Allied Arts, echoing the Enlightenment vision of

Egypt; in 1929 a pharaonic Balsinger Ford car showroom was built in nearby Klamath Falls in a style more reminiscent of contemporaneous cinema architecture.[106]

Popular literature provided an interpretative frame for the meticulous and highly scientific clearance of the tomb of Tutankhamun, with the invention of the story of the curse (although Haggard denounced this as 'superstition').[107] The front page of the *Sunday Times* (Sydney) read: ' "THE CURSE OF OSIRIS": Superstitious Legend round Lord Carnarvon's Death. MARIE CORELLI'S POISON THEORY. Conan Doyle Puts Suspicion on Tut-ankh-Amen'.[108] As other newspaper articles noted, 'it is only a novelist's fancy';[109] 'there is fine material for a romancer of the type the late Guy Boothby or Sir Rider Haggard in the record of death which has pursued the participants in the opening and exploration of Tut-Ankh-Amen's tomb'.[110] Such narratives have nevertheless provided an academic and aesthetic paradigm that can still remain influential, as seen in the tendency for academics to wear 'Indiana Jones' hats in both media documentaries and faculty webpages.[111] New power-inequalities and concerns with scientificity have since developed in the academic world that can further hinder the empathetic response, so advocated by Forster.[112] Only occasionally has western modernism engaged with ancient Egyptian culture; one example is the minimalist setting of the *Great Hymn to the Sundisk* from c. 1350 BC by Philip Glass in his opera *Akhnaten* (1984), which inspired a highly engaged and engaging performance by Anthony Roth Costanzo in 2016 (Fig. 12.4).[113] In the face of Budge's persistent legacy, such 'human' works are a welcome reminder that these 'old objects' do not have to speak only to ears that are dead. As Forster's essay implies by challenging the reader's own response to Budge's yarns, how such objects are 'used' remains a political, ethical and individual choice.

Figure 12.4 Anthony Roth Costanzo as Akhnaten, at the English National Opera, 2016. © Richard Hubert Smith.

CHAPTER 13
WOMEN SURREALISTS AND EGYPTIAN MYTHOLOGY: SPHINXES, ANIMALS AND MAGIC
Sabina Stent

> I have taken Nadja, from the first day to the last, for a free genius, something like one of those spirits of the air which certain magical practices momentarily permit us to entertain but which we can never overcome. As for her, I know that in every sense of the word, she takes me for a god, she thinks of me as the sun. I also remember ... having appeared black and cold to her, like a man struck by lightning, lying at the feet of the Sphinx.[1]

The East, the orient, magic and myth have always enticed the Surrealists. Over time, in the work of both male and female artists, this attraction has manifested through paintings, photography, fashion and costumes. Ancient Egypt, through various incarnations, is a notable influence on the work of certain women Surrealists, less frequently discussed than their male counterparts.[2] Nevertheless, some work on these figures has laid the groundwork for such consideration. In her essay 'La Feminité triomphante: Surrealism, Leonor Fini, and the Sphinx', for example, Alyce Mahon explores Fini's self-constructed image and alignment with the mythical Egyptian creature. With reference to Claude Lévi-Strauss and canonical Surrealists texts, Mahon notes that 'for the Surrealists, ... [mythology] offered a fantastic discourse with which to champion the irrational'.[3] She continues,

> the myth of the sphinx was especially attractive, providing the perfect metatext for an exploration of forbidden desire, as well as encompassing the fantasy of the femme fatale, the potential of the city for the marvellous encounter, and a means of self-questioning by which logic and riddle can be set against each other.[4]

From Fini's challenge of traditional sphinx imagery via tropes of the divinity which interrogate the patriarchal nature of canonical Surrealism, to the goddesses, deities and mysticism abundant in the works of Leonora Carrington and Remedios Varo, a particular unity exists between Surrealism and the ancient world. For these women, early Egyptian myth and symbolism was rich and potent: magic reinforcing feminine power and agency that contrasted with the more violent, powerless depictions of 'castrated' and dismembered women's bodies as depicted by male artists. Women painted animals, totems and alchemical imagery, recognized the majesty of the natural world as both creator and destroyer, and invoked symbols which do not seem to belong to this world but rather of a bygone era, of an historic land or parallel universe. They reinvent the sphinx, the goddess Isis, and Egyptian queens, and bring them forth to do their bidding through the canvas, realigning both the powerful nature of the past world and the inherently feminist tradition that is woven throughout the culture of classical Egypt.[5]

In this essay I explore the various ways that Egypt and the orient were incorporated into the work of women Surrealists, paying specific attention to animals, goddess imagery, and interpretations of nature and maternity. Using material written by Surrealist scholars, as well as historians and experts on mythology and magic, I unpack how various artists used hermetic tradition, art history, and folklore to subvert masculine assumptions of femininity in their work. The women whom I have chosen as the basis of this study, whether through detailed analysis or with brief reference, all have the same thread running through their art: an interest in forging a connection with the 'other', the exotic, the unexplored, the untarnished, and to align themselves with a higher power.

Although these themes have been touched upon in previous scholarly analysis, I group together a set of artists who are usually treated independently or in different groupings. In doing so, I present my findings in a way which pulls together previous analysis concerning Surrealism, the esoteric and the autonomous – and sometimes erotic – woman, as viewed through an Egyptian lens. This allows for a greater interdisciplinary reading of these works while creating a space for topics under-represented in traditional or canonical 'male' Surrealism. Women artists forged their own space by adapting and creating new narratives of established themes both in and around the movement, which is demonstrated throughout this exploration.

The first section analyses how women artists used Egyptian mythology to fuel their work and enforce personal feminist autonomy. I begin with a brief examination of key Surrealist themes exploring how, through alchemical symbolism, women Surrealists fought against male oppression and the stigmatization of the 'problematic female' to seek both personal and artistic freedom and independent creative license and expression. With reference to Lee Miller's Egyptian photography, produced in a period of her life widely considered to be that of her most evocative and enduring work, we see how the land of the ancient worlds possessed a transformative quality for both art and artist in forging their own art and adventures away from the trappings of male partnership and 'muse' identities.

The next section examines Fini's reinvention of iconic sphinx imagery. Fini's uncensored art channelled the iconography in the sphinx, which, in turn, allowed her to exhibit and 'perform' a part of her psyche. Renowned for her sartorial flamboyance, Fini – in her adoption of the sphinx as her totem and personal spirit animal – both infused new meaning into the myth and provided the base of her own identity: self-governing, sexual and erotic, yet maintaining a guise of non-acquiescence.

The final sections of this essay explore the work of Remedios Varo and Leonora Carrington, two artists who, despite falling prey to Surrealist categorization, display a noted affinity for magic and esotericism. With additional reference to Fini, and using selected artworks, I determine how their interpretations of animal totems (in contrast to the sphinx), goddesses, lunar symbolism and themes of maternity depict the dominance of and respect for female deities and queens. My conclusion emphasizes how these women artists presented ancient Egyptian myth through a lens that was not only Surrealist, but autonomous, determined and unmovable.

A Surrealist mythology

Fantasies, dreams, literature and unconscious imagery based on the irrational 'woman' – or the 'problematic woman' – are so ingrained in patriarchal Surrealist history that it is easy to see why ancient Egypt – a land of myth and alchemical potency – was held in such high esteem by these artists. As Fiona Bradley has noted, in works created by male Surrealists, 'woman is presented as being in closer touch than man with the desired irrationality of the dream'.[6] Therefore, male Surrealists usually appear to be 'searching for the woman, following her as she turns away from the creative "forest" of the marvellous'.[7]

One artist who began to dismantle these enduring depictions of women was Dorothea Tanning, who Paula Lumbard has pronounced 'an archaeologist of the human psyche' who 'carefully removes debris from areas within her unconscious, catalogs the shards of memory, fantasy, and prophecy, and then displays them in paintings that are alarmingly beautiful'.[8] Tanning's 'alarmingly beautiful', and often explicitly erotic, depictions of female sexuality brazenly confronted the depiction of women enforced by male Surrealists. André Breton, the self-styled 'Pope' of the movement who had 'adopted the word surrealism to describe the literary and artistic practice of himself and his "friends"',[9] wrote that the Surrealist woman was 'born out of Freud's ambivalent and dualistic positioning of woman at the center of the creative and the subversive powers of the love instinct in her incompatible roles as mother and the bearer of life, and destroyer of man'.[10] It is retaliation against this idea, and ability to subvert and disarm the seemingly mundane and ordinary, that made the work of women artists in the movement captivating, arresting and provocative, as was their ability to invert traditional stereotypes imposed on them by the group's founding members. In relation to traditional myth, 'Breton turned to the sphinx as a means of reinforcing his knight-muse fantasy, Max Ernst and Salvador Dalí turned to the sphinx as the seductive intermediary between gods and humans, fantasy and the real, with an emphatic Freudian emphasis on the tale.'[11] On numerous occasions Breton incorporated the sphinx into his writings, most famously in his seminal novel *Nadja*, set in an encounter between himself and his eponymous doomed heroine in the Hotel Sphinx in Paris. She is his sphinx: beautiful, forbidden, desired and a flawed femme fatale. She is also his fantasy, his mystical apparition whom he likens to a mythic creature with an unfeasible ability to still him and render him helpless. He is in awe of her, yet when she descends into madness his self-created fallacy is tarnished. She is no longer his exotic, marvellous creature. She has shattered his illusion, and therefore is no longer desirable. This is at odds with the romanticism surrounding men when they were overcome by mental affliction: celebrated, cheered, elevated. The woman, meanwhile, was destroyed, cast out, victimized and all but forgotten.

Breton had already written an ode to the orient four years prior to *Nadja*, 1927's *Discours sur le peu de réalité* (*Introduction to the Discourse of the Dearth of Reality*). Mahon refers to this as 'his orientalist gaze', something that 'reinforces the erotic appeal of the sphinx'.[12] He would rekindle this theme in his 1937 tome, *L'Amour Fou* (*Mad Love*), a novel wherein his description of the desert – his orient – is as erotically charged as a woman's body. He yearns to explore the land as he would the female physique, making notable comparisons between the desert and a young woman's flesh. However, as Mahon states, his evocations 'allow Breton to simultaneously portray the male artist as valiant lover and explorer and the female as perpetually elusive'.[13] Breton's rendition of the male adventurer and the subdued female in need of rescuing are problematic for many reasons, particularly when we note how intrepid, fearless and resourceful the women associated with the movement were during their lives. Weary of their roles as muses, and the victims of misogyny and patriarchal rule, women artists shook up the movement through their actions and art, walking away from stifling situations and refusing to live their lives on anyone's terms but their own.

Leonor Fini is a prime example of a woman artist refusing to relinquish her power. Instead, this self-styled 'Sphinx of Surrealism' inverted the erotic appeal of the sphinx, transforming it from a sexually objectified figure of male desire to one of empowered female sexuality, commenting:

> I wanted to be like the sphinx I saw in the garden of Miramar Castle in Trieste. I wanted to think like it, to be strong and eternal, to be a living sphinx. Later, I felt that the combination of half-animal, half-human was the ideal state. I identified with the hybrid. The sphinx is a living being who dominates men in a calm way and has pity for them. But it can also be dangerous.[14]

Fini's autonomous art was unyielding, and she worked to transform this erotic entity into something that was sensual, alluring and, as in all her work, as deeply attuned to mysticism, magic and femininity as it was to the ethos of Surrealism. Born in Argentina but raised in her mother's home town Trieste since she was eighteen months old, Fini became synonymous with her semi-autobiographical depictions of powerful, autonomous women revelling in a dynamic agency. She did not subscribe to Breton's declaration that 'the problem of woman is the most wonderful and disturbing problem there is in the world',[15] and despised his inherent misogyny. To Fini, no such 'problem' existed. She lived a life of unashamed sexuality evidenced in her art, painting sphinxes that were self-governing, non-acquiescent, seductive and often predatory. To quote Mahon:

> Intrinsic to the surrealists' stance on the sphinx as a poetic representation was a gendered view of desire, of course. Paradoxically, woman was famed as a peculiarly initiatory and healing power on the one hand and as a fatal seductress on the other.[16]

Fini's determinism and strident independence may have inspired male artists, and, on occasion, she may have been an intermittent, reluctant muse, yet she never fell prey to the label as did other women. Raised in an educated, wealthy household by her mother and grandparents, she was encouraged in her artistic pursuits, and never felt the need to rebel in the traditional sense. While Fini's defiance was a response to the depiction of women as passive sexual objects, other female Surrealists had their own methods for rebelling, perfectly encapsulated by Leonora Carrington, the debutante who defied her family to run away with the older Surrealist artist Max Ernst in order to explore a life of creativity and independence. As Carrington maintained, 'I didn't have time to be anyone's muse. … I was too busy rebelling against my family and learning to be an artist.'[17] Lee Miller, meanwhile, the model who became a muse, Man Ray's collaborator and once of the most renowned photographers of the twentieth century, embarked on her second rebellion post-surrealism and prior to her career as a renowned documentary and war photographer: a solo car journey into the Egyptian desert which resulted in some of the most striking photography of her career.

Following her separation from Man Ray, and with the waning of her artistic vocation, Miller married the wealthy Egyptian businessman Aziz Eluoi Bey. They met while she was recovering from pleurisy in St Moritz, but they were two opposing personalities within the same marriage, and she remained indifferent and dismayed by his lifestyle and routine, which largely consisted of orchestrating his large rota of domestic staff or indulging in his favourite sporting pastimes. To escape this unfamiliar lifestyle – and maybe regain a sense of the exciting, vibrant life she once knew – she seized her camera and drove into the Egyptian desert. Their short marriage ended soon before the Second World War when Miller left Eloui Bey for Roland Penrose. Georgiana M. M. Colville has considered this period in Miller's life, and how she 'found an inner freedom in photographing the desert landscape',[18] referring to how 'Carolyn Burke reads "a latent sexual energy" into Miller's Egyptian work at a time when, according to her letters, she longed for her absent lover.'[19] The photographs hint at Dadaism through their abstraction, as she highlights and reflects light to create a series of geometric shapes that imply loneliness, longing and escape.

The unleashing of bound-up sexual anxiety and repressed emotions is continually documented and explored in the work of numerous female artists, but less noted in the work of men. Women's art tends to be read alongside biography and as such it can be difficult, when needed, to separate an artist's personal life from the work itself. Renée Riese Hubert explores this idea in *Magnifying Mirrors: Women, Surrealism, & Partnership* (1994): 'self-portraits and autobiographical writings are genres abundantly practiced by women and in particular by women artists associated with Surrealism, whose female representations strongly deviate from generic conventions'.[20]

The sphinx of Surrealism

This deviation is pertinent when discussing the adoption of the sphinx by Leonor Fini, whose subversion of this creature both bewitches and entices, corresponding with her own sexual prowess. She painted the sphinx many times in various settings, however the underlying thread was that depicting the creature was an act of self-portraiture; this was her animal. By portraying herself as this entity she was aligning herself with all its mythical symbolism; she saw this imposing beast as nurturer and destroyer, a maternal creator with the ability to wreak havoc and destroy life as much as create. As historically Egyptian sphinxes are male and Greek sphinxes female, Fini's alignment to the Egyptian model allowed her to rework disparate mythologies and recreate her own interpretation of the model as representative of self-governed, sexually dominant femininity, and charged with many more totemic associations in the process.

The historical associations of Fini's totem vary according to country. For example, 'the Egyptian sphinx was viewed as benevolent, a guardian, whereas the Greek sphinx was invariably malevolent towards people'.[21] Fini plays with variation, sexual dynamics, gender expectations and forges her own tradition. Rather than depicting female sphinxes as violent or threatening, she emboldened her sphinxes as non-subservient women unleashing their potency through art and alchemy. Her sphinxes are women who decline to be silent; they can be wild and untamed. As Chadwick notes, 'Fini's sphinx ... poses a question not about man, but about the woman artist's place in the natural and metamorphic process that lies at the heart of the Surrealist vision of an art of fantasy, magic and transformation.'[22] This is because Fini and her sphinxes, rather like the various women Surrealists themselves, refuse to be categorized. Instead, as enigmatic figures, they have the potential to invoke magic.

Fini's sphinxes are always in control; any surrounding males are submissive, subservient and non-threatening docile pets, worshipping her in adulation. Sometimes, in retaliation to the violence inherent in so much Freudian imagery, they are asleep. Fini projects her affection for the theatrical onto her female sphinxes, and they stand as proud, beautiful and bejewelled as Egyptian goddesses. As Leon Kochnitsky has noted, 'Fini combines the portrait with the fantasy setting in her work and is herself "the imperious shepardess of a herd of sphinxes [who] [sic] really creates a new myth; these are other Arianes [sic], Andromedas, Cleopatras – although they do not have these names." '[23] This is because they are all named Fini.

Fini began to paint sphinxes in 1943. Her first painting in this series, *Petit sphinx gardien* (*Little Guardian Sphinx*) (1943–4) was painted while staying on the isle of Giglio, and she continued the theme after returning to Rome. Chadwick has discussed Fini's fusions – masculine and feminine, human and bestial, wilderness and civilization – in work that is often darker, symbolically alluding to the forces underneath the veneer of civilization: the murky goings on that linger beneath any glossy surface.[24] She refers to *Petit sphinx gardien* and how it 'recalls the figure of the sphinx as sorceress and image of death. Here representations of necromancy and death surround the hybrid creature: a triangle, broken eggs, and a hermetic text'.[25] The painting depicts a woman with abundant feline hair (similar to Fini's own leonine mane), cat-like facial features and naked bosom with eggshells scattered about her. Behind her is a dark, foreboding sky tinged with red and green, a depiction of chaos and doom (impending or retreating) in the background. There is a large crack on the plinth on which her sphinx resides. The image raises a multitude of questions connecting to Fini's interest in sorcery and the occult, subjects that interested so many women Surrealists. What has hatched from the eggs, or, what has been destroyed in them? While in Egyptology eggs may refer to the 'Cosmic Egg' discussed in creation myths, in Surrealism they were often painted in both a physical and literal sense to connote an artist's creativity and fertility. They were also nourishment, the all-powerful feminine, and as magical apparatus, one of the oldest symbols of fertility in pagan religions and essential to the alchemical and magical.[26]

Drawn to the roll of script – similar to a papyrus text or an ancient scroll – at the forefront of the painting, the viewer may contemplate what the sphinx is invoking. What is the pink material draped on the branches behind her? The branches on which the cloth rests appear to have grown from underneath the ground, brought forth from the underworld by the sphinx's bidding, implying that she is not on a pedestal, but rather on a tomb. Whose tomb was this, what is this force she has raised, and why is she so intent on causing destruction? Such questions may also be asked of *Self Portrait with Scorpion* (1938).

In this self-portrait Fini stands side-on, facing the viewer's gaze, hair up, wearing a long-sleeved dress and single grey glove. The glove bears similarities to a hunter's glove, and here the tiniest of details is the most symbolic: the tail of a scorpion protrudes (or escapes) and dangles from her wrist. Notable also are the tears at her right elbow and on her left arm above the spot from where the creature dangles. Is the scorpion a part of her, her pet, her totem, or has she called on this stinging creature to do her bidding? It evokes the scorpions of the Egyptian desert, the goddess Isis, and of the myths connecting the two:

> A story inscribed on the Metternich Stela tells how Isis and her seven magical scorpions took refuge in a remote marsh village. She is refused hospitality by a rich woman but taken in by a fisherwoman. The scorpions sting the rich woman's child in revenge. Isis cures the child after the rich woman gives her wealth to the fisherwoman.[27]

This is a curious image, associating Fini with Isis and in doing so imbuing her with the potential to harm all who cross her. Fini's assumption of the magical potency of Isis strengthens her reputation – and self-representation – as a powerful woman attuned to sorcery. Pinch describes Isis as a magician, but some would maybe call her an enchantress with the ability to restore and cast spells.[28] After Seth dismembers her husband Osiris, she and Ra restore him: 'Isis had to search for the decomposed body of Osiris and restore it with her magic.'[29] More significantly to Surrealism, she severs the hands of Horus before preceding to make him a new pair. Even when she herself is beheaded she gains the head of the cow goddess. These mutilations are referred to in Surrealism as castrations, and something the male Surrealists inherently feared as a threat to their masculinity. It also aligns with the pleasure and pain principle through the depiction of hands (hands could invoke trauma or create immense pleasure) a theme that has been explored and reworked by many women artists. In this example Isis, in restoring Horus's hands, creates manhood: she is the giver of life, a magician with the ability to create the male phallus, and as such to be feared; she is the bringer of life and pleasure, and the bringer of chaos and pain. Egyptian goddesses were formidable women and forces to be reckoned with, in life as well as in myth. As Pinch asserts, 'in general, goddesses were more feared than gods; there were no meek divine housewives in the Egyptian pantheon'.[30]

Fini's personal potency was expressed through such references to Isis and other female deities; her animalistic attributes were also solidified in her association with and deep affection for cats, also held as sacred in ancient Egyptian religion. Whether domestic, wild or mythic, Fini can often be seen (whether in photographs or self-portraits) bedside one of her feline companions, her devotion to, and adoption of, this particular animal strengthening her bond with the ancient Egyptians. As a young girl who often slept in her mother's bed, she would recall her dreams of cosmic felines:

> I dreamed about the forest where I met the enormous cat who kissed me and sang the song of the white lamb who was promised that his coat would never be shorn; sometimes it was I who sang the song to the big cat; this was real happiness.[31]

Her grandmother's cat – Cioci – was the first cat she ever saw. Peter Webb notes that she was immediately enamoured of the huge white Persian who became 'her friend and confidant for the next ten years'; 'Leonor remained devoted to cats ever after'.[32]

Fini began questioning the hypocrisy of religion when she was eight years old and, preparing for her first communion, pilfered communion wafers. She lied about the number she had eaten, telling her mother she had had only one instead of the multitude of biscuits she had spent the afternoon delicately consuming, practicing her technique in fear of damaging the body of Christ with her teeth. Realizing that lying was easy, and could be deployed whenever she wished, she decided to test religion further by accosting the reproduction of Carlo Dolci's *Virgin and Child* that hung on the wall of her Uncle's house to see if the Madonna would reprimand her vulgar words.[33] Having received no reaction, she refused to submit to religious doctrine; 'she remained a confirmed atheist all her life, believing only in the cat god'.[34] As Webb records:

> From Cioci in Trieste to countless numbers in her various homes in France, cats dominated Leonor's life. She often said that she preferred cats to humans, seeing them as wiser and also more absolute and total in their affection, loyalty and devotion.[35]

Fini's self-image is so entwined with felines (both household and mythical) that her artistic transmutation is akin to mythological animal transformations, such as the story of the Roman goddess Diana, wishing to escape from giants, choosing to hide herself in the form of a cat. Frank Hamel has noted how the most frequent transformations in the ancient world were of humans into cats. This was because 'the cat, as appears from many legends, easily holds the place amongst mystic animals that the serpent has among reptiles, partly no doubt because of its close relationship with sorcerers and witches'.[36]

Fini's commitment to cats is attuned to how animal gods and goddesses – particularly Sekhmet and Bast – were honoured and depicted in Egyptian mythology, and of their quick tempers when provoked. One is reminded of the series of photographs, taken by André Ostier, in which Fini wears several cat-like masks (she frequently wore masks for balls and other society functions), while striking casual yet ferocious feline poses. Ostier's images form part of a series in which Fini appears not so much sphinx but lioness, with wild mane and imposing presence, a Surrealist Sekhmet, a transformation paralleling Ra's metamorphosis:

> When Ra sent his eye to destroy humanity for the crime of rebellion, she was transformed into the raging lioness, Sekhmet. She devoured all the evil humans and had to be tricked by Ra into sparing the rest.[37]

Fini's interpretation of Egyptian mythology incorporated animals and magic to weave an assertive female-centric mythology, transforming sphinxes from unreadable entities into imposing female forces exuding dominant sexual desires and embodying female sorcery. In her self-created identity, she imbued herself with the characteristics she so admired in both the sphinxes and felines of the ancient world, projecting a self-curated eroticism to the outside world and becoming a hybrid creature: a Surrealist sphinx and feline queen who ruled and dominated the subservient men who crossed her path. However, there were other ways that women Surrealists paid tribute to the ancient world through animals and their bodies, as they twisted and adapted traditional mythology for their own ends.

Surrealist shapeshifters and animal magic

Magic, sorcery and Egyptian myth were not themes solely adopted by Fini; they frequently appear in the works of other women Surrealists. Leonora Carrington and Remedios Varo were especially well-versed in esoteric phenomena. Varo's art seamlessly blends physics and metaphysics to create a world in which opposing universes and creatures co-exist harmoniously. The Spanish-Mexican artist had a unique ability to align the natural world with the scientific, the mystical and the esoteric. As the daughter of a hydraulics engineer, she was familiar with scientific apparatus and devices. As Lois Zamora writes, 'Varo's idiosyncratic iconography includes fantastical machines that facilitate metaphysical voyages to other shores, other worlds.'[38] These other worlds are historic and futuristic: both parallel universes located in the present. There is a historic quality to her paintings yet something that is esoteric and untouchable, as though she has access to information out of reach to others. With her great friend Carrington (both women lived together in Mexico for many years), their art, themes and biographies are entwined and aligned. Like Fini, both saw truth in the notion of the goddess and made art to restore that magic by locating 'the origins of woman's creative consciousness in this ancient [goddess] tradition'.[39]

Varo, a passionate animal lover, is striking in her depiction of animal totems. Whether cats, birds or androgynous deities, they are presented warmly and with affection: to be greeted rather than feared. They are active autobiographical self-portraits, granting the artist the ability to shapeshift, create and pioneer her own inventions. In Varo's well-known painting *The Creation of The Birds* (1958) an owl, with many of the characteristics of a human, sits at a desk to partake in a scientific experiment. The viewer supposes that this is a female owl on account of her large eyes, slim feathered legs and elegant bare feet (more human than bird-like); the owl is not dissimilar to Varo herself and very like the other female protagonists that populate her paintings. She holds a triangular magnifying glass, denoting occult symbolism and there is dark sky outside the arched non-glass window. Hamel notes that 'in the north country [of ancient Egypt] the owl was … said to be of royal descent, perhaps of birth even as high as the child of a Pharaoh',[40] while Nadia Choucha specifies that owls are symbols of wisdom. She continues, 'in Egyptian symbolism, it is related to death, and the idea of the "seer in the darkness", and images of Lillith also show her accompanied by a barn owl'.[41]

The owl – evocative of these and other associations – smiles knowingly, gazing at her hand-held prism, while the animated egg-timer to her side (whether vessel or assistant) alludes, similarly to Fini, to the symbolism of the hermetic egg. It reflects Varo's respect for science and nature working in tandem, alongside art and nurturing, positioning her as the creator of her own myths. She is the embodiment of the wise owl goddess – suggesting Athena or Minerva in Greek and Roman mythology respectively – uniting scientific and mystical knowledge, perhaps even knowledge of the Egyptian underworld in her creation of birds, evoking the Bâ: the part of the human soul that could fly between the world of the living and that of the dead. Varo's owl has twin powers over life and death.

The emphasis on female deities and their connection to animals, whether directly or indirectly, is also prominent in Varo's *La Llamada (The Call)* (1961), an especially rich painting with regards to mythology and symbolism. Laced with astrological references, *La Llamada* accentuates Varo's links to ancient worlds, deities and magic. Varo's painting glows with deep amber tones: hues of orange, red, and yellow. In astrological terms, gold is emblematic of the sun, the ruler of the Leo sign, and lord of the solar system. However, rather than present the masculine lion as the incarnation of the sign, Varo has painted her interpretation of the goddess Sekhmet to represent those ruled by this section of the chart under the dominance of the sun, equating her with the incarnation of strength.

There are also suggestions of the pyramids here, in the geometric patterns beneath the goddess's feet (appearing as pyramids as seen from above) 'pointing' up to celestial bodies. As Ian Shaw observes,

> It has long been suggested that the so-called 'air-vents' in the Great Pyramid served some astronomical function, since they are evidently carefully aligned with various stars, including the constellation of Orion (the Egyptian god Sah), which might have been the intended destination of the king's *ba*, when he ascended to take his place among the unpopular stars.[42]

Various static onlookers gaze upon the figure as she walks along the corridor, their eyes following in awe, adoration or worship. Whether these are levitating apparitions or ancient statues, carved from stone or wood, they appear deeply embedded into the surrounding walls and bear a striking likeness to Egyptian and Incan goddesses, their alternating headdresses possibly referencing the ancient worlds or other universes from whence they came. Additional visual references, including the alchemical vessel placed in the subject's hand (alchemy being a reoccurring theme in Varo's paintings) suggests an extension of Varo's interest in mythology and folklore that stretched beyond her usual references to Celtic iconography. It hints at a reworking of the symbolism of Isis and Osiris, with Isis as the sun goddess rather than Osiris as the sun god.[43]

As Fini altered Egyptian sphinxes to infuse them with femininity, Varo reversed the traditional notion of the male sun presiding over his solar kingdom. Again, the feminization of tradition does not result in a reduction of power, but rather highlights Varo's ability to extricate and draw out the hidden motifs, and previously ignored symbolism, so richly abundant in Egyptian myth. Her figure in *La Llamada*, with its sharp, angular face is androgynous, ethereal and not of this world, while the loose clothing draped around the figure's body signals pregnancy, illuminating the connection between the ancient world, goddesses and maternity.

The mythology of maternity

Certain women Surrealists viewed childbearing with the same philosophy as the ancient Egyptians – demonstrative of female strength, elevation, and empowerment – while others viewed it as a hindrance, and as something that would stifle their creativity. Maternity is a recurring theme in the work of women artists as a topic that conflicts with orthodox male-produced Surrealism and, indeed, to the work of many women Surrealists.[44] A particular anxiety certainly seems to revolve around the subject. In Surrealism, this worry can be traced to the patriarchal roots of the movement, and the desire for a woman to forever remain as *femme-enfant*. A pregnant woman would often be seen as desexualized and unwomanly.

Returning to Varo, Zamora describes *Still Life Reviving* (1963) as a birth of sorts, and a gestation of cosmic creation rather than a traditional pregnancy:

> The whirling table spins around a cosmic center, a center that is reiterated by the circles expanding outward centrically from it. Centrifugal force sends planetary fruit and saucers into orbit: on the left, a pomegranate (symbol of fertility and maternity in medieval Jewish and Christian iconography) bursts; on the right, other fruits collide, their seeds falling to Earth like meteorites.[45]

The fruit in the image is emblematic of the solar system. Bright, full, fertile oranges (representing femininity) rotate around the phallic flame and shatter the pomegranate.[46] The image is Varo's attack on patriarchy, and the tension of being a woman suspended in a male-centred (phallocentric) universe.⁴⁷ Cosmic imagery is present in the earlier painting *Nacer de Nuevo* (*Born Again*) (1960), with the pregnant figure noted by Zamora as 'witness to the symbolic source of the cosmic force generated by the painting's centric system – eyes, breast, table, moon, bowl, moon'.⁴⁸ The painting contains not one but two moons: one in the chalice of water on the table at which the figure – or deity – is gazing, the other visible in the fractured ceiling above her head. The being stands in the middle, bookended by the double cosmic alignments, perhaps implying that she (or an apparition of herself) was created from the moon: she is a lunar child and has taken on the system's properties. Although the crescent moon in the liquid may be a reference to the ancient Egyptian Khonsu, the creator moon god and controller of fate who wore a headdress with an inverted crescent moon, we are reminded, too, of certain Egyptian moon goddesses. One of the best-known goddesses, Isis, widely revered for her powers of witchcraft, is considered both solar and lunar deity, while Sefket (partner of the lunar god Thoth), was the lunar deity of time, the stars and architecture.

The painting also references female creation and fertility. As the subject bursts through the wall, the lower half of her body is covered by the tears in this partition, while her exposed breasts signify the life-force emanating from the painting. Brambles and branches – like the ones seen in the open air outside the arch – sprout from the table, plunge into the room and creep down from the ceiling, in a show of life and movement. Is she a lunar deity, a goddess of creation bringing forth this life-force? Or, is she a moonchild birthed by this celestial crescent?

More reworking of goddess imagery can be explored in Leonora Carrington's 1946 painting *Palatine Predella*, considered by Chadwick to be an untraditional rendering of the goddess Isis despite evoking the Roman goddess Proserpina's return from the underworld:

> The figure may not be a specific representation of this goddess, but there are a number of images in the painting that indicate references to this myth, long viewed as a parable of life and spiritual quest. The image of the Egyptian Isis, the goddess of the moon, sister and spouse of the moon God Osiris, was revived during Hellenistic times as one of the mystery cults; in ancient Egypt, the Book of the Dead contained instruction in the mystery religion of Osiris. Osiris, who died and went to the underworld, was later restored to life by the power of Isis, who had wandered the earth searching for the dead god.⁴⁹

Usually associated with Celtic mythology and Mexican magic rather than Egyptian influences, Carrington's interest in mysticism can also be fruitfully explored from an Eastern perspective. She herself encourages this, referencing 'the other' in *Professional Ethics* (1955), 'where the presence of a horned cow bearing the moon and a black-robed figure casting a spell outside a sick child's bedroom recall the black-robed Egyptian goddess who was reported to brew a medicine that could raise the dead'.⁵⁰ By extracting this element of Carrington's work, we are able to focus the lenses through which we read her in Surrealist, esoteric, and mystic canons.

Again, it is interesting to consider the duality of goddesses in relation to both Egyptian mythology and art history and how the aforementioned women spun a fresh perspective on the independence of these figures. Pinch has discussed how goddesses' identities were often dependent on their relationships with a male deity; even if they were worshipped as a couple, her level of importance would be second to his. Maternity, however, was different, because 'if the goddess was playing a maternal role, the child deity was given the inferior position'.[51] She continues, 'the maternal role was more important for goddesses than the paternal role was for most gods. Romantic love is almost entirely absent from Egyptian myth, but maternal love was consistently portrayed as one of the most powerful forces in the universe'.

The notion of maternity is intriguing when considered alongside Fini's depiction of women, as well as her own personal views. While the maternal role elevated the goddess, pregnancy was vehemently opposed in Fini's world, as she aligned herself with darker entities, emphasized in her comment: 'myself, I know that I belong with the idea of Lilith, the anti-Eve, and that my universe is that of the spirit. Physical maternity instinctively repulses me'.[52] Instead, her world was filled with autonomous, powerful women who were goddesses, deities and mystical beings who flaunted their potent non-reproductive sexuality. Choucha observes that many artistic women, faced with the dearth of women in their field, turned to all-powerful feminine and goddesses of the occult.[53] As Gloria Orenstein has noted, 'Leonor Fini's world is a Matriachy. Her love of cats in both her painting and her life is partially related to her worship of the Goddess, for in Egypt the cat was linked with the moon and sacred to the Goddesses Isis and Bast.'[54] It is the goddess – not her progeny – which was of interest to Fini.

As much as Fini's world was matriarchal, it was non-maternal and she maintained a vehemently childless stance throughout her life. Therefore, the male Surrealists may have viewed her as what we may call a 'complete woman'. Pregnancy would both desexualize and defetishize a woman's body; therefore by remaining childless, her body was physically 'whole': she had not 'given' any of herself, either physically or emotionally, to a child. She remained a complete, sexual woman. However, even without producing offspring, a woman's body might become 'desexualised' or viewed as less erotic. This was something that Fini experienced for herself, coping with her trauma through art.

In 1947 Fini painted *Petit sphinx ermite* (*Little Hermit Sphinx*) following her hysterectomy. It is a dark painting of imposing destruction, with an aura of doom and desolation. Although she had painted eggs many times before – as in *Petit sphinx gardien* – the broken eggs in this painting have greater autobiographical suggestion. Commenting on the painting she declared: 'they [the eggs] represent destruction. It was no longer possible for me to have children, therefore I thought the eggs contained children. It looks very good like that because the eggs are very pretty.'[55] Even though Fini did not want children, through this painting she mourns the loss of her body's ability to procreate. The issue here was the limitation Western culture placed on women by categorizing them as maiden, mother or whore, Fini's childlessness seemingly confining her to this final category. Eastern philosophies differed in the sense of elevating the feminine to a higher power, however, and this allowed the women of Surrealism (Fini, Carrington and Varo) instead to follow this path. As Choucha asserts, 'Leonor Fini, an imperious and theatrical individual, must receive special credit for her attempts to subvert these crude roles and define a powerful female image in her life as well as her art'.[56] She believed that 'men were more ordinary, limited, unimaginative, while women were more mythic, closer to their origins, in tune with the natural order',[57] commenting to Webb that 'women have been mistreated for so long, no wonder they are cruel'.[58]

Fini's visible association with witches and Egyptian mythology functions on both an artistic and aesthetic level. She admired Jules Michelet's Medieval text *La Sorcière* (*The Witch*) with its 'beautiful, rebellious, clever' witches, owned a copy of Grillot de Givry's *Le Musée des sorcière* (*The Witch Museum*), and on 24 June 1932 attended Tristan Tzara's party to celebrate the witches' sabbath dressed in her trademark flamboyant attire of 'knee-length white leatherette boots and a cape of white feathers. Blue feathers and tinsel dust were sprinkled in the curls of her hair'.[59] Aside from the connections to ancient Egyptian sorcery already addressed in this essay, there are further examples in her work: her 1938 painting *Personnages sur une terrace* (*Characters on a Terrace*) features three young, Fini-esque women with a conspicuous broomstick in the background; in 1957, she created a series of sketches for Jacques Audiberti's *Le Sabbat* (*The Sabbath*); and in 1980 produced another series of pencil-drawn witches. Everything about Fini – from her lifestyle to her persona and artwork – screams conjurer, her feline association suggesting witches' familiars. Malcolm Gaskill has written that 'wicked female magicians were known to the Egyptians and Babylonians',[60] and goes on to elaborate on the connections between witchcraft and the ancient world. The following observation is especially apt, as Fini draws on themes including the rational (or the irrationality that formed the foundations of Surrealism), 'femaleness' and magic:

> Rituals, spells, and taboos were endemic, and the frontier between this world and the next elaborately constructed. Greece and Rome followed the Egyptian lead. For all its grandeur and glory, the classical world was steeped in the dark manipulation of spirits; here was a means to alleviate anxiety, deploy anger, and satisfy desire. Nor was this residual or eccentric, a precursor to the arts and sciences later celebrated by an ascending West. Magic was part of an excepted and vibrant reality integral to everyone's culture and mentality. When tracing our social ancestry back to the ancients, we should take the rough with the smooth – that is, the superstitious with the rational.[61]

Much like the ancient mystical tradition of the classical world, the women examined here filled their lives with magic, transforming chores into alchemical rituals. Carrington's *The House Opposite* (1945) is a wonderful example of the 'Alchemical Kitchen', while Fini manifested desire through provocative art and flamboyant clothing. All regular occurrences and actions were imbued with new meanings, and held as a continuation of regular magic. These artists made themselves goddesses, brimming with magical potency.

As with the women artists I have considered in this essay, ancient Egyptian goddesses, and the mythology of the ancient world, cannot be reduced to any one form. Through a combination of traditional Surrealism, Egyptian mythology and demonstrations of female agency, the artworks produced by these women are multi-faceted and complex, filled with symbolic content, shifting, merging and re-shaping under scrutiny. I have endeavored to demonstrate how Varo's, Carrington's and Fini's personal interests in the esoteric went beyond the aesthetic: these were women who incorporated magical practices and methods into their daily lives, and whose knowledge of mythology and alchemy inhabited their work as if manifested in their canvases. Usually critics emphasize Carrington's Celtic connections, the Mexican influences she shared with Varo, Varo's interest in Sufi mysticism, and Fini's high fashion as a form of alchemy and witchery, but rarely has this work been examined through an Egyptian lens. Each artist had their own interpretations of ancient Egypt, yet there is a common theme running throughout. While Fini's inclination to personalize the Sphinx of Giza transformed the traditional symbol into one of beguiling eroticism, Varo and Carrington spun new stories around ancient familial models, reinventing traditional narratives with feminist flair while including themes of motherhood and domesticity. Their reimagining of tales usually told in very similar ways both re-direct mythology and allow for greater interdisciplinary reading. By utilizing and resisting the patriarchal framework of canonical Surrealism, and aligning themselves with Egyptian mythology, women Surrealists took on the properties of the deities they chose to embody. This re-reading, re-positioning and re-creating of well-known myths resulted in a totemic manifestation of strength and power.

To conclude, I wish to turn to one final image. There is a captivating photograph of Fini by Adrian de Menasce, where she can be seen beside the Great Sphinx of Giza. It is an arresting sight, not because it is loud and overstated, nor because we see her entire frame dressed in one of her dynamic, flamboyant ensembles, but because it is quiet and introspective. Her eyes are downcast, and only her upper body is visible, mirroring the pose of the sphinx that looms vast and imposing above her. She wears a black wide-brimmed hat, similar to an explorer's, while her pussy-bow blouse and billowy black sleeves hint at her flare for the dramatic. It is a rare opportunity to see Fini so quiet, so still, and enchants because we see the self-styled sphinx alongside the very structure that bears her name. It is royal and majestic, a contrast to her assertive self-portraiture, while her calm demeanor implies that she is meditating, absorbing the majesty that surrounds her, settling herself so that her pose mirrors the Great Sphinx. It is quite an image, the Sphinx of Surrealism together with that which she adores. Which of them, one cannot help but wonder, is most in awe of the other?

CHAPTER 14
EGYPTIAN EXCESSES: TAYLOR, BURTON AND *CLEOPATRA*
Siv Jansson

To this day *Cleopatra* (1963) remains one of the most expensive films ever made, nearly bankrupting 20th Century Fox. The film also scandalized the world with the very public affair of its two major stars, Elizabeth Taylor and Richard Burton. Rarely has there been such synergy between the lives of the main characters in a film and the actors playing them. Cleopatra and Mark Antony – and the Egyptian court over which they presided – have become bywords for excess in the ancient Egyptian world; the marriage of Burton and Taylor was also an index of extravagance and hedonism. Both couples were, and still are, stars and celebrities.

The commonly told story of the movie's historic characters has become legendary: the seductive Egyptian queen wrests the Roman hero Antony away from his official duties and, in so doing, takes on the Roman Empire,[1] and their suicides crown a classic romantic narrative. This version of Cleopatra and Antony's relationship was largely derived from Roman sources,[2] and therefore is unsurprisingly hostile towards the Egyptian queen. As such, this biased history has become *the* story of Cleopatra and Antony. Cleopatra's gifts as a politician, her ruthlessness with her enemies and her intellectual qualities are all excluded from these accounts. Cleopatra won Julius Caesar's support, no mean achievement when dealing with such a wily leader and general; she ruled Egypt alone after her brother and sisters were eliminated; and she retained control over her death in the face of Octavian's determination to humiliate her. The 'Roman' Cleopatra, however, is wanton, an emblem of her sensual and undisciplined country, and largely to blame for the fall of Antony as well as her own misfortunes. It is true that Cleopatra made little effort to vanquish this perception, and she certainly cultivated an excessive lifestyle: Egypt was a very wealthy country, one of the reasons why it was of interest to Rome. Yet, Cleopatra was much more complex than this reductive image.

Some 2,000 years later, in 1963, the equally excessive behaviour of the two stars who were to play Cleopatra and Antony in a Hollywood incarnation of their story also became a legend, not only through a passionate love affair so intense that it blurred the lines between film and reality,[3] but also through the supposed suicide attempts, wounded spouses and even the involvement of 'Rome' in the form of the Vatican, who condemned the affair.[4] Both couples shocked and appalled their respective audiences, both played out dramatic peaks and troughs in their professional and private lives, and both remain stars, celebrities and legends, constantly reconstructed through biography, drama, books and photographic and artistic images. In this essay, I consider the ways in which Taylor and, to a lesser extent, Burton have become synonymous with their film characters, to the extent that the popular cultural concept of Antony and Cleopatra is interchangeable with the identities and lifestyles of the two stars, and how this has resulted in, and perpetuated, a mutual act of 'celebrification' between the two couples.

Celebrity and legend

There are several threads to unravel in pursuing the connections between Cleopatra and Antony and their movie star 'doppelgangers'. Chris Rojek has pointed out that 'celebrity status always implies a split between a private self and a public self';[5] in this case, both couples comprise a collection of 'selves'. Firstly, there are the 'real' characters of Cleopatra and Antony, constructed through historical research, ancient artefacts and a few textual accounts from their own time. Enclosed within these are differing biographical versions: Cleopatra the astute ruler and Cleopatra the manipulative 'harlot', Antony the effective general and Antony the weak and besotted lover.[6] There is the culturally familiar 'Antony and Cleopatra', most famously represented in Shakespeare's 1606 play of the same name, but also characterized in other works by John Dryden and George Bernard Shaw, and in opera by Handel. In addition, there are many biographies and novels, numerous paintings and films and a Cleopatra industry: a trawl through Amazon UK reveals the availability of Cleopatra wigs, costumes, jewellery, t-shirts, children's toys and, rather surprisingly, glue. Replicas of Egyptian artefacts which mimic Cleopatra, or items from her reign, can be obtained in museum shops across the globe, as well as online. The emphasis on Cleopatra rather than Antony in this range of cultural 're-visions' indicates that it is the Egyptian queen who has continued to fascinate the public imagination, paradoxically because of her representation as little more than a beautiful vamp. There are other legendary Egyptian icons of the ancient civilization– Nefertiti, Ahkenhaten, Rameses II and, of course, Tutankhamun – but Cleopatra leads them all, and by some distance.

This emphasis on the female half of a legendary partnership is, to some extent, replicated in the Taylor-Burton marriage, and exemplifies the parallels that exist between the historic couple and their 1963 counterparts. A search through scholarly and popular literature reveals many more sources on Taylor than Burton. Taylor had a longer and more spectacular life than Burton: her eight marriages, immense jewellery collection and her latter-day campaigning for AIDS charities provide a more gripping narrative, and her long film career satisfies the public's insatiable interest in the Hollywood of the past. Of course, biographies of either Taylor or Burton inevitably become biographies of both, although he is a player in her story more frequently than the reverse.[7] Those who have written on Burton alone have brought him out from the shadow of his two marriages to Taylor, but these biographies are relatively few. This difference is mimicked in the number of narratives available on Cleopatra in comparison to Antony,[8] which encompass serious biography, novels, children's books and history. Such comparisons do not necessarily reflect significance or talent: both Burton and Antony were highly gifted and intelligent men. It is rather that scandalous women attract a more consistent, and often more prurient, interest; historically, women have not been expected or permitted to be scandalous. A disregard for public outrage is shared by Cleopatra and Taylor, and is an important part of their legend: to live without modifying one's behaviour to please others is a luxury few can afford. Both, therefore, are fantasy figures, as much for women as for men.

The copious biographical sources on both Taylor and Burton mean that, like Cleopatra and Antony, they have a range of 'characterizations'. There are the 'real' individuals, their public personas,[9] and the collective entity known as 'Taylor and Burton' or 'Liz and Dick':

> Above all, everyone knew that *Cleopatra* had given the world 'Liz and Dick,' the adulterous pairing of Elizabeth Taylor and Richard Burton, irresistibly cast as Cleopatra and Mark Antony. ... It was during the making of *Cleopatra* that [Taylor] truly transcended the label of mere 'movie star' and became, once and for all, *Elizabeth Taylor*, the protagonist in a still-running extra-vocational melodrama of star-crossed romance, exquisite jewelry, and periodic emergency hospitalizations.[10]

Taylor has attained mythical status, which transcends the work which originally brought her to the public's attention and mostly comprises her off-screen activities rather than her on-screen roles.[11] Although the above quotation refers to 'Liz *and* Dick', Burton's subsidiary role suggests that his movie star status was initially derived from his connection with her, a factor to which some attribute his subsequent acting choices and his heavy drinking (prior to this Burton had been seen as a potentially great classical stage actor).[12] In another instance of historical parallel, Antony was a respected figure in Rome before he met Cleopatra, having most famously eulogized the dead Caesar and sought out his murderers: he was one of the Roman Triumvirate and a successful general. His abandonment of this in favour of Cleopatra and Egypt was blamed exclusively on the queen by contemporary historians, while a more modern view recognizes that this was indicative of Antony's choices rather than Cleopatra's seductive abilities. Similarly, Burton's decision to pursue a film rather than stage career (though he continued to work on stage periodically) may have been because the ambitions which others had for him were ones he did not share: his diaries demonstrate that his great love was writing, not acting.[13] Therefore, the synergy of these two couples may also lie in the ways they have been misperceived and constructed in the public mind to serve a narrative imposed upon them, though it was a narrative which neither couple did much to dispel.

The 'real' Cleopatra

The historic identification of Cleopatra and Egypt with excess has been noted by several historians: for example, Rivka Ullmer observes that Cleopatra was both an icon and a symbol of Egyptian indulgence.[14] Lucy Hughes-Hallett, however, sees Cleopatra's 'displays' as affirmations of power:

> Her barge may have been faced with ebony, trimmed with gold and hung with purple silk, as story-tellers were later to assert; if it was, its splendour was designed not for Cleopatra's own sensual pleasure but as a symbol of her royal magnificence.[15]

Hughes-Hallett makes a connection between increasing hostility to Cleopatra's extravagance and the development of her relationship with Antony, thus suggesting that reports of 'Egyptian excess' were politically motivated, designed to discredit the queen and Antony alike. Similarly, Mary Hamer speaks of the public events which the queen 'stage-managed', indicating that while the popular perception of ancient Egypt as embodied by Cleopatra is one of conspicuous consumption, the queen had clear and politically motivated reasons for such displays; Hamer also recognizes that most of the accounts of Cleopatra's excesses come from hostile observers.[16]

Ironically, however, for a figure who has historically typified Egypt, Cleopatra was not Egyptian: the Ptolemies were Greek/Macedonian. Cleopatra VII came from a long line of powerful male and female rulers. She was married to her brother, Ptolemy XIII, when she was eighteen and he much younger,[17] and her childhood years were consumed by the various rivalries existing within her family. At nineteen, having been forcibly deposed by her brother/husband, she sought Julius Caesar's aid through the now famous device of infiltrating his quarters rolled up in some bedding;[18] the 'legend' of Cleopatra began.

The Cleopatra myth, as the archetypal femme fatale, has overshadowed her many talents. Biographers suggest that her two most famous alliances, with Caesar and Antony, were largely politically motivated,[19] and that later generations have lost sight of the fact that Cleopatra's life consisted of far more than just these two affairs. She was a cunning queen and a ruthless operator; she despatched her enemies, including her siblings, without sentiment; she lost and then regained the throne of Egypt through her recognition of the importance of alliances and her ability to manipulate them. She was also economically very successful, at one point being 'the wealthiest monarch in the world',[20] and Egypt's riches were one of the factors which attracted both Caesar and Antony, who needed financial assistance from outside Rome to maintain their power and fight various wars. As Stacy Schiff observes: '[e]xcess had put the Ptolemies on the map, where Cleopatra fully intended the dynasty to remain'.[21] The wealth built by the Ptolemaic dynasty is described in studies of Cleopatra's court:

> The opulence and luxury of Cleopatra's court was thought to be unusual even within the standards of Hellenistic royalty. ... Lucan, in a detailed description, recounted the banquet that Cleopatra gave for Caesar in 48 BC. It is a world of gold table service, jewelled glassware, crystal water pitchers, exotic foods, flowers everywhere, and even the best Italian wine.[22]

Clearly, Cleopatra deliberately flaunted her wealth; she had ample resources and knew the power which such display could exert. Hughes-Hallett suggests that Cleopatra's 'luxury ... without limit' has 'a kind of magnificence' which is not necessarily a negative facet of her legend.[23] Her 'excess' was reviled by Roman observers, but certainly neither Caesar nor Antony was repelled.

Nowhere is Cleopatra's acumen better illustrated than in her determination to define the mode of her death. Following Antony's suicide, Cleopatra sought to negotiate with Octavian to retain her throne; any grief for Antony did not obscure her survival instinct. Upon being made aware that Octavian intended to parade her in chains through the Roman streets she staged her own death and comprehensively outwitted him. While this may seem a Pyrrhic victory for the Egyptian queen – she was unable to secure the succession for her son and therefore Egypt passed into Roman hands – she not only cemented her own legend, but also Antony and Cleopatra as star-crossed lovers: defeated by the coldly calculating Octavian, but joined eternally in memory.

While this is an over-simplified account of Cleopatra's story, it does indicate how, and why, the 1963 film and the life of its female star have become so imbricated with the historic Cleopatra. As Hughes-Hallett records:

> The world's favourite Cleopatra story of the early sixties was not contained in the film: it is about the film's making. Taylor is Cleopatra, and Burton Antony, far more effectively in their off-set personae, in the gossip columns and paparazzi pictures, than they are on the screen.[24]

Hughes-Hallett's observation of the blurred lines between Taylor/Cleopatra and Burton/Antony is reflected in the use of Taylor's Cleopatra image as archetypical: Francesca Royster, questioning the historic 'whiteness' of popular cultural Cleopatras, uses a picture of Taylor on the cover of her book to indicate the extent to which Cleopatra and Taylor have merged in the public mind, resulting in a fixed concept of Cleopatra as white.[25] While it is not within the scope of this essay to discuss Cleopatra's ethnicity,[26] the possibility of a black Cleopatra, while explored in more recent scholarship, was never (as far as we know) considered by the film's producers: the other actresses in line for the role were all white. This is no doubt due, in part, to the widely held assumption at that time that a black performer could not 'carry' a major film,[27] but also suggests that Taylor, representing a classic version of white Western beauty as well as being a box-office draw, would be a less challenging Cleopatra for 1963 Western audiences.[28]

Taylor and Burton: Hollywood excess

Like Cleopatra's biography, narratives of Taylor's life contain copious descriptions of excess. Even before 'Liz and Dick', Taylor's marriage to Mike Todd was marked by extraordinary extravagance.[29] Taylor's next two husbands, Eddie Fisher and Richard Burton, struggled to keep up with the largesse of Todd, and often spent well beyond their means to gratify Taylor's love of expensive gems.[30] The Burtons' lifestyle both fascinated and appalled observers: the film critic Alexander Walker commented that '[t]hey lived on a scale few hereditary rulers except the despots of Africa or Arabia thought prudent for either their people to witness or their treasuries to support'.[31] Walker's analogy to despotic rulers, while scarcely flattering to the Burtons, further suggests links to the hedonism of Cleopatra and Antony.[32]

The connections between the actress and the role she played are more complex than simple external trappings, however, as suggested by one of her biographers, William J. Mann:

> Elizabeth Taylor – for her performances both good and bad, for her innocence, sexiness, rebellion, honesty, and sheer life force – has been called the greatest movie star of all. She has become a cultural artefact that transcends temporal value judgements and the hectoring of the moralists who plagued her career. Her life was made into art, soap opera, scandal, tragedy, and even a bit of myth … an icon of desire, of gusto, of appetites passionately sated, of candour, of courage, of never saying no to big bad life.[33]

If Taylor's name is replaced with Cleopatra's, much of Mann's description could remain unchanged.[34] Like Cleopatra, Taylor conducted illicit relationships and scandalized her world: she enjoyed luxury and wealth, and was not shy about displaying it; she was also a shrewd manager of her life and career, able to negotiate excellent deals on her films, and very aware of how to 'stage' herself; she was gutsy, courageous and not easily intimidated.[35] Both women understood the value of allure, even more than beauty, and had no qualms about using it. Most historians now agree that Cleopatra was not beautiful in our modern understanding of the term. Joyce Tyldesley, for example, speculates that Cleopatra had bad teeth, short stature, a prominent nose and a thick neck, all details taken from her coinage, which are the only confirmed images we have of the real Cleopatra.[36] The relative absence of such images make the queen something of a *tabula rasa* in her physicality: she can be made into anything. However, what she certainly had was unmistakable energy, charisma, intelligence and a will to survive. Taylor, by comparison, undoubtedly had spectacular beauty, but did not want to build her career around this sole commodity, taking on many challenging film roles. The visible allure of Taylor and the imagined allure of Cleopatra have conflated into a populist concept whereby, in the absence of any contradictory images, Cleopatra can 'be' Elizabeth Taylor, and her Egypt can be the Egypt of Hollywood.[37]

This connection is further strengthened by the role played by money in the lives of both women. As the association of Cleopatra with Taylor was established, so wealth – in Cleopatra's time, a sign of success and power also signified decadence, indiscipline, indulgence and utter disregard for the rules of 'proper' behaviour. Cleopatra and Antony, by all accounts, spent money freely and staged many spectacular parties and events: the lifestyle of Taylor and Burton served to cement images of excess in the public mind that became intertwined with their historic counterparts. In the film,

Taylor performs Cleopatra's self-staging and 'her' Cleopatra indicates a sharp grasp not only of the visual impact of displays of wealth, but of the political and social power it wields. The lengthy and very famous scene of the procession into Rome to greet Julius Caesar slowly builds to the entrance of the queen atop a sphinx pulled by slaves. This could just have been a further visual marker of the film's spectacular credentials, except for the way it ends. Cleopatra, kneeling before Caesar, looks up at him and winks. What has been a rather ponderous, though highly colourful, episode in the film becomes a self-reflexive private joke which the audience are invited to share. It makes Taylor's Cleopatra a modern, 1960s girl: sassy, irreverent, making a gesture to the trick she is playing on Rome with the collusion of Caesar and the audience. Alongside this, however, the historic Cleopatra's self-staging ability is made explicit: this is a queen fully aware of the power of spectacle and the use of wealth to manipulate others, including Caesar. Thus, the implication in the film that the enormous procession is a piece of deliberate theatre to create effect and intimidate the Romans aligns Taylor's queen more closely with her original than the filmmakers most probably understood.[38]

Although the film has some reference to Cleopatra's political acumen, many scenes remain ultimately shaped by exploitation of Taylor's celebrity and notoriety; hearing of Caesar's approach while she is relaxing in her palace, Taylor/Cleopatra determines to arrange a spectacular 'performance' for him which will confirm her bad reputation in Rome, allowing him to find her nearly naked and surrounded by her attendants. The emphasis on Cleopatra as the prototypical 'bad girl', when combined with Taylor's reputation as a 'home-wrecker', further established the Taylor/Cleopatra synergy and the image of ancient Egypt as an enormous, opulent playground.[39] Taylor remained relatively undamaged by 'Le Scandale' (Burton's nickname for their affair) despite the moral condemnation she received: for her, 'bad behaviour brought not cost, but profit'.[40]

The same cannot be said of Burton/Antony. Burton's relationship with Taylor elicited disapproving responses from his family and many of his friends, and even temporarily severed some of those friendships.[41] Similarly, Antony lost alliances and friendships; he was increasingly seen as in thrall to his 'strumpet', as Philo describes her at the opening of Shakespeare's play.[42] Burton and Antony were heavy drinkers.[43] Both are often portrayed as having sacrificed their abilities for love and/or celebrity.[44] Antony made increasingly poor decisions, not the least of which was agreeing to fight Octavian on water, not land.[45] Moreover, by publicly 'flaunting' his relationship with Cleopatra – at least as perceived by Roman eyes – and neglecting his duties in Rome, he not only insulted his wife Octavia and her brother, but also became 'Egyptian' and not 'Roman', thus betraying his identity as part of the Triumvirate and as a Roman leader, identifying himself instead with the 'sensual' and 'irrational' Egypt. Similarly, Burton's film career was perceived by some as a betrayal of his potential as a stage or classical actor.[46] Therefore, Antony, and the actor who was to play him so memorably, shares much in terms of the effect of one significant relationship on their lives, careers and subsequent historical perception.

Ancient Egypt in the Modern Imagination

The 1963 *Cleopatra*

In some ways, the style of the 1963 *Cleopatra* owed a debt to previous onscreen portrayals of Egypt: *The Egyptian* (1954) and *Land of the Pharaohs* (1955) both attempted to show something of the vitality of the ancient civilization.[47] What these films lacked was the global myth of a central character and global notoriety surrounding at least one of their stars. The 1963 *Cleopatra* had both.

Taylor was not the only actress considered for the lead role: Susan Hayward, Gina Lollobrigida and Joan Collins were in the running,[48] and Collins was considered as an option to take over the role when Taylor was unwell.[49] There were pitfalls associated with Taylor: aside from her notoriety and health issues, she lacked the exotic appeal of Theda Bara or the playfulness of Claudette Colbert and Vivien Leigh, all previous incarnations of the queen. In addition, her voice was always one of her weakest qualities, easily ascending to shrillness. Yet, as a global star and a 'dangerous' femme fatale, casting her as one of history's most notorious women was not only logical but also potentially a major financial boost for 20th Century Fox.

The sense of serendipity in the casting decisions is reinforced when one considers that neither Rex Harrison nor Richard Burton were the original choices as Caesar and Antony; recasting became necessary after extensive production delays played havoc with the shooting schedule.[50] Prior to filming, Taylor's private life was already a feature of the global media. In the aftermath of the death, in 1958, of Mike Todd, she 'stole' Eddie Fisher from his wife Debbie Reynolds and their two young children, thus becoming established as a predatory sex-goddess. The media comparisons between the apparently homely Debbie and the recently widowed Elizabeth reinforced Taylor's 'man-eater' image, although, according to Fisher's account, his marriage to Reynolds was already over prior to the affair with Taylor.[51] This increases the links between Taylor and Cleopatra: both Caesar and Antony were married to virtuous Roman wives. Caesar, of course, never married Cleopatra or showed any inclination to do so, but he maintained his relationship with her until his murder in 44 BC, and they had a son, Caesarion. Octavia outlived both her husband and his Egyptian queen and adopted their children.

While Taylor received some negative public response to the Fisher affair, it was not sufficient to seriously damage her career in the long-term and it also made her a 'natural' to be cast as history's most famous vamp.[52] Mann describes the approach taken by the film's producers to persuade Taylor to take the role:

> 'It is important for Liz to know that Cleopatra was considered a goddess, directly divine, by herself, as well as by the Egyptians', writer Paddy Chayevsky advised the producers. The Egyptian Queen was sensual, aristocratic, clever and impulsive. Call it a match or a revision of history or just pure invention, but Cleopatra was becoming the latest incarnation of Elizabeth Taylor.[53]

The similarities of an Egyptian goddess/queen to a Hollywood goddess/queen are obvious: neither believe that the rules of 'ordinary' behaviour apply to them.[54] Part of Taylor's ability to rise above the scandal of her marriage to Fisher was her refusal to apologize for what she had supposedly done: when quizzed by Hollywood gossip columnist Hedda Hopper on the subject, she reportedly snapped, 'Mike's dead, and I'm alive. What do you expect me to do? Sleep alone?'[55]

While she would become embroiled in an even bigger scandal during the making of *Cleopatra*, the blueprint for excess that the film was to become was already in motion:

> To understand the scale of the budgetary and box-office double-whammy that did for Joseph L Mankiewicz's elephantine 1963 version of *Cleopatra*, it's worth noting that of the 50 most expensive movies ever made, adjusted for inflation, *Cleopatra* is the only one on the list that was released before 1998 – and at no. 15, it's still a major contender. The budget was around $44m ($320m in today's money), the kind of outlay that might have helped NASA put a man on the moon by 1966.[56]

The film began planning in 1959 and Taylor was on board by 1961. She would later describe the role as 'unplayable',[57] but she was the box-office attraction and was also being paid a historic million-dollar fee for her involvement; this was a further component of the cost of the film and another index of the extravagance which linked the star to the role. While she was not the first star to be paid this figure, she was the most publicized and high-profile.[58] The film's budget was set at $20 million initially, but had spiralled to $44 million by its conclusion, and the Alexandrian set was the largest ever built for a film.[59] The push for scale and spectacle was to be a costly choice.

Burton's involvement had been reluctant at first and his initial disrespect for his co-star is evident in his references to her as 'Miss Tits'.[60] The two had, in fact, met some years earlier, but the relationship sparked when Taylor helped Burton through a hangover on set and found herself falling for him. Although obviously attracted to Taylor, Burton could not have been ignorant of the profile which such an affair – and marriage – could give him: Bragg suggests that 'he was knocked out by Taylor's stardom and saw the association with her as a very useful leg-up'.[61] There were other benefits to the relationship: biographers have suggested that he learned how to act for the camera by watching her, and eventually developed a great respect for her grasp of the nature of film performance.[62] While their marriage certainly helped to put his name in lights, and he made occasional forays onto the classical stage, the sense that Burton sacrificed his potential for Hollywood glamour always dogged him,[63] as Maureen Dowd pointed out in this obituary in *The New York Times*:

> Sir John Gielgud said that Mr. Burton should have been in the same rank as Laurence Olivier, 'but he was very wild and had a scandal around him all the time and I think in theater circles that would not be approved of.' It was a note that was often struck in the reactions to Mr. Burton's death, and it was an albatross he had carried with him for two decades: his lost promise, or as was said about Hamlet, one of his most famous roles, 'what a falling-off was there.' His career was

dazzlingly erratic. He was the most nominated actor who never won an Oscar and the most famous British actor who was never knighted.[64]

Antony was also dazzling and erratic, and never fulfilled his promise as a Roman ruler. The Roman historian Plutarch described Antony as completely in thrall to Cleopatra:

> He allowed the queen to carry him off to Alexandria, where he indulged himself in a waste of childish sports, squandering on idle pleasures what Antiphon calls the most precious of commodities, which is time. For they gathered around them a group of friends whom they called the Inimitable Livers, and they gave banquets for one another of extraordinary expense.[65]

The most notable of Antony's damaging choices was made at the Battle of Actium. Antony was a formidable land general but no naval commander, thus meeting Octavian on water, apparently at the behest of Cleopatra who had an extensive and expensive navy, compounded the sense (in Rome at any rate) that he was weak and led by his Egyptian lover.[66]

The comparative lack of wealth of both men in contrast to their female partners also contributed to some of their career choices and, perhaps, their downfall. Even before their liaison, Plutarch refers to Antony's excessive extravagance and irresponsibility,[67] while Burton demonstrated his love for Taylor through the acquisition of many expensive gems (he also bought her a plane),[68] even though, in the early stages of his film career, he was earning far less than her.

At the beginning of the affair, Burton's actress wife Sybil refused to take the relationship seriously, but eventually emerged, like Antony's wife Octavia, as the wronged wife who was behaving immaculately, with support from Burton's family and friends.[69] According to Michael Munn, Burton's marriage to Sybil could have been saved had he abandoned Taylor – she was not his first extra-marital love affair – but neither could sustain a separation:

> It was art imitating life. This was the way it had been, on film and in history. Mark Antony giving up everything for the woman he could not live without. And maybe that's what, today, makes the film of *Cleopatra* so spellbinding – because Richard had made Antony become him, and Elizabeth Taylor was Cleopatra after all.[70]

Joe Mankiewicz, *Cleopatra*'s director, thought that Burton was 'overawed by her sheer power in Hollywood', and that he found Taylor's potent mix of 'sexual and economic power' irresistible.[71] Burton described Taylor as 'intoxicating',[72] suggesting a loss of control, power or will. The 'intoxicating' effect of Cleopatra/Taylor evokes the impact of their personal qualities as well as the party lifestyle enjoyed by both couples. It also implies that 'intoxicated' men slough off responsibility for their behaviour, thus fuelling the destructive imagery associated with both women.

The studio, meanwhile, was struggling to cope with the level of publicity once the affair went public, and was also undecided as to whether it was beneficial to the film or not.[73] Initially they perceived the potential for the success of the film of by linking Taylor with Cleopatra in promotional material, but as the affair became public, the studio lost control of the narrative and its increasingly negative tone.[74] In addition, there were difficulties long before the eruption of 'Le Scandale'. Mankiewicz's original intention was to make two three-hour films: the first focusing on, and entitled, *Caesar and Cleopatra*, the second, *Antony and Cleopatra*. He shot six hours of footage but the film's increasing costs and some negative audience reaction at previews led to a cut to four hours, then to three, as cinema chains complained about its length. These cuts were also enforced after a boardroom coup at 20th Century Fox, when legendary mogul Darryl F. Zanuck took back control of the company and insisted that *Cleopatra* be edited to a more economical length. Mankiewicz never fully recovered from what he felt was the ruination of his masterpiece and both Burton and Taylor felt that the film had been weakened by the cuts; indeed, Burton refused to watch it.[75]

If Cleopatra's Egypt was awash with wealth and gold, the film certainly sought to replicate this, though unfortunately without the necessary funds to shoulder such cost. One actress who played a small role in the film commented on the extravagant production values:

> The sets were as lavish in real life as they appear on screen – no wonder the budget soared out of control. I wore an antique headdress made of beaten gold and coral that belonged in a museum. Whenever my shoot was finished they'd whip it off me and lock it in a safe.[76]

Other examples of excess include the 26,000 costumes created for the film; Taylor had sixty-five costume changes, a record for a motion picture at the time, and was allocated a massive $194,800 (£123,000) wardrobe budget.[77] Costume designers Renie Conley, Irene Sharaff and Vittorio Nino Novarese won an Oscar for Taylor/Cleopatra's fabulous wardrobe: the clothes were designed to focus on glamour and sexual allure rather than historical fidelity, structured as they were to emphasize Taylor's curves and her fabulous face.[78] Taylor's erratic health, as well as rows and break-ups between the two lovers which resulted in loss of filming days, exacerbated the problem of cost, which had begun with issues concerning where the film should be shot and were compounded by in-fighting among those in control at 20th Century Fox.[79]

Cleopatra: The aftermath

Cleopatra, as with many cultural/historical texts, tells us more about the period in which it was produced and the Hollywood which produced it than the period it purports to represent.[80] Scrutinized now, the film seems a last gasp of the soon-to-be-defunct

Hollywood 'star' system, while the gossip, scandal, public 'flaunting' by its stars and the involvement of the Italian paparazzi in the exposure of the Taylor/Burton affair is a foretaste of the 'tell-all' celebrity culture with which the public is now so familiar. There are, however, other cultural inflections. In *The Accidental Feminist* (2012), M. G. Lord suggests that the portrayal of Cleopatra in the film was influenced by the lack of strong female leaders on the world stage, and by the post-war emphasis, particularly in America, on a particular type of homebound femininity, well-represented during the breaking of 'Le Scandale' by the public persona of the 'wronged' Debbie Reynolds.[81] As Lord points out, 1963 was also the year of Betty Friedan's *The Feminine Mystique*: however, conservative expectations of women's adherence to a domestic role remained powerful.[82] While there is no attempt in the film to 'domesticate' Cleopatra – indeed, casting Taylor would make no sense in such a context – the film draws upon ultimately traditional models for her characterization and thus disables some of the strength which Taylor can only reveal in particular scenes (e.g. the map scene with Caesar early in the film). With the introduction of Antony, the film focuses on love: Cleopatra strives to win the world for her lover and her son, rather than to increase her own power and secure her survival. This differentiates Taylor's Cleopatra not only from the historic queen but from Taylor's own innate career drive: even in the most intense periods of the love affair with Burton, Taylor never took her eye off her own interests. Thus, the film operates in two halves, both literally and thematically: one in which Cleopatra the politician and leader is given a very limited profile and the other in which Cleopatra the lover is prioritized.

The importance of colour for the 1963 film cannot be overemphasized. Firstly, as Lord observes, this was to compete with the rise of television.[83] The fixation on colour and spectacle was to remind the public that television could not provide this kind of scale and visual impact, being, of course, in black and white and with a much smaller screen (previous films featuring Cleopatra had also been shot in black and white). Secondly, colour is important in the marketing of Taylor as Cleopatra. As Joyce Tyldesley has suggested, the queen's ethnicity was highly likely to have made her at least olive-skinned;[84] Taylor's porcelain skin and violet eyes represent a 'Westernised' Cleopatra for a Hollywood market. While the previous film Cleopatras were presented in black and white, the technicolour presentation of the 1963 film, designed for visual impact, emphasizes the Eurocentric model of allure to which Taylor's Cleopatra conforms. It also established a style which influenced and continues to shape fashion and makeup: firms brought out cosmetics to create 'Egyptian eyes'. Revlon, for example, promoted what they called Cleopatra 'Sphinx Eyes',[85] and fashion writer Tove Hermandson points out that 'the liquid-liner experiments of the mod 1960s and the geometric Vidal Sassoon hairdos come through in Liz'.[86] Evie Leathem explores the style of Taylor's makeup in the film and refers to the 'new wave of Egyptomania that still resonates now':

> Even Kim Kardashian has taken up the role of the Queen of the Nile for her cover shoot with American *Harper's Bazaar* in March 2011, wearing one of Taylor's original Cleopatra gowns in photographs by Terry Richardson.[87]

In 2013, *Time Magazine* published '50 Years Later: How *Cleopatra* Continues to Influence Fashion Today', featuring fashion scholar and historian, Hazel Clark, on the film's (and Taylor's) fashion impact:

> 'In the contemporary imagination, the [1963 Elizabeth Taylor/Richard Burton] movie powerfully brought images of Cleopatra which are still very present and seductive.... That image ... was very much linked to the early 1960s. I think there's been a revived interest in the early 1960s, with the popularity of *Mad Men* and stores like Banana Republic picking up the look. ... The whole celebrity fascination or obsession was very much what caught the public's imagination – not just with Elizabeth Taylor as Cleopatra, but with Elizabeth Taylor as Elizabeth Taylor.' The persistent mythology of this powerful female pharaoh combined with the allure of the beautiful violet-eyed actress who personified her onscreen, make the figure of Cleopatra an enduring sartorial influence.[88]

In celebration of the film's re-release in 2013, several articles emerged focusing on its enduring fashion impact. The *Express* opined that '[d]raped in stunning golden cloaks and impeccably made up with shimmering metallics, emerald greens, heavily-lined eyes and plaited hair, Taylor is forever synonymous with the young queen of Egypt'.[89] In their November 2014 issue, *Vogue* presented a selection of photos depicting 'fashion's obsession with ancient Egypt',[90] and *Harper's Bazaar* listed Cleopatra as number eight in the top ten of 'the most important movies by decade – from the 1950s to today – that every fashion lover should see'.[91]

While recognizing the film's impact on fashion, none of these celebratory responses acknowledge the possibility of cultural appropriation: such glamourization and 'fashion iconicity' as applied to ancient Egypt, and Cleopatra as its most famous representative, pays scant attention to the meaning or significance of history, instead focusing on its role in Western fashion trends. For example, colours, frequently referenced in articles on the film's fashion influence, were highly meaningful in the ancient civilization, because 'they revealed the true essence of a person or a thing, [and] could provide them with protection or other magical properties'.[92] The popular cultural response of the mass media is focused on opulence, magnificence, colour as decoration, and, most importantly, how to 'get' the Cleopatra 'look'. It might be argued that this approach trivializes one of the most sophisticated societies of the ancient world, and objectifies Cleopatra as played by Taylor so that both women are fashion-plates rather than powerful women. However, Taylor/Cleopatra was fully aware of the importance of image and how to exploit it.[93] In their hands, clothes and cosmetics become tools of power, modes of manipulation.

The film received some unenthusiastic notices: Judith Crist commented that 'The mountain of notoriety has produced a mouse',[94] while *The New Statesman* opined that 'Miss Taylor is monotony in a slit skirt, a pre-Christian Elizabeth Arden with sequinned eyelids and occasions constantly too large for her.'[95] In *The Classical World*, Bernard Dick not only criticized Taylor's performance ('about as much vitality as an amateur's still life') but also her 'blatant aloofness from the historical text',[96] and is equally scathing about Burton. He is also unable to resist a sly dig at the two stars:

> The film is a dubious bargain: two pictures for the price of one. The first is definitely worthwhile, but the second is the painfully familiar tale of a femme fatale, her dissipated lover, and their tawdry affair. And any resemblance to persons living or dead is purely coincidental.[97]

Variety, however, was more positive, referring to the 'giant panorama', 'spectacle scenes' and 'acute' personal story, though it observed that 'some of the weaker moments in the film are the love scenes between Liz and Dickie'.[98]

Several factors contributed to the artistic failure of the film.[99] Everything about the movie is big: rooms are like halls; the eye constantly wanders.[100] There is little intimacy, despite the background scandal, and limited psychological complexity. In addition, while the Taylor/Burton affair added much interest to the making of the film, it is a distraction when watching, overshadowing the characters. The lynchpin is Taylor, but the focus on spectacle disallowed her from giving a more intimate and subtle performance. It also strained her voice – already suffering by comparison with Burton's sonorous tones – requiring her to shout to match the largeness of the setting.[101] There *are* some sparkling moments: at the end, Octavian tells the defeated Cleopatra, 'I suppose you are still beautiful', to which she replies, 'You flatter me'. He responds: 'My interest is impersonal: if you had any intention …', and she interrupts him: 'Now you flatter yourself'.[102] Although considered a commercial failure, with reissues, DVD and TV rights, *Cleopatra* eventually made a small profit.[103]

But, of course, it was – and is – the off-screen affair which dominates the movie,[104] as Richard Brody's comment in *The New Yorker* reveals:

> The fact that Taylor and Burton had become an item is obvious from watching the film; the passion that they generate on-screen has a thrillingly spontaneous, electric ardor. The production was cursed – and yet, in this regard, it was, perhaps more than any other, blessed.[105]

The 'epic movie' could find no better or more appropriate setting than the spectacular landscape of ancient Egypt, and no more epic subject-matter than Cleopatra and Antony/Liz and Dick. But, more than this, the film and its gossip-laden background raised the curtain on the modern cult of 'celebrification'. The audience could feel an intimacy with the stars of the film through the media coverage and the 'performance' of love which the film contains.[106] Daniel Williams sees this as a forerunner of the contemporary blurring of boundaries between the real and the imagined or artificial:

> Art in general comments on life by exaggerating it and they seemed to exaggerate life in their own lives and on the screen simultaneously. *Cleopatra* seems absolutely ridiculous now, but if there's anything in there that retains any interest it is the

passion on-screen between them. ... *Cleopatra* exaggerates this idea of them as almost godlike mythic figures. There's an element of that about the two of them I guess, as actors, beautiful people, representing that.[107]

Thus, Burton and Taylor are early exemplars of current celebrity culture, where 'the world of celebrity is a place where the real and the unreal intermingle'.[108] Ellis Cashmore's recent study of Taylor and her fame confirms her significance in the history of celebrity,[109] something which Kashner and Schoenberger make explicit when they write that 'Elizabeth and Richard's grand passion launched a new industry: celebrity culture on a scale never seen before'.[110]

When the couple reunited professionally to perform Noel Coward's *Private Lives* on tour in the United States in 1983, the possibility of a third Burton-Taylor marriage surfaced as an additional narrative:

> WJ Wetherby, who reviewed the play for *The Guardian* when it reached Broadway, called it 'the show business event of the season,' as tabloids filled their columns with gossip and will they-won't they rumours of a third marriage surfaced. Burton emphatically scotched those when, during a break in performances in July 1963 (Taylor was unwell), he married girlfriend Sally Hay.[111]

Although the romantic desire for a further reunion never came to pass, and although both Taylor and Burton remarried more than once after their second divorce, the sense of a couple 'destined' to be together, the narrative of a 'great love story', persists.[112]

Thus, whatever the myths and legends that have become associated with Taylor and Burton's relationship, there remains an inextricable connection between the historical characters they played in 1963 and their own lives, one which also ties the extremities of the film in terms of budget, spectacle and salaries to the 'excess' of ancient Egypt and the extravagances of the Burtons. The making of *Cleopatra* has acquired the same mythical status in movie-making history as its subjects have acquired in ancient history, a myth-making that began almost as soon as the film began shooting. Nadine Liber, writing for *Life Magazine* at the time, noted that in her scenes, Taylor showed:

> an immediate and right understanding of what the director Mankiewicz expects from her. ... As someone said about Liz, 'that woman has more power than Cleopatra ever had.' Maybe that is why while Rex Harrison [Julius Caesar] and Richard Burton [Mark Antony] intellectualize and study their parts, Liz seems to let herself be herself.[113]

It was almost as if Liz and Cleopatra were 'one'.

It may be that the glamour and extravagance of *Cleopatra* provided escapism in a time of anxiety (the Cuban Missile crisis occurred while the film was in production), but it is likely that the off-screen narrative diverted audiences more than the film itself. Jon Solomon argues that the financial disaster it brought on 20th Century Fox dissuaded filmmakers from adopting the epic style in later films,[114] but more significantly, the move towards social realism in 1960s cinema, and the development of political and youth movements, such as civil rights and the anti-Vietnam protests, made the extravagant glamour of *Cleopatra*-type films seem outdated, and, perhaps more damagingly, inappropriate.[115]

The implications of the film in terms of popular cultural influence are relatively easy to see (although fascination with the time of the pharaohs, of course, predates *Cleopatra*), but its impact on perceptions of Egypt and Egyptology is more difficult to assess. The representation of Egypt in the Western imagination has been distorted as well as enlightened by the discoveries of tombs and artefacts and widespread cultural fascination with them: as Peter Hessler, in an article for *The Guardian* in April 2019, points out, the pharaohs, pyramids and all the other aspects of ancient Egyptian culture so loved by the West are regarded more ambivalently in Egypt itself:

> The national relationship with the past is complicated. Average citizens take pride in pharaonic history, but there's also a disconnect because the tradition of the Islamic past is stronger and more immediate. This is captured by the design of Egypt's currency. Every denomination follows the same pattern: on one side of a bill, words are in Arabic and there's an image of some famous Egyptian mosque. The other side pairs English text with a pharaonic statue or monument. The implication is clear: the ancients belong to foreigners, and Islam belongs to us.[116]

The disconnect identified here reflects on what some scholars, such as Bernard Dick (quoted elsewhere in this essay) see as the 1963 film's tawdry version of Egypt, preoccupied with gratification, excess, love affairs, monuments and display. However, the purpose of a film is to entertain, rather than instruct, and ancient Egypt was an entirely suitable period for twentieth-century Hollywood precisely because, like Hollywood, it was a mix of business, politics, money, pleasure, grandiose gestures, inequality in terms of power and a devotion to enjoyment, at least if you had the economic and social wherewithal to sustain it. The extreme grandeur of the film might be derided, but it connects to the historic period it purports to represent in ways other than the illicit love affairs of its leading characters.[117]

As a documentary portrayal of history, or of ancient Egypt, *Cleopatra* is too much in thrall to its stars – or its star – and the Hollywood style which produced it to focus on authenticity. There was some historical research behind the writing of the script,[118] and the film's magnificence was an accurate mirror of the extent of ancient Egypt's wealth. But its most memorable legacy is not its qualities as a piece of cinema or art, but the mutual act of 'celebrification' between its fictional and real couples which it commemorates, the version of both the story and the setting which it established, and the imagery of ancient Egypt – or at least, its most famous female – which became embedded in popular culture.[119] Allison Berry, writing about the film's influence on fashion, quotes fashion historian and scholar Hazel Clark on Taylor's and the film's impact:

Much as 'the discovery of Tutankhamun's tombs [sic] in 1922 served as inspiration for the Art Deco movement,' Clark points out, our image of Cleopatra from the film revived interest in the styles of ancient Egypt. And the fact that Taylor herself was a well-known actress and personality fuelled this: 'The whole celebrity fascination or obsession was very much what caught the public's imagination – not just with Elizabeth Taylor as Cleopatra, but with Elizabeth Taylor as Elizabeth Taylor.' The persistent mythology of this powerful female pharaoh combined with the allure of the beautiful violet-eyed actress who personified her onscreen, make the figure of Cleopatra an enduring sartorial influence.[120]

Taylor's performance, in and outside the film, secured her 'as' Cleopatra in the public mind, and the focus on the love affairs of both women eclipsed the shrewdness and acumen with which they ran their lives.[121] Both became women who 'gave all for love'; whether this was the case in reality became irrelevant. The intensely glamourous version of Cleopatra which Taylor provided not only granted additional star quality to her character but also showed ancient Egypt as a colourful, exciting place, where Taylor's dazzling costumes, makeup and headdresses are emblematic of a fascinating civilization. In this way, one might argue that the film did a service to perceptions of ancient Egypt. There are scenes set in Rome, but many are interiors or take place in the Forum, and the only major external scene is the procession, where the focus is on Egyptian rather than Roman magnificence.

The 1963 *Cleopatra* also located ancient Egypt in the genre of adventure and romance, distancing it – for a time – from recent previous associations with the supernatural. The off-screen action was as exciting a narrative as that onscreen: in fact, more exciting, since no one could script the ending. The film confirmed the popular perception of Egypt, whose magnificence was demonstrated by the exhibition of the Tutankhamun treasures at the British Museum in 1972. More recently, cinema has seemingly built upon the basis which Taylor's film provided. The highly successful *Mummy* franchise combines the 'horror' element, which was maintained by Hammer Films throughout the 1950s and 1960s, with romance, spectacle and comedy, and CGI has enabled film directors to dispense with actors wrapped in bandages or expensive sets with thousands of extras. Although Taylor's performance was panned by many critics, all acknowledged the film's visual power, and it is *her* image which remains the iconic popular culture Cleopatra, one to which all others are likely to be compared.

Above all, the 1963 film had an element which no producer could have arranged, making it a legend in ways which its excessive cost and visual magnificence could not.[122] Even those who worked on the 2013 restoration of the original movie acknowledge that nothing eclipses the fascination of the parallel love stories, as these comments from Susan King's 2013 article in the *LA Times* illustrate, written as the restored film was about to be released:

'The movie is so beautiful to look at – the costumes and the production design,' said Schawn Belston, senior vice president of library and technical services at

Fox, who was responsible for the restoration of 'Cleopatra.' 'But I think you can't separate the experience of seeing the film from at least knowing about the scandal between the two lovers.'

'I think what happened is that the movie came out and it was so overwhelmed by their relationship,' said Kate Burton, the actress daughter of Richard Burton. 'It basically became "we are watching them fall in love for the first time."'[123]

The link between the chief characters in the story and two of the great celebrities of the twentieth century was beyond the engineering capabilities of any publicist. Both couples conducted stormy public affairs; they flaunted wealth and power, and 'met', as it were, on the set of a Hollywood movie, itself a site of fantasy and make-believe. In the present culture of celebrity, Liz and Dick would be a 'brand', and the film would have an extensive marketing campaign of associated products. In the somewhat more moralizing atmosphere of the early 1960s, the producers were unable to openly exploit this kind of capital: it was left to commercial interests to pursue this, focusing on Liz/Cleopatra rather than Taylor/Burton. However, such contrived attention was superfluous. Taylor and Burton's love of excess and subsequent marriage allowed the film's story to continue,[124] for 'Cleopatra' and 'Antony' to fulfil the (temporarily) 'happy' ending denied to the historical characters,[125] while providing an indelible image for those characters and the ancient civilization they inhabited.[126] Finally, *Cleopatra* gave, and still gives, a moment of ultimate satisfaction for a voyeuristic and celebrity-obsessed audience: it made it possible to see the love affair of these two great stars actually played out in the guise of their roles. There was no need for 'sources close to the couple' or any of the other euphemisms used in gossip magazines: the public could view the affair as, literally, an entertainment, and the continuance of 'Liz and Dick' as an entity simply extended it, offering, whether intentionally or not, their very own soap opera. The colour and drama of Egypt suited a Hollywood epic, in an industry trying to compete with the increasing power of television, but, beyond that, the dramatic excesses of Taylor and Burton as Cleopatra and Antony, and vice versa, remain a watershed moment in celebrity culture, and a film legend.[127]

CHAPTER 15
THE MUMMY, THE PRIESTESS AND THE HEROINE: EMBODYING AND LEGITIMATING FEMALE POWER IN 1970S GIRLS' COMICS
Nickianne Moody

The use of ancient Egypt as an exotic location, an immediately recognizable visual iconography through which to construct supernatural beings or monsters and a rationale for the use of magic, has long been noted in the graphic novel.[1] The following discussion, however, is interested in a specific version of this popular medium: the British girls' comic of the 1970s. Stephanie Moser's survey of reception studies published in the *Journal of Archaeological Method and Theory* in 2015 considers how the creative exploration of antiquity generates knowledge about the past.[2] Following this methodological perspective, and taking as its focus 'When the Mummy Walks', serialized in *Spellbound* between 25 September and 27 November 1976, and 'The Cult of the Cat', serialized in *Misty* between 4 February and 22 April 1978, this essay examines the context in which readers in the 1970s encountered the comic strip, the interaction expected between the reader and the polysemy of the narrative, and how the iconography of these representations of ancient Egypt can tell the stories of girlhood, maturity and the acquisition of power and responsibility in the late twentieth century.

Both stories examined here use the visual register of ancient Egypt to render high-quality artwork: of the reanimated mummy and priestess in 'When the Mummy Walks', written by Esteban Maroto and illustrated by Norman Lee, and the temple, use of magic, transmogrification and ancient Egyptian characters in 'The Cult of the Cat', likely written by *Misty*'s sub-editor Bill Harrington and illustrated by Honeriu Romeu.[3] Moser remarks upon how the decorative arts and popular media or performance convey distinct qualities of 'monumentality, strength and immortality' which are evident in both of these cultural products, particularly the latter.[4] This fiction uses the intrusion of antiquity in a neo-Victorian and a contemporary setting respectively to explore women's influence, intelligence and agency, using ideas about women's status and authority in a specific imagined past as a nexus for the creative engagement with ancient Egypt.[5]

During the late 1970s, comics and young adult fiction for girls was subject to intense academic debate, especially in the newly emerging field of cultural and media studies. Key to this discussion is Angela McRobbie's initial publication through the Centre for Contemporary Cultural Studies at the University of Birmingham which argued that popular magazines were forms of socialization for women's understanding of feminine gender norms. She examined a publication which was aimed at older adolescent girls; the role of comics for younger readers remained contentious as they focussed on adventure, resilience and middle-class aspiration, which was then countered by relinquishment of such independence later in a woman's reading career. McRobbie was interested in how adolescent publications framed the world for their readers. She claimed:

> In fact women's and girls' weeklies offer a privileged position. Addressing themselves solely to a female market, their concern is with providing a feminine culture for their readers. They define and shape a woman's world, spanning every age form childhood to old age. From *Mandy*, *Bunty* and *Judy* to *House and Home* the exact nature of the woman's role is spelt out in detail, according to her age.[6]

The publications considered in this discussion are for girls (approximately from the ages of eight to thirteen) and their stories focus on mystery and adventure. Twentieth-century girls' comics embraced a variety of genres and the imagination of different backgrounds and situations. These stories usually narrativized crisis and its resolution through personal resilience. These publications sit outside adolescent concerns regarding romance but they do concern themselves with making sense of the adult world. Rivalry between girls and experiences of isolation are often present in these stories, but so is collective feminine identity. This is very different to McRobbie's location of a preoccupation with accepting heteronormative behaviour, valour and ambition in popular magazines for teenage and older readers.

Martin Barker, in his survey of research and approaches to studying comics, begins by addressing the development of this argument concerning the social function of comics in preparing young women for adolescent sexuality and the ideology of heterosexual romance under patriarchy found in the work of McRobbie and Valerie Walkerdine.[7] Such publications are identified as talking to those areas of girls' lives where dreams, hopes, ambitions, fears and desires are formed. The narratives play out existing tensions and propose consensual resolutions. Walkerdine's argument is uniquely interesting; she considers how readers consume texts, seeking 'to show that cultural products for girls, by exploring those dynamics in symbolic form, may be of strategic importance in presenting psychic conflicts lived out in fantasy situations, and also in presenting resolution and potential resolutions for these conflicts'.[8] Looking at *Bunty* and *Tracy*, she focuses on how the heroines of these narratives become 'victims' because the stories validate passivity and do not allow them access to feelings of anger which are instead projected onto others.[9]

Barker refutes Walkerdine's account by looking at one of the most popular stories in *Judy* (1960–91), a publication for the relevant pre-teen age group. He does find the shared characteristics that Walkerdine observes, such as cruelty, being in receipt of injustice, loss, being misunderstood and the importance of the family, but not the same organizing principles which allow for different narrative pleasures and engagement. Barker argues that it is the heroine's struggle to understand what is happening around her when those in positions of authority or responsibility cannot or will not that determines the narrative.[10] This pursuit of understanding a disrupted world is also acknowledged as an organizing principle of bestselling horror films of the 1980s. The shift in genre, the alignment with other popular media forms and the representation of experience is important in understanding how comics were received and consumed. The endings of these stories are also significant because the restoration of stable family units, explanations and final resolutions to the psychic dilemmas are not uniform.

Moreover, in a similar fashion to detective fiction, the endings are not the focus of the narrative engagement. Barker argues more forcefully that the endings are unmotivated by these stories making the serial development of the narrative and the fictional diegesis that it creates more important to the reader.[11] Barker feels that:

> these stories are unresolved dramas of the class experience of working class girls rather than desire, knowledge and its relation to action. And the readers are not implicated in the stories; they are watchers of stories, seeing dramatised in front of themselves their own typified experience.[12]

The stories that we are considering which use the ancient Egyptian diegesis feature the acquisition of Egyptological knowledge that empowers the heroine and sets her apart from the mundane world but still leaves her functional within it. She can identify with role models from an ancient civilization and move beyond the roles and stereotypes associated with being a daughter because the diegesis posits matriarchal structures and access to feminine power which meets with social approval.

In a later study of children's television viewing, which draws on these earlier debates, David Buckingham theorized how young people made sense of fiction and factual programming. Using empirical method, he concluded that there were complex relationships between mediated experience and lived culture. Children are bound to be drawn to texts that speak to their fear of loss and abandonment, of disgrace and humiliation and offer them ways of coming to terms with them.[13] Therefore, they are interested in the ambiguous pleasures that were evident in the girls' comics of the 1970s such as the disruption of the family, pity towards those presented as vulnerable and defenceless and the negotiation of violence. Horror is therefore a significant genre for young adult fiction as it allows for the extrapolation of how the reader will react to the experience of the adult world and to question the strangeness of adult values, attitudes, agency and decision making.

Marie Messenger-Davies, in her summary of the distinctiveness of British children's television during this period, notes that it is less constrained than programming for adults, employing magic, fantasy, fairy tale and slapstick.[14] These are qualities that it shared with the comic culture which it was replacing. The carnivalesque subverts the respectability of adult authority. It is told from the point of view of the child. Stylistic features include brightly coloured sets, vivid graphics, multimedia presentations and glamorous young presenters; it offered a direct address to the audience and incorporated both wackiness and animation.[15] And, through this style, it could provide a treatment of painful issues. Both the heroines that I consider are making tentative steps towards deciding on their future and independent life.

Ancient Egypt in the Modern Imagination

Across the twentieth century, girls' comics, usually for primary school age readers, focussed on girlhood as a time of adventure. Adventure was local, international, investigative or historical with typically fourteen weekly episodes based on school, work, sport or animal welfare scenarios. These stories were occasionally fantastic, but largely mimetic. However, in the 1970s several short lived but popular comics experimented with narratives for girls that focussed on horror, mystery and the supernatural.[16] Foremost of these were DC Thomson's *Spellbound* (1976-7) and Fleetway's *Misty* (1978-80), which differed from the more established publications such as *Bunty* (1958-2001). Both of these titles, in contrast to formidable competition in the shape of *Bunty* among others, lasted only a short while; it appears that *Misty* was introduced specifically to compete with *Spellbound*, but by the time of its inaugural issue *Spellbound* has already folded. *Spellbound* merged with *Debbie* in 1977, and *Misty* with *Tammy* in 1980. The reasons for these titles' demise are unclear, though they were certainly competitively priced (*Bunty* cost 6 pence in 1976, rising to 7 pence by 1978, while *Spellbound* and *Misty* were introduced at 7 and 8 pence, respectively). It is possible that the supernatural and mystery focuses of both magazines was a factor, especially as both merged with more 'mainstream' comics. As Julia Round observes, however, the 1970s saw the market for British comics – especially those marketed to girls – nosedive, for several reasons, of which comics' economic performance was but one.[17]

Both *Spellbound* and *Misty* featured the first instalment of an ancient Egyptian-themed story in their debut issues, perhaps indicating the perceived popularity of ancient Egyptian-inspired narratives in a competitive market on the part of the comics' editors. The narrative imperatives of these stories are adventure and investigation; horror is evoked through the destructive force of the reanimated mummy and the cult of Bast which wants to lay claim to the young heroine. They draw on older narrative structures associated with storytelling about ancient Egypt: the malevolent mummy, the evil priestess, revenge, possession, a curse, magic, transmogrification and the work of the Egyptologist. However, these elements are reinterpreted by the narrative. In each case, the heroine must question the perilous supernatural environment in which she finds herself and then aligns herself with the ancient Egyptian quest for justice, asserting her own moral worth in the process.

Ancient Egypt as a narrative setting

Vera Vasiljević argues that ancient Egypt is a well-established location for graphic novels,[18] which may bring the characters into the contemporary world or leave them in a fantastic and stereotypical historical one. She identifies three recurrent stereotypes: the wisdom of the Egyptians, the revived (evil) mummy and the misuse of visual signifiers for characters all of which are predicated on a longer historical interest in ancient Egypt stretching back to Plato and the Renaissance.[19] She illustrates the last stereotype with three examples, one from the 1930s and two from the 1970s, analysing the artists' inaccuracies and errors which she argues have become standardized in the media form. Despite her preoccupation with historic inaccuracy, the tropes that she identifies are interesting when applied to the examples considered by this discussion.

Knowledge is a prominent issue in both the girls' stories, but it is the protagonists rather than ancient Egyptians who demonstrate their learning, intuition or acquire self-knowledge. The revived mummy which appears in the girls' comic contrasts greatly with the ones that Vasiljević discusses. She places an emphasis on the motif of a young man reviving a female mummy, and the romantic narrative which ensues, tracing its origin to Théophile Gautier.[20] In 'When the Mummy Walks', however, the supernatural creature has been animated by an older female Egyptologist in order to acquire power and riches, evoking – rather than Gautier – Arthur Conan Doyle's short story 'Lot No. 249' (1892).[21] The mummy's longing for revenge is answered by the younger heroine, who pits her wits and knowledge of Egyptology against the criminal to bring her to justice and set the mummy free. Romance does occur between the heroine and her lower-status male sidekick but is present almost as comic relief. The final stereotype which focuses on popular representation is less useful but connects the iconography in both narratives with the rich heritage of ancient Egypt found in nineteenth-century visual media. This is particularly the case in 'The Cult of the Cat' with regards to the clothes of the priestesses. The inappropriate use of regnal symbols on their headdresses corresponds with Vasiljević's concern with critiquing inaccuracy in narratives which use an ancient Egyptian diegesis. More interestingly, the heroine in this story spends time trying to understand the metaphorical meaning of the eternal battle between cats and snakes. Both publications use random hieroglyphic symbols to advertize and promote the serials while they were running.

The most useful element of Vasiljević's analysis is the consideration of narrative mechanism and whether the ancient past intrudes upon the contemporary (or in this instance also the neo-Victorian) world. Revivification of the mummy – a conceit that originates with Jane Webb Loudon's *The Mummy: Or a Tale of the Twenty-Second Century* (1827)[22] – allows for a commentary on the present and evaluation of contemporary civilization, its science, mores, social organization and gendered politics. Both of the narratives considered here are meaningful to their young audiences because they envisage girls' futures, their work, the value of their education, their secret lives and the roles that they will play in wider society.

Before we look more closely at these stories there are two other concepts that ancient Egypt is frequently used to explore in popular culture: imagery representing justice and the feminine divine. Although Kathryn E. Slanski discusses a Mesopotamian law stele, her interest in the enduring visual representation of justice and its association with the feminine divine found in the art of the ancient world is also applicable to ancient Egypt.[23] She explores the compelling motifs in the visual iconography of justice which emphasizes its divine origin and the obligation of the elite 'to execute and maintain lasting just ways for their people'.[24] Rather than returning wholeheartedly to her family and putting her adventure behind her, the heroine in 'The Cult of the Cat' accepts the need to become part of a matriarchy dedicated to resolving injustice.

The representation of older women and ageing is also important to both narratives. Deborah Sweeney discusses the difficulties of representing women and authority in her detailed examination of women's ageing in ancient Egyptian art: 'to appropriate images of experience and wisdom, they also had to depart from the socially dictated female norm of youth and beauty and risk being associated with the strange and the laughable – a problem which is still with us'.[25] Images of men could positively use characteristics of ageing to connote authority and experience but for women youth and beauty are the definitive representational norm in formal Egyptian art. In particular, old age is absent from the visual repertoire of the female afterlife.

Sweeney does find a variety of interesting examples of female ageing depicted in a third dynasty relief of Hathorneferhotep on a pillar on the portico of her pyramid complex, an Old Kingdom figurine of a miller housed in the Louvre, a First Intermediate Period false door portrait of Hemy-Re in the Fitzwilliam Museum, and a sculpture from the workshop of Thutmose found at El Amarna. It is more usual, however, for artists to overlook the gendered life course in female representation. These examples 'appropriated aspects of the Egyptian images of successful male ageing to express female power and experience'.[26] Moreover, she agrees with Dorothea Arnold that the signs of ageing in representations of Queen Tiy and Nefertiti act as 'a deliberate attempt to provide a female parallel to the image of the venerable and experienced older male'.[27]

Both of the protagonists of the girls' comic stories find themselves in direct conflict with older women who have amassed power and experience.[28] These relationships are negotiated in very different ways, demonstrating the importance of requiring the reader to engage and empathize with the narrative. In 'The Cult of the Cat' the high priestess is depicted as being in extreme old age. She frightens and disconcerts the heroine who perceives her to be evil. The older woman wants to recruit the next priestess to replace her as she feels that she is nearing death: 'the seeds of my ninth life run through the hands of Ra. Before another moon she the chosen of Ra the blessed of Bast must be brought here!'[29] The heroine fears for her life and sanity in confrontation with the ageing skeletal and capable woman. The horrifying visual representation of the elderly priestess and the character's increasing decrepitude as the story develops makes us empathize with the heroine. In contrast, the older woman who gains power over the mummified priestess in 'When the Mummy Walks' is corpulent and middle aged. She is a bully and the heroine is nervous about this new boss. The heroine suspects her superior and investigates her nefarious activities. The mummy alternates between a frightening supernatural entity amok on the streets of London and a young priestess in search of justice and revenge. Each page of the story is given a title which draws out aspects of the text upon which it invites the reader to focus. During the final battle on the penultimate page of the story 'The Mummy Believes Me' this emphasis is placed on the mummy accepting the moral worth of the heroine.[30] The heroine assumes the older woman's magical ability, controls the mummy and restores order so that she can continue her career.

The Mummy, the Priestess and the Heroine

Ancient Egyptian iconography in girls' comics

These stories use the ancient Egyptian diegesis in different ways to explore the experience of girlhood. The opening page to 'The Cult of the Cat' is a spectacular scene of temple worship with rows of priestesses, pillars covered in hieroglyphs and a central statue of Bast. 'When the Mummy Walks' also uses immediate ancient Egyptian signification. The title page has the mask-like head of the priestess looking over the steam train taking the heroine to her new job in London. 'The Cult of the Cat' starts very traditionally with the heroine Nicola Scott practicing for the Interschools Challenge Swimming Cup. She is admired for her prowess by her school friends. After practice she finds and takes home a stray cat and subsequently develops a fear of heights and water which means that she cannot dive; the school loses the cup to her utter humiliation.

She suffers greater anxiety when taunted by her rival about her failure. The illustration of this scene shows Nicola react. The artwork shows her holding her hands out – the fingers shaped like claws – with the outline of a cat's head behind her own. The readers have already been reminded in the recap at the beginning of this episode, 'It's no ordinary cat, it's an emissary from a select group who practice their rites within the most secret and sacred pyramids.'[31] The high priestess instructs another to go to Britain and seek the chosen one. We are shown a cartouche which contains a line of women. The figure that she points to is in a swimming costume. In front of that figure is one in futuristic dress and behind them older styles, most strikingly Tudor women represented side on in a parody of ancient Egyptian art. The cult is immortal and the priestesses – throughout time – are endowed with physical ability and strength.

Nicola dreams of the priestesses' rituals and their desire for her to join them. In her ordinary life she wakes up to find a ring on her finger and experiences changes in her behaviour that appear to be feline. This brings her into conflict with her mother and female teachers who are represented as significantly older. The illustration emphasizes her fear that she is transforming into a cat. Throughout her ordeal she remains resilient and determined to understand what is happening to her.[32]

On a school trip to the British Museum she can recite knowledge of ancient Egypt, pronouncing that 'the cat goddess is known as Bast and is an extremely popular deity and has been since the second dynasty particularly in the Valley of Bubastis.'[33] She presents the activities of the cult as contemporary, and the style of drawing uses shadows and a slow focus on her face to emphasize the horror of being able to know something beyond her own understanding or experience. The title pages for each instalment reiterate the temple, the rites and the imaginative dress of the priestesses, which is based on different representations of ancient Egyptian goddesses. A monumental statue of Bast dominates the scene but the face is always an ordinary serene cat until there is danger that Nicola will not complete the initiation. Then the eyes glow.

Nicola fears for her sanity and contemplates running away but discovers that she has gained physical abilities to jump and fight which save her in perilous, though ordinary, situations. The narrative illustrates disturbing dream sequences and hallucinations which intensify and exaggerate the ageing body of the high priestess. Nicola appears at times to be subsumed by her and taken in by the cult against her will. She ends up in hospital and male doctors consider her a case of lycanthropy; her friends feel that due to shock and strain she has 'flipped her lid'.[34]

In response to the younger priestess who has been sent to protect her and oversee the initiation, Nicola accepts the transformation: 'And that secret self, that secret Nicola, that lay deep within her and could travel distances in seconds was greeted by those who waited at Bubastis.'[35] At the resolution to the narrative, the police return Nicola to her mother. Mother and daughter embrace, and Nicola promises to return to normal. However, a newly mature version of the heroine looks out at the audience with a more cynical response. The final frame informs us that 'Nicola knew now she was a very special person. The chosen of Bast … and the cats of Bast must be ever watchful.'[36] At the bottom of this image 'The End' as a final caption is appended with a question mark.

The horror in 'When the Mummy Walks' is externalized and more traditional in the narrative conventions that it uses for representing ancient Egyptian stereotypes and characters. Jenny Hunt is also negotiating the adult world and her place in it. She has taken a job in a neo-Victorian London where she discovers that the head curator is able to reanimate an Egyptian mummy: the Golden Priestess of Manaton.[37] Miss Brisson is using her control over the mummy to steal treasures from eminent archaeologists. After a visit from the mummy they contract a mysterious illness referred to as the Curse of Manaton. Brisson alternates in the illustrations from an ordinary older woman to a witch-like crone (complete with bulbous nose). The mummy is also a skeletal, powerful monster in some scenes, while other representations which focus on her mask-like face show her as youthful, slender and attractive. Jenny works out that magic is being used, appropriates the ability and challenges Brisson for control of the mummy in a dramatic conclusion. However, the mummy must choose between them and in a final display of force destroys both Miss Brisson and the amulet used to control the priestess.

During the run of the story, many of the covers for *Spellbound* feature stylized images of the priestess, and Jenny on her own or with Bob, the odd job boy at the museum, either investigating or running away from the mummy. The title pages also concentrate on adventure. Jenny and Bob search underground for the hidden treasure. They feel unable to tell the authorities about the supernatural nature of the crimes. The narrative uses many more actual artefacts which exist and can be activated in the neo-Victorian diegesis. There is a scarab ring of protection, an amulet shaped like a jackal, different shapes and figures of gods and goddesses in the Egyptian room, libraries and ancient lore, and a preoccupation with trailing and abandoned mummy wrappings. Both publications also offered free gifts – a ring and a pendant, that tied in with these stories – inviting other cultural practices of play and imagination beyond the text.

The stories use the artwork to emphasize and dwell on the power held by the priestesses which is directed towards violence. This is a feminine power which must be contained by the heroines and is beyond the acknowledgement of male authorities. The heroines cannot turn to their friends or families for support while they deal with these personal problems and their public manifestations. To understand the occurrences, they must recognize their own newfound abilities, demonstrate knowledge beyond that of their peers and make moral decisions. The ancient Egyptian diegesis is a parallel world and one which is available to merge horror and adventure tropes. It sets the heroines apart from their peers, provides a sophisticated account of aspirational beauty, authority and meaningful adult life in the figure of the younger priestesses and provides a creative space to contemplate the further ramifications of adolescent identity. Notably, the evil that the matriarchy opposes is undefined and left to the readers' imagination. Jenny's career in the museum after Miss Brisson disappears is also left open to speculation.

These narratives draw on an older tradition of popular and commercial story telling which used the ancient Egyptian diegesis across the eighteenth, nineteenth and twentieth centuries. The experience of the phantasmagoria from its origins in post-revolutionary France used a bricolage of technology and performance regimes which took the audience into a supernatural and terrifying world.[38] Its spectacular staging encouraged a sense of immersion and inclusion within a fictional and narrative landscape. This was one in which the presence and absence of light, a confusing sense of scale, the sudden appearance of monstrous figures looming over or rushing towards the audience and the use of a fantastic narrative to hold these encounters together is similar to the artwork in the girls' comics. Like the phantasmagoria, the artwork for the girls' comics renders scenes of spectacle and action and utilizes the significance of light and shadow. Highlighting, flame and the movement of light in the illustrations emphasize the supernatural elements and use of magic.

The phantom show and the exhibition of Egyptiana in the early nineteenth century were near neighbours in the entertainment on offer in London and the provinces. Alongside stories of terror, the prose and dramatization given by performers and travellers like Giovanni Belzoni (1778–1823) shared extraordinary experiences, emphasizing action, adventure and Gothic sensationalism.[39] This approach to narrative drew on the many circulating images of the archaeological remains of ancient Egypt illuminating the darkness of temples and tombs with potential stories of rites, divine beings and magic.

One of the figures to emerge in the popular Victorian imagination of ancient civilizations is the priestess, who has a more ambiguous meaning than a princess or queen.[40] The priestess is undeniably pagan, she is learned and more likely to exist within matriarchal rather than patriarchal social relations. The knowledge with which she is credited forms a relationship with the divine and the use of magic. This has enabled representational art to consider the priestess' acquisition of self-knowledge, aesthetic sensibility and a spiritual independence.

Antonia Lant, a cinema historian who is interested in proto-cinematic experience, makes the argument that Egypt in the popular imagination is important to the development of popular narrative, especially early cinema.[41] This is evident in the display of magic and illusion which used the allusion to ancient Egypt as a narrative structure for stage performance. *The Haunted Curiosity Shop* (1901) directed by the magician Walter Booth and the pioneering British film maker R. W. Paul draws directly on these traditions and imagery. In this film an antiquarian is confronted by various bizarre encounters including a living mummy of a woman whose flesh dissolves to reveal a skeleton. These early films follow two main forms of narrative: the resurrection of a mummy or someone pretending to be a mummy for a joke. The first full-length horror film produced in Britain, *The Wraith of the Tomb* (1915), featured the ghost of an ancient Egyptian princess searching for her murderous, severed, mummified hand, adapting for a new medium the narratives tropes of Edgar Allan Poe, Théophile Gautier, Arthur Conan Doyle and Bram Stoker. The complexity and moral ambiguity of ancient Egyptian women, especially the priestess, and the use of the ancient Egyptian diegesis which features magic, adventure, destiny and woman's power is well established by the time that it is used by girls' comics in the 1970s.

It is significant that in both instances the matriarchal cult and the museum as an institution mean that the heroine is entering an adult world outside of the family home. The necessity to move beyond the ordinary world of school or home is part of the adventure. The older women with whom they find themselves in conflict are removed, leaving them with both the capacity to act and knowledge about the world around them. They appropriate the place of male adventurers and are able to keep the parallel world a secret in order to continue with their ordinary lives. Despite the fear of being controlled by adult social order, both young women are able to overcome their fears and find their place in an exciting and uncertain future. Moreover, the stereotype of the public service spinster and the crone abdicating after a lifetime of service do not deter the heroines from choosing the same path.

The mummy in girls' comics

Jasmine Day considers 'mummymania' – a fascination with the ambulatory mummy found in the horror genre and children's popular culture – a subfield of Egyptomania.[42] Through an extensive study of literature, cultural practice, popular culture and consideration of archaeology, Day argues that this phenomenon is 'not a mere collection of bric-a-brac but a cohesive system of ideas and images rooted in the history of colonialization, archaeology and the media'.[43] She identifies shifting periods of popular understanding and cultural preoccupations with the mummy. The pre-classical (1800–1931) used romantic narrative structures and instigates a particular association of the mummy with supernatural curses visited upon the despoilers of tombs. For the classical period (1932–71) she analyses the operating principle of Universal and Hammer horror films and finds that 'along with corpse like attributes, violence explains why classic mummies are almost exclusively male'.[44] The use of the mummy is a signifier of the abject which has the potential to threaten 'social order, moral standards, hygiene, conventional gender roles, economic stability, authority or the rule of law'.[45] However, by the post-classic period (1972–present) 'derivative works referenced the contrasting paradigms of previous eras and the collapsing credibility of horror mummies relegated them to children's culture'.[46]

Her analysis of a broader spectrum of popular culture allows her to offer an understanding of how the stories that we have examined here run counter to the prevailing narrative use of the ancient Egyptian diegesis. The stories for the inaugural issues of these girls' comics in the 1970s use horror, feature a female mummy, hold an ambivalent attitude to the abject and reject the curse as a meaningful structuring device as well as inherently evil ancient Egyptian characters. Day is able to confirm through her interviews with museum visitors 'that ambiguity underlies the status of mummies'.[47] Ambiguity and the ability to raise questions about shared cultural values is why the mummy remains such a valid imaginative construct in popular fiction. They hold 'the power to instantly signify age, decay, pollution, death, and difference'.[48] In narratives where the commonly affirmed beliefs and values associated with this form of signification is challenged or negated, then the use of the ancient Egyptian diegesis is particularly interesting.

Day characterizes the period in which the two girls' comics were published as one where mummies were most prevalent in children's television, especially cartoons. She sees the development of three distinct mummy character types marked by 'malevolence, stupidity or obsolescence'.[49] These attributes develop in strength and cultural recognition throughout the late twentieth century. In contrast, the artwork of the girls' stories associates the female mummy with stylized visualizations of magical power. 'When the Mummy Walks' retains the climatic rampage of the classical period, depicted in several episodes, but it does not portray the mummy as the 'loathsome creature deprived of the moral high ground'.[50] Therefore, rather than adopting the predominant characterization of popular media for the period, the comics invite their readers to consider female authority, erudition, ageing and engagement with ancient civilizations in a very different way.

It is when she looks at the late twentieth century that Day considers the cinematic fiction of the pre-classic period. She does not do this in depth, instead characterizing these films as comedies, magic sketches and fantasies.[51] In the first quarter of the twentieth century the mummy is incorporated into mystery stories which Day feels are concerned with 'the triumph of the detective logic over superstition'.[52] The girls' stories combine investigation with the revelation of the supernatural and the divine. The priestess is the conduit to this marvellous discovery and its normalization. As we have seen, fictional ancient Egyptian priestesses sometimes take over from the princess and become their own avengers. They exist in 'The Cult of the Cat' as a purposeful sorority. If the reader does not want to identify with the heroine she can speculate instead on the life of these young women. In Victorian narrative art the priestess is an ambivalent figure because she is pagan. Moreover, in the twentieth century her role in society is associated with the villainy of the High Priest Im-Ho-Tep, a character in the originating narrative of the classic period *The Mummy* released by Universal Pictures in 1932.[53] Unlike the girls at school the priestesses are united, they understand the world around them and are supportive of the new recruit. The girls' stories also overturn the abject repulsive physical traits of the supernatural mummy, the associations of dilapidation and obsolescence that it shares with old age and the subjection of the female mummy or heroine to male domination. In revisiting the moral worth of these characters, the visual impact of this fiction resisted the imagery and narrative logic which Day identifies as the shared characteristics of the evolving mummy story as it stood in the 1970s.

Most of these comics reject the romance narrative. Day notes that gender in the pre-classical stories precipitates moral crises and anxieties about sexual misconduct through the exposure of the beautiful and nubile ancient woman.[54] The passive mummy of this period could be manipulated and controlled, its only recourse to justice being the feminized older civilization's use of the curse. The curse in 'When the Mummy Walks' is quickly brushed aside. The heroine does not fear it and is instead preoccupied with the mummy's destructive force and the actions of the specifically female modern-day villain. The heroine in 'The Cult of the Cat' similarly must reinterpret the actions of the matriarchy as beneficial and noble rather than evil in order to understand her place in the new world. As such, this story takes on the structure of the thriller, rather than horror, and presents neither a stable nor a consensual conclusion.

Conclusion

The late 1970s in Britain were a time of high unemployment and changing educational attitudes for young women. Higher education was made possible through grants, the opening up of the sector and the understanding that entry into service industries rather than manufacturing would require qualifications. Acknowledgement of these opportunities and the encouragement to take advantage of them is found in Mel Gibson's interviews with women readers of girls' comics of this period.[55] It was also a decade of equal rights legislation which had an impact on educational strategies and the experience of employment. Gibson finds that the representation of girlhood in these comics 'offered tensions, contradictions, complexity and change' rather than stable and inflexible narratives.[56] The ancient Egyptian diegesis retained a resonance that allowed young female readers to think about prospective worlds beyond school and the family home. The pleasures of the text were not the childish interest in filth and the unclean, or luxury and the exotic, but the wielding of female power and the assuaging of guilt for holding that capacity.

In a recent contribution to *Frontiers in Psychology* Khalil et al. argue for the importance of female role models from Egypt's ancient history.[57] Concerned with how to intervene in prevailing female gender role norms that currently exist in Egypt and Middle Eastern countries, they are interested in providing relevant cultural role models for Egyptian schools which would contrast with gender-based disparity and inequality. The remarkable ancient Egyptian women that they review, particularly pioneers in science, medicine and the middle-class privilege of public participation in the arts, employment, religion, decision making about marriage, legal, financial and educational rights offer suitable role models for contemporary school children.

They perceive ancient Egyptian women to be 'privileged, as they were able to seek their dreams, strengthen their family life, study, and achieve progress in their work'.[58] They also identify the importance of female divinities in this outlook: 'Seemingly, the goddess Bastet, a champion around the vast majority of Egyptian gods, figured out how to enhance women's well-being, security and labor.'[59] Through their review, they feel that knowledge about their abilities and achievements is appropriate to realign contemporary notions about desirable behaviour attributable to girls and women. The use of women's history is very apparent in British girls' comics, especially examples which open up speculation about opportunities for careers, expression or contribution to the community using the same technique proposed by Khalil et al. These are role models that emphasize the existence of an ancient past which operated a social organization and might have been superior to the current one. Knowledge of its existence invites debate and imaginative engagement. Both *Spellbound* and *Misty* in the 1970s chose an ancient Egyptian diegesis and used its effective visual imagery in order to emphasize the depth of the perspective it offered to explore female justice, exercise of power and maturing adolescent identity.

NOTES

Introduction

1. The volumes in the *Encounters with Ancient Egypt* series are David O'Connor and Andrew Reid (eds), *Ancient Egypt in Africa* (London, 2007), John Tait (ed.), *Views of Ancient Egypt since Napoleon Bonaparte: Imperialism, Colonialism and Modern Appropriations* (London, 2007), David O'Connor and Stephen Quirke (eds), *Mysterious Lands* (London, 2007), Jean-Marcel Humbert and Clifford Price (eds), *Imhotep Today: Egyptianizing Architecture* (London, 2003), Peter J. Ucko and Timothy Champion (eds), *The Wisdom of Egypt: Changing Visions through the Ages* (London, 2003), Roger Matthews and Cornelia Roemer (eds), *Ancient Perspectives on Egypt* (London, 2003); and Sally MacDonald and Michael Rice (eds), *Consuming Ancient Egypt* (London, 2003). See also William Carruthers (ed.), *Histories of Egyptology: Interdisciplinary Measures* (London, 2014).

2. Stephanie Moser, *Wondrous Curiosities: Ancient Egypt at the British Museum* (Chicago, 2006); Stephanie Moser, *Designing Antiquity: Owen Jones, Ancient Egypt and the Crystal Palace* (London, 2012), Stephanie Moser, *Painting Antiquity: Ancient Egypt in the Art of Lawrence Alma-Tadema, Edward Poynter and Edwin Long* (Oxford, 2019); David Gange *Dialogues with the Dead: Egyptology in British Culture and Religion, 1822–1922* (Oxford, 2013); Donald Malcolm Reid, *Whose Pharaohs?: Archaeology, Museums, and Egyptian National Identity from Napoleon to World War I* (Los Angeles, 2007); Elliott Colla, *Conflicted Antiquities: Egyptology, Egyptomania, Egyptian Modernity* (London, 2007).

3. Dominic Montserrat, *Akhenaten: History, Fantasy and Ancient Egypt* (London, 2001).

4. Florian Ebeling, *The Secret History of Hermes Trismegistus: Hermeticism from Ancient to Modern Times*, trans. David Lorton (Ithaca, 2007); Roger Luckhurst, *The Mummy's Curse: The True History of a Dark Fantasy* (Oxford, 2012); Caroline Tully, 'Walk like an Egyptian: Egypt as authority in Aleister Crowley's reception of *The Book of the Law*', *Pomegranate: International Journal of Pagan Studies* 12 (2010), pp. 20–47; Steve Vinson and Janet Gunn, 'Studies in esoteric syntax: The enigmatic friendship of Aleister Crowley and Battiscombe Gunn', in William Carruthers (ed.), *Histories of Egyptology: Interdisciplinary Measures* (New York, 2015). See also Maria Fleischhack, 'Possession, trance, and reincarnation: Confrontations with ancient Egypt in Edwardian fiction', *Victoriographies* 7.3 (2017), pp. 257–70; Eleanor Dobson, 'The sphinx at the séance: Literature, Spiritualism and psycho-archaeology', in Eleanor Dobson and Gemma Banks (eds), *Excavating Modernity: Physical, Temporal and Psychological Stratification in Literature, 1900–1930* (London, 2018).

5. James Stevens Curl, *The Egyptian Revival: Ancient Egypt as the Inspiration for Design Motifs in the West* (New York, 2005).

6. Molly Youngkin, *British Women Writers and the Reception of Ancient Egypt, 1840–1910: Imperialist Representations of Ancient Egyptian Women* (Basingstoke, 2016); Judith E. Tucker, *Women in Nineteenth-Century Egypt* (Cambridge, 2009).

7. Jasmine Day, *The Mummy's Curse: Mummymania in the English-Speaking World* (London, 2006); Jasmine Day, 'The rape of the mummy: Women, horror fiction and the Westernisation of the curse', in Pablo Atoche-Peña, Conrado Rodríguez-Martin and Ángeles Ramírez-Rodríguez (eds), *Mummies and Science: World Mummies Research, Proceedings of the VI World*

Congress on Mummy Studies (Santa Cruz de Tenerife, 2008); Nolwenn Corriou, '"A woman is a woman, if she had been dead five thousand centuries!": Mummy fiction, imperialism and the politics of gender', *Miranda* 11 (2015), available at http://journals.openedition.org/miranda/6899.

8. Bradley Deane, 'Mummy fiction and the occupation of Egypt: Imperial striptease', *English Literature in Transition, 1880–1920* 51.4 (2008), pp. 381–410; Lynn Meskell, 'Consuming bodies: Cultural fantasies of ancient Egypt', *Body & Society* 4.1 (1998), pp. 63–76; Angie Blumberg, 'Strata of the soul: The queer archaeologies of Vernon Lee and Oscar Wilde', *Victoriographies* 7.3 (2017), pp. 239–56; Eleanor Dobson, 'Cross-dressing scholars and mummies in drag: Egyptology and queer identity', *Aegyptiaca: Journal of the History of the Reception of Ancient Egypt* 4 (2019), pp. 33–54.

1 'Wonderful Things' in Kingston upon Hull

1. For more on the aftermath of the Tutankhamun excavations, see Chapter 8 of this volume written by Lizzie Glithero-West.
2. The subject of replicas does not exclude the casts that are found in museums across the world (a particularly prominent collection in the UK is found, e.g. at the Ashmolean Museum in Oxford), but the focus here is on replicas more generally and so will not delve into the question of casts in depth.
3. See, for example, Donald Malcolm Reid, *Contesting Antiquity in Egypt: Archaeologies, Museums, and the Struggle for Identities from World War I to Nasser* (Cairo, 2015), pp. 74–5. Reid notes the political situation that led to the inclusion of the replicas, and discusses Carter's attempt to prevent the opening of the exhibition, but of the objects themselves notes simply that they were 'only replicas'. Thomas Garnett Henry James provides a little more information, noting 'the great gilded bed, the thrones ... the king's mannequin', and recording the claim that 'the smallest hieroglyphs were reproduced so faithfully that they could be read by Egyptologists', but the focus of his discussion is the work of Howard Carter rather than the exhibition; Thomas Henry Garnett James, *Howard Carter: The Path to Tutankhamun* (London, 2006), pp. 354–6.
4. Tutankhamun Archive, Griffith Institute, University of Oxford, TAA i.2.1, p. 25. Available at http://www.griffith.ox.ac.uk/discoveringTut/journals-and-diaries/season-1/journal.html (accessed 30 January 2018).
5. At this time a system of finds division, or partage, meant that excavated objects must be reported to the Egyptian Museum in Cairo, who had first refusal (all excavated objects being the property of the state and needing a permit for export). The remaining objects could then be removed from the country by the excavator, after which they were often donated to institutions who had funded the excavations in return for their sponsorship. Through this system, thousands of important antiquities were distributed to museums and institutions across the world, often with little regard for the integrity of site archives. See, for example, 'Artefacts of Excavation: Destinations'. Available at http://egyptartefacts.griffith.ox.ac.uk/destinations (accessed 14 April 2019) for destinations of objects excavated by the Egypt Exploration Fund (now Society). Additionally, despite this supposed control of exports, objects continued to be taken out of the country by individuals (often part of excavation teams), and many pieces found their way into private hands where they were, to all intents and purposes, lost. This subject is much larger than the remit of this article and deserves far greater attention than can be given here; a good introduction to the subject can be found in

Alice Stevenson, *Scattered Finds: Archaeology, Egyptology and Museums*. Available at https://ucldigitalpress.co.uk/Book/Article/73/97/5453/ (accessed 14 April 2019).

6. Weigall, for example, notes this increasing tension between the excavators and the press in his *Daily Mail* article of 9 February 1923, writing that this 'trafficking in publicity rights' might mean that a 'commercial precedent will be established and all excavation in Egypt will have to end'; Arthur Weigall, 'Trafficking in "Publicity" Rights', *Daily Mail*, 9 February 1923.
7. Tutankhamun Archive, TAA i.2.3, p. 3. Available at http://www.griffith.ox.ac.uk/discoveringTut/journals-and-diaries/season-4/journal.html (accessed 30 January 2018).
8. Arthur Weigall, 'Inscription from the Golden Shrine', *Daily Mail*, 20 February 1923.
9. Allegra Fryxell, 'Tutankhamun, Egyptomania, and temporal enchantment in interwar Britain', *Twentieth Century British History* 27.4 (2017), pp. 516–54 (p. 530).
10. Amelia Deffries, 'At Wembley', *The American Magazine of Art* 15.7 (1924), pp. 386–7 (p. 387).
11. See, for example, Julie Hankey, *A Passion for Egypt: Arthur Weigall, Tutankhamun and the Curse of the Pharaohs* (London, 2007), pp. 209–44, which details his time working in theatre and film and his success in carving out a career in set design.
12. As well as designing sets, Weigall had also worked in films (even writing his own scripts) and had been a film critic for the *Daily Mail*.
13. The dramatic appeal of Egypt in the nineteenth and early twentieth centuries is clear, for example, in the vast amount of popular fiction with Egyptian themes; see Maria Fleischhack, *Narrating Ancient Egypt: The Representation of Ancient Egypt in Nineteenth-Century and Early Twentieth-Century Fantastic Fiction* (Frankfurt, 2015).
14. Arthur Weigall, 'Laying Bare a Royal Tomb', *Daily Mail*, 4 December 1922.
15. In later seasons, the burial chamber was excavated as well as a small side chamber and an annexe. For a plan of the tomb, see Howard Carter Collection, Griffith Institute, University of Oxford, Carter MSS i.G.3. Available at http://www.griffith.ox.ac.uk/gri/4camaps.html (accessed 30 January 2018).
16. Many of these images can now be viewed on the website of the Griffith Institute Archive, University of Oxford. See 'Tutankhamun: Anatomy of an excavation', *The Griffith Institute*. Available at http://www.griffith.ox.ac.uk/gri/carter/gallery/ (accessed 30 January 2018).
17. C. Rodmell, 'Treasures of Tutankhamun's tomb', *Ours* 17.11 (1936), pp. 563–73 (p. 563).
18. See, for example, Fryxell, 'Tutakhamun, Egyptomania', p. 531.
19. See Christopher Frayling, *The Face of Tutankhamun* (London, 1992), p. 32.
20. I use the 'authenticity' without meaning to refer to many of the same connotations as the term has at most heritage sites today. Here, the colonial attitude towards other nations, and lack of understanding of other cultures, is patently clear.
21. See, for example, Julie Hankey, *A Passion for Egypt*, pp. 287–8.
22. *Ours* magazine notes Aumonier's War Memorial Fountain as well as his bust of T. R. Ferens, created for the Ferens Art Gallery, and the Stuart memorial on Holderness Road; see Rodmell, 'Treasures of Tutankhamun', p. 563.
23. The Mortimer Museum was founded in 1929 to display the excellent archaeological collections of the local archaeologist J. R. Mortimer, after whom the museum was named. The majority of this collection was eventually moved to the Museum of Archaeology and Transport in the 1950s and is now housed at Hull and East Riding Museum in Hull's Old Town.
24. The Municipal Museum on Albion Street suffered a direct hit in one of the many bombing raids and many of the collections were destroyed, while other warehouses and stores also suffered the same fate.

Notes to pages 18–23

25. Howard Carter Collection, Carter no. 091. Available at http://www.griffith.ox.ac.uk/gri/carter/091.html (accessed 30 January 2018).
26. A 'uraeus' is the rearing cobra often seen on the headdresses of Egyptian royalty and gods.
27. There is a multitude of literature on the Aten cult of Akhenaten. Good overviews are provided in: Jacobus Van Dijk, 'The Amarna Period and the later New Kingdom (c. 1352–1069 BC)', in I. Shaw (ed.), *The Oxford History of Ancient Egypt* (Oxford, 2000); Barry Kemp, *Ancient Egypt: Anatomy of a Civilisation* (London, 2006).
28. Howard Carter Collection, Carter no. 091.08. Available at http://www.griffith.ox.ac.uk/gri/carter/091-c091-08.html (accessed 30 January 2018).
29. This crown is also referred to as a *hemhem*-crown.
30. Howard Carter Collection, Carter no. 091.06. Available at http://www.griffith.ox.ac.uk/gri/carter/091-c091-06.html (accessed 30 January 2018). See also Howard Carter Collection, Burton photograph p0154a. Available at http://www.griffith.ox.ac.uk/gri/carter/091-p0154a.html (accessed 30 January 2018).
31. Howard Carter Collection, Carter no. 083. Available at http://www.griffith.ox.ac.uk/gri/carter/ (accessed 30 January 2018).
32. Howard Carter Collection, Carter no. 083.01. Available at http://www.griffith.ox.ac.uk/gri/carter/083-c083-1.html (accessed 1 January 2018).
33. For example, Johannes Dümichen, *Historische Inschriften Altägyptischer Denkmäler* (Leipzig, 1869).
34. See Howard Carter Collection, Burton photograph p0353. Available at http://www.griffith.ox.ac.uk/gri/carter/083-p0353.html (accessed 30 January 2018).
35. Howard Carter Collection, Carter no. 108.1. Available at http://www.griffith.ox.ac.uk/gri/carter/108-c108-01.html (accessed 30 January 2018).
36. Howard Carter Collection, Burton photographs p0313-p0317. Available at http://www.griffith.ox.ac.uk/gri/carter/108.html (accessed 30 January 2018).
37. Howard Carter Collection, Carter no. 108.5. Available at http://www.griffith.ox.ac.uk/gri/carter/108-c108-05.html (accessed 30 January 2018).
38. Howard Carter Collection, Carter no. 108b. Available at http://www.griffith.ox.ac.uk/gri/carter/108b.html (accessed 30 January 2018). See also Howard Carter Collection, Carter no. 108c. Available at http://www.griffith.ox.ac.uk/gri/carter/108c.html (accessed 30 January 2018).
39. See, for example, Randy Moore, *Dinosaurs by Decades: A Chronology of the Dinosaur in Science and Popular Culture* (Santa Barbara, 2014), p. 127, for an image of the recently removed Dippy the Diplodocus, a well-known and popular cast. The public outcry when the museum announced that Dippy was to be removed from display demonstrates its popularity.
40. See Rosmarie Beier de Haan, 'You can always get what you want: History, the original, and the endless opportunities of the copy', in *Original, Copy, Fake, On the significance of the object in History and Archaeology Museums, 22nd ICOM General Conference in Shanghai, China, 7–12nd November 2010* (Shanghai, 2010), p. 3. Available at http://network.icom.museum/fileadmin/user_upload/minisites/icmah/publications/Actes-Shanghai-complet2.pdf (accessed 30 January 2018).
41. The archaeological practice of restoring objects using modern materials is addressed, for example, in Philippos Mazarakis-Ainian, 'Archaeological copies: A scientific aid, a visual reminder or a contradiction in terms?', in *Original, Copy, Fake, On the Significance of the*

Object in History and Archaeology Museums, 22nd ICOM General Conference in Shanghai, China, 7–12nd November 2010 (Shanghai, 2010). Available at http://network.icom.museum/fileadmin/user_upload/minisites/icmah/publications/Actes-Shanghai-complet2.pdf (accessed 30 January 2018). Mazarakis-Ainian suggests that the definition of 'copy' should be approached differently when looking at archaeological as opposed to other museum collections due to the need for restoration and preservation techniques.

42. These items are catalogued under British Museum numbers EA 550, EA 551 and EA 552.
43. For a discussion of the various approaches to site preservation, including reconstruction, replication and the removal of a site to a new location, see Bai Yan, 'Significance of originals and replicas in archaeological site museums with a case study of the Han Dynasty Site Museums in China', in *Original, Copy, Fake, On the Significance of the Object in History and Archaeology Museums, 22nd ICOM General Conference in Shanghai, China, 7–12nd November 2010* (Shanghai, 2010). Available at http://network.icom.museum/fileadmin/user_upload/minisites/icmah/publications/Actes-Shanghai-complet2.pdf (accessed 30 January 2018). Yan notes that 'A basic tenet is that every effort should be made to protect relics at their original sites and in their original state', p. 10.
44. Although one could argue that visitors are not always aware of such alterations to sites, which may explain their lack of concern over replicated artefacts or change of location.
45. As opposed, for example, to ancient replicas, such as Roman copies of older Greek objects that are found in many collections.
46. See, for example, Yan, 'Significance of Originals', pp. 15–19.
47. Details of the drums can be found on the British Museum website. See 'The Folkton drums', *The British Museum*. Available at www.britishmuseum.org/research/collection_online/collection_object_details.aspx?objectId=814086&partId=1 (accessed 30 January 2018).
48. 'Modigliani VR: The Ochre Atelier' was displayed at the Tate Modern from November 2017 to April 2018.
49. Beier de Haan, 'You can always get what you want', p. 1. She notes the ICOM guidelines which state the importance of permanently marking replicas as such, so that there is no risk that they might later be confused with the original object.
50. Walter Benjamin, *The Work of Art in the Age of Its Technological Reproducibility, and Other Writings on Media*, Michael Jennings, Brigit Doherty and Thomas Levin (eds), trans. Edward Jefcott (Cambridge, MA, 2008), p. 22.
51. Ibid., p. 21. Benjamin refers to this concept as the 'aura'; 'what, then, is the aura? A strange tissue of space and time: the unique apparition of a distance, however near it may be. To follow with the eye – while resting on a summer afternoon – a mountain range on the horizon or a branch that casts its shadow on the beholder is to breathe the aura of those mountains, of that branch'; p. 24.
52. Anthony Hughes, 'Authority, authenticity and aura: Walter Benjamin and the case of Michelangelo', in Anthony Hughes and Erich Ranfft (eds), *Sculpture and Its Reproductions* (London, 1997), pp. 30–1.
53. See, for example, Hillel Schwartz, *The Culture of the Copy: Striking Likenesses, Unreasonable Facsimiles* (Cambridge, MA, 1996), p. 320.
54. Indeed, they can be seen not only as result of the rise of Tutmania, but as actually furthering its effects through providing an opportunity for more people to experience the 'wonder' of the tomb. One is, therefore, left with the question of whether the 'authenticity' of an object is of any real relevance in creating phenomena such as Egyptomania in the modern world.

2 'Let Sleeping Scarabs Alone': When Egypt Came to Stonehenge

Thanks to Adrian Green at Salisbury and South Wiltshire Museum for access to the scarabs and correspondence held there, and to David Dawson of Wiltshire Museum, Devizes, for access to the museum archives and for efforts to find the missing scarab. Thanks also to the editors for their patience.

1. The literature here is considerable. Some recent summaries of (mis)uses of ancient Egypt can be found in Robin Derricourt, *Antiquity Imagined: The Remarkable Legacy of Egypt and the Ancient Near East* (London, 2015), and Ronald H. Fritze, *Egyptomania: A History of Fascination, Obsession and Fantasy* (London, 2016). Examples of recent literature arguing for an Egyptian presence in prehistoric Britain include Lorraine Evans, *Kingdom of the Ark: The Startling Story of How the Ancient British Race Is Descended from the Pharaohs* (London, 2000), and Ralph Ellis, *Scota: Egyptian Queen of the Scots* (Cheshire, 2006). A rival tradition also exists, which sees civilization introduced to Egypt from ancient Britain. An example is Laird Scranton, *The Mystery of Skara Brae: Neolithic Scotland and the Origins of Ancient Egypt* (Vermont, 2017).
2. George Engleheart and Percy Newberry, 'Two scarabs found in Wiltshire', *Man* 35 (1935), pp. 120-1; George Engleheart and Pierre L. Collignon, 'Two Egyptian limestone scarabs found in Wiltshire', *Wiltshire Archaeological and Natural History Magazine* 47.164 (1936), pp. 412-19 (p. 416). Bibliographically speaking, these two papers are not straightforward. The article in *Man* comprises a report on the scarabs by George Engleheart, to which two brief additional notes by Percy Newberry have been added. The article in the *Wiltshire Archaeological Magazine* consists of separate reports by the two named authors, plus a lengthy explanatory footnote by E. H. Goddard, the *Magazine*'s editor.
3. In fact, almost all the correspondence is in Salisbury and South Wiltshire Museum. The Wiltshire Museum, Devizes, appears to hold just two relevant items. Neither the Salisbury Museum nor the Devizes Museum currently has catalogue numbers for correspondence collections, as reflected in subsequent references.
4. For more on the cultural impact of Grafton Elliot Smith, see Chapter 3 of this volume, written by Edward Chaney.
5. Key works include Grafton E. Smith, *The Migration of Early Culture: A Study of the Significance of the Geographical Distribution of the Practice of Mummification as Evidence of the Migrations of Peoples and the Spread of Certain Customs and Beliefs* (Manchester, 1915); Grafton E. Smith, *The Evolution of the Dragon* (Manchester, 1919), Grafton E. Smith, *Elephants and Ethnographers* (London, 1924); Grafton E. Smith, *Human History: A History of Primitive Man* (London, 1930); William J. Perry, *The Megalithic Culture of Indonesia* (Manchester, 1918); William J. Perry, *The Origin of Magic and Religion* (London, 1923); William J. Perry, *The Children of the Sun: A Study of the Egyptian Settlement of the Pacific* (Kempton, IL, 2004), originally published in 1923; William J. Perry, *Gods and Men: The Attainment of Immortality* (London, 1927). The term 'hyperdiffusionists' was coined some time later, but is used here, somewhat anachronistically, as a convenient label.
6. Adam Stout, *Creating Prehistory: Druids, Ley Hunters and Archaeologists in Pre-War Britain* (Oxford, 2008). Stout provides the kind of contextualized approach to the work of Smith, Rivers and Perry that is markedly absent from most other discussions of the episode.
7. Ibid., p. 74.
8. Ibid., p. 108.
9. Glyn Daniel questioned in one of his discussions of hyperdiffusionism, 'Why does the world tolerate this academic rubbish…?'; see Glyn Daniel, *The Idea of Prehistory* (Harmondsworth,

Notes to pages 31–33

1964), p. 97. Adam Stout describes key elements of the criticism offered by Daniel and others as a 'travesty'; see Stout, *Creating Prehistory*, pp. 109–10.

10. Perry, for example, claimed that the dolmen 'is nothing more or less than a degenerate Egyptian mastaba tomb'; *Origin of Magic and Religion*, p. 64.

11. Osbert Guy Stanford Crawford, generally known by his initials 'O. G. S.', sometimes pronounced 'Ogs', was a hugely influential figure in the development of archaeology and, particularly, prehistory between the wars. He is perhaps best known as founder/editor of the journal *Antiquity*, and as a pioneer in the use of aerial survey and aerial photography in archaeology. See Kitty Hauser, *Bloody Old Britain* (London, 2008).

12. Osbert G. S. Crawford, 'The origins of civilization', *Edinburgh Review* 239 (1924), pp. 101–16 (p. 101).

13. Perry, *Children of the Sun*, pp. 8–9.

14. Ibid., p. 9.

15. Osbert G. S. Crawford, 'Prehistoric geography', *Geographical Review* 12.2 (1922), pp. 257–63 (p. 258).

16. Osbert G. S. Crawford, *Man and His Past* (Oxford, 1921), p. 120.

17. Ibid.

18. For a discussion of Crawford's geographical approaches to prehistory, see Martyn Barber, 'Crawford in 3-D', *AARGNews* 51 (2015), pp. 32–47. For an account of the social contexts in which Crawford's ideas developed, see Helen Wickstead, '"Wild worship of a lost and buried past": Enchanted archaeologies and the cult of Kata, 1908–1924', *Bulletin of the Prehistory of Archaeology* 27.1 (2017), pp. 1–18.

19. Massingham wrote about his time working with Smith and Perry in his memoir; see Harold J. Massingham, *Remembrance: An Autobiography* (London, 1942), p. 56.

20. Stout, *Creating Prehistory*, p. 92. For a brief biographical account of Harris and his biblical researches, see Alessandro Falcetta, 'James Rendel Harris: A life on the quest', *Quaker Studies* 8.2 (2003), pp. 208–25.

21. James R. Harris, *The Builders of Stonehenge* (Cambridge, 1932). Harris churned out numerous pamphlets during the 1920s and 1930s on the subject of cultural migration and Egyptians in Britain (and elsewhere). Most were published by the Woodbrooke Institute in Birmingham, where he had been Director of Studies for some years prior to retirement. His books were published by the likes of Blackwells and the University of London Press, among others.

22. For the place-name 'Egypt', see, for example, Harris, *Builders of Stonehenge*, pp. 38–9. As an example of Harris's approach, he argued that the place-name Totnes derived from Thothmes: 'If we further suppose that the Thothmes referred to is the first king of the eighteenth dynasty … we shall have a date for the first settlement, between the years B.C. 1551 and 1501; this is not very remote from the building of Stonehenge'; James R. Harris, *Egypt in Britain* (Cambridge, 1927), pp. 15–16.

23. Pierre L. Collignon, 'Egyptian place names in relation to the diffusion of culture', *Atlantean Research* 2.2 (1949), pp. 24–30 (p. 25). The idea that the faience beads found in British round barrows may be of Egyptian origin had a long history, although this was seldom acknowledged. When A. H. Sayce published his note on 'The date of Stonehenge' in the first volume of the *Journal of Egyptian Archaeology* in 1914, he seems to have been completely unaware of this. He described a visit to Devizes Museum where he saw some of these beads, insisting that they were 'well-known Egyptian beads of Egyptian faience and coated with Egyptian blue glaze … which belong to … the latter part of the age of the Eighteenth Dynasty

and he earlier part of that of the Nineteenth Dynasty'; Archibald H. Sayce, 'The date of Stonehenge', *Journal of Egyptian Archaeology* 1.1 (1914), p. 18. Meanwhile in 1938, in his classic paper 'The early Bronze Age in Wessex', which introduced the idea of the 'Wessex Culture' to British prehistory, Stuart Piggott unequivocally accepted the idea that these beads were of Egyptian manufacture; Stuart Piggott, 'The early Bronze Age in Wessex', *Proceedings of the Prehistoric Society* 4.1 (1938), pp. 52–106.

24. For Engleheart, see, for example, 'Mr. G. H. Engleheart', *The Times*, 18 March 1936.
25. Engleheart and Newberry, 'Two scarabs', p. 120.
26. Ibid.
27. Biographical details on Collignon come mainly from Collignon, 'Egyptian place names'; and Keble College records, Keble College, Oxford, University of Oxford, KC/ACA 1 A/5 Collections Register, 1910–1919. Access to the latter was provided courtesy of Eleanor Ward, Archivist and Records Manager, Keble College, Oxford.
28. P. L. Collignon, 'The ritual significance of water' (University of London Ph.D. thesis, 1927). I would like to thank the various librarians at UCL who helped track down what proved to be a remarkably elusive item.
29. Collignon, 'Egyptian place names', p. 25: 'There had been rumours that Egyptian scarabs and other objects had been found in many places in these islands, especially of the scarabs found on Salisbury Plain. I conducted an exhaustive enquiry and found that there never has been any genuine find of an Egyptian object here except in association with foreign burials.' He never published this research. A letter from Collignon was printed in the *Yorkshire Post* on 18 January 1935 discussing a scarab and vase said to have been 'dug up at Darlington', while correspondence with Engleheart in Salisbury Museum refers to a scarab from 'Gloucestershire' of uncertain provenance; Salisbury Museum, Engleheart to Collignon, 30 October 1934. Collignon and O. G. S. Crawford also corresponded about a scarab from Durham; Salisbury Museum, Collignon to Crawford, 13 January 1935.
30. Salisbury Museum, Engleheart to Crawford, 6 February 1935. Engleheart appears to have been unaware that Collignon was already in touch with Crawford at this point.
31. Engleheart and Newberry, 'Two scarabs', p. 120.
32. For a detailed account of the appearance and disappearance of this aerodrome, see Martyn Barber, *Stonehenge Aerodrome and the Stonehenge Landscape* (Swindon, 2014).
33. Engleheart and Newberry, 'Two scarabs', p. 120. 'Shepherd's Crown' refers to fossil sea urchins, commonly found in chalk, the name inspired by their appearance. They have attracted a fair amount of folklore.
34. Engleheart and Collignon, 'Two Egyptian limestone scarabs', p. 412.
35. Ibid.
36. Ibid., p. 418.
37. Salisbury Museum, Wright to Engleheart, 16 February 1933. On the envelope, Engleheart has written 'Letter re scarab from Mr W.E. Wright, School Inspector, who gave me the scarabs. G.H.E.'
38. Salisbury Museum, note from Collignon dated 10 January 1935. It is not clear who this note was written for. It contains a single paragraph on each scarab, summarising Collignon's assessment of their respective provenances and circumstances of discovery. Collignon has signed the note and dated it '10.1.35', stating, 'The above is a bald statement of the facts and findings. The evidence will follow later on.'

Notes to pages 37–41

39. Salisbury Museum, anon, note dated 6 June 1935. This anonymous note states that 'the lad found the scarab on his shovel', that is, that it was among the rubble being backfilled in to the foundation trenches.
40. Engleheart and Collignon, 'Two Egyptian limestone scarabs', p. 418.
41. Ibid.
42. Engleheart and Newberry, 'Two scarabs', p. 120.
43. Ibid., pp. 120–1.
44. Engleheart and Collignon, 'Two Egyptian limestone scarabs', p. 416.
45. Salisbury Museum, Mr James, note in pencil. This note is undated, but its position in the sequence of correspondence (assuming, of course, that it has not been moved in the last 80 years or so) as well as its contents suggest it post-dates Collignon's visit to Wiltshire. The location in relation to both Fairoak Gate and the earthwork is impossible. The distances cannot reflect actual measurement and are presumably guesses, possibly as much as seven years after the event. The earthwork, a lengthy, approximately north-south holloway running across Chute Down, is the most visible element of a field system of probable later prehistoric or Roman date (Historic England: National Record of the Historic Environment monument number 224343). I have not found any other reference to it being known locally as 'Grimsditch'.
46. Ibid.
47. Engleheart and Collignon, 'Two Egyptian limestone scarabs', pp. 416–17.
48. Ibid., p. 417.
49. Ibid., p. 419.
50. Ibid., p. 417. There is no indication that Collignon sought more detail about the boat-shaped 'metal thing'.
51. One of Engleheart's archaeological claims to fame was the discovery of a hoard of Roman pewter objects at Appleshaw, Hampshire, which he sold to the British Museum. Some of the letters in Salisbury Museum hint at the possibility that Mr Fuzzard may have been aware of this. James, for example, raised the matter of the Appleshaw find in a letter to Engleheart dated 9 January 1933 when discussing problems with the Fuzzards' stories. James also claimed that 'I managed to get [Alec] Fuzzard to write a full account of the discovery, but this was destroyed before reaching me, by his parents'; Salisbury Museum, James to Engleheart, 15 January 1933.
52. Salisbury Museum, James to Engleheart, 15 January 1933.
53. Engleheart and Newberry, 'Two scarabs', p. 121.
54. Ibid.
55. Engleheart and Collignon, 'Two Egyptian limestone scarabs', p. 413.
56. Ibid.
57. Ibid.
58. Engleheart and Newberry, 'Two scarabs', p. 121. For a discussion of 'modern antiques' from Thebes, see Kees Van der Spek, 'Faked antikas and "modern antiques"', *Journal of Social Archaeology* 8 (2008), pp. 163–89.
59. Engleheart and Collignon, 'Two Egyptian limestone scarabs', p. 419.
60. Herbert H. Thomas, 'The source of the stones of Stonehenge', *Antiquaries Journal* 3 (1923), pp. 239–60.

Notes to pages 41–44

61. Engleheart and Newberry, 'Two scarabs', p. 121.
62. Salisbury Museum, Thomas to Engleheart, 17 February 1935.
63. Salisbury Museum, Goddard to Stevens, 27 January 1936. The letter begins, 'The scarab business is rather a nightmare to me.'
64. Salisbury Museum, George Engleheart, typescript, 'Two scarabs found in Wiltshire'. For the Alton scarab see 'Hampshire Cultural Trust acc. no. Alton 1891.2.
65. Salisbury Museum, Engleheart to Collignon, 30 October 1934.
66. Salisbury Museum, Crawford to Collignon, 14 January 1935.
67. Engleheart and Collignon, 'Two Egyptian limestone scarabs', p. 419. The 'somebody who lives near Salisbury' may well have been Engleheart.
68. Ludwig Glanert, 'Scarabs in Wiltshire', *Man* 35 (1935), p. 176.
69. Engleheart and Collignon, 'Two Egyptian limestone scarabs', p. 419.
70. Devizes Museum, Passmore to Goddard, 20 June 1936. For a biographical account of Passmore, see Laura Phillips, 'An investigation into the life of A.D. Passmore, "a most curious specimen"', *Wiltshire Archaeology and Natural History Magazine* 97 (2004), pp. 273–92.
71. Devizes Museum, Passmore to Goddard, 20 June 1936.
72. Ibid.
73. Salisbury Museum, Cunnington to Goddard, 2 June 1936. 'Mr. E. sent them to us on his own initiative', wrote Maud; 'we never asked him for them, but he said he was tired of them.' She added a postscript to the letter: 'I kept all the letters in case there was ever a fuss made about the ownership.'
74. Salisbury Museum, Cunnington to Goddard, 2 June 1936. In another note held by Salisbury Museum, James had written a rather terse note, dated 5 March 1935, insisting that the Ludgershall scarab 'is my property, and I have twice expressed the wish that it should be deposited in the Blackmore [Salisbury] Museum as that museum can be easily visited by Ludgershall school children'.
75. Salisbury Museum, Cunnington to Goddard, 2 June 1936.
76. Ibid. Engleheart seems to have deposited the scarabs at Devizes sometime between mid-January and early March 1935, presumably in the wake of Collignon's investigation into their circumstances and authenticity. Maud Cunnington seems to have wanted Engleheart's agreement to the idea of sending two of the scarabs to Salisbury, adding, 'I think Mr Engleheart would agree to the other one remaining here …, at least for the present.' The transfer appears not to have happened until after Engleheart's death.
77. Martyn Barber, '"It shouldn't have been found there": The trouble with Canon Greenwell's axe' (forthcoming).
78. Salisbury Museum, Engleheart to Crawford, 6 February 1935.
79. Crawford's own personal archives, at the Bodleian Library, Oxford, contain nothing relating to the scarabs. Neither did Crawford ever refer to them in print. Among the collection of correspondence at Salisbury Museum, the earliest letter from Engleheart to Collignon is dated 6 February 1935, with a reply from Crawford dated five days later. However, the earliest letter from Collignon to Crawford is dated 13 January 1935, but is in response to a letter that Crawford apparently sent to Collignon on January 9. This letter is not among those at either Salisbury or Devizes Museum. The contents of the letters noted here suggest that contact – at least with Collignon – may have begun some time earlier, perhaps in connection with his wider research into Egyptian objects.

80. Crawford, 'Origins of civilization', p. 116.
81. O. G. S. C., 'Sir Grafton Elliot Smith: A biographical record by his colleagues. Edited by Warren R. Dawson. Cape, 1938. 12s 6d', *Antiquity* 13.49 (1939), pp. 120–1. This article was actually a short review of a posthumous festschrift written and published by a number of Smith's colleagues. Crawford wrote it as an obituary: 'Those who had the pleasure of knowing him personally recognised his genius, urbanity and essential kindheartedness .... It is right that his life should be recorded and the book here reviewed is both worthy of its subject and eminently readable'; p. 121.
82. Harold Peake's correspondence with O. G. S. Crawford during the First World War contains numerous references to Smith, Perry and Rivers, the earliest dated 7 September 1915. These letters are contained within the Crawford Archive, Bodleian Library, Oxford, MSS Crawford Special Collection box 2. Unfortunately, Crawford's letters to Peake do not survive.
83. O. G. S. Crawford, 'Egypt as a place-name', *Notes & Queries* 10.258 (1908), pp. 447–8. *The Eye Goddess* (London, 1957) was published just a few weeks before his death. A return to the kind of ideas that characterized his early interests, and to the kind of diffusionist framework that was falling from favour, his surviving correspondence at the Bodleian Library shows considerable support from peers and contemporaries while the book was being researched and written. Professionally and academically, its publication was barely acknowledged.
84. Daniel, *The Idea of Prehistory*, p. 96.
85. See, for example, Robin Derricourt, *Inventing Africa: History, Archaeology and Ideas* (London, 2011); Derricourt, *Antiquity Imagined*.
86. Vere G. Childe, *The Prehistory of European Society* (Harmondsworth, 1958), p. 34. Childe's connection with Smith and Perry is discussed in Stout, *Creating Prehistory*, p. 105.
87. Vere G. Childe, 'Changing methods and aims in prehistory', *Proceedings of the Prehistoric Society* 1 (1935), pp. 1–15 (p. 7).
88. Glyn Daniel, *A Hundred Years of Archaeology* (London, 1950), p. 317.
89. For a discussion of Keiller's obelisks and fondness for concrete, see Helen Wickstead and Martyn Barber, 'Concrete prehistories: The making of megalithic modernism', *Journal of Contemporary Archaeology* 2.1 (2015), pp. 195–216. The Stonehenge Museum design can be seen in Lynda Murray, *Alexander Keiller: A Zest for Life* (Swindon, 1999).

3 'Mummy First: Statue After': Wyndham Lewis, Diffusionism, Mosaic Distinctions and the Egyptian Origins of Art

1. Edward Chaney, 'Wyndham Lewis: The modernist as pioneering anti-modernist', *Modern Painters*, 3.3 (1990), pp. 106–9 and idem in note 24 below, but see above all, Paul Edwards, *Wyndham Lewis: Painter and Writer* (New Haven; London, 2000). I am very grateful to Dr Edwards for generous assistance with this article and indeed for having published his superb account of this 'most fascinating personality of our time', as T. S. Eliot called him. I would also like to thank Katy Budge, Hugo Evans, Cy Fox, Tim Champion, David Gange and the editors of this volume for timely assistance.
2. Wyndham Lewis, *Creatures of Habit and Creatures of Change: Essays on Art, Literature and Society 1914–1956*, Paul Edwards (ed.) (Santa Rosa, 1989), p. 147.
3. For more on Smith, see Chapter 2 of this volume, written by Martyn Barber.
4. 'And Moses was learned in all the wisdom of the Egyptians' (Acts, 7: 22).

5. Plato, *Laws*. Available at: http://classics.mit.edu/Plato/laws.2.ii.html (accessed 1 July 2018). Aristotle praised the Egyptian-trained Thales as the first philosopher in the Greek tradition (*Metaphysics Alpha*, 983b18).
6. Freud Museum, *Leaving Today: The Freuds in Exile*, Julia Hoffbrand (ed.) (London, 2018), p. 63.
7. Edward Chaney, 'Egypt in England and America: The cultural memorials of religion, royalty and revolution', in Maurizio Ascari and Adriana Corrado (eds), *Sites of Exchange European Crossroads and Faultlines* (Amsterdam; New York, 2006), pp. 39–74.
8. Ibid., p. 45, citing Jan Assmann, *Moses the Egyptian: The Memory of Egypt in Western Monotheism* (Cambridge, 1997), p. 167: 'By making Moses an Egyptian, [Freud] deemed himself able to shift the sources of negativity and intolerance out of Judaism and back to Egypt, and to show that the defining fundamentals of Jewish mentality came from outside it.' For Assmann's more recent thoughts on this and 'the Mosaic Distinction', see Jan Assmann, *The Price of Monotheism* (Stanford, 2010).
9. Breasted was as appalled by what he called 'the World War' as Elliot Smith had been, writing in the foreword to his *Dawn of Conscience* that: 'man has been fashioning destructive weapons for possibly a million years, whereas conscience emerged as a social force less than five thousand years ago'; James Henry Breasted, *The Dawn of Conscience* (New York, 1933), p. ix. Freud's copy of Breasted is still in his London house, neatly underlined in places. I thank Dr Michael Molnar for permission to inspect it. See also Marsha Bryant and Mary Ann Eaverly, 'Egypto-Modernism: James Henry Breasted, H. D., and the new past', *Modernism/modernity* 14.3 (2007), pp. 435–53.
10. Paul Crook, *Grafton Elliot Smith: Egyptology and the Diffusion of Culture: A Biographical Perspective* (London, 2012), pp. 35–7. See also Jan Assmann, 'Monotheism and polytheism', in Sarah Iles Johnston (ed.), *Ancient Religions* (Cambridge, MA, 2007). For a very useful (and balanced) account of diffusionism, see Tim Champion, 'Egypt and the diffusion of culture', in David Jeffreys (ed.), *Views of Egypt since Napoleon Bonaparte* (London, 2003). For a recent, more general and sceptical account of diffusionism, predicated on the commonplace that the present influences our view of the past, see Robin Derricourt, *Antiquity Imagined: The Remarkable Legacy of Egypt and the Ancient Near East* (London, 2015).
11. Exodus 20:3–5; *cf.* Deuteronomy 7:5.
12. To some extent invited by Copts opposed to Byzantine rule as distinct from Pharaonism.
13. The major figure in countering the counter-religious early Christian iconoclasts was St John of Damascus, who spent the first part of his life in the service of the Muslim Caliph.
14. Wyndham Lewis, *Time and Western Man*, Paul Edwards (ed.) (Santa Rosa, 1993), p. 527. For the prevalence of Byzantine iconoclasm (in part a response to the Islamic variety), see John Haldon and Leslie Brubaker, *Byzantium in the Iconoclast era c. 680–850* (Cambridge, 2011). For Lewis's 1912 watercolour, *Russian Madonna*, see 'Russian Madonna', *V&A*. Available at http://collections.vam.ac.uk/item/O185918/russian-madonna-drawing-lewis-wyndham/ (accessed 31 July 2018). See also the now lost image reproduced in Lisa Tickner, 'A lost Lewis: The *Mother and Child* of 1912', *Wyndham Lewis Annual* 2 (1995), pp. 2–11. For the 'Mother of God cult' as a regression and 'failure to live up to the abstract (masculine) rigor of Judaic monotheism', see Richard H. Armstrong, *A Compulsion for Antiquity: Freud and the Ancient World* (Ithaca, NY, 2005), p. 245. It has also been argued that: 'the iconography and ideology of divine kingship [were] the ancient Egyptians' greatest inventions'; see Toby Wilkinson, *The Rise and Fall of Ancient Egypt* (London, 2010), p. 509. Julius Caesar and Augustus seem likely to have derived their aspirations to divine status from Egyptian example, as ultimately did also therefore, the early Stuarts, with fatal consequences.

Notes to pages 49–50

15. The Christian idea of the soul is surely derived from that of the *Ka* (see below), just as the Last Judgement seems to have evolved from the *Book of the Dead's* weighing of the heart against a feather, the latter surviving in Hilliard's Fitzwilliam miniature of the 'Wizard' Earl of Northumberland. Even the Christian Trinity seems to owe something to the Egyptian equivalent. By its omission from his account, John Gray's *Seven Types of Atheism* (London, 2018) underestimates the authenticity (and legacy) of 'belief' in ancient Egypt.

16. Sigmund Freud, *Moses and Monotheism* (London, 1939), pp. 19–20.

17. Wyndham Lewis, *The Diabolical Principle and the Dithyrambic Spectator* (London, 1931), pp. 179–80. This statement reminds one of Adrian Stokes's 'All perfection is close to death'; see Philip Head, 'Death and the monad', *The Wyndham Lewis Society*. Available at www.wyndhamlewis.org/images/WLA/2001/wla-2001-head.pdf (accessed 20 March 2017).

18. This despite the fact that the more neo-Platonically inclined Renaissance humanism focussed upon the 'Prisca theologia and [thereby] the Abolition of the Mosaic Distinction', to cite a section of Assmann's *The Price of Monotheism*, pp. 76–84.

19. Edward Chaney, *The Grand Tour and the Great Rebellion* (Geneva, 1985), pp. 56, 318–19. Interestingly, the Egyptologist Margaret Murray devoted much of her life to maintaining the notion of a widespread fertility-based religion in ancient Europe; see Margaret Alice Murray, *The Witch-Cult in Western Europe* (London, 1921). As Professor at UCL she failed to get Smith and Flinders Petrie to speak to each other; David Gange, *Dialogues with the Dead: Egyptology in British Culture and Religion, 1822–1922* (Oxford, 2013), p. 316. Where America was concerned Lewis believed that 'the average descendant of the original Puritan feels nearer to the Jew than he does to the Catholic'; Wyndham Lewis, *America, I Presume* (London, 1940), p. 95.

20. Ian Straughn, 'Ancient Egyptian icons next target of Islamists' (30 November 2012), *Albuquerque Journal*. Available at www.abqjournal.com/main/2012/11/23/opinion/ancient-egyptian-icons-next-target-of-islamists.html (accessed 20 March 2018). Al-Gohary insists that the 'idols and statues that fill Egypt must be destroyed' and boasts of the destruction of the colossal Bamiyan Buddhas in Afghanistan, blown up by the Taliban in 2001.

21. For the negative results of which 'political religions' see the writings of Eric Voegelin. See also Jan Assmann's criticisms as summarized by Werner Ustorf, 'The missiological roots of the concept of "political religion"', in Roger Griffin, Robert Mallett and John Tortorice (eds), *The Sacred in Twentieth-Century Politics: Essays in Honour of Professor Stanley G. Payne* (London, 2018), pp. 49–50.

22. Ernst H. Gombrich, *In Search of Cultural History* (Oxford, 1969). Cf. Paul Edwards, 'Wyndham Lewis and Nietzsche: How much truth does a man require?', in Giovanni Cianci (ed.), *Wyndham Lewis: Letteratura/Pittura* (Palermo, 1982). For Hegel and Egypt, see Jon Stewart, *Hegel's interpretation of the Religions of the World* (Oxford, 2018).

23. Janine Burke, *The Sphinx on the Table: Sigmund Freud's Art Collection and the Development of Psychoanalysis* (New York, 2006), pp. 246–8.

24. See the consideration of Lewis's 1932 *Physics of the Not-Self* (appended to *The Enemy of the Stars*, for which see below) in Edwards, *Wyndham Lewis*, pp. 300–11. Lewis shared with Yeats an enthusiasm for George Berkeley for his attempt 'to destroy the myth of the superiority of the "abstract" over the immediate and individual' and his awareness of the mind's creativity in perception; Wyndham Lewis, *Time and Western Man* (London, 1928), p. 168.

25. For the personal consequences of which see Edward Chaney, 'Lewis and the Men of 1938: Graham Bell, Kenneth Clark, Read, Reitlinger, Rothenstein, and the mysterious Mr Macleod: A discursive tribute to John and Harriet Cullis', *Journal of Wyndham Lewis Studies* 7 (2016), pp. 34–147 (p. 78). For Kitaj puncturing the ponderous Greenberg on the missing

ingredients in the abstraction he was promoting, see the video recording of the latter's lecture to the Architectural Association on 17 January 1976: AA School of Architecture, 'Clement Greenberg – lecture', *YouTube*. Available at https://www.youtube.com/watch?v=hk5Nzo2qzro (accessed 31 July 2018).

26. Ironically Bell was more anti-Semitic than Lewis, as was his sister-in-law, Virginia Woolf despite her marriage and the Hogarth Press's publication of Freud's works.

27. Roger Fry, *Last Lectures* (London, 1939), p. 83. See also Chaney, 'Lewis and the men of 1938', passim for Clark, Graham Bell and their reservations about extreme abstraction.

28. October 1913 circular signed by Lewis and three other leavers; quoted in Virginia Woolf, *Roger Fry: A Biography* (London, 1940), p. 192. On being excluded from a commission by Fry, Lewis's published a round robin, referring in all but name to Fry: 'the Pecksniff-shark, a timid but voracious journalistic monster, unscrupulous, smooth-tongued and, owing chiefly to its weakness, mischievous'; see Frances Spalding, *Roger Fry: Art and Life* (London, 1980), p. 187.

29. Gaudier Brzeska, 'Vortex', *Blast: Review of the Great English Vortex* 1 (1914), pp. 155–8.

30. Ibid., pp. 156–7. Where India is concerned Gaudier-Brzeska is presumably referring to the influence of Egypt via Alexander the Great's invasion. Gaudier came to be regarded 'as surely a genius as D. H. Lawrence was, or William Blake'; see Edward Chaney, *Genius Friend: G.B. Edwards and The Book of Ebenezer le Page* (London, 2015), p. 152.

31. T. E. Hulme, *Speculations*, Herbert Read (ed.) (London, 1924), p. 83; part of this is quoted by Philip Head, *Engaging the Enemy: The Gentle Art of Contradiction in the Work of Wyndham Lewis* (Borough Green, 2001), p. 40, but he does not point out that Hulme introduces this passage as 'practically an abstract of Worringer's views'. (Hulme says he met the Munich-based art historian Worringer and heard him give a lecture). Worringer cited Alois Riegl's notion that the Mycenaeans derived their plant ornament from the Egyptians while defending the latter against Riegl's notion that 'the Egyptians' capacity for ornamental achievement was exhausted'; see Wilhelm Worringer, *Abstraction and Empathy: A Contribution to the Psychology of Style*, trans. Michael Bullock (Chicago, 1997), pp. 68–9.

32. Wyndham Lewis, 'Review of contemporary art', *Blast* 2 (1915), pp. 38–47 (p. 43).

33. Edward Wadsworth, 'Inner necessity', *Blast* 1 (1914), pp. 119–25 (p. 119). Michael Sadler's translation, *The Art of Spiritual Harmony* (later *Concerning the Spiritual in Art*), appeared in the same year.

34. Ibid., p.120. For a discussion of the Egyptian influence on Kandinsky and others as also for his enthusiasm for Theosophy and Steiner, see Moshe Barasch, *Modern Theories of Art 3: From Impressionism to Kandinsky* (New York, 2000), pp. 293–369. Barasch was the dedicatee of Assmann's *Moses and Monotheism*.

35. See Edward Chaney, 'The Vasari of British art: Sir John Rothenstein … and the importance of Wyndham Lewis', *Apollo* 132.345 (1990), pp. 322–6 (p. 322). Kandinsky's first abstract was probably not done until 1913, albeit back-dated to 1910 with a view to future art history.

36. 'Review of contemporary art', p. 42.

37. Ibid., p. 47.

38. See Rowan Williams, 'Freudian psychology', in Alan Richardson and John Bowden (eds), *A New Dictionary of Christian Theology* (London, 1983), p. 220; *cf.* the similarly dismissive remarks regarding Freud's 'pseudo-factual nonsense' by Paul Johnson in *A History of the Jews* (London, 1987), p. 29.

39. Assmann, *Moses the Egyptian*, pp. 146–8: 'If the history of this discourse, from the early oral beginnings after the breakdown of the Amarna revolution until modernity, can be reconstructed as a story of remembering and forgetting, Sigmund Freud is the one who restored the suppressed evidence'; *cf.* Assmann's revised thoughts in *The Price of Monotheism*, pp. 4–6.
40. Lewis, *Time and Western Man*, p. 275.
41. Lewis remained genuinely concerned about artistic patronage both on a social and personal level, commenting in 1949, a decade after Mark Gertler's suicide, that he 'gassed himself, quite simply because no one would buy his pictures, and he had no money'. A year later he praised the then still-living John Minton, who nevertheless committed suicide in 1957 partly for related reasons; see Wyndham Lewis, *Wyndham Lewis on Art*, Walter Michel and C. J. Fox (eds) (London, 1969), pp. 405, 412. On patronage and 'progress' more generally, see Chaney, 'Lewis and the men of 1938'.
42. Chaney, 'Lewis and the men of 1938', pp. 36, 104.
43. 'The art collector and educator Katherine Dreier commissioned *Tu m'* to be hung over a bookcase in her library, hence the unusual shape of the work. Executed in 1918, it is Duchamp's last painting on canvas and sums up his previous artistic concerns'; 'Tu m', *Yale University Art Gallery*. Available at https://artgallery.yale.edu/collections/objects/50128 (accessed 20 March 2018); but *cf.* Glyn Thompson, 'Stereotypical perspective', *The Jackdaw* 139 (2018), pp. 30–4.
44. They visited the Louvre's Egyptian galleries together in the summer of 1911; see Anna Akhmatova, *Memoirs of Modigliani* cited in Nancy Ireson and Simonetta Fraquelli, *Modigliani* (London, 2017), p. 200. Lewis, however, criticized Modigliani as 'stylistic caricature'; Lewis, *Wyndham Lewis on Art*, p. 450.
45. Jonathan Jones, 'Modigliani review – "a gorgeous show about a slightly silly artist"', *Guardian*, 21 November 2017. Available at https://www.theguardian.com/artanddesign/2017/nov/21/modigliani-review-tate-modern-a-gorgeous-show-about-a-slightly-silly-artist (accessed 31 July 2018).
46. Gange, *Dialogues with the Dead*, pp. 320–2, citing in particular Norma Lorimer's 1918 novel about an archaeologist inspired by Akhenaten: *There was a King in Egypt*. For Lewis's anti-imperialism, where nineteenth- and twentieth-century British attitudes to Egypt were concerned, see Wyndham Lewis, *The Mysterious Mr Bull* (London, 1938), pp. 242, 249, 252.
47. The XVIII dynasty of Egypt was the first dynasty of the New Kingdom period, c. 1550–1292 BC in the middle of which period, almost a century after Queen Hatshepsut, Akhenaten, Nefertiti and Tutankhamun reigned. The giant scarab representing Khepri, the sun reborn at dawn, situated by the Sacred Lake at Karnak is XVIII dynasty. The even larger one in the British Museum, that Lewis is most likely to have known, dates from almost a millennium later.
48. Wyndham Lewis, *The Caliph's Design* (London, 1919), p. 29.
49. Ibid.
50. Ibid.; *cf.* the revised version in *Wyndham Lewis on Art*, p. 151.
51. Section 143 of Nietzsche, *The Gay Science* (first published 1882). See also Wyndham Lewis, *Left Wings over Europe: Or, How to Make a War about Nothing* (London, 1936), pp. 260–4 and Daniel Schenker, *Wyndham Lewis: Religion and Modernism* (Tuscalosa; London, 1992), pp. 116–17. Regarding Nietzsche and Freud, see Edward Chaney, review of Armstrong, 'A compulsion for antiquity', *Psychoanalysis and History* 9.1 (2007), pp. 123–30.
52. These sculptures were the subject of scholarly debate at this time. See Jean Capart, 'Some remarks of the Sheikh el-Beled', *Journal of Egyptian Archaeology* vi/4 (1920), pp. 225–33;

and A. Weidemann, 'Agyptische religion', *Archiv fur Religions-Wissenschaft* 21 (1922), p. 457, which is subsequently cited for having called attention to the occasional double entombment of pharaohs in Ernst H. Kantorowicz, *The King's Two Bodies: A Study in Mediaeval Political Theology* (Princeton, 1957), pp. 497–8, n. 6. Kantorowicz also mentions the fact that the *Ka*, of great interest to Lewis also, 'would lead ipso facto to duplication', citing Rameses II inaugurating his own sanctuary and worshipping his own image. Ka-Aper features in Kenneth Clark's superb 1975 (post *Civilisation*) TV film *In the Beginning*: 'I wanted it to make people reflect on what I believe to be the greatest miracle in history. By the year 2750 Egypt had developed nearly all the qualities that we value or used to value, in our own civilization: a belief in the individual as moral being: pride in the merciful execution of justice, a well organized system of government, a sense of the beauty and dignity of man, who had a soul that would survive him after death; an awareness of animals as something very close to ourselves, which could be lovable as well as useful; geometry and its application to stone architecture; and above all an art that combined grandeur with humanity'; *In the Beginning*, dir. Michael Gill, *BBC*, 29 September 1975. It may be more than a coincidence that Clark used the same title as Smith's 1932 contribution to 'The Thinker's Library': *In the Beginning* (subtitle: *The Origins of Civilization*).

53. This picture now belongs to ING Commercial Banking. It was reproduced in the Tauris Parke reprint of Cy Fox's edition of Lewis's *Journey into Barbary* of 2013.
54. Edwards, *Wyndham Lewis*, p. 237. Fry's head of Clive Bell could indeed be said to resemble a pumpkin.
55. Lucian Freud was sensitive about this comparison and withheld permission when I wished to publish paintings of his daughters or indeed his mother in supinely psychoanalytical mode in Edward Chaney, 'Freudian Egypt', *The London Magazine* (April/May 2006), pp. 62–9 and Chaney, 'Egypt in England and America'.
56. Michael Brenson, 'Egyptian art is alive and well in the West', *The New York Times*, 31 December 1989. Available at www.nytimes.com/1989/12/31/arts/art-gallery-view-egyptian-art-is-alive-and-well-in-the-west.html (accessed 20 March 2018).
57. See John Russell, *Francis Bacon* (New York, 1979), p. 99.
58. Gilles Deleuze, *Francis Bacon: The Logic of Sensation* (New York; London, 2003), p. 123. For dismissal of Deleuze (though his position is slightly weakened by his argument that 'bas-relief is not really particular to Egypt'), see Ben Davis, 'Bacon, half-baked', *Artnet*. Available at www.artnet.com/magazineus/reviews/davis/francis-bacon-gilles-deleuze7-28-09.asp (accessed 20 March 2018).
59. Wyndham Lewis, 'Round the London galleries', *The Listener* 42.1086 (1949), p. 860. See Jan Cox, 'Wyndham Lewis and Francis Bacon', *Universidad de la Rioja*. Available at www.unirioja.es/listenerartcriticism/essays/essay-Wyndham-Lewis-and-Francis-Bacon.htm (accessed 30 July 2018).
60. Wyndham Lewis, *The Demon of Progress in the Arts* (London, 1954), p. 50.
61. 'Plaster mask from the workshop of Thutmose'; one of a pair used by Lucian Freud, this one perhaps of Amenhotep III, from Breasted's book, which was described as having been Bacon's source when his *Three Studies for a Self-Portait* sold for £13,761,250. See 'Contemporary art evening auction', *Sotheby's*. Available at www.sothebys.com/en/auctions/ecatalogue/2013/contemporary-art-evening-auction-l13020/lot.11.lotnum.html (accessed 20 March 2018).
62. Freud's *Egyptian Book* of 1994 explicitly refers to Breasted's monograph. See 'The Egyptian Book', *The Metropolitan Museum of Art*. Available at www.metmuseum.org/art/collection/search/360169 (accessed 20 March 2018).

63. Lewis reviewed Grafton Elliot Smith and Warren R. Dawson, *Egyptian Mummies* (London, 1924), which builds on the former's scrupulously scientific analysis of *The Royal Mummies*, first published by the Service des Antiquités de l'Égypte. For Smith's account of the mummy of Amenhotep III, see Grafton Elliot Smith, *The Royal Mummies* (Paris, 1912), pp. 46–51. In analysing the materials used in this mummification Smith is fully aware that by the early days of the reign of Akhenaten: 'the old conventions in the Arts, as well as in worship, were being overthrown'; p. 50. Smith also analysed the mummy discovered in 1907 that is almost certainly that of Akhenaten himself; pp. 51–6.
64. Chaney, 'Egypt in England and America', p. 44; Chaney, 'Freudian Egypt', p. 67, fig. 5; *cf.* Richard Nathanson (citing William Feaver), 'Lucian Freud, "Portrait with horses" 1939'. Available at https://richardnathanson.co.uk/publications/12/ (accessed 20 March 2018).
65. He had indeed visited his grandfather in Vienna with his architect father, Ernst, in August 1935, after they had migrated to England; Chaney, 'Egypt in England and America', p. 43.
66. Chaney, 'Egypt in England and America', p. 45.
67. Cynthia Lewiecki-Wilson, *Writing Against the Family: Gender in Lawrence and Joyce* (Carbondale, 1994), pp. 179–82. See also the discussion in Eleanor Dobson, 'Literature and culture in the golden age of Egyptology' (University of Birmingham Ph.D. thesis, 2016), pp. 182–3.
68. Lewis, *Left Wings over Europe*, p. 260.
69. Lewis, *The Demon of Progress in the Arts*, p. 32; *cf.* Chaney, 'Lewis and the men of 1938', p. 78.
70. Lewis, *Left Wings over Europe*, p. 261.
71. Assmann, *Moses the Egyptian*, p. 7.
72. Acts 7: 22.
73. It may have been to avoid the risk of Moses being deified that led to the Haggadah, despite being an account of the Exodus, including only one passing reference to him.
74. That is, in 1909; Chaney, 'Egypt in England and America', p. 45; and *idem*, review of Armstong, *A Compulsion to Antiquity*, p. 108. For Jung's account of him and Freud arguing about whether Akhenaten's iconoclasm was patricidal, see Emanuel Rice, *Freud and Moses: The Long Journey Home* (New York, 1990), p. 157
75. Instead Freud focussed instead upon the case of seventeenth-century artist Christoph Haizmann; Chaney, 'Egypt in England and America', p. 42.
76. See below, note 150.
77. H. D., *Tribute to Freud* (Manchester, 1985), p. 42. The figures were more likely made by lost-wax casting and few if any 'predynastic'. H. D. was married to Lewis's friend Richard Aldington.
78. Kitaj expressed his preference for Moses when I facetiously suggested he resembled Father Christmas in a National Gallery video in February 2002. One of his late paintings is entitled *Moses contra Freud*. For surprisingly understudied connections between Freud and Warburg, see Edward Chaney, 'R.B. Kitaj (1932–2007): Warburgian artist', 30 November 2013, *emaj*, p. 7. Available at https://emajartjournal.com/2013/11/30/edward-chaney-r-b-kitaj-1932-2007-warburgian-artist/ (accessed 20 March 2018). Perhaps the most fascinating pre-Freudian figure to identify with Moses in an Egyptian context was Florence Nightingale, who is indeed clearer (franker?) than Freud on those sources, Manetho, who brought Moses and Akhenaten (in all but name) together, and Strabo, who had already speculated on his having been 'a priest of Heliopolis'; Chaney, 'Egypt in England and America', pp. 59–62.

79. Chaney, 'R.B. Kitaj (1932–2007)', p. 24.
80. R. B. Kitaj, *Second Diasporist Manifesto* (New Haven, 2007), no. 70.
81. See, for example, York Art Gallery's *Egyptian Head disappearing into Descending Clouds* of 1961.
82. Marco Livingstone, 'Introduction', in David Hockney, *Egyptian Journeys: Palace of Arts, Cairo, 16 January to 16 February 2002* (Cairo, 2002). Hockney wrote to Kitaj about this journey; see Christopher Simon Sykes, *Hockney: The Biography: Vol. 2. 1975-2012* (London, 2014), pp. 134–5.
83. David Hockney, *That's the Way I See It: David Hockney*, Nikos Stangos (ed.) (London, 1993), p. 36; *cf.* Philip McCouat, 'Lost masterpieces of ancient Egyptian art from the Nebamun tomb-chapel', 2015, *Journal of Art in Society*. Available at http://www.artinsociety.com/lost-masterpieces-of-ancient-egyptian-art-from-the-nebamun-tomb-chapel.html (accessed 31 July 2018).
84. Jessica Dismorr, 'London notes', *Blast* 2 (1915), p. 66. The attribution to Jessica Dismorr is based on the contents page, given that the only other evidence that this and the succeeding pages are by her is her name at the foot of a poem on p. 65. It seems she did not become Lewis's mistress as did her friend and fellow contributor to *Blast*, Helen Saunders. Both women subsequently suffered breakdowns; Paul O'Keeffe, *Some sort of Genius: A Life of Wyndham Lewis* (London, 2000). Dismorr committed suicide in 1939; Brigid Peppin, 'Women that a movement forgot', *Tate Etc* 22 (2011). Available at http://www.tate.org.uk/context-comment/articles/women-movement-forgot (accessed 31 July 2018). Saunders died of accidental gas poisoning in 1963.
85. Despite its modest appearance in the 'Home University Library, Lewis pronounced Lethaby's *Architecture* as: 'the best treatise I have so far come across'; Lewis, *The Caliph's Design*, p. 23. See also Godfrey Rubens, *William Richard Lethaby: His Life and Work 1857-1931* (London, 1986), p. 256. Interestingly, though the earlier work is very detailed on Egypt, his *Form in Civilization* (1922), is not, despite the substantial epigram on its title-page epigraph being a eulogy of Egyptian art by Flinders Petrie. Earliest of all is Lethaby's *Architecture, Mysticism and Myth* (London, 1892) which on p. 234 features the relevant line: 'These men of Egypt loved the same sky that we also love.'
86. T. S. Eliot, *The Letters of T.S. Eliot*, Vol. 2, Valerie Eliot and Hugh Haughton (eds) (London, 2009), pp. 154–5. Eliot seems not to have been conscious of the extent to which Smith was critical of Frazer and his influence. In a long footnote in his *Evolution of the Dragon*, Smith critiques Frazer's dependence upon 'the modern ethnological dogma of independent evolution of similar customs and beliefs without cultural contact between the different localities where such similarities make their appearances'. He quotes Alan Gardiner's criticisms of Frazer's misinterpretation of the myth of Osiris ('Osiris is always a *dead* king') and concludes this note by expressing surprise that 'Professor J.H. Breasted should have accepted Sir James Frazer's views'; Smith, *Evolution of the Dragon*, pp. 24–5. Frazer was defended by the Oxford anthropologist (albeit from Jersey), Robert Marett who accused Smith of 'premature dogmatism'; Paul Crook, *Grafton Elliot Smith, Egyptology and the Diffusion of Culture: A Biographical Perspective* (Brighton, 2012), pp. 85–6.
87. Eliot, *Letters*, Vol. 2, pp. 340–1, 501.
88. Ibid., p. 548.
89. Ibid., p. 580, n. 2.
90. Lewis, *Creatures of Habit*, p. 108.
91. Ibid., p. 112.

92. Ibid.
93. Warren R. Dawson, *Sir Grafton Elliot Smith: A Biographical Record by His Colleagues* (London, 1938), p. 33.
94. Lewis, *The Diabolical Principle*, p. 179.
95. Raymond A. Dart, 'Sir Grafton Elliot Smith and the *Evolution of Man*', in A. P. Elkin and N. W. G. Macintosh (eds), *Grafton Elliot Smith: The Man and his Work* (Sydney, 1974), p. 29. For the extraction of all Lewis's teeth. see O'Keeffe, *Some Sort of Genius*, pp. 550–5. As well as the Egyptian books, Lewis owned Smith's *Evolution of Man* (Oxford, 1924), with its then authoritative section on 'the human brain'; this copy now resides in the Harry Ransom Library, University of Texas at Austin.
96. Ed Pilkington and Mark Tran, 'Tooth solves Hatshepsut mummy mystery', *Guardian*, 27 June 2007. Available at www.theguardian.com/world/2007/jun/27/egypt.science (accessed 20 March 2018). See also Jo Marchant, *The Shadow King: The Bizarre Afterlife of King Tut's Mummy* (London, 2013), pp. 171–9.
97. Jeffrey Meyers, *The Enemy: A Biography of Wyndham Lewis* (London, 1980), p. 21.
98. Andrew Causey, 'The hero and the crowd: The art of Wyndham Lewis in the twenties', in Paul Edwards (ed.), *Volcanic Heaven: Essays on Wyndham Lewis's Painting and Writing* (Santa Rosa, 1996), p. 95.
99. Edwards, *Wyndham Lewis*, pp. 419–20. Giorgio de Chirico, whose paintings influenced Lewis and who shared an interest in 'creative dreaming', likewise denied the influence of Freud.
100. One wonders whether Lewis thought of Akhenaten when choosing the title of Athanaton for two works, dating 1927 and 1933, subtitled: 'Immortality of the Soul' and 'Immortality' respectively. In Reginald Scot's *Discoverie of Witchcraft* of 1584, Athanaton is a demonic leader who had 'the power of the east'.
101. Edwards, *Lewis*, p. 42, crediting Richard Humphreys. In *The Growth of Civilization*, Perry was particularly keen to emphasize Peru's supposed indebtedness to ancient Egypt, both in the arts and more basic phenomena such as irrigation. Lewis's heavily annotated copy of Perry's book is in the Harry Ransom Library; see Peter Carracciolo and Paul Edwards,'In fundamental agreement: Yeats and Wyndham Lewis', *Yeats Annual* 13 (1998), pp. 110–57. In private communication Professor Tim Champion confirms his admiration for (particularly the later chapters that relate to the avoidance of war) Perry's *Growth of Civilization*.
102. 'The making of meaning', *Living with the Gods*, BBC Radio 4, 15 November 2017. MacGregor states that Peruvian custom of mummification of ancestors 'predates the better-known tradition in Egypt by some way'.
103. Lewis, *Creatures of Habit*, p. 112.
104. Edwards, *Wyndham Lewis*, p. 423. Lewis paraphrases William J. Perry, *Children of the Sun* (London, 1923), pp. 130–202, on the coronation of the pharaoh when 'the ka, the double of the hawk, which bird was intimately associated with Horus, descended from the sky and incarnated itself in the king. … When the dead king died, his ba, or soul, which was his breath, went to the sky, in the form of a bird, there to join the ka, or afterbirth, that had gone there when he was born'. Lewis references the ka when he has Victor describing Margot as having 'arrived like the Egyptian symbol of the psyche'; Wyndham Lewis, *The Revenge for Love*, R. W. Dasenbrock (ed.) (Santa Rosa, 1991), p. 310. I thank Paul Edwards for this reference.
105. For the most detailed account with relevant illustrations, see Herbert Broderick, *Moses the Egyptian in the Illustrated Old English Hexateuch* (Notre Dame, IN, 2017).

106. It seems that the potter's wheel was used some three hundred years before a wheel was used on a vehicle. As late as 1970 Thor Heyerdahl was still trying to prove the diffusionist case when he sailed from the West Coast of Africa to Barbados on his papyrus reed boat, appropriately named *Ra II*. His first boat, the Kon Tiki dated from the 1940s when Lewis was still alive.

107. Lewis, *The Dithyrambic Spectator*, pp. 192–5.

108. Ibid., p. 199.

109. Smith, *Evolution of the Dragon*, p. 45.

110. Ibid., p. 20.

111. Lewis, *The Dithyrambic Spectator*, p. 187.

112. E. H. Gombrich, *The Story of Art* (London, 1950), p. 34. Gombrich cites Lewis in agreement with *The Demon of Progress in the Arts*, specifying historicism as the principal culprit; see E. H. Gombrich, *Meditations on a Hobby Horse*, 2nd edn (London, 1971), pp. 106, 118. Gombrich also shared Lewis's critical view of Bergson. For his being further persuaded by my advocacy of *Time and Western Man*, see Chaney, 'Lewis and the men of 1938', pp. 126–7. For further expressions of admiration for the Egyptian 'eternity of art' in which context Gombrich, as Lewis had done, quotes Keats's *Ode to a Grecian Urn*, see E. H. Gombrich, *Art and Illusion* (London, 1960), pp. 101–7; *cf.* Head, 'Death and the monad', p. 64.

113. See Smith, *Evolution of the Dragon*, p. 25. Smith quotes his *The Migrations of Early Culture*, in which he writes that 'Dr Alan Gardiner has kindly given me the following note in reference to this matter'; G. E. Smith, *The Migrations of Early Culture; A Study of the Significance of the Geographical Distribution of the Practice of Mummification as Evidence of the Migrations of Peoples and the Spread of Certain Customs and Beliefs* (Manchester, 1915), p. 42.

114. There is increasing evidence of the widespread practice of mummification. See, most recently, St John Simpson, 'Scythians, ice mummies and burial mounds', 23 August 2017, *British Museum*. Available at http://blog.britishmuseum.org/scythians-ice-mummies-and-burial-mounds/ (accessed 20 March 2018).

115. Wyndham Lewis, 'Essay on the objective of plastic art in our time', *The Tyro: A Review of the Arts of Painting, Sculpture and Design* 2 (1922), pp. 21–37 (p. 23); *cf.* T. S. Eliot, 'Art never improves', cit. in Chaney, 'Lewis and the Men of 1938', p. 103.

116. Wyndham Lewis, *Men without Art*, Seamus Cooney (ed.) (Santa Rosa, 1987), p. 96. For all its fascination, the British Museum's *Rodin and the Art of Ancient Greece* (London, 2018) confirms Lewis's line on this 'master of the Flux', reminding one of the fact that Rodin didn't participate in the revival of direct carving associated with Brancusi, Gaudier and Epstein, all three of whom were celebrated by Ezra Pound with reference to ancient Egyptian sculpture; see Jack Quin, 'W.B. Yeats and the sculpture of Brancusi', *International Yeats Studies* 2.1 (2017), pp. 45–63. Brancusi's *Wisdom of the Earth* (1906) seems to be inspired by an Egyptian 'block statue' of a male figure with his knees drawn up. Brancusi eventually visited Egypt in 1938; see Sanda Miller, *Constantin Brancusi: A Survey of his Work* (Oxford, 1995), p. 126.

117. Ibid., p. 99. Lewis returned to the comparison in *Blasting and Bombadiering* (p. 103) referring to Hulme: 'both he and I preferred to the fluxions in stone of an Auguste Rodin (following photographically the lines of nature) the more concentrated abstractions-from nature of the Egyptians.'

118. Ibid., p. 103.

119. Lewis was aware of Smith's critics but wrote that 'whatever the ultimate fate of his theory of Egyptian cultural priority, there is nothing *behind* Egypt that has been so far discovered that

can be said to interfere with its claim to origination', which in terms of what survives and from the artistic point of view, is surely true; see Lewis, *The Dithyrambic Spectator*, p. 195.

120. Wyndham Lewis, *Filibusters in Barbary* (London, 1932), p. 4. It was Cy Fox rather than Lewis who dedicated his edition of *Journey into Barbary* (Santa Barbara, 1983), 'to Froanna who also made the journey'. When I visited her in 1973 she was upset that her copy of this and another volume seemed to have been purloined by a previous visitor to her Torquay apartment. I subsequently tracked the volume down to a certain Covent Garden bookshop, identified by an unusually affectionate handwritten dedication to her, but the proprietors were able to demonstrate that they had acquired it through respectable means and concluded that she may have been confused.

121. Grafton Elliot Smith, *The Ancient Egyptians and the Origins of Civilization*, 2nd edn (London, 1923), pp. 5–6 and the 1911 edition, p. 176. On pp. 157–8 Smith discusses the 'bonds of affinity that link the Berber population of North Africa to the Egyptians', based on Randall-MacIver's *Libyan Notes*, but largely on the basis of his analysis of skull shapes, disagrees with his source's conclusion regarding priority.

122. Inigo Jones, *The Most Notable Antiquity of Great Britain Vulgarly Called Stonehenge* (London, 1655), p. 34. Jones's sixteenth-century Italian edition of Herodotus (at Worcester College, Oxford) is annotated on the subject of obelisks or 'guglie'. He also talks of Sixtus V's campaign to re-erect Rome's obelisks, for which see Edward Chaney, 'Roma Britannica and the cultural memory of Egypt: Lord Arundel and the Obelisk of Domitian', in David R. Marshall, Susan Russell and Karin Wolfe (eds), *Roma Britannica: Art Patronage and Cultural Exchange in Eighteenth-Century Rome* (Rome, 2011), pp. 147–70. For Colin Renfrew's discounting Mycenean influence on Stonehenge because carbon-dating showed it to be 'several centuries older (than 1500 B.C.)', see Dart, 'Sir Grafton Elliot Smith', p. 165.

123. Chaney, 'Lewis and the men of 1938', appendix and cover illustration.

124. Lewis, *Journey into Barbary*, p. 118; uncatalogued but listed on p. 233 as belonging to a 'private collection'. The clumsy depiction of both the figure and the Kasbah raise questions regarding its authenticity.

125. The 'Koubah' presumably refers to the twelfth-century Koubba, south of the mosque of Ben Youssef, the only surviving example of Almoravid architecture in Marrakesh, though elsewhere Lewis talks of 'the Koubahs' swarming everywhere and being based on a 'saint's tomb'.

126. Lewis, *Journey into Barbary*, p. 214. Further down the page Lewis says of 'the Berber' that: 'As many as *fourteen times*, he apostasized from Islam. Today he is only a Moslem out of habit, no doubt – and he might as well be that as anything else. His heart is more in the great Confréries, with their magical basis in a pre-Islamic past, or in the pagan deities that survive, their sanctuaries masquerading as a maraboutic shrine.'

127. Ibid., p. 218.

128. Ibid., p. 208. Gautier's book was *L'Islamisation de l'Afrique du Nord: les Siècles obscurs du Maghreb* (Paris, 1927).

129. Ibid., p. 219.

130. Ibid.

131. In his coins and elsewhere Alexander has himself depicted as wearing the ram's horns of the son of Zeus-Ammon; see Robin Lane Fox, *Alexander the Great* (London, 1971), pp. 200–09.

132. Lewis, *Journey into Barbary*, p. 220.

133. Ibid.
134. Wyndham Lewis, *Blasting and Bombardiering* (London, 1937), p. 254.
135. Lewis, *Time and Western Man*, p. 36. Amusingly, my copy of this, the first American edition, has the ownership signature of Sidney J. Perelman, scriptwriter for the Marx brothers and promoter of Joseph Heller's *Catch-22* (1961).
136. For this and Freud's remarks on Catholicism as 'the enemy of all thought', see Chaney, 'Egypt in England and America', pp. 45–6. In a letter to H. D. dated 5 March 1934, Freud reported on week's civil war in Vienna but that 'I expect no salvation from Communism. So we could not give our sympathy to either side of the combatants'; H. D., *Tribute to Freud*, p. 192. 'In the Dritte Reich, as conceived by Hitler' wrote Lewis, 'that great Jewish man of science, Einstein, would, I think, be honoured as he deserves'. 'Luckily', writes D. G. Bridson, 'Einstein did not stay to put the matter to the test'; see D. G. Bridson, *The Filibuster: A Study of the Political Ideas of Wyndham Lewis* (London, 1972), p. 113.
137. Lewis, *Filibusters*, p. 4.
138. See Chaney, 'Wyndham Lewis', p. 106. Lewis's title provocatively referenced a now forgotten book entitled: *The English: Are They Human?* by Gustaaf Johannes Renier, published in 1935. His copy is now in the Harry Ransom Library, Austin Texas; cf., Meyers, *The Enemy*, p. 106.
139. Lewis, *The Mysterious Mr. Bull*, p. 117. For useful discussion, including of Smith and Rivers, see Graham Richards, *Race, Racism and Psychology: Towards a Reflexive History* (London, 1997).
140. Edwards, *Wyndham Lewis*, p. 477.
141. Bernard Lafourcade, 'The taming of the wild body', in Jeffrey Meyers (ed.), *Wyndham Lewis: A Revaluation* (London, 1980), p. 83; *cf.* Lewis, *The Mysterious Mr. Bull*, p. 118 and G. Elliot Smith, 'Freud's speculations in ethnology', *The Monist* 33/1 (1923), pp. 81–97. Though Nietzsche is probably the principal influence here, this may also reflect a reminiscence of his original interest in Bergson who wrote a book on *Laughter*, published in 1900, the same year as Freud's on *The Interpretation of Dreams*. Lewis's attitude to Freud may be favourably compared with Pound's February 1940 letter to his friend from Italy, commenting critically on his *Hitler Cult*, and 'wonderin' whether … was done 89% to get yr /boat fare OUT of Judaea? … Proust and Freud are unmitigated shit / they pass for intelligentsia because their shit is laid out in most elaborate arabesques: the ideas which they have swiped'; Wyndham Lewis and Ezra Pound, *Pound/Lewis: The Letters of Ezra Pound and Wyndham Lewis*, Timothy Materer (ed.) (London, 1985), pp. 217–18. Smith cites Freud on dreams but is at pains to point out that his own interpretation of myth is 'almost diametrically opposed to that suggested by Freud, and pushed to a reduction ad absurdum by his more reckless followers, and especially by Yung' [sic]; Smith, *Evolution of the Dragon*, pp. 76–7. Smith quotes and spells Jung correctly elsewhere.
142. Ironically Freud's chow, Jofi, brought out his sense of humour (he wrote a poem to his daughter on her birthday supposedly from the dog) and occasional irritation on the part of some of his patients, not least H. D. who remembered that 'the Professor was more interested in Jofi than he was in my story' (much of which was based on dreams of Egypt, the opening of tombs and so on); see H. D., *Tribute to Freud*, and Susan Stanford Freidman (ed.), *Analysing Freud: Letters of H.D. Bryher and their Circle* (New York, 2002).
143. Chaney, 'Lewis and the Men of 1938', and Gill Hedley's forthcoming biography of Arthur Jeffress (I am most grateful to her for this reference).
144. Hugh Kenner, 'Hoodopip', *Agenda* 7.3-8.1 (1969–1970), p. 183.

145. I am extremely grateful to Dr Paul Edwards for these timely transcriptions from the manuscript of *Hoodopip* which is in the Wyndham Lewis Collection, Cornell University Library, Division of Rare and Manuscript Collections, box 9, folder 20, chapter I, fol. 3.

146. Paul Edwards kindly informs me of a note among the Cornell papers which indicates that Lewis intended that the Scot, Douglas/Macrob who emerges in decayed condition from the Netherworld in Lewis's 1927 novel, *Childermass*, was destined to reintegrate, 'quite on the pattern of Osiris'; Box 5, fol. 72.

147. Cornell University Library's Division of Rare and Manuscript Collections, chap. V, folder 20, fol. 5.

148. Wyndham Lewis, *Enemy of the Stars* (London, 1927), pp. 12, 27.

149. Ibid., pp. 28–9.

150. Ibid., p. 43. Hotshepsot does not appear in the 1914 edition of the play and is presumably therefore, like the references in *Hoodopip*, a product of Lewis's Egyptian interest of the 1920s.

151. Such a reading is cautiously suggested by Paul Scott Stanfield, 'The betrayed father: Wyndham Lewis, homosexuality, and *Enemy of the Stars*', *Journal of Modern Literature* 40.3 (2017), pp. 84–101, an argument which is curiously paralleled by Freud's relationship with his father as suggested by Emanuel Rice in 'Freud, Moses, and the religions of Egyptian antiquity: A journey through history', *Psychoanalytical Review* 86 (1999), pp. 223–43. It seems likely that Lewis's reluctance to subscribe to Frazerian/Freudian notions of filial antagonism towards the father-figure related to his increasingly anti-futurist respect for traditional continuities and especially Egyptian art, the Oedipal notion of killing the father encouraging instead the Bloomsbury tendency of traducing one's elders, as satirized in *The Apes of God* (London, 1930).

152. Lewis, *Enemy of the Stars*, p. 44 and Chaney, 'Egypt in England and America', pp. 48–50. I demonstrate that *pace* both Shelley and Belzoni's standard biographies, the British Museum bust arrived in London just too late for Shelley to have seen it and that far from 'Ozymandias' being forgotten, thanks to Champollion and others, as Rameses II, he managed to maintain just the kind of immortality he is ridiculed for having failed to achieve.

153. Zahi Hawass, 'The search for Hatshepsut and the discovery of her mummy', June 2007, *Guardian's Egypt*. Available at www.guardians.net/hawass/hatshepsut/search_for_hatshepsut.htm (accessed 20 March 2018).

154. Lewis, *The Enemy of the Stars*, p. 45. Though it seems unlikely to have been known by Lewis, the British Museum possess a wooden model adze bearing the incised cartouche of Hatshepsut which could conceivably have inspired him. See 'Model/foundation-deposit/adze', *British Museum*, museum no. EA 26278. Available at www.britishmuseum.org/research/collection_online/collection_object_details.aspx?objectId=118442&partId=1&searchText=%22Pharaoh%3A+King+of+Egypt%22&page=1 (accessed 20 March 2018). Smith discusses Hatshepsut from time to time, not least in discussing the sailing exhibition to Punt in his discussion of the feasibility of diffusionist journeys further afield in, for example, Grafton Elliot Smith, *The Ancient Egyptians and their Influence upon the Civilization of Europe* (London; New York, 1911), p. 75.

155. See the first chapter in this book, written by Gabrielle Heffernan.

156. For the best account, see Roger Luckhurst, *The Mummy's Curse: The True History of a Dark Fantasy* (London, 2012), pp. 3–24. On one aspect of the cultural influence of the discovery, see Chapter 8 of this volume, written by Lizzie Glithero-West.

157. Wyndham Lewis, *Paleface: The Philosophy of the 'Melting-Pot'* (London, 1929), p. 4.

158. See Richard Humphreys' catalogue entry on 'Tut' in the Fundacion Juan March catalogue: *Wyndham Lewis (1882–1957)* (Madrid, 2010), p. 229.

159. As the son of Akhenaten, Tutankhamon was originally named Tutankhaten, meaning 'Living Image of Aten', the change in his name symbolizing the abandonment of monotheism (and return of the temporarily repressed old religion) after the death of his father.
160. Tut-Ankh-Aten was changed to Tut-Ankh-Amon after the demise of his father/father-in-law and demoting of the Aten.
161. Wyndham Lewis, 'The war baby', *Art and Letters* 2.1 (1918–1919), pp. 14–41 (p. 30). See also Jamie Wood, '"A third method": Lewis and sympathy in the aftermath of war', *Journal of Wyndham Lewis Studies* 7 (2017), pp. 148–74.
162. There is a parallel here with the experience of Lewis himself, who had fathered Iris Barry's children in this period.
163. Lewis, 'The war baby', p. 39.
164. Martin Stannard, *Evelyn Waugh: The Early Years 1903–1939* (London, 1986), p. 174. The father of Waugh's second wife, Aubrey Herbert, died within months of his half-brother, Lord Carnarvon, also from septicaemia, but in this case the result of having all his teeth removed due to a similarly false diagnosis to that which Lewis received a little later.
165. Hoover named his Belgian shepherd dog, King Tut, soon after the discovery of the tomb. This Tut died in late 1929 at the age of eight.
166. Grafton Elliot Smith, *Tutankhamen and the Discovery of his Tomb by the late Earl of Carnarvon and Mr. Howard Carter* (London, 1923), pp. 17–18.
167. O'Keeffe, *Some Sort of Genius*, p. 313.
168. Paul Edwards observes that the earliest of the two drawings he illustrates is reminiscent of Sung dynasty art, also greatly admired by Lewis; *Wyndham Lewis*, p. 394. This was acquired by Valerie Eliot in 1967 and sold in November 2013; see Christie's *A Life's Devotion: The Collection of the Late Mrs. T.S. Eliot*, Vol. 2 (London, 2013). p. 82. Christie's has previous sold another version of 'The Seal Dog (Tut)' on 27 June 2007. For Lewis's best drawing of an Egyptian-influenced Kasbah, reproduced in *The Architectural Review* for January 1933, see Edwards, *Wyndham Lewis*, fig. 218 and Lewis, *Journey into Barbary*, p. 216.
169. It seems they only escaped being torpedoed thanks to Froanna not wishing to travel on a Friday which necessitated taking a later boat; O'Keeffe, *Some Sort of Genius*, p. 401.
170. Lewis (letter to Felix Giovanelli) in *Letters*, pp. 375–6.
171. The description of Lewis is W. H. Auden's.
172. William Shakespeare, *Timon of Athens*, 4.3. Available at http://shakespeare.mit.edu/timon/full.html (accessed 31 July 2018). See Paul Edwards, 'Wyndham Lewis's Timon of Athens portfolio: The emergence of Vorticist abstraction', *Apollo* (October 1998), pp. 34–40. Like 'The Thebaid' itself, Timon's epitaph is appropriately ambivalent, in this case because derived from Plutarch who reproduced both that supposedly provided by Timon himself as well as the one 'in general circulation' by Callimachus, the Alexandrian protégé of the Ptolemys: Plutarch, *Antony*, Bernadotte Perrin (ed.), *Perseus Digital Library*. Available at http://www.perseus.tufts.edu/hopper/text?doc=Perseus%3Atext%3A2008.01.0007%3Achapter%3D70 (accessed 31 July 2018). *cf.* Susan A. Stephens, *Seeing Double: Intercultural Poetics in Ptolemaic Alexandria* (Los Angeles, 2003). The Egyptophile Plutarch was a favourite of Lewis's, providing him with the epigraph from the *Moralia* he used in each of the three issues of *The Enemy*: 'A man of understanding is to benefit by his enemies. ... He that knoweth that he hath an enemy will look circumspectly about him to all matters, ordering his life and behavior in better sort.' Finally, Stephen Gosson's *School of Abuse* (London, 1579), springs to mind, the attack on plays by an ex-playwright: 'I will imitate the

dogs of Egypt, which coming to the banks of Nylus [the Nile] to quench their thirst, sip and away, drink running lest they be snapped short for a prey to crocodiles.'

4 Ancient Egypt in William S. Burroughs's Novels

1. See Chapters 6, 7 and 8 of this volume by Jolene Zigarovitch, Nichola Tonks and Lizzie Glithero-West, respectively, in which ancient Egyptian imagery is also evoked to convey a sense of immortality.
2. Barry Miles, *William S. Burroughs: A Life* (London, 2014), p. 90.
3. Ibid., p. 68.
4. Ibid., p. 14.
5. Oliver Harris, *William Burroughs and the Secret of Fascination* (Carbondale, 2003), p. 25.
6. Miles, *William S. Burroughs*, pp. 177–8.
7. Riccardo Gramantieri, *Metafisica dell'evoluzione in A. E. van Vogt* (Bologna, 2011).
8. William H. Patterson Jr., *Robert A. Heinlein: In Dialogue with His Century*, Vol 1 (New York, 2010), p. 225.
9. Alfred Korzybski, 'The role of language in the perceptual process', in Robert R. Blake and Glenn V. Ramsey (eds), *Perception: An Approach to Personality* (New York, 1951), p. 97.
10. See, for example, Akfred Korzybski, *Science and Sanity: An Introduction to Non-Aristotelian Systems and General Semantics*, 5th edn (New York, 2000), p. 71.
11. William S. Burroughs, *Nova Express* (London 1968), p. 12.
12. William S. Burroughs, *Naked Lunch: The Restored Text* (New York, 2001), p. 21.
13. William S. Burroughs, *The Ticket That Exploded* (London, 1987), p. 52.
14. William S. Burroughs, *The Adding Machine* (New York, 1993), p. 52.
15. RiccardoGramantieri, 'William Burroughs e il complotto contro l'umanità', in Riccardo Gramantieri and Giuseppe Panella, *Ipotesi di complotto* (Chieti, 2012), pp. 99–118.
16. Burroughs, *The Ticket That Exploded*, p. 116.
17. William S. Burroughs and Daniel Odier, *The Job: Interviews with William S. Burroughs* (London, 1989), p. 59.
18. William S. Burroughs and Brion Gysin, *The Third Mind* (New York, 1978), p. 186.
19. Alfred Wiedemann, *The Ancient Egyptian Doctrine of the Immortality of the Soul* (London, 1895), p. 2.
20. Erik Hornung, *The Ancient Egyptian Books of the Afterlife*, trans. David Lorton (Ithaca; London, 1999), p. 7.
21. Guy Rachet, *Le livre des morts des anciens égyptiens* (Paris, 1996).
22. Giuseppe Botti, 'Il *Libro del respirare* e un suo nuovo esemplare nel *Papiro Demotico n. 766* del Museo Egizio di Torino', *The Journal of Egyptian Archaeology* 54 (1986), pp. 223–30.
23. James Baikie, *The Story of the Pharaohs* (London, 1908), p. 347.
24. Eva von Dassow (ed.), *The Egyptian Book of the Dead: The Book of Going Forth by Day*, trans. Raymond O. Faulkner (San Francisco, 1998), p. 143.
25. Henri Frankfort, *Ancient Egyptian Religion: An Interpretation* (New York, 2012).

26. William S. Burroughs, *The Western Lands* (New York, 1988), p. 190.
27. Ibid., p. 113.
28. Miles, *William S. Burroughs*, p. 590.
29. Harold Bloom, 'Norman in Egypt', *The New York Review of Books*, 28 April 1983.
30. Nigel Leigh, *Radical Fictions and the Novels of Norman Mailer* (Berlin, 1990), p. 168.
31. Kathryn Hume, 'Books of the dead: Postmodern politics in novels by Mailer, Burroughs, Acker, and Pynchon', *Modern Philology* 97.3 (2000), pp. 417–44 (p. 418).
32. Raymond O. Faulkner, *The Egyptian Book of the Dead: The Book of Going Forth by Day* (San Francisco, 2008), p. 140.
33. Burroughs, *The Western Lands*, pp. 4–5.
34. William S. Burroughs, *Burroughs Live: The Collected Interviews of William S. Burroughs, 1960–1997* (New York, 2001), p. 754.
35. Algebra of need, the mechanism of desire for drugs, is reflective of American Capitalism. See Allan Johnston, 'Consumption, addiction, vision, energy: Political economies and utopian visions in the writings of the Beat Generation', *College Literature* 32.2 (2005), pp. 103–26.
36. Burroughs, *Burroughs Live*, p. 646.
37. AlexHouen, 'William S. Burroughs's Cities of the Red Night Trilogy: Writing outer space', *Journal of American Studies* 40.3 (2006), pp. 523–49.
38. Burroughs, *The Western Lands*, p. 241.
39. Salomon Resnik, *The Theatre of the Dream* (London, 2005), p. 234.
40. Burroughs, *Burroughs Live*, p. 646.
41. William S. Burroughs, *My Education: A Book of Dreams* (London, 1996), p. 11.
42. Ibid., p. 5.
43. Ibid., p. 174.
44. Timothy S. Murphy, *Wising Up the Marks: The Amodern William Burroughs* (Berkeley, 1997), p. 192.
45. Burroughs, *The Western Lands*, p. 257.

5 Between Success and Controversy: Christian Jacq and the Marketing of 'Egyptological' Fiction

1. Didier Sénécal, 'Christian Jacq', *L'Express*, 1 December 1994.
2. Roger Caratini, *L'égyptomanie, une imposture* (Paris, 2002), p. 35; Carole Vantroys, 'Italien-Coréen comme Christian Jacq', *L'Express*, 1 May 1998.
3. Pierre Vavasseur, 'Christian Jacq joue à nous faire très peur', *Le Parisien*, 29 October 2016. Jacq claims to have sold approximatively 35 million copies; see Pascale Zimmermann, 'Jacq, le pharaon du livre', *La Tribune de Genève*, 23 November 2013.
4. Claudie Voisenat and Pierre Lagrange, *L'ésotérisme contemporain et ses lecteurs: Entre savoirs, croyances et fictions* (Paris, 2005), p. 153.
5. On this subject, see Bernadette Schnitzler, 'Hijacked images: Ancient Egypt in French commercial advertising', in Sally MacDonald and Michael Rice (eds), *Consuming Ancient Egypt* (New York, 2016).

6. Philippe Nourry 'Heurs et malheurs', *Le Point*, 22 December 2000.
7. Annette Lévy-Willard, 'Christian Jacq, le nouveau pharaon', *Libération*, 9 May 1996.
8. Gianfranco Rubino, *Voix du contemporain: histoire, mémoire et réel dans le roman français d'aujourd'hui* (Rome, 2006), p. 29.
9. Françoise Monier, 'Scribe best-seller', *L'Express*, 3 August 2000.
10. Raphaël Draï, 'Egyptologues ou bibliocastes? Christian Jacq, Christiane Desroches Noblecourt, Jan Assmann', *Pardès* 38.1 (2005), pp. 153–69 (p. 156).
11. Daniel Bermond, 'Il était une fois sur les bords du Nil …', *L'Histoire* cxc (1995), pp. 20–1 (p. 20).
12. See 'La culture du mystère et de l'étranger', in Pierre-André Taguieff, *La foire aux 'Illuminés': ésotérisme, théorie du complot, extrémisme* (Paris, 2005).
13. These controversies are discussed in Lévy-Willard, 'Christian Jacq'; Pierre Louis, *Main basse sur une loge maçonnique. Vers un nouveau Temple Solaire?* (Valence d'Albigeois, 2012); Renaud Marhic, 'Christian Jacq, la dérive du pharaon à deux balles', *Le Vrai Papier Journal*, 1 September 2000; Xavier Pasquini, 'Christian Jacq, le pharaon des bacs à sable', *Charlie Hebdo*, 3 April 1996; Vantroys, 'Italien-Coréen comme Christian Jacq'. For more on ancient Egypt in the context of modern occult groups and secret societies, see Chapter 9 of this volume, written by Caroline Tully.
14. Monier, 'Scribe best-seller'.
15. Vavasseur, 'Christian Jacq'.
16. See Draï, 'Egyptologues ou bibliocastes?', pp. 153–69.
17. Brian M. Stableford, *Science Fact and Science Fiction: An Encyclopedia* (New York, 2006), p. 27.
18. Monier, 'Scribe best-seller'.
19. Ibid.
20. Amy Tao, 'Christian Jacq' (10 August 2010), *Encyclopaedia Britannica*. Available at www.britannica.com/biography/Christian-Jacq (accessed 21 March 2018).
21. Monier, 'Scribe best-seller'.
22. Lévy-Willard, 'Christian Jacq'.
23. 'Christian Jacq', *XO Editions*. Available at www.xoeditions.com/en/auteurs/christian-jacq-en/ (accessed 21 March 2018).
24. Ibid.
25. The last two pen names are a tribute to the Scottish explorer of the Nile, David Livingstone (1813–1873), and the English Egyptologist Howard Carter (1874–1939).
26. Philippe Chauveau, 'Christian Jacq – Les enquêtes de Setna, la tombe maudite', *Web Tv Culture*, 10 December 2014. Available at www.web-tv-culture.com/les-enquetes-de-setna-la-tombe-maudite-de-christian-jacq-724.htlm (accessed 17 December 2016).
27. These are: *Le Juge d'Egypte* (*The Judge of Egypt*, 1993–4, 3 vols); *Ramsès* (*Rameses*, 1995–6, 5 vols); *La Pierre de lumière* (*The Stone of Light*, 2000, 4 vols); *La Reine Liberté* (*Queen Liberty*, 2001–2, 3 vols); *Les Mystères d'Osiris* (*The Mysteries of Osiris*, 2003–4, 4 vols); *La Vengeance des dieux* (*The Vengeance of the Gods*, 2005–7, 2 vols); *Et l'Egypte s'éveilla* (*The Rise of Egypt*, 2010–11, 3 vols); and *Les enquêtes de Setna* (*Setna*, 2014–15, 4 vols). For a brief description of these series, see Ronald H. Fritze, *Egyptomania: A History of Fascination, Obsession and Fantasy* (London, 2016), p. 350.
28. These sales figures are provided by Jacq's current publisher, XO Editions.

29. Monier, 'Scribe best-seller'; Laure Mentzel, 'Docteur Christian et le mystère Jacq', *Le Figaro*, 6 November 2010.
30. Emilie Grangeray, 'Christian Jacq, la saga du "petit scribe"', *Le Monde*, 20 March 2009.
31. Donald M. Reid, 'Remembering and forgetting Tutankhamun: Imperial and national rhythms of archaeology, 1922–1972', in William Carruthers (ed.), *Histories of Egyptology: Interdisciplinary Measures* (London, 2014), p. 168.
32. Jean-Claude Perrier, 'Le mystère editorial des grandes pyramides', *Livres Hebdo*, 24 October 1998.
33. Thiébault Dromard, 'Christian Jacq ou le bon filon de Bernard Fixot', *Le Figaro*, 15 February 2013.
34. Grangeray, 'Christian Jacq'.
35. This frantic rate of writing led to speculations that Jacq might have turned to ghostwriters for assistance; see Christian Cannuyer's criticism in Dominique Legrand, 'Les recettes de Christian Jacq', *Le Soir*, 13 February 2010.
36. Christophe Mangelle, 'Christian Jacq nous parle du tome 1 de sa nouvelle saga: *Les enquêtes de Setna*', *La fringale Culturelle*, 13 December 2014.
37. Legrand, 'Les recettes'.
38. Sénécal, 'Christian Jacq'.
39. See Michel Grodent, 'A la foire du livre: Christian Jacq et *L'affaire Toutankhamon*, vive le romanesque!', *Le Soir*, 22 April 1993.
40. Cécile Lecoultre, 'Christian Jacq, le pharaon s'encanaille dans le techno-thriller', *La Tribune de Genève*, 12 November 2016.
41. See criticism from Egyptologists Desroches Noblecourt in Bermond, 'Il était une fois'; and Cannuyer in Legrand, 'Les recettes'.
42. Blaise de Chabalier, 'Christian Jacq dans la peau d'un scribe', *Le Figaro*, 29 January 2009.
43. Mangelle, 'Christian Jacq'.
44. Michel Lisse, 'La fiction: prothèse de l'histoire', *Interférences littéraires* ii (2002), pp. 58–68 (p. 59).
45. Christian Jacq, *Ramsès: Le Fils de la lumière* (Paris, 1995), p. 8.
46. All translations are the author's unless otherwise noted.
47. Mentzel, 'Docteur Christian'.
48. In *Ramsès*, dialogues are musically punctuated by a vivid, fast tempo, reminiscent of Mozart's Allegro; see Legrand, 'Les recettes'. Jacq wrote extensively on Mozart and *The Magic Flute* whose major influence was Terrasson's *Sethos* and his central notion of 'Egyptian mysteries'.
49. Lévy-Willard, 'Christian Jacq'.
50. Legrand, 'Les recettes'.
51. Christian Jacq, *Ramsès: Sous l'acaccia d'occident* (Paris, 1996), p. 17.
52. Isabelle Durieux, 'Christian Jacq: Avec la bénédiction des pharaons', *L'Express*, 6 March 1997.
53. Christian Jacq, *Ramsès: La Bataille de Kadesh* (Paris, 1996), p. 22.
54. See Michel Serceau, *Le mythe, le miroir et le divan: pour lire le cinéma* (Villeneuve d'Ascq, 2009), p. 34.

55. See Michel Grodent, 'Le Temple des millions d'années, la fiction fait des enfants à l'histoire', *Le Soir*, 3 April 1996.
56. Pierre Verdaguer, 'Manipulating the past: The role of history in recent French detective fiction', in Barry Rothaus (ed.), *Proceedings of the Western Society for French History: Selected Papers of the 1998 Annual Meeting* (Greeley, 2000), p. 37.
57. Caratini, *L'égyptomanie*, p. 98.
58. See Philippe Nourry, 'Christian Jacq: Les offrandes du pharaon', *Le Point*, 17 August 1996.
59. Bérangère Adda, 'Christiane Desroches Noblecourt: 80 ans de passion pour l'Egypte', *Le Parisien*, 30 May 2003.
60. Amelia B. Edwards, *A Thousand Miles Up the Nile*, 2nd edn (London, 1888), p. 265.
61. Miriam Lichtheim, *Ancient Egyptian Literature*, Vol. 2 (Berkeley, 2006), pp. 58–60.
62. Herodotus's claim that Helen was in Egypt for the duration of the Trojan War was taken up by Euripides in his play *Helen* (412 BC).
63. Jacq, *Ramsès: Soul l'accacia d'occident*, p. 54.
64. See 'La culture du mystère et de l'étranger', in Taguieff, *La foire aux 'Illuminés'*.
65. For a definition of magic in ancient Egypt, see Emily Teeter, *Religion and Ritual in Ancient Egypt* (New York, 2011), pp. 161–2.
66. Legrand, 'Les recettes'.
67. Sénécal, 'Christian Jacq'.
68. Jacq, *Ramsès: Sous l'acaccia d'occident*, p. 342.
69. Jacq, *Ramsès: Le Fils de la lumière*, p. 83.
70. See François Cavaignac, *Balades maçonniques en littérature* (Namur, 2014).
71. Legrand, 'Les recettes'.
72. Durieux, 'Christian Jacq'.
73. Durieux, 'Christian Jacq'; Lévy-Willard, 'Christian Jacq'; Vantroys, 'Italien-Coréen'.
74. See Pasquini, 'Christian Jacq'.
75. See Louis, *Main basse*.
76. Lévy-Willard, 'Christian Jacq'.
77. See Isabelle Falconnier, 'Christian Jacq: un Egyptien à Blonay', *L'Hebdo*, 18 December 2014.
78. Verdaguer, 'Manipulating the Past', p. 37.
79. Draï, 'Egyptologues ou bibliocastes?', p. 163.
80. Jacq, *Ramsès: Sous l'acaccia d'occident*, p. 307.
81. See Colosimo's view on the subject in Monier, 'Scribe best-seller'.
82. Leila Fares wrote extensively on this subject in her doctoral thesis: Leila Fares, 'Féminisme et anachronisme dans les romans de Christian Jacq sur l'Egypte ancienne' (University of Florida Ph.D. thesis, 2009).
83. Jacq, *Ramsès: Sous l'acaccia d'occident*, p. 267.
84. Lecoultre, 'Christian Jacq'; Vavasseur, 'Christian Jacq'.
85. Sénécal, 'Christian Jacq'.
86. Draï, 'Egyptologues ou bibliocastes?', p. 157.

Notes to pages 101–107

87. Ibid., pp. 160–1.
88. Lévy-Willard, 'Christian Jacq'.
89. Jacq, *Ramsès: Sous l'acaccia d'occident*, p. 373.
90. Legrand, 'Les recettes'.

6 Egyptomania, English Pyramids and the Quest for Immortality

My special thanks to The Mausolea & Monuments Trust and Charles Saumerez Smith CBE for their generous permission to use their images. I am grateful for the anonymous reviewers' suggestions and comments.

1. British political interest in Egypt would go on to have a long history. Egypt would find itself under the British from 1882, when it was occupied by British forces during the Anglo-Egyptian War, until 1956, when the last British forces withdrew in accordance with the Anglo-Egyptian agreement of 1954 after the Suez Crisis.
2. See also Chapter 7 in this volume, written by Nichola Tonks, for a case study of ancient Egypt in funerary culture of the nineteenth century.
3. Clare Gittings, *Death, Burial and the Individual in Early Modern England* (London, 1984), p. 104.
4. Ibid.
5. John Hadley, 'An account of a Mummy, inspected at London 1763', *Philosophical Transactions*, 54 (1764), pp. 1–14.
6. Ibid., p. 1.
7. John Frederick Blumenbach, 'Observations on some Egyptian Mummies opened in London', *Philosophical Transactions*, 84 (1794), pp. 177–95.
8. Smart Lethieullier's cousin, Captain (later Colonel) William Lethieullier, had a small collection of Egyptian mummies that he eventually donated to the British Museum following Sir Hans Sloane's donation, which formed the British Museum in 1753. In fact, Lethieullier donated his first mummy (no. 6696), which had been in the country thirty-three years, a few years after the founding of the Museum. An older mummy (no. 6957) was the property of Nell Gwyn, but not presented to the Museum until 1837. William Lethieullier's interest in mummification may have led to Smart's interest in corporeal preservation. For a list of the mummified items, see Warren R. Dawson and P. H. K. Gray, *Catalogue of Egyptian Antiquities in the British Museum*, Vol. 1 (London, 1968), pp. 1–40. See also, Alexander Gordon, *An Essay Towards Explaining the Hieroglyphical Figures, on the Coffin of the Ancient Mummy Belonging to Capt. William Lethieullier* (London, 1737); and, for a fascinating description of Egyptian motifs and symbols, Alexander Gordon, *Essay towards Explaining the Hieroglyphical Figures, on the Egyptian Mummy, in the Museum of Doctor Mead, Physician in Ordinary to his Majesty* (London, 1737).
9. Thomas Greenhill, Νεκροκηδεία: *or, the Art of Embalming: Wherein is Shewn the Right of Burial, the Funeral Ceremonies, and the several Ways of Preserving Dead Bodies in Most Nations of the World* (London, 1705), p. 107. '*Nekpokhdeia*' or '*Nekrokedia*' are acceptable English spellings of the title.
10. Ibid., p. 133.
11. Quoted in Robert W. Habenstein and William M. Lamers, *The History of American Funeral Directing* (Milwaukee, 1955), p. 109. The term 'undertaker', in its modern sense, goes back

Notes to pages 107–109

to at least 1698 at which date its present usage was recorded in a parish register. The term does not seem to have come into use to designate a funeral contractor until the beginning of the eighteenth century. See Habenstein and Lamers, *History of American Funeral Directing*, pp. 102–6.

12. For a brief history of the Barber-Surgeons see Habenstein and Lamers, *History of American Funeral Directing*, pp. 100–10.
13. Sidney Young, *Annals of the Barber-Surgeons of London* (London, 1980), pp. 111–12.
14. In 1745, the surgeons and barbers ended their joint relationship and again became two separate organizations. During the barber–surgeons period they were permitted to be the sole agency for embalming and for performing anatomical dissections in the city of London, although there is no record of any of the bodies for anatomy being embalmed. In 1745, the surgeons formed a separate company of surgeons, which later became the Royal College of Surgeons.
15. Richard Steele, *The Funeral, or Grief-a-la-Mode* (London, 1701), p. 16.
16. According to Olivia Bland, the undertaker, Mr Harcourt, produced a bill for £43 9s. 6d. Harcourt laid out the corpse, provided the coffin, winding sheet, and 'two wooden urns covered with lead and lined with silk for ye Bowels', and 'six men to move the Body under the canopy'; Olivia Bland, *The Royal Way of Death* (London, 1986), p. 100.
17. For further discussion of early embalming practices, see Jolene Zigarovich, 'Preserved remains: Embalming in eighteenth-century England', *Eighteenth-Century Life*, 33.3 (2009), pp. 65–104.
18. Pettigrew still staged public mummy unrolling in the 1830s and 1840s. For more information about the history of the Hamilton Mausoleum, see Aidan Dodson, 'Duke Alexander's sarcophagi', *Archiv Orientální*, 70 (2002), pp. 329–36; Aidan Dodson, 'Legends of a sarcophagus', in Thomas Schneider and Kasia Maria Szpakowska (eds), *Egyptian Stories: A British Egyptological Tribute to Alan B. Lloyd* (Münster, 2007); 'Hamilton Mausoleum (South Lanarkshire)', *The Mausolea & Monuments Trust*. Available at http://www.mmtrust.org.uk/mausolea/view/501/Hamilton_Mausoleum_South_Lanarkshire (accessed 28 January 2018).
19. Francis Bancroft, *A True Copy of the remarkable Last Will and Testament of Mr. Francis Bancroft, Citizen and Draper of London* (London, 1728), p. 6.
20. Ibid.
21. Ibid., p. 7.
22. 'An account of Mr. Francis Bancroft, so far as relates to his monument and burial', *The Ladies Magazine, Or, The Universal Entertainer*, 22 August 1752.
23. As the practice most likely began in France, it has always been most popular in that country, but there are many instances of British royals and religious figures having their hearts and viscera separately buried. See Bertram S. Puckle, *Funeral Customs: Their Origin and Development* (London, 1926), and C. A. Bradford, *Heart Burial* (London, 1933), for detailed histories of heart burial and notable British figures who had their hearts embalmed.
24. See R. C. Finucane's 'Sacred corpse, profane carrion: Social ideals and death rituals in the later Middle Ages', in Joachim Whaley (ed.), *Mirrors of Mortality: Studies in the Social History of Death* (New York, 1981), pp. 40–60 for a discussion of attempts to embalm in the Middle Ages.
25. Quoted in Bradford, *Heart Burial*, p. 235. For a detailed account of the ceremony, see R. Chambers (ed.) *The Book of Days*, Vol. 2 (London: W. and R. Chambers, 1869), p. 418.
26. Recent comparative studies have shown that the number and types of organs removed from the body during the evisceration process was more variable than previously thought. As

an example, elites and commoners were having organs preserved and replaced in the body cavity by the Third Intermediate Period. For a helpful study of these variations, including the discovery that the heart was not universally retained in situ, see A. D. Wade and A. J. Nelson, "Radiological evaluation of the evisceration tradition in ancient Egyptian mummies." *HOMO-Journal of Comparative Human Biology*. 64 (2013), pp. 1–28. My thanks to the anonymous reader for recommending this source.

27. See Bodo Neuss, 'The Funerary of Thomas Willson', *Architectural Association*, 18 (2014), pp. 88–92.
28. Catharine Arnold, *Necropolis: London and its Dead* (London, 2006), p. 139.
29. William Justyne, *Guide to Highgate Cemetery* (London, 1865), p. 33.
30. David Gange, *Dialogues with the Dead: Egyptology in British Culture and Religion, 1822–1922* (Oxford, 2013), p. 96.
31. Ibid., p. 219.
32. Ibid., p. 220.
33. The secular mausoleum was built for Charles Howard, 3rd Earl of Carlisle (d. 1738). In a letter to George Selwyn (dated 12 August 1772), Horace Walpole famously described it as a building which 'would tempt one to be buried alive'. See 'Howard Mausoleum (North Yorkshire)', *The Mausolea & Monuments Trust*. Available at http://www.mmtrust.org.uk/mausolea/view/199/Howard_Mausoleum_North_Yorkshire (accessed 28 January 2018).
34. A copy of Douce's will was printed in an obituary that appeared in *The Gentleman's Magazine* in 1834. See 'Francis Douce, Esq. F.S.A.', *The Gentleman's Magazine*, ii (1834), pp. 212–17 (pp. 216–17). Quoted by Matthew Craske, in 'Entombed like an Egyptian: An eighteenth-century surgeon's extravagant mausoleum to preserve his mortal remains', *Church Monuments*, 15 (2000), pp. 71–88 (p. 85).
35. Craske, 'Entombed like an Egyptian'. For other examples of burial vaults, see Julian Litten, 'Tombs fit for kings: Some burial vaults of the English aristocracy and landed gentry of the period 1650–1850', *Church Monuments*, 14 (1999), pp. 104–28.
36. For a full discussion of Egypt and Europe, and the history of the Egyptianizing of European architecture, see James Stevens Curl's *Egyptomania: The Egyptian Revival, A Recurring Theme in the History of Taste* (Manchester, 1994).
37. See David Winpenny, *Up to a Point: In Search of Pyramids in Britain and Ireland* (York, 2009).
38. See Augustus Welby Northmore Pugin, *An Apology for the Revival of Christian Architecture in England* (London, 1843).
39. Jurgis Baltrušaitis, *Aberrations: An Essay on the Legends of Forms*, trans. Richard Miller (Cambridge, MA, 1989), p. 191. Quoted in Rodney Stenning Edgecombe's 'James Murphy, Shelley and a Stanza in *Adonais*', *Keats-Shelley Review*, 15.1 (2001), pp. 86–7 (p. 86).

7 Obituaries and Obelisks: Egyptianizing Funerary Architecture and the Cemetery as a Heterotopic Space

1. Brian Masters, *The Dukes: Origins, Ennoblement and History of Twenty-Six Families* (London, 2011) p. 267.
2. For the cultural precursors to the practices considered in this chapter, see Chapter 6 of this volume, written by Jolene Zigarovich.

Notes to pages 117–121

3. Pat Jalland, *Death in the Victorian Family* (Oxford, 1996), p. 194.
4. Edwin Chadwick, *A supplementary report on the results of a spiecal (sic) inquiry into the practice of interment in towns*, 1843, p. 70.
5. Ibid., p. 69.
6. For more on the intricacies of the costs of Victorian funerals see Julie Rugg, 'The rise of cemetery companies in Britain 1820–1853', PhD Thesis, University of Stirling, 1992 and James Stevens Curl, *The Victorian Celebration of Death* (London, 1972).
7. The notion of a 'good death' was 'signified by a calm fearlessness rather than an ecstatic "parade."' Pat Jalland, *Death in the Victorian Family*, p. 24. For more on this notion see *Death in the Victorian Family*, Chapters 1 and 2.
8. Michel Foucault, 'Of other spaces, heterotopias', *Foucault, Info*. Available at https://foucault.info/doc/documents/heterotopia/foucault-heterotopia-en-html (accessed 26 June 2018).
9. For more on this notion see Edward Said, *Orientalism* (New York, 1978).
10. On jewellery, see, for instance, Chapter 8 of this volume, written by Lizzie Glithero-West. Glithero-West argues, as I do here, for a more nuanced understanding of the use of ancient Egyptian iconography in the modern world that goes beyond mere 'fashion'.
11. Robert Southey, *Don Manuel Evarez Espriella: Letters from England – Translated from the Spanish* (New York, 1836), p. 275. It is important to note that Southey is not the translator of this text; Don Manuel Evarez Esperiella was his pseudonym.
12. Noreen Doyle, 'The earliest known uses of "l'égyptomanie"/"Egyptomania" in French and English', *Journal of Ancient Egyptian Interconnections* 8 (2016), pp. 122–5 (p. 122).
13. James Stevens Curl, *Egyptomania: The Egyptian Revival, A Recurring Theme in the History of Taste* (Manchester, 1994); James Stevens Curl, *The Egyptian Revival: Ancient Egypt as the Inspiration for Design Motifs in the West* (New York, 2005).
14. Ronald H. Fritze, *Egyptomania: A History of Fascination, Obsession and Fantasy* (London, 2016), pp. 10–11.
15. Ibid., p. 10. The term 'Egyptopath' was coined by Jean-Marcel Humbert and Clifford Price to describe those who are 'completely crazy about anything and everything to do with Ancient Egypt' and was intended for use instead of 'egyptomaniacs', though they do not offer an explanation as to why this sounds better than Egyptomaniac. Jean-Marcel Humbert and Clifford Price, 'Introduction: An architecture between dream and meaning' in Jean-Marcel Humbert and Clifford Price (eds), *Imhotep Today: Egyptianizing Architecture* (London, 2003), p. 1.
16. Fritze, *Egyptomania*, p. 10.
17. Eleanor Dobson, 'Gods and ghost-light: Ancient Egypt, electricity, and X-rays', *Victorian Literature and Culture* 45.1 (2017), pp. 119–35 (p. 121). See also Eleanor Dobson, 'Literature and culture in the golden age of Egyptology' (PhD thesis, University of Birmingham, 2016).
18. Dobson, 'Gods and ghost-light', pp. 121–2.
19. Sara Brio, *Prefiguring the Cross: A Typological Reading of H. Rider Haggard's* Cleopatra in Eleanor Dobson (ed.), *Victorian Literary Culture and Ancient Egypt* (Manchester, 2020).
20. Matthew Coniam, *Egyptomania Goes to the Movies: From Archaeology to Popular Craze to Hollywood Fantasy* (Jefferson, NC, 2017), p. 22.
21. Ibid., p. 3.
22. Sarah Rutherford, *The Victorian Cemetery* (Oxford, 2013), pp. 5–10.
23. Harold Mytum, *Recording and Analysing Graveyards* (York, 2000), p. 44.

24. A total of five acts were passed within a decade (1852, 1853, 1855, 1857, and 1859).
25. Hazel Conway, *People's Parks: The Design and Development of Victorian Parks in Britain* (Cambridge, 1991) p. 215.
26. Rutherford, *The Victorian Cemetery*, p. 31.
27. Ibid., p. 5.
28. Lee Jackson, *Dirty Old London: The Victorian Fight Against Filth* (New Haven, 2014), p. 107.
29. The Royal College of Surgeons Archive, Royal College of Surgeons. *Prospectus of the General Cemetery Company: for providing places of interment, secure from violation, inoffensive to public health and decency, and ornamental to the metropolis: with papers illustrative of the subject* (London, 1830), p. 6.
30. Ibid., p. 32.
31. In 1838, John Finch stated to the Select Committee on Drunkenness that he thought the idea that public parks and cemeteries where people may 'amuse themselves innocently' were closed on Sundays was 'absurd' as the only other option for recreation was the public house. Quoted in Conway, *People's Parks*, p. 31.
32. *Prospectus of the General Cemetery Company*, p. 28.
33. Ibid., p. 31.
34. For more on the development of Victorian commercial cemeteries see Rugg, 'The rise of cemetery companies in Britain 1820–1853'.
35. Alasdair Douglas-Hamilton, *Lord of the Skies*, 2nd edn (London, 2015), p. 34.
36. 'Alexander, 10th Duke of Hamilton', *The Douglas Archives*. Available at http://www.douglashistory.co.uk/history/alexander10thdukeofhamilton.htm (accessed 26 June 2018); Bryan Crawford, *Letters My Grandfather Wrote Me: Family Origins* (Bloomington, IN, 2011).
37. It also seems that the Duke made a habit of falling off his horse; a similar instance is recorded in *The Standard* less than a year later. See also 'Accident to the Duke of Hamilton', *Morning Post*, 26 September 1849; 'Serious accident to His Grace the Duke of Hamilton', *Standard*, 13 July 1850; 'Duke of Hamilton recovering', *Morning Post*, 31 July 1850.
38. Godfrey Evans, 'Alexander, 10th Duke of Hamilton (1767–1852) as patron and collector' (PhD thesis, University of Edinburgh, 2009), p. ii.
39. Aidan Dodson, 'Duke Alexander's sarcophagi', *Archiv Orientální* 70 (2002), pp. 329–36 (p. 329); Thomas Pettigrew, *A History of Egyptian Mummies* (London, 1834), p. xi.
40. 'Will of Alexander Hamilton Hamilton of Stevenston, Ayrshire', The National Archives, Reference: PROB 11/2175/410, 25 July 1853.
41. Matt Cardin, *Mummies Around the World: An Encyclopedia of Mummies in History, Religion, and Popular Culture* (London, 2014), p. 342.
42. 'Obituary of the Duke of Hamilton', *The Gentleman's Magazine, and Historical Chronicle, for the Year 1852* 38 (1852), p. 425; Catherine Caufield, *The Man Who Ate Bluebottles: And Other Great British Eccentrics* (London, 2006), p. 71.
43. 'Obituary of the Duke of Hamilton', p. 426.
44. Dodson, 'Duke Alexander's sarcophagi', p. 333.
45. 'Hamilton Mausoleum (South Lanarkshire)', *The Mausolea & Monuments Trust*. Available at http://www.mmtrust.org.uk/mausolea/view/501/Hamilton_Mausoleum_South_Lanarkshire (accessed 26 June 2018).
46. 'Obituary of the Duke of Hamilton', p. 426.

47. Ibid.
48. Rosalie David, *The Pyramid Builders of Ancient Egypt: A Modern Investigation of Pharaoh's Workforce* (London, 2002), p. 63.
49. Ibid.

8 Tutankhartier: Death, Rebirth and Decoration; Or, Tutmania in the 1920s as a Metaphor for a Society in Recovery after World War One

1. Howard Carter and A. C. Mace, *The Discovery of the Tomb of Tutankhamen* (New York: 1977), p. 95. For more on the cultural impact of this discovery, see Chapter 1 of this volume, written by Gabrielle Heffernan.
2. Bridget Elliott, 'Art Deco worlds in a tomb: Reanimating Egypt in Modern(ist) visual culture', *South Central Review* 25.1 (2008), pp. 114–35 (p. 133).
3. Kate Denny McKnight, 'The persistence of Egyptian traditions in art and religion after the pharaohs', *Art and Archaeology*, 17 January/February 1924, p. 43.
4. Vivien Raynor, 'Art; A bounty of Egyptian imagery.' *The New York Times*, 25 February 1990. Available at www.nytimes.com/1990/02/25/nyregion/art-a-bounty-of-egyptian-imagery.html (accessed 3 February 2018).
5. Daniel Miller, 'Artefacts and the meaning of things', in Tim Ingold (ed.), *Companion Encyclopaedia of Anthropology* (London, 1994), p. 408.
6. Notable exceptions are Elliott, 'Art Deco worlds'; Michael North, *Reading 1922: A Return to the Scene of the Modern* (New York, 1999); and Christopher Frayling, *The Face of Tutankhamun* (London, 1992).
7. Examples include James Stevens Curl, *The Egyptian Revival: Ancient Egypt as the Inspiration for Design Motifs in the West* (London, 2005); Micki Forman, 'Tutmania', *Dress* 4 (1982), pp. 7–16; Jean-Marcel Humbert, Michael Pantazzi, and Christiane Zeigler, *Egyptomania: Egypt in Western Art 1730–1930* (Ottawa, 1994); Bob Brier *Egyptomania: Our Three Thousand Year Obsession with the Land of the Pharaohs* (New York, 2013) and Dominic Montserrat, *Akhenaten: History, Fantasy and Ancient Egypt* (London, 2001).
8. Stephanie Moser explores the more general theme of context in Reception Studies in her paper 'Reconstructing ancient worlds: Reception studies, archaeological representation and interpretation of ancient Egypt' in *Journal of Archaeological Method and Theory* 22.4 (2015), pp. 1263–308. Jasmine Day *The Mummy's Curse: Mummymania in the English Speaking World* (London, 2006) and Roger Luckhurst *The Mummy's Curse: The True History of a Dark Fantasy* (Oxford, 2012) both examine the idea of the curse in context, including its roots and manifestations in literature and film.
9. Helen Whitehouse, 'Review article: 'Egyptomanias', *American Journal of Archaeology* 101.1 (1997), pp. 158–61 (p. 161).
10. See also Chapter 11 of this volume, written by Mara Gold, which deals with women's fashion.
11. Joanna Bourke, *Dismembering the Male: Men's Bodies, Britain and the Great War* (Chicago, 1999), p. 229.
12. Ibid., p. 226.
13. See Jay Winter, *Sites of Memory, Sites of Mourning* (Cambridge, 1995), pp. 22–8 for greater detail.

14. For earlier Egyptianizing burials and memorials, see Chapters 6 and 7 of this volume, written by Jolene Zigarovich and Nichola Tonks respectively.
15. Winter, *Sites of Memory, Sites of Mourning*, p. 67.
16. Bourke, *Dismembering the Male*, p. 230.
17. Clifford Geertz, *The Interpretation of Cultures: Selected Essays* (New York, 1973), cited in Richard Huntington and Peter Metcalf, *Celebrations of Death: The Anthropology of Mortuary Ritual* (Cambridge, 1979), p. 5.
18. Daniel Sherman, 'Monuments, mourning and masculinity in France after World War I', *Gender and History* 8.1 (1996), pp. 82–107 (p. 83).
19. Winter, *Sites of Memory*, p. 2.
20. Charles Morice, 'Nécessité présente du travail intellectual', *L'Homme Libre*, 20 December 2017, trans. in Kenneth E. Silver, *Esprit de Corps: The Art of the Parisian Avant-Garde and the First World War, 1914–1925* (London, 1989), pp. 33, 165.
21. For in-depth detail on the post-war mood, see Ric Burns and James Sanders, *New York: An Illustrated History* (New York, 2003).
22. Charlotte Benton and Tim Benton, 'The style and the age', in Charlotte Benton, Tim Benton and Ghislaine Wood (eds), *Art Deco 1910–1939* (London, 2003), p. 13.
23. James Laver, *Women's Dress in the Jazz Age* (London, 1964), p. 6.
24. David Cannadine, 'War and death, grief and mourning in modern Britain', in Joachim Whaley (ed.), *Mirrors of Mortality: Studies in the Social History of Death* (London, 1981), p. 230.
25. Ibid., p. 218.
26. Cited in Thomas Hoving, *Tutankhamun: The Untold Story* (London, 1979), p. 200. Hoving does not provide further source information.
27. Carter and Mace, *Discovery of the Tomb of Tutankhamen*, p. 141.
28. Initially songs such as 'Old King Tut' envisioned Tutankhamun as an old man; it was his 1925 autopsy which revealed that he was between 17 and 19 when he died. However, many of the items in his tomb (published as early as 1923) depicted a young man. Likewise, 1923 saw the publication of two Tutankhamun romance novels, which imagine the king in early adulthood.
29. Bourke, *Dismembering the Male*, p. 220.
30. Ibid., p. 215.
31. Geoffrey Gorer, *Death, Grief and Mourning in Contemporary Britain* (Salem, 1965), p. 6, cited in Jenny Hockey, 'Changing death rituals', in Jenny Hockey, Jeanne Katz and Neil Small (eds), *Grief, Mourning and Death Ritual* (Buckingham, PA, 2001), p. 188.
32. See Bourke, *Dismembering the Male*, p. 216.
33. 'Pharaoh's shrine is rare treasure: Closer examination reveals 'Naos' is one of the finest monuments ever discovered', *The New York Times*, 10 February 1923.
34. 'What the great "find" in Egypt may bring: A 3000-year old pharaoh "coming forth into the day," with the contemporary garlands which adorned his mummy', *Illustrated London News*, 16 December 1922, p. 977.
35. 'Tutankhamen's statue sentinels: Robbers scared away by superstition', *Manchester Guardian*, 27 January 1923. This quotation is attributed to Harry Burton, the archaeological photographer working on the excavation of the tomb.
36. Howard Carter, *The Tomb of Tutankhamen* (London, 1972), p. 89.

37. Joanna Bourke, *Dismembering the Male*, p. 252.
38. Frayling, *The Face of Tutankhamun*, p. 63.
39. 'Ancient Egyptian styles to dominate jewelry and dress', *The Jewelers' Circular*, 21 February 1923, p. 79. The anonymous author refers to an interview in *The New York Times* of 18 February 1923 with J. M. Gidding.
40. L. Reid, 'Paris jewelry fashions', *The Jewelers' Circular*, 19 September 1923, p. 99.
41. Philippe Trétiack, *Cartier*, trans. Jane Brenton (London, 1997), p. 6. From 1904 to 1939, 15 warrants were signed appointing Cartier as 'official purveyor' to monarchies, including Egypt.
42. Gilberte Gautier, *Cartier: The Legend* (London, 1983), p. 203.
43. Kathryn Bonanno Patrizzi, 'The magnificent period of Mauboussin', *Kathryn Bonnano: Fine Collectable Jewels & Rare Gems*. Available at www.kathrynbonannogems.com/assets/magnificent-period-of-maubossin_small.pdf (accessed 3 February 2018).
44. Judy Rudoe 'Exoticism in Cartier jewels: The influence of Egypt, Persia, India and the Far East', in Nuno Vassalo e Silva and João Cavalho Dias (eds), *Cartier 1899-1949: The Journey of a Style* (Milan, 2007), p. 41.
45. Ibid., p. 43.
46. Tracy Kendrick, *Cartier Viewed by Sottsass* (Houston, 2005), p. 3.
47. François Chaille, *Cartier: Innovation Through the 20th Century* (Paris, 2007), p. 50.
48. Rudoe, 'Exoticism in Cartier jewels', p. 42.
49. See Francois Chaille and Eric Nussbaum, *The Cartier Collection: Jewellery* (Paris, 2004), p. 136.
50. Iya, Lady Abdy owned a couple of such items, and Linda Lee Porter commissioned a piece comprising an ancient scarab.
51. Martin Battersby, *The Decorative Twenties* (London, 1974), p. 117.
52. Marilyn Francis, 'Form follows fashionable function: The look of the Egyptian XVIII Dynasty', *Dress* 4.1 (1982), pp. 1–6 (p. 6).
53. Susan D. Cowie and Tom Johnson, *The Mummy in Fact, Fiction and Film* (Jefferson, NC, 2002), p. 22.
54. See also Vivienne Becker, *Antique and Twentieth Century Jewellery* (Colchester, 1987), p. 170.
55. See Carol Andrews, *Ancient Egyptian Jewellery* (London, 1990) for detailed references.
56. Andrews, *Ancient Egyptian Jewellery*, pp. 7–30.
57. Clement W. Coumbe, 'Egyptian decorative motifs', *The Jewelers' Circular*, 18 April 1923, p. 69.
58. Bourke, *Dismembering the Male*, p. 221.
59. John T. Irwin, *American Hieroglyphics: The Symbol of the Egyptian Hieroglyphics and the American Renaissance* (Baltimore, 1980), p. 147.
60. Eleanor Dobson, 'The sphinx at the séance: Literature, Spiritualism and psycho-archaeology', in Eleanor Dobson and Gemma Banks (eds), *Excavating Modernity: Physical, Temporal and Psychological Stratification in Literature, 1900-1930* (London, 2018).
61. 'Black magic: Sir H. Rider Haggard and dangerous nonsense', *Daily Mail*, 7 April 1923, cited in Frayling, *The Face of Tutankhamun*, p. 47.
62. Ibid., p. 53.
63. Ibid., p. 239.
64. Rudoe, *Cartier 1900-1939*, p. 152.

65. Ibid.
66. Thomas Moore, *Alciphron, A Poem* (Philadelphia, 1840), p. 13. Available at: www.forgottenbooks.com/en/books/Alciphron_10503901 (accessed 3 February 2018).
67. In 1923 the face of Tutankhamun had yet to be uncovered. Inspiration must have come, instead, from models or wall paintings.
68. See Wallis Budge, *The Egyptian Book of the Dead (Abridged)* (London, 2001), p. 66.
69. Andrews, *Ancient Egyptian Jewellery*, p. 37.
70. Even Vladimir Lenin was mummified after he died in January 1924.
71. North, *Reading 1922*, p. 24.
72. Tag Gronberg, *Designs on Modernity* (Manchester, 1998), p. 39.
73. Ibid., p. 23.
74. This is explored in Mary Louise Roberts, 'Samson and Delilah revisited', in Whitney Chadwick and Tirza True Latimer (eds), *The Modern Woman Revisited: Paris Between the Wars* (London, 2003).
75. Sydney Tremayne, 'A career for women: Being beautiful', *Vogue London*, Early September 1923, p. 19.
76. Gronberg, *Designs on Modernity*, p. 47.
77. North, *Reading 1922*, p. 27.

9 Celtic Egyptians: Isis Priests of the Lineage of Scota

1. For more on nineteenth-century esoteric uses of ancient Egypt and their cultural ripples in the late twentieth century, see Chapter 10 in this volume, written by Eleanor Dobson.
2. Reginald Eldred Witt, *Isis in the Ancient World* (Baltimore, 1971); Richard H. Wilkinson, *The Complete Gods and Goddesses of Ancient Egypt* (London, 2003), pp. 79, 146-7.
3. Sarolta A. Takács, *Isis and Sarapis in the Roman World* (Leiden, 1995), pp. 32-51; Robert Turcan, *The Cults of the Roman Empire* (Oxford, 1997), pp. 75-129.
4. Outside of Italy Isis worship was not a mystery religion. See Miranda Green, 'Isis at Thornborough', *Recs of Bucks* 25 (1983), pp. 139-41.
5. Robert A. Wortham, 'Urban networks, deregulated religious markets, cultural continuity and the diffusion of the Isis cult', *Method and Theory in the Study of Religion* 18.2 (2006), pp. 103-23.
6. Champollion incorporated the work of British scholar, Thomas Young. Arab scholars had already begun to decipher the language as early as the Middle Ages, unbeknownst to Europeans. See Okasha El Daly, *Egyptology: The Missing Millennium: Ancient Egypt in Medieval Arabic Writings* (London, 2005); Charles Burnett, 'Images of ancient Egypt in the Latin Middle Ages', in Peter J. Ucko and Timothy Champion (eds), *The Wisdom of Egypt: Changing Visions Through the Ages* (London, 2003), pp. 65-99.
7. Plutarch, *Plutarch's De Iside Et Osiride*, trans. John Gwyn Griffith (Swansea, 1970).
8. Diodorus Siculus, *Library of History*. Available at http://penelope.uchicago.edu/Thayer/E/Roman/Texts/Diodorus_Siculus/home.html (accessed 3 March 2019).
9. Paraskevi Martzavou. 'Isis aretalogies, initiations and emotions: The Isis aretalogies as sources for the study of emotions', in Angelos Chaniotis (ed.), *Unveiling Emotions: Sources and Methods*

for the Study of Emotions in the Greek World (Stuttgart, 2012), pp. 267–91; Garth Fowden, *The Egyptian Hermes: A Historical Approach to the Late Pagan Mind* (Princeton, 1986).

10. Florian Ebeling, *The Secret History of Hermes Trismegistus: Hermeticism from Ancient to Modern Times* (Ithaca, 2007), pp. vi–xiii.
11. Giovanni Boccaccio, *Famous Women*, trans. Virginia Brown (Cambridge, 2001).
12. Daniel Stolzenberg, *Egyptian Oedipus: Athanasius Kircher and the Secrets of Antiquity* (Chicago, 2013), p. 37.
13. Jean Terrasson, *Life of Sethos*, trans. Thomas Lediard (London, 1732).
14. The Neo-Platonic writer Proclus (410–85 BC) had added 'The fruit I bore was the sun'. See Jan Assmann, *Moses the Egyptian: The Memory of Egypt in Western Monotheism* (Cambridge, 1997), pp. 118–25; Pierre Hadot, *The Veil of Isis: An Essay on the History of the Idea of Nature* (Cambridge, 2006).
15. Erik Hornung, *The Secret Lore of Egypt: Its Impact on the West* (Ithaca, 2001), pp. 1, 3.
16. Ibid.
17. Ellic Howe, *The Magicians of the Golden Dawn* (London, 1972), p. 1.
18. All the Golden Dawn temples had Egyptian names: the Isis-Urania Temple in London, the Osiris Temple in Weston-super-Mare, the Horus Temple in Bradford, the Amen-Ra Temple in Edinburgh and the Ahathoor Temple in Paris.
19. Israel Regardie, *The Complete Golden Dawn System of Magic*, Vol. 6 (Scottsdale, 1990), pp. 18, 5–22; Apuleius, *The Golden Ass*, trans. Joel C. Relihan (Indianapolis, 2007), p. 249; Raymond O. Faulkner, *The Ancient Egyptian Book of the Dead* (New York, 1985), pp. 44–50.
20. Regardie, *Complete Golden Dawn*, Vol. 7, p. 53.
21. Regardie, *Complete Golden Dawn*, Vol. 7, p. 151; Regardie, *Complete Golden Dawn*, Vol. 8, pp. 17–19; Caroline Tully, 'Egyptosophy in the British Museum: Florence Farr, the Egyptian adept and the ka', in Christine Ferguson and Andrew Radford (eds), *The Occult Imagination in Britain, 1875 – 1947* (London, 2018).
22. Regardie, *Complete Golden Dawn*, Vol. 7, pp. 8, 1–13; Regardie, *Complete Golden Dawn*, Vol. 6, p. 84; Caroline Tully, 'Walk like an Egyptian: Egypt as authority in Aleister Crowley's reception of *The Book of the Law*', *Pomegranate: International Journal of Pagan Studies* 12 (2010), pp. 20–47.
23. Née Bergson. Moina was the sister of French philosopher Henri Bergson. Originally 'Mina', she would later change her name to the more Celtic 'Moina'. See Mary Katherine Greer, *Women of the Golden Dawn: Rebels and Priestesses* (Rochester, 1995), pp. 41–2.
24. Ibid., p. 55.
25. Ibid., p. 191.
26. Christopher McIntosh, *Eliphas Lévi and the French Occult Revival* (London, 1972); James Webb, *The Occult Underground* (Illinois, 1974), pp. 153–90; Tobias Churton, *Occult Paris: The Lost Magic of the Belle Époque* (Rochester, 2016). In Paris in 1891 MacGregor had allegedly met a Higher Adept, Frater Lux E Tenebris, who gave him materials for constructing higher degree rituals for the Golden Dawn; Greer, *Women of the Golden Dawn*, p. 102.
27. They were reliant in Paris on the financial beneficence of their wealthy friend Annie Horniman until mid-1896, after which they struggled financially. There is no evidence that Horniman or anyone else paid for them to visit Egypt. See Greer, *Women of the Golden Dawn*, pp. xviii, 155, 174, 207. Contra Colquhoun who fails to provide any evidence; Ithell Colquhoun, *The Sword of Wisdom: Macgregor Mathers and the Golden Dawn* (New York, 1975), p. 86.

Notes to pages 148–149

28. André Gaucher, 'Isis à Montmartre', *L'Echo du merveilleux: Revue bimensuelle* 94, 95 (1900), pp. 446–53, 470–3 (pp. 446–9). I am grateful to Christopher Kimberley for his translation of this article.
29. Colquhoun, *Sword of Wisdom*, pp. 84, 88.
30. Ella Young, *Flowering Dusk: Things Remembered Accurately and Inaccurately* (New York, 1945), p 105; Greer, *Women of the Golden Dawn*, pp. 200, 314.
31. Frederic Lees, 'Isis worship in Paris: Conversations with the Hierophant Rameses and the High Priestess Anari', *The Humanitarian* 16/2 (1900), pp. 82–7. Paraphrased by Greer, *Women of the Golden Dawn*, p. 222.
32. Young, *Flowering Dusk*, pp. 105–6.
33. Lees, 'Isis Worship in Paris', p. 86.
34. W. B. Yeats, William H. O'Donnell (eds), *The Speckled Bird by William Butler Yeats: An Autobiographical Novel, with Variant Versions. New Edition, Incorporating Recently Discovered Manuscripts* (London, 2003), p. 185, n. 27.
35. Colquhoun, *Sword of Wisdom*, p. 86.
36. Lees, 'Isis worship in Paris', p. 83.
37. Ibid., p. 84.
38. Caroline Tully, 'Samuel Liddell MacGregor Mathers and Isis', in Dave Evans and Dave Green (eds), *Ten Years of Triumph? Academic Approaches to Studying Magic and the Occult: Examining Scholarship into Witchcraft and Paganism Ten Years after Ronald Hutton's Triumph of the Moon* (Harpenden, 2009), pp. 64–8.
39. Young, *Flowering Dusk*, p. 105.
40. Yeats, *Speckled Bird*, p. 78.
41. Moina was a native French speaker. See Greer, *Women of the Golden Dawn*, p. 42.
42. Lees, 'Isis worship in Paris', pp. 85–6.
43. Gaucher, 'Isis à Montmartre', pp. 446–9. Quoted in Greer, *Women of the Golden Dawn*, pp. 248–50.
44. O'Donnell, *Speckled Bird*, p. 79.
45. Lees, 'Isis worship in Paris', p. 86.
46. George Mills Harper, *Yeats's Golden Dawn* (London, 1974), p. 202.
47. John Brodie-Innes, 'MacGregor Mathers: Some personal reminiscences', *Occult Review* 29.5 (1919), pp. 284–6. Cited in R. A. Gilbert, *The Golden Dawn Scrapbook* (York Beach, 1997), p. 112.
48. James Stevens Curl, *The Egyptian Revival: Ancient Egypt as the Inspiration for Design Motifs in the West* (New York, 2005), p. 345. Dourgnon also designed the Egyptian Museum in Cairo.
49. Butler, *Victorian Occultism*, p. 8.
50. Greer, Women of the Golden Dawn, p. 75.
51. Ibid., pp. xvi–xvii, 115.
52. Colquhoun, *Sword of Wisdom*, p. 85.
53. O'Donnell, *Speckled Bird*, p. 194, n. 90.
54. Greer, *Women of the Golden Dawn*, p. 42.
55. Jeanne Sheehy, *The Rediscovery of Ireland's Past: the Celtic Revival 1830–1930* (London, 1980), p. 95. The Celtic Revival was different to, although overlapped with, the Occult Revival, an

increasing interest evident since the eighteenth century in knowledge and use of supernatural beings.
56. Susan Johnston Graf, *W. B. Yeats Twentieth Century Magus* (York Beach, 2000), pp. 6–7.
57. Greer, *Women of the Golden Dawn*, p. 196.
58. Greer, *Women of the Golden Dawn*, p. 196; O'Donnell, *Speckled Bird*, p. 186.
59. O'Donnell, *Speckled Bird*, p. 194, n. 89; Greer, *Women of the Golden Dawn*, pp. 196–8; Mark Williams, *Ireland's Immortals: A History of the Gods of Irish Myth* (Princeton, 2016), pp. 332–41.
60. O'Donnell, *Speckled Bird*, p. 194, n. 89.
61. Ibid., p. x.
62. O'Donnell, *Speckled Bird*, p. x; Greer, *Women of the Golden Dawn*, pp. xviii, 76–9.
63. Greer, *Women of the Golden Dawn*, p. 189; Young, *Flowering Dusk*, p. 106.
64. Richard J. Finneran, George Mills Harper, William M. Murphy and Alan B. Himber (eds), *Letters to W. B. Yeats* (London, 1977), pp. 29–30.
65. Greer, *Women of the Golden Dawn*, pp. 189, 201–2, 207, 318.
66. Lucy Shepard Kalogera, *Yeats's Celtic Mysteries* (Florida, 1977); Graf, *Twentieth Century Magus*, pp. 40–2.
67. Jed Z. Buchwald and Diane Greco Josefowicz, *The Zodiac of Paris* (Princeton 2010), pp. 52–53, 63.
68. Hornung, *Secret Lore of Egypt*, pp. 132–4; Kevin M. McGeough, *The Ancient Near East in the Nineteenth Century: Appreciations and Appropriations*, Vol. 1 (Sheffield, 2015), pp. 29, 51.
69. The ship on the Paris coat of arms, which dates to the thirteenth century, actually refers to the importance of shipping on the Seine. King Louis XVIII changed the coat of arms back to the old design in 1817.
70. Timothy Champion, 'The Celt in archaeology', in Terrence Brown (ed), *Celticism* (Leiden, 1996), p. 74.
71. Cunliffe, *The Ancient Celts* (London, 1997), pp. 13–14.
72. Joep Leerssen, 'Celticism', in Terence Brown (ed.), *Celticism* (Amsterdam, 1996), p. 4; Barry Cunliffe, *Ancient Celts*, p. 13.
73. Gaucher, 'Isis à Montmartre', p. 449.
74. William Matthews, 'The Egyptians in Scotland: The political history of a myth', *Viator* 1 (1971), pp. 289–306; Edward J. Cowan, 'Myth and identity in early Medieval Scotland', *The Scottish Historical Review* 63.176 (1984), pp. 111–35; John Collis, *The Celts: Origins, Myths, Inventions* (Stroud, 2003), pp. 30, 32–3; Ralph Ellis, *Scota, Egyptian Queen of the Scots* (Cheshire, 2006), p. xiv; Joseph Lennon, *Irish Orientalism: A Literary and Intellectual History* (Syracuse, 2004).
75. Collis, *The Celts*, p. 30.
76. McGeough, *Ancient Near East*, p. 3.
77. Ellis, *Scota*, p. xiv.
78. Lawrence and Olivia are descents of the first Lord Esmonde who built the castle in 1625. They were also cousins of another major influence on British Paganism, Robert Graves (1895–1985).
79. Olivia claimed that her first spiritual awakening from Isis dated back to 1946. See Olivia Robertson, 'Isis of alchemy, transformation through the goddess', *Fellowship of Isis*. Available at www.fellowshipofisis.com/liturgy/alchemyintro.html (accessed 18 March 2017).

80. Catherine Maignant, 'Irish base, global religion: The Fellowship of Isis', in Olivia Cosgrove, Laurence Cox, Carmen Kuhling and Peter Mulholland (eds), *Ireland's New Religious Movements* (Newcastle upon Tyne, 2011), p. 267.
81. Maignant, *Irish Base, Global Religion*, p. 270.
82. 'The Fellowship of Isis manifesto', *Fellowship of Isis*. Available at www.fellowshipofisis.com/manifesto.html (accessed 24 February 2017).
83. Maignant, *Irish Base, Global Religion*, p. 265.
84. 'Fellowship of Isis enrollment', *Fellowship of Isis*. Available at www.fellowshipofisis.com/joinform.html (accessed 6 April 2017).
85. Maignant, *Irish Base, Global Religion*, p. 269.
86. 'The Fellowship of Isis manifesto'.
87. 'Introduction to the Fellowship of Isis', *Fellowship of Isis*. Available at www.fellowshipofisis.com/intro.html (accessed 24 February 2017).
88. Maignant, *Irish Base, Global Religion*, p. 269.
89. Ibid., p. 265.
90. Caroline Wise (ed.), *Olivia Robertson: A Centenary Tribute* (London, 2017), p.10.
91. Ellen Evert Hopman, *A Legacy of Druids: Conversations with Druid Leaders of Britain, the USA and Canada, Past and Present* (Winchester: 2016), p. 49.
92. Mr Fox had served in Egypt in the British Egyptian Expedition with General Edmund Allenby in World War I. See 'Druid Clan of Dana – the faery seat', *Fellowship of Isis Central Website*. Available at www.fellowshipofisiscentral.com/druid-clan-of-dana--the-faery-seat (accessed 25 February 2017).
93. 'Noble Order of Tara', *Fellowship of Isis*. Available at www.fellowshipofisis.com/nobleorderoftara.html (accessed 14 April 2017).
94. 'Druid Clan of Dana', *Fellowship of Isis*. Available at www.fellowshipofisis.com/druidclanofdana.html (accessed 14 April 2017).
95. Maignant, *Irish Base, Global Religion*, p. 265; 'The Circle of Brigid', *Fellowship of Isis*. Available at www.fellowshipofisis.com/circleofbrigid.html (accessed 13 April 2017).
96. Maignant, *Irish Base, Global Religion*, p. 273.
97. Vivianne Crowley, 'Olivia Robertson: Priestess of Isis', in Inga Bårdsen Tøllefsen and Christian Guidice (eds), *Female Leaders in New Religious Movements* (Basingstoke, 2017), pp. 152-3.
98. Olivia Robertson (ed.), *The Handbook of the Fellowship of Isis* (London, 1992), pp. 4-6.
99. Olivia Robertson, 'Ordination of priestesses and priests', *Fellowship of Isis*. www.fellowshipofisis.com/liturgy/ordainpref.html (accessed 24 February 2017). See also 'Fellowship of Isis priesthood', *Fellowship of Isis*. Available at www.fellowshipofisis.com/priesthood.html (accessed 24 February 2017).
100. Olivia cites the *Lebor Gabála Érenn* and the *Scotichronicon* as her sources. See 'College of Isis – training of priestesses and priests', *Fellowship of Isis Central Website*. Available at www.fellowshipofisiscentral.com/college-of-isis---training-of-priestesses-and-priests (accessed 11 December 2016).
101. 'Quick key to the cosmic web', *Fellowship of Isis*. Available at www.fellowshipofisis.com/keyalch.html (accessed 24 February 2017). See also Olivia Robertson, 'FOI online liturgy: Fortuna, creation through the goddess', *Fellowship of Isis*. Available at www.fellowshipofisis.com/liturgy/fortuna6.html (accessed 24 February 2017). 'Cesara' refers to

Notes to pages 159–164

Cessair who features in the *Lebor Gabála Érenn* as the female leader of the first group of settlers in Ireland; Collis, *The Celts*, pp. 30, 32–3; Olivia Robertson, 'Sphinx, goddess myths and mysteries', *Fellowship of Isis*. Available at www.fellowshipofisis.com/liturgy/sphinx.html (accessed 24 February 2017).

102. 'Druid Clan of Dana groves', *Fellowship of Isis*. Available at www.fellowshipofisis.com/directory_groves.html (accessed 24 February 2017). See also 'Clan Donnachaidh – Robertson: Barony of Strathloch', *Fellowship of Isis*. Available at www.fellowshipofisis.com/coatofarms.html (accessed 24 February 2017).

103. 'Changing faces of the temple' (24 March 2011), *Fellowship of Isis Homepage*. Available at www.foihomepage.blogspot.com.au/2011/03/changing-faces-of-temple_24.html (accessed 23 February 2017). See also 'Changing faces of the temple' (13 June 2011), *Fellowship of Isis Homepage*. Available at www.foihomepage.blogspot.com.au/2011/06/changing-faces-of-temple.html (accessed 23 February 2017). For more images, see 'New temple photos' (27 May 2013), *Fellowship of Isis Homepage*. Available at www.foihomepage.blogspot.com.au/2013/05/new-temple-photos.html (accessed 23 February 2017).

10 Jack the Ripper and the Mummy's Curse: Ancient Egypt in *From Hell*

1. Alan Moore and Eddie Campbell, *From Hell: Being a Melodrama in Sixteen Parts* (London, 2016), ch. 5, p. 0. As pagination begins anew with each chapter in *From Hell*, I provide references to the text which provide chapter number and page number. As the first page of each chapter is unnumbered I refer to these as p. 0.
2. 'The unlucky mummy', *The British Museum*. Available at www.britishmuseum.org/research/collection_online/collection_object_details.aspx?objectId=117233&partId=1 (accessed 25 February 2018).
3. For more on nineteenth-century esoteric uses of ancient Egypt, see Chapter 9 in this volume, written by Caroline Tully.
4. For more on ancient Egyptian symbolism in graphic texts, see Chapter 15 in this volume, written by Nickianne Moody.
5. Christine Ferguson, 'Victoria-arcana and the misogynistic poetics of resistance in Iain Sinclair's *White Chappell Scarlet Tracings* and Alan Moore's *From Hell*', *LIT: Literature Interpretation Theory* 20.1–2 (2009), pp. 45–64 (p. 46).
6. Ruth Hoberman, *Museum Trouble: Edwardian Fiction and the Emergence of Modernism* (Charlottesville, VA, 2011), p. 3.
7. Ibid., p. 7.
8. Alan Moore, 'Annotations to the chapters', in Moore and Campbell, *From Hell*, appendix 1, p. 19.
9. Moore and Campbell, *From Hell*, ch. 5, p. 0.
10. Moore, 'Annotations to the chapters', p. 19.
11. J. A. Brooks, *Ghosts of London: The West End, South and West* (Norwich, 1982), p. 50. Brooks capitalizes 'War', while Moore does not.
12. Ibid.
13. Ibid., p. 41.
14. Moore and Campbell, *From Hell*, ch. 5, p. 18.

15. Ibid., ch. 5, p. 15. Despite there being no known mummy associated with this wooden board, the object is presented as a mummy throughout *From Hell*. Moore himself uses 'mummy' and 'mummy case' interchangeably to refer to this object (despite the artefact being neither of these things); see, e.g., Moore, 'Annotations to the chapters', p. 19.
16. Moore and Campbell, *From Hell*, ch. 5, p. 18.
17. Roger Luckhurst, *The Mummy's Curse: The True History of a Dark Fantasy* (Oxford, 2012), p. 26.
18. Ibid., pp. 31–2. Luckhurst quotes G. St. Russell, 'The mysterious mummy', *Pearson's Magazine* 28 (1909), pp. 162–72 (pp. 163–4). Luckhurst also relates a similar account with minor differences; pp. 33–4.
19. 'Lot No. 249' is often cited as the earliest tale in which an Egyptian mummy is magically rather than scientifically reanimated though, as Jasmine Day notes, an 1862 anonymously authored short story, 'The Mummy's Soul', features an ambulatory mummy reanimated by magic. This example is also the first known ambulatory mummy since Loudon's precedent, and the first female such character. See Jasmine Day, *The Mummy's Curse: Mummymania in the English-Speaking World* (London, 2006), p. 46.
20. Most sources spell 'Nichols' with a single 'l', though Moore uses 'Nicholls'.
21. Moore and Campbell, *From Hell*, ch. 9, p. 13.
22. Ibid., ch. 9, p. 14.
23. Luckhurst, *The Mummy's Curse*, p. 27.
24. Alan Moore and Eddie Campbell, *The From Hell Companion* (London, 2013), p. 168.
25. See Eleanor Dobson, 'Literature and culture in the golden age of Egyptology' (PhD thesis, University of Birmingham, 2017), pp. 304–6.
26. Alex Owen, *The Place of Enchantment: British Occultism and the Culture of the Modern* (Chicago, 2004), p. 61; Lynn Parramore, *Reading the Sphinx: Ancient Egypt in Nineteenth-Century Literary Culture* (Basingstoke, 2008), p. 112.
27. Moore and Campbell, *The From Hell Companion*, p. 169.
28. Ibid.
29. Moore, 'Annotations to the chapters', p. 31.
30. Monika Pietrzak-Franger, 'Envisioning the Ripper's visions: Adapting myth in Alan Moore and Eddie Campbell's *From Hell*', *Neo-Victorian Studies* 2.2 (2009/2010), pp. 157–85 (p. 174).
31. Elizabeth Ho, 'Postimperial landscapes: "Psychogeography" and Englishness in Alan Moore's graphic novel *From Hell: A Melodrama in Sixteen Parts*', *Cultural Critique* 63 (2006), pp. 99–121 (p. 113).
32. Rob Vollmar, 'Northampton calling: A conversation with Alan Moore', *World Literature Today* 111.1 (2017), pp. 28–34 (p. 30). I am grateful to Daniel Moore for his insights on this subject.
33. Niall Martin, *Iain Sinclair: Noise, Neoliberalism and the Matter of London* (London, 2015), p. 60. See also Michel Foucault, 'Of other spaces, heterotopias', *Foucault, Info*. Available at <https://foucault.info/doc/documents/heterotopia/foucault-heterotopia-en-html> (accessed 16 April 2017).
34. Martin, *Iain Sinclair*, p. 65.
35. Brian Baker, *Iain Sinclair* (Manchester, 2007), pp. 122–3.
36. Moore and Campbell, *From Hell*, ch. 4, p. 12.

37. Ibid., ch. 4, p. 13.
38. Obelisks are notable in *From Hell* at, for example, ch. 7, pp. 21, 31, ch. 9, p. 45, ch. 10, p. 34.
39. Moore, 'Annotations to the chapters', p. 25.
40. Moore and Campbell, *From Hell*, ch. 2, p. 15.
41. Moore 'Annotations to the chapters', p. 42.
42. Ibid., p. 14.
43. Moore and Campbell, *From Hell*, ch. 4, pp. 20-1.
44. Ibid., ch. 4, p. 19. Campbell drew the sphinx from an image that Moore had sent to him; see Moore and Campbell, *The From Hell Companion*, p. 82. The photograph can be seen in the unnumbered plates section in this volume.
45. Moore and Campbell, *The From Hell Companion*, p. 84.
46. Ibid.
47. James Stevens Curl, *Egyptomania: The Egyptian Revival, A Recurring Theme in the History of Taste* (Manchester, 1994), p. 200.
48. Moore and Campbell, *From Hell*, ch. 4, pp. 20-1.
49. Ibid., ch. 4, p. 21; ch. 14, p. 8. One of Moore's sources, *London's Secret History*, records that these objects were buried in 'two earthenware jars', suggestive of canopic jars. See Peter Bushell, *London's Secret History* (London, 1983), p. 146.
50. Moore and Campbell, *From Hell*, ch. 4, p. 21.
51. Ibid., ch. 3, p. 12.
52. In the film adaptation of the graphic novel, Polly Nichols is murdered as she looks at Cleopatra's Needle; see *From Hell*, dir. the Hughes Brothers (2001).
53. Moore, 'Annotations to the chapters', p. 18.
54. Moore and Campbell, *From Hell*, ch. 14, p. 8.
55. Sigmund Freud, *Civilization and Its Discontents*, trans. Joan Riviere (London, 1982), p. 7.
56. Moore and Campbell, *The From Hell Companion*, p. 269.
57. Moore and Campbell, *From Hell*, ch. 14, p. 8.
58. Moore and Campbell, *The From Hell Companion*, p. 269.
59. Moore and Campbell, *From Hell*, ch. 14, p. 8.
60. Moore and Campbell, *The From Hell Companion*, p. 271.
61. Ibid.
62. Moore and Campbell, *From Hell*, ch. 14, p. 22.
63. Paul Harrison, *The Curse of the Pharaohs' Tombs: Tales of the Unexpected Since the Days of Tutankhamun* (Barnsley, 2017), p. 58.
64. Moore and Campbell, *From Hell*, ch. 11, p. 0.
65. Ibid. Moore misspells 'Belgrave' as 'Belgrade'.
66. Francis King, *Modern Ritual Magic: The Rise of Western Occultism* (Bridport, 1989), p. 43; Owen, *The Place of Enchantment*, pp. 53-54.
67. Moore relates that 'Drs Woodford [Woodman] and Westcott, besides being doctors with Freemasonic connections of that period, were included because of their association with the only recently founded Order of the Golden Dawn and my own fondness for introducing arcane historical celebrities at the drop of a hat'; Moore, 'Annotations to the chapters', p. 40. For Westcott and Woodman's appearance, see Moore and Campbell, *From Hell*, ch. 12, p. 21.

68. Owen, *The Place of Enchantment*, pp. 62–3.
69. Caroline Tully, 'Florence and the mummy', in Brandy Williams (ed.), *Women's Voices in Magic* (Stafford, 2009), pp. 15–16.
70. Moore and Campbell, *From Hell*, ch. 2, p. 17.
71. Ibid., ch. 9 p. 33.
72. Ibid., ch. 9, p. 15.
73. Alan Moore and Eddie Campbell, 'Dance of the gull catchers', in Moore and Campbell, *From Hell*, appendix 2, p. 3.
74. Mabel Collins, *The Story of Sensa: An Interpretation of the Idyll of the White Lotus* (New York, 2013), pp. 2–3.
75. Owen, *The Place of Enchantment*, pp. 32, 45.
76. Moore and Campbell, *From Hell*, ch. 9, p. 4.
77. Ibid., ch. 9, p. 0.
78. Harrison, *The Curse of the Pharaohs' Tombs*, p. 57.
79. In Craig Fischer and Charles Hatfield's foreword to *The From Hell Companion*, they misidentify Horus as Thoth; Craig Fischer and Charles Hatfield, 'Foreword', in Alan Moore and Eddie Campbell, *The From Hell Companion* (London, 2013), p. 6.
80. Pietrzak-Franger, 'Envisioning the Ripper's visions', p. 174.
81. Samuel Sharpe was a key figure in comparisons between ancient Egyptian religion and Christianity in the nineteenth century. See David Gange, *Dialogues with the Dead: Egyptology in British Culture and Religion, 1822–1922* (Oxford, 2013), pp. 90–114.
82. Moore and Campbell, *From Hell*, ch. 14, p. 23.
83. Moore and Campbell, 'Dance of the gull catchers', p. 12. For ancient Egypt and late nineteenth- and early twentieth-century spiritualism, see Eleanor Dobson, 'The sphinx at the séance: Literature, Spiritualism and psycho-archaeology', in Eleanor Dobson and Gemma Banks (eds), *Excavating Modernity: Physical, Temporal and Psychological Strata in Literature, 1900–1930* (London, 2018).
84. Moore and Campbell, *From Hell*, ch. 4, p. 30.
85. Ibid., prologue, p. 5.
86. Ibid., epilogue, p. 10.
87. Harrison, *The Curse of the Pharaohs' Tombs*, p. 37.
88. John Maclauchlan, 'Presidential address', *Museums Journal* 7 (1907–8), pp. 4–17 (p. 15). Quoted in Hoberman, *Museum Trouble*, p. 14.

11 From Sekhmet to Suffrage: Ancient Egypt in Early Twentieth-Century Women's Culture

1. Edward Said, *Orientalism* (New York, 1978); Meyda Yeğenoğlu, *Colonial Fantasies: Towards a Feminist Reading of Orientalism* (Cambridge, 1998), p. 1.
2. Dúnlaith Bird, 'Disorienting eyes: Women travellers to the Orient from 1880–1930' (MPhil thesis, Oxford University, 2006), pp. 1–3; Billie Melman, *Women's Orients: English Women and the Middle East* (Basingstoke, 1995); Yeğenoğlu, *Colonial Fantasies*, pp. 1, 13.

3. Melman, *Women's Orients*. See also Chapters 13 and 14 of this volume, written by Sabina Stent and Siv Jansson, respectively.
4. Sara Mills, *Discourses of Difference: An Analysis of Women's Travel Writing and Colonialism* (London, 1991); Mary Louise Pratt, *Imperial Eyes: Travel Writing and Transculturation* (London, 2008).
5. Bird, 'Disorienting eyes', p. 3; Yeğenoğlu, *Colonial Fantasies*, p. 78.
6. See also how these themes translate for younger audiences in the 1970s, as detailed in the Chapter 15 of this volume, written by Nickianne Moody.
7. Bob Brier, *Egyptomania: Our Three Thousand Year Obsession with the Land of the Pharaohs* (New York, 2013); Paola Bono, 'Rewriting the memory of a queen: Dido, Cleopatra, Elizabeth I', *European Journal of English Studies*, x/2 (2006), pp. 117–30 (p. 121).
8. Jasmine Day, *The Mummy's Curse: Mummymania in the English-Speaking World* (London, 2006), p. 43.
9. Jasmine Day, 'The rape of the mummy: Women, horror fiction and the Westernisation of the curse', in Pablo Atoche-Peña, Conrado Rodríguez-Martin and Ángeles Ramírez-Rodríguez (eds) *Mummies and Science: World Mummies Research, Proceedings of the VI World Congress on Mummy Studies* (Santa Cruz de Tenerife, 2008), pp. 617–21.
10. I use 'positive' here to differentiate between women's own constructions of femininity as a source of power and 'negative' concepts of femininity, which include weakness (as in the subjugation of the East) and dangerous, sexual 'excess femininity' (as in Cleopatra). For the professionalization of Egyptology leading up to and concurrent with the period I consider, see Philippa Levine, *The Amateur and the Professional: Antiquarians, Historians and Archaeologists in Victorian England 1838-1886* (Cambridge, 1986), and David Gange, *Dialogues with the Dead: Egyptology in British Culture and Religion, 1822-1922* (Oxford, 2013).
11. Karin J. Bohleke, 'Mummies are called upon to contribute to fashion: Pre-Tutankhamun Egyptian revivalism in dress', *Dress*, 40.2 (2014), pp. 93–115 (pp. 95–6).
12. Adam Geczy, *Fashion and Orientalism: Dress, Textiles and Culture from the 17th to the 21st Century* (London, 2013), pp. 80–1; Valerie D. Mendes, *Fashion Since 1900* (London, 2010), pp. 63–4.
13. Elizabeth Ewing and Alice Mackrell, *History of Twentieth Century Fashion* (London, 2001), pp. 119–20.
14. See, for instance, Chapter 8 of this volume, written by Lizzie Glithero-West.
15. James Stevens Curl, *The Egyptian Revival: Ancient Egypt as the Inspiration for Design Motifs in the West* (New York, 2005), p. 195.
16. Judith Butler, *Gender Trouble: Feminism and the Subversion of Identity* (London, 2014).
17. Bono, 'Rewriting the memory', p. 117; Christine Peltre, *Orientalism in Art* (New York, 1998), p. 206.
18. Peter Roger Stuart Moorey, *A Century of Biblical Archaeology* (Cambridge, 1991), pp. 2–3.
19. Peltre, *Orientalism in Art*, p. 206.
20. The last time the Cleopatra theme was so popular in entertainment was during the reign of Queen Elizabeth I, likely in response to popular insecurity regarding a female sovereign. Perhaps, then, Cleopatra's revival was somewhat related to Britain's second female monarch, Queen Victoria; see Bono, 'Rewriting the memory', p. 126.
21. Peltre, *Orientalism in Art*, pp. 206–9.

Notes to pages 185–190

22. Juliet Bellow, 'Fashioning *Cléopâtre*: Sonia Delaunay's New Woman', *Art Journal*, 68.2 (2009), pp. 6–25 (pp. 7–8).
23. Ibid., p. 8.
24. For examples of such mummy masks see 'Mummy of Amenhotep the First', *Global Egyptian Museum*, Cairo Museum inventory no. JE 26211. Available at http://www.globalegyptianmuseum.org/detail.aspx?id=15871 (accessed 27 January 2018). See also 'Mummy mask / cartonnage', *British Museum*, museum no. EA 29770. Available at http://www.britishmuseum.org/research/collection_online/collection_object_details.aspx?objectId=6415&partId=1 (accessed 27 January 2018).
25. Bellow, 'Fashioning *Cléopâtre*', p. 8; Jill Fields, 'Fighting the corsetless evil: Shaping corsets and culture, 1900–1930', *Journal of Social History*, 33.2 (1999), pp. 355–84 (p. 358); 'The "New Woman" anticipated by centuries', *Leeds Mercury*, 25 January 1911.
26. Bellow, p. 8.
27. Ibid.
28. Tatjana Petzer, 'Veils in action: The "Oriental other" and its performative destruction in modern fashion and art', in Ulrike Brunotte, Anna-Dorothea Ludewig and Axel Stähler (eds), *Orientalism, Gender, and the Jews: Literary and Artistic Transformations of European National Discourses* (Berlin, 2015), p. 256.
29. Ibid.
30. Ibid.
31. Ibid.
32. Cheryl Buckley and Hilary Fawcett, *Fashioning the Feminine: Representation and Women's Fashion from the Fin de Siècle to the Present* (London, 2002), p. 74.
33. Ibid., p. 75.
34. Ibid.
35. Geczy, *Fashion and Orientalism*, p. 151.
36. Sarah Berry, *Screen Style: Fashion and Femininity in 1930s Hollywood* (Minneapolis, 2000), p. 132.
37. Berry, *Screen Style*, p. 132; 'Pharaoh's daughters had a facial', *Evening Despatch*, 14 July 1939.
38. 'Cleopatra sets a fashion', *Essex Newsman*, 15 September 1934. For comparison, see 'Mummy mask/cartonnage'.
39. Jacky Stacey, *Star Gazing: Hollywood Cinema and Female Spectatorship* (London, 1994), p. 99; Berry, pp. 130–4.
40. Statistic taken from Jeffrey Richards, *The Age of the Dream Palace: Cinema and Society in 1930s Britain* (London, 2010), p. 13.
41. Stacey, *Star Gazing*, p. 99.
42. Ibid.
43. Ibid., p. 97.
44. 'The Thebes stool', *Victoria and Albert Museum*, CIRC.439-1965. Available at http://collections.vam.ac.uk/item/O7878/the-thebes-stool-stool-william-birch-ltd/ (accessed 1 August 2017).
45. Helena Hayward, *World Furniture: An Illustrated History* (London, 1965), p. 13. For original, see 'Chair', *British Museum*, museum no. EA 2480. Available at http://www.britishmuseum.

org/research/collection_online/collection_object_details.aspx?objectId=119024&partId=1 (accessed 27 January 2017).

46. Diane Lawrence, *Genteel Women: Empire and Domestic Material Culture, 1840–1910* (Manchester, 2012); Jane Hamlett, *Material Relations: Domestic Interiors and Middle-Class Families in England, 1850–1910* (Manchester, 2010); Deborah Cohen, *Household Gods: The British and their Possessions* (New Haven, 2006).

47. 'Desert fashions', *Yorkshire Evening Post*, 3 January 1923.

48. Judy Giles, *The Parlour and the Suburb: Domestic Identities, Class, Femininity and Modernity* (Oxford, 2004), p. 139; 'Some precious household goods in glass and silver', *Courier*, 13 February 1926.

49. Ruth Iskin, 'Material women: The department-store fashion poster in Paris, 1880–1900', in Maureen Goggin and Beth Tobin (eds), *Material Women, 1750–1950: Consuming Desires and Collecting Practices* (Farnham, 2009), p. 35.

50. Elsie M. Lang, *British Women in the Twentieth Century* (London, 1929), pp. 272–3; Helen Wang, 'Stein's recording angel – Miss F. M. G. Lorimer', *Journal of the Royal Asiatic Society*, 8.2 (1998), pp. 207–28 (pp. 223–4).

51. Lang, *British Women in the Twentieth Century*, pp. 33–55.

52. Kathy Peiss 'Making faces: The cosmetics industry and the cultural construction of gender, 1890–1930', *Genders*, 7 (1990), pp. 143–69 (p. 159). Quoted in Berry, *Screen Style*, p. 132. This shying away from the classical is a common theme, with examples ranging from the Orientalization of Cleopatra (a Hellenistic rather than a native Egyptian ruler), to female archaeologists preferring to avoid classical subjects due to their perceived masculinity.

53. Curl, *Egyptian Revival*, p. 197.

54. Sydney V. Wilson, 'The jewels of the ancients', *Vogue*, 15 September 1926.

55. For a more in-depth examination of the influence of ancient Egypt on modern British architecture, see Curl, *Egyptian Revival*, pp. 195–211.

56. This is explored in more detail in Chapter 8 of this volume, by Lizzie Glithero-West.

57. Judy Rudoe, *Cartier 1900–1939* (London, 1998), p. 135.

58. 'The "Tutankhamen" influence in modern jewellery', *Illustrated London News*, 26 January 1924.

59. Terri Baker, 'The record of a life: Nation and narrative in Victorian women's collections', in Kevin M. Moist and David Banash (eds), *Contemporary Collecting: Objects, Practices, and the Fate of Things* (Lanham, 2013), pp. 173–4.

60. Wilson, 'The jewels of the ancients', p. 106.

61. Some examples include Mary W. Hogg, 'The position of women four millenniums ago in Egypt and Babylonia', *The Englishwoman*, 21.7 (1910), pp. 268–76; Florence G. Fidler, 'The position of women under the Hammurabi Code', *English Review*, 15 (1913), pp. 422–9 (p. 422); 'Antique feminine culture', *Evening News*, 20 January 1920. While most of the articles referenced specifically refer to equal political rights to make a point about women's suffrage, other important women's issues were also covered, such as Babylonian women's education as a justification for women's colleges in 'Antique feminine culture'.

62. Billie Melman, 'Gender, history and memory: The invention of women's past in the nineteenth and early twentieth centuries', *History and Memory*, 5.1 (1993), pp. 5–41.

63. Jill Matthews, 'Feminist History', *Labor History*, 50 (1986), pp. 147–53 (pp. 147–8).

64. Barbara Caine, *Victorian Feminists* (Oxford, 1992), p. 251.

Notes to pages 195–199

65. Evelyn Cobbold, 'The first suffragette', in *Wayfarers in the Libyan Desert* (London, 1912).
66. 'The "New Woman" anticipated by centuries'.
67. In particular, see 'The "New Woman" anticipated by centuries'; Hogg, 'The positions of women four millenniums ago'; Miller, 'Women in ancient Egypt'.
68. Michelle Tusan, 'Inventing the New Woman: Print culture and identity politics during the fin-de-siecle:', *Victorian Periodicals Review*, 31.2 (1998), pp. 169–82 (p. 176).
69. Hogg, 'The positions of women four millenniums ago', p. 274.
70. 'One of the most beautiful women in history', *Illustrated London News*, 31 December 1927; 'A feminist of 1375 B.C.', *Equal Rights*, 19 February 1933.
71. 'The ancient Egyptian type of beauty', *Illustrated London News*, 17 February 1923.
72. 'The loveliest woman of antiquity? A rival to Helen', *Illustrated London News*, 13 December 1924; 'Ancient Egypt's queen of beauty: A newly found quartzite head of Nefertiti from Tell-Amarna', *Illustrated London News*, 6 May 1933.
73. 'Be subtle with your make-up', *Evening Telegraph*, 31 July 1933; 'A feminist of 1375 B.C.'.
74. 'A feminist of 1375 BC'.
75. 'Turning afflictions into attractions', *Evening Telegraph*, 10 July 1939.
76. 'The strange face of beauty', *Vogue*, 1 November 1939.
77. Ibid.
78. Ibid.
79. Melinda K. Hartwig, *A Companion to Ancient Egyptian Art* (Oxford, 2015), p. 340.

12 'The Use of Old Objects': Ancient Egypt and English Writers around 1920

1. For Lisa Montagno Leahy, with fond memories of the Oxford of the Witch-queen, and for my father, a boyhood reader of H. Rider Haggard and Sax Rohmer. Versions of this paper were given at the conference 'Modernity and the Shock of the Ancient: The Reception of Antiquity in the Late 19th and Early 20th Century', Oxford, 10 June 2016, and at the Queen's College Seminar, 24 October 2016. My thanks are due to Ellie Dobson, Chris Hollings, Jennifer Ingleheart, James Ivory, Clare Lewis, Eva Miller, Emily Taylor and Helen Whitehouse. I write as a former curator in the British Museum, and as a former holder of the Lady Wallis Budge Junior Research Fellowship at University College, Oxford.
2. E. M. Forster, *The Uncollected Egyptian Essays of E. M. Forster*, Hilda D. Spear and Abdel Moneim Aly (eds) (Dundee, 1988), p. 52.
3. For example, Evelyn Silber, *The Sculpture of Epstein: With a Complete Catalogue* (Oxford, 1986), pp. 20–3; Emma Chambers, *Paul Nash* (London, 2016), p. 26.
4. E. M. Forster, *Abinger Harvest* and *England's Pleasant Land*, Elizabeth Heine (ed.) (London, 1996), pp. 280–6.
5. Joseph Allen Boone, *The Homoerotics of Orientalism* (New York, 2015), p. 164.
6. Western Manuscripts, British Library, Add mss 25639 f. 88 (44 vso) (unpublished).
7. Nicholas Frankel, '"The Sphinx," by Oscar Wilde, with decorations by Charles Ricketts (1894)', *Open Stax*. Available at: http://cnx.org/contents/TuaO_Mx2@2/The-Sphinx-by-Oscar-Wilde-with (accessed 25 March 2018). Some illustrations are included in Stephen

Calloway, *Charles Ricketts, Subtle and Fantastic Decorator* (London, 1979), pp. 44–9. On the style of the illustrations in general see, for example, Jeremiah Romano Mercurio, 'Faithful infidelity: Charles Ricketts' illustrations for two of Oscar Wilde's poems in prose', *Victorian Network* 3.1 (2011), pp. 3–21, esp. pp. 4–5.

8. Charles Ricketts, 'Head in Serpentine of Amenemmes III in the possession of Oscar Raphael, Esq.', *Journal of Egyptian Archaeology* 4 (1917), pp. 211–12; Charles Ricketts, 'Head of Amenemmēs III in obsidian: From the collection of the Rev. W. MacGregor, Tamworth', *Journal of Egyptian Archaeology* 4 (1917), pp. 71–3; Charles Ricketts, 'Bas-relief figure of a king of the Ptolemaic period in blue faience', *Journal of Egyptian Archaeology* 5 (1918), pp. 77–8; Charles Ricketts, 'Two faience chalices at Eton College from the collection of the Late Major W. J. Myers', *Journal of Egyptian Archaeology* 5 (1918), pp. 145–7. On his collecting, see Joseph Darracott, *The World of Charles Ricketts* (London, 1980), p. 117.

9. Nicholas Frankel, 'Second series of sphinx illustrations (1923)', *Open Stax*. Available at: https://cnx.org/contents/0nqwZZGI@1/Second-Series-of-Sphinx-Illust (accessed 25 March 2018). Some are illustrated in Calloway, *Charles Ricketts*, pp. 86–91.

10. See, for example, Eugène Warmenbol (ed.), *Sphinx: Les gardiens de l'Égypte* (Brussels, 2006).

11. Oscar Wilde, *The Sphinx*, ll. 171–4, in *The Complete Works of Oscar Wilde*, Vol. 1: *Poems and Poems in Prose*, Bobby Fong and Karl Beckson (eds) (Oxford, 2000), p. 194.

12. See, for example, Maria Fleischhack, *Narrating Ancient Egypt: The Representation of Ancient Egypt in Nineteenth-century and Early-Twentieth-century Fantastic Fiction* (Frankfurt, 2016).

13. H. Rider Haggard, *She*, Daniel Karlin (ed.) (Oxford, 1991). See Fleischhack, *Narrating Ancient Egypt*, pp. 89–92, 168–73; Lynn Parramore, *Reading the Sphinx: Ancient Egypt in Nineteenth-Century Literary Culture* (New York, 2008), pp. 103–9.

14. Charles Kerr 'Up above them towered his beautiful pale face', in H. Rider Haggard, *She: A History of Adventure* (London, 1911), p. 103. Available at: www.visualhaggard.org/illustrations/526 (accessed 25 March 2018). For Haggard's encounters with Egypt see, for example, Roger Luckhurst, *The Mummy's Curse: The True History of a Dark Fantasy* (Oxford, 2012), pp. 190–9.

15. Haggard, *She*, pp. 23, 277–9 n. 32, 41. See Luckhurst, *The Mummy's Curse*, pp. 202–4; Shirley M. Addy, *Rider Haggard and Egypt* (Accrington, 1998).

16. The object measures 25 cm × 19.5 cm.

17. For occultism, and specifically the goddess Isis as imagined in the nineteenth century and subsequently, see Chapter 9 of this volume, written by Caroline Tully.

18. Guy Boothby, 'A professor of Egyptology', *The Graphic: An Illustrated Weekly Magazine*, 10 December 1904, pp. 773–5; see R. B. Parkinson, *Reading Ancient Egyptian Poetry: Among Other Histories* (Chichester, 2009), pp. 248–9; Fleischhack, *Narrating Ancient Egypt*, pp. 107–8.

19. William M. Flinders Petrie, *Egyptian Tales: Translated from the Papyri*, Vol. 1: *IVth to XIIth Dynasty* (London, 1895); W. L. Alden, 'The hunter', *The Idler: An Illustrated Monthly Magazine*, 7 July 1895, pp. 424–5; Parkinson, *Reading Ancient Egyptian Poetry*, pp. 231–3.

20. Two cartouches with epithets of the heroine in Middle Egyptian featured on the title page.

21. 'Have you read?', *The World's News* (Sydney), 13 June 1925. Available at: http://trove.nla.gov.au/newspaper/article/130620902 (accessed 2 March 2018).

22. Luckhurst, *The Mummy's Curse*, pp. 168–71.

23. Sax Rohmer, *The Brood of the Witch-Queen* (London, 1918). Available at: http://www.gutenberg.org/files/19706/19706-h/19706-h.htm (accessed 25 March 2018). On Rohmer's Egyptian fiction see, for example, Luckhurst, *The Mummy's Curse*, pp. 168–71.
24. Luckhurst, *The Mummy's Curse*, p. 169.
25. Rohmer, *The Brood of the Witch-Queen*, p. 1.
26. Ibid., p. 2. 'Queer' meaning 'homosexual' is listed with attestations before 1918 in the Oxford English Dictionary, as both adjective and noun. See 'Queer, adj.1', *Oxford English Dictionary*. Available at: www.oed.com/view/Entry/156236 (accessed 2 March 2018). See also 'Queer, n.2', *Oxford English Dictionary*. Available at: www.oed.com/view/Entry/156235 (accessed 2 March 2018).
27. Rohmer, *Brood of the Witch-Queen*, p. 8.
28. Ibid., p. 200. The term 'unnatural' recurs on pp. 94, 98, 204.
29. Ibid., pp. 28–9.
30. Ibid., pp. 22, 196–7, 180, 210–12; see Francis Llewellyn Griffith, *Stories of the High Priests of Memphis: The Sethon of Herodotus and The Demotic Tales of Khamuas*, Vol. 1 (Oxford, 1900).
31. Rohmer, *Brood of the Witch-Queen*, pp. 188–98; see, for example, R. B. Parkinson, 'Hordjedef', in Donald B. Redford (ed.), *The Oxford Encyclopedia of Ancient Egypt*, Vol. 2 (New York, 2001), p. 114.
32. Rohmer, *Brood of the Witch-Queen*, p. 212.
33. John Baines and Liam McNamara, 'The twin stelae of Suty and Hor', in Zahi A. Hawass and Janet E. Richards (eds), *The Archaeology and Art of Ancient Egypt: Studies in Honor of David B. O'Connor*, Vol. 1 (Cairo, 2007), pp. 63–79. For an Egyptological suggestion that they were lovers, see Steven Blake Shubert, '*Double entendre* in the stela of Suty and Hor', in Gary N. Knoppers and Antoine Hirsch (eds), *Egypt, Israel, and the Ancient Mediterranean World: Studies in Honor of Donald B. Redford* (Leiden, 2004), pp. 143–65.
34. Aleister Crowley, 'The twins', in *The Winged Beetle* (privately printed, 1910), pp. 99–101, ll. 25–9, 55–62. I am grateful to Emily Taylor for drawing this poem to my attention.
35. Steve Vinson and Janet Gunn, 'Studies in esoteric syntax: The enigmatic friendship of Aleister Crowley and Battiscombe Gunn', in William Carruthers (ed.), *Histories of Egyptology: Interdisciplinary Measures* (London, 2014), pp. 96–112; Gange, *Dialogues with the Dead*, pp. 262–9. On Gunn, see Morris L. Bierbrier, *Who Was Who in Egyptology* (London, 2012), pp. 232–3.
36. J. Gwyn Griffiths, 'Some claims of xenoglossy in the ancient languages', in *Atlantis & Egypt with Other Selected Essays* (Cardiff, 1991), pp. 266–90 (p. 277); also cited in Christopher Frayling, *The Face of Tutankhamun* (London, 1992), pp. 255–8.
37. Vinson and Gunn, 'Studies in esoteric syntax', p. 100; Jan Assmann, *Moses the Egyptian: The Memory of Egypt in Western Monotheism* (Cambridge, 1997), p. 22. See Gange, *Dialogues with the Dead*, pp. 215–19, 268–9.
38. For example, Heidi Stalla, 'William Bankes: Echoes of Egypt in Virginia Woolf's *To the Lighthouse*', *Woolf Studies Annual* 14 (2008), pp. 21–34.
39. Virginia Woolf, *Jacob's Room*, Kate Flint (ed.) (Oxford, 2008), p. 224.
40. Virginia Woolf, *To the Lighthouse*, Stella McNichol (ed.) (London, 2000), p. 57. I am grateful to Ellie Dobson for drawing this passage to my attention.
41. According to a newspaper story, cited (without reference or date) in Frayling, *The Face of Tutankhamun*, pp. 49–50. See also Jasmine Day, *The Mummy's Curse: Mummymania in*

Notes to pages 204–205

the English-speaking World (London, 2006), pp. 50-1. The specific curse on the tablet is surprisingly elusive in accessible newspapers: the earliest citation I know of is the *Dundee Courier*, 31 December 1929, p. 5.

42. Arthur Weigall, *Tutankhamen and Other Essays* (London, 1923), p. 110.
43. 'No curse of pharaohs: Ludicrous superstition', *Telegraph* (Brisbane), 10 April 1930, p .4.
44. Virginia Woolf, *The Waves*, Michael Herbert and Susan Sellers (eds) (Cambridge, 2011), pp. 161, 51 (with note on pp. 291–2). The motif recurs throughout the novel: pp. 7, 51, 75, 100, 133, 161, 180; it is taken up by Bernard on p. 227.
45. T. S. Eliot, 'The burial of the dead', ll. 43–5, in T. S. Eliot, *The Poems of T.S. Eliot*, Vol 1: *Collected and Uncollected Poems*, Christopher Ricks and Jim McCue (eds) (London, 2015), p. 56; on the sources for the name Sosostris, see pp. 610–11. Egypt had also featured in Ezra Pound's early work before his interest turned to China: see, for example, Angus Fletcher, 'Ezra Pound's Egypt and the origin of the "Cantos"', *Twentieth Century Literature* 48.1 (2002), pp. 1–21.
46. See also Chapter 3 of this volume, written by Edward Chaney, for ancient Egypt in the work of the modernist writer and artist Wyndham Lewis.
47. See E. M. Forster and Constantine P. Cavafy, *The Forster-Cavafy Letters: Friends at a Slight Angle*, Peter Jeffreys (ed.) (Cairo, 2009). On the limited role of pharaonic history in Forster's guide see Hala Halim, *Alexandrian Cosmopolitanism: An Archive* (New York, 2013), pp. 131–2, 137–8, 161, 163.
48. E. M. Forster, *Alexandria: A History and a Guide; and, Pharos and Pharillon*, Miriam Allott (ed.) (London, 2004). On other material, see Forster, *Uncollected Egyptian Essays*; Hilda D. Spear, 'E. M. Forster's Alexandrian Essays', in Norman Page and Peter Preston (eds), *The Literature of Place* (Basingstoke, 1993), pp. 122–31; Halim, *Alexandrian Cosmopolitanism*, pp. 120–78; Muhammad A. Deeb, 'Alexandria as E.M. Forster's rainbow bridge to the Middle East & India: A comparative inquiry', *Canadian Review of Comparative Literature* 37 (2010), pp. 10–23.
49. E. M. Forster, *Selected letters of E. M. Forster*, Vol. 1: *1879–1920*, Mary Lago and P. N. Furbank (eds) (London, 1983), p. 233. Quoted in, for example, *Alexandria*, p. xxiii. In general, see P. N. Furbank, *E. M. Forster: A Life*, Vol. 2 (New York, 1978), pp. 18–63.
50. E. M. Forster, *A Passage to India*, Oliver Stallybrass (ed.) (London, 1978), p. 2. This passage was written before the letter: Forster, *Alexandria*, p. xxiii.
51. Furbank, *E.M. Forster: A Life II*, pp. 59–63; see also Alexandria, pp. 322–46; Robert Aldrich, *Colonialism and Homosexuality* (London and New York: Routledge 2003), pp. 308–19
52. In *The Egyptian Mail*, 13 January 1918 and 21 October 1917: Forster, *Uncollected Egyptian Essays*, pp. 52, 53, 37.
53. Forster, *A Passage to India*, p. xv. See, for example, Donald Watt, 'Mohammed el Adl and *A Passage to India*', *Journal of Modern Literature* 10.2 (1983), pp. 311–26; Halim, *Alexandrian Cosmopolitanism*, pp. 177–8.
54. Forster, *A Passage to India*, pp. 17, 253, 270; see Furbank, *E.M. Forster: A Life* II, pp. 70, 103–4; Forster, *Alexandria*, pp. 323–4.
55. Forster, *A Passage to India*, p. 270.
56. E. M. Forster, *Aspects of the Novel, and Related Writings*, Oliver Stallybrass (ed.) (London, 1974), pp. 110, 131.
57. For example, Dominic Montserrat, *Akhenaten: History, Fantasy and Ancient Egypt* (London, 2001), pp. 168–70.
58. E. M. Forster, 'The objects', *The Athenaeum*, 7 May 1920, pp. 599–600.

59. E. A. Wallis Budge, *By Nile and Tigris: A Narrative of Journeys in Egypt and Mesopotamia on Behalf of the British Museum Between the Years 1886 and 1913*, 2 vols (London, 1920); Forster, *Abinger Harvest*, pp. 280–6.

60. Fleischhack, *Narrating Ancient Egypt*, pp. 110–13. See Joanna Paul, '"Time is Only a Mode of Thought, You Know": Ancient history, empire, and imagination in E. Nesbit's stories for children', in Lisa Maurice (ed.), *The Reception of Ancient Greece and Rome in Children's Literature: Eagles and Heroes* (Leiden, 2015); Ruth Hoberman, 'In quest of a museal aura: Turn of the century narratives about museum-displayed objects', *Victorian Literature and Culture* 31.2 (2003), pp. 467–82; Virginia Zimmerman, 'Excavating children: Archaeological imagination and time-slip in the early 1900s', in Eleanor Dobson and Gemma Banks (eds), *Excavating Modernity: Physical, Temporal and Psychological Strata in Literature, 1900–1930* (London, 2018).

61. Luckhurst, *The Mummy's Curse*, p. 195.

62. Mark Smith, 'Budge, Sir Ernest Alfred Thompson Wallis (1857–1934)' (2004), *Oxford Dictionary of National Biography*. Available at: www.oxforddnb.com/view/article/32161 (accessed 2 March 2018). See also a recent biography: Matthew Ismail, *Wallis Budge: Magic and Mummies in London and Cairo* (Kilkerran, 2011).

63. Forster, *Abinger Harvest*, p. 280.

64. Ibid.

65. Ibid.

66. E. M. Forster, *Maurice*, P. Gardner (ed.) (London, 1999), p. 191. For Forster's attitude to museums see, for example, Jennifer Ingleheart, 'Responding to Ovid's Pygmalion episode and receptions of same-sex love in classical antiquity: Art, homosexuality, and the curatorship of classical culture in E. M. Forster's "The Classical Annex"', *Classical Receptions Journal* 7.2 (2014), pp. 141–58.

67. For the papyrus see, for example, John H. Taylor, *Journey Through the Afterlife: Ancient Egyptian Book of the Dead* (London, 2010).

68. Budge, *By Nile and Tigris*, Vol. 1, p. 136. See, for example, Carol A. R. Andrews, 'Pharaoh trampler of Egypt's enemies: A new amuletic form', in Jacke Phillips (ed.), *Ancient Egypt, the Aegean, and the Near East: Studies in Honour of Martha Rhoads Bell*, Vol. 1 (San Antonio, 1997), p. 41; nothing connects the supposed cosmetic box of Ani's wife Tutu with the supposed tomb (EA 24708: PM I.2², 838). For another example of Budge's unsubstantiated claims of provenance, see R. B. Parkinson, 'Two or three literary artefacts: EA 41650/47896, and 22878–9', in W. V. Davies (ed.), *Studies in Egyptian Antiquities: A Tribute to T. G. H. James* (London, 1999), pp. 49–57, esp. p. 52.

69. This must have been drawn in part from other sources, since Budge's account simply listed some of Ani's titles: Budge, *By Nile and Tigris*, Vol. 1, p. 137.

70. Bierbrier, *Who Was Who*, p. 223. On Forster's misspelling, see Forster, *Abinger Harvest*, p. 438.

71. Forster, *Abinger Harvest*, p. 280.

72. 'Have you read?', p. 12.

73. E. M. Forster, 'Malconia Shops', *Independent Review*, November 1903; reprinted in Forster, *Abinger Harvest*, pp. 163–5 (p. 165).

74. Forster, *Abinger Harvest*, pp. 281–2.

75. Ibid., p. 282.

76. Ibid.

Notes to pages 208–210

77. Luckhurst, *The Mummy's Curse*, p. 197.
78. See Halim, *Alexandrian Cosmopolitanism*, p. 163.
79. Forster, *Abinger Harvest*, p. 283.
80. 'The younger Memnon', *British Museum*, museum no. EA 19. Available at http://www.britishmuseum.org/research/collection_online/collection_object_details.aspx?objectId=117633&partId=1&searchText=Younger+Memnon&page=1 (accessed 2 March 2018). See, for example, John Rodenbeck, 'Travelers from an antique land: Shelley's inspiration for "Ozymandias"', *Alif: Journal of Comparative Poetics* 14 (2004), pp. 121–48.
81. Forster, *Abinger Harvest*, p. 283.
82. 'Statue', *British Museum*, museum no. GR1859,1226.26. Available at: www.britishmuseum.org/research/collection_online/collection_object_details.aspx?objectId=460416&partId=1 (accessed 2 March 2018). See Andrew D. Radford, *The Lost Girls: Demeter-Persephone and the Literary Imagination, 1850-1930* (Amsterdam, 2007), pp. 172–223.
83. E. M. Forster, 'Cnidus', *Independent Review*, March 1904; reprinted in Forster, *Abinger Harvest*, pp. 166–70 (pp. 167, 168).
84. Forster, *Abinger Harvest*, p. 284.
85. Ibid., p. 286. A parallel distrust of museums was voiced by D. H. Lawrence in 'Volterra' (1932), in D. H. Lawrence, *Etruscan Places: Travels through Forgotten Italy* (London, 2011), pp. 197–8.
86. Forster, *Abinger Harvest*, pp. 283–4.
87. Ibid., p. 283.
88. Ibid., p. 282.
89. Ibid., p. 284. See Halim, *Alexandrian Cosmopolitanism*, pp. 167–9 on specifically local social pressures.
90. Forster, *Abinger Harvest*, p. 282.
91. Forster, *Alexandria*, pp. 340–1.
92. Letter of 29 March 1919: Furbank, *E.M. Forster: A Life*, Vol. 2, pp. 57–8; Halim, *Alexandrian Cosmopolitanism*, pp. 172–4.
93. *The Government of Egypt: Recommendations by a Committee of the International Section of the Labour Research Department* ([London], 1920), pp. 3–12; summary in *Alexandria*, pp. 360–71; Halim, *Alexandrian Cosmopolitanism*, pp. 174–6.
94. Donald Malcolm Reid, *Whose Pharaohs? Archaeology, Museums, and Egyptian National Identity from Napoleon to World War I* (Los Angeles, 2007), pp. 205–12.
95. See Halim, *Alexandrian Cosmopolitanism*, p. 167.
96. Forster, *Alexandria*, p. 331.
97. John Murray, *A Handbook for Travellers in Lower and Upper Egypt* (London, 1891), pp. 308–9; H. Rider Haggard, *Ayesha: The Return of She* (London, 2013), p. 211.
98. Forster, *A Passage to India*, p. 72. In Forster's *Goldsworthy Lowes Dickinson*, the Maharajah asks 'Oh, when will Krishna come and be my friend?'; E. M. Forster, *Goldsworthy Loves Dickinson* (London, 1973), p. 115. On 'friend' see *Maurice*, p. 171.
99. Forster, *A Passage to India*, pp. 17, 301.
100. Forster, *Alexandria*, p. 190.
101. Letter of 4 July 1917: Lago and Furbank, *Selected Letters*, Vol. 1, p. 261.

102. Forster's is not a genuine Egyptian obelisk, though Cleopatra's Needle is mentioned. See E. M. Forster, *The Life to Come, and Other Stories*, Oliver Stallybrass (ed.) (London, 1972), pp. 113–29, esp. pp. 127, 128.
103. For example, Paul Collins and Liam McNamara, *Discovering Tutankhamun* (Oxford, 2014), pp. 62–87.
104. Carter Lupton, '"Mummymania" for the masses: Is Egyptology cursed by the mummy's curse?', in Sally MacDonald and Michael Rice (eds), *Consuming Ancient Egypt* (London, 2003), pp. 35–6. For the cultural impact of the Tutankhamun discovery as explored elsewhere in this volume, see Chapter 1 by Gabrielle Heffernan and Chapter 8 by Lizzie Glithero-West.
105. Forster, *Aspects of the Novel*, p. 112.
106. 'Hope Abbey Mausoleum', *Eugene Masonic Cemetery*. Available at: www.eugenemasoniccemetery.org/mausoleum.html (accessed 2 March 2018). The showroom was demolished in 2016. See 'Isiger Ford Building (Klamath Falls, Oregon), *Oregon Digital*. Available at: https://oregondigital.org/catalog/oregondigital:df67qh08t (accessed 2 March 2018). I am grateful to James Ivory for making me aware of these buildings.
107. Frayling, *The Face of Tutankhamun*, pp. 47–8; Luckhurst, *The Mummy's Curse*, p. 186. Budge likewise said it was 'bunkum': 'Egypt's black arts: Scientists ridicule theory', *Daily Herald* (Adelaide), 9 April 1923, p. 3.
108. 'The curse of Osiris', *Sunday Times* (Sydney), 20 May 1923; Collins and McNamara, *Discovering Tutankhamun*, p. 83. On Conan Doyle and the mummy's curse see Frayling, *The Face of Tutankhamun*, pp. 46–8.
109. 'Lord Carnarvon', *Leeds Mercury*, 6 April 1923, p. 8.
110. 'The curse of the pharaohs', *Dundee Courier*, 31 December 1929, p. 4.
111. On the hat see, for example, Kate Thomas, 'Using history to sell clothes? Don't try it with the pharaohs' (2011), *The New York Times*. Available at: www.nytimes.com/2011/04/19/arts/design/egyptian-antiquities-official-defends-fashion-line.html (accessed 2 March 2018). Recent images of Egyptologists in a hat include 'John Darnell', *Yale Macmillan Centre*. Available at: http://cmes.macmillan.yale.edu/people/john-darnell (accessed 2 March 2018).
112. On the potential role of empathy in Egyptology see Parkinson, *Reading Ancient Egyptian Poetry*, pp. 270–8.
113. Anthony Roth Costanzo, 'Becoming Akhenaten', *YouTube*. Available at: www.youtube.com/watch?v=U0mjrcrXmp4 (accessed 2 March 2018). For an Egyptological perspective on the opera, see Paul John Frandsen, 'Philip Glass's "Akhnaten"', *The Musical Quarterly* 77.2 (1993), pp. 241–67.

13 Women Surrealists and Egyptian Mythology: Sphinxes, Animals and Magic

1. André Breton, *Nadja*, trans. Mark Polizzotti (London, 1999), p. 111.
2. Although some artists I discuss in this essay were opposed to being labelled 'Surrealists', their work and social involvement within and on the periphery of the group sees their continued association with the movement. Therefore, for ease, I refer to them as such. Some connections between particular Surrealists and ancient Egypt are more deeply embedded in their personal histories than others. The Surrealist couturier Elsa Schiaparelli

descended from a long line of scholars on her father's side including an Egyptologist, Ernesto Schiaparelli, who 'discovered the grave of Nefertari in the Valley of the Queens, then founded a museum to display his treasures in Turin'; see Meryle Seacrest, *Elsa Schiaparelli: A Biography* (London, 2014), p. 5.

3. Alyce Mahon, 'La feminité triomphante: Surrealism, Leonor Fini, and the sphinx', *Dada/Surrealism* 19.1 (2013), pp. 1–20 (p. 1). Available at http://ir.uiowa.edu/cgi/viewcontent.cgi?article=1274&context=dadasur (accessed 24 April 2017).
4. Ibid.
5. For more on gender and female power, especially with regards to occultism, see Chapters 9 and 15 of this volume, written by Caroline Tully and Nickianne Moody respectively.
6. Fiona Bradley, *Movements in Modern Art: Surrealism* (London, 1997), p. 47.
7. Ibid.
8. Paula Lumbard, 'Dorothea Tanning: On the threshold to a darker place', *Woman's Art Journal* 2.1 (1981), pp. 49–52 (p. 49).
9. Bradley, *Movements in Modern Art*, p. 6.
10. Whitney Chadwick, *Women, Art and Society* (London, 2007), p. 310.
11. Mahon, 'La feminité triomphante', p. 3.
12. Ibid., p. 2.
13. Ibid.
14. Peter Webb, *Sphinx: The Life and Art of Leonor Fini* (New York, 2009), p. 102.
15. André Breton, *Manifestoes of Surrealism*, trans. Richard Seaver and Helen R. Lane (Ann Arbor, 1990), p. 180.
16. Mahon, 'La feminité triomphante', p. 1.
17. Whitney Chadwick, *Women Artists and the Surrealist Movement* (London, 1991), p. 66.
18. Georgiana M. M. Colville, 'Women artists, Surrealism, and animal representation', in Patricia Allmer (ed.), *Angels of Anarchy: Women Artists and Surrealism* (Munich, 2009), p. 68.
19. Ibid.
20. Renée Riese Hubert, *Magnifying Mirrors: Women, Surrealism, & Partnership* (Lincoln, 1994), p. 19.
21. Manfred Lurker, *The Gods and Goddesses of Ancient Egypt* (London, 1980), p. 114.
22. Chadwick, *Women Artists*, p. 180.
23. Mahon, 'La feminité triomphante', p. 8.
24. Chadwick, *Women Artists*, p. 188.
25. Ibid., p. 189.
26. Rowena Sheperd and Robert Sheperd, *1000 Symbols: What Shapes Mean in Art and Myth* (London, 2002), p. 599.
27. Geraldine Pinch, *Egyptian Myth: A Very Short Introduction* (Oxford, 2004), p. 61.
28. Ibid., p. 97.
29. Ibid.
30. Ibid., p. 38.
31. Webb, *Sphinx*, p. 10.
32. Ibid., p. 8.

33. Ibid., p. 11.
34. Ibid.
35. Ibid., p. 25.
36. Frank Hamel, *Werewolves, BirdWomen, TigerMen and Other Human Animals* (New York, 2007), p. 189.
37. Pinch, *Egyptian Myth*, p. 37.
38. Lois Parkinson Zamora, 'The magical tables of Isabel Allende and Remedios Varo', *Comparative Literature* 44.2 (1992), pp. 113–43 (p. 115).
39. Chadwick, *Women Artists*, p. 187.
40. Hamel, *Werewolves*, p. 207.
41. Nadia Choucha, *Surrealism and the Occult* (Oxford, 2016), p. 150.
42. Ian Shaw, *Ancient Egypt: A Very Short Introduction* (Oxford, 2004), pp. 141–2.
43. Carolyn Merchant, 'Isis' consciousness raised', *The History of Social Science* 73.3 (1982), pp. 398–409 (p. 398).
44. Chadwick, *Women, Art and Society*, p. 315.
45. Zamora, 'The magical tables', p. 131.
46. Ibid.
47. Ibid.
48. Ibid., p. 130.
49. Chadwick, *Women Artists*, p. 214.
50. Ibid.
51. Pinch, *Egyptian Myth*, p. 37.
52. Xavière Gauthier, *Léonor Fini* (Paris, 1973), quoted in Chadwick, *Women Artists*, p. 130.
53. Choucha, *Surrealism and the Occult*, p. 116.
54. Gloria Orenstein, 'Women of Surrealism', *Feminist Art Journal* 2.2 (1973), pp. 15–21 (p. 16), quoted in Webb, *Sphinx*, p. 166.
55. Webb, *Sphinx*, p. 135.
56. Choucha, *Surrealism and the Occult*, p. 120.
57. Webb, *Sphinx*, p. 135.
58. Ibid.
59. Julian Levy, *Memoir of an Art Gallery* (New York, 1977), p. 178, quoted in Webb, *Sphinx*, p. 45.
60. Malcolm Gaskill, *Witchcraft: A Very Short Introduction* (Oxford, 2010), p. 30.
61. Ibid., p. 10.

14 Egyptian Excesses: Taylor, Burton and *Cleopatra*

1. Lucy Hughes-Hallett has traced the evolution of Cleopatra's image and its inconsistencies: e.g., she points out that in the medieval period she was portrayed as a virtuous and good woman; see Lucy Hughes-Hallett, *Cleopatra: Queen, Lover, Legend* (London, 2006), p. 147. Lynn Parramore suggests that Shakespeare's use of Plutarch as a source for *Antony and Cleopatra*

re-visioned the queen in the vampish role she has occupied since; see Lynn Parramore, *Reading the Sphinx: Ancient Egypt in Nineteenth-Century Literary Culture* (Basingstoke, 2008), p. 11.

2. See, e.g., Plutarch's *Life of Antony* (75 CE), C. Suetonius Tranquillus, *The Lives of the Caesars* (121 CE), or Pliny the Elder's *Natural History* (77–79 CE), which tells the famous story of the pearls.

3. For example, Jack Brodsky (assistant publicity manager) described how kissing would often continue in a scene after the director had yelled 'cut'. He refers to Joe Mankiewicz commenting to the pair, 'I feel as if I'm intruding' after one such episode. See Jack Brodsky and Nathan Weiss, *The Cleopatra Papers: A Private Correspondence* (New York, 1963), p. 59.

4. The Vatican described Taylor as living a life of 'erotic vagrancy'. For more detail see Walter Wanger, *My Life with Cleopatra* (London, 1963), pp. 46–8.

5. Chris Rojek, *Celebrity* (London, 2001), p. 3.

6. The following are some of the available biographies of Cleopatra: Lucy Hughes-Hallett, *Cleopatra*; Joyce Tyldesley, *Cleopatra: Last Queen of Egypt* (London, 2008); Stacy Schiff, *Cleopatra: A Life* (London, 2010); Michael Foss, *The Search for Cleopatra* (London, 1997); Duane W. Roller, *Cleopatra: A Biography* (Oxford, 2010).

7. Sam Kashner and Nancy Shoenberger's *Furious Love* (2010) focuses on their relationship and marriages, and thus is a joint biography; see Sam Kashner and Nancy Schoenberger, *Furious Love: Elizabeth Taylor, Richard Burton, The Marriage of the Century* (London, 2010). There have also been two 'biopics' on the couple, *Liz and Dick* (2012, dir. Lloyd Kramer) and *Burton and Taylor* (2013, dir. Richard Laxton) as well as a film drama focused on Taylor.

8. A quick and by no means exhaustive online search reveals about 18 biographies (of various sorts) on Cleopatra, compared to five on Antony.

9. Hughes-Hallett points out that, in the myth that grew around Taylor and Burton during and after *Cleopatra*, 'everything they did seemed somehow grander, looser, more extreme, than the same action or experience could have been to ordinary mortals … a passion which ends twice in divorce must cause both parties as much wretchedness as joy. But such dreary facts concern the real Taylor and Burton. In the legend of 'Elizabeth Taylor' and 'Richard Burton' they have no place. In the fantasies of their public, Taylor-Cleopatra and Burton-Antony were exultant rebels'; Hughes-Hallett, *Cleopatra*, pp. 359–60.

10. David Kamp, 'When Liz met Dick', *Vanity Fair*, April 1998. Available at www.vanityfair.com/news/1998/03/elizabeth-taylor-199803 (accessed 2 September 2016).

11. Maria Wyke and Dominic Montserrat refer to 'Cleomania' in their study of popular cultural Cleopatras, and 'Lizpatra' as a description of Taylor's 'new superstar image' in the role; Maria Wyke and Dominic Montserrat, 'Glamour girls: Cleomania in mass culture', in Margaret M. Miles (ed.), *Cleopatra: A Sphinx Revisited* (Berkeley, CA, 2011), p. 189.

12. Burton himself had a somewhat cynical view of these expectations, and indeed disputed them. He wrote in his diaries: 'The press have been sounding the same note for many years – ever since I went to Hollywood in the early fifties, in fact – that I am or was potentially the greatest actor in the world and the successor to Gielgud, Olivier, etc., but that I had dissipated my genius, etc., and 'sold out' to films and booze and women. An interesting reputation to have and by no means dull but by all means untrue'; Richard Burton, *The Richard Burton Diaries*, Chris Williams (ed.) (New Haven, 2012), p. 437.

13. Commenting upon the criticism he and Taylor received for their lifestyle and its supposed effect on his acting career, Burton wrote that 'my "first love" … is not the stage. It is a book with lovely words in it'; Burton, *The Richard Burton Diaries*, p. 257.

14. Rivka Ullmer, *Egyptian Cultural Icons in Midrash* (Berlin, 2009), p. 242.
15. Hughes-Hallett, *Cleopatra*, pp. 103–4.
16. See Mary Hamer, *Signs of Cleopatra* (London, 1993), pp. 16–17. Such displays fuelled Roman hostility to the queen because of the apparent 'flaunting' of wealth which they signified.
17. Sources give different ages for Ptolemy XIII at the time of this marriage.
18. Tyldesley notes that the rug story emanates from Plutarch, not the most reliable commentator on Cleopatra's life, and instead refers to 'the bed-roll' story; Tyldesley, *Cleopatra*, pp. 53–5.
19. See, e.g., M. G. Lord, *The Accidental Feminist: How Elizabeth Taylor Raised Our Consciousness and We Were Too Distracted by Her Beauty to Notice* (New York, 2012), p. 97.
20. Tyldesley, *Cleopatra*, p. 162.
21. Schiff, *Cleopatra*, p. 70.
22. Roller, *Cleopatra*, pp. 130–1.
23. Hughes-Hallett, *Cleopatra*, p. 90.
24. Ibid., p. 345.
25. Francesca T. Royster, *Becoming Cleopatra: The Shifting Image of an Icon* (Basingstoke, 2003).
26. Sally-Ann Ashton considers the significance of Cleopatra's Greek Macedonian heritage against the fact of her family's lengthy residence in Egypt, concluding that perhaps she looked 'Egyptian' rather than African or Greek and that she 'wanted to be seen as an Egyptian in her own country'; Sally-Ann Ashton, *Cleopatra and Egypt* (Oxford, 2008), p. 3. Ashton does not describe what this 'look' might have implied, however.
27. Sarfraz Manzoor points out that the emergence of black actors such as Sidney Poitier in the 1950s was a major factor in the development of black cinema and the increasing profile of black performers in Hollywood, however, there has still been no black Cleopatra in a major film, though many have played her on stage; Sarfraz Manzoor, 'The slow rise of black cinema', *Guardian*, 21 September 2014. Available at www.theguardian.com/film/2014/sep/21/slow-rise-black-cinema-african-american-hollywood (accessed 26 January 2018). In the 1920s, Josephine Baker was known as 'the Jazz Cleopatra' but did not perform the role on screen; in the 1970s the film *Cleopatra Jones* (1973, dir. Jack Starrett) gestured towards the image of a powerful black woman but is chiefly remembered as part of the 'blaxploitation' genre. Shirea L. Carroll, on the possible casting of Angelina Jolie as the 'next' Cleopatra, asked, 'Why does Hollywood think it's even slightly plausible to cast white women in roles that would be more sensible to cast a black actress for?'; Shirea L. Carroll, 'Commentary: Another white actress to play Cleopatra?', *Essence*, 14 June 2010. Available at https://www.essence.com/2010/06/14/commentary-angelina-jolie-to-play-cleopa (accessed 26 January 2018).
28. According to James Grout in the online *Encyclopaedia Romana*, Roman views of Cleopatra's beauty were mixed, suggesting that the more common concept of Cleopatra as 'beautiful' is tied to assumptions about the source of her power: Dio (*Roman History* XLII.34.4–6) described her as 'a woman of surpassing beauty' while in Plutarch's *Life of Antony* her looks are referred to as 'not at all incomparable' (XXVII.2–3). The only Roman commentator who could have provided a description based on having seen her in Rome was Cicero, and he does not mention her looks, instead choosing to attack her 'arrogance' possibly based upon the failure by Cleopatra to honour a promise made to him of a gift (*Letters to Atticus*, XV.15). Later Roman views of Cleopatra are entirely negative: she was a 'whore queen' (Propertius, *Poems*, III.11.39), a 'fatal monster' (Horace, *Odes*, I.37.21), and 'Egypt's shame' by Lucan (*Pharsalia*, X.59). For more discussion of these and other historic views of Cleopatra's beauty, see James Grout, 'Was Cleopatra beautiful?', *Encyclopaedia Romana*. Available at http://

penelope.uchicago.edu/~grout/encyclopaedia_romana/miscellanea/cleopatra/bust.html (accessed 29 April 2019). Alastair Sooke's article on the BBC website about an exhibition of Egyptian artefacts, *Beyond Beauty* (2016), uses a large photo of Taylor and quotes biographer Joyce Tyldesley as saying 'we have decided that [Cleopatra] was beautiful and that she has to look like Elizabeth Taylor. I think that the idea of Cleopatra, rather than Cleopatra herself, has influenced us'; Alastair Sooke, 'How ancient Egypt influenced our idea of beauty', *BBC Culture*, 4 February 2016. Available at http://www.bbc.com/culture/story/20160204-how-ancient-egypt-shaped-our-idea-of-beauty (accessed 26 January 2018).

29. David Bret, *Elizabeth Taylor: The Lady, the Lover, the Legend: 1932–2011* (London, 2011), p. 104.
30. For example, Burton's purchase of the Krupp diamond, which cost $307,000 (about $2 million today).
31. Bret, *Elizabeth Taylor*, p. 191. Bret does not provide further reference details for this source.
32. Melvyn Bragg also comments on the Taylor-Burton love of excess: 'how they flaunted it, even as they stepped out not so gingerly on the Via Veneto and began their act on the public stage. Jewellery for her; a $257,000 Van Gogh from her to him. ... She took 300 dresses with her to Rome and then sent to Paris for more'; Melvyn Bragg, *Rich: The Life of Richard Burton* (London, 1988), p. 165. Kitty Kelley suggests Burton's pursuit of wealth at the expense of artistic credibility was fuelled by the poverty of his childhood; Kitty Kelley, *Elizabeth Taylor: The Last Star* (London, 1981), p. 154.
33. William J. Mann, *How to Be a Movie Star: Elizabeth Taylor in Hollywood* (London, 2009), p. 14.
34. Maria Wyke and Dominic Montserrat make the astute observation that 'stars are cast in Hollywood's histories not as characters but in character and thus they people the represented past with the present, while extracinematic discourses about them and about the moment of film production further extend the temporality of the time represented into the here-and-now'; Wyke and Montserrat, *Cleopatra: A Sphinx Revisited*, p. 189.
35. The idea of 'performing' or staging is explored by Suzanne Leonard: 'Taylor and Burton thus consistently appeared both on screen and in their personal lives to be performing, and quite convincingly at that, the role of great lovers'; Suzanne Leonard, 'The true love of Elizabeth Taylor and Richard Burton', in Vicki Callahan (ed.), *Reclaiming the Archive: Feminism and Film History* (Detroit, 2010), p. 75.
36. Tyldesley, *Cleopatra*, p. 54. Tyldesley also mentions that Cleopatra would have been dark haired and olive-skinned. Commenting to the BBC on the 'Beyond Beauty' exhibition in London, Tyldesley observed that 'We still find ancient Egyptian civilisation very seductive ... we have decided that [Cleopatra] was beautiful and that she has to look like Elizabeth Taylor. I think that the idea of Cleopatra, rather than Cleopatra herself, has influenced us'. See Sooke, 'How ancient Egypt shaped our idea of beauty'.
37. Such a conflation is facilitated, of course, by the 'reach' of a Hollywood movie in comparison to historical biographies or even Shakespeare: far more of the public will be acquainted with Cleopatra-as-Taylor than with Cleopatra as herself. Taylor's notorious romantic life, in this instance, had a significant if inadvertent effect on perceptions of Cleopatra when she was cast to play her, helping to confirm in the public mind the historic – and biased – view of the queen. Bret, e.g., refers to her as 'perfection itself in the role of the celebrity harlot'; Bret, *Elizabeth Taylor*, p. 162.
38. Nathan Weiss, the film's publicity manager, hated the wink, writing to his assistant, Jack Brodsky, that it was 'just awful'; see Brodsky and Weiss, *The Cleopatra Papers*, p. 97. In fact, Weiss hated the whole procession scene, as he comments in the same letter.

39. Egypt's excessive, potentially 'corrupting' sensuality, is also detailed in Chapter 12 of this volume, written by R. B. Parkinson.
40. Hughes-Hallett, *Cleopatra*, p. 341.
41. His mentor, Philip Burton, from whom he took his surname, severed their friendship for some years: he fell out with his brother Ifor and other members of his family. Friends, such as Stanley Baker, took Sybil's side, although Baker told Walter Wanger that he 'understood' why Burton had been drawn to Taylor; Wanger, *My Life with Cleopatra*, p. 155.
42. William Shakespeare, *Antony and Cleopatra*, I. 1. Available at http://shakespeare.mit.edu/cleopatra/full.html (accessed 3 September 2017).
43. Kashner and Schoenberger quote Eddie Fisher as expressing concern over Taylor's drinking even prior to the affair with Burton; Kashner and Shoenberger, *Furious Love*, p. 2.1 Biographies describe their many alcohol-fuelled rows.
44. Rachael Thompson describes Burton's Antony as a 'Byronic aspirant who seeks the comfort of alcohol to anaesthetize his masculine failings'; Rachel Thompson, *Mark Antony and Popular Culture: Masculinity and the Construction of an Icon* (London, 2014), p. 257.
45. Schiff, *Cleopatra*, p. 254.
46. Kelley, *Elizabeth Taylor*, p. 154; Ellis Cashmore, *Elizabeth Taylor: A Private Life for Public Consumption* (New York, 2016), p. 110.
47. The Western fascination with Egypt, and particularly with Cleopatra, dates back many centuries, as does the perception that Egypt was a place of abundance and extreme consumption. Diego Saglia, e.g., has written about Egypt as an image in Romantic poetry: 'The traditional figuration of Egypt as a geography of abundance bordering on excess was the theme for a 15-minute sonnet-writing competition between Keats, Shelley and Leigh Hunt on 4 February 1818'; Diego Saglia, 'Consuming Egypt: Appropriation and the cultural modalities of Romantic luxury, *Nineteenth Century Contexts* 24.3 (2002), pp. 317–32 (p. 317). Camille Paglia, meanwhile, has commented that 'Egypt invented glamour, beauty as power and power as beauty. Egyptian aristocrats were the first Beautiful People'; Camille Paglia, *Sexual Personae: Art and Decadence from Nefertiti to Emily Dickinson* (New Haven, 1990), p. 59. This assertion suggests why Egypt, Cleopatra and Antony were such fertile ground for a Hollywood struggling to maintain the dying 'star-system' and wanting to remind the public (against the backdrop of the rise of television) that only cinema could do the 'spectacular'.
48. Bret, *Elizabeth Taylor*, p. 137. All of these actresses were presumably considered for their physical resemblance to the producers' idea of Cleopatra: none however, had Taylor's reputation or, at that time, her star-power.
49. Discussions about replacing Taylor at various points in the production of the film are related by Wanger, the film's producer, in *My Life with Cleopatra* (1963). He describes how he was blamed for the film's spiralling costs for casting Taylor, who suffered from persistent ill-health and was consequently often unable to work.
50. Peter Finch and Stephen Boyd were replaced by Harrison and Burton.
51. Kashner and Schoenberger refer to Fisher's comment that his marriage to Debbie Reynolds 'was mostly studio-arranged and had never been a love-match'; Kashner and Schoenberger, *Furious Love*, p. 8.
52. Leonard suggests that the ability to transcend the scandal was heavily reliant on 'a public reinterpretation of the affair as motivated by destiny, rather than whim'; Leonard, 'The true love', p. 84. Such a sense of inevitability, as suggested by Leonard, would allow the public to 'forgive' the errant stars more easily, since they were thought to be in the throes of emotions beyond their control.

53. Mann, *How to be a Movie Star*, p. 14.
54. Dick Hanley – Taylor's secretary – observed that 'A great star sees the world very differently than you or I. That's not good, that's not bad. It just is'; Mann, *How to Be a Movie Star*, p. 23.
55. This comment was claimed in Hedda Hopper's memoirs; Taylor later disputed that she had said these exact words; see Bret, *Elizabeth Taylor*, p. 116.
56. John Patterson, 'Cleopatra, the film that killed off big-budget epics', *Guardian*, 15 July 2013. Available at https://www.theguardian.com/film/2013/jul/15/cleopatra-killed-big-budget-epics (accessed 4 September 2016).
57. Michael Munn, *Richard Burton: Prince of Players* (London, 2008), p. 125.
58. Mary Pickord signed a contract with Adolph Zukor and Paramount in 1916 which was worth a million dollars; Ben Judge, '24 June 1916: Mary Pickford becomes Hollywood's first million-dollar actress', *Moneyweek Magazine*, 24 June 2015. Available at https://moneyweek.com/24-june-1916-mary-pickford-becomes-hollywoods-first-million-dollar-actress/ (accessed 26 January 2018). Taylor was the first woman to receive that amount for a single film; Mann, *How to be a Movie Star*, p. 270.
59. The film's producers, facing a financial disaster, sought, in the year following its release, to sue Taylor and Burton on the grounds that their affair had materially damaged the film's prospects by 'depreciating the commercial value of the movie by their "scandalous" conduct before and during the filming. … The suit also seeks to enjoin Miss Taylor from continuing to impugn the quality of the picture'; Edward Ranzal, 'Miss Taylor and Burton sued for $50 million on "Cleopatra"', *The New York Times*, 23 April 1964. The last sentence refers to Taylor's view that many of the best scenes were cut, particularly scenes involving Burton: Michael Munn quotes Burton saying that Taylor 'hated' the film; Munn, *Richard Burton*, p. 126. The stars then countersued and eventually won their case; C. David Heymann, *Liz: An Intimate Biography of Elizabeth Taylor* (London, 1995), p. 249.
60. Bragg, *Rich*, p. 145.
61. Ibid., p. 152.
62. Munn, *Richard Burton*, p. 118; Kashner and Schoenberger, *Furious Love*, pp. 20–1.
63. Daniel Williams rejects the idea that Taylor was somehow 'harmful' to Burton, arguing that this plays to 'sexist' assumptions about the 'siren female'. While agreeing that Burton was drawn to Hollywood glamour, and that Taylor, 'in a simplistic way' represented that, Williams asserts that 'I wouldn't blame her for it'; Kirstie McCrum, 'Exploring Richard Burton and Elizabeth Taylor's chemistry on and off-screen', *Wales Online*, 20 July 2013. Available at http://www.walesonline.co.uk/whats-on/film-tv/exploring-richard-burton-elizabeth-taylors-5151010 (accessed 2 December 2017).
64. Maureen Dowd, 'Richard Burton, 58, is dead; Rakish stage and screen star', *The New York Times*, 6 August 1984.
65. Plutarch, *Antony*, trans. John Dryden. Available at http://classics.mit.edu/Plutarch/antony.html (accessed 5 December 2017). Plutarch was, of course, writing nearly a hundred years after Antony's death: the *Parallel Lives* was written in approximately AD 125, whereas Antony died in 30 BC. His version of Antony and his relations with Cleopatra influenced Shakespeare's play about the couple and has remained a significant element in understanding the relationship of Cleopatra and Antony.
66. Ibid.
67. Ibid.
68. Burton, *The Richard Burton Diaries*, p. 183.

69. Taylor met Burton's family in Wales once their affair was established and they apparently grew very fond of her. However, Burton had a fight with his brother Ifor over his treatment of Sybil, and many of his family and friends shunned him, some for years. See Munn, *Richard Burton*, p. 128.

70. Munn, *Richard Burton*, p. 128.

71. Ibid., p. 117.

72. Ibid., p. 119. Bragg also uses this word in his biography of Burton to describe Burton's feelings for Taylor; Bragg, *Rich*, p. 150.

73. Munn, *Richard Burton*, p. 123. It is striking how many times different people involved in the film talk of the two actors as 'really' being the characters: Wanger, e.g., describes Taylor in his early meetings with her as 'really, a modern Cleopatra' and further on, when describing how he is informed of the affair, quotes Mankiewicz as saying, 'Liz and Burton are not just playing Antony and Cleopatra'; Wanger, *My Life with Cleopatra*, pp. 11, 121. Kashner and Schoenberger, meanwhile, in describing the beginning of the affair, make further explicit connections between the historical characters and the movie stars: 'It was not just Elizabeth Taylor who was casting her spell over [Burton], it was Cleopatra herself. ... Taylor already identified with Cleopatra. She felt that "Mike Todd ... had been to her what Julius Caesar had been to Cleopatra. Now Mark Antony – Burton – would take his place"'; Kashner and Schoenberger, *Furious Love*, p. 23.

74. Wyke and Montserrat point out that the Taylor/Cleopatra links initially nurtured by the studio came to 'signify not glamour and luxury but wastefulness and adultery'; Wyke and Montserrat, *Cleopatra: A Sphinx Revisited*, p. 189.

75. Munn, *Richard Burton*, p. 126.

76. Anna Tims, 'How we made *Cleopatra*', *Guardian*, 15 July 2013. Available at https://www.theguardian.com/film/2013/jul/15/how-we-made-cleopatra (accessed 4 September 2018).

77. See Cathy Whitlock, 'The set designs of *Cleopatra*, Elizabeth Taylor's classic movie', *Architectural Digest*, 31 December 2012. Available at https://www.architecturaldigest.com/gallery/cleopatra-elizabeth-taylor-set-design-50th-anniversary-cannes-slideshow/all (accessed 5 December 2017). See also Deborah Arthurs, 'Cape worn by Elizabeth Taylor for iconic scenes in 1963 film Cleopatra could fetch over £100k at auction', *Daily Mail*, 21 March 2012. Available at http://www.dailymail.co.uk/femail/article-2118243/Cape-worn-Elizabeth-Taylor-iconic-scenes-1963-film-Cleopatra-fetch-100k-auction.html (accessed 4 December 2017).

78. Kate Scheyer comments on this: 'Critics grumbled at some of the designers' unhistorical artistic flourishes, such as a bodice-wrapping rope on Cleopatra, or a laurel leaf on one of Mark Antony's (Richard Burton) equally clingy tunics. But who cares? Moviegoers were there to see the day's biggest stars at their most unattainably, superlatively beautiful. So, naturally, Taylor was to be bedecked in her body weight's worth of jewelry'; Kate Scheyer, 'Classic Hollywood style: Cleopatra', *Vanity Fair*, 20 April 2010. Available at https://www.vanityfair.com/hollywood/2010/04/classic-hollywood-style-cleopatra (accessed 3 December 2017). Elizabeth A. Ford and Deborah Mitchell suggest this further reinforces the conflation of actress and character: 'Taylor could have worn most of these gowns off the set. ... Cleopatra's style *is* Taylor's style'; Elizabeth A. Ford and Deborah Mitchell, *Royal Portraits in Hollywood: Filming the Lives of Queens* (Lexington, 2009), p. 106.

79. Hollywood, London and Italy were all locations at various times. Ultimately, the film was made in and around Rome.

80. Lord makes a similar point: 'It teaches us not about 48 to 31 BC but about AD 1958 to 1963'; Lord, *Accidental Feminist*, p. 100. However, it is this factor that makes the period of

the film so appropriate as a cinematic choice. Monica Silveiro Cyrino observes: 'The final years of the Roman Republic offer an arresting gallery of real human characters and critical historical events ideal for epic cinematic portrayal: the dictatorship and assassination of Julius Caesar, the rivalry between his successors, Antony and Octavian, that gave rise to the Roman Empire, and in particular, the fascinating figure of the brilliant Egyptian queen who shaped the course of history'; Monica Silveira Cyrino, *Big Screen Rome* (Oxford, 2005), p. 136. The film also made connections (deliberate or otherwise) to contemporary American politics: as Cyrino points out, Cleopatra's words to Caesar about 'one world, one nation, living in peace' resonate with the words of John F. Kennedy in his Inauguration Address in 1961 and Martin Luther King's 'I have a dream' speech of 1963. Other elements of the Cleopatra/Antony story made it attractive to the filmmakers: although neither were young when they began their relationship, they symbolized rebellion against conventional mores and glorified the notion that 'love conquers all', a message that was becoming more appealing at the beginning of the 1960s and which reached its climax in the hippie movement and youth protests at the end of the decade, as Margaret Malamud comments: 'The promotion for *Cleopatra* ... plays on the boom-time prosperity, the shifts in sexual attitudes, and the loosening of restraints on self-gratification and the pursuit of pleasure which characterized the 1960s'; Margaret Malamud, *Ancient Rome and Modern America* (Oxford, 2009), p. 233. Cyrino observes, 'The opulence and decadence of ancient Rome and Egypt were reborn in the early 1960s on the streets of modern Rome, nicknamed "Hollywood on the Tiber." Because of this uniquely well-exposed conjunction between life and art, Mankiewicz's *Cleopatra* had an unrivalled impact upon the public imagination'; Cyrino, *Big Screen Rome*, p. 136.

81. Lord, *Accidental Feminist*, pp. 100–1.
82. Betty Friedan, *The Feminine Mystique* (New York, 1963), p. 16, discussed in Lord, *Accidental Feminist*, pp. 100–1.
83. Lord, *Accidental Feminist*, p. 103.
84. Francesca T. Royster, meanwhile, suggests that Cleopatra was probably black. See Royster, *Becoming Cleopatra*, p. 35.
85. Jennifer Grayer Moore, *Fashion Fads Through American History: Fitting Clothes into Context* (Santa Barbara, 2010), p. 41.
86. Tove Hermanson, 'Cleopatra and Egyptian fashion in film', *Huffington Post*, 4 June 2010. Available at https://www.huffingtonpost.com/tove-hermanson/cleopatra-and-egyptian-fa_b_447708.html (accessed 17 February 2018).
87. Evie Leathem, 'Beauty flashback: Elizabeth Taylor, *Cleopatra* 1963', *Daily Telegraph*, 12 June 2015. Available at http://www.telegraph.co.uk/beauty/people/Elizabeth-Taylor-beauty-Cleopatra/ (accessed 26 January 2018).
88. Alison Berry, '50 years later: How *Cleopatra* continues to influence fashion today', *Time Magazine*, 12 June 2013. Available at http://style.time.com/2013/06/12/50-years-later-how-cleopatra-continues-to-influence-fashion-today/ (accessed 17 February 2018).
89. Emma Kniveton, 'The enduring influence of *Cleopatra*', *Express*, 27 May 2013. Available at https://www.express.co.uk/life-style/style/402820/The-enduring-influence-of-Cleopatra (accessed 27 January 2018). Kniveton also comments on the impact of Taylor's Bulgari-designed jewellery.
90. Laird Borrelli-Persson, 'A King named Tut and his influence on fashion', *Vogue*, 4 November 2014. Available at https://www.vogue.com/slideshow/king-tut-ancient-egypt-fashion (accessed 27 January 2018). See also Chapter 11, written by Mara Gold.

91. Lauren Alexis Fisher, 'The '60s films that every fashion girl should watch', *Harper's Bazaar*, 27 January 2015. Available at http://www.harpersbazaar.com/culture/film-tv/a9768/fashion-films-from-the-1960s/ (accessed 27 January 2018). Margaret Malamud, meanwhile, has written about the influence of ancient Egyptian imagery in Las Vegas, a city which subsists chiefly on gratification, excess and spectacle and calls itself 'the entertainment capital of the world'. She refers to 'the Luxor Casino' where, claims its publicity, 'the mysteries of ancient Egypt meet the modern-day excitement of Las Vegas', the Chicago Exhibition of 1893 which featured in its Midway section a 'Streets of Cairo' construction, and Grauman's Egyptian Theatre, built in Los Angeles in 1922; Margaret Malamud, 'Pyramids in Las Vegas and in outer space: Ancient Egypt in twentieth century American architecture and film', *The Journal of Popular Culture* 34.1 (2004), pp. 31–47 (p. 32). This further suggests that glamour, pleasure and hedonism became intrinsically connected to twentieth-century perceptions of Egypt, the 1963 film being the pinnacle of this association.

92. Anita Stratos, 'Breaking the color code', *Tour Egypt*. Available at http://www.touregypt.net/featurestories/colorcode.htm (accessed 27 January 2018). See also J. Hill, 'Colour in ancient Egypt', *Ancient Egypt Online*. Available at http://ancientegyptonline.co.uk/colour.html (accessed 27 January 2018).

93. Taylor did her own makeup for the film, and there are stills showing her practising different 'looks', as well as a scene in the film where Cleopatra is shown applying make-up. In an interview in 2006, she said that 'Alberto De Rossi prepared the sketches, but his back went out before filming began, and he had to have surgery. I had studied his techniques, so I copied what I had seen him do'; Michael Kors, 'Michael Kors talks to Dame Elizabeth Taylor', *Harper's Bazaar*, 23 March 2011. Available at http://www.harpersbazaar.com/celebrity/latest/news/a699/michael-kors-talks-to-elizabeth-taylor/ (accessed 27 January 2018). Joyce Tyldesley suggests that the 'plain' image on Cleopatra's coins was deliberately chosen to signify power more effectively, thus further indicating that she was fully aware of the uses of appearance; Sooke, 'How ancient Egypt shaped our idea of beauty'.

94. Judith Crist, 'Cleopatra: A monumental mouse', *New York Herald Tribune*, 13 June 1963. Available at http://centennial.journalism.columbia.edu/1963-the-movies-as-art/index.html (accessed 6 September 2016).

95. Ibid.

96. Bernard F. Dick, 'In the entertainment world: *Cleopatra*', *The Classical World* 57.1 (1963), pp. 35–6 (p. 35).

97. Ibid., p. 36.

98. Munn, *Richard Burton*, p. 124. This is an interesting comment in view of the love affair which underpinned the film. It implies that, rather than adding to the dynamic of passion between the two characters, the off-screen affair may have undermined it, and the focus on spectacle diminished the possibility for subtlety or psychological truth. It might also be the result of raised expectations: as Suzanne Leonard puts it, '*Cleopatra* thereby positioned itself as a film that teased audiences with what was at best a barely concealed notion that it contained the "truth" of the romance between Taylor and Burton'; Leonard, 'The true love', p. 80.

99. Julie Ponzi makes an interesting alternative suggestion as to the source of the film's artistic failure: '[Taylor's] performance falls flat and – not unlike the actual story of Cleopatra – ends in bitter disappointment. Does it show Taylor's inability to live up to a Shakespearean erotic ideal or does it, merely, demonstrate (in four painful hours) the impossibility of becoming one's own goddess? A true goddess has no need for self-control, but a mere mortal playing a goddess may find that high drama creeps in when she proves unable to control others or

Notes to pages 242–244

100. the events around her'. Julie Ponzi, 'Drama Queens: Elizabeth Taylor, Camille Paglia, and the Purposes of Female Power', Ashbrook Centre at Ashland University, 2011. Available at https://ashbrook.org/publications/oped-ponzi-11-dramaqueens/.
100. Lord observes that 'nearly every set could double as an airplane hanger'; Lord *The Accidental Feminist*, p. 105.
101. *Cleopatra*, dir. by Joseph Mankiewicz (20th Century Fox, 1963).
102. Ibid.
103. See Constantine Santas, James M. Wilson, Maria Colavito and Djoymi Baker, *The Encyclopaedia of Epic Films* (Lanham, 2014), p. 141.
104. Leonard comments that 'Taylor and Burton lent verisimilitude to the historical romance; likewise, Antony and Cleopatra's fated relation gave credence to the affair between the two stars. … The public construction of Taylor and Burton's affair … was thus consistently filtered through the narrative of *Cleopatra*'; Leonard, 'The true love', p. 78.
105. Richard Brody, 'The case for *Cleopatra*', *New Yorker*, 2013. Available at https://www.newyorker.com/culture/richard-brody/the-case-for-cleopatra (accessed 2 December 2017).
106. This could also be seen as an early manifestation of 'parasocial' behaviour, a term used by Chris Rojek to describe fans' perception of 'closeness' to idols. See Chris Rojek, *Presumed Intimacy: Parasocial Interaction in Media, Society and Celebrity Culture* (London, 2015).
107. McCrum, 'Exploring Richard Burton and Elizabeth Taylor's chemistry'.
108. David R. Croteau, and William D. Hoynes, *Media/Society: Industries, Images, and Audiences* (Thousand Oaks, CA, 2002), p. 296.
109. Cashmore, *Elizabeth Taylor*.
110. Kashner and Schoenberger, *Furious Love*, p. 35. Munn, meanwhile, observes that 'Liz and Dick' became 'a franchise'; Munn, *Richard Burton*, p. 132.
111. Katy Stoddard, 'Burton and Taylor, private lives played out in public', *Guardian*, 22 July 2013. Available at https://www.theguardian.com/theguardian/from-the-archive-blog/2013/jul/22/elizabeth-taylor-richard-burton-archive (accessed 7 January 2018).
112. Sally Hay, Burton's fourth wife, has dismissed the suggestion that this was a 'perfect match': 'Yes, they were in love, but they got divorced twice – that means their marriage didn't work'; ChristopherWilson, 'Richard Burton never wrote that "last love letter"', *Daily Telegraph*, 9 November 2011. Available at http://www.telegraph.co.uk/culture/film/starsandstories/8877223/Richard-Burton-never-wrote-that-last-love-letter.html (accessed 5 January 2018). In the same article, Hay also rejects the story that Burton wrote a 'final love letter' to Taylor, which was buried with her.
113. Liz Ronk, 'Liz Taylor and Richard Burton on the set of Cleopatra: Rare and classic photos', *Time Magazine*, 10 June 2013. Available at http://time.com/3877380/cleopatra-rare-photos-of-liz-taylor-richard-burton-on-set-in-1962/ (accessed 3 September 2016).
114. Jon Solomon, 'In the wake of "Cleopatra": The ancient world in the cinema since 1963', *The Classical Journal* 91.2 (1995–6), pp. 113–40.
115. Nathan Weiss made an interesting comment on this in a letter to Jack Brodsky at the end of *The Cleopatra Papers*: 'For surely *Cleopatra* will come to mark the end of a Hollywood era – Hollywood as we knew it as kids, as the world has come to have an image of it. I think with this film it can be seen that the whole system finally breaks down under its own weight'; Weiss, *The Cleopatra Papers*, pp. 167–8.
116. Peter Hessler, 'Into the pharaoh's chamber: How I fell in love with ancient Egypt' *The Guardian*, 26 April 2019. Available at https://www.theguardian.com/news/2019/apr/

26/ancient-egypt-amarna-akhenaten-rebel-king-arab-spring-revolution (accessed 29 April 2019).

117. Ronald H. Fritze argues that the film does an acceptable job of portraying ancient Egypt, at least in the context of 'Egyptomania': 'as a work of historical fiction and Egyptomania, the film is quite good. ... Scenes depicting Alexandria show a city where Hellenistic and Egyptian architecture jostle with each other for prominence and the great Lighthouse is shown in the background.... Interior décor is Egyptianised as are the dark and mysterious temples'; Ronald H. Fritze, *Egyptomania: A History of Fascination, Obsession and Fantasy* (London, 2016), p. 346. Lynn Meskell suggests that concern with authenticity in such portrayals is superfluous: 'It seems that invoking historical Egypt is unnecessary, since it is our (re)construction of Egypt which has become the powerful and evocative vehicle of contemporary desires'; Lynn Meskell, 'Consuming bodies: Cultural fantasies of ancient Egypt', *Body & Society* 4/1 (1998), pp. 63–76 (p. 63).

118. A key source was fictional: Carlo Maria Franzero's 1957 novel, *Cleopatra*. There was some historical research: W. Robert LaVine and Florio Allen observe that 'to achieve historical accuracy in *Cleopatra*, research for the outfits was done from early Egyptian bas-reliefs, tomb paintings, and sculpture'; W. Robert LaVine and Florio Allen, *In a Glamorous Fashion: The Fabulous Years of Hollywood Costume Design* (New York, 1980), p. 139. The film's publicity material makes references to Plutarch, Dion Cassius, and Suetonius as sources; see, e.g., https://www.nyu.edu/projects/wke/press/cleopatra/cleopatra.pdf. However, there are few details on the extent of the research or what was used or discarded.

119. Alison Berry reminds us that 'the black kohl eyeliner Cleopatra (and many other Egyptian women) wore in a cat-eye style has stood the test of time; the smoky, heavily-lined eye is still popular today'; Berry, '50 years later: How *Cleopatra* continues to influence fashion today'. Margaret Malamud further suggests that 'Americans have constructed images of Egypt and exploited those Egypts as terms in their own political and cultural self-definition'; Malamud, 'Pyramids in Las Vegas and in outer space', p. 31.

120. Berry, '50 Years Later'.

121. *Time Magazine*, discussing the affair in August 1962, speculated that 'If [Burton] marries her, he will be the Oxford boy who became the fifth husband of the Wife of Bath. If she loses him, she loses her reputation as a fatal beauty, an all-consuming man-eater, the Cleopatra of the twentieth century'; Heymann, *Liz*, p. 255. Heymann provides no further reference details for the article.

122. Nathan Weiss commented at the time of the film's release that 'Everybody, but everybody, will go to see this picture to say that they can see on screen what's going on off it'; Weiss, *The Cleopatra Papers*, p. 55. Walter Wanger's account of the making of the film recounts a number of episodes suggesting that this is exactly what viewers *will* see, as follows: 'Cleopatra comes in to see Antony who is in the bath. ... They commence a beautiful love scene. JLM's dialogue is right out of real life, with Cleopatra telling how she will feel if Antony leaves her. ... It was hard to tell whether Liz and Burton were reading lines or living the parts'; Wanger, *My Life with Cleopatra*, p. 134. Wanger's biographer suggested that he embellished some of his recollection of this aspect of *Cleopatra* to create publicity for the film (his diary was published before its release), but the analogies in between the historic and contemporary couple were not his creation.

123. Susan King, '*Cleopatra*, a spectacle on- and off-screen', *Los Angeles Times*, 20 May 2013. Available at http://articles.latimes.com/2013/may/20/entertainment/la-et-mn-classic-hollywood-cleopatra-20130520 (accessed 6 January 2018).

124. Vivien Sobchack examines *Cleopatra* through the impact of Taylor and Burton on the film and the reasons for casting stars in epic films. She sees it as a way of extending and even

mimicking the historical moment of the film: 'Consider how Taylor and Burton's illicit extratextual romance– and their magnitude as stars – mimicked the historical situation of the text in which they were imitating Cleopatra and Antony and extended the produced History of the past into the present moment of historical production. ... This extension of temporality is also one of the functions, I would suggest, of casting highly recognizable stars to represent historical figures ... their presence functions as a sign of temporal transcendence. Elizabeth Taylor outlives the end of History as it was writ by Cleopatra'; Vivien Sobchack, ' "Surge and splendour": A phenomenology of the Hollywood historical epic', *Representations* 29 (1990), pp. 24–49.

125. Taylor and Burton eventually divorced in 1974, remarried in 1975, and divorced again in 1976. In a TV interview in 1988, Taylor was asked whether she regretted the fact that she and Burton never reunited. Her response – 'I'm sure we will be, one day' – received a lengthy round of applause; *Aspel & Company*, season 5 episode 5, ITV, 6 February 1988.

126. As noted earlier, Wyke and Montserrat observe that 'Stars are cast in Hollywood histories not as characters, but in character, and thus they people the represented past with the present, while extracinematic discourses about them and about the moment of film production further extend the temporality of the time represented into the here-and-now'; Wyke and Montserrat, 'Glamour girls', p. 189. They also relate the republication of Carlo Maria Franzero's 1957 novel, *Cleopatra*, the main source for the film, with stills taken both on and offset, as if 'Taylor had lived Cleopatra offset as well as on'; p. 190.

127. Cashmore refers to this as 'the period in history when voyeurism became respectable'; Cashmore, *Elizabeth Taylor*, p. 161.

15 The Mummy, the Priestess and the Heroine: Embodying and Legitimating Female Power in 1970s Girls' Comics

1. Vera Vasiljević, '*Princess Ru* and *Papyrus*: Stereotypes on ancient Egypt in graphic novels', *Issues in Ethnology and Anthropology* 7.3 (2012), pp. 763–88 (p. 764).

2. Stephanie Moser, 'Reconstructing ancient worlds: Reception studies, archaeological representation and the interpretation of ancient Egypt', *Journal of Archaeological Method and Theory* 22.4 (2015), pp. 1263–308 (p. 1263).

3. 'When the Mummy Walks' was published by DC Thompson in *Spellbound* for ten issues from 25 September to 27 November 1976. The 'The Cult of the Cat' was published by Fleetway in *Misty* for 12 issues from 4 February to 22 April 1978. Neither of these comics were paginated. While the authorship of 'The Cult of the Cat' is uncertain, Julia Round, in her database of *Misty* stories, proposes Bill Harrington as its writer.

4. Moser, 'Reconstructing ancient worlds', p. 1277.

5. Comics and the reception of the Classical world have been the subject of several recent academic studies, most notably George Kovacs and C. W. Marshall (eds), *Classics and Comics* (Oxford, 2011) and George Kovacs and C. W. Marshall (eds), *Son of Classics and Comics* (Oxford, 2015). Ancient Egypt in comics and graphic novels has been the subject of relatively scant academic study, with the exception of Vasiljević's '*Princess Ru* and *Papyrus*', this chapter, and Chapter 10 of this volume by Eleanor Dobson.

6. Angela McRobbie, 'Jackie: An ideology of adolescent femininity', *Centre for Contemporary Cultural Studies Stencilled Occasional Paper*, 'Women series' 53 (1978).

7. Martin Barker, *Comics: Ideology, Power and the Critics* (Manchester, 1989).

8. Valerie Walkerdine, 'Some day my prince will come: Young girls and the preparation for adolescent sexuality', in Angela McRobbie and Mica Nava (eds), *Gender and Generation* (London, 1984), p. 163.
9. Ibid.
10. Barker, *Comics*, p. 231.
11. Ibid., p. 237.
12. Ibid., pp. 233–4.
13. David Buckingham, *Moving Images: Understanding Children's Emotional Responses to Television* (Manchester, 1996), p. 3.
14. Marie Messenger-Davies, 'Children's television', in Glen Creeber (ed.), *The Television Genre Book* (London, 2008), pp. 96–7.
15. Ibid.
16. *Misty*, for instance, sold approximately 170,000 copies a week on launch, a figure that is – like most girls' comics – higher than comparable figures for boys' comics. See Pat Mills, 'Misty lives!', *Pat Mills*, 6 September 2016. Available at https://patmills.wordpress.com/2016/09/06/misty-lives/ (accessed 3 June 2019).
17. See Jenkins, Henry, 'Cult conversations: Interview with Julia Round', *Confessions of an Aca-Fan*, 15 November 2018. Available at http://henryjenkins.org/blog/2018/11/9/cult-conversations-interview-with-julia-round-part-ii.
18. Vasiljević, '*Princess Ru* and *Papyrus*', p. 764.
19. Ibid., p. 777.
20. Ibid., p. 779.
21. The plot of 'When the Mummy Walks', with a person reanimating and directing a mummy to carry out evil deeds, is an archetype that has been traced back to Arthur Conan Doyle's short story 'Lot No. 249' (1892). While he did not invent ambulatory mummies, he was the first major male author to depict one; he was the first, however, to portray the mummy as having no mind of its own and being able to be manipulated via magic by a living person. This idea was the uncredited but obvious origin of the High Priest characters in Universal Pictures' 1940s films (the Kharis saga), who controlled the murderous mummy Kharis with 'tana leaf' brew. Hammer Films went on to use the 'mummy puppet' motif with the mummy being controlled via a magic scroll (*The Mummy*, dir. Terence Fisher [1959]) or magic spells on a shroud (*The Mummy's Shroud*, dir. Joh Gilling [1967]). See Day, *The Mummy's Curse: Mummymania in the English-Speaking World* (London, 2006), especially the second and third chapters. Doyle's narrative, perhaps via the Kharis and Hammer films, is the probable origin of the 'mummy puppet' motif in 'When the Mummy Walks'.
22. Vasiljević, '*Princess Ru* and *Papyrus*', p. 779.
23. Kathryn E. Slanski, 'The Law of Hammurabi and its audience', *Yale Journal of Law and the Humanities* 24.1 (2012), pp. 97–110 (p. 97).
24. Ibid., p. 98.
25. Deborah Sweeney, 'Forever young? The representation of older and ageing women in ancient Egyptian art', *Journal of the American Research Centre in Egypt* 41 (2004), pp. 67–84 (p. 86).
26. Ibid., p. 72.
27. Ibid., p. 74. See also Dorothea Arnold, *The Royal Women of Amarna: Images of Beauty from Ancient Egypt* (New York, 1996).

28. On the subject of female occult authority, see Julia Round's analysis of witches in *Misty*; Julia Round, '*Misty, Spellbound* and the lost Gothic of British girls' comics', *Palgrave Communications* 3 (2017). Available at https://doi.org/10.1057/palcomms.2017.37 (accessed 2 June 2019).
29. 'The cult of the cat', *Misty*, 4 February 1978.
30. 'When the mummy walks', *Spellbound*, 25 September 1976.
31. 'The cult of the cat', *Misty*, 11 February 1978.
32. As Julia Round notes, *Misty*'s 'longer serials have girls thrown into threatening situations or discovering some unwanted or uncanny ability and ultimately coming to terms with this', suggesting, as a result, that they might be understood as *Bildungsromane*. 'The Cult of the Cat' is therefore – in terms of its narrative – typical of the comic. See Round, '*Misty, Spellbound* and the lost Gothic of British girls' comics'.
33. 'The cult of the cat', *Misty*, 25 February 1978.
34. 'The cult of the cat', *Misty*, 8 April 1978.
35. 'The cult of the cat', *Misty*, 22 April 1978.
36. Ibid.
37. 'When the mummy walks', *Spellbound*, 25 September 1976.
38. Terry Castle, 'Phantasmagoria: Spectral technology and the metaphorics of modern reverie', *Critical Inquiry* 15.1 (1988), pp. 26–61 (pp. 27, 30).
39. John Whale, 'Sacred objects and the sublime ruins of art', in Stephen Copley and John Whale (eds), *Beyond Romanticism: New Approaches to Texts and Contexts 1780–1832* (London, 1992), p. 231.
40. For more on women and mysticism with reference to ancient Egypt, see Chapters 9 and 13 of this volume, written by Caroline Tully and Sabina Stent respectively.
41. Antonia Lant, 'The curse of the pharaoh, or how cinema contracted Egyptomania', *October* 59 (1992), pp. 86–112.
42. Day, *The Mummy's Curse*, p. 4.
43. Ibid., p. 3.
44. Ibid., p. 86.
45. Ibid., p. 55.
46. Ibid., p. 8.
47. Ibid., p. 172.
48. Ibid.
49. Ibid., p. 98.
50. Ibid., p. 93.
51. Ibid., p. 64.
52. Ibid., p. 102.
53. *The Mummy*, dir. Karl Freund (1932).
54. Day, *The Mummy's Curse*, p. 40.
55. Mel Gibson, *Remembered Reading: Memory, Comics and Postwar Constructions of British Girlhood* (Leuwen, 2015).
56. Ibid., p. 38.

57. Radwa Khalil, Ahmed A. Moustafa, Marie Z. Moffat and Ahmed A. Karim, 'How knowledge of ancient Egyptian women can influence today's gender role: Does history matter in gender psychology', *Frontiers in Psychology* 7 (2017), pp. 1–7.
58. Ibid., p. 3.
59. Ibid.

BIBLIOGRAPHY

'A feminist of 1375 B.C.', *Equal Rights*, 19 February 1933.
AA School of Architecture, 'Clement Greenberg—Lecture', *YouTube*. Available at https://www.youtube.com/watch?v=hk5Nzo2qzro.
'Accident to the Duke of Hamilton', *Morning Post*, 26 September 1849.
Adda, Bérangère, 'Christiane Desroches Noblecourt: 80 ans de passion pour l'Egypte', *Le Parisien*, 30 May 2003.
Addy, Shirley M., *Rider Haggard and Egypt* (Accrington, 1998).
Alden, W. L., 'The hunter', *The Idler: An Illustrated Monthly Magazine*, 7 July 1895.
'Alexander, 10th Duke of Hamilton', *The Douglas Archives*. Available at http://www.douglashistory.co.uk/history/alexander10thdukeofhamilton.htm.
'An account of Mr. Francis Bancroft, so far as relates to his monument and burial', *The Ladies Magazine, Or, The Universal Entertainer*, 22 August 1752.
'Ancient Egypt's queen of beauty: A newly found quartzite head of Nefertiti from Tell-Amarna', *Illustrated London News*, 6 May 1933.
'Ancient Egyptian styles to dominate jewelry and dress', *The Jewelers' Circular*, 21 February 1923.
Andrews, Carol, *Ancient Egyptian Jewellery* (London, 1990).
Andrews, Carol, 'Pharaoh trampler of Egypt's enemies: A new amuletic form', in Jacke Phillips (ed.), *Ancient Egypt, the Aegean, and the Near East: Studies in Honour of Martha Rhoads Bell*, Vol. 1 (San Antonio, 1997).
'Antique feminine culture', *Evening News*, 20 January 1920.
Apuleius, *The Golden Ass*, trans. Joel C. Relihan (Indianapolis, 2007).
Armstrong, Richard H., *A Compulsion for Antiquity: Freud and the Ancient World* (Ithaca, NY, 2005).
Arnold, Catharine, *Necropolis: London and its Dead* (London, 2006).
Arnold, Dorothea, *The Royal Women of Amarna: Images of Beauty from Ancient Egypt* (New York, 1996).
Arthurs, Deborah, 'Cape worn by Elizabeth Taylor for iconic scenes in 1963 film Cleopatra could fetch over £100k at auction', *Daily Mail*, 21 March 2012. Available at http://www.dailymail.co.uk/femail/article-2118243/Cape-worn-Elizabeth-Taylor-iconic-scenes-1963-film-Cleopatra-fetch-100k-auction.html.
Ashton, Sally-Ann, *Cleopatra and Egypt* (Oxford, 2008).
Aspel & Company, season 5 episode 5, ITV, 6 February 1988.
Assmann, Jan, 'Monotheism and polytheism,' in Sarah Iles Johnston (ed.), *Ancient Religions* (Cambridge, MA, 2007).
Assmann, Jan, *Moses the Egyptian: The Memory of Egypt in Western Monotheism* (Cambridge, 1997).
Assmann, Jan, *The Price of Monotheism* (Stanford, 2010).
Baikie, James, *The Story of the Pharaohs* (London, 1908).
Baines, John, and Liam McNamara, 'The twin stelae of Suty and Hor', in Zahi A. Hawass and Janet E. Richards (eds), *The Archaeology and Art of Ancient Egypt: Studies in Honor of David B. O'Connor*, Vol. 1 (Cairo, 2007).
Baker, Brian, *Iain Sinclair* (Manchester, 2007).

Bibliography

Baker, Terri, 'The record of a life: Nation and narrative in Victorian women's collections', in Kevin M. Moist and David Banash (eds), *Contemporary Collecting: Objects, Practices, and the Fate of Things* (Lanham, 2013).
Baltrušaitis, Jurgis, *Aberrations: An Essay on the Legends of Forms*, trans. Richard Miller (Cambridge, MA, 1989).
Bancroft, Francis, *A True Copy of the remarkable Last Will and Testament of Mr. Francis Bancroft, Citizen and Draper of London* (London, 1728).
Barasch, Moshe, *Modern Theories of Art 3: From Impressionism to Kandinsky* (New York, 2000).
Barber, Martyn, 'Crawford in 3-D', *AARGNews* 51 (2015), pp. 32–47.
Barber, Martyn, '"It shouldn't have been found there": The trouble with Canon Greenwell's axe' (forthcoming).
Barber, Martyn, *Stonehenge Aerodrome and the Stonehenge Landscape* (Swindon, 2014).
Barker, Martin, *Comics: Ideology, Power and the Critics* (Manchester, 1989).
Battersby, Martin, *The Decorative Twenties* (London, 1974).
'Be subtle with your make-up', *Evening Telegraph*, 31 July 1933.
Becker, Vivienne, *Antique and Twentieth Century Jewellery* (Colchester, 1987).
Bellow, Juliet, 'Fashioning *Cléopâtre*: Sonia Delaunay's New Woman', *Art Journal* 68.2 (2009), pp. 6–25.
Bermond, Daniel, 'Il était une fois sur les bords du Nil...', *L'Histoire* 190 (1995), pp. 20–1.
Berry, Sarah, *Screen Style: Fashion and Femininity in 1930s Hollywood* (Minneapolis, 2000).
Beier de Haan, Rosmarie, 'You can always get what you want: History, the original, and the endless opportunities of the copy', in *Original, Copy, Fake, On the significance of the object in History and Archaeology Museums, 22nd ICOM General Conference in Shanghai, China, 7–12nd November 2010* (Shanghai, 2010). Available at www.network.icom.museum/fileadmin/user_upload/minisites/icmah/publications/Actes-Shanghai-complet2.pdf.
Benjamin, Walter, *The Work of Art in the Age of Its Technological Reproducibility, and Other Writings on Media*, Michael Jennings, Brigit Doherty and Thomas Levin (eds), trans. Edward Jefcott (Cambridge, MA, 2008).
Benton, Charlotte, and Tim Benton, 'The style and the age', in Charlotte Benton, Tim Benton and Ghislaine Wood (eds), *Art Deco 1910–1939* (London, 2003).
Berry, Alison, '50 years later: How *Cleopatra* continues to influence fashion today', *Time Magazine*, 12 June 2013. Available at http://style.time.com/2013/06/12/50-years-later-how-cleopatra-continues-to-influence-fashion-today/.
Bierbrier, Morris L., *Who Was Who in Egyptology* (London, 2012).
Bird, Dúnlaith, 'Disorienting eyes: Women travellers to the Orient from 1880–1930' (MPhil thesis, Oxford University, 2006).
'Black magic: Sir H. Rider Haggard and dangerous nonsense', *Daily Mail*, 7 April 1923.
Bland, Olivia, *The Royal Way of Death* (London, 1986).
Bloom, Harold, 'Norman in Egypt', *The New York Review of Books*, 28 April 1983.
Blumberg, Angie, 'Strata of the soul: The queer archaeologies of Vernon Lee and Oscar Wilde', *Victoriographies* 7.3 (2017), pp. 239–56.
Blumenbach, John Frederick, 'Observations on some Egyptian mummies opened in London', *Philosophical Transactions* 84 (1794), pp. 177–95.
Boccaccio, Giovanni, *Famous Women*, trans. Virginia Brown (Cambridge, 2001).
Bohleke, Karin J., 'Mummies are called upon to contribute to fashion: Pre-Tutankhamun Egyptian revivalism in dress', *Dress* 40.2 (2014), pp. 93–115.
Bono, Paola, 'Rewriting the memory of a queen: Dido, Cleopatra, Elizabeth I', *European Journal of English Studies* 10.2 (2006), pp. 117–30.
Boone, Joseph Allen, *The Homoerotics of Orientalism* (New York, 2015).

Bibliography

Boothby, Guy, 'A professor of Egyptology', *The Graphic: An Illustrated Weekly Magazine*, 10 December 1904, pp. 773–5.

Borrelli-Persson, Laird, 'A King named Tut and his influence on fashion', *Vogue*, 4 November 2014. Available at https://www.vogue.com/slideshow/king-tut-ancient-egypt-fashion.

Botti, Giuseppe, 'Il *Libro del respirare* e un suo nuovo esemplare nel *Papiro Demotico n. 766* del Museo Egizio di Torino', *The Journal of Egyptian Archaeology* 54 (1986), pp. 223–30.

Bourke, Joanna, *Dismembering the Male: Men's Bodies, Britain and the Great War* (Chicago, 1999).

Bradford, C. A., *Heart Burial* (London, 1933).

Bradley, Fiona, *Movements in Modern Art: Surrealism* (London, 1997).

Bragg, Melvyn, *Rich: The Life of Richard Burton* (London, 1988).

Breasted, James Henry, *The Dawn of Conscience* (New York, 1933).

Brenson, Michael, 'Egyptian art is alive and well in the West', *The New York Times*, 31 December 1989. Available at www.nytimes.com/1989/12/31/arts/art-gallery-view-egyptian-art-is-alive-and-well-in-the-west.html.

Bret, David, *Elizabeth Taylor: The Lady, the Lover, the Legend: 1932–2011* (London, 2011).

Breton, André, *Manifestoes of Surrealism*, trans. Richard Seaver and Helen R. Lane (Ann Arbor, 1990).

Breton, André, *Nadja*, trans. Mark Polizzotti (London, 1999).

Bridson, D. G., *The Filibuster: A Study of the Political Ideas of Wyndham Lewis* (London, 1972).

Brier, Bob, *Egyptomania: Our Three Thousand Year Obsession with the Land of the Pharaohs* (New York, 2013).

Brio, Sara, 'Prefiguring the cross: A typological reading of H. Rider Haggard's *Cleopatra*' in Eleanor Dobson (ed.), *Victorian Literary Culture and Ancient Egypt* (Manchester, 2020).

British Museum, *Rodin and the Art of Ancient Greece* (London, 2018).

Broderick, Herbert, *Moses the Egyptian in the Illustrated Old English Hexateuch* (Notre Dame, IN, 2017).

Brodie-Innes, John, 'MacGregor Mathers: Some personal reminiscences', *Occult Review* 29.5 (1919), pp. 284–6.

Brodsky, Jack, and Nathan Weiss, *The Cleopatra Papers: A Private Correspondence* (New York, 1963).

Brody, Richard, 'The case for *Cleopatra*', *New Yorker*, 2013. Available at https://www.newyorker.com/culture/richard-brody/the-case-for-cleopatra.

Brooks, J. A., *Ghosts of London: The West End, South and West* (Norwich, 1982).

Bryant, Marsha, and Mary Ann Eaverly, 'Egypto-Modernism: James Henry Breasted, H.D., and the new past', *Modernism/modernity* 14.3 (2007), pp. 435–53.

Brzeska, Gaudier, 'Vortex', *Blast: Review of the Great English Vortex* 1 (1914), pp. 155–8.

Buchwald, Jed Z. and Diane Greco Josefowicz, *The Zodiac of Paris* (Princeton, 2010).

Buckingham, David, *Moving Images: Understanding Children's Emotional Responses to Television* (Manchester, 1996).

Buckley, Cheryl and Hilary Fawcett, *Fashioning the Feminine: Representation and Women's Fashion from the Fin de Siècle to the Present* (London, 2002).

Budge, E. A. Wallis, *By Nile and Tigris: A Narrative of Journeys in Egypt and Mesopotamia on Behalf of the British Museum Between the Years 1886 and 1913*, 2 vols (London, 1920).

Budge, E. A. Wallis, *The Egyptian Book of the Dead (Abridged)* (London, 2001).

Burke, Janine, *The Sphinx on the Table: Sigmund Freud's Art Collection and the Development of Psychoanalysis* (New York, 2006).

Burnett, Charles, 'Images of ancient Egypt in the Latin Middle Ages', in Peter J. Ucko and Timothy Champion (eds), *The Wisdom of Egypt: Changing Visions through the Ages* (London, 2003).

Bibliography

Burns, Ric, and James Sanders, *New York: An Illustrated History* (New York, 2003).
Burroughs, William S., *Burroughs Live: The Collected Interviews of William S. Burroughs, 1960–1997* (New York, 2001).
Burroughs, William S., *My Education: A Book of Dreams* (London, 1996).
Burroughs, William S., *Naked Lunch: The Restored Text* (New York, 2001).
Burroughs, William S., *Nova Express* (London 1968).
Burroughs, William S., *The Adding Machine* (New York, 1993).
Burroughs, William S., *The Ticket That Exploded* (London, 1987).
Burroughs, William S., *The Western Lands* (New York, 1988).
Burroughs, William S., and Brion Gysin, *The Third Mind* (New York, 1978).
Burroughs, William S., and Daniel Odier, *The Job: Interviews with William S. Burroughs* (London, 1989).
Bushell, Peter, *London's Secret History* (London, 1983).
Burton, Richard, *The Richard Burton Diaries*, Chris Williams (ed.) (New Haven, 2012).
Butler, Judith, *Gender Trouble: Feminism and the Subversion of Identity* (London, 2014).
Caine, Barbara, *Victorian Feminists* (Oxford, 1992).
Calloway, Stephen, *Charles Ricketts, Subtle and Fantastic Decorator* (London, 1979).
Cannadine, David, 'War and death, grief and mourning in modern Britain', in Joachim Whaley (ed.), *Mirrors of Mortality: Studies in the Social History of Death* (London, 1981).
Capart, Jean, 'Some remarks of the Sheikh el-Beled', *Journal of Egyptian Archaeology* 6.4 (1920), pp. 225–33.
Caratini, Roger, *L'égyptomanie, une imposture* (Paris, 2002).
Cardin, Matt, *Mummies around the World: An Encyclopedia of Mummies in History, Religion, and Popular Culture*: (London, 2014).
Carracciolo, Peter, and Paul Edwards, 'In fundamental agreement: Yeats and Wyndham Lewis', *Yeats Annual* 13 (1998), pp. 110–57.
Carroll, Shirea L., 'Commentary: Another white actress to play Cleopatra?', *Essence*, 14 June 2010. Available at www.essence.com/2010/06/14/commentary-angelina-jolie-to-play-cleopa.
Carruthers, William (ed.), *Histories of Egyptology: Interdisciplinary Measures* (London, 2014).
Carter, Howard, *The Tomb of Tutankhamen* (London, 1972).
Carter, Howard, and A. C. Mace, *The Discovery of the Tomb of Tutankhamen* (New York, 1977).
Cashmore, Ellis, *Elizabeth Taylor: A Private Life for Public Consumption* (New York, 2016).
Castle, Terry, 'Phantasmagoria: Spectral technology and the metaphorics of modern reverie', *Critical Inquiry* 15.1 (1988), pp. 26–61.
Caufield, Catherine, *The Man Who Ate Bluebottles: And Other Great British Eccentrics* (London, 2006).
Causey, Andrew, 'The hero and the crowd: The art of Wyndham Lewis in the twenties', in Paul Edwards (ed.), *Volcanic Heaven: Essays on Wyndham Lewis's Painting and Writing* (Santa Rosa, 1996).
Cavaignac, François, *Balades maçonniques en littérature* (Namur, 2014).
Chabalier, Blaise de, 'Christian Jacq dans la peau d'un scribe', *Le Figaro*, 29 January 2009.
Chaille, François, *Cartier: Innovation Through the 20th Century* (Paris, 2007).
Chaille, Francois, and Eric Nussbaum, *The Cartier Collection: Jewellery* (Paris, 2004).
'Chair', British Museum, museum no. EA 2480. Available at www.britishmuseum.org/research/collection_online/collection_object_details.aspx?objectId=119024&partId=1.
Chambers, Emma, *Paul Nash* (London, 2016).
Chambers, R. (ed.), *The Book of Days*, Vol. 2 (London: W. and R. Chambers, 1869).
Champion, Tim, 'Egypt and the diffusion of culture', in David Jeffreys (ed.), *Views of Egypt since Napoleon Bonaparte* (London, 2003).

Chaney, Edward, 'Egypt in England and America: The cultural memorials of religion, royalty and revolution', in Maurizio Ascari and Adriana Corrado (eds), *Sites of Exchange European Crossroads and Faultlines* (Amsterdam; New York, 2006).
Chaney, Edward, 'Freudian Egypt', *The London Magazine* (April/May 2006), pp. 62–9.
Chaney, Edward, *Genius Friend: G.B. Edwards and The Book of Ebenezer le Page* (London, 2015).
Chaney, Edward, 'Lewis and the Men of 1938: Graham Bell, Kenneth Clark, Read, Reitlinger, Rothenstein, and the mysterious Mr Macleod: A discursive tribute to John and Harriet Cullis', *Journal of Wyndham Lewis Studies* 7 (2016), pp. 34–147.
Chaney, Edward, 'R.B. Kitaj (1932–2007): Warburgian artist', 30 November 2013, *emaj*, p. 7. Available at https://emajartjournal.com/2013/11/30/edward-chaney-r-b-kitaj-1932-2007-warburgian-artist/.
Chaney, Edward, review of Armstrong, 'A compulsion for antiquity', *Psychoanalysis and History* 9.1 (2007), pp. 123–30.
Chaney, Edward, '*Roma Britannica* and the cultural memory of Egypt: Lord Arundel and the Obelisk of Domitian' in David R. Marshall, Susan Russell and Karin Wolfe (eds), *Roma Britannica: Art Patronage and Cultural Exchange in Eighteenth-Century Rome* (Rome, 2011).
Chaney, Edward, *The Grand Tour and the Great Rebellion* (Geneva, 1985).
Chaney, Edward, 'The Vasari of British art: Sir John Rothenstein . . . and the importance of Wyndham Lewis', *Apollo* 132.345 (1990), pp. 322–6.
Chaney, Edward, 'Wyndham Lewis: The modernist as pioneering anti-modernist', *Modern Painters* 3.3 (1990), pp. 106–9.
'Changing faces of the temple' (24 March 2011), *Fellowship of Isis Homepage*. Available at www.foihomepage.blogspot.com.au/2011/03/changing-faces-of-temple_24.html.
'Changing faces of the temple' (13 June 2011), *Fellowship of Isis Homepage*. Available at www.foihomepage.blogspot.com.au/2011/06/changing-faces-of-temple.html.
Chauveau, Philippe, 'Christian Jacq – *Les enquêtes de Setna, la tombe maudite*', *Web Tv Culture*, 10 December 2014. Available at www.web-tv-culture.com/les-enquetes-de-setna-la-tombe-maudite-de-christian-jacq-724.htlm.
Childe, Vere G., 'Changing methods and aims in prehistory', *Proceedings of the Prehistoric Society* 1 (1935), pp. 1–15.
Childe, Vere G., *The Prehistory of European Society* (Harmondsworth, 1958).
Choucha, Nadia, *Surrealism and the Occult* (Oxford, 2016).
'Christian Jacq', *XO Editions*. Available at www.xoeditions.com/en/auteurs/christian-jacq-en/.
Christie's, *A Life's Devotion: The Collection of the Late Mrs. T.S. Eliot*, Vol. 2 (London, 2013).
Churton, Tobias, *Occult Paris: The Lost Magic of the Belle Époque* (Rochester, 2016).
'Clan Donnachaidh – Robertson: Barony of Strathloch', *Fellowship of Isis*. Available at www.fellowshipofisis.com/coatofarms.html.
Cleopatra, dir. by Joseph Mankiewicz (20th Century Fox, 1963).
'Cleopatra sets a fashion', *Essex Newsman*, 15 September 1934.
Cobbold, Evelyn, 'The first suffragette', in *Wayfarers in the Libyan Desert* (London, 1912).
Cohen, Deborah, *Household Gods: The British and their Possessions* (New Haven, 2006).
Colla, Elliott, *Conflicted Antiquities: Egyptology, Egyptomania, Egyptian Modernity* (London, 2007).
'College of Isis – training of priestesses and priests', *Fellowship of Isis Central Website*. Available at www.fellowshipofisiscentral.com/college-of-isis-training-of-priestesses-and-priests.
Collignon, Pierre L., 'Egyptian place names in relation to the diffusion of culture', *Atlantean Research* 2.2 (1949), pp. 24–30.
Collignon, Pierre L., 'The ritual significance of water' (PhD thesis, University of London, 1927).
Collins, Mabel, *The Story of Sensa: An Interpretation of the Idyll of the White Lotus* (New York, 2013).

Bibliography

Collins, Paul, and Liam McNamara, *Discovering Tutankhamun* (Oxford, 2014).
Collis, John, *The Celts: Origins, Myths, Inventions* (Stroud, 2003).
Colquhoun, Ithell, *The Sword of Wisdom: Macgregor Mathers and the Golden Dawn* (New York, 1975).
Colville, Georgiana M. M., 'Women artists, Surrealism, and animal representation', in Patricia Allmer (ed.), *Angels of Anarchy: Women Artists and Surrealism* (Munich, 2009).
Coniam, Matthew, *Egyptomania Goes to the Movies: From Archaeology to Popular Craze to Hollywood Fantasy* (Jefferson, NC, 2017).
'Contemporary art evening auction', *Sotheby's*. Available at www.sothebys.com/en/auctions/ecatalogue/2013/contemporary-art-evening-auction-l13020/lot.11.lotnum.html.
Conway, Hazel, *People's Parks: The Design and Development of Victorian Parks in Britain* (Cambridge, 1991).
Corriou, Nolwenn, '"A woman is a woman, if she had been dead five thousand centuries!": Mummy fiction, imperialism and the politics of gender', *Miranda* 11 (2015). Available at http://journals.openedition.org/miranda/6899.
Costanzo, Anthony Roth, 'Becoming Akhenaten', *YouTube*. Available at: www.youtube.com/watch?v=U0mjrcrXmp4.
Coumbe, Clement W., 'Egyptian decorative motifs', *The Jewelers' Circular*, 18 April 1923.
Cowan, Edward J., 'Myth and identity in early Medieval Scotland', *The Scottish Historical Review* 63.176 (1984), pp. 111–35.
Cowie, Susan D., and Tom Johnson, *The Mummy in Fact, Fiction and Film* (Jefferson, N C, 2002).
Cox, Jan, 'Wyndham Lewis and Francis Bacon', *Universidad de la Rioja*. Available at www.unirioja.es/listenerartcriticism/essays/essay-Wyndham-Lewis-and-Francis-Bacon.htm.
Craske, Matthew, 'Entombed like an Egyptian: An eighteenth-century surgeon's extravagant mausoleum to preserve his mortal remains', *Church Monuments* 15 (2000), pp. 71–88.
Crawford, Bryan, *Letters My Grandfather Wrote Me: Family Origins* (Bloomington, IN, 2011).
Crawford, Osbert G. S., 'Egypt as a place-name', *Notes & Queries* 10.258 (1908), pp. 447–8.
Crawford, Osbert G. S., 'Prehistoric geography', *Geographical Review* 12.2 (1922), pp. 257–63.
Crawford, Osbert G. S., 'Sir Grafton Elliot Smith: A biographical record by his colleagues. Edited by Warren R. Dawson. Cape, 1938. 12s 6d.', *Antiquity* 13.49 (1939), pp. 120–1.
Crawford, Osbert G. S., 'The origins of civilization', *Edinburgh Review* 239 (1924), pp. 101–16.
Crist, Judith, 'Cleopatra: A monumental mouse', *New York Herald Tribune*, 13 June 1963. Available at http://centennial.journalism.columbia.edu/1963-the-movies-as-art/index.html.
Crook, Paul, *Grafton Elliot Smith: Egyptology and the Diffusion of Culture: A Biographical Perspective* (Brighton, 2012).
Croteau, David R., and William D. Hoynes, *Media/Society: Industries, Images, and Audiences* (Thousand Oaks, CA, 2002).
Crowley, Aleister, 'The twins', in *The Winged Beetle* (privately printed, 1910).
Crowley, Vivianne, 'Olivia Robertson: Priestess of Isis', in Inga Bårdsen Tøllefsen and Christian Guidice (eds), *Female Leaders in New Religious Movements* (Basingstoke, 2017).
Cunliffe, Barry, *The Ancient Celts* (London, 1997).
Curl, James Stevens, *Egyptomania: The Egyptian Revival, A Recurring Theme in the History of Taste* (Manchester, 1994).
Curl, James Stevens, *The Egyptian Revival: Ancient Egypt as the Inspiration for Design Motifs in the West* (New York, 2005).
Cyrino, Monica Silveira, *Big Screen Rome* (Oxford, 2005).
Daniel, Glyn, *A Hundred Years of Archaeology* (London, 1950).
Daniel, Glyn, *The Idea of Prehistory* (Harmondsworth, 1964).
Darracott, Joseph, *The World of Charles Ricketts* (London, 1980).

Dart, Raymond A., 'Sir Grafton Elliot Smith and the *Evolution of Man*, in A. P. Elkin and N. W. G. Macintosh (eds), *Grafton Elliot Smith: The Man and his Work* (Sydney, 1974).
David, Rosalie, *The Pyramid Builders of Ancient Egypt: A Modern Investigation of Pharaoh's Workforce* (London, 1992).
Davis, Ben, 'Bacon, half-baked', *Artnet*. Available at www.artnet.com/magazineus/reviews/davis/francis-bacon-gilles-deleuze7-28-09.asp.
Dawson, Warren R., *Sir Grafton Elliot Smith: A Biographical Record by His Colleagues* (London, 1938).
Dawson, Warren R. and P. H. K. Gray, *Catalogue of Egyptian Antiquities in the British Museum*, Vol. 1 (London, 1968).
Day, Jasmine, *The Mummy's Curse: Mummymania in the English-Speaking World* (London, 2006).
Day, Jasmine, 'The rape of the mummy: Women, horror fiction and the Westernisation of the curse', in Pablo Atoche-Peña, Conrado Rodríguez-Martin and Ángeles Ramírez-Rodríguez (eds), *Mummies and Science: World Mummies Research, Proceedings of the VI World Congress on Mummy Studies* (Santa Cruz de Tenerife, 2008).
Deane, Bradley, 'Mummy fiction and the occupation of Egypt: Imperial striptease', *English Literature in Transition, 1880–1920* 51.4 (2008), pp. 381–410.
Deeb, Muhammad A., 'Alexandria as E.M. Forster's rainbow bridge to the Middle East & India: A comparative inquiry', *Canadian Review of Comparative Literature* 37 (2010), pp. 10–23.
Deffries, Amelia, 'At Wembley', *The American Magazine of Art* 15.7 (1924), pp. 386–7.
Deleuze, Gilles, *Francis Bacon: The Logic of Sensation* (New York; London, 2003).
Derricourt, Robin, *Antiquity Imagined: The Remarkable Legacy of Egypt and the Ancient Near East* (London, 2015).
Derricourt, Robin, *Inventing Africa: History, Archaeology and Ideas* (London, 2011).
'Desert fashions', *Yorkshire Evening Post*, 3 January 1923.
Devizes Museum, Passmore to Goddard, 20 June 1936.
Dick, Bernard F., 'In the entertainment world: *Cleopatra*', *The Classical World* 57.1 (1963), pp. 35–6.
Dismorr, Jessica, 'London notes', *Blast* 2 (1915), p. 66.
Dobson, Eleanor, 'Cross-dressing scholars and mummies in drag: Egyptology and queer identity', *Aegyptiaca: Journal of the History of the Reception of Ancient Egypt* 4 (2019), pp. 1–22.
Dobson, Eleanor, 'Gods and ghost-light: Ancient Egypt, electricity, and X-rays', *Victorian Literature and Culture* 45.1 (2017), pp. 119–35.
Dobson, Eleanor, 'Literature and culture in the golden age of Egyptology' (PhD thesis, University of Birmingham, 2016).
Dobson, Eleanor, 'The sphinx at the séance: Literature, Spiritualism and psycho-archaeology', in Eleanor Dobson and Gemma Banks (eds), *Excavating Modernity: Physical, Temporal and Psychological Stratification in Literature, 1900–1930* (London, 2018).
Dodson, Aidan, 'Duke Alexander's sarcophagi', *Archiv Orientální* 70 (2002), pp. 329–36.
Dodson, Aidan, 'Legends of a sarcophagus', in Thomas Schneider and Kasia Maria Szpakowska (eds), *Egyptian Stories: A British Egyptological Tribute to Alan B. Lloyd* (Münster, 2007).
Douglas-Hamilton, Alasdair, *Lord of the Skies*, 2nd edn (London, 2015).
Dowd, Maureen, 'Richard Burton, 58, is dead; Rakish stage and screen star', *The New York Times*, 6 August 1984.
Doyle, Noreen, 'The earliest known uses of "l'égyptomanie"/"Egyptomania" in French and English', *Journal of Ancient Egyptian Interconnections* 8 (2016), pp. 122–5.
Draï, Raphaël, 'Egyptologues ou bibliocastes? Christian Jacq, Christiane Desroches Noblecourt, Jan Assmann', *Pardès* 38.1 (2005), pp. 153–69.
Dromard, Thiébault, 'Christian Jacq ou le bon filon de Bernard Fixot', *Le Figaro*, 15 February 2013.

Bibliography

'Druid Clan of Dana', *Fellowship of Isis*. Available at www.fellowshipofisis.com/druidclanofdana.html.

'Druid Clan of Dana groves', *Fellowship of Isis*. Available at www.fellowshipofisis.com/directory_groves.html.

'Druid Clan of Dana – the faery seat', *Fellowship of Isis Central Website*. Available at www.fellowshipofisiscentral.com/druid-clan-of-dana--the-faery-seat.

'Duke of Hamilton recovering', *Morning Post*, 31 July 1850.

Dümichen, Johannes, *Historische Inschriften Altägyptischer Denkmäler* (Leipzig, 1869).

Durieux, Isabelle, 'Christian Jacq: Avec la bénédiction des pharaons', *L'Express*, 6 March 1997.

Ebeling, Florian, *The Secret History of Hermes Trismegistus: Hermeticism from Ancient to Modern Times* (Ithaca, 2007).

Edgecombe, Rodney Stenning, 'James Murphy, Shelley and a Stanza in *Adonais*', *Keats-Shelley Review* 15.1 (2001), pp. 86–7.

Edwards, Amelia B., *A Thousand Miles Up the Nile*, 2nd edn (London, 1888).

Edwards, Paul, *Wyndham Lewis: Painter and Writer* (New Haven; London, 2000).

Edwards, Paul, 'Wyndham Lewis and Nietzsche: How much truth does a man require?', in Giovanni Cianci (ed.), *Wyndham Lewis: Letteratura/Pittura* (Palermo, 1982).

Edwards, Paul, 'Wyndham Lewis's Timon of Athens portfolio: The emergence of Vorticist abstraction', *Apollo* (October 1998), pp. 34–40.

'Egypt's black arts: Scientists ridicule theory', *Daily Herald* (Adelaide), 9 April 1923.

El Daly, Okasha, *Egyptology: The Missing Millennium: Ancient Egypt in Medieval Arabic Writings* (London, 2005).

Eliot, T. S., 'The burial of the dead', in T. S. Eliot, *The Poems of T.S. Eliot*, Vol 1: *Collected and Uncollected Poems*, Christopher Ricks and Jim McCue (eds) (London, 2015).

Eliot, T. S., *The Letters of T.S. Eliot*, Vol. 2, Valerie Eliot and Hugh Haughton (eds) (London, 2009).

Elliott, Bridget, 'Art Deco worlds in a tomb: Reanimating Egypt in Modern(ist) visual culture', *South Central Review* 25.1 (2008), pp. 114–35.

Elliot Smith, G. 'Freud's speculations in ethnology', *The Monist* 33.1 (1923), pp. 81–97.

Elliot Smith, G., *The Ancient Egyptians and the Origin of Civilization* (London; New York, 1911).

Ellis, Ralph, *Scota, Egyptian Queen of the Scots* (Cheshire, 2006).

Engleheart George, and Pierre L. Collignon, 'Two Egyptian limestone scarabs found in Wiltshire', *Wiltshire Archaeological and Natural History Magazine* 47.164 (1936), pp. 412–19.

Engleheart, George, and Percy Newberry, 'Two scarabs found in Wiltshire', *Man* 35 (1935), pp. 120–1.

Evans, Godfrey, 'Alexander, 10th Duke of Hamilton (1767–1852) as patron and collector' (PhD thesis, University of Edinburgh, 2009).

Evans, Lorraine, *Kingdom of the Ark: The Startling Story of How the Ancient British Race is Descended from the Pharaohs* (London, 2000).

Ewing, Elizabeth and Alice Mackrell, *History of Twentieth Century Fashion* (London, 2001).

Falcetta, Alessandro, 'James Rendel Harris: A life on the quest', *Quaker Studies* 8.2 (2003), pp. 208–25.

Falconnier, Isabelle, 'Christian Jacq: un Egyptien à Blonay', *L'Hebdo*, 18 December 2014.

Fares, Leila, 'Féminisme et anachronisme dans les romans de Christian Jacq sur l'Egypte ancienne' (PhD thesis, University of Florida, 2009).

Faulkner, Raymond O., *The Ancient Egyptian Book of the Dead* (New York, 1985).

Faulkner, Raymond O., *The Egyptian Book of the Dead: The Book of Going Forth by Day* (San Francisco, 2008).

'Fellowship of Isis enrollment', *Fellowship of Isis*. Available at www.fellowshipofisis.com/joinform.html.

'Fellowship of Isis priesthood', *Fellowship of Isis*. Available at www.fellowshipofisis.com/priesthood.html.

Ferguson, Christine, 'Victoria-arcana and the misogynistic poetics of resistance in Iain Sinclair's *White Chappell Scarlet Tracings* and Alan Moore's *From Hell*', *LIT: Literature Interpretation Theory* 20.1–2 (2009), pp. 45–64.

Fidler, Florence G., 'The position of women under the Hammurabi Code', *English Review* 15 (1913), pp. 422–9.

Fields, Jill, 'Fighting the corsetless evil: Shaping corsets and culture, 1900–1930', *Journal of Social History* 33.2 (1999), pp. 355–84.

Finneran, Richard J., George Mills Harper, William M. Murphy and Alan B. Himber (eds), *Letters to W. B. Yeats* (London, 1977).

Finucane, R. C. 'Sacred corpse, profane carrion: Social ideals and death rituals in the later Middle Ages', in Joachim Whaley (ed.), *Mirrors of Mortality: Studies in the Social History of Death* (New York, 1981).

Fischer, Craig, and Charles Hatfield, 'Foreword', in Alan Moore and Eddie Campbell, *The From Hell Companion* (London, 2013).

Fisher, Lauren Alexis, 'The '60s films that every fashion girl should watch', *Harper's Bazaar*, 27 January 2015. Available at http://www.harpersbazaar.com/culture/film-tv/a9768/fashion-films-from-the-1960s/.

Fleischhack, Maria, *Narrating Ancient Egypt: The Representation of Ancient Egypt in Nineteenth-century and Early-Twentieth-century Fantastic Fiction* (Frankfurt, 2016).

Fleischhack, Maria, 'Possession, trance, and reincarnation: Confrontations with ancient Egypt in Edwardian fiction', *Victoriographies* 7.3 (2017), pp. 257–70.

Fletcher, Angus, 'Ezra Pound's Egypt and the origin of the "Cantos"', *Twentieth Century Literature* 48.1 (2002), pp. 1–21.

Ford, Elizabeth A., and Deborah Mitchell, *Royal Portraits in Hollywood: Filming the Lives of Queens* (Lexington, 2009).

Forman, Micki, 'Tutmania', *Dress* 4 (1982), pp. 7–16.

Forster, E. M., *A Passage to India*, Oliver Stallybrass (ed.) (London, 1978).

Forster, E. M., *Abinger Harvest* and *England's Pleasant Land*, Elizabeth Heine (ed.) (London, 1996).

Forster, E. M., *Alexandria: A History and a Guide; and, Pharos and Pharillon*, Miriam Allott (ed.) (London, 2004).

Forster, E. M., *Aspects of the Novel, and Related Writings*, Oliver Stallybrass (ed.) (London, 1974).

Forster, E. M., 'Cnidus', *Independent Review*, March 1904.

Forster, E. M., *Goldsworthy Loves Dickinson* (London, 1973).

Forster, E. M., 'Malconia Shops', *Independent Review*, November 1903.

Forster, E. M., *Maurice*, P. Gardner (ed.) (London, 1999).

Forster, E. M., *Selected letters of E. M. Forster*, Vol. 1: *1879–1920*, Mary Lago and P. N. Furbank (eds) (London, 1983).

Forster, E. M., *The Life to Come, and Other Stories*, Oliver Stallybrass (ed.) (London, 1972).

Forster, E. M., 'The objects', *The Athenaeum*, 7 May 1920, pp. 599–600.

Forster, E. M., *The Uncollected Egyptian Essays of E. M. Forster*, Hilda D. Spear and Abdel Moneim Aly (eds) (Dundee, 1988).

Forster, E. M., and Constantine P. Cavafy, *The Forster-Cavafy Letters: Friends at a Slight Angle*, Peter Jeffreys (ed.) (Cairo, 2009).

Foss, Michael, *The Search for Cleopatra* (London, 1997).

Foucault, Michel, 'Of other spaces, heterotopias', *Foucault, Info*. Available at https://foucault.info/doc/documents/heterotopia/foucault-heterotopia-en-html.

Bibliography

Fowden, Garth, *The Egyptian Hermes: A Historical Approach to the Late Pagan Mind* (Princeton, 1986).
Fox, Robin Lane, *Alexander the Great* (London, 1971).
'Francis Douce, Esq. F.S.A.', *The Gentleman's Magazine* 2 (1834), pp. 212–17.
Francis, Marilyn, 'Form follows fashionable function: The look of the Egyptian XVIII Dynasty', *Dress* 4.1 (1982), pp. 1–6.
Frankel, Nicholas, 'Second series of sphinx illustrations (1923)', *Open Stax*. Available at: https://cnx.org/contents/0nqwZZGI@1/Second-Series-of-Sphinx-Illust.
Frankel, Nicholas, '"The Sphinx," by Oscar Wilde, with decorations by Charles Ricketts (1894), *Open Stax*. Available at: http://cnx.org/contents/TuaO_Mx2@2/The-Sphinx-by-Oscar-Wilde-with.
Frankfort, Henri, *Ancient Egyptian Religion: An Interpretation* (New York, 2012).
Frandsen, Paul John, 'Philip Glass's "Akhnaten"', *The Musical Quarterly* 77.2 (1993), pp. 241–67.
Frayling, Christopher, *The Face of Tutankhamun* (London, 1992).
Freud Museum, *Leaving Today: The Freuds in Exile*, Julia Hoffbrand (ed.) (London, 2018).
Freud, Sigmund, *Civilization and Its Discontents*, trans. Joan Riviere (London, 1982).
Freud, Sigmund, *Moses and Monotheism* (London, 1939).
Friedan, Betty, *The Feminine Mystique* (New York, 1963).
Freidman, Susan Stanford (ed.), *Analysing Freud: Letters of H.D. Bryher and their Circle* (New York, 2002).
Fritze, Ronald H., *Egyptomania: A History of Fascination, Obsession and Fantasy* (London, 2016).
From Hell, dir. the Hughes Brothers (2001).
Fry, Roger, *Last Lectures* (London, 1939).
Fryxell, Allegra, 'Tutankhamun, Egyptomania, and temporal enchantment in interwar Britain', *Twentieth Century British History* 27.4 (2017), pp. 516–54.
Furbank, P. N., *E. M. Forster: A Life*, Vol. 2 (New York, 1978).
Gange, David, *Dialogues with the Dead: Egyptology in British Culture and Religion, 1822–1922* (Oxford, 2013).
Gaskill, Malcolm, *Witchcraft: A Very Short Introduction* (Oxford, 2010).
Gaucher, André, 'Isis à Montmartre', *L'Écho du merveilleux: Revue bimensuelle* 94 & 95 (1990), pp. 446–53, 470–3.
Gautier, Gilberte, *Cartier: The Legend* (London, 1983).
Gautier, Émile-Félix, *L'Islamisation de l'Afrique du Nord: les Siecles obscurs du Maghreb* (Paris, 1927).
Gauthier, Xavière, *Léonor Fini* (Paris, 1973).
Geczy, Adam, *Fashion and Orientalism: Dress, Textiles and Culture from the 17th to the 21st Century* (London, 2013).
Geertz, Clifford, *The Interpretation of Cultures: Selected Essays* (New York, 1973).
Gibson, Mel, *Remembered Reading: Memory, Comics and Postwar Constructions of British Girlhood* (Leuwen, 2015).
Gilbert, R. A., *The Golden Dawn Scrapbook* (York Beach, 1997).
Giles, Judy, *The Parlour and the Suburb: Domestic Identities, Class, Femininity and Modernity* (Oxford, 2004).
Gittings, Clare, *Death, Burial and the Individual in Early Modern England* (London, 1984).
Glanert, Ludwig, 'Scarabs in Wiltshire', *Man* 35 (1935), p. 176.
Gombrich, Ernst H., *Art and Illusion* (London, 1960).
Gombrich, Ernst H., *In Search of Cultural History* (Oxford, 1969).
Gombrich, Ernst H., *Meditations on a Hobby Horse*, 2nd edn (London, 1971).
Gombrich, Ernst H., *The Story of Art* (London, 1950).

Gordon, Alexander, *An Essay Towards Explaining the Hieroglyphical Figures, on the Coffin of the Ancient Mummy Belonging to Capt. William Lethieullier* (London, 1737).
Gordon, Alexander, *Essay Towards Explaining the Hieroglyphical Figures, on the Egyptian Mummy, in the Museum of Doctor Mead, Physician in Ordinary to His Majesty* (London, 1737).
Gorer, Geoffrey, *Death, Grief and Mourning in Contemporary Britain* (Salem, 1965).
Gosson, Stephen, *School of Abuse* (London, 1579).
Graf, Susan Johnston, *W. B. Yeats Twentieth Century Magus* (York Beach, 2000).
Gramantieri, Riccardo, *Metafisica dell'evoluzione in A. E. van Vogt* (Bologna, 2011).
Gramantieri, Riccardo, 'William Burroughs e il complotto contro l'umanità', in Riccardo Gramantieri and Giuseppe Panella, *Ipotesi di complotto* (Chieti, 2012).
Grangeray, Emilie, 'Christian Jacq, la saga du "petit scribe"', *Le Monde*, 20 March 2009.
Gray, John, *Seven Types of Atheism* (London, 2018).
Green, Miranda, 'Isis at Thornborough', *Recs of Bucks* 25 (1983), pp. 139–41.
Greenhill, Thomas, Νεκροκηδεία, *or The Art of Embalming; Wherein Is Shewn the Right of Burial, the Funeral Ceremonies, and the Several Ways of Preserving Dead Bodies in Most Nations of the World* (London, 1705).
Greer, Mary Katherine, *Women of the Golden Dawn: Rebels and Priestesses* (Rochester, 1995).
Griffith, Francis Llewellyn, *Stories of the High Priests of Memphis: The Sethon of Herodotus and The Demotic Tales of Khamuas*, Vol. 1(Oxford, 1900).
Griffiths, J. Gwyn, 'Some claims of xenoglossy in the ancient languages', in *Atlantis & Egypt with Other Selected Essays* (Cardiff, 1991).
Grodent, Michel, 'A la foire du livre: Christian Jacq et *L'affaire Toutankhamon*, vive le romanesque!', *Le Soir*, 22 April 1993.
Grodent, Michel, '*Le Temple des millions d'années*, la fiction fait des enfants à l'histoire', *Le Soir*, 3 April 1996
Grout, James, 'Was Cleopatra beautiful?', *Encyclopaedia Romana*. Available at http://penelope.uchicago.edu/~grout/encyclopaedia_romana/miscellanea/cleopatra/bust.html.
Gombrich, E. H., *Art and Illusion* (London, 1960).
Gombrich, E. H., *Meditations on a Hobby Horse*, 2nd edn (London, 1971).
Gombrich, E. H., *The Story of Art* (London, 1950).
Gronberg, Tag, *Designs on Modernity* (Manchester, 1998).
Gautier, Théophile, *L'Islamisation de l'Afrique du Nord: les Siecles obscurs du Maghreb* (Paris, 1927).
Habenstein, Robert W. and William M. Lamers, *The History of American Funeral Directing* (Milwaukee, 1955).
Hadley, John, 'An account of a mummy, inspected at London 1763', *Philosophical Transactions* 54 (1764), pp. 1–14.
Hadot, Pierre, *The Veil of Isis: An Essay on the History of the Idea of Nature* (Cambridge, 2006).
Haggard, H. Rider, *She*, Daniel Karlin (ed.) (Oxford, 1991).
Haggard, H. Rider, *Ayesha: The Return of She* (London, 2013).
Haldon, John, and Leslie Brubaker, *Byzantium in the Iconoclast era c. 680-850* (Cambridge, 2011).
Halim, Hala, *Alexandrian Cosmopolitanism: An Archive* (New York, 2013).
Hamer, Mary, *Signs of Cleopatra* (London, 1993).
Hamel, Frank, *Werewolves, BirdWomen, TigerMen and Other Human Animals* (New York, 2007).
'Hamilton Mausoleum (South Lanarkshire)', *The Mausolea & Monuments Trust*. Available at www.mmtrust.org.uk/mausolea/view/501/Hamilton_Mausoleum_South_Lanarkshire.
Hamlett, Jane, *Material Relations: Domestic Interiors and Middle-Class Families in England, 1850-1910* (Manchester, 2010).
Harper, George Mills, *Yeats's Golden Dawn* (London, 1974).

Bibliography

Harris, James R., *Egypt in Britain* (Cambridge, 1927).
Harris, James R., *The Builders of Stonehenge* (Cambridge, 1932).
Harris, Oliver, *William Burroughs and the Secret of Fascination* (Carbondale, 2003).
Harrison, Paul, *The Curse of the Pharaohs' Tombs: Tales of the Unexpected Since the Days of Tutankhamun* (Barnsley, 2017).
Hartwig, Melinda K., *A Companion to Ancient Egyptian Art* (Oxford, 2015).
Hauser, Kitty, *Bloody Old Britain* (London, 2008).
'Have you read?', *The World's News* (Sydney), 13 June 1925. Available at: http://trove.nla.gov.au/newspaper/article/130620902.
Hawass, Zahi, 'The search for Hatshepsut and the discovery of her mummy', June 2007, *Guardian's Egypt*. Available at www.guardians.net/hawass/hatshepsut/search_for_hatshepsut.htm.
Hayward, Helena, *World Furniture: An Illustrated History* (London, 1965).
H.D., *Tribute to Freud* (Manchester, 1985).
Head, Philip, 'Death and the monad', *The Wyndham Lewis Society*. Available at www.wyndhamlewis.org/images/WLA/2001/wla-2001-head.pdf.
Head, Philip, *Engaging the Enemy: The Gentle Art of Contradiction in the Work of Wyndham Lewis* (Borough Green, 2001).
Hermanson, Tove, 'Cleopatra and Egyptian fashion in film', *Huffington Post*, 4 June 2010. Available at https://www.huffingtonpost.com/tove-hermanson/cleopatra-and-egyptian-fa_b_447708.html.
Hessler, Peter, 'Into the pharaoh's chamber: How I fell in love with ancient Egypt', *Guardian*, 26 April 2019. Available at https://www.theguardian.com/news/2019/apr/26/ancient-egypt-amarna-akhenaten-rebel-king-arab-spring-revolution.
Heymann, C. David, *Liz: An Intimate Biography of Elizabeth Taylor* (London, 1995).
Hill, J., 'Colour in ancient Egypt', *Ancient Egypt Online*. Available at http://ancientegyptonline.co.uk/colour.html.
Ho, Elizabeth, 'Postimperial landscapes: "Psychogeography" and Englishness in Alan Moore's graphic novel *From Hell: A Melodrama in Sixteen Parts*', *Cultural Critique* 63 (2006), pp. 99–121.
Hoberman, Ruth, 'In quest of a museal aura: Turn of the century narratives about museum-displayed objects', *Victorian Literature and Culture* 31.2 (2003), pp. 467–82.
Hoberman, Ruth, *Museum Trouble: Edwardian Fiction and the Emergence of Modernism* (Charlottesville, VA, 2011).
Hockey, Jenny, 'Changing death rituals', in Jenny Hockey, Jeanne Katz and Neil Small (eds), *Grief, Mourning and Death Ritual* (Buckingham, PA, 2001).
Hockney, David, *That's the Way I See It: David Hockney*, Nikos Stangos (ed.) (London, 1993).
Hogg, Mary W., 'The position of women four millenniums ago in Egypt and Babylonia', *The Englishwoman* 21.7 (1910), pp. 268–76.
'Hope Abbey Mausoleum', *Eugene Masonic Cemetery*. Available at: www.eugenemasoniccemetery.org/mausoleum.html.
Hopman, Ellen Evert, *A Legacy of Druids: Conversations with Druid Leaders of Britain, the USA and Canada, Past and Present* (Winchester, 2016).
Hornung, Erik, *The Ancient Egyptian Books of the Afterlife*, trans. David Lorton (Ithaca; London, 1999).
Hornung, Erik, *The Secret Lore of Egypt: Its Impact on the West* (Ithaca, 2001).
Houen, Alex, 'William S. Burroughs's Cities of the Red Night Trilogy: Writing outer space', *Journal of American Studies* 40.3 (2006), pp. 523–49.
Hoving, Thomas, *Tutankhamun: The Untold Story* (London, 1979).

Bibliography

Howard Carter Collection, Griffith Institute, University of Oxford, Burton photograph p0154a. Available at www.griffith.ox.ac.uk/gri/carter/091-p0154a.html.
Howard Carter Collection, Burton photographs p0313-p0317. Available at www.griffith.ox.ac.uk/gri/carter/108.html.
Howard Carter Collection, Burton photograph p0353. Available at www.griffith.ox.ac.uk/gri/carter/083-p0353.html.
Howard Carter Collection, Carter no. 083. Available at www.griffith.ox.ac.uk/gri/carter/.
Howard Carter Collection, Carter no. 091. Available at www.griffith.ox.ac.uk/gri/carter/091.html.
Howard Carter Collection, Carter no. 108. Available at www.griffith.ox.ac.uk/gri/carter/108.html.
Howard Carter Collection, Carter MSS i.G.3. Available at www.griffith.ox.ac.uk/gri/4camaps.html.
'Howard Mausoleum (North Yorkshire)', *The Mausolea & Monuments Trust*. Available at www.mmtrust.org.uk/mausolea/view/199/Howard_Mausoleum_North_Yorkshire.
Howe, Ellic, *The Magicians of the Golden Dawn* (London, 1972).
Hubert, Renée Riese, *Magnifying Mirrors: Women, Surrealism, & Partnership* (Lincoln, 1994).
Hughes, Anthony, 'Authority, authenticity and aura: Walter Benjamin and the case of Michelangelo', in Anthony Hughes and Erich Ranfft (eds), *Sculpture and its Reproductions* (London, 1997).
Hughes-Hallett, Lucy, *Cleopatra: Queen, Lover, Legend* (London, 2006).
Hulme, T. E., *Speculations*, Herbert Read (ed.) (London, 1924).
Humbert, Jean-Marcel, Michael Pantazzi, and Christiane Zeigler, *Egyptomania: Egypt in Western Art 1730–1930* (Ottawa, 1994).
Humbert, Jean-Marcel and Clifford Price, 'Introduction: An architecture between dream and meaning', in Jean-Marcel Humbert and Clifford Price (eds), *Imhotep Today: Egyptianizing Architecture* (London, 2003).
Hume, Kathryn, 'Books of the dead: Postmodern politics in novels by Mailer, Burroughs, Acker, and Pynchon', *Modern Philology* 97.3 (2000), pp. 417–44.
Humphreys, Richard, 'Tut', in *Wyndham Lewis (1881–1957)* (Madrid, 2010).
Huntington, Richard, and Peter Metcalf, *Celebrations of Death: The Anthropology of Mortuary Ritual* (Cambridge, 1979).
In the Beginning, dir. Michael Gill, *BBC*, 29 September 1975.
Ingleheart, Jennifer, 'Responding to Ovid's Pygmalion episode and receptions of same-sex love in classical antiquity: Art, homosexuality, and the curatorship of classical culture in E. M. Forster's "The Classical Annex"', *Classical Receptions Journal* 7.2 (2014), pp. 141–58.
'Introduction to the Fellowship of Isis', *Fellowship of Isis*. Available at www.fellowshipofisis.com/intro.html.
Ireson, Nancy, and Simonetta Fraquelli, *Modigliani* (London, 2017).
Irwin, John T., *American Hieroglyphics: The Symbol of the Egyptian Hieroglyphics and the American Renaissance* (Baltimore, 1980).
'Isiger Ford Building (Klamath Falls, Oregon), *Oregon Digital*. Available at: https://oregondigital.org/catalog/oregondigital:df67qh08t.
Iskin, Ruth, 'Material women: The department-store fashion poster in Paris, 1880–1900', in Maureen Goggin and Beth Tobin (eds), *Material Women, 1750–1950: Consuming Desires and Collecting Practices* (Farnham, 2009).
Ismail, Matthew, *Wallis Budge: Magic and Mummies in London and Cairo* (Kilkerran, 2011).
Jackson, Lee, *Dirty Old London: The Victorian Fight Against Filth* (New Haven, 2014).
Jacq, Christian, *Ramsès: La Bataille de Kadesh* (Paris, 1996).
Jacq, Christian, *Le Fils de la lumière* (Paris, 1995).
Jacq, Christian, *Ramsès: Sous l'acaccia d'occident* (Paris, 1996).
Jalland, Pat, *Death in the Victorian Family* (Oxford, 1996).

Bibliography

James, Thomas Henry Garnett, *Howard Carter: The Path to Tutankhamun* (London, 2006).

Jeffreys, David (ed.), *Views of Ancient Egypt since Napoleon Bonaparte: Imperialism, Colonialism and Modern Appropriations* (London, 2007).

Jenkins, Henry, 'Cult conversations: Interview with Julia Round', *Confessions of an Aca-Fan*, 15 November 2018. Available at http://henryjenkins.org/blog/2018/11/9/cult-conversations-interview-with-julia-round-part-ii.

'John Darnell', *Yale Macmillan Centre*. Available at: http://cmes.macmillan.yale.edu/people/john-darnell.

Johnson, Paul, *A History of the Jews* (London, 1987).

Johnston, Allan, 'Consumption, addiction, vision, energy: Political economies and utopian visions in the writings of the Beat Generation', *College Literature* 32.2 (2005), pp. 103–26.

Jones, Inigo, *The Most Notable Antiquity of Great Britain Vulgarly Called Stonehenge* (London, 1655).

Jones, Jonathan, 'Modigliani review – "a gorgeous show about a slightly silly artist"', *Guardian*, 21 November 2017. Available at https://www.theguardian.com/artanddesign/2017/nov/21/modigliani-review-tate-modern-a-gorgeous-show-about-a-slightly-silly-artist.

Judge, Ben, '24 June 1916: Mary Pickford becomes Hollywood's first million-dollar actress', *Moneyweek Magazine*, 24 June 2015. Available at https://moneyweek.com/24-june-1916-mary-pickford-becomes-hollywoods-first-million-dollar-actress/.

Justyne, William, *Guide to Highgate Cemetery* (London, 1865).

Kalogera, Lucy Shepard, *Yeats's Celtic Mysteries* (Florida, 1977).

Kamp, David, 'When Liz met Dick', *Vanity Fair*, April 1998. Available at www.vanityfair.com/news/1998/03/elizabeth-taylor-199803.

Kantorowicz, Ernst H., *The King's Two Bodies: A Study in Mediaeval Political Theology* (Princeton, 1957).

Kashner, Sam, and Nancy Schoenberger, *Furious Love: Elizabeth Taylor, Richard Burton, The Marriage of the Century* (London, 2010).

Keble College records, Keble College, Oxford, University of Oxford, KC/ACA 1 A/5 Collections Register, 1910–1919.

Kelley, Kitty, *Elizabeth Taylor: The Last Star* (London, 1981).

Kemp, Barry, *Ancient Egypt: Anatomy of a Civilisation* (London, 2006).

Kendrick, Tracy, *Cartier Viewed by Sottsass* (Houston, 2005).

Kenner, Hugh, 'Hoodopip', *Agenda* 7.3-8.1 (1969–70), p. 183.

Kerr, Charles, 'Up above them towered his beautiful pale face', in H. Rider Haggard, *She: A History of Adventure* (London, 1911), p. 103. Available at: www.visualhaggard.org/illustrations/526.

Khalil, Radwa, Ahmed A. Moustafa, Marie Z. Moffat and Ahmed A. Karim, 'How knowledge of ancient Egyptian women can influence today's gender role: Does history matter in gender psychology', *Frontiers in Psychology* 7 (2017), pp. 1–7.

King, Francis, *Modern Ritual Magic: The Rise of Western Occultism* (Bridport, 1989).

King, Susan, '*Cleopatra*, a spectacle on- and off-screen', *Los Angeles Times*, 20 May 2013. Available at http://articles.latimes.com/2013/may/20/entertainment/la-et-mn-classic-hollywood-cleopatra-20130520.

Kitaj, R. B., *Second Diasporist Manifesto* (New Haven, 2007).

Kors, Michael, 'Michael Kors talks to Dame Elizabeth Taylor', *Harper's Bazaar*, 23 March 2011. Available at http://www.harpersbazaar.com/celebrity/latest/news/a699/michael-kors-talks-to-elizabeth-taylor/.

Korzybski, Alfred, *Science and Sanity: An Introduction to Non-Aristotelian Systems and General Semantics*, 5th edn (New York, 2000).

Bibliography

Korzybski, Alfred, 'The role of language in the perceptual process', in Robert R. Blake and Glenn V. Ramsey (eds), *Perception: An Approach to Personality* (New York, 1951).
Kovacs, George, and C. W. Marshall (eds), *Classics and Comics* (Oxford, 2011).
Kovacs, George, and C. W. Marshall (eds), *Son of Classics and Comics* (Oxford, 2015).
Kniveton, Emma, 'The enduring influence of *Cleopatra*', *Express*, 27 May 2013. Available at https://www.express.co.uk/life-style/style/402820/The-enduring-influence-of-Cleopatra.
Lafourcade, Bernard, 'The taming of the wild body', in Jeffrey Meyers (ed.), *Wyndham Lewis: A Revaluation* (London, 1980).
Lang, Elsie M., *British Women in the Twentieth Century* (London, 1929).
Lant, Antonia, 'The curse of the pharaoh, or how cinema contracted Egyptomania', *October* 59 (1992), pp. 86–112.
'Last will and Testament of Alexander Hamilton, Duke of Hamilton and Brandon
Laver, James, *Women's Dress in the Jazz Age* (London, 1964).
LaVine, W. Robert, and Florio Allen, *In a Glamorous Fashion: The Fabulous Years of Hollywood Costume Design* (New York, 1980).
Lawrence, D. H., *Etruscan Places: Travels through Forgotten Italy* (London, 2011).
Lawrence, Diane, *Genteel Women: Empire and Domestic Material Culture, 1840–1910* (Manchester, 2012).
Leathem, Eviem 'Beauty flashback: Elizabeth Taylor, *Cleopatra* 1963', *Daily Telegraph*, 12 June 2015. Available at http://www.telegraph.co.uk/beauty/people/Elizabeth-Taylor-beauty-Cleopatra/.
Lecoultre, Cécile, 'Christian Jacq, le pharaon s'encanaille dans le techno-thriller', *La Tribune de Genève*, 12 November 2016.
Leerssen, Joep, 'Celticism', in Terence Brown (ed.), *Celticism* (Amsterdam, 1996).
Lees, Frederic, 'Isis worship in Paris: Conversations with the Hierophant Rameses and the High Priestess Anari', *The Humanitarian* 16.2 (1900), pp. 82–7.
Legrand, Dominique, 'Les recettes de Christian Jacq', *Le Soir*, 13 February 2010.
Leigh, Nigel, *Radical Fictions and the Novels of Norman Mailer* (Berlin, 1990).
Lennon, Joseph, *Irish Orientalism: A Literary and Intellectual History* (Syracuse, 2004).
Leonard, Suzanne, 'The true love of Elizabeth Taylor and Richard Burton', in Vicki Callahan (ed.), *Reclaiming the Archive: Feminism and Film History* (Detroit, 2010).
Lethaby, William, *Architecture, Mysticism and Myth* (London, 1892).
Levine, Philippa, *The Amateur and the Professional: Antiquarians, Historians and Archaeologists in Victorian England 1838–1886* (Cambridge, 1986).
Levy, Julian, *Memoir of an Art Gallery* (New York, 1977).
Lévy-Willard, Annette, 'Christian Jacq, le nouveau pharaon', *Libération*, 9 May 1996.
Lewiecki-Wilson, Cynthia, *Writing Against the Family: Gender in Lawrence and Joyce* (Carbondale, 1994).
Lewis, Wyndham, 'Review of contemporary art', *Blast* 2 (1915), pp. 38–47.
Lewis, Wyndham, *America, I Presume* (London, 1940).
Lewis, Wyndham, *Art and Letters* 2.1 (1918–1919).
Lewis, Wyndham, *Blasting and Bombardiering* (London, 1937).
Lewis, Wyndham, *Creatures of Habit and Creatures of Change: Essays on Art, Literature and Society 1914–1956*, Paul Edwards (ed.) (Santa Rosa, 1989).
Lewis, Wyndham, *Enemy of the Stars* (London, 1927).
Lewis, Wyndham, 'Essay on the objective of plastic art in our time', *The Tyro: A Review of the Arts of Painting, Sculpture and Design* 2 (1922), pp. 21–37.
Lewis, Wyndham, *Filibusters in Barbary* (London, 1932).
Lewis, Wyndham, *Left Wings over Europe: Or, How to Make a War about Nothing* (London, 1936).

Bibliography

Lewis, Wyndham, *Men without Art*, Seamus Cooney (ed.) (Santa Rosa, 1987).
Lewis, Wyndham, *Paleface: The Philosophy of the 'Melting-Pot* (London, 1929).
Lewis, Wyndham, 'Round the London galleries', *The Listener* 42.1086 (1949), p. 860.
Lewis, Wyndham, *The Caliph's Design* (London, 1919).
Lewis, Wyndham, *The Demon of Progress in the Arts* (London, 1954).
Lewis, Wyndham, *The Diabolical Principle and the Dithyrambic Spectator* (London, 1931).
Lewis, Wyndham, *The Mysterious Mr Bull* (London, 1938).
Lewis, Wyndham, *The Tyro: A Review of the Arts of Painting, Sculpture and Design* 2 (1922).
Lewis, Wyndham, *The Revenge for Love*, R. W. Dasenbrock (ed.) (Santa Rosa, 1991).
Lewis, Wyndham, 'The war baby', *Art and Letters* 2.1 (1918–1919), pp. 14–41.
Lewis, Wyndham, *Time and Western Man*, Paul Edwards (ed.) (Santa Rosa, 1993).
Lewis, Wyndham, *Wyndham Lewis on Art*, Walter Michel and C.J. Fox (eds) (London, 1969).
Lewis, Wyndham, and Ezra Pound, *Pound/Lewis: The Letters of Ezra Pound and Wyndham Lewis*, Timothy Materer (ed.) (London, 1985).
Lichtheim, Miriam, *Ancient Egyptian Literature*, Vol. 2 (Berkeley, 2006).
Lisse, Michel, 'La fiction: prothèse de l'histoire', *Interférences littéraires* 2 (2002), pp. 58–68.
Litten, Julian, 'Tombs fit for kings: Some burial vaults of the English aristocracy and landed gentry of the period 1650–1850,' *Church Monuments* 14 (1999), pp. 104–28.
Livingstone, Marco, 'Introduction', in David Hockney, *Egyptian Journeys: Palace of Arts, Cairo, 16 January to 16 February 2002* (Cairo, 2002).
'Lord Carnarvon', *Leeds Mercury*, 6 April 1923.
Lord, M. G., *The Accidental Feminist: How Elizabeth Taylor Raised Our Consciousness and We Were Too Distracted by Her Beauty to Notice* (New York, 2012).
Louis, Pierre, *Main basse sur une loge maçonnique. Vers un nouveau Temple Solaire?* (Valence d'Albigeois, 2012).
Luckhurst, Roger, *The Mummy's Curse: The True History of a Dark Fantasy* (Oxford, 2012).
Lumbard, Paula, 'Dorothea Tanning: On the threshold to a darker place', *Woman's Art Journal* 2.1 (1981), pp. 49–52.
Lupton, Carter, ' "Mummymania" for the masses: Is Egyptology cursed by the mummy's curse?', in Sally MacDonald and Michael Rice (eds), *Consuming Ancient Egypt* (London, 2003).
Lurker, Manfred, *The Gods and Goddesses of Ancient Egypt* (London, 1980).
MacDonald, Sally, and Michael Rice (eds), *Consuming Ancient Egypt* (London, 2003).
Maclauchlan, John, 'Presidential address', *Museums Journal* 7 (1907–8), pp. 4–17.
Mahon, Alyce, 'La feminité triomphante: Surrealism, Leonor Fini, and the sphinx', *Dada/Surrealism* 19.1 (2013), pp. 1–20. Available at www.ir.uiowa.edu/cgi/viewcontent.cgi?article=1274&context=.
Maignant, Catherine, 'Irish base, global religion: The Fellowship of Isis', in Olivia Cosgrove, Laurence Cox, Carmen Kuhling and Peter Mulholland (eds), *Ireland's New Religious Movements* (Newcastle upon Tyne, 2011).
Malamud, Margaret, *Ancient Rome and Modern America* (Oxford, 2009).
Malamud, Margaret, 'Pyramids in Las Vegas and in outer space: Ancient Egypt in twentieth century American architecture and film', *The Journal of Popular Culture* 34.1 (2004), pp. 31–47.
Mangelle, Christophe, 'Christian Jacq nous parle du tome 1 de sa nouvelle saga: *Les enquêtes de Setna*', *La fringale Culturelle*, 13 December 2014.
Mann, William J., *How to Be a Movie Star: Elizabeth Taylor in Hollywood* (London, 2009).
Manzoor, Sarfraz, 'The slow rise of black cinema', *Guardian*, 21 September 2014. Available at www.theguardian.com/film/2014/sep/21/slow-rise-black-cinema-african-american-hollywood.
Marchant, Jo, *The Shadow King: The Bizarre Afterlife of King Tut's Mummy* (London, 2013).

Marhic, Renaud, 'Christian Jacq, la dérive du pharaon à deux balles', *Le Vrai Papier Journal*, 1 September 2000.
Martin, Niall, *Iain Sinclair: Noise, Neoliberalism and the Matter of London* (London, 2015).
Martzavou. Paraskevi, 'Isis aretalogies, initiations and emotions: The Isis aretalogies as sources for the study of emotions', in Angelos Chaniotis (ed.), *Unveiling Emotions: Sources and Methods for the Study of Emotions in the Greek World* (Stuttgart, 2012).
Massingham, Harold J., *Remembrance: An Autobiography* (London, 1942).
Masters, Brian, *The Dukes: Origins, Ennoblement and History of Twenty-Six Families* (London, 2011).
Matthews, Jill, 'Feminist History', *Labor History* 50 (1986), pp. 147–53.
Matthews, Roger, and Cornelia Roemer (eds), *Ancient Perspectives on Egypt* (London, 2003).
Matthews, William, 'The Egyptians in Scotland: The political history of a myth', *Viator* 1 (1971), pp. 289–306.
Mazarakis-Ainian, Philippos, 'Archaeological copies: A scientific aid, a visual reminder or a contradiction in terms?', in *Original, Copy, Fake, On the Significance of the Object in History and Archaeology Museums, 22nd ICOM General Conference in Shanghai, China, 7–12nd November 2010* (Shanghai, 2010). Available at www.network.icom.museum/fileadmin/user_upload/minisites/icmah/publications/Actes-Shanghai-complet2.pdf.
McCouat, Philip, 'Lost masterpieces of ancient Egyptian art from the Nebamun tomb-chapel', 2015, *Journal of Art in Society*. Available at http://www.artinsociety.com/lost-masterpieces-of-ancient-egyptian-art-from-the-nebamun-tomb-chapel.html.
McCrum, Kirstie, 'Exploring Richard Burton and Elizabeth Taylor's chemistry on and off-screen', *Wales Online*, 20 July 2013. Available at http://www.walesonline.co.uk/whats-on/film-tv/exploring-richard-burton-elizabeth-taylors-5151010.
McGeough, Kevin M., *The Ancient Near East in the Nineteenth Century: Appreciations and Appropriations*, Vol. 1 (Sheffield, 2015).
McIntosh, Christopher, *Eliphas Lévi and the French Occult Revival* (London, 1972).
McKnight, Kate Denny, 'The persistence of Egyptian traditions in art and religion after the pharaohs', *Art and Archaeology*, 17 January/February 1924.
McRobbie, Angela, 'Jackie: An ideology of adolescent femininity', *Centre for Contemporary Cultural Studies Stencilled Occasional Paper*, 'Women series' 53 (1978).
Melman, Billie, 'Gender, history and memory: The invention of women's past in the nineteenth and early twentieth centuries', *History and Memory* 5.1 (1993), pp. 5–41.
Melman, Billie, *Women's Orients: English Women and the Middle East* (Basingstoke, 1995).
Mendes, Valerie D., *Fashion since 1900* (London, 2010).
Mentzel, Laure, 'Docteur Christian et le mystère Jacq', *Le Figaro*, 6 November 2010.
Merchant, Carolyn, 'Isis' consciousness raised', *The History of Social Science* 73.3 (1982), pp. 398–409.
Mercurio, Jeremiah Romano, 'Faithful infidelity: Charles Ricketts' illustrations for two of Oscar Wilde's poems in prose', *Victorian Network* 3.1 (2011), pp. 3–21.
Meskell, Lynn, 'Consuming bodies: Cultural fantasies of ancient Egypt', *Body & Society* 4.1 (1998), pp. 63–76.
Messenger-Davies, Marie, 'Children's television', in Glen Creeber (ed.), *The Television Genre Book* (London, 2008).
Meyers, Jeffrey, *The Enemy: A Biography of Wyndham Lewis* (London, 1980).
Miles, Barry, *William S. Burroughs: A Life* (London, 2014).
Miller, Daniel, 'Artefacts and the meaning of things', in Tim Ingold (ed.), *Companion Encyclopaedia of Anthropology* (London, 1994).
Miller, Sanda, *Constantin Brancusi: A Survey of His Work* (Oxford, 1995).

Bibliography

Mills, Pat, 'Misty lives!', *Pat Mills*, 6 September 2016. Available at https://patmills.wordpress.com/2016/09/06/misty-lives/.

Mills, Sara, *Discourses of Difference: An Analysis of Women's Travel Writing and Colonialism* (London, 1991).

'Model/foundation-deposit/adze', *British Museum*, museum no. EA 26278. Available at www.britishmuseum.org/research/collection_online/collection_object_details.aspx?objectId=118442&partId=1&searchText=%22Pharaoh%3A+King+of+Egypt%22&page=1.

Monier, Françoise, 'Scribe best-seller', *L'Express*, 3 August 2000.

Montserrat, Dominic, *Akhenaten: History, Fantasy and Ancient Egypt* (London, 2001).

Moore, Alan, 'Annotations to the chapters', in Moore and Campbell, *From Hell*, appendix 1.

Moore, Alan, and Eddie Campbell, 'Dance of the gull catchers', in Moore and Campbell, *From Hell*, appendix 2.

Moore, Alan, and Eddie Campbell, *From Hell: Being a Melodrama in Sixteen Parts* (London, 2016).

Moore, Alan, and Eddie Campbell, *The From Hell Companion* (London, 2013).

Moore, Jennifer Grayer, *Fashion Fads Through American History: Fitting Clothes into Context* (Santa Barbara, 2010).

Moore, Randy, *Dinosaurs by Decades: A Chronology of the Dinosaur in Science and Popular Culture* (Santa Barbara, 2014).

Moore, Thomas, *Alciphron, A Poem* (Philadelphia, 1840). Available at www.forgottenbooks.com/en/books/Alciphron_10503901.

Moorey, Peter Roger Stuart, *A Century of Biblical Archaeology* (Cambridge, 1991).

Morice, Charles, 'Nécessité présente du travail intellectual', *L'Homme Libre*, 20 December 2017, trans. in Kenneth E. Silver, *Esprit de Corps: The Art of the Parisian Avant-Garde and the First World War, 1914–1925* (London, 1989).

Moser, Stephanie, *Designing Antiquity: Owen Jones, Ancient Egypt and the Crystal Palace* (London, 2012).

Moser, Stephanie, *Painting Antiquity: Ancient Egypt in the Art of Lawrence Alma-Tadema, Edward Poynter and Edwin Long* (Oxford, 2019).

Moser, Stephanie, 'Reconstructing ancient worlds: Reception studies, archaeological representation and the interpretation of ancient Egypt', *Journal of Archaeological Method and Theory* 22.4 (2015), pp. 1263–308.

Moser, Stephanie, *Wondrous Curiosities: Ancient Egypt at the British Museum* (Chicago, 2006).

'Mr. G. H. Engleheart', *The Times*, 18 March 1936.

'Mummy mask / cartonnage', *British Museum*, museum no. EA 29770. Available at www.britishmuseum.org/research/collection_online/collection_object_details.aspx?objectId=6415&partId=1.

'Mummy of Amenhotep the First', *Global Egyptian Museum*, Cairo Museum inventory no. JE 26211. Available at www.globalegyptianmuseum.org/detail.aspx?id=15871.

Munn, Michael, *Richard Burton: Prince of Players* (London, 2008).

Murphy, Timothy S., *Wising Up the Marks: The Amodern William Burroughs* (Berkeley, 1997).

Murray, John, *A Handbook for Travellers in Lower and Upper Egypt* (London, 1891).

Murray, Lynda, *Alexander Keiller: A Zest for Life* (Swindon, 1999).

Murray, Margaret Alice, *The Witch-Cult in Western Europe* (London, 1921).

Mytum, Harold, *Recording and Analysing Graveyards* (York, 2000).

Nathanson, Richard, 'Lucian Freud, "Portrait with horses" 1939'. Available at https://richardnathanson.co.uk/publications/12/.

Neuss, Bodo, 'The funerary of Thomas Willson', *Architectural Association* 68 (2014), pp. 88–92.

'New temple photos' (27 May 2013), *Fellowship of Isis Homepage*. Available at www.foihomepage.blogspot.com.au/2013/05/new-temple-photos.html.

'No curse of pharaohs: Ludicrous superstition', *Telegraph* (Brisbane), 10 April 1930.
'Noble Order of Tara', *Fellowship of Isis*. Available at www.fellowshipofisis.com/nobleorderoftara.html.
North, Michael, *Reading 1922: A Return to the Scene of the Modern* (New York, 1999).
Nourry, Philippe, 'Christian Jacq: Les offrandes du pharaon', *Le Point*, 17 August 1996.
Nourry, Philippe, 'Heurs et malheurs', *Le Point*, 22 December 2000.
O'Connor, David, and Stephen Quirke (eds), *Mysterious Lands* (London, 2007).
O'Connor, David, and Andrew Reid (eds), *Ancient Egypt in Africa* (London, 2007).
O'Keeffe, Paul, *Some Sort of Genius: A Life of Wyndham Lewis* (London, 2000).
'Obituary of the Duke of Hamilton', *The Gentleman's Magazine, and Historical Chronicle, for the Year 1852* 38 (1852), p. 425.
'One of the most beautiful women in history', *Illustrated London News*, 31 December 1927.
Orenstein, Gloria, 'Women of Surrealism', *Feminist Art Journal* 2.2 (1973), pp. 15–21.
Owen, Alex, *The Place of Enchantment: British Occultism and the Culture of the Modern* (Chicago, 2004).
Paglia, Camille, *Sexual Personae: Art and Decadence from Nefertiti to Emily Dickinson* (New Haven, 1990).
Parkinson, R. B., 'Hordjedef', in Donald B. Redford (ed.), *The Oxford Encyclopedia of Ancient Egypt*, Vol. 2 (New York, 2001).
Parkinson, R. B., *Reading Ancient Egyptian Poetry: Among Other Histories* (Chichester, 2009).
Parkinson, R. B., 'Two or three literary artefacts: EA 41650/47896, and 22878–9', in W. V. Davies (ed.), *Studies in Egyptian Antiquities: A Tribute to T. G. H. James* (London, 1999).
Parramore, Lynn, *Reading the Sphinx: Ancient Egypt in Nineteenth-Century Literary Culture* (Basingstoke, 2008).
Pasquini, Xavier, 'Christian Jacq, le pharaon des bacs à sable', *Charlie Hebdo*, 3 April 1996.
Patrizzi, Kathryn Bonanno, 'The magnificent period of Mauboussin', *Kathryn Bonnano: Fine Collectable Jewels & Rare Gems*. Available at www.kathrynbonannogems.com/assets/magnificent-period-of-maubossin_small.pdf.
Patterson, John, 'Cleopatra, the film that killed off big-budget epics', *Guardian*, 15 July 2013. Available at https://www.theguardian.com/film/2013/jul/15/cleopatra-killed-big-budget-epics.
Patterson, William H., Jr., *Robert A. Heinlein: In Dialogue with His Century*, Vol. 1 (New York, 2010).
Paul, Joanna, '"Time is Only a Mode of Thought, You Know": Ancient history, empire, and imagination in E. Nesbit's stories for children', in Lisa Maurice (ed.), *The Reception of Ancient Greece and Rome in Children's Literature: Eagles and Heroes* (Leiden, 2015).
Peiss, Kathy, 'Making faces: The cosmetics industry and the cultural construction of gender, 1890–1930', *Genders* 7 (1990), pp. 143–69.
Peltre, Christine, *Orientalism in Art* (New York, 1998).
Peppin, Brigid, 'Women that a movement forgot', *Tate Etc* 22 (2011). Available at http://www.tate.org.uk/context-comment/articles/women-movement-forgot.
Perrier, Jean-Claude, 'Le mystère editorial des grandes pyramides', *Livres Hebdo*, 24 October 1998.
Perry, William J., *Children of the Sun* (London, 1923).
Perry, William J., *Gods and Men: The Attainment of Immortality* (London, 1927).
Perry, William J., *The Children of the Sun: A Study of the Egyptian Settlement of the Pacific* (Kempton, IL, 2004).
Perry, William J., *The Megalithic Culture of Indonesia* (Manchester, 1918).
Perry, William J., *The Origin of Magic and Religion* (London, 1923).

Bibliography

Petrie, William M. Flinders, *Egyptian Tales: Translated from the Papyri*, Vol. 1: *IVth to XIIth Dynasty* (London, 1895).
Pettigrew, Thomas, *A History of Egyptian Mummies* (London, 1834).
Petzer, Tatjana, 'Veils in action: The "Oriental other" and its performative destruction in modern fashion and art', in Ulrike Brunotte, Anna-Dorothea Ludewig and Axel Stähler (eds), *Orientalism, Gender, and the Jews: Literary and Artistic Transformations of European National Discourses* (Berlin, 2015).
'Pharaoh's daughters had a facial', *Evening Despatch*, 14 July 1939.
'Pharaoh's shrine is rare treasure: Closer examination reveals "Naos" is one of the finest monuments ever discovered', *The New York Times*, 10 February 1923.
Phillips, Laura, 'An investigation into the life of A.D. Passmore, "a most curious specimen"', *Wiltshire Archaeology and Natural History Magazine* 97 (2004), pp. 273–92.
Pietrzak-Franger, Monika, 'Envisioning the Ripper's visions: Adapting myth in Alan Moore and Eddie Campbell's *From Hell*', *Neo-Victorian Studies* 2.2 (2009/2010), pp. 157–85.
Piggott, Stuart, 'The early Bronze Age in Wessex', *Proceedings of the Prehistoric Society* 4.1 (1938), pp. 52–106.
Pilkington, Ed, and Mark Tran, 'Tooth solves Hatshepsut mummy mystery', *Guardian*, 27 June 2007. Available at www.theguardian.com/world/2007/jun/27/egypt.science.
Pinch, Geraldine, *Egyptian Myth: A Very Short Introduction* (Oxford, 2004).
Plato, *Laws*. Available at: http://classics.mit.edu/Plato/laws.2.ii.html.
Plutarch, *Antony*, trans. John Dryden. Available at http://classics.mit.edu/Plutarch/antony.html.
Plutarch, *Antony*, Bernadotte Perrin (ed.), *Perseus Digital Library*. Available at http://www.perseus.tufts.edu/hopper/text?doc=Perseus%3Atext%3A2008.01.0007%3Achapter%3D70.
Plutarch, *Plutarch's De Iside Et Osiride*, trans. John Gwyn Griffith (Swansea, 1970).
Ponzi, Julie, 'Drama Queens: Elizabeth Taylor, Camille Paglia, and the purposes of female power' (March 2011), *Ashbrook Centre at Ashland University*. Available at https://ashbrook.org/publications/oped-ponzi-11-dramaqueens/.
Puckle, Bertram S., *Funeral Customs: Their Origin and Development* (London, 1926).
Pugin, Augustus Welby Northmore, *An Apology for the Revival of Christian Architecture in England* (London, 1843).
'Queer, adj.1', *Oxford English Dictionary*. Available at: www.oed.com/view/Entry/156236.
'Queer, n.2', Oxford English Dictionary. Available at: www.oed.com/view/Entry/156235.
'Quick key to the cosmic web', *Fellowship of Isis*. Available at www.fellowshipofisis.com/keyalch.html.
Quin, Jack, 'W.B. Yeats and the sculpture of Brancusi', *International Yeats Studies* 2.1 (2017), pp. 45–63.
Rachet, Guy, *Le livre des morts des anciens égyptiens* (Paris, 1996).
Radford, Andrew D., *The Lost Girls: Demeter-Persephone and the Literary Imagination, 1850–1930* (Amsterdam, 2007).
Ranzal, Edward, 'Miss Taylor and Burton sued for $50 million on "Cleopatra"', *The New York Times*, 23 April 1964.
Raynor, Vivien, 'Art; A bounty of Egyptian imagery' *The New York Times*, 25 February 1990. Available at www.nytimes.com/1990/02/25/nyregion/art-a-bounty-of-egyptian-imagery.html.
Regardie, Israel, *The Complete Golden Dawn System of Magic*, Vols 6–8 (Scottsdale, 1990).
Reid, Donald Malcolm, *Contesting Antiquity in Egypt: Archaeologies, Museums, and the Struggle for Identities from World War I to Nasser* (Cairo, 2015).
Reid, Donald Malcolm, 'Remembering and forgetting Tutankhamun: Imperial and national rhythms of archaeology, 1922–1972', in William Carruthers (ed.), *Histories of Egyptology: Interdisciplinary Measures* (London, 2014).

Reid, Donald Malcolm, *Whose Pharaohs? Archaeology, Museums, and Egyptian National Identity from Napoleon to World War I* (Los Angeles, 2007).
Reid, L., 'Paris jewelry fashions', *The Jewelers' Circular*, 19 September 1923.
Resnik, Salomon, *The Theatre of the Dream* (London, 2005).
Rice, Emanuel, *Freud and Moses: The Long Journey Home* (New York, 1990).
Rice, Emanuel, 'Freud, Moses, and the religions of Egyptian antiquity: A journey through history', *Psychoanalytical Review* 86 (1999), pp. 223–43.
Richards, Graham, *Race, Racism and Psychology: Towards a Reflexive History* (London, 1997).
Richards, Jeffrey, *The Age of the Dream Palace: Cinema and Society in 1930s Britain* (London, 2010).
Ricketts, Charles, 'Bas-relief figure of a king of the Ptolemaic period in blue faience', *Journal of Egyptian Archaeology* 5 (1918), pp. 77–8.
Ricketts, Charles, 'Head in Serpentine of Amenemmes III in the possession of Oscar Raphael, Esq.', *Journal of Egyptian Archaeology* 4 (1917), pp. 211–12.
Ricketts, Charles, 'Head of Amenemmēs III in obsidian: From the collection of the Rev. W. MacGregor, Tamworth', *Journal of Egyptian Archaeology* 4 (1917), pp. 71–3.
Ricketts, Charles, 'Two faience chalices at Eton College from the collection of the Late Major W. J. Myers', *Journal of Egyptian Archaeology* 5 (1918), pp. 145–7.
Roberts, Mary Louise, 'Samson and Delilah revisited', in Whitney Chadwick and Tirza True Latimer (eds), *The Modern Woman Revisited: Paris between the Wars* (London, 2003).
Robertson, Olivia, 'FOI online liturgy: Fortuna, creation through the goddess', *Fellowship of Isis*. Available at www.fellowshipofisis.com/fortuna6.html.
Robertson, Olivia, 'Isis of alchemy, transformation through the goddess', *Fellowship of Isis*. Available at www.fellowshipofisis.com/liturgy/alchemyintro.html.
Robertson, Olivia, 'Ordination of priestesses and priests', *Fellowship of Isis*. Available at www.fellowshipofisis.com/liturgy/ordainpref.html.
Robertson, Olivia, 'Sphinx, goddess myths and mysteries', *Fellowship of Isis*. Available at www.fellowshipofisis.com/liturgy/sphinx.html.
Robertson, Olivia (ed.), *The Handbook of the Fellowship of Isis* (London, 1992).
Rodenbeck, John, 'Travelers from an antique land: Shelley's inspiration for "Ozymandias"', *Alif: Journal of Comparative Poetics* 14 (2004), pp. 121–48.
Rodmell, C., 'Treasures of Tutankhamun's tomb', *Ours* 17.11 (1936), pp. 563–73.
Rohmer, Sax, *The Brood of the Witch-Queen* (London, 1918). Available at: http://www.gutenberg.org/files/19706/19706-h/19706-h.htm.
Rojek, Chris, *Celebrity* (London, 2001).
Rojek, Chris, *Presumed Intimacy: Parasocial Interaction in Media, Society and Celebrity Culture* (London, 2015).
Roller, Duane W., *Cleopatra: A Biography* (Oxford, 2010).
Ronk, Liz, 'Liz Taylor and Richard Burton on the set of Cleopatra: Rare and classic photos', *Time Magazine*, 10 June 2013. Available at http://time.com/3877380/cleopatra-rare-photos-of-liz-taylor-richard-burton-on-set-in-1962/.
Round, Julia, '*Misty*, *Spellbound* and the lost Gothic of British girls' comics', *Palgrave Communications* 3 (2017). Available at https://doi.org/10.1057/palcomms.2017.37.
Royster, Francesca T., *Becoming Cleopatra: The Shifting Image of an Icon* (Basingstoke, 2003).
Rubens, Godfrey, *William Richard Lethaby: His Life and Work 1857–1931* (London, 1986).
Rubino, Gianfranco, *Voix du contemporain: histoire, mémoire et réel dans le roman français d'aujourd'hui* (Rome, 2006).
Rudoe, Judy, *Cartier 1900–1939* (London, 1998).

Bibliography

Rudoe, Judy, 'Exoticism in Cartier jewels: The influence of Egypt, Persia, India and the Far East', in Nuno Vassallo e Silva and João Cavalho Dias (eds), *Cartier 1899-1949: The Journey of a Style* (Milan, 2007).
Rugg, Julie, 'The rise of cemetery companies in Britain 1820-1853' (PhD thesis, University of Stirling, 1992).
Russell, *Francis Bacon* (New York, 1979).
'Russian Madonna', *V&A*. Available at http://collections.vam.ac.uk/item/O185918/russian-madonna-drawing-lewis-wyndham/.
Rutherford, Sarah, *The Victorian Cemetery* (Oxford, 2013).
Saglia, Diego, 'Consuming Egypt: Appropriation and the cultural modalities of Romantic luxury', *Nineteenth Century Contexts* 24.3 (2002), pp. 317-32.
Said, Edward, *Orientalism* (New York, 1978).
Salisbury Museum, anon, note, 6 June 1935.
Salisbury Museum, Collignon to Crawford, 13 January 1935.
Salisbury Museum, Crawford to Collignon, 14 January 1935.
Salisbury Museum, Cunnington to Goddard, 2 June 1936.
Salisbury Museum, Engleheart to Collignon, 30 October 1934.
Salisbury Museum, Engleheart to Crawford, 6 February 1935.
Salisbury Museum, Engleheart, George, typescript, 'Two scarabs found in Wiltshire'.
Salisbury Museum, Goddard to Stevens, 27 January 1936.
Salisbury Museum, James to Engleheart, 15 January 1933.
Salisbury Museum, James, Mr, note in pencil, undated.
Salisbury Museum, Thomas to Engleheart, 17 February 1935.
Salisbury Museum, Wright to Engleheart, 16 February 1933.
Salisbury Museum, Collignon, Pierre Louis, note, 10 January 1935.
Santas, Constantine, James M. Wilson, Maria Colavito and Djoymi Baker, *The Encyclopaedia of Epic Films* (Lanham, 2014).
Sayce, Archibald H., 'The date of Stonehenge', *Journal of Egyptian Archaeology* 1.1 (1914), p. 18.
Schenker, Daniel, *Wyndham Lewis: Religion and Modernism* (Tuscalosa; London, 1992).
Scheyer, Kate, 'Classic Hollywood style: Cleopatra', *Vanity Fair*, 20 April 2010. Available at https://www.vanityfair.com/hollywood/2010/04/classic-hollywood-style-cleopatra.
Schiff, Stacy, *Cleopatra: A Life* (London, 2010).
Schnitzler, Bernadette, 'Hijacked images: Ancient Egypt in French commercial advertising', in Sally MacDonald and Michael Rice (eds), *Consuming Ancient Egypt* (New York, 2016).
Schwartz, Hillel, *The Culture of the Copy: Striking Likenesses, Unreasonable Facsimiles* (Cambridge, MA, 1996).
Scott Stanfield, Paul, 'The betrayed father: Wyndham Lewis, homosexuality, and *Enemy of the Stars*', *Journal of Modern Literature* 40.3 (2017), pp. 84-101.
Scranton, Laird, *The Mystery of Skara Brae: Neolithic Scotland and the Origins of Ancient Egypt* (Vermont, 2017).
Seacrest, Meryle, *Elsa Schiaparelli: A Biography* (London, 2014).
Sénécal, Didier, 'Christian Jacq', *L'Express*, 1 December 1994.
Serceau, Michel, *Le mythe, le miroir et le divan: pour lire le cinéma* (Villeneuve d'Ascq, 2009).
'Serious accident to His Grace the Duke of Hamilton', *Standard*, 13 July 1850.
Shakespeare, William, *Antony and Cleopatra*. Available at http://shakespeare.mit.edu/cleopatra/full.html.
Shakespeare, William, *Timon of Athens*. Available at http://shakespeare.mit.edu/timon/full.html.
Shaw, Ian, *Ancient Egypt: A Very Short Introduction* (Oxford, 2004).
Sheehy, Jeanne, *The Rediscovery of Ireland's Past: the Celtic Revival 1830-1930* (London, 1980).

Sheperd, Rowena and Robert Sheperd, *1000 Symbols: What Shapes Mean in Art and Myth* (London, 2002).
Sherman, Daniel, 'Monuments, mourning and masculinity in France after World War I', *Gender and History* 8.1 (1996), pp. 82–107.
Shubert, Steven Blake, 'Double entendre in the stela of Suty and Hor', in Gary N. Knoppers and Antoine Hirsch (eds), *Egypt, Israel, and the Ancient Mediterranean World: Studies in Honor of Donald B. Redford* (Leiden, 2004).
Siculus, Diodorus, *Library of History*. Available at http://penelope.uchicago.edu/Thayer/E/Roman/Texts/Diodorus_Siculus/home.html.
Silber, Evelyn, *The Sculpture of Epstein: With a Complete Catalogue* (Oxford, 1986).
Simpson, St John, 'Scythians, ice mummies and burial mounds', 23 August 2017, *British Museum*. Available at http://blog.britishmuseum.org/scythians-ice-mummies-and-burial-mounds/
Slanski, Kathryn E., 'The Law of Hammurabi and its audience', *Yale Journal of Law and the Humanities* 24.1 (2012), pp. 97–110.
Smith, Grafton E., *Elephants and Ethnographers* (London, 1924).
Smith, Grafton E., 'Freud's speculations in ethnology', *The Monist* 33.1 (1923), pp. 81–97.
Smith, Grafton E., *Human History: A History of Primitive Man* (London, 1930).
Smith, Grafton E., *The Ancient Egyptians and Their Influence upon the Civilization of Europe* (London; New York, 1911).
Smith, Grafton E., *The Ancient Egyptians and the Origins of Civilization*, 2nd edn (London, 1923).
Smith, Grafton E., *The Evolution of the Dragon* (Manchester, 1919).
Smith, Grafton E., *The Migration of Early Culture: A Study of the Significance of the Geographical Distribution of the Practice of Mummification as Evidence of the Migrations of Peoples and the Spread of Certain Customs and Beliefs* (Manchester, 1915).
Smith, Grafton E., *The Royal Mummies* (Paris, 1912).
Smith, Grafton E., *Tutankhamen and the Discovery of his Tomb by the late Earl of Carnarvon and Mr. Howard Carter* (London, 1923).
Smith, Mark, 'Budge, Sir Ernest Alfred Thompson Wallis (1857–1934)' (2004), *Oxford Dictionary of National Biography*. Available at: www.oxforddnb.com/view/article/32161.
Sobchack, Vivien, '"Surge and splendour": A phenomenology of the Hollywood historical epic', *Representations* 29 (1990), pp. 24–49.
Solomon, Jon, 'In the wake of "Cleopatra": The ancient world in the cinema since 1963', *The Classical Journal* 91.2 (1995–1996), pp. 113–40.
'Some precious household goods in glass and silver', *Courier*, 13 February 1926.
Sooke, Alastair, 'How ancient Egypt shaped our idea of beauty', *BBC Culture*, 4 February 2016. Available at www.bbc.com/culture/story/20160204-how-ancient-egypt-shaped-our-idea-of-beauty.
Southey, Robert, *Don Manuel Evarez Espriella: Letters from England – Translated from the Spanish* (New York, 1836).
Spalding, Frances, *Roger Fry: Art and Life* (London, 1980).
Spear, Hilda D., 'E. M. Forster's Alexandrian essays', in Norman Page and Peter Preston (eds), *The Literature of Place* (Basingstoke, 1993).
St. Russell, G., 'The mysterious mummy', *Pearson's Magazine* 28 (1909), pp. 162–72.
Stableford, Brian M., *Science Fact and Science Fiction: An Encyclopedia* (New York, 2006).
Stacey, Jacky, *Star Gazing: Hollywood Cinema and Female Spectatorship* (London, 1994).
Stalla, Heidi, 'William Bankes: Echoes of Egypt in Virginia Woolf's *To the Lighthouse*', *Woolf Studies Annual* 14 (2008), pp. 21–34.
Stanfield, Paul Scott, 'The betrayed father: Wyndham Lewis, homosexuality, and *Enemy of the Stars*', *Journal of Modern Literature* 40.3 (2017), pp. 84–101.

Bibliography

Stanford Freidman, Susan (ed.), *Analysing Freud: Letters of H.D. Bryher and Their Circle* (New York, 2002).
Stannard, Martin, *Evelyn Waugh: The Early Years 1903–1939* (London, 1986).
'Statue', *British Museum*, museum no. GR1859,1226.26. Available at: www.britishmuseum.org/research/collection_online/collection_object_details.aspx?objectId=460416&partId=1.
Steele, Richard, *The Funeral, or Grief-a-la-Mode* (London, 1701).
Stephens, Susan A., *Seeing Double: Intercultural Poetics in Ptolemaic Alexandria* (Los Angeles, 2003).
Stewart, Jon, *Hegel's Interpretation of the Religions of the World* (Oxford, 2018).
Stoddard, Katy, 'Burton and Taylor, private lives played out in public', *Guardian*, 22 July 2013. Available at www.theguardian.com/theguardian/from-the-archive-blog/2013/jul/22/elizabeth-taylor-richard-burton-archive.
Stolzenberg, Daniel, *Egyptian Oedipus: Athanasius Kircher and the Secrets of Antiquity* (Chicago, 2013).
Stout, Adam, *Creating Prehistory: Druids, Ley Hunters and Archaeologists in Pre-War Britain* (Oxford, 2008).
Stratos, Anita, 'Breaking the color code', *Tour Egypt*. Available at http://www.touregypt.net/featurestories/colorcode.htm.
Straughn, Ian, 'Ancient Egyptian icons next target of Islamists' (30 November 2012), *Albuquerque Journal*. Available at www.abqjournal.com/main/2012/11/23/opinion/ancient-egyptian-icons-next-target-of-islamists.html.
Sweeney, Deborah, 'Forever young? The representation of older and ageing women in ancient Egyptian art', *Journal of the American Research Centre in Egypt* 41 (2004), pp. 67–84.
Sykes, Christopher Simon, *Hockney: The Biography: Vol. 2. 1975–2012* (London, 2014).
Taguieff, Pierre-André, *La foire aux 'Illuminés': ésotérisme, théorie du complot, extrémisme* (Paris, 2005).
Tait, John (ed.), *Never Had the Like Occurred: Egypt's View of its Past* (London, 2007).
Takács, Sarolta A., *Isis and Sarapis in the Roman World* (Leiden, 1995).
Tao, Amy, 'Christian Jacq' (10 August 2010), *Encyclopaedia Britannica*. Available at www.britannica.com/biography/Christian-Jacq.
Taylor, John H., *Journey Through the Afterlife: Ancient Egyptian Book of the Dead* (London: 2010).
Teeter, Emily, *Religion and Ritual in Ancient Egypt* (New York, 2011).
Terrasson, Jean, *Life of Sethos*, trans. Thomas Lediard (London, 1732).
'The ancient Egyptian type of beauty', *Illustrated London News*, 17 February 1923.
'The Circle of Brigid', *Fellowship of Isis*. Available at www.fellowshipofisis.com/circleofbrigid.html.
'The cult of the cat', *Misty*, 4 February 1978.
'The cult of the cat', *Misty*, 11 February 1978.
'The cult of the cat', *Misty*, 25 February 1978.
'The cult of the cat', *Misty*, 8 April 1978.
'The cult of the cat', *Misty*, 22 April 1978.
'The curse of Osiris', *Sunday Times* (Sydney), 20 May 1923.
'The curse of the pharaohs', *Dundee Courier*, 31 December 1929.
'The Egyptian Book', *The Metropolitan Museum of Art*. Available at www.metmuseum.org/art/collection/search/360169.
'The Fellowship of Isis manifesto', *Fellowship of Isis*. Available at www.fellowshipofisis.com/manifesto.html.
'The Folkton drums', *The British Museum*. Available at www.britishmuseum.org/research/collection_online/collection_object_details.aspx?objectId=814086&partId=1.

The Government of Egypt: Recommendations by a Committee of the International Section of the Labour Research Department ([London], 1920).
'The loveliest woman of antiquity? A rival to Helen', *Illustrated London News*, 13 December 1924.
'The making of meaning', *Living with the Gods*, BBC Radio 4, 15 November 2017.
The Mummy, dir. Terence Fisher (1959).
The Mummy, dir. Karl Freund (1932).
The Mummy's Shroud, dir. Joh Gilling (1967).
'The "New Woman" anticipated by centuries', *Leeds Mercury*, 25 January 1911.
'The strange face of beauty', *Vogue*, 1 November 1939.
'The Thebes stool', *Victoria and Albert Museum*, CIRC.439–1965. Available at www.collections.vam.ac.uk/item/O7878/the-thebes-stool-stool-william-birch-ltd/.
'The "Tutankhamen" influence in modern jewellery', *Illustrated London News*, 26 January 1924.
'The unlucky mummy', *The British Museum*. Available at www.britishmuseum.org/research/collection_online/collection_object_details.aspx?objectId=117233&partId=1.
'The younger Memnon', *British Museum*, museum no. EA 19. Available at http://www.britishmuseum.org/research/collection_online/collection_object_details.aspx?objectId=117633&partId=1&searchText=Younger+Memnon&page=1.
Thomas, Herbert H., 'The source of the stones of Stonehenge', *Antiquaries Journal* 3 (1923), pp. 239–60.
Thomas, Kate, 'Using history to sell clothes? Don't try it with the pharaohs' (2011), *The New York Times*. Available at: www.nytimes.com/2011/04/19/arts/design/egyptian-antiquities-official-defends-fashion-line.html.
Thompson, Glyn, 'Stereotypical perspective', *The Jackdaw* 139 (2018), pp. 30–4.
Thompson, Rachel, *Mark Antony and Popular Culture: Masculinity and the Construction of an Icon* (London, 2014).
Tickner, Lisa, 'A lost Lewis: The *Mother and Child* of 1912', *Wyndham Lewis Annual* 2 (1995), pp. 2–11.
Tims, Anna, 'How we made *Cleopatra*', *Guardian*, 15 July 2013. Available at https://www.theguardian.com/film/2013/jul/15/how-we-made-cleopatra.
Tremayne, Sydney, 'A career for women: Being beautiful', *Vogue London*, Early September 1923.
Trétiack, Philippe, *Cartier*, trans. Jane Brenton (London, 1997).
'Tu m'', *Yale University Art Gallery*. Available at https://artgallery.yale.edu/collections/objects/50128.
Tucker, Judith E., *Women in Nineteenth-Century Egypt* (Cambridge, 2009).
Tully, Caroline, 'Egyptosophy in the British Museum: Florence Farr, the Egyptian adept and the ka', in Christine Ferguson and Andrew Radford (eds), *The Occult Imagination in Britain, 1875–1947* (London, 2018).
Tully, Caroline, 'Florence and the mummy', in Brandy Williams (ed.), *Women's Voices in Magic* (Stafford, 2009).
Tully, Caroline, 'Samuel Liddell MacGregor Mathers and Isis', in Dave Evans and Dave Green (eds), *Ten Years of Triumph? Academic Approaches to Studying Magic and the Occult: Examining Scholarship into Witchcraft and Paganism Ten Years after Ronald Hutton's Triumph of the Moon* (Harpenden, 2009).
Tully, Caroline, 'Walk like an Egyptian: Egypt as authority in Aleister Crowley's reception of *The Book of the Law*', *Pomegranate: International Journal of Pagan Studies* 12 (2010), pp. 20–47.
Turcan, Robert, *The Cults of the Roman Empire* (Oxford, 1997).
'Turning afflictions into attractions', *Evening Telegraph*, 10 July 1939.
Tusan, Michelle, 'Inventing the New Woman: Print culture and identity politics during the fin-de-siecle:', *Victorian Periodicals Review* 31.2 (1998), pp. 169–82.

Bibliography

'Tutankhamun: Anatomy of an excavation', *The Griffith Institute*. Available at www.griffith.ox.ac.uk/gri/carter/gallery/).

Tutankhamun Archive, Griffith Institute, University of Oxford, TAA i.2.1, p. 25. Available at www.griffith.ox.ac.uk/discoveringTut/journals-and-diaries/season-1/journal.html.

Tutankhamun Archive, TAA i.2.3, p. 3. Available at www.griffith.ox.ac.uk/discoveringTut/journals-and-diaries/season-4/journal.html.

'Tutankhamen's statue sentinels: Robbers scared away by superstition', *Manchester Guardian*, 27 January 1923.

Tyldesley, Joyce, *Cleopatra: Last Queen of Egypt* (London, 2008).

Ucko, Peter J., and Timothy Champion (eds), *The Wisdom of Egypt: Changing Visions Through the Ages* (London, 2003).

Ullmer, Rivka, *Egyptian Cultural Icons in Midrash* (Berlin, 2009).

Ustorf, Werner, 'The missiological roots of the concept of "political religion"', in Roger Griffin, Robert Mallett and John Tortorice (eds), *The Sacred in Twentieth-Century Politics: Essays in Honour of Professor Stanley G. Payne* (London, 2018).

Van der Spek, Kees, 'Faked antikas and "modern antiques"', *Journal of Social Archaeology* 8 (2008), pp. 163–89.

Van Dijk, Jacobus, 'The Amarna Period and the later New Kingdom (c. 1352–1069 BC)', in I. Shaw (ed.), *The Oxford History of Ancient Egypt* (Oxford, 2000).

Vantroys, Carole, 'Italien-Coréen comme Christian Jacq', *L'Express*, 1 May 1998.

Vasiljević, Vera, '*Princess Ru* and *Papyrus*: Stereotypes on ancient Egypt in graphic novels', *Issues in Ethnology and Anthropology* 7.3 (2012), pp. 763–88.

Vavasseur, Pierre, 'Christian Jacq joue à nous faire très peur', *Le Parisien*, 29 October 2016.

Verdaguer, Pierre, 'Manipulating the past: The role of history in recent French detective fiction', in Barry Rothaus (ed.), *Proceedings of the Western Society for French History: Selected Papers of the 1998 Annual Meeting* (Greeley, 2000).

Vinson, Steve, and Janet Gunn, 'Studies in esoteric syntax: The enigmatic friendship of Aleister Crowley and Battiscombe Gunn', in William Carruthers (ed.), *Histories of Egyptology: Interdisciplinary Measures* (London, 2014).

Voisenat, Claudie and Pierre Lagrange, *L'ésotérisme contemporain et ses lecteurs: Entre savoirs, croyances et fictions* (Paris, 2005).

Vollmar, Rob, 'Northampton calling: A conversation with Alan Moore', *World Literature Today* 91.1 (2017), pp. 28–34.

Von Dassow, Eva (ed.), *The Egyptian Book of the Dead: The Book of Going Forth by Day*, trans. Raymond O. Faulkner (San Francisco, 1998)

Wadsworth, Edward, 'Inner necessity', *Blast* 1 (1914), pp. 119–25.

Walkerdine, Valerie, 'Some day my prince will come: Young girls and the preparation for adolescent sexuality', in Angela McRobbie and Mica Nava (eds), *Gender and Generation* (London, 1984).

Wanger, Walter, *My Life with Cleopatra* (London, 1963).

Wang, Helen, 'Stein's recording angel – Miss F. M. G. Lorimer', *Journal of the Royal Asiatic Society* 8.2 (1998), pp. 207–28.

Warmenbol, Eugène (ed.), *Sphinx: Les gardiens de l'Égypte* (Brussels, 2006).

Watt, Donald, 'Mohammed el Adl and *A Passage to India*', *Journal of Modern Literature* 10.2 (1983), pp. 311–26.

Webb, James, *The Occult Underground* (Illinois, 1974).

Webb, Peter, *Sphinx: The Life and Art of Leonor Fini* (New York, 2009).

Weidemann, A., 'Ägyptische religion', *Archiv fur Religions-Wissenschaft* 21 (1922), p. 457.

Weigall, Arthur, 'Laying bare a royal tomb', *Daily Mail*, 4 December 1922.

Weigall, Arthur, 'Trafficking in "publicity" rights', *Daily Mail*, 9 February 1923.

Weigall, Arthur, *Tutankhamen and Other Essays* (London, 1923).
Weigall, Arthur, 'Inscription from the golden shrine', *Daily Mail*, 20 February 1923.
Western Manuscripts, British Library, Add mss 25639 f. 88 (44 vso) (unpublished).
Whale, John, 'Sacred objects and the sublime ruins of art', in Stephen Copley and John Whale (eds), *Beyond Romanticism: New Approaches to Texts and Contexts 1780–1832* (London, 1992).
'What the great "find" in Egypt may bring: A 3000-year old pharaoh "coming forth into the day," with the contemporary garlands which adorned his mummy', *Illustrated London News*, 16 December 1922.
'When the mummy walks', *Spellbound*, 25 September 1976.
Whitehouse, Helen, 'Review article: "Egyptomanias", *American Journal of Archaeology* 101.1 (1997), pp. 158–61.
Whitlock, Cathy, 'The set designs of *Cleopatra*, Elizabeth Taylor's classic movie', *Architectural Digest*, 31 December 2012. Available at https://www.architecturaldigest.com/gallery/cleopatra-elizabeth-taylor-set-design-50th-anniversary-cannes-slideshow/all.
Whitney, Chadwick, *Women Artists and the Surrealist Movement* (London, 1991).
Whitney, Chadwick, *Women, Art and Society* (London, 2007).
Wickstead, Helen, ' "Wild worship of a lost and buried past": Enchanted archaeologies and the cult of Kata, 1908–1924', *Bulletin of the Prehistory of Archaeology* 27.1 (2017), pp. 1–18.
Wickstead, Helen, and Martyn Barber, 'Concrete prehistories: The making of megalithic modernism', *Journal of Contemporary Archaeology* 2.1 (2015), pp. 195–216.
Wiedemann, Alfred, *The Ancient Egyptian Doctrine of the Immortality of the Soul* (London, 1895).
Wilde, Oscar, *The Sphinx*, in *The Complete Works of Oscar Wilde*, Vol. 1: *Poems and Poems in Prose*, Bobby Fong and Karl Beckson (eds) (Oxford, 2000).
Wilkinson, Richard H., *The Complete Gods and Goddesses of Ancient Egypt* (London, 2003).
Wilkinson, Toby, *The Rise and Fall of Ancient Egypt* (London, 2010).
'Will of Alexander Hamilton Hamilton of Stevenston, Ayrshire', *The National Archives*, Reference: PROB 11/2175/410, 25 July 1853.
Williams, Mark, *Ireland's Immortals: A History of the Gods of Irish Myth* (Princeton, 2016).
Williams, Rowan. 'Freudian psychology', in Alan Richardson and John Bowden (eds), *A New Dictionary of Christian Theology* (London, 1983).
Wilson, Christopher, 'Richard Burton never wrote that "last love letter" ', *Daily Telegraph*, 9 November 2011. Available at www.telegraph.co.uk/culture/film/starsandstories/8877223/Richard-Burton-never-wrote-that-last-love-letter.html.
Wilson, Sydney V., 'The jewels of the ancients', *Vogue*, 15 September 1926.
Winpenny, David, *Up to a Point: In Search of Pyramids in Britain and Ireland* (York, 2009).
Winter, Jay, *Sites of Memory, Sites of Mourning* (Cambridge, 1995).
Wise, Caroline (ed.), *Olivia Robertson: A Centenary Tribute* (London, 2017).
Witt, Reginald Eldred, *Isis in the Ancient World* (Baltimore, 1971).
Wood, Jamie, ' "A third method": Lewis and sympathy in the aftermath of war', *Journal of Wyndham Lewis Studies* 7 (2017), pp. 148–74.
Woolf, Virginia, *Jacob's Room*, Kate Flint (ed.) (Oxford, 2008).
Woolf, Virginia, *The Waves*, Michael Herbert and Susan Sellers (eds) (Cambridge, 2011).
Woolf, Virginia, *To the Lighthouse*, Stella McNichol (ed.) (London, 2000).
Woolf, Virginia, *Roger Fry: A Biography* (London, 1940).
Wortham, Robert A., 'Urban networks, deregulated religious markets, cultural continuity and the diffusion of the Isis cult', *Method and Theory in the Study of Religion* 18.2 (2006), pp. 103–23.
Worringer, Wilhelm, *Abstraction and Empathy: A Contribution to the Psychology of Style*, trans. Michael Bullock (Chicago, 1997).

Bibliography

Wyndham Lewis Collection, Cornell University Library, Division of Rare and Manuscript Collections.

Wyke, Maria, and Dominic Montserrat, 'Glamour girls: Cleomania in mass culture', in Margaret M. Miles (ed.), *Cleopatra: A Sphinx Revisited* (Berkeley, CA, 2011).

Yan, Bai, 'Significance of originals and replicas in archaeological site museums with a case study of the Han Dynasty Site Museums in China', in *Original, Copy, Fake, On the significance of the object in History and Archaeology Museums, 22nd ICOM General Conference in Shanghai, China, 7–12nd November 2010* (Shanghai, 2010). Available at www.network.icom.museum/fileadmin/user_upload/minisites/icmah/publications/Actes-Shanghai-complet2.pdf.

Yeats, W. B., *The Speckled Bird by William Butler Yeats: An Autobiographical Novel, with Varian Versions. New Edition, Incorporating Recently Discovered Manuscripts*, William H. O'Donnell (ed.) (London, 2003).

Yeğenoğlu, Meyda, *Colonial Fantasies: Towards a Feminist Reading of Orientalism* (Cambridge, 1998).

Young, Ella, *Flowering Dusk: Things Remembered Accurately and Inaccurately* (New York, 1945).

Young, Sidney, *Annals of the Barber-Surgeons of London* (London, 1980).

Youngkin, Molly, *British Women Writers and the Reception of Ancient Egypt, 1840–1910: Imperialist Representations of Ancient Egyptian Women* (Basingstoke, 2016).

Zamora, Lois Parkinson, 'The magical tables of Isabel Allende and Remedios Varo', *Comparative Literature* 44.2 (1992), pp. 113–43.

Zigarovich, Jolene, 'Preserved remains: Embalming in eighteenth-century England', *Eighteenth-Century Life* 33.3 (2009), pp. 65–104.

Zimmermann, Pascale, 'Jacq, le pharaon du livre', *La Tribune de Genève*, 23 November 2013.

Zimmerman, Virginia, 'Excavating children: Archaeological imagination and time-slip in the early 1900s', in Eleanor Dobson and Gemma Banks (eds), *Excavating Modernity: Physical, Temporal and Psychological Strata in Literature, 1900–1930* (London, 2018).

INDEX

Abney Park cemetery 112
Abu Simbel 23, 96
Abydos 96
afterlife 4, 31, 80–2, 83, 88, 109, 115, 139, 252
Akhenaten 19, 48–9, 50, 55, 56, 57, 70, 91, 92, 196, 197, 205, 210, 211, 230
alchemy 147, 213, 214, 215, 218, 219, 223, 226–7
Alexandria 65, 146, 171, 204
Amarna 19, 48, 56, 91, 197, 210, 252
animal 8, 21, 48, 106, 213, 214, 220
Ankhesenamun 19, 92, 133, 142–3
Antony, Mark 8, 73, 142, 229–31, 232, 233, 234, 235, 236, 238, 240, 246
Anubis 81, 146, 169, 175
Apophis 81
Apuleius 147, 152
architecture 3, 5, 25, 33, 47, 58, 62, 64, 65, 66, 97, 105, 110, 113, 115, 117, 121, 153, 190, 210–11
Ashmolean Museum 196, 262 n.2
Aswan Dam 23
Aten 19, 48
Atum 169, 171
Aumonier, William 16–17, 21, 263 n.22

Bacon, Francis 55–6
Ballets Russes 134, 186
Bara, Theda 188, 236
Bast 221, 225, 253, 254, 258
beauty 137, 139, 142, 143, 154, 188, 193, 195–7, 209, 215, 218, 230, 233, 234, 241, 242–3, 255, 258, 320 n.28
Bell, Clive 50
Belzoni, Giovanni 109, 110, 255
Benjamin, Walter 27
Bernhardt, Sarah 185, 186
Bes 69
bird 60, 83, 178, 222
  see also duck; hawk; ibis; owl
Blake, William 169
Blavatsky, Helena 165, 179
Bonaparte, Napoleon 93, 112, 155
Bonomi Jr, Joseph 112, 113
Book of the Dead 81, 86, 136, 147, 202, 208
Booth, Walter 255
Boothby, Guy 200, 211
Breasted, James 48, 50, 56, 272 n.9
Breton, André 215–16
British Empire 7, 15, 105, 184, 201

British Empire Exhibition 3, 13, 15–17, 19, 21, 24, 26, 27, 28, 70
British Museum 1, 6, 24, 25, 40, 58, 106, 109, 130, 139, 147, 161, 163, 164, 165, 166–8, 175, 180, 185, 191, 196, 202, 204, 205, 208, 245, 253, 275 n.47, 283 n.154, 290 n.8
Bubastis 253, 254
Budge, E. A. Wallis 6, 41, 161, 162, 163, 164, 167, 175, 205, 206, 207, 208, 209, 211
burial 5, 81, 91, 105, 106, 108–11, 112, 115, 117, 118, 120–2, 123, 125, 126, 128, 136
Burroughs, William 4, 75, 76, 77–80, 82–8
Burton, Harry 16, 296 n.35
Burton, James 199
Burton, Richard 8, 229–31, 233–4, 235, 236, 237–8, 239, 240, 242–3, 246
Butler, Judith 185
Byron, Lord George 109

Caesar, Julius 58, 229, 231, 232, 233, 235, 236, 239, 240
Cairo 14, 24, 42, 59, 69, 91, 165, 207, 208
Campbell, Eddie 6, 161–3, 167, 168, 173, 175
Carnarvon, 5th Earl of 14, 15, 70, 92, 130, 135, 138, 203, 211
Carrington, Leonora 213, 214, 217, 221, 224, 225, 227
Carter, Howard 3, 13, 14, 15–17, 21, 26, 28, 70, 92, 127, 130, 131, 133, 204, 262 n.3
Cartier 6, 128, 133–5, 137, 138, 139, 140, 141, 142, 143, 144, 193
cat 218, 220–1, 222, 225, 226, 251, 253
celebrity 8, 229, 230, 235, 240, 242–3, 244, 245, 246
Cestius, Caius 109
Champollion, Jean-François 92, 93, 101, 146, 298 n.6
Christ 49, 106, 147, 171, 177, 220
Christianity 5, 33, 34, 47, 48, 49, 50, 51, 53, 57, 82, 91, 101, 106, 107, 109, 110, 113, 115, 118, 120, 121, 122, 124, 126, 146, 147, 149, 155, 156, 157, 178, 200, 220, 223, 229
Christie, Agatha 92
cinema 188–90, 191, 197, 211, 229–31, 233–46, 255
Cleopatra VII 8, 9, 58, 73, 142, 171, 184, 185, 186, 188–9, 196, 229–33, 234–5, 236, 238, 239, 240, 241, 242, 243, 245, 246, 307 n.20, 318 n.1, 320 n.28
Cleopatra's Needle 6, 161, 164, 168–9, 170–3, 174, 175, 177, 180, 305 n.52

Index

cobra 18
Colbert, Claudette 188, 189, 236
Collignon, Pierre Louis 33, 34–5, 37–9, 40, 41, 42, 44, 46
Collins, Mabel 177
Corelli, Marie 167, 211
Costanzo, Anthony Roth 211
cow 219, 224
Crawford, O. G. S. 31–2, 35, 42, 44, 45, 46, 267 n.11
crocodile 81, 119
Crowley, Aleister 177, 202–3

Daily Mail 14
Dalí, Salvador 215
death 5, 7, 49, 54, 61–2, 81, 83, 84–7, 88, 105, 106, 107, 108, 110, 115, 117–18, 120, 122, 123, 124, 126, 127, 128–30, 131, 136, 137–8, 139, 142, 143, 144, 154, 164, 168, 169, 172, 173, 176, 178, 218, 222, 224, 229, 233, 257
decadence 8, 9, 10, 63, 90, 185, 186, 188, 196, 199, 234
Defoe, Daniel 169
Denon, Vivant 93
Devizes Museum 35, 42, 43
diffusionism
    see hyperdiffusionism
Douce, Francis 105, 110, 111, 115
Douglas, Lord Alfred 173
Doyle, Arthur Conan 92, 165, 211, 251, 256
dream 57, 61, 86, 149, 172, 174, 178, 179, 204, 215, 220, 253
Dryden, John 73, 230
Duchamp, Marcel 53, 54
duck 20
Dumas, Alexandre 97
Durdin-Robertson, Lawrence 6, 145, 157, 158–9, 160
Durdin-Robertson, Olivia 6, 145, 157–8, 159, 160
Durdin-Robertson, Pamela 6, 145, 157, 158, 160

Ebers, Georg 89
Egypt Exploration Fund 195, 196, 262 n.5
Egyptian Museum, Cairo 262 n.5, 300 n.48
Egyptology 2, 3, 4, 8, 10, 14, 16, 48, 59, 60, 65, 70, 80, 81, 89, 90, 91, 92, 93, 94, 95, 98, 101, 102, 105, 109, 110, 120, 147, 153, 165, 176, 193, 194, 199, 200, 201, 203, 204, 205, 207, 210, 219, 244, 249, 250, 251
Egyptomania 4, 9, 72, 89, 93, 105, 115, 118, 119, 120, 128, 184, 240, 256, 265 n.54
el-Adl, Mohammed 204, 205, 209, 210
Eliot, T. S. 54, 58, 59, 204
embalming 105, 106, 107, 108, 109, 110, 115, 123
Engleheart, George 34, 35, 37, 39, 40–1, 43, 44, 46
Epstein, Jacob 199

Ernst, Max 215, 217
esotericism 6, 89, 90, 91, 98, 101, 214, 221, 224, 227

Farr, Florence 153, 167, 175
fashion 5, 7, 8, 118, 127, 128, 130, 131, 133–5, 138, 139, 140, 141, 143–4, 149, 150, 184, 185–6, 188, 191, 193, 196, 197, 213, 227, 240–1, 244–5
Fellowship of Isis 6, 145, 157–9, 160, 219–20
feminism 8, 9, 15, 100, 130, 143, 183, 184, 191, 193–4, 195–6, 197, 214, 216, 227, 240, 258
Fini, Leonor 8, 214, 216–20, 225–6, 227
First World War 6, 15, 31, 34, 36, 42, 51, 54, 127, 128–9, 131, 133, 137–8, 139, 143, 144, 163, 164, 179, 184, 188, 204
Fisher, Eddie 233, 236, 237
Fitzwilliam Museum 252
Forster, E. M. 8, 199, 204–5, 207–10, 211
Foucault, Michel 118, 168
Fox, Cyril 32
Frazer, Sir James 34, 58, 59, 69, 278 n.86
Freemasonry 33, 90, 91, 99–100, 145, 146, 147, 161, 162, 165, 168, 171, 173, 174–6, 177–8
Freud, Ernst 48
Freud, Lucian 48, 55, 56
Freud Museum 48
Freud, Sigmund 48, 49, 50, 53, 55, 56, 57, 61, 67, 68, 69, 70, 72, 129, 130, 172, 215, 218, 272 n.9
Fry, Roger 50–1, 55

Gardiner, Alan 61, 62
Gaudier-Brzeska, Henri 51, 52, 53
Gautier, Théophile, 90, 96, 251, 256
Geertz, Clifford 129
gender 7, 9, 100, 138, 143, 183, 184, 185, 190, 197, 199, 213, 215, 216–17, 218, 221, 223, 224, 225, 227, 247–8, 258
Geological Survey of Great Britain 41
Ginsberg, Allen 76, 86
Giza 96, 171
Glass, Philip 211
Goddard, E. H. 41
Gonne, Maud 151
Gray, Terence 68
Great Sphinx of Giza 171, 227
Grébaut, Eugène 207, 209
Greenhill, Thomas 105, 110
Gunn, Battiscombe 203

Haggard, H. Rider 120, 138, 200, 205, 207, 208, 210, 211
Hall, Henry 40, 204
Hamilton, 10th Duke of 5, 108, 117, 118, 123–6
Handel, George Frideric 230
Hands on History 3, 13, 17, 25, 27
Harrington, Bill 247

Index

Harris, J. Rendel 33, 35, 45, 267 n.21
Harrison, Rex 236, 243
Hathor 81
Hatshepsut 8, 20, 60, 68, 69–70, 186, 194, 195, 283 n.154
hawk 84
Hawksmoor, Nicholas 110, 166–7, 169
Hegel, Georg Wilhelm Friedrich 50, 52
Heliopolis 169, 171
hermeticism 5, 147, 151, 154, 172, 214, 218
Hermetic Order of the Golden Dawn 6, 145, 147, 148, 151, 153, 154, 167, 175, 176, 177, 178, 179, 203
Herodotus 64, 98
hieroglyphs 21, 75, 76, 79–80, 87, 88, 91, 92, 93, 99, 112, 123, 125, 146, 162, 169, 170, 251, 253
Highgate cemetery 109–10, 112
Hitler, Adolf 67, 164
Hockney, David 58
Homer 95, 98
Horus 6, 49, 68, 135, 146, 147, 149, 159, 161, 177, 178, 180, 202, 219
Hulme, T. E. 51, 52, 274 n.31
hyperdiffusionism 3, 30–5, 44, 47, 53, 54, 59, 60, 63, 65, 73

ibis 81, 106, 139
Imhotep 62
immortality 7
imperialism 7, 13, 25, 93, 105, 110, 112, 115, 155, 183, 185, 188, 197, 199, 200, 205, 208, 209, 210, 256, 263 n.20, 290 n.1
   see also British Empire
Ireland 6, 145, 154, 156–7, 159, 160
Isis 49, 68, 73, 140, 145–7, 149–52, 154, 155, 158, 159, 160, 175, 177, 202, 210, 214, 223, 224, 225
Islam 48, 49, 64, 82, 244

Jack the Ripper 6, 161, 173, 174, 175, 177
jackal 169, 254
Jacob, Edgar P. 90
Jacq, Christian 4, 89–102
Jahbulon 161, 175, 176
James, Henry 205
jewellery 6, 22, 127, 128, 133–4, 135, 137, 138–9, 140, 141, 143, 191–3, 218, 230, 254
Jones, Inigo 64
Joyce, James 56, 144
Judaism 48, 49, 53, 56, 57–8, 67, 82, 101
Jung, Carl 48, 57

Kandinsky, Wassily 52, 55
Karnak 96, 138
Kircher, Athanasius 146
Khepri 135

Khonsu 224
Kitaj, R. B. 57, 58
Korzybski, Alfred 75, 76, 77

Langtry, Lily 185
Lascaux Caves 25
Lawrence, D. H. 53, 56
Lee, Norman 247
Leigh, Vivien 236
leopard 20–1, 23, 150
Lévi-Strauss, Claude 213
Lewis, Wyndham 3, 47, 48, 49, 51–2, 53, 54–7, 58, 59, 60, 61, 62–4, 65, 66, 67, 68–70, 72–3
lion 19, 221
London 6, 15, 16, 17, 25, 106, 107, 109, 112, 122, 129, 134, 135, 147, 154, 161, 162, 163, 167, 168, 172, 174, 175, 177, 178, 191, 196, 252, 253, 254, 255
lotus 6, 135, 139, 144, 150, 202
Luxor 17, 40–1, 96, 130

magic 6, 8, 9, 34, 62, 75, 80–1, 83, 92, 98, 120, 136, 138, 139, 146, 147, 149, 154, 160, 161, 162, 165, 173, 174, 175, 178, 202, 213, 214, 216, 218–19, 224, 226, 227, 247, 249, 250, 252, 254, 255, 256, 257
Mailer, Norman 83
Mariette, Auguste 55, 93
Maroto, Esteban 247
Massingham, H. W. 33
maternity 143, 145–6, 157, 158, 164, 196, 214, 215, 218, 223, 225
Mathers, Moina 6, 145, 147, 148, 149–53, 154–5, 160
Mathers, Samuel Liddell MacGregor 6, 145, 147, 148, 149–56, 160
matriarchy 9, 169, 249, 252, 255, 256, 258
medicine 105–6, 107
Memphis 96
Memphis Museum 91
Merlin 33
Mertz, Barbara 89
Metropolitan Museum of Art 76
Miller, Lee 8, 214, 217
Misty 9, 247, 250, 259
modernism 42, 53, 127, 199, 203
monkey 81
moon 83, 215, 224, 225
Moore, Alan 6, 161–3, 167–8, 169, 172, 173, 175, 177, 178
Moses 48, 56, 57, 61, 68, 101, 156, 157
mummy 3, 5, 31, 47, 54, 60, 61–2, 82, 84, 85, 88, 105, 106, 107, 108, 115, 119, 120, 123, 130, 131, 165, 184, 189, 247, 250, 251, 252, 254, 255, 256–7, 277 n.63, 290 n.8, 330 n.21
   see Unlucky Mummy

363

Index

mummy's curse 70, 92, 130, 138, 163, 165, 166, 167, 178, 203–4, 211, 250, 254, 256, 257, 258
Murray, Margaret 3, 40, 273 n.19
Musée du Louvre 93, 133, 134, 193, 252, 275 n.44
museum 3, 13, 17, 23, 28, 49, 69, 106, 163, 190, 199, 230, 256
mythology 4, 6, 75, 82, 87, 88, 140, 145, 161, 162, 171, 207, 213, 214, 215, 218, 219–20, 221, 223, 225, 226–7, 232, 243

Nash, Paul 199
Natural History Museum 23
Nefertari 93, 100, 317 n.2
Nefertiti 8, 142, 143, 196–7, 230, 252
Nesbit, Edith 167, 205, 207
New York 53, 54, 67, 69, 70, 86, 129, 134, 139
Newberry, Percy 3, 40, 41
Nietzsche, Friedrich 55, 56, 59, 68, 71
Nile 139, 165
Noblecourt, Christiane Desroches 93, 98
Norwich Castle Museum 200

obelisk 46, 64, 92, 93, 109, 111–12, 122, 129, 155, 169–70, 174, 179, 180, 210, 271 n.89
see also Cleopatra's Needle
occultism 5, 6, 75, 145, 148, 160, 162, 167, 173, 174, 176, 177, 178, 180, 200, 201, 202, 203, 204, 205, 207, 210, 218–19, 222, 225
orientalism 6, 183, 184, 185, 186, 197, 201, 202, 216
Osiris 6, 33, 57, 81, 139–40, 145, 146, 147, 149, 152, 159, 161, 175, 176, 180, 202, 219, 223, 224, 283 n.145
Ostier, André 221
owl 222

paganism 49, 56, 110, 113, 154, 155, 157, 158, 159, 160, 166, 168, 177, 179, 219, 255, 257
Paris 6, 67, 90, 93, 121, 122, 129, 134, 141, 143, 145, 148, 149, 150, 151, 152, 153, 154, 155, 160, 196, 215
Passmore, A. D. 42–3
Paul, R. W. 256
Père Lachaise cemetery 121
Perry, William 3, 30–3, 34, 35, 44, 45, 59, 60, 61, 63, 68
Perth Museum, Australia 42
Petrie, Flinders 50, 200
Pettigrew, Thomas 108, 123
photography 16, 17, 21, 59, 144, 167, 171, 213, 214, 217, 220, 221, 227
Piranesi, Giovanni 109
Pirenne, Jacques 91
Plutarch 73, 146, 147, 238
Poe, Edgar Allan 255
Pound, Ezra 51, 313 n.45

priesthood 9, 48, 60, 145, 149–50, 157, 158, 159, 160, 247, 250, 251, 252, 253, 254, 255, 256, 257
Proclus 146
psychogeography 161, 162, 168, 169, 172
Ptahhotep 95
pyramid 5, 29, 50, 58, 105, 109, 110, 111, 113, 115, 121, 123, 125, 126, 155, 202

Ra 33, 81, 219, 221, 252
ram 19, 66
Rameses II 83, 69, 91, 93, 96, 99, 100, 101, 173, 177, 230
Ray, Man 217
Reckitt, Albert 17, 25
religion 4, 5, 6, 34, 48, 51, 65, 80, 82, 87, 90, 91, 101, 110, 120, 145, 146, 147, 148, 149, 151, 155, 157, 158, 167, 177, 178, 220
Renouf, Peter le Page 167
replica 3, 4, 13, 15–24, 25, 26–7, 28, 70, 196, 230, 262 n.2, 265 n.49
Reynolds, Debbie 236, 240
Ricketts, Charles 199–200
Rivers, W. H. R. 30–1, 59, 61
Rohmer, Sax 8, 201, 210
Romeu, Honeriu 247
Rosetta Stone 26
Royal Anthropological Society 30
Royal Society 106, 108

Salisbury Museum 43
sarcophagus 5
scarab 3, 6, 30, 34, 35, 36, 37–9, 40, 41–4, 46, 135–7, 138, 139, 254, 268 n.29
scorpion 219
Scota 6, 145, 156–7, 159, 160
Scotland 6, 153, 155–7, 159
sculpture 3, 23, 27, 28
Second World War 17, 48, 56, 67, 164, 179
Sekhmet 58, 135, 138, 221
Seth 68, 81, 147, 202, 219
sexuality 7, 9, 10, 78, 183, 184, 185, 188, 189, 196, 199, 200, 202, 203, 204, 205, 209, 210, 214, 215, 216, 217, 218, 221, 223, 225, 227, 229, 231, 234, 235, 236, 238, 239, 241, 245, 248, 258, 325 n.80
Shakespeare, William 73, 185, 230
Shaw, George Bernard 230
Shelley, Percy 69, 109, 208
Siculus, Diodorus 146
Sinclair, Iain 168
Sloane, Hans 105
Smith, Grafton Elliot 3, 30–3, 35, 44, 45–6, 47, 49, 54, 56, 58–60, 61, 62, 63, 64, 66, 68, 70, 72
snake 22, 81, 220, 251
see also cobra
Soane, Sir John 119

Index

Society of Antiquaries 34
Sotheby's 164
Southey, Robert 119
Spellbound 9, 247, 250, 254, 259
sphinx 8, 76, 139, 155, 169, 171, 172, 199–200, 213, 214, 215, 217–18, 221, 227, 235
  see also Great Sphinx of Giza
spiritualism 129, 138, 157, 177, 178
Stoker, Bram 120, 256
Stonehenge 3, 29, 33, 35, 36, 37, 41, 42, 44, 46, 64
sun 19, 21, 48, 144, 169, 171, 177, 222, 223, 224
Surrealism 8, 213–15, 216, 217–27

Tanning, Dorothea 215
Taylor, Elizabeth 8, 229–31, 233–5, 236–7, 238, 239, 240, 241–3, 244, 245, 246
The Times 14
Thames 173
Thebes 40, 165, 168
Theosophy 154, 165, 177, 178, 179, 274 n.34
Thoth 49, 81, 224
Tiy 252
Todd, Mike 233, 236, 237
tourism 24–6, 30, 40, 41, 42, 96, 109, 165, 183
Tutankhamun 3, 6, 10, 13, 14, 15–17, 19, 20, 21, 23, 24, 25, 26, 27, 28, 70, 72, 92, 93, 97, 127, 128, 130, 131, 133, 135, 136, 138, 139, 140, 143, 144, 184–5, 193, 203, 210, 211, 230, 245, 296 n.28
Tuthmosis III 3, 30, 41, 171

Unlucky Mummy 6, 161, 163, 164–8, 170, 172, 175, 179, 180, 304 n.15
uraeus 18, 19, 23, 66

Valley of the Kings 13, 26, 96, 125
van Gennep, Arnold 129
Varo, Remedios 8, 213, 214, 221–3, 225, 227
Victoria and Albert Museum 188

Warburg, Aby 51, 54, 57
Webb, Jane 165, 251
Weigall, Arthur 14, 16, 21, 89, 204, 263 nn.6, 11, 12
Westcott, William Wynn 147, 175, 305 n.67
Westminster Abbey 115, 169
Wiedemann, Alfred 80
Wilde, Oscar 161, 173–4, 199–200
Wiltshire Archaeological Society 30
Woodman, William Robert 147, 175, 305 n.67
Woolf, Virginia 203–4

Yeats, William Butler 149, 153, 154, 155, 158
York Cathedral 115

www.ingramcontent.com/pod-product-compliance
Lightning Source LLC
Chambersburg PA
CBHW070009010526
44117CB00011B/1485